Handbook in Diagnostic-Prescriptive Teaching

Stiles

Philip H. Mann
University of Miami, Coral Gables, Florida

Patricia A. Suiter
House of Learning, Miami, Florida

Rose Marie McClung
University of Miami, Coral Gables, Florida

Handbook in Diagnostic-Prescriptive Teaching

ABRIDGED SECOND EDITION

Allyn and Bacon, Inc.
Boston London Sydney Toronto

Library of Congress Cataloging in Publication Data

Mann, Philip H
Handbook in diagnostic-prescriptive teaching.

First ed. by P. H. Mann and P. Suiter published in 1974 under title: Handbook in diagnostic teaching.
Bibliography: p.
Includes index.
1. Remedial teaching—Handbooks, manuals, etc.
2. Reading—Remedial teaching—Handbooks, manuals, etc.
I. Suiter, Patricia, joint author. II. McClung, Rose Marie, joint author. III. Title.

LB1029.R4M362 1979 372.1'1'02 79-11169
ISBN 0-205-06673-9
10 9 8 7 6 5 85 84

Production Editor: Rowena Dores
Design Editor: Paula Carroll
Manufacturing Buyer: Win Benner

Printed in the United States of America

Contents

Preface

This edition of the *Handbook* has been changed to meet the growing needs of today's educators, who are becoming more precise in their efforts to develop programs for students who exhibit learning and behavior difficulties in school. The diagnostic-prescriptive approach to individualizing instruction is becoming more prevalent as teachers begin to observe earlier and to understand more about the cause-effect relationships within their classrooms. As was true of the first edition, the purpose of the *Handbook* is to provide educators with a comprehensive practical guide to diagnostic-prescriptive teaching.

Teacher education programs are modernizing their training programs at different levels to include in-service as well as pre-service so that teachers, administrators, and support personnel will be better able to meet the needs of students who must accommodate and adjust to a changing society. Any new knowledge that is communicated to teachers through various training programs must reflect the combined pooling of information from individuals in various disciplines to include psychology, medicine, and social work, as well as the various areas within the discipline of education itself. To share responsibility for students exhibiting variability, special education and regular classroom teachers must first have the kind of training that will foster a common language, develop a common core of competencies, and provide opportunities for working together to achieve the best and most appropriate educational climate for students. This sharing of responsibility for the learning handicapped students who are failing in our schools must become the new model for providing the best possible educational service system.

By delineating the developmental skills necessary for success in the language arts areas and arithmetic, teachers trained in the diagnostic-prescriptive teaching approach (with support from other professionals within the school) will be better able to identify the students' strengths in the language arts and other subject areas, as well as the problems that prevent the students from being successful in the given tasks. Teachers who have alternatives will be better able to adjust the curriculum and therefore provide appropriate programs for their students.

In keeping with today's emphasis on minimum achievement standards and accountability by educators for the progress of their students, teacher training institutions must become more responsive to the needs of students and their teachers, as well as to the changing needs of the communities they serve. Future-looking programs must develop in teachers at different levels the skills necessary to assess needs (both personally and with others) and to select and apply the methodology necessary to develop, implement, and evaluate educational curriculum.

Many students are being called lazy and stupid. The teachers who are trying to educate these students are looking for materials that will do the job instead of looking at the children for clues as to how they may best learn. It can be said that they are "material centered" rather than "student centered" in their approach to teaching. This handbook was developed to fill the gap between what teachers may already know about teaching students and what they need to know to teach those who have difficulty in learning. It is also designed to create both an awareness of, and a desire for, additional knowledge that will lead to the improvement of present-day educational programs for students exhibiting learning and behavior difficulties.

Chapter 1 of the book presents a frame of reference for examining learning and provides a rationale for why children fail. Following this theoretical framework are chapters that describe diagnostic procedures and contain specific assessment devices. Also included are chapters that give specific suggestions related to the areas of developmental skills as well as to the subject areas such as language arts and arithmetic. Chapter 10 discusses social-emotional development, to enable the reader to better understand and meet the needs of students with behavior difficulties. The chapter that follows contains specific suggestions for educational management, which includes classroom and materials organization and working with parents and paraprofessionals. The last chapter deals with individual educational programming.

Dr. Philip H. Mann

Foreword to First Edition

Since the advent of the educational measurements movement about a half century ago, teachers have been given advice by testers and diagnosticians of many kinds. Unfortunately, the teachers more often have been intimidated by the psychometrics than helped by the results. Much of the testing has been too peripheral to the instructional situation or too general to be useful. On the basis of test results teachers have often been advised, for example, that a child may be "expected" to achieve well or that he is "reading below capacity." At best, such information is fraught with error, but the more fundamental difficulty is that it fails even to approach the kind of specificity required to organize instruction. The teacher's work is to influence the development of children through detailed and continuing instruction, and it is in the interior of that process that help is needed.

Lately, teachers have pressed their claim for more helpful consultation and technical assistance at the level of specific instructional decisions for individual children. Some genuinely helpful and promising developments have emerged, such as the work on criterion-referenced testing, program evaluation, task analysis, and "precision teaching." In a broader context, new systems for managing assessments and instruction in classroom settings are being developed, for example, the individually Guided Education (IGE) program advanced by the University of Wisconsin R & D Center. It is hoped that we are at the dawn of a new day in which the technicians and theorists will address the critical and detailed aspects of instruction to meet the individual needs of children.

Another main thrust in education is in the ways schools treat children who present exceptional needs of various kinds. Currently, the trend is to provide for such children by enhancing their regular classroom situations whenever possible, rather than displacing them to special classes or centers. This effort—*mainstreaming*—permits the bypassing of many of the stigmatizing labeling and segregating processes of more traditional approaches. However, mainstreaming also requires that regular classroom teachers know more about instruction of children with different learning patterns.

The Mann-Suiter book makes the contribution of adapting instruction to individual learning differences. The authors present a broad set of detailed and practical procedures by which the learning needs of individual children can be assessed and instruction in basic skills adapted. Diagnosis and teaching are made integral in a way that teachers can understand and will appreciate. Although the book assembles many ideas that are already on the educational scene, Mann and Suiter have creatively enlarged, synthesized, and organized them in a valuable format.

The authors know very well that mainstreaming requires strong efforts to enhance the functioning of regular school programs. With their Miami colleagues they have been strong figures in pioneering methods by which regular classroom teachers and those who work with them are enabled to serve exceptional children in acquiring the basic tools of our culture within the mainstream of the community.

The ideas and techniques presented in this volume were developed and tested in practical teaching situations that involved both children and teachers.

Heretofore, the ideas have been available only at conferences or through film; now the authors have made them available in an expanded form to a wider audience.

Mann and Suiter present no grand theory on the learning problems of children, nor do they claim to present a final word on any topic. Indeed, the publication format—in looseleaf binding—suggests their openness to additions and refinement. The reader who reviews this book systematically will find herein a marvelously useful set of tools in finished form and others in suggestions that teachers can adapt to create their own improvements in instruction.

Maynard C. Reynolds
Professor, Special Education
University of Minnesota

Handbook in Diagnostic-Prescriptive Teaching

Chapter 1 Theoretical and Philosophical Perspectives

HISTORICAL BACKGROUND

Some years ago, before special education as we know it today, *general educators* were responsible for all the students in their classes. The obviously severely handicapped were for the most part excluded from school, while other students exhibiting problems related to learning and behavior were labeled by such terms as *slow, immature, incorrigible,* and *unmanageable.* Special education as a movement slowly changed the entire structure of education and, to some extent, the attitudes of most teachers toward students who fail in school.

Labels such as learning disabled were devised to describe those students who, although they were more like their nonhandicapped peers than different from them, were nevertheless thought of as "different" by virtue of their inability to accomplish academically what was expected of them in school settings. Legislation—combined with highly motivated and well-intentioned parents, professionals, and others in the community—gave impetus to the development of special services.

Over a period of years, changes have occurred in the delivery of educational services to students with learning and behavior problems, as well as in the delineation of responsibility for those implementing the service delivery system. The special education teachers' responsibility has shifted from self-contained separatism (individual responsibility) to alternating responsibility and, more recently, shared responsibility.

Individual Responsibility

Not too many years ago, the persons who were titled special educators were expected to assume total individual responsibility for labeled students. They were supported by ancillary personnel, but, for the most part, they assumed primary responsibility for diagnosis, curriculum, behavior management, and educational management of learning handicapped students in self-contained classrooms. In many school systems where self-contained classrooms were the mode, students were segregated physically, socially, and academically from their nonhandicapped agemates. Any interaction with their nonhandicapped peers was accomplished mainly by chance, such as eating in the same cafeteria at the same time as "normal" students or taking physical education at the same time as "normal" students. Special educators were, by and large, expected to be experts in the particular handicapping conditions manifested by their students. These educators were expected to design a "different curriculum."

Alternating Responsibility

Demands for change, along with the efforts of forward-looking administrators and teachers, began some years ago to encourage the integration of handicapped students into regular classes, bringing about an alternating responsibility for educational programming. This approach was, and still is, somewhat loosely defined and poorly structured in many school systems. The success of this approach depends upon the competencies and public relations abilities of the special education teacher, the attitudes of the principal and his or her key teachers, and the attitudes of the regular teachers who are also responsible for the handicapped students.

Alternating responsibility roles are currently assumed in two situations by special education personnel: the self-contained classroom teacher and the resource teacher. The fundamental difference between the two is that a resource teacher moves from classroom to classroom or removes students from the classroom for specific instructional purposes while primary responsibility for the students rests with the regular educator; the special education teacher with a self-contained classroom, on the other hand, assumes primary responsibility for the students, but they attend regular classes for part of the school day. Some school systems refer to the resource teacher's efforts as an "integrated program" approach. Others are calling the resource teacher model their "mainstream program." They say that as long as the students are in the regular classroom part of the day, and as long as they are the primary responsibility of the regular classroom teacher, they are being mainstreamed. Regardless of what the alternating responsibility approach is called and who assumes more responsibility in which situation, there are some serious problems with the approach in terms of role delineation. This system of serving students appears to be the most popular one in public schools today, but little research, if any, is available to support its efficacy. It is apparent that the following situations need to be investigated or at least considered with respect to alternating responsibility.

1. Students with learning and behavior disabilities who are resourced out of the regular classroom may be overloaded with too many programs; for example, two reading programs offered simultaneously by different teachers may be conflicting for the learner.
2. Poor or inadequate communication between resource and regular classroom teachers may result in a lack of cooperative planning.
3. Constant movement of the student in and out of the regular class without appropriate communication between the resource and regular teacher can result in negative feelings because the regular teacher may not want the student to be out of the room at a given time.
4. The shifting of responsibility back and forth, based on discrete academic areas of concern, often results in no one's accepting full responsibility for the student's progress.
5. The alternating responsibility approach can result in the student's being involved in academic work for the resource period but sitting around doing little or nothing for the rest of his or her regular classroom time.
6. The responsibility for explaining the student's placements, progress, and educational performance may become too diffuse in an alternating responsibility program. The parent may be forced to communicate with educators who, as a rule, do not communicate with each other.
7. The ongoing evaluation process may break down as the student begins to exhibit strengths and weaknesses within the educational prescription as it was originally designed for him or her. Individual educational plans may not be updated or reevaluated because formal procedures have not been set up by the school to accomplish this task.
8. Students may feel that they are being shifted from one teacher to another and that the responsibility for much of the communication between the resource and regular teacher is being channeled through them (e.g., "John, what are you doing in Mrs. Brown's class in reading?")

Mutual/Shared Responsibility

Recently, school systems have adopted a more shared, or mutual, responsibility approach to serving learning handicapped students. This is in keeping with recent mandates (Public Law 94–142) for ongoing evaluation as part of individual educational planning for students exhibiting learning or behavior difficulties.

The mutual responsibility concept appears to be the most progressive in the continuum of diagnostic-prescriptive teaching. The most cogent aspect of mutual responsibility is the one that suggests that all teachers, regular and special, operating as a team, must bring to the learning situation all the skills, competencies, and attitudes that will enable shared responsibility to become a reality. In a sense, this means that one must stop thinking of oneself as just a third grade teacher or just a teacher of social studies and bring all one's strengths to the task of providing for more input into comprehensive programs for students with learning difficulties. There are some teachers, for example, who have excellent backgrounds in reading and language that may never surface or become known unless these individuals are called upon to exhibit their strengths in team-oriented situations.

The implications for diagnostic-prescriptive teaching using this approach are at once apparent. Before one can successfully provide for the educational needs of students with wide ranges of individual variation, one must consider the skills that must be present or developed in teachers so that the interaction between regular and special education personnel will bring about optimal growth and result in maximum efficiency of learning for each student. Diagnostic-prescriptive teaching therefore becomes a natural outgrowth of utilizing "sound" educational principles and effective individualization of instruction and is not merely a "new approach." To be successful, it must be a total school effort, with all the support systems operating together to provide for the varying needs of all students—not only the identified and labeled students, but also the students in regular classes who are not receiving special services because of lack of program funds or poor educational management. The main idea in the whole approach is that the special education teacher and the regular class teacher together plan, coordinate, and evaluate a program for each particular student, so that one teacher is not teaching by using one approach or method while the other is teaching the same subject using a conflicting approach. Handwriting is a good example.

Under a mutual responsibility "umbrella program," students exhibiting learning and behavior disorders participate in regular classes for as much of the day as possible, depending on their abilities to function in a regular educational setting. They spend the rest of the day with a special education teacher. Some students may spend most of the day with a trained special education teacher; others may be able to remain in the regular classroom for most of the day. The degree of change accomplished in reality depends upon the effective utilization of time, the number of students in the classroom, the physical environment, the attitudes and skills of educators, and the support services and material resources of a given school. Physical manipulation of students can be mandated in many ways, but growth can only come about through a thorough knowledge and understanding of what it is that needs to be changed.

Whether our present system is worthwhile for the majority of students with learning problems is not an issue in this book. The purpose of this volume is to identify the content and the processes that may be relevant to improving the delivery of services to students who are failing. Eventually, however, several issues will need to be resolved. They deal with the following:

1. The notion that special education nas become a vehicle by which regular classroom teachers move students who are failing or misbehaving in their classes out of their rooms into essentially segregated situations. This involves a labeling process with all the concomitant concerns and repercussions.
2. The idea that the labels we use provide for a classification or categorization of students that connotes that these students must have an essentially different curriculum that a regular classroom teacher cannot provide within traditional classroom settings and size.
3. The belief that labeling offers a rationale for considering certain students different to the extent that they would inhibit the learning of nonhandicapped students if they were permitted to study in the same programs.
4. The belief in the almost infallibility of tests and what they purport to measure or predict, since the basis for making judgments in many cases is standardized or formal tests as opposed to observational procedures.

Diagnostic-Prescriptive Orientation

School-community advocacy of improved educational programming has become an important new trend in education. Communities, concerned about the poor academic achievement of many learners, are demanding accountability in the public schools and, to a lesser degree, in the institutions of higher education. Anticipated are higher levels of performance by teachers, with concomitant increases in academic achievements of students, in order to meet the requirements imposed by accepted academic standards. Those who are involved in programmatic decisions will of necessity be more cognizant of the variability in performance of students in our schools.

Diagnostic-prescriptive teaching as an instructional alternative for students exhibiting learning and behavior disorders has received wide recognition by special, as well as general, educators. This approach, which is inherently a more individualized approach to education than the traditional one, recognizes that educational programs must fulfill students' needs and protect their rights, providing for success in school while simultaneously preserving the dignity of the learners.

Diagnostic-prescriptive teaching lends itself to shared responsibility and to implementation in many different educational settings. Traditional as well as open school settings can readily adapt diagnostic-prescriptive teaching techniques as long as the basic philosophy of the school incorporates the principle of individualized instruction. (A school that is modern in its physical facilities only—that concerns itself primarily with the "learners," omitting the atypical student from the mainstream of education—has a lesser educational program than a one-room red-brick schoolhouse where the teacher develops appropriate educational programs for all students, including the learning handicapped.)

The diagnostic-prescriptive approach to teaching students can be called *eclectic* in that it pulls together the best of all available resources. It can also be described as *humanistic* in that it attempts to change the life-style of students who have been failures in school, changing their attitude toward learning from one of "failure-avoiding" to one of "success-striving." This approach emphasizes success. The teacher, after reaching a point of failure in instruction, must then drop down to the last success and leave the student with a successful achievement or an accurate model.

Diagnostic-prescriptive teaching is a *behavioral analysis* approach in that analyzing individual behavior in relation to the physical setting and tasks to be learned is imperative to the development of appropriate educational strategies for students.

DIFFERENTIAL LEARNERS

For years, teachers have referred to the *learning styles* of particular students. It is recognized that students can be served in a variety of settings. The prevailing philosophy today is that all students should be served in as "normal" an environment as possible, given both their abilities and disabilities. A great deal has also been written about the *life-styles* of individuals, which to a large degree are formed by habit, economics, and life experiences that are either positive or negative. More recently it has been observed that *learning style* and *life-style* are interrelated; that is, behaviors observed in some learners in school (such as distractibility, hyperactivity, and poor memory) tend to be seen in the same learners in other situations, including at home. For example, individuals who are easily distracted in a school or classroom (considered to be a high visual stimulus environment) tend to wear conservative, not too colorful, clothes and live in a house or room that is relatively free from excessive visual stimulation such as busy wallpaper and pictures. Persons who like to study alone and are distracted by noise in the classroom may also desire a "quiet" place in their homes, or they may avoid situations that "overload" them auditorily. Some teachers and children find it difficult to work in large "open classrooms" because of the noise level, movement, and other distractions present. They become easily fatigued or anxious by the end of the day. They expend more than the usual amount of energy in attempting to attend to many different tasks with excessive auditory or visual stimulation present.

A number of learners have difficulty in processing information that is presented to them auditorily or visually. Some cannot learn or perform a particular task efficiently when their auditory, visual, and tactual-kinesthetic processes are not synchronized to operate as a functional unit. By the same token, learning occurs in many students who have moderate deficiencies in certain processes that involve perception, imagery, language, and motor abilities, while some students who are only mildly involved fail at the same tasks. One explanation could be that the former compensate more effectively for the disability.

Students exhibiting learning problems may be impeded by intra- or inter-channel disorders.

A student with an *intra-channel disorder* may have difficulty in processing information that is mainly within one learning modality, that is, more visual or more auditory in nature. For example a student may be unable to discriminate between symbols visually (*a* from *o*) or auditorily (sound of *f* from *v*) at the level of perception.

A student with an *inter-channel disorder* may have difficulty using auditory and visual clues simultaneously and in concert with each other. For example, the student may understand what is required (reception), but be unable to respond with a motor act (expression).

Compensatory Processing

Some individuals may be deficient in a particular learning process (auditory-sequential memory, for example) that is necessary for the successful performance of a specific task. They will often compensate for their deficiency by utilizing related abilities or processes to a greater degree. For problems involving auditory-sequential memory, the students may use more visual associations to help them to remember rather than relying completely on auditory memory. For example, they may always write down phone numbers instead of depending solely on auditory memory. However, compensatory processing depends on certain conditions:

1. The processes used to compensate must be intact. If students are using visual clues or processes to compensate for poor auditory memory, for example, their visual skills must be operating efficiently.
2. The learners must be motivated enough to want to compensate for their disability. Where there is no will to learn, there will be little learning.
3. The school must provide the learners with oppor-

tunities to use their intact learning skills. Associative clues should be included whenever possible to reinforce learning. This means that objects, pictures, movement (tactual-kinesthetic), and opportunities to use manipulative materials such as clay and anagrams must be integrated as reinforcers into each of the skill or task level areas to be learned. For example, whenever possible, the instructor should furnish the students with visual representations (i.e., concrete objects or pictures) of the symbols they are learning so that they can associate the words with their visual referents.

Program Assumptions and Rationale

Relying upon intact processing abilities (for example, depending mainly upon visual clues for learning when auditory learning processes are deficient) may result in a minimal utilization of the deficient learning processes for new skill acquisition. For example, individuals who depend chiefly upon visual input because their auditory processing abilities are deficient may never really develop good auditory skills. They may, in fact, never trust their listening abilities. Opportunities for developing such deficient skills must be provided. However, if the teacher concentrates only upon reducing the disabilities, the students may have little opportunity to receive instruction in reading, writing, or arithmetic. Thus, they may take years to become "ready" to learn. There is little evidence to support the contention that teaching to the deficits alone will result in significantly increased performance in reading, for example.

It is recommended that the students' strengths and weaknesses both be considered in setting up an instructional program. The teacher must be responsive to the needs of each student. The term *open channel* is familiarly associated with Anne Sullivan who discovered that Helen Keller could learn from input given through the sense of touch. The teacher must "decode" the student to discover the open channels. Simultaneously, closed channels must be opened whenever possible for more integrated learning. In the daily education program, the teacher must work with the strengths in the subject areas as well as with the problems in the developmental skills areas.

It is not illogical to conclude that reliance primarily upon intact learning abilities or correlates to the extent that deficient learning processes receive minimal utilization during the formative years results in an adult life-style that stabilizes a pattern of learning reflecting this early disuse. As educators, we must each recognize that individuals learn differently. To better understand ourselves, we should try to decode our own learning styles or patterns. But we must try not to impose our own learning styles on others. One teacher, a strong visual learner, required her students to "look up" and "focus in" before she presented a lesson. Her feeling was that "if they are not looking at me, they are not learning." However, problems began to arise when she received a student teacher who was a strong auditory learner. He insisted that the students "tune in" and "listen up." Sometimes students listen better when they are not looking at you. The important thing to consider is "Are they learning?"

There is presently a deep concern over how to teach language (reading, writing, spelling, arithmetic) to children who appear to have near average, average, or above average intelligence, but who have difficulty in learning. Although the basic integrity of their sensory input systems, such as auditory and visual acuity, is within normal range and their speech and motor performance are adequate, the children do not learn at a normal pace. Thus, many learners have been described as exhibiting a "maturational lag." These students have been labeled *neurologically impaired, perceptually handicapped, educationally handicapped,* or *dyslexic* or they are said to have specific learning disabilities.

The most obvious symptom, common to all these learners, is the discrepancy in their learning between expected and actual achievement. They have been referred to as exhibiting a pattern of "hills and valleys" in their development, very high in some areas and very low in others. Many educators are recognizing that there is too much variability in their development to simply label them retarded or slow learners. These students display one or more significant deficits in essential learning processes and require specific educational techniques for initial, as well as for remedial, instruction.

In evaluating learning difficulties, the teacher needs to look at each child's level of development, determining where the child breaks down in the learning process and what specific problem areas prevent him or her from learning a given task. Although the students may seem to have normal achievement possibilities and the potential to learn in some areas, in other areas they may be weak, needing special instruction or remediation that takes into account their specific problems.

To do an effective job of program planning or diagnostic teaching, the teacher needs to understand the components of each student's behavior patterns and the appropriate academic achievement levels for learners of different ages. The teacher must also be prepared to utilize contributions from related disciplines such as medicine, psychology, and social work.

Why Students Fail

Educators must be continually aware that each learner is an individual, uniquely different in physical characteristics, personality, and general capacity. On the other hand, they must also always consider physiological and social-emotional likenesses, so that concern for differences is kept in the proper perspective.

Every student is capable of learning something and of making a contribution.

It has become apparent to many educators that sometimes they wait too long for *readiness* to occur for particular students. It is questionable whether overall readiness is necessary for a student to learn a specific task. It is also obvious that some students need help to become ready. Some teachers are attempting to facilitate readiness by providing students with activities that will better prepare them to become efficient learners. Since failure rather than success in school becomes the mode for so many students, it is necessary that we intervene as early as possible. This does not mean that teachers should impose inappropriate activities but rather that they cannot wait for an overall state of readiness in every area before starting to teach a student. Care must be taken, on the other hand, not to push the student too fast, as this may result in the habituation of faulty learning responses as the student attempts to meet the expectations of parents, teachers, and peers.

We need to find out where the student breaks down in the learning process and understand how a perceptual, memory, or language disability, for example, can interfere with other areas of learning. Learning is a multidimensional phenomenon. It is important to understand the relationships between the various processing areas and how they function with each other to enable a student to learn a given task. The teacher needs to ask the right questions, such as "What kinds of problems does the student have?" and "To which areas do I need to give priority in terms of where and how to begin to teach?" The answers to these questions will aid the teacher in determining the rate of input, the amount of input, and the sequence of input for each student. This, in effect, is individualizing instruction for the student who has learning problems.

The following concepts deal with some of the dynamics of why students fail.

PRINCIPLE OF "PLATEAU"

The principle of *plateau* implies that the student shall not remain at the same level of skill development for an extended period of time, without justifiable explanation. Success must become continual for students who have been accustomed to failure. This can be achieved by teachers who escape from the bonds of traditional or prescribed curriculum methodologies and adjust the rate, amount, and sequence of input according to the needs of each student.

RATE OF INPUT

It is essential that the teacher determine the rate of input that is appropriate for each learner. Some students are *slow learners.* They need more time for acquiring a skill and are often penalized by timed tests. By trying to go too fast, the teacher may produce anxiety and frustration in these children. Many teachers tend to speed up the rate of input in an attempt to follow the textbook. Unfortunately, when developing materials for use in schools, most authors do not take into consideration the learner who has a slower rate of learning. A more moderate rate would permit the repetition and reinforcement necessary to help the student better stabilize that which has been learned. Learning is more efficient when new material is tied in associatively to what has already been retained. This is especially true for students who exhibit learning difficulties. Children exhibiting problems in auditory discrimination skills require a slower rate of oral input.[1]

AMOUNT OF INPUT

Many students are jammed, or overloaded, by too much input given at one time. Sometimes that extra spelling word or that extra arithmetic problem may cause the student to forget much of what has already been taught. In controlling the amount of input, the teacher must be careful to leave the learner with a successful experience. The key words for directed activities that will leave students with success are "show me," "give me," and "tell me." When doing these types of activities, they can more readily correct their own errors. Self-correction of errors is a more efficient learning technique than merely listening to the right answer given by another student. Overloading is discussed further on page 7.

SEQUENCE OF MODALITY OF INPUT

One of the critical variables of input is the order of presentation. The teacher must identify the open channel, that is, the *modality* (auditory, visual, or tactual) that enables each student to learn best. By utilizing the open channels, the teacher can apply associative principles to instruction. For example, students with a visual channel problem may learn best

1. R. L. McCroskey and H. W. Thompson, "Comprehension of Rate Controlled Speech by Children with Special Learning Disabilities," *Journal of Learning Disabilities* 6 (December 1973): 621–627.

through an auditory-to-visual-plus-tactual (listen, look, and feel) association rather than by a visual-to-auditory (look and listen) association. Learners who have difficulty learning how to hold a pencil by observing the teacher demonstrating a series of actions may learn best by listening to the teacher describe the action with their eyes shut as they mold their hands around their pencils. They can then visualize the sequence in their mind's eye. The following modality input sequences are recommended for specific channel deficits:

1. *Auditory Channel Problems* (sensory, perception, memory, language) Visual to Auditory plus Tactual-Kinesthetic, if necessary

   $$(V \longrightarrow A + TK)$$

2. *Visual Channel Problems* (sensory, perception, memory, language) Auditory to Visual plus Tactual-Kinesthetic, if necessary

   $$(A \longrightarrow V + TK)$$

3. *Visual and Auditory Channel Problems* (sensory, perception, memory, language) Visual to Auditory to Tactual-Kinesthetic, automatically included

   $$(V \longrightarrow A \longrightarrow TK)$$

OPTIMAL TEACHING TIME

It is important to know when during the day the learner is most responsive to input from the teacher, peers, paraprofessionals, and volunteers. Those who regularly work with the student can ascertain these periods of time by clocking the number of seconds or minutes the learner stays on task during selected times during the day. The observer should also note where, and with whom, the learner has the maximum learning time. The implications of teaching students with a short attention span include the following:

1. the scheduling of teacher-directed and independent study. If a student cannot sit for thirty minutes in a group, the most appropriate number of minutes for group activity has to be considered, along with backup activities for reinforcement.
2. the transition of activities. Some students cannot easily move from an active physical education or music activity to a quiet self-directed activity. Intervening activities should be considered, and the time it takes for the learner to become ready for a task should be noted.
3. the time for review of new learning during the day. Students who do not retain new material easily may need short segments of review time during the day at optimal teaching moments. For example, reviewing new reading vocabulary during a school day may be more appropriate than relying totally on after-school review at home.

OVERLOADING

Students with learning difficulties are often expected to learn too much material too fast, and they tend to become "overloaded," or saturated, to the extent that they cannot stabilize (learn) or retain new material. For example, students who are taught two or even three different reading programs simultaneously may stabilize little or none of the words from any of those programs. Since each book series or program essentially unfolds different words with some overlap, they tend to "wipe each other out," or displace each other, when they are taught concurrently. The students appear to be able to "hold," or retain, just so many words in a given period of time, and those words must be continually reinforced in different ways in order to be stabilized. The rate must be carefully controlled when adding new words to a student's program. Often, for each new word taught, the overloaded student may forget words that were previously thought to have been learned.

Controlling for Overloading. The following procedures will enable the instructor to more specifically control the rate of input and to make better decisions about how to introduce new learning to a particular student.

The teacher can order the concepts or skills to be learned, designating them as being either equivalent or hierarchical.

1. *Equivalent.* Concepts, behaviors, or skills that are of the same difficulty are equivalent. For example, for most individuals, learning the meaning of the word *house* is equivalent in difficulty to learning the meaning of the word *car.*
2. *Hierarchical.* Concepts, behaviors, or skills, that can be ordered from simple to complex, easy to hard, or prerequisite critical skills to higher-level activities are hierarchical in nature. For example, before you can learn to blend sounds together to make words you need to learn the sounds that represent particular symbols.

Learners bring previous learning to school tasks. Before teaching, teachers should know, or attempt to find out, what the students already know. Given the task of identifying (word recognition) twenty words, for example, it is first important for the teacher to find out how many of the words the student can already read. This establishes a baseline for the learning of the twenty words (sight read). The teacher should divide

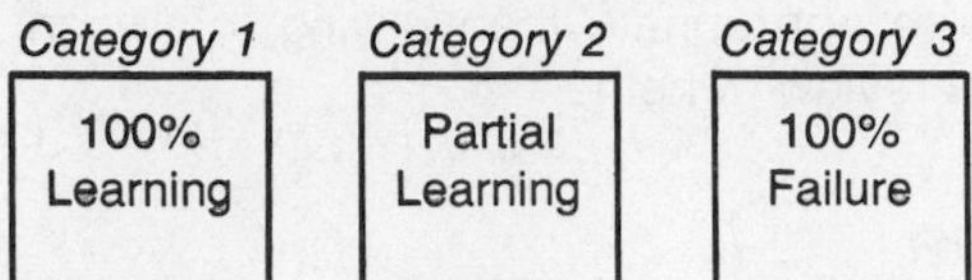

Figure 1-1 Categories of Word Recognition

the words into three categories (Figure 1-1), as follows:

1. Show the student all twenty words and find out how many of the words he or she can read easily and with no hesitation or prompting. The words the student reads easily are considered 100 percent learning, or mastery (Category 1). The words in this category can be used by the student at the independent level. That is, the student can write with these words and can read them in books. These sight words have a high degree of associative value in that they can be combined with new words to be learned, enabling the learner to use the process of association in stabilizing the new sight words.
2. Identify the words that the learner reads with difficulty, correctly on one occasion and incorrectly at others (Category 2). With these words, learners may, for example, hesitate, attempt to sound out the words, or close their eyes and struggle to remember. This category of sight words can be called partial learning. We learn a lot about individual learners as we observe them in their attempt to read these words. We find out what they do to try to identify the words that they do not immediately recognize. We note the trial-and-error behavior and how much prompting they need. This kind of observation gives us a clue to possible learning problems. Partially learned words are also called *leverage* words. Leverage words are the ones that are ready to be learned and should be taught first.
3. Identify the words that are a complete frustration to the student (Category 3). They are the words that are totally unknown and misread on repeated occasions. Category 3 is the level of 100 percent failure; the student just rejects the words. This is the area that is of most concern in terms of overloading. Many programs tend to unfold too many words or concepts that are at the 100 percent failure level simultaneously, resulting in overloading with little or no learning.

The following is an example of how to apply the concept of overloading to word recognition.

After the teacher has tested the student on his or her sight recognition of twenty words and assigned the words to one of the three categories, the teacher and the student can plot the words on a graph and talk about the results. According to the sample graph in Figure 1-2, the learner has already learned five words.

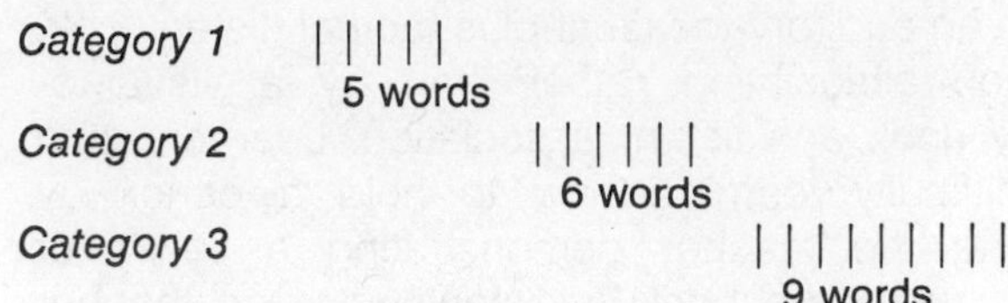

Figure 1-2 Sample Graph of Twenty Words

These words can be put on a word card or on a folder and dated.

The next step is to teach the Category 2 (leverage) words, in the following manner:

1. Introduce each word one at a time and in context, using the student's sight vocabulary and one or more of the Category 1 words that he or she already knows. The Category 2 words should never be introduced in isolation, only in context.

   Example:
   Category 1 Word (100% learning) = *experiment*
   Category 2 Word (partial learning) = *beaker*

The word *beaker* is taught associatively in context, using a writing or typing approach. The student writes the sentence "The boy used the *beaker* in his experiment." The student can underline the word beaker if desired.

2. Additional reinforcement can be utilized as appropriate. For example, the teacher can have the student prepare a self-checking word card (Figure 1-3) with the word on one side and an illustration of the word on the other. The student can draw the picture or cut it from a magazine and then paste it on the card.

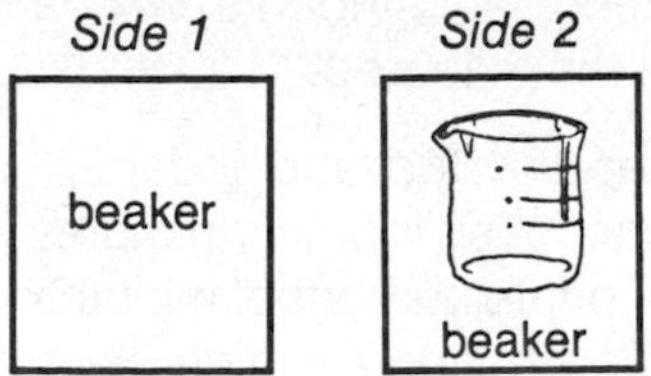

Figure 1-3 Word Card

3. Other reinforcers include tracing the word, writing the word in a sentence, typing, and using other media.

As Category 2 words are learned, the instructor can begin to introduce Category 3 (100 percent failure) words one at a time and only in context. Care must be taken not to overload the student by introducing too many of these words at one time. As Category 2 words are established and begin to become part of Category 1, and as some Category 3 words become Category 2 words, the student's learning profile should begin to change in appearance.

Table 1-1 Sample Learning Profile

	1st week	3rd week	5th week
Category 1	5 words	8 words	12 words
Category 2	6 words	7 words	6 words
Category 3	9 words	5 words	2 words

Table 1-1 is a sample profile. According to that example, the biggest changes are taking place in Categories 1 and 3, with Category 2 functioning as leverage words between Categories 1 and 3.

By plotting in this way, the teacher and the student can begin to see a pattern of learning and can regulate the rate accordingly. The same approaches for dealing with overloading can be used for other areas of learning, such as word meaning or vocabulary, oral production of sounds and words, spelling, writing, arithmetic, and other areas of language development.

EXPLANATION OF DESIGN OF CORRELATES FOR THE ANALYSIS OF LEARNING AND BEHAVIOR

Figure 1-4 depicts the learning design and the important parameters that pertain to the learning patterns of students. It provides the teacher with a framework within which to identify strengths and weaknesses in the learning processes. After identifying these learning and behavior correlates as they pertain to particular students, the teacher can develop specific educational strategies for each learner.

Verbal Learning Systems

Most of what occurs in school can be termed *verbal learning.* By this, we mean speech, reading, writing, spelling, and arithmetic. We are concerned in verbal learning with the student's ability to deal with symbols at different levels.

SENSATION

Sensory aspects of learning involve both verbal and nonverbal learning systems. The teacher must determine early in the school year whether the learners are able to see and hear (acuity). This can be done through tests of auditory and visual acuity or by merely lining the students up at the back of the room and asking them to respond to their names (auditory) or to symbols on the chalkboard in the teacher's everyday writing (visual). The student who cannot respond appropriately should be referred for further evaluation. Ocular motor disorders and other disorders of vision may also affect learning.

The tactual (touch), olfactory (smell), and gustatory (taste) modalities can also be used in teaching. The teacher should determine whether or not the students can acquire accurate information through haptic processes. This can be done by experimenting with the students' ability to identify different textures sight unseen. Students should be able to describe familiar objects just by touching them and be able to ascertain whether their textures are different or similar.

Sometimes the most obvious problem is overlooked in our attempt to seek complex reasons for learning failure. Sensation is the most primitive level of learning, and the possibility of sensory dysfunction should be considered in all cases where learners react atypically to auditory or visual stimuli.

Auditory Acuity. Students with an auditory acuity problem may exhibit any or all of the following:

1. They may be restless and exhibit poor behavior, often disturbing other students in their attempt to get the information they missed.
2. They may have difficulty in following directions and ask for repetitions from the teacher and others. (Check auditory memory.)
3. They may miss a great deal if the teacher speaks while facing the chalkboard, or if they sit in the back of the room.

It is important to note that even a minor uncorrected hearing loss may be a problem if the student is seated too far away from the teacher or if the student's better ear is facing the wall. If the teacher will line up all the students at the back of the room at the beginning of the school year and call their names in his or her usual voice, the teacher will quickly identify those who cannot hear from the rear of the room. Further evaluation and referral may save a student from a great deal of frustration. Some students may have hearing aids but refuse to wear them for cosmetic reasons.

Visual Acuity. There are a number of visual disabilities a teacher should be aware of in attempting to teach a problem learner.

1. The student may exhibit difficulty with near- or far-point vision.
2. Suppression of vision may occur if the "bad eye" interferes with the "good eye," causing the student to see a double image. Check unusual head tilt in reading.

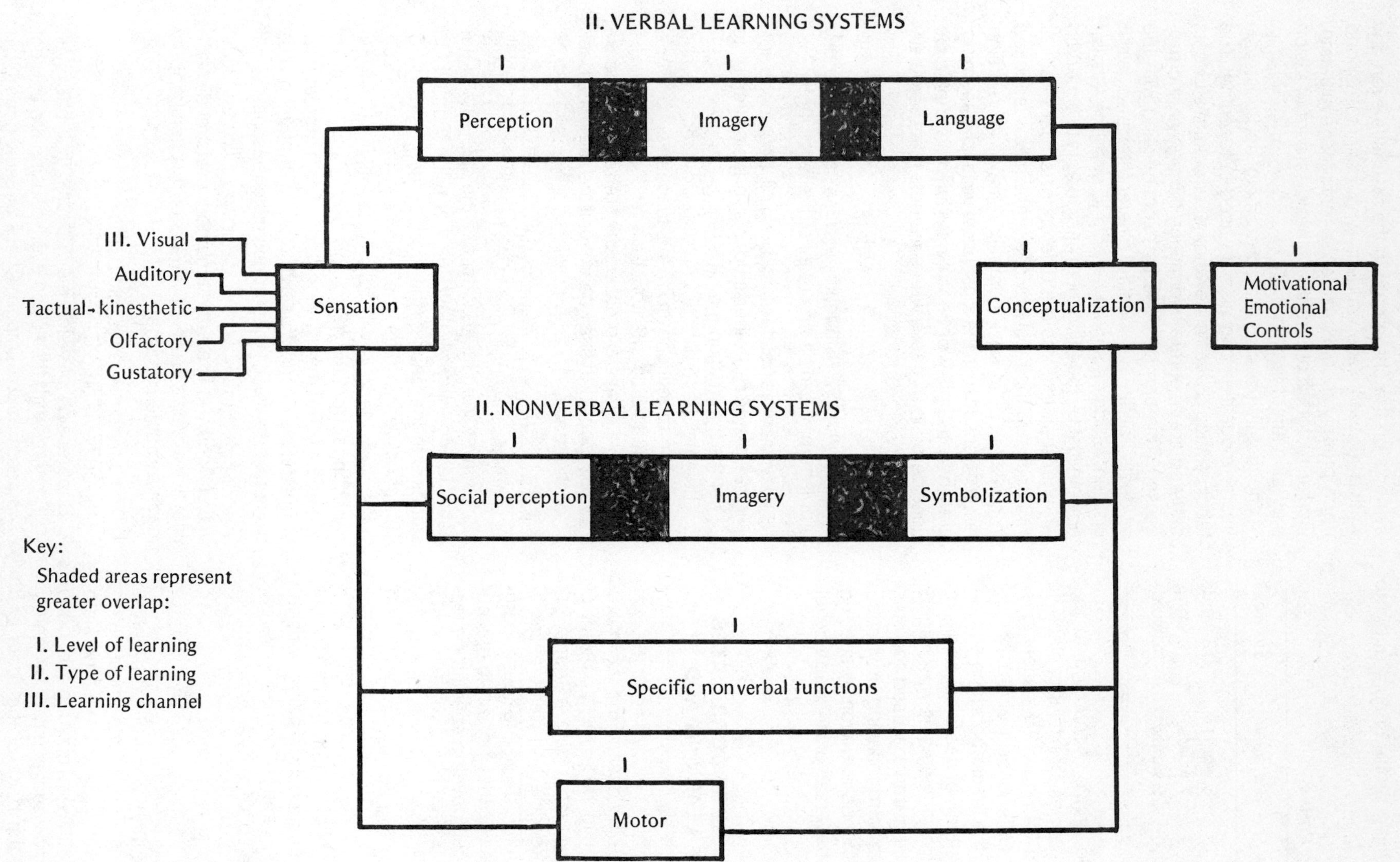

Figure 1-4 Design of Correlates for the Analysis of Learning and Behavior

3. Convergence difficulties may result from muscle imbalance in that the student cannot focus on a given task for a period of time.
4. Scanning or ocular pursuit problems may interfere with visual tracking and reading.
5. The following signs also need special attention: blinking; crossed eyes; unusual head tilt; tearing, redness, or inflammation of the eye; and fatigue.

PERCEPTION

In viewing perception, we are leaving the realm of the senses alone and entering into processes that involve other brain functions. The area of perception includes the following sub-categories:

1. *Discrimination.* Seeing or hearing likenesses and differences in sounds and symbols.
2. *Object recognition.* The ability to view objects, geometric shapes, letters, numerals, and words and recognize the nature of these visual stimuli with a high degree of constancy.
3. *Figure-ground.* The ability to separate what one wishes to attend to visually or auditorily from the surrounding environment.
4. *Localization and attention.* The ability to locate and attend to stimuli in one's environment.
5. *Closure.* The ability to recognize objects even when parts of the objects are missing, to synthesize sounds (auditory) and symbols (visual), or go from the parts to the whole. (In reading, this can be called blending.)

Auditory Discrimination. Students with problems in auditory discrimination may be unable to hear fine differences between letter sounds. They may be unable to differentiate the following:

1. Sounds such as *f–v, p–b, t–d.*
2. Vowels or consonants in spelling. Students may omit these in words. For example, they may spell *varnish* as *vrnsh.* (Check visual memory.)
3. Similarities in sounds within a word. For example, students may not be able to discriminate that the *and* in *hand* and *sand* are the same sounds.
4. Similar beginning or ending sounds in words, such as *man–mat* or *pant–rat.*
5. Short vowel sounds, such as the *i* in the word *bit* or the *e* in the word *bet.*
6. The second consonant in consonant clusters, such as the *l* in *fl* or the *t* in *st.*
7. The quiet consonant. Students may drop it in blends and in spelling words. For example, they may read *rust* as *rut.*

Visual Discrimination. The student with problems in visual discrimination may be unable to distinguish fine differences between letters such as *n* and *h* and *e* and *o.* Therefore, they fail to note details of words such as *snip* and *ship* or *red* and *rod.* Some students with this difficulty may not be able to match letters accurately. Of course, some students make visual discrimination errors because they "look too quickly"; they do not have actual visual discrimination problems.

Object Recognition. Children with difficulties in recognizing an object cannot efficiently integrate visual stimuli into a uniform whole. Their attention is drawn to the parts rather than to the entire configuration. This condition is known as *central blindness.*

Auditory Figure-Ground. Students with auditory figure-ground difficulties may exhibit forced attention to noises or sounds in their environment. They may attend to irrelevant sounds and may not be able to concentrate on the task at hand or to the speech of others. It has been said that "They hear too well." For example, the student may hear the police siren or fire engines long before anyone else does. One student stated that he could not concentrate on what the teacher was saying with the other students sharpening pencils and shuffling their feet. Appropriate seating and a reduced auditory stimulus environment should be considered in setting up a program for these students.

Visual Figure-Ground. Students who cannot distinguish an object from the general irrelevant stimuli in the background and find it difficult to hold an image while scanning the total pattern may have a visual figure-ground disability. Often teachers complain that these students appear to have difficulty completing their work. The learners may lose their place in the book easily or skip sections of a test. The students may not complete material presented on a crowded paper. Therefore, teachers should avoid using books or workbooks that have a lot on a page, with small print and very few "white spaces" in which students may write. Material that is too colorful or distracting should also be avoided.

Auditory Localization and Attention. A child with problems in auditory localization and attention may have difficulty in locating the source and direction of sound. Some teachers sometimes give instructions from behind students. In order to attend, the student with a localization problem must first locate the source of sound. Attention may be affected by excessive auditory or visual stimuli in the environment. Anxiety will also affect attention.

Auditory Closure (Blending). Sometimes a student

may be unable to break a word into syllables or individual sounds and blend them back into a word. An example of this type of problem with synthesis is the inability to form *cat* from *c a t*.

Visual Closure. A student may not be able to retain a visual image of a whole word. If given the word in parts as in a puzzle, he may be unable to put it together again correctly. This disability becomes a problem when teachers attempt to teach blending using letters printed in the center of cards, like this: a n

instead of using letters printed at the edges of the cards, like this: a n

IMAGERY

Imagery involves overall memory whereby learners are required to remember that which they have heard, seen, or felt. It also involves retaining auditory, visual, and tactual stimuli in sequence. Memory entails both long-term and short-term processes. Other aspects of memory that are also a part of language association are auditory language symbol associations and visual language symbol association. The former is the ability to relate a sound to a sound (for example, generalizing the sound of "*m*" in *man* to be the same as the sound of *m* in *map*), and the latter is the ability to integrate sounds to symbols (such as relating the sound *m* to the symbol *m*).

Auditory Imagery (Memory). Some students may have difficulty with the rhyming of word sounds. They may be unable to hear one word and think of another word with the same ending. For example, given the word *mouse,* they cannot respond with a word like *house.* This difficulty may display itself in the inability to associate a letter with its sound, or auditory referent. Watching a student to see if he or she can associate the sound *m* with the symbol *m,* for instance, also may reveal an auditory language association problem. This inability may be evident in bizarre spelling patterns such as writing letters randomly for words or writing just one word for everything (say, *cat* for each word given on a spelling test). Technically, this condition is referred to as an inability to form phoneme-grapheme relationships.

A student may have problems in drawing auditory to visual relationships. One way of testing for this disability is to see if given the sounds tap-tap-tap, the student can draw the right amount of corresponding dots, . . ., or the numeral 3. In this case, it is also important to check auditory language association.

Some students may have difficulty remembering the sounds of letters given orally. They may be unable to remember the sequence of sounds in a word.

Visual Imagery (Memory) or Memory-Sequence. Students may be able to remember the letters of a word, but not the visual sequence, so that a simple word can be misspelled, sometimes several different ways on the same paper. For example, the student may write the word *not* as *ont* or *ton* (*a variable response*), or he or she may spell it *ont* consistently (*a fixed response*). It appears easier to remediate a variable response than a fixed response whereby the student has stabilized an incorrect pattern. Even though students may know a word in one context, when it is presented in a new situation, they think they have never seen it before. Some students exhibit reversals in reading and writing, such as confusing *b* for *d* and *was* for *saw.* Inversions such as *m* for *w* can be observed when *me* and *we* are taught together. When writing, students may either forget to punctuate or make odd punctuation marks. For example, they may write $ for ? or write ⸮ for ?. Sometimes when writing, students may not remember some lower case letters and substitute capital letters in the middle of a word. In all cases of reversals, however, it is a good idea to check visual discrimination as another possible causative factor.

LANGUAGE SYMBOLIZATION

In the area of language, we are concerned with whether or not individuals can apply meaning to words based on their experiences. Are they just word callers? Can they express themselves meaningfully and sequentially? Does a student have a speech impediment, such as an articulation defect or a stuttering pattern?

Receptive Language. Good receptive ability enables students to relate speech and words to meaning; they not only can hear and see words but also can understand them. Students with receptive problems may not be able to relate spoken or written words to the appropriate unit of experience. For example, a student might have difficulty in relating the word *bridge* to the concrete object. Students may be frustrated in conversation and not be able to "decode" input coming in visually and auditorily at a normal rate. The more specific problem areas under language receptivity are the following:

1. *Visual language classification.* Students with difficulty in this area often cannot understand difference and sameness by category classification of objects presented visually. For example, when a

student is shown a picture of a car and asked whether it belongs with a picture of a pen, knife, hat, or truck, he or she cannot discern the correct classification. In this case, it is vehicles or transportation; therefore, car belongs with truck.

2. *Visual language association.* Students with difficulty in this area are unable to understand non-categorical relationships between objects or pictures of objects presented to them visually. For example, when a student is shown a picture of a dog and asked whether it belongs with a picture of a bone, car, hat, or crayon, he or she cannot discern the correct association. In this case, dog is associated with bone.
3. *Visual language symbol association.* Students with difficulties in this area are unable to deal with symbols used in the process of decoding that includes relating letters to words to ideas. They may be able to deal with relationships at the object and picture level, but when ideas or concepts are translated into words they have difficulty.
4. *Auditory language classification.* Students with problems in this area often cannot understand difference and sameness by category classification of objects presented orally. For example, when a student is asked whether a boy belongs with a lamp, dress, man, or door, he or she cannot discern the correct association of boy with man.
5. *Auditory language association.* Students who exhibit difficulty in this area are unable to understand noncategorical relationships between words presented orally. For example, when a student is asked whether an oar belongs with a door, sky, lamp, or boat, he or she cannot discern the correct association of oar with boat.

Expressive Language. Learners should be able to use words that describe, show action, or characterize. But students with expressive disorders cannot do that. Their difficulties may be motor or verbal. In speech, their verbal expressions may be unclear, unintelligible, and nonsequential, involving a great deal of gesturing and pantomiming. Students may have difficulty retrieving words or performing the motor act of speech. In writing, the students may exhibit difficulty in expressing ideas in a logical sequence. Some students have difficulty with writing simple sentences; others cannot summarize by writing the content of material presented to them.

MOTOR LANGUAGE EXPRESSION. Motor language expression includes the following sub-categories:

1. *Manual language expression.* Students with difficulty in manual expression may be unable to discern the function of an object even though, when asked, they may be able to identify it from among other objects. For example, a student may be able to identify a spoon from among other objects but be unable to show you what to do with it manually.
2. *Speech (oral production).* Students may exhibit poor speech patterns. They may have difficulties articulating; omit initial, medial, or final sounds; substitute (*wabbit* for *rabbit*); distort (lisp, sloppy *s*, or hissing); or add sounds to words *(sumber* for *summer).*
3. *Written expression (visual language graphic association).* Students exhibiting a disorder in this area of encoding have problems with writing words to express ideas or concepts. Some cannot write a sentence that indicates a complete thought or write a paragraph on a theme. Others cannot write definitions of words or record in a meaningful sequence an event or real life experience.

VERBAL LANGUAGE EXPRESSION. Students exhibiting a disorder in this area may be able to identify a pencil from among other objects presented visually and may be able to show you what can be done with it, but they are unable to talk about it in a meaningful way or describe its function. They may be unable to retrieve words for speaking. Verbal expression disorders also include syntax and formulation problems, which are characterized by difficulty with the smooth and natural flow of the English language. The students may be unable to structure their thoughts into grammatically correct verbal units or sentences. A contributing factor to poor syntax utilization and to poor listening skills in kindergarten children may be auditory discrimination deficiencies (e.g., discriminating among sounds).[2]

INNER-LANGUAGE. Inner-language is the language with which one thinks. It serves to integrate experiences with a native spoken language. Inner-language can also be thought of as *inner-speech.* Inner-speech, in this sense, relates to thinking; outer, or external, speech provides for communication between people.

Students who read well may not be able to understand the meaning of what they read. They may have difficulty transforming experiences into symbols. If English is their second language, they may think in their native tongue. Difficulty may arise in their trying to take an examination in English while thinking out the problems in Spanish, for example. Inner-language

2. T. P. Marquardt, and J. H. Saxman, "Language Comprehension and Auditory Discrimination in Articulation Deficient Kindergarten Children," *Journal of Speech and Hearing Research* 15 (June 1972): 382–389.

conflict may result from the unwillingness of a student to give up his or her native language or dialect for standard English.

Nonverbal Learning Systems

SOCIAL PERCEPTION

Some students have difficulty in gleaning meaning from gestures and expressions or from what others think are easily discernible cause-effect relationships. They are unable to understand the significance of the behavior of others and, in some cases, appear to be emotionally disturbed or exhibit strange behavior patterns.

IMAGERY

Imagery in this sense refers to an ability to recall places or events that do not involve symbols, such as how something looks or sounds as part of an experience. Students with difficulty in this area may not be able to describe their visit to the circus or the way their room looks.

SYMBOLIZATION

Nonverbal symbolic language refers to deriving meaning from symbols or symbolic representations other than words. Students with difficulty in this area have problems assigning meaning to such nonverbal, abstract subjects as art, religion, music, holidays, or patriotism. There is a language of art and music from which the individual cannot derive meaning. It appears that this disorder is sometimes accompanied by problems in the spatial area, such as having difficulty in understanding measurement and exhibiting a poor sense of direction.

SPECIFIC NONVERBAL FUNCTIONS

Nonverbal aspects of learning that have been recognized as important to verbal learning are *body image, spatial-temporal orientation, laterality,* and *directionality (left-right orientation).* Spatial readiness has been considered by many to be one of the prerequisites for many of the academic functions that are called reading, writing, and arithmetic. A good body image enables the students to relate themselves to their environment. Adequate *spatial-temporal* orientation appears to be important to arithmetical operations and in learning to tell time.

Body Image. Learners with poor body image often indicate this in their human figure drawings. They tend to draw distorted or asymmetrical figures, for example, feet coming out of the head or facial features in the wrong places. This may be due to the students' unfamiliarity with the locations of different parts of the body. The students may not be able to organize themselves physically for a task and may exhibit concomitant difficulties with spatial concepts.

Spatial-Temporal Orientation. The student with spatial-temporal difficulties may not understand such concepts as *before, after, left,* and *right* or even simple words such as *in* and *out.* Sometimes reversals of letters and numerals are evident, along with difficulties in doing arithmetical operations beyond rote memory. Students may exhibit poor alignment of numerals and inadequate spacing in writing. Watch for the student whose number alignment is erratic on such activities as numbering for a spelling test. Students may have difficulty in understanding measurements, maps, and graphs; they may have a poor sense of direction. Learning how to tell time is often a problem for learners with spatial-temporal difficulties.

Laterality and Directionality. Laterality, or sidedness, that is not established, may be evident in students who cannot relate themselves physically to an object in space. They may not be able to tell how far or how near something is in relation to themselves. Directionality also pertains to making spatial judgments about object-to-object relationships in space. Directionality problems are manifested by poor left-right orientation.

MOTOR

Teachers have become more aware recently of the importance of gross motor and fine motor efficiency for handwriting as well as for many other motor activities that are required in school. It is also apparent that the clumsy or awkward children often become socially unacceptable to their parents, their teachers, and their peers.

Gross Motor. The students may exhibit poor coordination, clumsiness, and general difficulty with large-muscle activities required in sports.

1. *Balance and coordination.* Students with balance and coordination problems have difficulty in using both sides of the body simultaneously, individually, or alternately. Poor coordination may affect self-concept, as well as inhibiting participation in motor activities.
2. *Body rhythm.* Students with body-rhythm difficulty may not be able to perform body rhythms to music or use band instruments effectively. They may have a dysrhythmic walk, which often accompanies coordination difficulties.

Fine Motor (Eye-Hand Coordination). The student may not be able to coordinate eye and hand movements to achieve a specific task. Handwriting, as well as other activities that involve fine movement (e.g., sorting, buttoning, doing puzzles, sewing), may be poor.

Fine Motor (Finger Strength). The student may lack the finger strength required to grasp a pencil or to hold an object. However, this may be maturational in young children.

CONCEPTUALIZATION

Conceptualization involves how a student thinks and uses good judgment. It is dependent upon the integrity of all the previously mentioned levels of learning, such as sensation, perception, and memory. The teacher must determine at what conceptual level the student is basically functioning. Examples of different levels of responses based on concept development are as follows:

Concrete-Level Response. An apple and an orange are both round.
Functional-Level Response. An apple and an orange can both be eaten.
Abstract-Level Response. An apple and an orange are both fruit.

By determining the primary response level of the learner, the teacher will be able to select material that is appropriate to the concept level of that student. The teacher may need to build classification-type activities into the curriculum so that learners can be taught to see relationships through the understanding of the concepts *difference* and *sameness.* It is important that students be asked to explain verbally how things are different or the same. It is through verbal expression that the teacher can determine how the learner thinks. The teacher can then relate that information to the concept level of the material that is to be learned. The developmental process in learning is speech (oral production), or verbal efficiency, then reading and writing. Writing is a higher-level language function.

Conceptualization is further delineated in other sections on language development (i.e., overloading, page 7; integrated learning, page 190; and auditory and visual language classification and association, pages 162–166 and 173–178).

MOTIVATIONAL, EMOTIONAL, AND CONTROL FACTORS

Success in school requires that students attain the basic skills of reading, writing, and arithmetic. Failure in acquiring these skills will, in most instances, result in learners who are unhappy about their inability to learn and who are unable to function usefully within a progressive adult society. The atypical or inefficient learner in our society is treated by many as a social outcast.

Teachers must understand that a failure to learn could be due to a combination of processing deficits and could also be accompanied by an unwillingness to learn. The will to learn is essential for success in any of the process areas previously mentioned. Another factor affecting learning is the emotions. A child with a learning problem who appears to be well adjusted may nevertheless have an emotional problem. Learning requires that many processes function in concert with each other. Educators, of necessity, must concern themselves with the effect of one system on all of the others.

Other factors that affect learning are associated with the students' inability to cope with school as it is presently set up. Learners may be easily distracted by stimuli that may be excessive for them. Students who are unable to use their "stop-and-go mechanism," or controls, efficiently may display perseverative behavior. Some students are carried away by their own thoughts and give inappropriate responses to questions. This is sometimes called disinhibited behavior. Others are hyperactive because of organic disorders or through learning in high stimulus environments. Frustration wlth teachers or the inability to cope with the way the task is presented often results in aggression. Students who are over-stimulated find it difficult to attend to the task or even retain what has been taught. Students who spend most of their time inhibiting their own behavior because of pressures of one kind or another sometimes have little energy left for learning. There are other children, however, who do not receive enough stimulation. These understimulated children need an environment that will challenge their abilities.

The following is a general classification of areas of social-emotional development that will be delineated and discussed in depth in Chapter 10.

Aggressive (acting out/passive)
Sensitive-withdrawn
Immature-dependent
Psychotic-neurotic
Delinquent-unorthodox
Social perception disorders
Control factors (distractibility, hyperactivity, perseveration, disinhibition, impulsivity)

MANN SELF-ASSESSMENT COMPETENCY INVENTORY

The Mann Self-Assessment Competency Inventory (Appendix) comprises a series of statements concerning needs perceived by the individual who is responding. The Inventory is included in this book because the authors feel that teachers need a vehicle by which they can determine their needs in different areas of diagnostic-prescriptive teaching when working with all the students within their area of responsibility, including students who exhibit a slower rate of development, learning problems, sensory impairments, behavior problems, physical disabilities, or any combinations of these and students who are gifted or talented.

The Mann Self-Assessment Competency Inventory was developed over a three-year period and represents input from approximately 200 teachers and administrators. The statements contained within were developed in the following manner. Approximately 800 statements concerning teacher skills or competencies were collected from teachers and administrators. These statements were categorized into the following general subareas: Diagnosis-Student Assessment (D-SA); Curriculum-Instruction (C-I); Educational Management (EM); Behavior Management (BM); and Special Education: School and Community (SE). Further refinement resulted in the sixty statements that make up the present Inventory.

Suggestions for Utilization

The Inventory can be used as

1. an assessment of self-perceived needs in each of the subareas (i.e., diagnosis-student assessment, curriculum-instruction; educational management, behavior management, special education: school and community)
2. a pre-post comparison of self-perceived needs that can be used for developing and evaluating courses, workshops, or institutes in the particular subareas of concern
3. a means of delineating the subareas for use in sections for particular areas of study
4. an aid in the development of objectives for a course, workshop, or institute
5. a way to organize the myriad of concerns and needs in the area of diagnostic-prescriptive teaching
6. an estimate of needs in planning activities for school staff development

Administering Mann Self-Assessment Competency Inventory

Respond to each of the statements in the inventory in the following manner:

1. For Part 1 (pages 331–334) circle the appropriate number.
2. For Part 2 (pages 335–336) rank the items within each subarea from 1 (the highest priority of personal need) to 10 (the lowest priority of personal need) as perceived by the individual taking the inventory.

Transfer the values for the 60 statements in Part 1 to the Summary Sheet (page 337), under the headings *a* and *b*. Then add the *a* and *b* figures together and write the totals under the heading *a* + *b*, which represents the combined value of responses to a particular need from different points of view.

1. All the *a* statements express a need for gaining information and knowledge.
2. All the *b* statements express a need for experiences and activity involving measurable performance.
3. Combined, *a* + *b* give a broader statement of need in terms of both knowledge and performance.

Part 2 is a suggested delineation of each of the subareas. This part can be used as written or modified as necessary to include other areas of concern. After the items are ranked by the respondents, they can be compared to the needs expressed in Part 1.

It is important to note that the inventory is not a test but merely a vehicle for precisely examining areas that may need further study and elaboration. The items for each of the subareas can be analyzed and interpreted accordingly.

The chapters that follow are designed to elaborate upon the concepts presented within the theoretical framework for diagnosis and prescriptive teaching purposes. Subjects will include developmental inventories, screening tests, a hierarchy of skills in specific areas of learning, and additional suggestions for both formal and informal evaluation. The assessment information, along with an array of educational strategies in the language arts area, arithmetic, science, and social studies, should give the classroom teacher and other professionals a basic fund of educational techniques necessary for meeting the needs of students who manifest a variety of learning problems.

Chapter 2 Introduction to Diagnosis

Diagnosis is viewed as a process of decoding learners to determine their individual learning and behavior characteristics for purposes of developing individualized prescriptive educational programs. In designing a diagnostic-prescriptive educational program, it is important to view learners within a dynamic environment. What are the forces that impinge upon them? What do they bring to learning situations? There is a tendency for parents and teachers to focus on the students' weaknesses, disregarding their strengths. Teachers sometimes forget that the students are more than a conglomerate of problems; they are human beings who have potential to develop and learn within an accommodating environment. The entire diagnostic process should focus more on what students can do rather than on what they cannot do. Two considerations need attention:

1. Why did the student perform as he or she did?
2. What did the student do to arrive at the observed response even though the response itself may have been incorrect?

Recent analysis of assessment practices suggests that it is no longer valid for those who evaluate students to record their performance in any form that denotes their capacity, placing limits on potential for achievement and on programming. It is more appropriate to interpret performance as a vehicle for determining aptitude. The student should be viewed as having various degrees of aptitude for acquiring certain knowledges and skills in prescribed programs.

If students' behavior can be interpreted in terms of aptitude, then teachers must assume responsibility for successful student experiences, developing programs that will accommodate to the students' learning styles. One of the responsibilities of educators is the modification of all existing programs, general education and special education, so that a better accommodation can be made to students who are failing in programs based on traditional approaches. This change would encompass a movement away from grouping according to the traditional norm-referenced interpretation of tests and concomitant labeling of students to more criterion-referenced evaluation and interpretation for individualized educational programming.

All of those involved with a particular student's education—from educators to paraprofessionals to supportive personnel—should help to evaluate the student's strengths and weaknesses. The regular classroom teacher or paraprofessional has the greatest potential for initial observation and ongoing evaluation in the classroom. As part of their daily routine, teachers can utilize observational techniques, including checklists, analyze achievement tests for criterion-referenced data, administer group and individual assessment inventories (e.g., reading, writing, spelling, and arithmetic), and use specialized screening devices, all of which are outlined in this volume. Even though many teachers in classrooms with high pupil-teacher ratios express concern about finding the time to participate in the evaluation process, it can be done. Administrators must plan with the teachers for the use of supportive personnel (counselor, special educator, parent volunteer, nurse, psychologist, social worker, librarian, member of the physical education staff, speech therapist, etc.) during the critical time when the teachers need help in the individual screening of students. After the initial screening, the specialists should evaluate only those students for whom additional information is necessary. If teachers have the relevant diagnostic skills and the ability to communicate information to ancillary personnel, they will make fewer inappropriate referrals, and they will not avoid responsibility when a student isn't learning and the pressure mounts for a solution to the problem. After a teacher has learned to use a framework to identify the strengths and weaknesses in students' learning processes, specific programs can be developed for initial teaching and amelioration.

Identification of students with learning and behavior problems is an ongoing process. The teacher must be able to identify potential failures early. This is true for younger children in initial learning situations as well as for students who have been accustomed to failure and have "plateaued" for an extended period of time. Initially, the teacher must be consciously aware of what is appropriate and what is inappropriate behavior, using as a basis the nature of the population of the particular class or school. For most educators this awareness will be a natural outcome of teaching and learning about the students in the process.

Inadequate learning and poor performance soon become associated with the *disesteemed* student (disesteemed in the sense that teachers, peers, and parents perceive the student in a negative manner). It is apparent that some learners just do not fit into groupings as they are presently constituted within classrooms in our public schools. It may well be that the behavior difficulties of particular students prevent them from learning and call excessive attention to them. This situation can be detrimental not only to the problem students but to the whole class. By screening, teachers can begin to identify, and attend to, particular learning and behavior characteristics of specific students. The general educator who may not wish to be burdened with screening an entire class may elect to screen just those stuents who have, as a part of the ongoing process of learning, indicated an apparent learning or behavior difficulty.

PLANNING DIAGNOSTIC PROCEDURES

Most effective planning for diagnostic procedures is accomplished as early in the school year as possible, preferably during the preplanning days. If at all possible, initial planning should begin in the spring for the fall of the next school year. Planning should be a total school process in which educators, by sharing information with each other about students and by writing cogent information into records, prepare for appropriate educational strategies, especially for *high-risk* students.

Planning an evaluation system can be simple or very complex and time-consuming, depending on the orientation of the staff and the resources available. Using a basic evaluation system, the classroom teacher may just be concerned about the educational needs of the students assigned to a particular class for a particular year. A total-school approach to planning diagnostic procedures may be based on the desire to identify all high-risk students in all classrooms in order to make early and appropriate decisions about how to utilize the myriad of services available within the school to meet particular students' individual needs. This type of planning involves a sharing of responsibility, or team approach, to maximize the development of a comprehensive, or full-service, program for each student. Students with learning and behavior difficulties will particularly benefit from this orientation. The full-service model by definition involves more than one person in the process of diagnosis and program planning. Those involved could include administrators, support staff such as resource people, psychologists, teachers, paraprofessionals, and parents. Together, they decide where, how, and by whom a student can best be served within existing alternative environments. A teacher should be able to say, "I've had it!" There should be an emotional climate in the school that will permit a teacher to admit failure and ask for help. The following questions should be considered before establishing procedures for referring students to special education or other programs outside the regular classroom or for changing the placement of a student.

1. How can high-risk students at any grade level who need additional or expanded services be identified according to a prearranged schedule? What alternatives have been designed other than the end-of-the-year-failure meeting?
2. Who will participate in the process of identification, screening, diagnosis, programming, and follow-up for these students?
3. How will due-process procedures be followed in applicable cases?
4. How will the parents or guardians be involved initially, and to what extent will they be consulted in accordance with a prescribed schedule?
5. Have the instructors evaluated their own motives as objectively as possible?
6. How will it be determined that individuals respon-

sible for setting up and maintaining a program for a particular student, which includes all the procedural concomitants, are competent and willing to accept this responsibility? In cases where weaknesses are determined, are staff development opportunities available on an ongoing basis so that individuals can become competent to deal with the different learning styles of their students?

7. Will attention to particular needs of students go beyond a good diagnostic program and in fact deal with effective curriculum programming and educational management?
8. Will the emphasis in the entire process be directed toward serving students in as "normal" an environment as possible or will the orientation be to design programs that will set students apart because of learning and behavior difficulties? Will the appropriate ancillary personnel give input about the student's problem before the student is referred to special education?
9. When will a student find out that a problem exists? Will students understand what is happening to them and, in fact, become part of the whole process of determining their educational program? Will they be protected by confidentiality of data or information related to them?
10. How will it be determined whether the program that has been designed for a particular student is in fact being carried out in an individualized manner and not just a report that has been put together to satisfy the requirement that a written prescription must be prepared?

These questions should be answered during open discussions between all those involved in planning, diagnosis, and programming for particular students.

SCREENING

A system of screening can be established in any learning situation and for any grade level. Screening, to be worthwhile, should provide a basis for initial teaching strategies and for further evaluation, not for labeling students. Accomplished as a part of everyday school activities, screening can provide the teacher with important input needed for total educational programming. Screening for potential school failures will provide initial information on all students, not only those exhibiting obvious learning and behavior difficulties. It will identify the "disesteemed" students who are not easily categorized but are nevertheless failing in school. These are the students who "fall into the cracks" and are not receiving any special services. Students who are already receiving supportive services are often fragmented to the extent that no one wants to assume full responsibility for them. They need appropriate screening so that better decisions can be made about how to coordinate the different programs provided for them.

Screening procedures should include the following:

1. All records of students, especially those of students who are exhibiting school failure, should be reviewed in the spring of the year by the teachers who will be getting the students in the fall of the next year. Special attention should be given to how the students were taught and what kinds of materials were used in the process, as well as to the vocabulary used to describe their behavior. Differentiation should be made between "name calling" and factual, important, relevant data about the quality and the level of the learner's performance.
2. In cases where screening is a formalized, individualized process, the parents should be made aware of what is taking place. They should be given a brief explanation of the rationale behind screening, and they should be told who will do the screening, how the screening will be used as a basis for future decisions, and how the parents will be involved. Parents can play an important role in screening by volunteering to be aides so that the teacher will have time to work more specifically with individual students.
3. Screening as a part of ongoing classroom activities can easily be done through the use of the observational checklists and screening devices found in this book. Although the checklists and screening devices are suggested for use primarily with younger students, they can also be used for older learners. Older students showing discrepancies in the areas indicated on the checklists and screening should receive further evaluation. Failure of older students in these areas tells us that the students cannot even perform the specific tasks at the level that is expected for younger learners.

A checklist is a good method of insuring that observation will encompass a broad range of behaviors. It should be used to identify strengths and weaknesses in different areas of development. Initial screening provides a backup system for the teacher, who can make comparisons between what is observed in the classroom and what is indicated through more formalized evaluation. In this way the teacher can accept or reject data, depending on whether they correlate or do not correlate with observed behavior. This enables the teacher to "buy in" to the evaluation process as an active participant in diagnostic team discussions or staffing for specific students.

Interpretation of data should consider local community norms as well as national standardized norms. Instrumentation used should assess strengths (abilities) as well as weaknesses (disabilities). Both of these areas should be reported and elaborated upon in terms of how the students' cognitive styles will accommodate to different educational tests. Individuals responsible for formal testing must provide a basic interpretation of the results to the parents or guardians in their native language whenever possible, indicating how this information will be used to benefit the student.

EXPANDED EVALUATION

Previous to, or simultaneous with, screening, the teacher should check the student's history. This can be accomplished by interviewing parents, interviewing the student, speaking to previous teachers, and checking the records. The teacher should be aware of the following:

1. Has the student been excessively absent?
2. Has the student been moved a great deal?
3. What have others (teachers, peers, administrators, other school workers, etc.) said about the student? What kind of words have been used to describe the student? Nebulous constructs such as *immature, lazy,* and *unmotivated* have little diagnostic value.
4. Who were the teachers who were successful with the student, and what did they do to provide for successful experiences?
5. How was the student initially taught, and what were the results? Has the student been continually taught in essentially the same manner, using the same basic approach in reading, for example?
6. Has the student ever had any serious emotional upheaval or traumatic experience? Has the student had any serious physical injury or disease? When was the last time vision or hearing was checked? Sometimes simple sensory problems have a lot to do with success in learning.
7. What kind of testing was done with the student, who did it, and what did they say? What action was taken as a result of past assessment, and was the action effective in promoting learning and good adjustment?

After screening using checklists or other observational techniques, the teacher can plot preliminary information on Analysis of Errors Worksheets (see Forms 6-1–6-4, pages 145–151).

The teacher should have access to the raw data from recent achievement testing for the student concerned. The observer or evaluator should be able to answer the following questions:

1. How much did the student accomplish in each subarea of the test before time was called? Was the student successful as far as he or she went? This information is important to determine whether the student is a "slow worker." Observing students taking a test is important because it tells us not only what they do but also how they do it. If possible, a student should be permitted to complete an alternate form of the test, an untimed test, or another timed test without timing, in order to get a more accurate level of performance.
2. Did the student just put down written responses without any rationale for what he or she did?
3. Did the student understand the directions and was he or she able to cope with the number of directions?
4. Were there any circumstances vitiating the student's performance, such as physical illness, excessive anxiety, general emotional lability, or poor motivation?

FORMAL TESTING

After screening, some students may require more formal testing. There is no one best way to test the learning and behavior characteristics of learners. Techniques presently in vogue are individual to particular programs or persons, and the extent, breadth, and depth of evaluation depends as well upon the time and resources available to the person doing the evaluation. To some degree, the underlying philosophy of the program can influence the instrumentation used in formal assessment. Someone once said, "If all you have is a hammer, the whole world looks like a nail." One must ask oneself, "What am I looking for?" Generally, however, there are situations, characteristics, and procedures that are common to most formal testing. Some of the requisites are as follows:

1. Tests should be appropriate to the student population in terms of age, sociocultural background, native language, experiences, and specific problem areas of concern.
2. The evaluators must determine whether or not they are in fact assessing the skills that are critical to success in the academic areas under concern. What are we measuring?
3. The individuals responsible for formal assessment must clearly understand why they are doing what

they are doing, and they must have previously indicated competency in using diagnostic instruments in real situations. Testing for labeling is not quite the same as testing for curriculum programming.
4. Whenever possible, students should be tested in their primary language.
5. The tester must provide an interpretation of the data, and even training in understanding this interpretation, for the teachers who will be translating the data into information that is useful for academic programming.

Note: A comprehensive list of formal tests is found in Chapter 6.

ROLE OF PARENTS IN DIAGNOSIS

Parents of potential school failures can play a role in diagnosis by providing the teacher with information about the student's life at home. This information will enable the teacher to verify or negate different aspects of the student's behavior in school. Educators must ask the right questions of parents. The following will provide important information.

1. How did the student's early development compare to that of other children in the family?
2. How does a specific student's rate of development compare with that of other children in the neighborhood or school? Some parents feel that their children are "late bloomers," or slow to mature. Parents often say, "My other children had similar problems, but they outgrew them."
3. Were there any early signs of delayed or inadequate development such as speech, language, or motor development? Did the child exhibit any early inappropriate behavior before coming to school? What did the parents do about any special problems or disorders in the child's life?
4. How do the parents discipline the child? This is especially important, since some parents resort to excessive physical punishment in order to modify behavior.
5. Do the parents view the learner as different from other children? How?
6. What kind of stimulation is provided the child at home? Is the student left alone for long periods of time? Who is with the child at home, and what kind of language interaction does he or she receive from adults and peers?
7. Viewed as a total environment, is the home a more negative or more positive force in the child's life?
8. How do the parents feel about the school and what the school's trying to do for their child? Is there an adversary relationship between the home and the school?

Note: A more comprehensive discussion of parental involvement in the educational process will be found in Chapter 11.

CONTINUOUS-PROGRESS EVALUATION

Continuous-progress evaluation is more than what goes on paper to substantiate gains in academics, because school is more than academics to students. It is where they spend a good part of their daily life. Continuous progress for each learner is based on his or her rate of learning. The teacher can generalize some realistic expectations based on the student's previous learning behavior within specific parameters (e.g., language arts, arithmetic, and subject level areas). Continuous progress from week to week can be assessed by observing relative changes in an obvious behavior such as school attendance, time on-task, ability to work in groups or independently in particular subject areas, or attitude toward peers, teachers, etc.

After establishing a rate of learning for subject level areas (for example, the number of new sight words learned over a two-week period or the number of words the student learns to define over two weeks or the number of stories the student reads over two weeks or the number of new math concepts learned over two weeks) the teacher can establish a baseline of learning in the most cogent academic areas. It is relatively easy then to make comparisons based on projected objectives for success. The section on overloading, page 7, covers this in more detail. The section on handwriting evaluation (pages 35, 223, and 227–228) will show how to get baseline data for continuous comparison for that area. The following are additional considerations in the area of continuous-progress evaluation:

1. Evaluation should be done when it needs to be done and not just to serve particular deadlines (e.g., reporting periods, promotion schedules, pre-post yearly evaluation).
2. The perceptive teacher is constantly evaluating, accepting, and rejecting and at the same time reprogramming in keeping with the student's needs at a particular time.
3. The teacher who is really into a continuous progress mode can differientate when a student is

taking a day off to daydream from when he or she is frustrated by the work or is emotionally upset for some reason. The perceptive teacher knows when to be there ahead of time and how to get the student back into academic activity.

4. Good observation must become a habit. Teachers who are not looking and listening all the time sometimes don't observe at all. In those situations, the "well-behaved" student with learning problems loses out and may be ignored until serious learning problems are observed in more formal testing.
5. One-time testing often gives spurious results, but continuous evaluation allows a teacher to look at students at different times in different ways while they are doing similar or the same activities.
6. By keeping an anecdotal record, or log, either daily or weekly for students exhibiting problems, the instructor can constantly document students' performances.
7. All testing doesn't have to be formal. Teachers must be organized and ready to test on the run. When an auspicious time occurs, they can have checklists, screening devices, and diagnostic materials ready for quick but informative sessions with individual students or small groups.
8. Teachers should encourage and train other people to observe for them as a part of the continuous evaluation of students. Paraprofessionals, volunteers, tutors, and the students themselves can be taught methods of charting progress.
9. The teacher can ask the students to evaluate their feelings about their progress in academics, their social adjustment, or their goals. A discrepancy between the teacher's evaluation and the student's evaluation should be constantly reevaluated and resolved.
10. One problem for a team of teachers involved in tracking the continuous progress of a student is finding time during the school day to get together to share records, classwork, testing, etc., and to discuss the student's progress. Early in the year, the school staff should establish a formal procedure by which volunteers, aides, or others can be used to free the teachers for urgent consultations. For less urgent cases, the teachers may have to share information by merely exchanging folders, clipboards, or summary sheets of progress. Management techniques, including a system of charting, may have to be devised to cope with the paperwork.

Note: Further discussion of the management of continuous evaluation and examples will be found in Chapter 11.

Chapter 3 Developmental Screening

This chapter discusses a developmental checklist, and a series of developmental screening devices in the learning process areas.

MANN-SUITER-McCLUNG DEVELOPMENTAL CHECKLIST

The Mann-Suiter-McClung Developmental Checklist (Form 3-1, pages 25–31) is a screening device that can be used to determine the presence or absence of prerequisite critical skills for task level learning in students. The checklist can be used in a variety of settings by anyone involved in the diagnostic-prescriptive process. Trained paraprofessionals, aides, parents, or volunteers can give the checklist. It can be used as a checklist only or as an ongoing evaluation of the student's progress. For ongoing evaluation, the examiner records the date on the list when it appears that the student has mastered or shown improvement in a task. Directions and items can be modified for a school in accordance with local norms or language. For example, for number 12, in the auditory section, examiners could prepare a tape of "Sounds of Things: Animal, Home, or Nature" for all of the classes at a particular grade level.

Suggestions for Observation Using the Checklist

It should be noted that items checked yes indicate difficulties in an area. Items checked no indicate no problem for the particular item. For younger children use good judgment. Only check items yes for them if the behavior appears to be excessive for their age group (speech is a good example).

Suggestions for using the checklist for one student or a group of students include the following.

1. Administer one section of the checklist at a time. During a segment of time (e.g., several days or a week), observe the particular students and check only *one* area, such as auditory. Place one or more copies of the auditory section on a clipboard and carry it from place to place. Also attach a list of all of the names of the students in a class or group. As you check a particular area for a few students, generally notice the behavior of all of the students. Star the names of those that may need more in-depth observation. Add additional sections as needed.
2. Observe one student or a few students and complete an entire checklist.
3. Have other people aid in checking selected items. The following support personnel, in addition to volunteers, parents, tutors, and aides, may assist in parts of the checklist:

   a. Auditory—speech and language teachers, music teachers, nurse
   b. Visual—nurse
   c. Motor—physical education teacher
   d. Speech—speech teacher
   e. Language—speech teacher, reading teacher
   f. Control Factors and Social-Emotional—counselors, psychologists

4. Counselors or social workers who make home visits can use selected items on the checklist when questioning the parents or guardians.
5. Use the checklist during parent-teacher conferences to gain input from the parent. Perhaps parts of the checklist can be sent home prior to the conference. The checklist will provide indications of both strengths and weaknesses that should be discussed. As an interpreter of data to parents, consider the language used in describing learning problems.
6. Use the checklist before a group discussion or school staff meeting concerning a student with learning or behavior problems. The specific items of a checklist will provide those discussing a student's problems with professional and accurate information to begin to seek a solution.
7. A checklist may give insight into areas of the curriculum that are being neglected. By quickly perusing the checklist, you may find areas where either diagnostic or curriculum materials are needed.
8. Many teachers direct interns or student teachers for their clinical or classroom teaching experiences. A checklist provides the beginning teacher with parameters of what to look for in students. This information will aid the student teacher in documenting observational experiences.
9. Use the checklist to discuss strengths and weaknesses with the student. It may not be necessary to actually show the student the checklist, but it will help you to remember to enumerate what the student *can* do. The self-concept of the student is especially important if he or she perceives that people are looking at areas that may be very sensitive and personal.
10. Use the checklist as a guide to additional screening and more formal testing. Time is a critical concern for most classroom teachers. Careful observation should help the teacher focus in on the critical next areas to be evaluated.
11. Under *Other,* list items that are specific to a particular classroom.

Performance Implications

1. Look for clusters of behavior within an area. This will provide a basis for additional screening of certain areas.
2. Focus on what is relevant. Some students may exhibit an overall immaturity, lack of readiness, or slower-than-normal rate of development. By being aware of certain critical areas it will be easier to provide an individualized educational program for the learner.
3. Match the checked items on the checklist to achievement testing and look for consistent or inconsistent patterns.
4. Wherever multiple causations are listed in parentheses after an item and you have doubts about what an item may mean, refer to Chapter 1 or the glossary for an explanation of the terms. The use of these terms by the authors is based on judgment and experience. The terms are to be used as a point of reference and a point of departure. What do we see and where do we go next? The descriptors are used merely to aid the observer in the decoding of a student and to provide a framework of language to communicate observations to others participating in the diagnostic-prescriptive process.
5. Notice that three sections of the Mann-Suiter-McClung Checklist (Auditory, Visual, and Motor) are divided into two levels: *Beginning Age 4* and *For Ages 6 and Over.*

Note: Prescriptive activities for the areas listed on the checklist may be found on the following pages:

Auditory	157–166
Visual	166–178
Motor	178–185
Speech	185–186
Language	185–189; 231–238
Control Factors	280–284
Social-Emotional	272–280

Form 3-1

MANN-SUITER-McCLUNG DEVELOPMENTAL CHECKLIST

EXAMINER ______________________________ DATE ______________

NAME ______________________________ ADDRESS ______________________

DATE OF BIRTH ______________________ SEX ________ RACE ________ PHONE ________

SCHOOL ______________________ TEACHER ______________________ GRADE ______

NUMBER IN FAMILY ____________ POSITION IN FAMILY ____________ GLASSES __ HEARING AID __

BILINGUAL ____ NATIVE LANGUAGE ______________________ NURSERY ______________

PERTINENT FACTS KNOWN IN PRE-SCHOOL HISTORY ______________________________

____

____

Auditory (Sensory, Perception, Memory)

BEGINNING AGE 4

	YES	NO
1. The child turns or cups one ear to the speaker. (hearing)	___	___
2. The child fails to answer to his or her name from behind. (hearing)	___	___
3. The child's voice is excessively loud.	___	___
(hearing) excessively soft.	___	___
monotone.	___	___
4. The child consistently asks to have words or directions repeated. (hearing)	___	___
5. The child fails to tell the difference between human and nonhuman sounds. (discrimination)	___	___
6. The child fails to tell when sounds are the same or different. (discrimination)	___	___
7. The child is unable to pay attention to speech or other activities when there is noise in the room or in the background. (figure-ground)	___	___
8. The child is unable to locate the source or direction of sound. (localization)	___	___
9. The child has difficulty repeating a clapped sequence (e.g., clap-clap—clap-clap). (memory-sequence)	___	___
10. The child fails to follow three directions. (memory-sequence)	___	___
11. The child fails to follow the rhythm in band playing activities. (memory-sequence)	___	___
12. The child fails to remember the sounds presented of two or more things: animal, home, school, street, nature. (memory)	___	___
13. The child fails to transfer sounds, for example, understanding that the sound *m* in the word *man* is the same as the sound *m* in the word *mop.* (auditory-auditory association)	___	___
14. The child is unable to identify most of the letter sounds. (visual-auditory associative memory)	___	___
15. The child is unable to identify most of the letter names. (visual-auditory associative memory)	___	___
16. Other ______________________________		
______________________________	___	___

FOR AGES 6 AND OVER, DO 1–16 AND ADD: YES NO

17. The student is unable to identify rhyming words. (discrimination) ___ ___
18. The student is unable to distinguish between similar sounding letters (*d/t, p/b*). (hearing/discrimination) ___ ___
19. The student is unable to identify same or different word endings. (hearing/discrimination) ___ ___
20. The student is unable to identify same or different medial sounds. (hearing/discrimination) ___ ___
21. The student fails to blend letter sounds into words (e.g., *c—a—t*). (closure/blending) ___ ___
22. The student fails to blend syllables into words (e.g., *ba—by*). (closure/blending) ___ ___
23. The student is unable to follow directions given orally in testing situations. (memory) ___ ___
24. The student fails to follow four or more directions in a sequence. (memory-sequence) ___ ___
25. The student fails to repeat a sequence of 5 digits presented orally. (memory-sequence) ___ ___
26. The student fails to state the days of the week and months of the year in sequence. (memory-sequence) ___ ___
27. The student fails to repeat complex word sentences in the correct sequence. (memory-sequence) ___ ___
28. Other ____ ___ ___

Visual (Sensory, Perception, Memory)

BEGINNING AGE 4

29. Squinting, redness, or watering of the eyes is present. (ocular-motor) ___ ___
30. The child's eyes appear to be crossed. (ocular-motor) ___ ___
31. The child works close to the paper or desk. (acuity/ocular-motor) ___ ___
32. The child is unable to use left-to-right eye movements. (ocular-motor) ___ ___
33. The child is unable to tell when objects are different or the same. (discrimination) ___ ___
34. The child is unable to match shapes or forms. (discrimination) ___ ___
35. The child is unable to do simple puzzles. (discrimination/closure) ___ ___
36. The child is unable to sort objects by color, size, and shape. (discrimination/motor or color vision disorder) ___ ___
37. The child is unable to match letters, numerals, and simple words. (discrimination) ___ ___
38. The child fails to find objects or pictures of objects hidden amongst an irrelevent background. (figure-ground) ___ ___
39. The child has difficulty in completing work presented on a crowded page. (figure-ground) ___ ___
40. The child is unable to identify missing parts in pictures of familiar objects. (closure) ___ ___
41. The child is unable to describe from memory the characteristics of pictures of objects that are shown and then removed. (memory) ___ ___
42. The child is unable to reproduce a simple bead pattern from memory. (memory-sequence) ___ ___
43. The child is unable to imitate three visual acts in a sequence (e.g., open the door, sharpen the pencil, and sit down). (memory-sequence) ___ ___
44. Other ____ ___ ___

FOR AGES 6 AND OVER, DO 29–44 AND ADD:

45. The student is unable to complete a form board with similar geometric forms such as a square, rectangle, circle, oval, triangle, and diamond. (discrimination) ___ ___
46. The student fails to match more complex geometric designs and words. (discrimination) ___ ___

	YES	NO
47. The student fails to keep his or her place on a page when reading material at the independent level. (figure-ground)	___	___
48. The student is unable to visually separate the foreground from the background and locate letters, numerals, or words embedded in figures, designs, or color. (figure-ground)	___	___
49. The student is unable to put letters together to make words within his or her reading vocabulary. (closure/blending)	___	___
50. The student is unable to copy from the chalkboard without excessive eye movements going from the chalkboard to the paper. (memory-vision)	___	___
51. The student fails to draw objects or geometric designs from recall. (memory)	___	___
52. The student is unable to recall five objects, letters, or numerals presented visually and then removed. (memory/memory-sequence)	___	___
53. The student is unable to reproduce complex bead patterns from memory. (memory-sequence)	___	___
54. The learner is unable to select from two or more choices the correct spelling of words that are within his or her independent reading vocabulary. (memory/memory sequence)	___	___
55. Other ______________________________	___	___

Motor (Gross, Fine, Body Image, Laterality, Spatial-Temporal)

BEGINNING AGE 4

56. The child fails to do the following: (gross motor) run ________ jump ________ hop ________ skip ________	___	___
57. The child is unable to throw a ball. (gross motor)	___	___
58. The child fails to swing his or her arms when walking or running. (gross motor)	___	___
59. The child is accident prone. (balance/coordination)	___	___
60. The child falls often. (balance/coordination)	___	___
61. The child is unable to climb a ladder. (balance/coordination)	___	___
62. The child excessively drops things (e.g., pencil, eraser). (fine motor)	___	___
63. The child is unable to pour from one container to another without spilling. (fine motor/spatial)	___	___
64. The child is unable to string beads. (fine motor/visual)	___	___
65. The child is unable to hold a pencil or crayon properly. (fine motor)	___	___
66. The child fails to color within boundaries. (fine motor)	___	___
67. The child fails to cut on the line. (fine motor)	___	___
68. The child fails to tie shoes and button buttons, etc. (fine motor)	___	___
69. The child fails to use one hand consistently. (handedness)	___	___
70. The child is unable to copy a circle. (fine motor/visual)	___	___
71. The child is unable to copy a square. (fine motor/visual)	___	___
72. The child is unable to print his or her name. (fine motor)	___	___
73. The child is unable to locate and name the different parts of his or her body. (body image)	___	___
74. The child is always stepping on someone's feet. (spatial)	___	___
75. The child is unable to estimate larger or smaller. (spatial)	___	___
76. The child tries to stuff big things into little places. (spatial)	___	___
77. Other ______________________________	___	___

FOR AGES 6 AND OVER, DO 56–77 AND ADD: YES NO

78. The student is unable to balance on one foot for 5 seconds. (balance/coordination) ___ ___
79. The student is unable to catch a ball. (gross motor) ___ ___
80. The student fails to jump rope in a coordinated manner. (balanced/coordination) ___ ___
81. The student is unable to identify left and right sides of the body. (laterality) ___ ___
82. The student fails to perform exercises and sports activities appropriate to his or her age group in a coordinated manner. (motor) ___ ___
83. The student is unable to draw a human figure with the body parts in proper position and in correct relationship. (body image) ___ ___
84. The student fails to estimate the size of objects in relation to each other. (spatial) ___ ___
85. The student is unable to indicate appropriate relationships between time, space, and geographic location. (spatial-temporal) ___ ___
86. The student fails to state the appropriate historical sequence utilizing an appropriate time reference. (spatial-temporal) ___ ___
87. The student is unable to tell time. (spatial-temporal) ___ ___
88. The student is unable to copy a diamond. (fine motor/visual) ___ ___
89. The student is unable to write letters, numerals, and words legibly. (fine motor/spatial) ___ ___
90. The student is unable to organize himself/herself in relation to daily activities (e.g., organizing school and homework and being where he/she is supposed to be). (spatial-temporal) ___ ___
91. Other ______________________________
______________________________ ___ ___

Speech

AGE 4 AND OVER

Articulation

92. The student distorts sounds or words (e.g., *shing/sing*). ___ ___
93. The student omits sounds (e.g., *hep/help*). ___ ___
94. The student substitutes one sound for another (e.g., *wead/read*). ___ ___
95. The student uses immature speech patterns (baby talk). ___ ___
96. The student exhibits sloppy speech. ___ ___
97. The student protrudes his or her tongue for *s* and *z* sounds. ___ ___

Voice

98. The student's voice is weak or soft and can hardly be heard. (volume/check hearing) ___ ___
99. The student speaks excessively loud. (volume/check hearing) ___ ___
100. The student's voice is husky, hoarse, nasal, breathy, or guttural. (quality) ___ ___
101. The student speaks in a monotonous voice. ___ ___

Fluency

102. The student repeats syllables, words, and phrases. ___ ___
103. The student's speech is irregular, exhibiting sudden starts or stops. ___ ___
104. The student talks too fast and therefore is difficult to understand. ___ ___
105. The student finds it difficult to get the words out. (looks like stuttering) ___ ___

Other Problems

106. The student stutters or stammers, which includes repetition of syllables or words, repetition and prolongation of sounds, and spasms and distortions of the face and organs of speech. ___ ___
107. The student exhibits cleft palate speech. (nasal quality) ___ ___
108. The student exhibits cerebral palsied speech (slow, labored, and spasmodic). ___ ___

	YES	NO
109. The student avoids speaking in classroom activities.	___	___
110. The student avoids speaking to peers.	___	___
111. The student's speech deteriorates under stress.	___	___
112. Other ______________________________	___	___

Language (Reception, Expression)

BEGINNING AGE 4

	YES	NO
113. The child consistently fails to understand directions. (reception)	___	___
114. The child is unable to associate common objects, such as a dog with a bone. (reception)	___	___
115. The child becomes confused by conversation. (reception)	___	___
116. The child is unable to classify objects by category, such as dogs, cats, vehicles. (reception)	___	___
117. The child fails to understand familiar sounds: horn, bell, etc. (reception)	___	___
118. The child fails to understand the language of space (e.g., *over, under, between, less*) and time (e.g., *early, late, soon, after*). (reception/spatial-temporal)	___	___
119. The child talks in disconnected phrases. (expression)	___	___
120. The child communicates with gestures and sounds. (expression)	___	___
121. The child speaks in single words or short phrases only. (expression)	___	___
122. The child fails to name familiar objects. (reception/expression)	___	___
123. The child is unable to state his/her full name, age, and home address. (reception/expression)	___	___
124. Other ______________________________	___	___

FOR AGES 6 AND OVER, DO 113–124 AND ADD:

	YES	NO
125. The student fails to recognize multiple meanings of words (e.g., *sail, sale*). (reception)	___	___
126. The student fails to interpret cause-effect situations or relationships. (reception)	___	___
127. The student uses words like *watchamacallit* or has strange words for common things within his/her experience. (expression)	___	___
128. The student fails to express himself/herself verbally in a meaningful manner. (reception/expression)	___	___
129. The student fails to express himself/herself in written communication in a meaningful manner. (reception/expression)	___	___
130. The student is unable to relate facts and a sequence of events about a past experience. (reception/expression)	___	___
131. The student is unable to read a paragraph or story at the independent level and orally paraphrase it. (reception/expression)	___	___
132. Other ______________________________	___	___

Control Factors (Distractibility, Hyperactivity, Impulsivity, Disinhibition, Perseveration)

BEGINNING AGE 4 AND OVER

	YES	NO
133. The child is easily distracted away from a task even though he/she appears motivated. (distractible)	___	___

	YES	NO
134. The learner is very active and easily over-stimulated. (distractible/hyperactive)	___	___
135. The learner is impulsive and unpredictable in his/her actions. (impulsivity)	___	___
136. The student has to do things one more time or repeat a previous act that is no longer appropriate. (perseveration)	___	___
137. The learner is unable to stay in his/her seat for a reasonable period of time. (distractible/hyperactive)	___	___
138. The student is unable to refrain from excessive movement. (hyperactive)	___	___
139. The learner responds too quickly and is more often wrong than not in his/her response. (impulsivity)	___	___
140. The student is easily carried away by his/her own thoughts, giving inappropriate answers to questions. (disinhibition)	___	___
141. Other ______________________________	___	___

Social-Emotional

BEGINNING AGE 4 AND OVER

Aggressive (Acting Out/Passive)

	YES	NO
142. The student is overtly or passively negative and does not do what is required of him/her.	___	___
143. The student is irritable and unhappy.	___	___
144. The student is destructive of his/her own belongings.	___	___
145. The student is destructive of other people's property.	___	___
146. The student is hot-tempered and flares up easily.	___	___
147. The student is disruptive (moves about excessively and bothers other children).	___	___
148. The student's behavior provokes unkind attitudes and expressions from others.	___	___
149. The student is poorly motivated and appears not to care about school.	___	___

Sensitive-Withdrawn

	YES	NO
150. The student exhibits feelings of insecurity.	___	___
151. The student becomes unhappy or cries easily.	___	___
152. The student likes to be left alone and withdraws from others.	___	___
153. The student is shy in social situations.	___	___
154. The student exhibits little self-confidence.	___	___

Immature-Dependent

	YES	NO
155. The student requires constant direction and relies a great deal on others.	___	___
156. The student prefers to play or interact with younger individuals.	___	___
157. The student does not attend to activities that require a degree of concentration.	___	___
158. The student is easily influenced by others.	___	___
159. The student appears to be absentminded or lost in thought to excess.	___	___

Psychotic-Neurotic

	YES	NO
160. The student enjoys inflicting physical pain on self and/or others.	___	___
161. The student feels that people want to physically hurt him/her.	___	___
162. The student exhibits compulsive behavior, such as excessive hand washing or door opening.	___	___
163. The student appears to be extremely nervous.	___	___
164. The student thinks that everyone is talking about and plotting against him/her.	___	___
165. The student exhibits *unusual* fears (e.g., water, heights, dirt, taking tests).	___	___

Delinquent-Unorthodox

	YES	NO
166. The student rejects figures representing authority.	___	___

	YES	NO
167. The student adheres to a gang's code of ethics and morality.	___	___
168. The student is often truant from school.	___	___
169. The student seeks the company of other delinquents.	___	___
170. The student does not express remorse for delinquent behavior.	___	___
171. Other ______________________________		
______________________________	___	___
Social Perception		
172. The student reacts inappropriately to situations, criticisms, and guidance from others.	___	___
173. The student fails to get meaning from gestures and expressions of others.	___	___
174. The student loses the essence of the event in the plot of stories read to him/her, films, stories on television, etc.	___	___
175. The student misunderstands motives (why people do what they do).	___	___
176. The student fails to associate an incident with its implications.	___	___
177. The student consistently says the inappropriate thing at the inappropriate time.	___	___
178. Other ______________________________		
______________________________	___	___

Comments:

MANN-SUITER DEVELOPMENTAL SCREENING

The Mann-Suiter developmental screening devices are designed to do the following:

1. Supply data to support the information accumulated through the use of the developmental inventories found in Chapters 4 and 5
2. Aid the teacher in focusing specifically on particular problem areas as they relate to language acquisition
3. Become the basis for the selection of more specific and sophisticated standardized testing in each of the processing areas when deemed necessary

The skill areas listed can be evaluated in total or in part as the teacher deems necessary for developing educational strategies for particular students. There is no total score. The screening devices are not designed as tests to measure the student's limit in a particular ability. Rather, they are designed to check for the minimum level of readiness abilities necessary for success in basic language tasks. It is our opinion that it is imperative that the teacher know if the student has the minimal critical skills needed for learning how to read, write, or do arithmetic. In screening of this nature the way the student performs and the quality of his or her response is just as important as the level of achievement, or score. The examiner must try to understand the student's learning style, or patterns of learning, and determine what it is that prevents him or her from learning a particular academic task.

After an extensive review of standardized tests, a criterion of minimal functioning in eighteen areas was identified. The areas (listed in Table 3-1) were pilot tested to eliminate and modify questionable items. The normative population consisted of 436 students, ages four through twelve, with borderline intelligence or above. The population contained students from all socioeconomic levels and from different ethnic and racial backgrounds. Of the 436, 291 were failing in school and 145 were making satisfactory progress, according to teacher reports.

The students were administered the appropriate subtests. The results were analyzed in relation to specific skills required for success in reading, writing, spelling, and arithmetic. For example, the majority of students who failed the visual motor screen also had difficulty in handwriting. All students who did not have difficulty in handwriting established the lower limit norms for success on the visual motor screen. Performance on the visual closure screen was compared with the student's performance in blending in reading. Visual memory was analyzed in relation to the learner's ability to remember objects, letters, or words, as well as to the learner's disabilities, such as reversals or inversions in reading, writing, spelling, and arithmetic. The same was done with all other subareas. The majority of the academically successful students met the minimum standard in all of the critical subareas, while the majority of failing students failed to meet them.

Initial content validity of the Mann-Suiter developmental screening devices was established by successive usage and review over a period of 2 years by over 200 teachers, counselors, and psychologists, who were requested to use the screening devices along with what they were already using to identify learning

Table 3-1 Index for the Mann-Suiter Developmental Screening Devices in This Book.

List of Screening Devices	*Page*	*Related Activities Page*
Visual:		
Visual motor	35	178
Visual figure-ground	35	168
Visual discrimination	39	167
Visual closure—Parts A and B	39	169
Visual memory	47	170
Auditory:		
Auditory discrimination	49	158
Auditory closure	49	160
Auditory memory (sentences)	52	161
Alphabet-Speech (auditory-visual association)	52	172
Language:		
Visual language classification	55	173
Visual language association	55	174
Auditory language classification	60	162
Auditory language association	62	163
Manual language expression	62	185
Speech	62	185
Verbal language expression	66	186
Written language expression	66	177, 187, 236
Nonverbal language	69	188

Form 3-2

MANN-SUITER DEVELOPMENTAL SCREENING RECORD FORM

NAME ______________________________ DATE ____________

DATE OF BIRTH ____________ EXAMINER ______________________________

Screen	*Minimal Requirements*	*Student's Response*	*Acceptance Yes*	*No*	*Date of Mastery*
Visual Motor	○, age 3	____	____	____	________
	▭, age 4	____	____	____	________
	△, age 5½	____	____	____	________
	◇, age 6	____	____	____	________
Visual Figure-Ground	10 correct responses, ages 4–5	____	____	____	________
	12 correct responses, age 6 or older	____	____	____	________
Visual Discrimination	2 errors, age 5 or older	____	____	____	________
Visual Closure (Part A)	5 errors, age 4	____	____	____	________
	3 errors, age 6	____	____	____	________
Visual Closure (Part B) (for students reading at level one or above)	2 errors, level one	____	____	____	________
	3 errors, other levels	____	____	____	________
Visual Memory	3 items, any order, age 5	____	____	____	________
	4 items, any order, age 6	____	____	____	________
Auditory Discrimination (Part A)	4 errors, age 6	____	____	____	________
Auditory Discrimination (Part B)	2 errors, age 7	____	____	____	________
Auditory Closure (blending)	9 errors, age 6	____	____	____	________
	4 errors, age 7	____	____	____	________
Auditory Memory (sentences)	7 item errors, age 5	____	____	____	________
	4 item errors, age 6	____	____	____	________
Alphabet-Speech:					
Alphabet sounds (letter)	4 errors, age 7 (Part A)	____	____	____	________
	1 error, age 8 (Part A)	____	____	____	________
Alphabet names (letter)	4 errors, age 7 (Part A)	____	____	____	________
	1 error, age 8 (Part A)	____	____	____	________
Alphabet digraphs	1 error, age 6 (Part B)	____	____	____	________

Screen	*Minimal Requirements*	*Student's Response*	*Acceptance Yes*	*No*	*Date of Mastery*
Visual Language Classification	4 errors, age 4–5				
	2 errors, age 6				
Visual Language Association	4 errors, 4–5				
	2 errors, age 6				
Auditory Language Classification	4 errors, age 4–5				
	2 errors, age 6				
Auditory Language Association	4 errors, ages 4–5				
	2 errors, age 6				
Manual Language Expression	4 errors, ages 4–5				
	2 errors, age 6				
Speech	3 item errors, age 4–6				
	2 item errors, age 7				
Verbal Language Expression	4 correct responses, age 6 (at least one per item)				
	6 correct responses, age 7 (at least one per item)				
Written Language Expression	teacher judgment				
Nonverbal Language	3 errors, age 4–6				
	1 error, age 7				

COMMENTS:

problems in children. They were requested to examine the contents carefully and, after using the devices, make suggestions regarding diagnosis, practicality, and applicability. Since 1974, when the Mann-Suiter screening devices were first published, thousands of educators have used them with students all over the United States and in foreign countries. A survey of many of these educators has indicated that developmental screening is a valuable instrument that can be used by classroom teachers, as well as support personnel, in the assessment of students with learning difficulties.

Table 3-1 is an index of all the Mann-Suiter developmental screening devices in this book.

The Mann-Suiter Developmental Screening Record Form (Form 3-2) can be utilized to summarize the data from the developmental screening devices.

MANN-SUITER VISUAL MOTOR SCREEN

Successful completion of the designs included in the Mann-Suiter Visual Motor Screen (Form 3-3) represents minimal standards for success in handwriting.[1]

Directions

The student is asked to copy a design exactly the way he or she sees it in each standard. The student is given three chances, but only the best effort is counted. Difficulty with these designs after age seven indicates a need for a program of comprehensive visual-motor activities to develop eye-hand readiness skills.

Normative Data (Ilg and Ames)

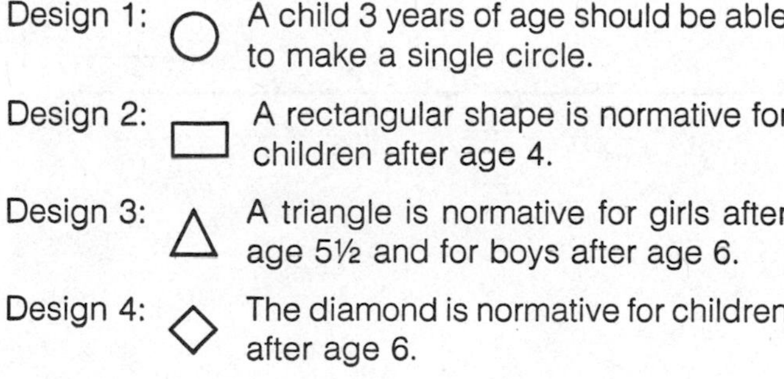

Design 1: A child 3 years of age should be able to make a single circle.

Design 2: A rectangular shape is normative for children after age 4.

Design 3: A triangle is normative for girls after age 5½ and for boys after age 6.

Design 4: The diamond is normative for children after age 6.

1. Frances L. Ilg and Louise Bates Ames, *School Readiness* (New York: Harper & Row, 1964), p. 127.

Scoring

Teachers must use good judgment to evaluate students' abilities on this examination. The following should be considered:

1. The lines should be fairly firm and not too erratic.
2. The angles should be good.
3. The basic shape should be easily recognizable and resemble the model.
4. Any minor imperfections should be overlooked. The following symbols should be used for correct and incorrect responses: ✓ = correct, ✓̸ = incorrect.

Things to Look For

1. Does the student switch hands?
2. Does the student make the circle counterclockwise? A counterclockwise circle is normative for (a) right-handed girls by age 5, (b) right-handed boys by age 5½, and (c) left-handed children by age 7–9.
3. Do the reproductions get worse or better with practice?

Note: If necessary, see Chapter 6 for more specific measuring criteria in this area.

MANN-SUITER VISUAL FIGURE-GROUND SCREEN

The Mann-Suiter Visual Figure-Ground Screen (Form 3-4) is designed to determine a student's ability to attend to a particular design (figure) while simultaneously screening out the irrelevant background (ground).

Directions

Using a blue, red, or green crayon, the teacher traces the standard in the upper left hand corner, saying to the student, "See how I trace this? You find all of the same thing in the big picture and trace them the way I did." The student is then handed the crayon. If the student cannot trace, he or she should color Designs 1, 3, and 4. If the student traces only one item, the teacher should say, "Can you find any more like it to trace?" If the student traces only part of each figure, the teacher should say, "Did you trace it all?" The teacher should not give any more clues. Note: Check for color blindness.

Form 3-3

MANN-SUITER VISUAL MOTOR SCREEN

NAME ______________________________ DATE ______________

DATE OF BIRTH __________ HAND USED ____________ EXAMINER ______________

RESPONSE

1. ____

2. ____

3. ____

4. ____

Form 3-4

MANN-SUITER VISUAL FIGURE-GROUND SCREEN

NAME ______________________________ DATE OF BIRTH __________

DATE ______________ EXAMINER ______________________________

RESPONSES

1. ___

2. ___

RESPONSE

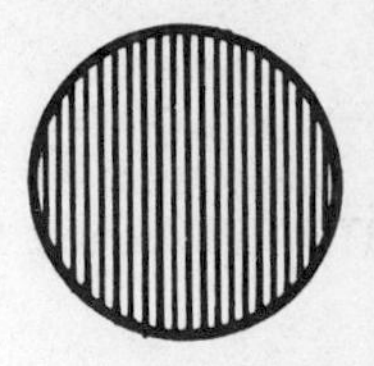

3. ____

4. ____

TOTAL ACCURATE RESPONSES: ____

Scoring

1. The entire figure must be traced (or colored) to be considered correct. Count crossover in tracing or coloring (part of the tree traced or colored, for example) correct if the student keeps the basic design intact.
2. Ten or more correct responses out of a possible fourteen for children ages 4–5 indicate intact visual figure-ground perception.

   Design 1—three possible correct responses
   Design 2—three possible correct responses
   Design 3—four possible correct responses
   Design 4—four possible correct responses

3. Twelve or more correct responses for students 6 and older suggest intact visual figure-ground perception.
4. Note visual-motor control and compare with the performance in the visual-motor screen.

Things to Look For

1. Does the student become confused and fail to attend to the task?
2. How does the student perform the task? Is the student specific or does he or she just point in a random fashion?
3. Does the student go off on a tangent as a result of the stimulus picture?

Note: See Chapter 6 for more specific evaluation in this area if necessary.

MANN-SUITER VISUAL DISCRIMINATION SCREEN

The Mann-Suiter Visual Discrimination Screen (Form 3-5) will enable the teacher to determine a student's ability to discriminate between designs or symbols that are similar in configuration.

Directions

With a practice example of five images in separate frames, the student should be asked to "Mark the one that looks the same as the first one." (To take this examination the student must understand the meaning of the word *same.*). If the practice response is incorrect, the student should be told which is the correct answer. The teacher should say, pointing, "See, this one is the same as the first one." If the response is correct, then the teacher should say, "Yes, this is the same as this," and point to the proper items. The student should be asked to do the rest by himself or herself and should be reinforced again only if necessary.

Scoring

1. Three or more errors suggest difficulty with visual discrimination for children age 5 or older.
2. The following symbols should be used: ✓= correct, ✓̸= incorrect.

Things to Look For

1. Does the student go back and forth many times before making a decision?
2. Does the student have a great deal of erasures?
3. Does the student anchor a finger on the first image as he or she peruses the rest?
4. Does the student verbalize as he or she proceeds through the task?

Note: See Chapter 6 for more specific measurement criteria in this area if necessary.

MANN-SUITER VISUAL CLOSURE SCREEN (PARTS A AND B)

Part A of the Mann-Suiter Visual Closure Screen (Form 3-6) will enable the instructor to determine the student's ability to complete designs and objects by matching and supplying missing parts. Part B tests the student's ability to take letters or letter groups that are somewhat apart from each other and put them together to make words.

Directions (Part A)

Part A of the Mann-Suiter Visual Closure Screen is appropriate for students who are at the readiness stage of development or reading below grade level 2 and exhibiting difficulties in parts-to-whole kinds of activities. Students who are having difficulty with blending in reading should be screened in this area. The instructor may find it valuable to give both Part A and Part B to students reading above grade level who are having difficulty in blending and reading in general. For items 1 through 5 the instructor should point to the standard and say to the student, "See this?"

Form 3-5

MANN-SUITER VISUAL DISCRIMINATION SCREEN

NAME ______________________________ DATE ____________

DATE OF BIRTH ____________ EXAMINER ______________________________

RESPONSE

Practice:

○	□	⬯	△	○	___

1.

M	T	M	P	O	___

2.

3	2	3	5	8	___

3.

H	M	N	U	H	___

RESPONSE

4. | b | D | P | b | G | ____

5. | ME | SHE | WE | HE | ME | ____

6. | SHIP | SNIP | SLIP | SHIP | SKIP | ____

7. | ARE | AIR | FIRE | ARE | ART | ____

8. | e | [illegible] | [illegible] | e | [illegible] | ____

TOTAL INCORRECT: ____

Form 3-6

MANN-SUITER VISUAL CLOSURE SCREEN

Part A

NAME ______________________________ DATE ______________

DATE OF BIRTH __________ EXAMINER ______________________________

RESPONSE

1. ______

2. ______

3. ______

4. ______

5. ______

6. ____________ 7. ____________ 8. ____________ 9. ____________

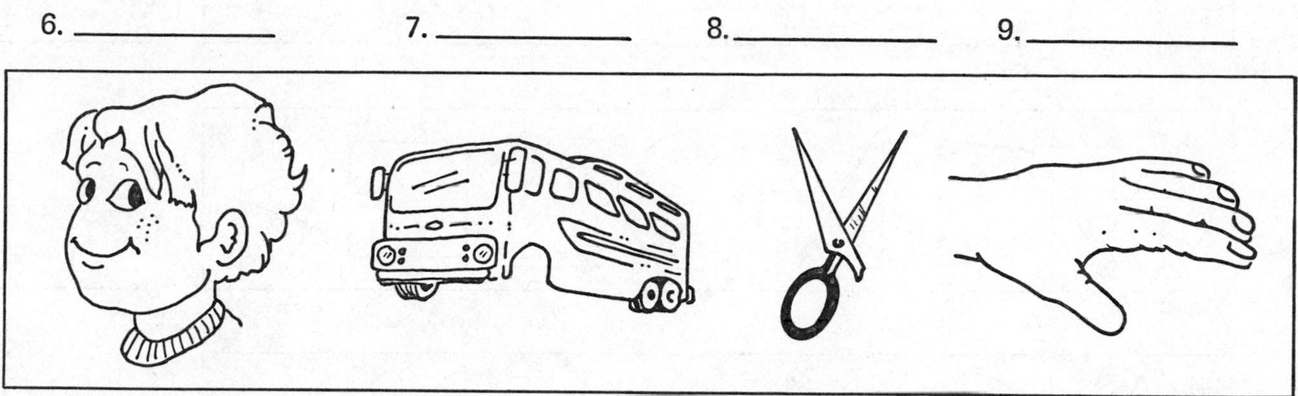

10. ____________ 11. ____________ 12. ____________ 13. ____________

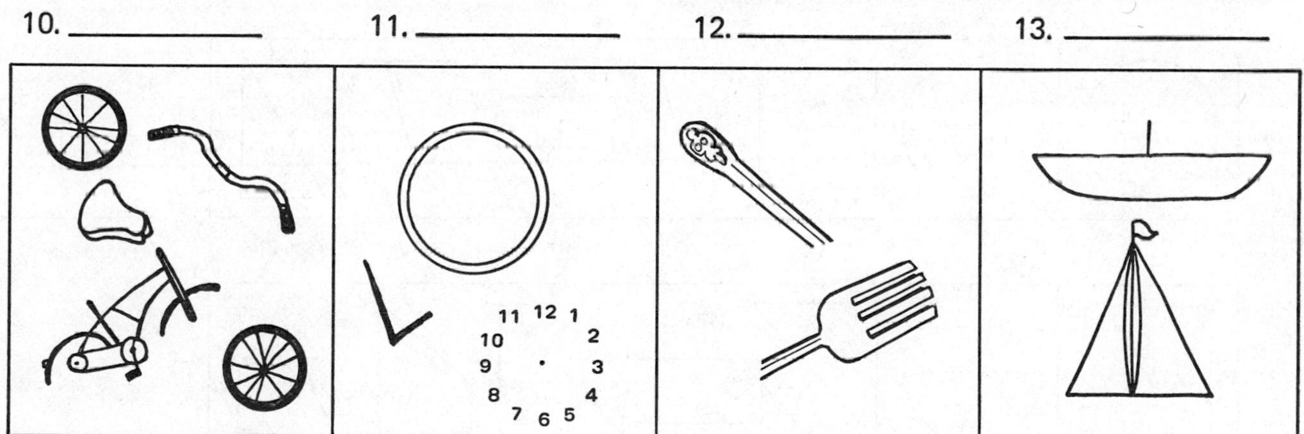

RESPONSE

14. ______

15. ______

16. ______

17. ______

18. ______

TOTAL INCORRECT: ______

Part B (Ages 6 And Over, Reading Above Level One)

NAME ______________________________ DATE ____________

DATE OF BIRTH ____________ EXAMINER ______________________________

LEVEL I	RESPONSE
c at	____
n o	____
r e d	____
a n d	____
y ou	____
th e	____
w e	____
i t	____
y e s	____
d og	____
b i g	____
li ke	____
h ave	____
w as	____

TOTAL INCORRECT: ____

LEVEL II	RESPONSE
p i t	____
f or	____
fu n	____
b y	____
so on	____
bab y	____
r i d e	____
d ow n	____
he ad	____
m other	____
ope n	____
ve ry	____
y e a r	____
ha ppy	____
lett er	____
n ext	____
mor ning	____
wit h	____

TOTAL INCORRECT: ____

LEVEL III	RESPONSE	LEVEL IV	RESPONSE
a l o n g	____	aw ake	____
gr and pa	____	gif t	____
ri ver	____	mi xed	____
bl ack	____	shir t	____
b at h	____	tu rn in g	____
pa rt	____	fa sten	____
f ix	____	lar ge st	____
foo d	____	r ained	____
wa lk	____	ta lks	____
cat ch	____	ca rry ing	____
t ai l	____	cof fee	____
s low	____	ju ice	____
tha n	____	s torm	____
p uppy	____	co r ners	____
la ugh ing	____	wri tes	____
f unny	____	doll ar	____
fa rm	____	hour s	____
s tar t	____	pe nn ies	____

TOTAL INCORRECT: ____ TOTAL INCORRECT: ____

Then, indicating the three alternatives, the instructor should say, "Point to the best one that will finish the picture." For items 6 through 9, the instructor should point to each item and say, "See this? Show or tell me what is missing from this picture." Repeat the same directions for each item (picture). For items 10 through 13, the instructor should point to each item and say, "These are parts of something. When you put the parts together, what will the picture be?" The directions should be repeated for each item (picture). For items 14 through 18, the instructor should say, pointing to the model, "See this? Which two of these [pointing to the alternatives] when put together will look like this one [pointing to the first one again]?" The directions should be repeated as necessary.

Scoring (Part A)

1. Six errors or more after age 4 and four errors or more at age 6 and older suggest difficulty with visual closure.
2. Symbols to be used are ✓= correct, ✓̸= incorrect.

Directions (Part B)

Part B of the Mann-Suiter Visual Closure Screen deals with words and is appropriate for students reading below grade five but above the primer level, since word-attack skills are generally well stabilized by the time students have attained at least primer level in reading. The teacher should begin the examination at the level at which the student has experienced 100% word recognition on the Developmental Word-Recognition Reading Inventory (pages 85–89). The teacher should say to the student, "Read the words as I point to them."

Scoring (Part B)

1. Three errors at level 1 or four errors at any other level suggest difficulty with visual closure.
2. Symbols to be used are ✓= correct, ✓̸= incorrect.

Things to Look For (Parts A and B)

1. Does the student exhibit guessing or trial-and-error behavior in Part A?
2. How much time does the student take to complete the task?
3. Does the student go back and forth from the standard to the choice excessively?
4. Which part of Part A does the student have difficulty with—matching, missing parts, etc.?
5. Is the student failing this screen also having difficulty dealing with spatial concepts in arithmetic?
6. Does the student know the letter sounds in Part B?
7. Can the learner read the blends in Part B?

Note: See Chapter 6 for more specific evaluation in this area if necessary.

MANN-SUITER VISUAL MEMORY SCREEN FOR OBJECTS

The Mann-Suiter Visual Memory Screen for Objects (Form 3-7) is designed to indicate a student's ability to revisualize pictures of common objects presented in groups.

Directions

The teacher says, "I am going to show you a row of little pictures. After I cover the pictures, I want you to tell me each time exactly what pictures you saw. Start at one end of the row each time and tell me all the pictures you saw. Try to tell them to me in the same order they were in a row."

Note: Number the sequence of the responses for diagnostic purposes to get an indication of the order of remembering even though this is not counted in the scoring.

Scoring

1. For children age 5, recalling three items in any order within a row suggests adequate visual memory.
2. For children age 6 and older, recalling four items in any order within a row suggests adequate visual memory.
3. Expose each row for approximately one second for each picture on it. Number one is a practice one and does not count. The order of response does not count in the scoring.
4. The exposure time for each row is as follows:

Row 1: 2 seconds
Row 2: 3 seconds
Row 3: 4 seconds
Row 4: 5 seconds

Form 3-7

MANN-SUITER VISUAL MEMORY SCREEN FOR OBJECTS

NAME ____ DATE ____________

DATE OF BIRTH __________ EXAMINER ______________________________________

RESPONSE

Practice:

____

____

____

____

____

LARGEST TOTAL IN ANY ROW IN ANY ORDER: ____

5. Use the following symbols to note responses: ✓ = correct, ✓̶ = incorrect.

Things to Look For

1. Note if the student remembers the pictures from left to right or from right to left.
2. Look for perseveration; that is, repeating the same objects over again from the preceding line.

Note: See Chapter 6 for more specific measurement in this area if necessary.

MANN-SUITER AUDITORY DISCRIMINATION SCREEN

Part A of the Mann-Suiter Auditory Discrimination Screen (Form 3-8) will enable the teacher to determine a student's ability to discriminate between words that are similar or different in the way they sound. It requires a comparison of sounds. Part B requires recall at another level of auditory discrimination.

Directions, Part A

1. The student must not see the teacher's face. The student can be turned around, or the teacher can cover his or her own face with a 3" x 5" card.
2. The teacher should say, "I am going to say some words and you tell me if they are the same or different." The student must understand the words *same* and *different.* If he or she does not, the teacher can call the student's name and another name for comparison. It is a good idea for the teacher to call the student's name and another name after every five responses or so to make sure the student is attending and understands what is required.
3. The teacher's voice quality must be consistent. It should not be allowed to drop on the second word.
4. On the first administration, an incorrect check mark should be put next to the wrong responses only (✓̶).
5. Only those responses that were wrong should be readministered immediately, marking them ✓̶ if wrong again or ✓ if correct.
6. If the learner corrects on the second administration, the response should be counted correct.

Scoring, Part A

Five or more uncorrected errors by children age 6 or older suggest difficulty with auditory discrimination and possible problems with learning through a phonetic approach.

Directions, Part B

Retaining instructions 1, 3, 4, and 6 from Part A, above, the teacher says the following: "The middle sound in the word *cat* is ă. What is the middle sound in the words *sad, bus, hot* . . . ?"

Scoring, Part B

Three or more errors at age 7 or older suggest difficulty with auditory analysis, or going from whole to parts, and may affect blending, or closure.

Note: More specific evaluation in this area can be found in Chapter 6.

Things To Look For

1. Does the student exhibit a short attention span?
2. Is the student just guessing?
3. Does the student close his or her eyes in order to listen better?
4. Does the student have a speech (articulation) problem?
5. Does the student appear to have a hearing loss (check acuity)?

MANN-SUITER AUDITORY CLOSURE (BLENDING) SCREEN

The Mann-Suiter Auditory Closure (Blending) Screen (Form 3-9) will indicate to the teacher a student's ability to combine sounds that are presented orally to make words.

Directions

The teacher begins by saying, "I am going to make some sounds that make a word. Tell me what the word is after I finish." The teacher says each sound of the word separately with about a second's pause after each sound. If the student's response is incorrect, the teacher repeats the sounds and then says each word and asks which word the sounds were most like. Correctly identifying the word from any three words is not part of the scoring.

Form 3-8

MANN-SUITER AUDITORY DISCRIMINATION SCREEN

NAME ______________________________ DATE __________

DATE OF BIRTH __________ EXAMINER ______________________________

Part A

Discrimination of Initial and Final Sounds (recognition)

		RESPONSE
1.	shine – sign	____
2.	tin – thin	____
3.	pine – pine	____
4.	mob – mop	____
5.	mud – mug	____
6.	life – like	____
7.	very – fairy	____
8.	ship – ship	____
9.	goal – coal	____
10.	moon – noon	____
11.	very – berry	____
12.	buff – tuff	____
13.	run – run	____
14.	robe – rode	____
15.	bus – buzz	____
16.	bill – mill	____
17.	brink – drink	____
18.	fling – cling	____
19.	lake – lake	____
20.	scream – stream	____
21.	and – end	____

Discrimination of Medial Vowel Sounds (recognition)

22.	mesh – mush	____
23.	slid – sled	____
24.	deck – dock	____
25.	band – bend	____

TOTAL INCORRECT: ____

Part B

Discrimination of Medial Sounds (recall analysis)

			RESPONSE
1.	a	sad	____
2.	u	bus	____
3.	o	hot	____
4.	e	pet	____
5.	e	team	____
6.	i	like	____
7.	o	boat	____
8.	u	mule	____
9.	i	bit	____
10.	a	cake	____

TOTAL INCORRECT: ____

Form 3-9

MANN-SUITER AUDITORY CLOSURE (BLENDING) SCREEN

NAME ______________________________ DATE ____________

DATE OF BIRTH __________ EXAMINER ______________________________

RESPONSE

1. g-oat (bell, good, goat) ____
2. sh-ip (push, shop, ship) ____
3. m-e (be, he, me) ____
4. t-ar (art, tar, rat) ____
5. sp-ot (spot, pot, stop) ____
6. dr-e-ss (grass, rage, dress) ____
7. d-us-t (stem, dust, stair) ____
8. br-i-ck (crib, brick, strip) ____
9. p-ai-l (same, pail, late) ____
10. b-a-g (gab, bag, back) ____
11. c-a-p (tack, pack, cap) ____
12. s-u-n (sun, mind, nuts) ____
13. s-l-a-p (black, rap, slap) ____
14. l-a-m-p (play, lamp, pack) ____
15. s-t-r-ing (string, green, rip) ____

TOTAL INCORRECT: ____

Scoring

1. Ten errors or more (excluding word recognition) at age 6 indicates possible difficulty with auditory closure (blending).
2. Five errors or more (excluding word recognition) at age 7 or older indicates possible difficulty with auditory closure (blending).
3. Symbols used for responses are √= correct, √^= incorrect.

Things to Look For

1. Is the student able to repeat the sounds, but not the word?
2. Does the student recognize the word from among the three words?
3. Did the student reverse the whole word—that is, was the sound the student heard last the one with which he or she started the word?
4. Did the student omit one sound of the consonant blend?
5. Did the student reverse part of the word?
6. Consistent failure and difficulties with the above suggests that the student may have difficulty with instruction that emphasizes a phonics approach.

Note: See Chapter 6 for more specific evaluation in this area.

MANN-SUITER AUDITORY MEMORY SCREEN (SENTENCES)

The Mann-Suiter Auditory Memory Screen (Sentences) (Form 3-10) is designed to determine a student's ability to repeat a sentence, a sequence of words that is characterized by a complete thought (meaning).

Directions

The teacher tells the student, "I am going to say something to you. When I finish, you say just what I said." The teacher proceeds to enunciate the sentences slowly, not repeating any. The teacher *administers all items* until the student exhibits one or more errors in eight sentences for age 5 or in five sentences for ages 6 and over.

Scoring

1. Record as errors words omitted and words added.
2. One or more errors in each of eight sentences (items) suggests difficulty with auditory memory in children age 5.
3. One or more errors in each of five sentences (items) suggests difficulty with auditory memory in students ages 6 and older.
4. Symbols for scoring are √= correct, √^= incorrect.

Things to Look For

1. Look for associative errors, such as saying *house* for *home*.
2. Note omission of endings such as *ed, ing,* and *s*. Do not record it as wrong if this appears to be a cultural phenomenon.
3. Although the student may have given the wrong sequence, note the fact that he or she gets the gist of the meaning.

Note: See Chapter 6 for more specific evaluation in this area if necessary.

MANN-SUITER ALPHABET-SPEECH SCREEN (AUDITORY-VISUAL ASSOCIATION)

Part A of the Mann-Suiter Alphabet-Speech Screen (Form 3-11) will indicate the student's ability to relate a symbol to its auditory referents, i.e., letter name and sound. Part B will indicate the student's ability to pronounce words containing digraphs.

Directions, Part A

1. The letters should be shown to the student in the order indicated. For children under age 6, the letters should be put on 3″ x 5″ cards.
2. The teacher should point to each letter, ask for the name of the letter, and then ask for the sound the letter makes.

Scoring, Part A

1. At age 7, five or more errors on either the letter names or the sounds indicate difficulty with sound-symbol (auditory-visual) associative relationships.
2. At age 8 or older, two or more errors on either the letter names or the sounds suggest difficulty with auditory-visual associations.
3. Symbols for scoring are √= correct, √^= incorrect.

Form 3-10

MANN-SUITER AUDITORY MEMORY SCREEN (SENTENCES)

NAME ______________________________ DATE __________

DATE OF BIRTH __________ EXAMINER ______________________________

RESPONSE

1. The boy has a big ball. ____
2. I like to ride in the car. ____
3. Mary is reading her new book. ____
4. John ran fast down the wide road. ____
5. It is time to go home from school. ____
6. Open the door, and let the dog out. ____
7. Last Sunday we went to the beach. ____
8. Pretty flowers come out in the spring. ____
9. Horses like to run wild in the fields. ____
10. The moon shone brightly in the sky at night. ____
11. The ship blew its horn when it passed under the bridge. ____
12. Mother put flowers on the table last night. ____
13. The bird built its nest high up in the shady tree. ____
14. He saw a car hit a pole on his way to school. ____
15. I like milk and crackers after school every day. ____
16. It was a dark and cloudy day, but Bill went swimming alone. ____
17. The dust was so thick you could hardly find your way around there. ____
18. Day after day, the dark clouds poured rain on the earth far below. ____
19. I was keeping it for a surprise, but I will show it now. ____
20. John went to Boston to see if he could pick up some good antiques. ____

TOTAL INCORRECT: ____

Form 3-11

MANN-SUITER ALPHABET-SPEECH SCREEN (AUDITORY-VISUAL ASSOCIATION)

NAME ______________________ DATE __________

DATE OF BIRTH ________ EXAMINER ______________________

Part A

Name	*Vowels & Consonants*	*Sound*	*Name*	*Vowels & Consonants*	*Sound*
____	M	____	____	T	____
____	S	____	____	H	____
____	P	____	____	G	____
____	C	____	____	E	____
____	L	____	____	K	____
____	R	____	____	Z	____
____	A	____	____	U	____
____	X	____	____	Y	____
____	F	____	____	W	____
____	O	____	____	D	____
____	B	____	____	N	____
____	Q	____	____	J	____
____	I	____	____	V	____
	TOTAL INCORRECT:	____		TOTAL INCORRECT:	____

Part B

DIGRAPH SCREEN

Word	*Picture*	*Response*	*Word*	*Picture*	*Response*
ch		____	th		____
ch		____	th		____
sh		____	wh		____
sh		____	th		____

TOTAL INCORRECT: ____

Directions, Part B

For children below age six who cannot read, the teacher may want to know how they pronounce words containing digraphs. The teacher should show the pictures in Part B and ask the student to name the objects.

Scoring, Part B

1. Two or more errors at age 6 or older suggest difficulty with digraph speech patterns.
2. Symbols for scoring are √ = correct, √̸ = incorrect.

Note: See Chapter 6 for more specific evaluation in this area if necessary.

Things to Look For

1. Does the student know more consonant than vowel sounds?
2. Does the student add a vowel sound (uh) to the consonant (buh for *b*)?
3. Is the student bilingual?
4. Does the student have a speech (articulation) problem?

MANN-SUITER VISUAL LANGUAGE CLASSIFICATION SCREEN

The Mann-Suiter Visual Language Classification Screen (Form 3-12) is designed to indicate a student's ability to classify pictures of objects by category when they are presented visually.

Directions

The teacher points to the first picture in the row (that of a cat, in the example) and says, "Look at this." Then the teacher points to each of the other pictures in that row and asks, "Which one of these is like this?" pointing to the first one again. If the student responds correctly, then the teacher says, "That's right," and continues to administer the rest of the items in the same way. If the response is incorrect, the teacher goes back and says, pointing, "See the cat. Here is another one." On completing the example, the teacher goes on to number one, repeating the directions, but giving no further help.

Scoring

1. Five errors or more for children ages 4–5 suggest difficulty with visual language classification.
2. Three errors or more for children age 6 or older suggest difficulty with visual language classification.
3. Symbols for scoring are √ = correct, √̸ = incorrect.

Key: (1) dog, (2) leaf, (3) cap, (4) woman, (5) truck, (6) chicken, (7) apple, (8) box, (9) knife, (10) airplane.

Things to Look For

1. How well does the student attend to the task?
2. Does the student verbalize while performing the task?
3. Does the student perseverate?
4. Does the student go off on a tangent as a result of the stimulus picture?
5. Does the student anchor by placing a finger on the first picture while he or she scans the rest?
6. Go back over some of the incorrect responses and ask the student why he or she chose the one he or she did. This may give you a clue as to how the student thinks.
7. Note any logical responses even though they may be incorrect in terms of the expected response.

Note: See Chapter 6 for more specific evaluation in this area if necessary.

MANN-SUITER VISUAL LANGUAGE ASSOCIATION SCREEN

The Mann-Suiter Visual Language Association Screen (Form 3-13) is designed to indicate a student's ability to formulate associative relationships between pictures of objects.

Directions

1. For the practice item and items 1–6, the teacher should point to the first picture and say, "Look at this," then point to each of the other pictures and say, "Point to the one it goes with," as he or she goes back and points to the first one again. If the student's response to the sample item is correct, the teacher should say, "That is right, doll goes with carriage," and administer the rest of the items. If

Form 3-12

MANN-SUITER VISUAL LANGUAGE CLASSIFICATION SCREEN

NAME ______________________________ DATE __________

DATE OF BIRTH __________ EXAMINER ______________________________

RESPONSE

Practice: ___

1. ___

2. ___

3. ___

4. ___

5. ___

RESPONSE

6. ____

7. ____

8. ____

9. ____

10. ____

TOTAL INCORRECT: ____

Form 3-13

MANN-SUITER VISUAL LANGUAGE ASSOCIATION SCREEN

NAME ______________________________ DATE ______________

DATE OF BIRTH __________ EXAMINER ______________________________

RESPONSE

Practice: ____

1. ____

2. ____

3. ____

4. ____

5. ____

RESPONSE

6.

7.

8.

9.

10.

TOTAL INCORRECT: ____

the answer is incorrect, the teacher should go back and say as he or she points, "See the doll—the doll goes with the carriage," then proceed to number one, repeat the directions, but give no further help.

2. For items 7–10, the teacher should point to each picture and say, "Fish goes with fish bowl as dog goes with ______?" If the response is incorrect, or if the student does not understand, the teacher should repeat the directions and add, pointing, "Which one of these goes under the dog?" The rest of the items are administered in the same manner.
3. All items should be administered.

Scoring

1. Five errors or more for children ages 4–5 suggest difficulty with visual language association.
2. Three errors or more for children age 6 and older suggest difficulty with visual language association.
3. Symbols used for recording responses are ✓ = correct, ✓^ = incorrect.

Key: (1) dress, (2) meat, (3) pants, (4) key, (5) mouse, (6) gun, (7) dog house, (8) rod and reel, (9) eye, (10) man on bed.

Things to Look For

1. Does the student attend to the task?
2. Does the student verbalize while performing the task?
3. Does the student perseverate?
4. Does the student go off on a tangent as a result of the stimulus picture?
5. Does the student anchor by placing his or her finger on the first picture while he or she scans the rest?
6. Incorrect responses should be reviewed and the student asked why he or she chose the one he or she did. This may give a clue about how he or she thinks.
7. Any logical responses should be written down even though they may be incorrect with regard to the expected response.

Note: See Chapter 6 for more specific evaluation in this area if necessary.

MANN-SUITER AUDITORY LANGUAGE CLASSIFICATION SCREEN

The Mann-Suiter Auditory Language Classification Screen (Form 3-14) is designed to indicate a student's ability to classify objects by category when they are presented orally.

Directions

The teacher asks, "Does boy go with dress or man?" If the response is correct, the teacher says, "Yes, boy goes with man," and continues to give the rest of the items in the same way. If it is incorrect, the teacher says, "boy goes with man" and continues without any further aid.

Scoring

1. Five errors or more for children ages 4–5 suggest difficulty with auditory language classification.
2. Three errors or more for children age 6 and older suggest difficulty with auditory language classification.
3. Symbols for scoring are ✓= correct, ✓^= incorrect.

Key: (1) radio, (2) cake, (3) tie, (4) chair, (5) water, (6) cat, (7) grapefruit, (8) notepad, (9) wool, (10) engine

Things to Look For

1. How well does the student attend to the task?
2. Does the student perseverate?
3. Does the student go off on a tangent as a result of the stimulus picture?
4. Incorrect responses should be reviewed and the student asked why he or she chose the one he or she did. This may give a clue about how the student thinks.
5. Record any logical responses even though they may be incorrect in terms of the expected response.

Note: See Chapter 6 for more specific evaluation in this area if necessary.

Form 3-14

MANN-SUITER AUDITORY LANGUAGE CLASSIFICATION SCREEN

NAME ______________________________ DATE __________

DATE OF BIRTH __________ EXAMINER ______________________________

			RESPONSE
Practice:	boy:	dress – man	____
1.	television:	radio – ball	____
2.	pie:	telephone – cake	____
3.	shirt:	tie – bread	____
4.	table:	pen – chair	____
5.	milk:	water – tree	____
6.	kitten:	cat – flower	____
7.	orange:	lettuce – grapefruit	____
8.	book:	glue – notepad	____
9.	hair:	wool – smoke	____
10.	motor:	sky – engine	____

TOTAL INCORRECT: ____

MANN-SUITER AUDITORY LANGUAGE ASSOCIATION SCREEN

The Mann-Suiter Auditory Language Association Screen (Form 3-15) is designed to indicate a student's ability to formulate associations between objects presented to him orally.

Directions

The teacher asks, "Does pencil go with wall or paper?" If the child answers correctly, the teacher says, "Yes, pencil goes with paper," and continues to give the rest of the items in the same way. If the response is incorrect, the teacher says, "Pencil goes with paper," and continues without any further aid.

Scoring

1. Five errors or more for children ages 4–5 suggest difficulty with auditory language association.
2. Three errors or more for children age 6 and older suggest difficulty with auditory language association.
3. Symbols for scoring are √= correct, √̸= incorrect.

Key: (1) eyes, (2) pants, (3) butter, (4) boat, (5) reel, (6) jelly, (7) wheel, (8) dress, (9) band, (10) rabbit

Things to Look For

1. Does the student attend to the task?
2. Does the student perseverate?
3. Does the student go off on a tangent as a result of the stimulus picture?
4. Incorrect responses should be reviewed and the student asked why he or she chose the one he or she did. This may give a clue about how the student thinks.
5. Record any logical responses even though they may be incorrect in terms of the expected response.

Note: See Chapter 6 for more specific evaluation in this area if necessary.

MANN-SUITER MANUAL LANGUAGE EXPRESSION SCREEN

The Mann-Suiter Manual Language Expression Screen (Form 3-16) will indicate to the instructor the student's ability to express the function of an object by his or her actions, without using words.

Directions

1. The teacher points to the ball and says, "Show me what you can do with this."
2. If the answer is correct, the teacher says, "Yes, now show me what you can do with this," pointing to the next picture.
3. If the student answers incorrectly, the teacher shows the student the motions of throwing and bouncing, then administers the rest of the items, giving no further aid.
4. All items should be administered.

Scoring

1. Five errors or more for children ages 4–5 suggest difficulty with manual language expression.
2. Three errors or more for children age 6 and older suggest difficulty with manual language expression.
3. Symbols for scoring are √= correct, √̸= incorrect.

Things to Look For

1. How well does the student attend to the task?
2. Does the student perseverate?
3. Does the student go off on a tangent as a result of the stimulus picture?
4. Incorrect responses should be reviewed and the student asked why he or she chose the one he or she did. This may give a clue about how the student thinks.
5. Write down any logical responses even though they may be incorrect in terms of the expected response.
6. Does the student verbalize the action as he or she performs it?

Note: See Chapter 6 for more specific evaluation in this area if necessary.

MANN-SUITER SPEECH SCREEN

The Mann-Suiter Speech Screen (Form 3-17) is designed to indicate the presence or absence of articulation defects and other types of nonfluencies (stuttering, etc.) in children.

Form 3-15

MANN-SUITER AUDITORY LANGUAGE ASSOCIATION SCREEN

NAME ______________________________ DATE ____________

DATE OF BIRTH __________ EXAMINER ____________________________

			RESPONSE
Practice:	pencil:	wall – paper	____
1.	look:	hand – eyes	____
2.	belt:	pants – plate	____
3.	bread:	ring – butter	____
4.	paddle:	car – boat	____
5.	rod:	reel – hat	____
6.	apple:	jelly – glass	____
7.	bicycle:	wheel – football	____
8.	button:	sail – dress	____
9.	drum:	envelope – band	____
10.	carrot:	rabbit – bush	____

TOTAL INCORRECT: ____

Form 3-16

MANN-SUITER MANUAL LANGUAGE EXPRESSION SCREEN

NAME ______________________________ DATE ____________

DATE OF BIRTH __________ EXAMINER ______________________________

RESPONSE

Practice: ____

____

____

____

____

____

____

RESPONSE

____

____

____

____

____

TOTAL INCORRECT: ____

Form 3-17

MANN-SUITER SPEECH SCREEN

NAME ______________________________ DATE ______________

DATE OF BIRTH __________ EXAMINER ______________________________

Speech Articulation	*Adds Sounds*	*Distorts Sounds*	*Omits Sounds*	*Substitutes Sounds*
1. The rabbit runs fast.	____	____	____	____
2. Theodore, the frog.	____	____	____	____
3. Blow the whistle.	____	____	____	____
4. She sees the ship.	____	____	____	____
5. Black bug's blood.	____	____	____	____
6. The quick brown fox.	____	____	____	____
7. Aluminum.	____	____	____	____
8. Methodist Episcopal.	____	____	____	____

TOTAL INCORRECT: ____

Check if appropriate

Stuttering ☐

Cleft Palate ☐

Other (explain) ☐

Directions

1. The teacher says,"I am going to say something and I want you to say it after me."
2. The teacher repeats each item as necessary.

Scoring

1. Check the appropriate box for specific types of errors.
2. Consider an item incorrect if only one error is made on it.
3. For students ages 4–6, four or more incorrect items suggest difficulty with speech articulation.
4. For students age 7 and older, three or more incorrect items suggest difficulty with speech articulation.
5. Underline the letter or word that is nonfluent.

Things to Look For

1. Does the student stutter or stammer?
2. Does the student have hesitations in his or her speech?
3. Does the student's tongue appear to be lost in his or her mouth?
4. Does the student perseverate?
5. Is it difficult for the student to attend to the task?
6. Does the student exhibit cleft palate speech?

Note: See Chapter 6 for more specific evaluation in this area if necessary.

MANN-SUITER VERBAL LANGUAGE EXPRESSION SCREEN

The Mann-Suiter Verbal Language Expression Screen (Form 3-18) is designed to indicate the student's ability to view pictures of common objects and formulate phrases or sentences that will describe or indicate a quality or function of the particular object presented.

Directions

The teacher should say, pointing to the car, "Tell me all you can about this." If the student does not understand, the teacher should say, "Tell me what it is and what it does or what you can do with it." No further aid should be given.

Scoring

1. List the number of responses in the response column. For children ages 4–6, less than four total responses (and at least one per item) suggests problems with verbal language expression. Count any logical response as correct.
2. For students age 7 and older, under six responses (and at least one per item) suggests difficulty in the area of verbal language expression.

Things to Look For

1. How well does the student attend to the task?
2. Does the student perseverate?
3. Does the student go off on a tangent as a result of the stimulus picture?
4. Does the student give one-word or short-phrase responses?
5. What is the quality of the student's verbal responses, considering the cultural and experiential background?

Note: See Chapter 6 for more specific evaluation in this area if necessary.

MANN-SUITER WRITTEN LANGUAGE EXPRESSION SCREEN (for students age 7 and older)

The Mann-Suiter Written Language Expression Screen (Form 3-19) is designed to indicate the student's ability to take dictation.

Directions

1. For the Dictation section, the teacher says, "I want you to write some sentences exactly as I say them." The teacher repeats the sentence as necessary.
2. For the Expression section, the teacher says, "Now I want you to write your own sentence using the word *girl*." The rest of the items are handled in the same manner.

Scoring

1. This screen is essentially for diagnostic purposes only.
2. Good teacher judgment is necessary in analyzing the responses.

Form 3-18

MANN-SUITER VERBAL LANGUAGE EXPRESSION SCREEN

NAME ______________________________ DATE ____________

DATE OF BIRTH __________ EXAMINER ______________________________

RESPONSES

____

____

____

TOTAL CORRECT RESPONSES: ____

Form 3-19

MANN-SUITER WRITTEN LANGUAGE EXPRESSION SCREEN

NAME ______________________________ DATE ______________

DATE OF BIRTH __________ EXAMINER ______________________________

(For Students Age 7 and Over)

DICTATION (ATTACH CHILD'S DICTATION RESPONSES)

1. The cat is big.
2. Mother likes to bake cookies.
3. John went to the store yesterday.

EXPRESSION

1. Write a sentence using the word *girl.*
2. Write a sentence using the word *walking.*
3. Write a sentence using the word *he.*
4. Write a paragraph about *school.*

Things to Look For

1. How many repetitions in presentation are necessary?
2. For 1–4, does the student reverse the order of the words?
3. Does the student verbalize as he or she writes?
4. Does the student perseverate?
5. Does the student write things that are totally irrelevant?
6. How is the student's handwriting?

Note: See Chapter 6 for more specific evaluation in this area if necessary.

MANN-SUITER NONVERBAL SYMBOLIC LANGUAGE SCREEN

The Mann-Suiter Nonverbal Symbolic Language Screen (Form 3-20, page 70) is designed to indicate the student's ability to associate meaning with objects or symbols that represent abstract constructs, such as art, music, and patriotism.

Directions

The teacher says, "Listen and tell me which one it is: A rabbit's foot brings you 'rain' or 'luck.'" The teacher repeats as necessary.

Scoring

1. For children ages 4–6, four or more errors suggest difficulty with nonverbal language.
2. For children age 7 and older, two or more errors suggest difficulty with nonverbal language.
3. Symbols for scoring are √= correct, √̸= incorrect.

Things to Look For

1. Does the student perseverate?
2. Does the student say things that are totally irrelevant?
3. Go back and question the incorrect responses. Look for logical answers.

Note: See Chapter 6 for more specific evaluation in this area if necessary.

Form 3-20

MANN-SUITER NONVERBAL SYMBOLIC LANGUAGE SCREEN

NAME ____ DATE ____________

DATE OF BIRTH ________ EXAMINER ____

		RESPONSE
1. A rabbit's foot brings you:	rain–luck	____
2. A flag means your:	home–country	____
3. A pumpkin goes with:	Easter–Halloween	____
4. We get snow in the:	winter–summer	____
5. Music can make you:	thirsty–happy	____
6. When people paint pictures, they tell you how they:	feel–hear	____
7. A statue of a person means he was:	old–famous	____
8. A badge tells what you can:	do–grow	____
9. Our national anthem means:	patriotism–mountains	____
10. A turkey goes with:	Thanksgiving–the President's birthday	____

TOTAL INCORRECT: ____

Chapter 4 Developmental Spelling Diagnosis

SCREENING USING A SPELLING INVENTORY

A spelling inventory can be used for individual assessment or as an aid in determining the range of reading abilities and possible problem areas of a large group of students. As a rule, students who have difficulty in reading have difficulty in spelling. A developmental spelling inventory can be made up of words taken from the basal spelling series used in the school. The inventory serves two purposes:

1. The nature of the spelling errors made indicates the weaker channel for learning. It also suggests the areas of learning that need to be further explored. Spelling inventory screening as a formal means of evaluation will either support or negate the judgments teachers make on the basis of informal observation.
2. A spelling inventory enables the teacher to determine at which point screening with developmental reading inventories ought to begin. With this in mind, the teacher testing for reading ability should begin one level below that at which the student failed in spelling. This will reduce the degree of failure for some students and also identify quickly the more advanced learners in the class.

DEVELOPING A SPELLING INVENTORY

Following is a simple procedure for setting up a spelling inventory.

1. Select a word sample from each basal spelling book of a given spelling series.
2. Take 15 words from the grade one speller.
3. Take 20 words from the spellers for grades 2 through 6. Note: To take a sample selection from grades 2 through 6, divide the number of words listed at the back of the spelling book by 20. If there are 300 words in the book, you would divide 300 by 20 giving you 15. Therefore, a word sample would consist of every fifteenth word in the speller. Should you decide not to develop your own inventory, you could use the Mann-Sulter Developmental Spelling Inventory. (Form 4-1).

MANN-SUITER DEVELOPMENTAL SPELLING INVENTORY

The Mann-Suiter Developmental Spelling Inventory (Form 4-1) consists of samples of several basal and linguistic spelling lists. Table 4-1 is an analysis of the spelling skills tested for. The lists represent different spelling programs. They have been randomly selected according to level of difficulty and general orientation, and they are stratified to achieve a balance in terms of different spelling patterns, prefixes and suffixes, and configurations of words. Trial testing involved approximately 345 students, grades 1 through 8. Their performances were compared to the level of their functioning as indicated by teachers. In approximately 80 percent of the cases, there was agreement between teacher estimates of student performance and student achievement on the Mann-Suiter Developmental Spelling Inventory.

Form 4-1

MANN-SUITER DEVELOPMENTAL SPELLING INVENTORY

Level I	*Level II*	*Level III*	*Level IV*
1. cat	1. nod	1. drank	1. strike
2. no	2. jug	2. swing	2. choke
3. red	3. get	3. bath	3. shook
4. see	4. sip	4. sheep	4. hobby
5. and	5. tab	5. each	5. age
6. you	6. sled	6. train	6. chopped
7. the	7. drop	7. lake	7. swimming
8. we	8. clip	8. third	8. hiding
9. it	9. ask	9. catch	9. folded
10. yes	10. shop	10. stick	10. studies
11. dog	11. thank	11. ducks	11. foolish
12. big	12. sing	12. child	12. highest
13. like	13. boat	13. jumping	13. ashes
14. have	14. home	14. shorter	14. sailor
15. was	15. doll	15. walk	15. tightly
	16. little	16. right	16. carrying
	17. father	17. puppy	17. doesn't
	18. down	18. uncle	18. through
	19. pretty	19. because	19. climb
	20. said	20. wash	20. listen

Level V	*Level VI*	*Level VII*	*Level VIII*
1. crime	1. scene	1. brief	1. genius
2. risky	2. hastened	2. phrase	2. ancient
3. ridge	3. trophy	3. delicious	3. variety
4. soldiers	4. whirl	4. seize	4. sphere
5. sauce	5. pierced	5. caution	5. receipt
6. ditch	6. noble	6. knowledge	6. tissue
7. address	7. ignorantly	7. museum	7. progression
8. trouble	8. rewarded	8. delaying	8. virtue
9. quietly	9. continued	9. glorious	9. noisier
10. thieves	10. enforcing	10. moisture	10. leisure
11. business	11. motoring	11. social	11. constitution
12. heroes	12. relation	12. initial	12. fiction
13. movies	13. shortage	13. request	13. angle
14. expect	14. chocolate	14. slight	14. essay
15. dismissed	15. canyon	15. citizen	15. union
16. studying	16. court	16. envy	16. schedule
17. joking	17. maples	17. banquet	17. muscles
18. reviewed	18. autograph	18. pursue	18. natural
19. ruins	19. earliest	19. league	19. technical
20. crept	20. heavens	20. average	20. cancel

Table 4-1 Analysis of Spelling Skills

LEVEL I

Words	Spelling Skill
1. cat	Basic sight words
2. no	" " "
3. red	" " "
4. see	" " "
5. and	" " "
6. you	" " "
7. the	" " "
8. we	" " "
9. it	" " "
10. yes	" " "
11. dog	" " "
12. big	" " "
13. like	" " "
14. have	" " "
15. was	" " "

LEVEL II

Words	Spelling Skill
1. nod	Short *o*
2. jug	Short *u*
3. get	Short *e*
4. sip	Short *i*
5. tab	Short *a*
6. sled	Short vowel and consonant blend *(sl)*
7. drop	Short vowel and consonant blend *(dr)*
8. clip	Short vowel and consonant blend *(cl)*
9. ask	Short vowel and consonant blend *(sk)*
10. shop	Short vowel and consonant digraph *(sh)*
11. thank	Short vowel and consonant digraph *(th)*
12. sing	Short vowel and consonant digraph *(ng)*
13. boat	Long *o* spelled with digraph *oa*
14. home	Vowel, consonant plus *e*
15. doll	Final consonant (double)
16. little	Ending *le*
17. father	Ending *er*
18. down	*ow* for *ou*
19. pretty	Sight word
20. said	Sight word

LEVEL III

Words	Spelling Skills
1. drank	Short vowel and consonant blend *(dr)*
2. swing	Short vowel and consonant blend *(sw)*
3. bath	Short vowel and consonant blend *(th)*
4. sheep	Long *e* spelled *ee*
5. each	Long *e* spelled *ea*
6. train	Long *a* spelled *ai*
7. lake	Vowel, consonant plus *e*
8. third	*th*, vowel, *r*
9. catch	*tch* spelling
10. stick	*k* sound after short vowel spelled *ck*
11. ducks	Plural, root plus *s*
12. child	*i* followed by *ld* makes vowel long
13. jumping	*ing* ending
14. shorter	*er* ending
15. walk	Silent *l*
16. right	Silent *gh*
17. puppy	*y* as short *i*
18. uncle	Irregular spelling of *kle*
19. because	Sight word
20. wash	Sight word

LEVEL IV

Words	Spelling Skills
1. strike	Vowel, consonant, plus *e*
2. choke	Vowel, consonant, plus *e*
3. shook	Short vowel sound of *oo*
4. hobby	*y* for short *i*
5. age	*j* sound as *ge*
6. chopped	Final consonant doubled and *ed*
7. swimming	Final consonant doubled and *ing*
8. hiding	*e* to *i* before adding *ng*
9. folded	Ending *ed*
10. studies	*y* to *i* before adding *es*
11. foolish	Root plus *ish*
12. highest	Root plus *est*
13. ashes	Plural, root plus *es*
14. sailor	Root plus *or*
15. tightly	Root plus *ly*
16. carrying	Root, final *y*, plus *ing*
17. doesn't	Contraction
18. through	Sight word
19. climb	Silent *b*
20. listen	Silent *t*

LEVEL V

Words	Spelling Skills
1. crime	Vowel, consonant, plus *e*
2. risky	*y* for short *i*
3. ridge	*j* sound as *dge*
4. soldiers	*j* sound as *di*
5. sauce	*s* sound of *c*
6. ditch	*tch* spelling
7. address	Final consonant (double)
8. trouble	The *ŭ* sound of *ou*
9. quietly	Root plus *ly*
10. thieves	*f* changed to *v* plus *es*
11. business	*ĭ* sound of *u*
12. heroes	Words ending in *o* add *es* for plural
13. movies	Plural, root, plus *s*
14. expect	Prefix *ex*
15. dismissed	Prefix *dis*
16. studying	Addition of *ing* following *y*

Table 4-1 Analysis of Spelling Skills (continued)

Words	Spelling Skill
17. joking	e to *i* before adding *ng*
18. reviewed	Addition of *ed*
19. ruins	Vowels adjacent but not blended
20. crept	Short vowel and consonant blend
LEVEL VI	
1. scene	Silent *c*
2. hastened	Silent *t*
3. trophy	*ph* digraph
4. whirl	Final *l* not doubled
5. pierced	*i* before *e* rule
6. noble	Ending *le*
7. ignorantly	*ly* ending
8. rewarded	*ed* ending
9. continued	*e* dropped for addition of *ed*
10. enforcing	*e* changes to *i* before adding *ng*
11. motoring	*ing* ending
12. relation	*shun* spelled *tion*
13. shortage	*ij* spelled *age*
14. chocolate	*it* spelled *ate*
15. canyon	Sight word
16. court	Silent *u*
17. maples	Plural, root, plus *s*
18. autograph	Addition of suffix *graph*
19. earliest	*y* to *i* and add *est*
20. heavens	short *e* sound of *ea*
LEVEL VII	
1. brief	*i* before *e* rule
2. phrase	*ph* digraph
3. delicious	*sh* spelled *ci*
4. seize	Breaks the *i* before *e* rule
5. caution	*shun* spelled *tion*
6. knowledge	*ij* spelled *edge*
7. museum	Vowels adjacent but not blended
8. delaying	Addition of *ing* following *y*
9. glorious	*y* changes to *i* before adding *ous*
10. moisture	*ch* spelled *tu*
11. social	*shul* spelled *cial*
12. initial	*shul* spelled *tial*
13. request	Prefix *re*
14. slight	Silent *gh*
15. citizen	*s* sound spelled as *c*
16. envy	*y* says long *e*
17. banquet	*kw* spelled *qu*
18. pursue	Long *u* sound of *ue*
19. league	Digraph *ue* silent
20. average	*ij* spelled *age*
LEVEL VIII	
1. genius	*yu* spelled as *iu*
2. ancient	*sh* spelled *ci*
3. variety	Vowels adjacent but not blended
4. sphere	*ph* digraph
5. receipt	*i* before *e* except after *c* rule
6. tissue	*sh* spelled *ss*
7. progression	*shun* spelled *sion*
8. virtue	*ch* spelled *tu*
9. noisier	*y* changes to *i* and adds *er*
10. leisure	*zh* spelled *s*
11. constitution	*shun* spelled *tion*
12. fiction	*shun* spelled *tion*
13. angle	*le* ending
14. essay	Double *ss*
15. union	*y* sound spelled as *i*
16. schedule	*sk* spelled *sch*
17. muscles	*c* has *s* sound
18. natural	*ch* spelled *tu*
19. technical	*k* spelled *ch*
20. cancel	*sul* spelled *cel*

SCREENING PROCEDURES

For grade four and below, begin testing by administering first-level spelling words. For fifth grade and above, begin testing with the third-level spelling words. Thus, for students who fail the third level there always remains a second level to which they can be dropped. In giving the test, except for the first twelve words of Level II, the teacher should (1) say the word, (2) use the word in a sentence, and (3) repeat the word again.

The twelve words of Level II are designed to tell the teacher whether or not the learner can hear short vowel sounds in CVC (Consonant-Vowel-Consonant) pattern words and in words combining blends or digraphs. The teacher should (1) say the word, (2) sound the word out (n–o–d), and (3) say the whole word again. These words are *not* to be used in sentences. This procedure will tell whether or not the student is hearing the sounds and whether he or she is able to write the symbol that stands for the sound.

In all testing, it is important that the teacher stress to

the students that even if they cannot spell a word, they should put down every sound they can hear in the word.

To screen a fourth grade class, the teacher should dictate words from Level I and Level II at the first sitting and then check the responses. At the second sitting, the teacher should test only those students who were able to successfully spell the words given at the first sitting, since there is no sense in testing those who have already failed the first two levels. To avoid continued frustration, a student who misses seven words at a level—which constitutes failure at that level—should not be tested any further. At the third sitting, the teacher should finish screening only those students who were successful with the previous words.

Children can usually spell only words they can read; therefore, by adding up the correct words on each paper and then placing the papers in an order from low to high, the teacher will have an immediate idea of the relative reading levels of the students. Spelling screens should occasionally be given on unlined white paper. This will give the teacher a sample of the student's handwriting, which can be analyzed for good spacing, letter production, and positioning of words on a page.

OBSERVING SPELLING BEHAVIOR

Spelling ability is viewed by some teachers and school administrators equally with other academic skills. Students who are good learners but poor spellers are inordinately penalized by them for poor spelling. But deficiency in spelling does not necessarily denote that the learners have a serious learning disorder. Many students, educators, and professionals in different fields are poor spellers. Therefore, if spelling is an isolated problem, many teachers and parents do not consider the students learning disabled.

When poor spelling occurs with poor reading and arithmetic, then there is reason for concern. It appears that many of the learning skills required for good spelling are also the ones that enable students to become good readers. It is axiomatic that poor readers are generally poor spellers.

In evaluating spelling, the teacher should observe the following:

1. Has the learner isolated sound-symbol relationships (i.e., correctly associating a visual symbol with its auditory referent)?
2. Does the learner sequence visual symbols (letters) and sounds of letters (auditory)?
3. Can the learner estimate the number of letters in a word?
4. Does the learner use a logical system to arrive at the spelling of a word correctly or incorrectly?
5. What is the overall memory ability of the student?
6. Is there a great discrepancy between spelling ability and other academic skills, such as reading?
7. Is spelling automatic to the student (spells words instantly, correctly or incorrectly) or has he or she developed a unique analytical attack for each word?
8. How rapidly does the student relate the sound of the word or letters to the visual association in his or her mind? Does the visual image appear as a word or just isolated letters? Can the student verbalize what is happening in his or her mind's eye?
9. Is there a discrepancy between the student's ability to spell isolated words and his or her ability to spell phrases or sentences from dictation?
10 What does the student do with unfamiliar words that are not part of the reading program?
11. Is poor spelling disguised by illegible or unorthodox handwriting?
12. In written expression, does the student with spelling difficulties tend to substitute simple for more complex words having the same meaning?
13. Is there a great discrepancy between short-term and long-term memory of how words are spelled, requiring a great deal of intermittent reinforcement throughout the school year?
14. Does the learner have right-left scanning eye movements during the reading process that may result in two-letter reversals in spelling?
15. Is a great deal of oral spelling sequencing necessary to correct a residual spelling problem even after the student has learned to read?
16. Is the student having difficulty associating the meaning of a word with the sounds or symbols that make up the spoken word?
17. Is spelling improvement commensurate with reading improvement, or is there a residual spelling problem after reading improves?
18. Does the student appear to learn better with words of similar spelling patterns (e.g., *fat, cat, sat, mat*)?
19 Have hearing and vision been checked recently and found to be withln normal limits?
20 Does the student improve with teacher-directed spelling activities? The student may need more carefully structured spelling activities. A part of the student's problem may be in the way spelling is taught and reinforced.

21. Has the student developed an emotional block to spelling due to continued failure and pressures from the home or the school?
22. What kinds of study skills does the student use for spelling in school and at home?
23. In evaluation, does the student select the spelled word from among choices (recognition) easier than he or she spells the word (recall)?
24. Is the student being confused or overloaded by the introduction of too many different phonics skills in the spelling and reading programs?
25. Does the student spell better aloud than in writing?
26. Does the student learn more words when fewer words are required to be learned in a given period of time (slower rate of input)?
27. Does the student "chunk" (use syllables or parts of words), or does he or she spell letter by letter?
28. Does the student pronounce words correctly?

SPECIFIC SPELLING ERRORS

Spelling Errors Primarily Due to Auditory-Channel Deficits

The misspellings are typically nonphonetic, because the students often lack phonetic skills.

1. Substitutes *t* for *d*, *f* for *v*, *sh* for *ch*. (Auditory discrimination or cultural)
2. Does not hear subtle differences in, or discriminate between, sounds and often leaves vowels out of two-syllable words—for example, spells *plsh* for *polish.* (Auditory acuity or discrimination)
3. Discerns the beginning or ending of a word but not the middle of the word, which may be missing or spelled wrong—for example, spells *hd* for *hand.* (Auditory acuity and/or discrimination)
4. Confuses vowels—for example, spells *bit* as *bet.* (Auditory discrimination)
5. Omits the second letter in blends, spelling *fled* as *fed.* (Auditory acuity and/or discrimination)
6. Uses a synonym, such as *house* for *home,* in spelling (Auditory-visual association)
7. Omits word endings such as *ed, s,* and *ing.* (Cultural or auditory discrimination)
8. Takes wild guesses with little or no relationship between the letters or words used and the spelling words dictated, such as spelling *dog* for *home* or writing *phe* for *home.* (Auditory-visual associative memory)

Spelling Errors Primarily Due to Visual Channel Deficits

The misspellings are typically phonetic and therefore often intelligible, although incorrect.

1. Visualizes the beginning or the ending of words but omits the middle of the word—for example, spells *hapy* for *happy.* (Visual memory)
2. Gives the correct letters but in the wrong sequence. The word *the* may be written as *teh* or *hte.* (Visual-memory sequence)
3. Reverses letters or words—for example, writes ƨ for *s, b* for *d, on* for *no,* or *was* for *saw.*
4. Inverts letters, writing *u* for *n, m* for *w.* (Usually visual memory but could also be either visual discrimination or spatial)
5. Mixes up capitals and small letters—cAt. This error is also evident in cursive writing. (Poor transitional teaching or visual memory.) Sometimes mixing of capitals and small letters is due to the student's attempt to compensate for not knowing the small letters by substituting a capital letter for the small letter he has not learned.
6. Spelling words phonetically that are nonphonetic in configuration—for example, *tuff* for *tough.* (Visual memory)

SUPPLEMENTARY SCREENING

After analyzing the student's errors, the examiner may want to gain further diagnostic information from the following screening devices:

Speech 62
Alphabet-Speech 52
Auditory Discrimination 49
Visual Memory 47
Handwriting 223, 227–228
Oral Reading 81
Silent Reading 94–95
Hearing (acuity) 143
Vision (acuity) 143

Note: Refer to the spelling section beginning on page 215 for prescriptive activities.

After screening the students with the developmental spelling inventory, the teacher can start testing for reading abilities. Testing for reading should begin with the students who made the lowest scores on the spelling inventory, since they are the students who will need a more accurate and comprehensive analysis of reading abilities.

It is suggested that in testing for reading with DWRI (Developmental Word Reading Inventory, Chapter 5) the teacher begin the evaluation by dropping down to one level below the student's last successful level in spelling. If the student cannot spell at all, then the following readiness skills should be assessed:

1. Does the student know the letter names and sounds?
2. Can the student match a letter sound with its visual symbol?
3. Can the student match a letter name with its visual symbol?

Chapter 5 Developmental Reading Diagnosis

The previous chapter discussed how to use the Mann-Suiter Developmental Spelling Inventory as a basal measurement device for the language arts. This chapter will provide specific suggestions for testing and for the formation and use of developmental reading inventories and screens. Information regarding informal reading inventories from professionals in the field indicate that although examiner judgment is an important factor, Informal Reading Inventories are a valid means of assessing reading levels and giving important diagnostic information.[1]

RATIONALE FOR DIAGNOSIS

In evaluating reading, educators must concern themselves with three levels of functioning:

1. Screening and differential diagnosis of the learning problems of the very young child are necessary to determine whether the child has the prerequisite skills for learning how to read. Early evaluation enables the school to make decisions that result in more appropriate approaches to initial teaching. Evaluation can be accomplished during the kindergarten year in the spring, in preparation for first grade placement in the fall. The areas to be examined would include those listed in the Mann-Suiter-McClung Developmental Checklist (Form 1-1) and in the estimated hierarchy of skills presented in Chapter 7. As a part of this early diagnosis of learning problems, the teacher can make decisions about specific programs and backup systems that would be appropriate for individual learners.
2. Learners who have plateaued or who have indicated a slow rate of learning will profit from an early evaluation of reading skills, because appropriate remedial programs can be instituted early by the instructor. The Mann-Suiter Developmental Reading Inventories can be utilized in this area.
3. A number of students are failing in reading because of insufficient motivation or inappropriate early teaching. These students may not indicate deficits in the learning correlates. Instead they have a history of poor motivation or behavior difficulties. In the case of the poorly taught student, a pattern of faulty learning and poorly stabilized reading skills is evident.

Students who have problems in the cognitive areas dealing with memory, perception, language, and spatial-temporal orientation will require specific analysis and a balanced program that will strengthen the weaknesses while simultaneously developing task level behaviors that educators refer to as reading skills.

1. Beatrice J. Levin, "The Informal Reading Inventory," *Reading Improvement* 8 (Spring 1971): 18–20, and Sheila K. Hollander, "Why's a Busy Teacher Like You Giving an IRI?" *Elementary English* 51 (September 1974): 905–907.

Table 5-1 Correlation between Spelling Inventory and Word-Recognition Reading Inventory

Spelling Inventory		Word-Recognition Reading Inventory
Level I	failed*	Start at preprimer 3 level†
Level II	failed but Level I passed	Start at primer level
Level III	failed but Level II passed	Start at first-reader level
Level IV	failed but Level III passed	Start at second-reader level
Level V	failed but Level IV passed	Start at third-reader level
Level VI	failed but Level V passed	Start at fourth-reader level

***A spelling level is considered failed when a learner misses seven or more at a particular level.**

†Regardless of the student's age or grade (beyond first grade), if the student fails the PP3 word-recognition and paragraph reading inventories, he or she is functioning on a beginning reading level and needs to be taught with initial teaching approaches.

INITIAL TESTING

If a teacher is testing a student for the first time, the following procedure is suggested, regardless of the age or grade of the learner who is beyond first grade.

Where to Start

Turn to page 74, use the screening procedures outlined, and give the student a spelling inventory. The spelling inventory will enable the teacher to determine at which point screening with developmental reading inventories should begin. In testing for reading ability, the teacher should begin one level below that at which the student failed in spelling. Table 5-1 indicates where to start testing on the Developmental Word-Recognition Inventory.

Testing a Student below the PP3 Level

The following procedure will enable the teacher to determine where to place the student in the preprimer materials. The first step is to find out how many of the words the learner can read in the PP1 series being used. The teacher puts all of the words introduced in the PP1 on 3″ x 5″ word cards and then shows the student all of the words, one at a time. As the student responds, the teacher places the cards into three groups: words read without hesitation, words sounded out and eventually read or read with noticeable hesitation, and words totally unknown. See pages 7–8 for a more complete description of the procedure.

The teacher will now have the following information:

1. *Group One* will be the words read without hesitation. These words are considered mastered. They have been learned and can be used by the student at the independent level.
2. *Group Two* will be the words read with difficulty. The student may have to sound them out, reads them correctly at one point and incorrectly at another, and exhibits hesitations. This category of sight words is called partial learning. These are also the "leverage" words, as they are the words that are ready to be learned and should be taught first.
3. *Group Three* words are unknown to the student. They are the words that are totally misread on repeated occasions. There is evidence of 100 percent failure and frustration.

After testing the student on his or her sight recognition of the PP1 words and placing the words into one of the three categories indicated above, the teacher can decide whether the student is possibly ready for the PP2 because enough of the PP1 material is known and review would suffice.

If the teacher feels that the student knows enough of the PP1 material to enable him or her to move on to PP2, the teacher uses the following method to determine where to start.

1. The teacher puts all of the words introduced in the PP2 on 3″ x 5″ word cards and tests the student, following the same procedure used for PP1.
2. If the student finds PP2 difficult because too many words are unknown, the teacher starts teaching at that level.

3. If the student passes the PP2 level the teacher proceeds to PP3 and tests to determine the starting point.

Most older students who fail the Mann-Suiter PP3 test have such a scattered vocabulary of known words that they find it difficult to fit into any Preprimer program. The above testing procedure will accurately place them in most reading systems.

Ongoing Evaluation—Under Primer Level

This type of ongoing evaluation is for students in established reading programs who are functioning under the primer level. When a learner completes a PP1, PP2, or PP3, he or she should be tested immediately on the words taught in that book and should not be moved on to the next book unless the words are known without hesitation. If the student has forgotten any words, they must be retaught in a different manner. All learning must be adjusted to a rate tolerable for each student, and only through ongoing testing is it possible to make sure the learner is "holding," or stabilizing, the material taught.

Ongoing Evaluation—Primer Level or Above

This type of ongoing evaluation is for students in an established reading program who are reading at the Primer level or above. Ongoing testing is an important part of any reading program. When a student finishes a reading book such as a primer or a 2^1 reader, the teacher needs to test to see whether the student is ready to be advanced to the next level or needs another book on the same level just completed. Some students need more than one book at each level. (At the primer and first grade level especially, some will need two or three.) Use the Mann-Suiter developmental reading inventories for this testing.

An alternative would be to select two or three paragraphs from the reader the student has just completed and informally observe how he or she reads. The teacher can ask the student questions about what he or she has read. Questions in the following areas should be included: (1) main ideas, (2) inference, (3) details, and (4) vocabulary.

At House of Learning we have found the following program most effective. Children reading below the primer level are taught in The Hilltop Series: An Individualized Program for Problem Readers.[2] This reading series consists of eight books, and the tests provided with them are used to test a child prior to starting a book and again upon completion.

Upon successfully completing the Hilltop Series the child is placed in another reading series at the primer level. Upon completion of the primer level the child is tested in the Mann-Suiter Developmental Reading Inventories and either moved on to the next book or placed in a parallel primer of an alternate book series. Upon completion of that book the student is again tested and is either placed in another primer or moved up to the next level.

OBSERVING READING BEHAVIORS

1. How does the student analyze problems and glean meaning?
2. Does the student have excessive body movements while reading?
3. Is the student penalized by slowness in reading?
4. Does the student prefer to read alone or in a group?
5. How does the student react to being tested? Will the student respond to an alternative type of evaluation?
6. Does the student avoid reading?
7. When the student reads, what types of material will he or she read?
8. Does the student read at home?
9. Does the student understand more after reading silently than after listening to someone read the material orally?
10. What are the student's strengths and weaknesses indicated on the Mann-Suiter-McClung Checklist (page 25)?
11. Does the student value reading?
12. Is the student's failure mechanical or is he or she deficient in comprehension?
13. Does the student substitute words that are appropriate in his or her dialect while reading?

PURPOSES OF THE DEVELOPMENTAL READING INVENTORIES

The purposes of the developmental reading inventories are as follows:

1. To aid the teacher in determining the three levels of reading that have been traditionally defined as *independent, instructional,* and *frustration* levels.
2. To provide the teacher with information at the task level in the language arts area, as well as to point

2. Philip H. Mann, Rose Marie McClung, and Patricia A. Suiter, The Hilltop Series: An Individualized Program for Problem Readers (Boston: Allyn and Bacon, 1977–1979).

out possible problems that result in failure in reading.

3. To indicate the students' strengths and weaknesses by analyzing their performance at the reading task. The results of these tests can become the basis for selecting appropriate educational strategies for particular students.

Three types of reading assessment are delineated in this chapter: (1) teacher-developed inventories based on the available language arts series, (2) the Mann-Suiter Developmental Reading Inventories, and (3) the Mann-Suiter General Reading Screening.

TEACHER-DEVELOPED WORD READING INVENTORY

To develop a word reading inventory, the teacher takes a sample of words from the back of basal reading books of each grade level. He or she selects 20 words from each level, beginning at the PP3 level (approximately every second or third word). The formula for extracting these words is similar to that described for the Mann-Suiter spelling inventory. For all grade levels, the teacher picks a sample of 20 words by dividing the number of words in the book by 20. Say there are 200 new words in the book. Two hundred divided by 20 would give 10; therefore, a sample selection would be every tenth word from the list in the back of the book. After selecting the words for each level, the teacher should go back and check that he or she has included the following:

For grade one:

1. A variety of vowel and consonant sounds in different positions.
2. Words that are similar and different in configuration (a few words may be exchanged in order to achieve this).

For grades two through six:

1. A variety of vowel and consonant sounds in different positions.
2. Words that are similar and different in configuration.
3. Words with prefixes such as *pre* and *re* and suffixes such as *ed* and *ing.*
4. Words that have abstract meanings, such as *liberty* and *justice,* as language development is also being tested.

Note: Proper nouns are not included. By convention, they are omitted.

Developing Scoring Sheets

After having selected a word sample from the various levels and made some adjustments as recommended (using good judgment), the teacher is now ready to make up his or her own word-recognition scoring sheets. Form 5-1 illustrates a teacher's copy of word-recognition scoring sheets.[3] The words are typed clearly and double spaced on white paper. These sheets are to be used only by the teacher and are designed to record each student's responses.

Developing a Tachistoscope

After selecting the vocabulary and making up the score, the teacher is ready to construct a device that can be used to present the words to the student. The words should be presented in a manual tachistoscopic fashion. The instructions for making a sample word-recognition tachistoscope are presented in Figures 5-1 and 5-2.[4]

Note: Primer type should be used for word list selections from PP3 through the first level.

MANN-SUITER DEVELOPMENTAL READING INVENTORIES

The Mann-Suiter Developmental Reading Inventory includes a word-recognition section and a paragraph reading section. Approximately 375 students, grades 1 through 8, were administered the entire inventory, and the results were compared to their level of functioning as specified by teachers. In approximately 85 percent of the cases there was agreement between the estimates of teachers and the students' performance on the Mann-Suiter Developmental Inventories.

Developmental Word-Recognition Inventory

The Developmental Word-Recognition Inventory was developed by sampling different basal and linguistic word lists. These lists were representative of many

3. M. Johnson and R. Kress discuss the development of word-recognition scoring sheets in *Informal Reading Inventories,* Reading Aid Series (Newark, Del.: International Reading Association, 1965.)

4. D. Durrell, *Improving Reading Instruction* (Yonkers-on-Hudson, N.Y.: World Book Co., 1956), pp. 200–201.

Form 5-1

TEACHER'S DEVELOPMENTAL WORD-RECOGNITION SCORING SHEET

NAME ______________________________ DATE ______________

√ = Correct √^ = Incorrect EXAMINER ______________

Flash	*Pre-Primer Stimulus*	*Untimed*	Flash	*Primer Stimulus*	*Untimed*
1. ____	the	____	1. ____	with	____
2. ____	red	____	2. ____	good	____
3. ____	see	____	3. ____	they	____
4. ____	to	____	4. ____	for	____
5. ____	house	____	5. ____	girl	____
6. ____	said	____	6. ____	all	____
7. ____	little	____	7. ____	duck	____
8. ____	big	____	8. ____	this	____
9. ____	not	____	9. ____	yellow	____
10. ____	ball	____	10. ____	away	____
11. ____	get	____	11. ____	home	____
12. ____	in	____	12. ____	are	____
13. ____	went	____	13. ____	but	____
14. ____	and	____	14. ____	like	____
15. ____	dog	____	15. ____	make	____
16. ____	mother	____	16. ____	come	____
17. ____	man	____	17. ____	my	____
18. ____	had	____	18. ____	one	____
19. ____	no	____	19. ____	want	____
20. ____	run	____	20. ____	what	____
____	Errors	____	____	Errors	____
____	Score	____	____	Score	____

5 points each 5 points each

Observations:

different reading programs and were selected according to level of difficulty. Some stratification was accomplished in order to achieve a balance of spelling patterns, prefixes and suffixes, and different configurations of words. Form 5-2 (pages 85–89) is the scoring sheet for the Developmental Word-Recognition Inventory.

ADMINISTERING DEVELOPMENTAL WORD-RECOGNITION INVENTORY

1. During the test, the teacher should sit opposite the student at a table.
2. The first word should be centered in the window of the tachistoscope but covered with a white unlined 3″ × 5″ index card. (Variations of presentations to students can be used, depending on teacher preference.)
3. After asking the student to watch, the teacher should expose the whole word clearly and quickly, making sure the student initially gets only a flash presentation of the word.
4. The timing for the complete movement on the flash showing of the word should be approximately that required to say "one thousand" at a normal rate.

   Note: No more than one flash exposure should be given. This means the examiner must *be sure that the student is ready and attending.*
5. If the student responds quickly, the examiner immediately records a check, ✓, in the flash response column and goes on to the next word.
6. If, however, the student gives an incorrect response, the examiner records a different check, √, in the flash column and notes everything that is said.
7. No clues should be given, but the student should be allowed to reexamine the word and answer if he or she can. No help should be given. The answer is then recorded in the untimed column.
8. When a student does not know a word, the teacher can obtain additional information by asking if he or she knows any part of the word. The teacher can cover part of the word, ask the student if he or she knows it, and then determine if the student can blend the parts. This step is optional but helpful diagnostically.
9. The teacher must record all responses immediately and continue testing until the student misses seven of the twenty words on an untimed section for a particular grade level.

   Note: The teacher must remember to cover the teacher scoring sheet with his or her arm so that the student cannot read the words ahead of time.
10. Table 5-2 is a compilation of commonly used notations that teachers can use to communicate their findings to each other.

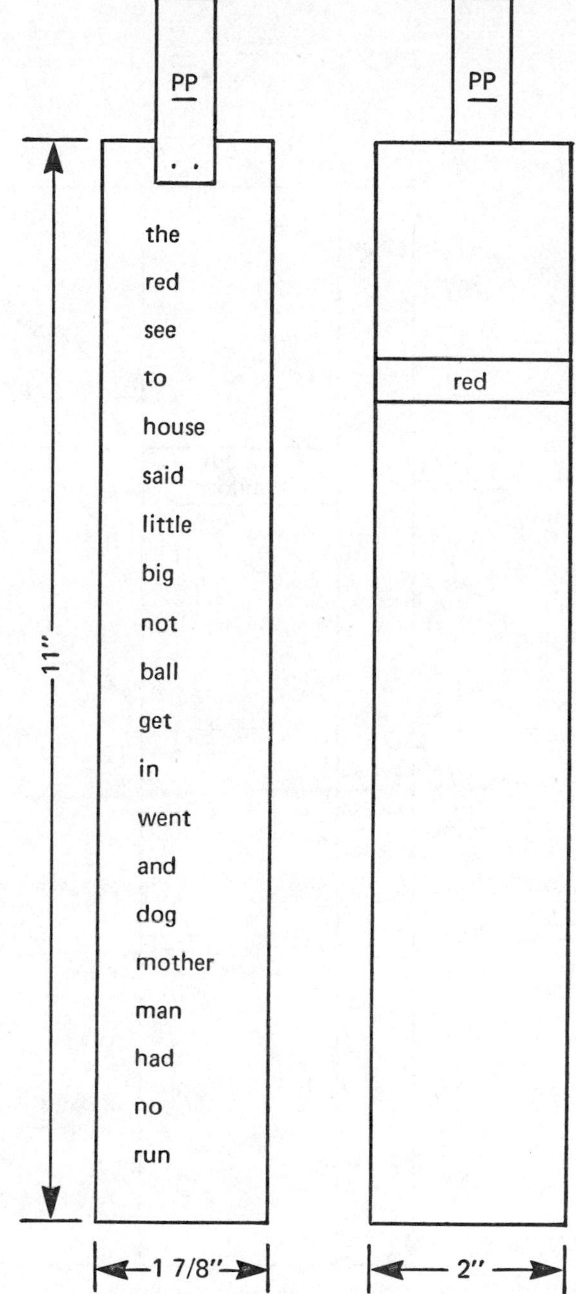

Figure 5-1 Instructions for Constructing a Tachistoscope: The Screen **A tab is stapled on top of the strip for ease of handling. All words should be double spaced. Primer type should be used for PP3 through level one words. A tachistoscope can be made from oak tag or strips cut from manila folders.**

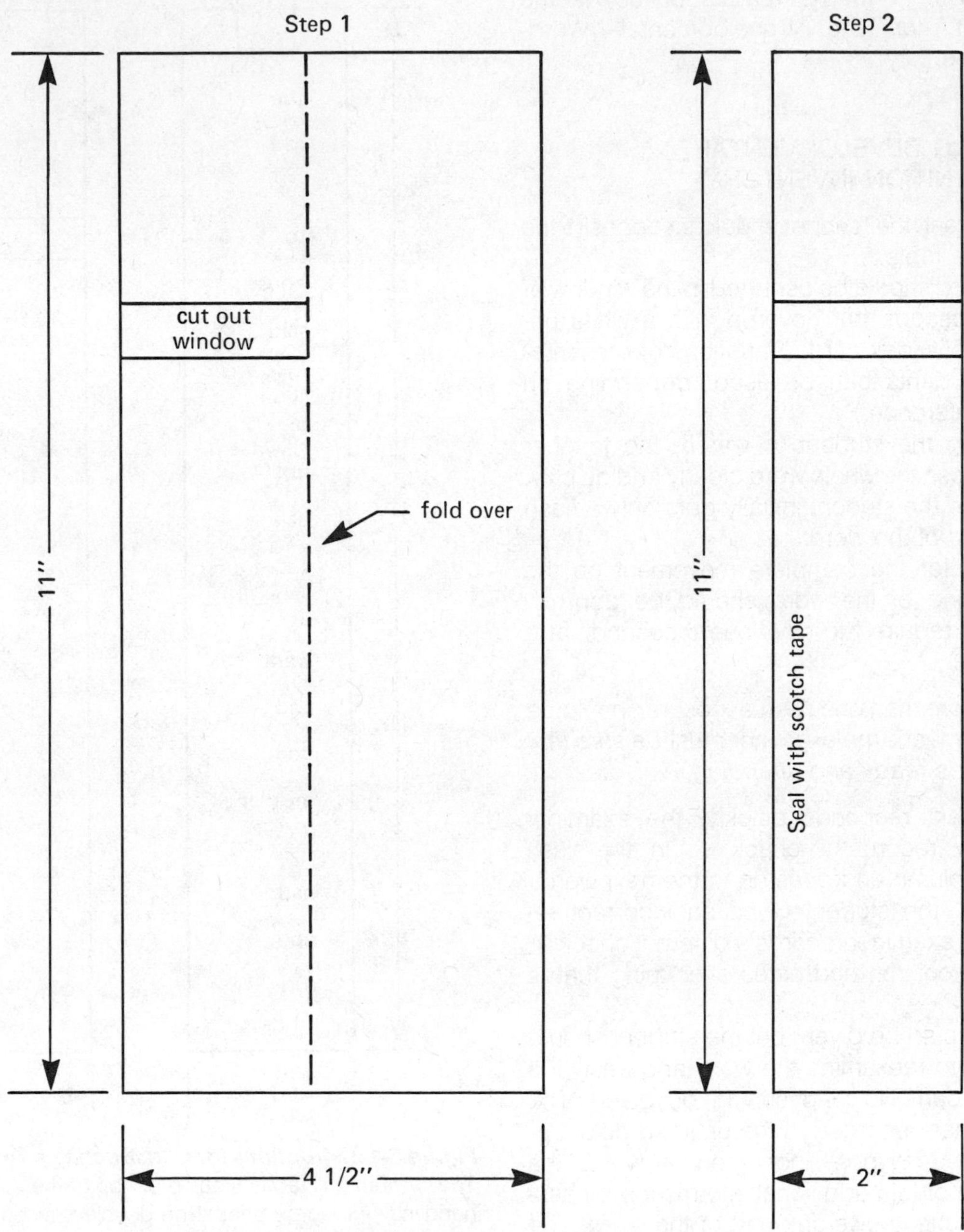

Figure 5-2 Instructions for Constructing a Tachistoscope: The Image Materials that can be used are oak tag or strips cut from a manila folder.

Form 5-2

MANN-SUITER DEVELOPMENTAL WORD-RECOGNITION SCORING SHEET (FORM A)

NAME ______________________________ DATE ______________

√ = Correct √ = Incorrect EXAMINER ______________

Pre-Primer

	Flash	Stimulus	Untimed
1.	____	the	____
2.	____	red	____
3.	____	see	____
4.	____	to	____
5.	____	house	____
6.	____	said	____
7.	____	little	____
8.	____	big	____
9.	____	not	____
10.	____	ball	____
11.	____	get	____
12.	____	in	____
13.	____	went	____
14.	____	and	____
15.	____	dog	____
16.	____	mother	____
17.	____	man	____
18.	____	had	____
19.	____	no	____
20.	____	run	____
	____	Errors	____
	____	Score	____

5 points each

Primer

	Flash	Stimulus	Untimed
1.	____	with	____
2.	____	good	____
3.	____	they	____
4.	____	for	____
5.	____	girl	____
6.	____	all	____
7.	____	duck	____
8.	____	this	____
9.	____	yellow	____
10.	____	away	____
11.	____	home	____
12.	____	are	____
13.	____	but	____
14.	____	like	____
15.	____	make	____
16.	____	come	____
17.	____	my	____
18.	____	one	____
19.	____	want	____
20.	____	what	____
	____	Errors	____
	____	Score	____

5 points each

Observations:

Mann-Suiter Developmental Word-Recognition Scoring Sheet (Form A)

NAME ____ DATE ______________

√= Correct √^= Incorrect EXAMINER ______________

First-Reader Level

Flash	*Stimulus*	*Untimed*
1. ____	many	____
2. ____	took	____
3. ____	feet	____
4. ____	please	____
5. ____	other	____
6. ____	drop	____
7. ____	their	____
8. ____	next	____
9. ____	over	____
10. ____	food	____
11. ____	hold	____
12. ____	again	____
13. ____	time	____
14. ____	when	____
15. ____	flag	____
16. ____	work	____
17. ____	thing	____
18. ____	going	____
19. ____	around	____
20. ____	frogs	____
____	Errors	____
____	Scores	____

5 points each

Second-Reader Level

Flash	*Stimulus*	*Untimed*
1. ____	head	____
2. ____	nice	____
3. ____	river	____
4. ____	string	____
5. ____	through	____
6. ____	side	____
7. ____	knew	____
8. ____	air	____
9. ____	grass	____
10. ____	floor	____
11. ____	drink	____
12. ____	while	____
13. ____	anything	____
14. ____	both	____
15. ____	leaves	____
16. ____	wash	____
17. ____	friend	____
18. ____	built	____
19. ____	ghost	____
20. ____	beautiful	____
____	Errors	____
____	Scores	____

5 points each

Observations:

Mann-Suiter Developmental Word-Recognition Scoring Sheet (Form A)

NAME ______________________________ DATE ______________

√ = Correct   √̸ = Incorrect   EXAMINER ______________

Third-Reader Level

	Flash	*Stimulus*	*Untimed*
1.	____	snail	____
2.	____	greatest	____
3.	____	eight	____
4.	____	lazy	____
5.	____	freeze	____
6.	____	gravel	____
7.	____	cousin	____
8.	____	path	____
9.	____	fifteen	____
10.	____	since	____
11.	____	awake	____
12.	____	shades	____
13.	____	scatter	____
14.	____	saddle	____
15.	____	journey	____
16.	____	chief	____
17.	____	tribe	____
18.	____	danger	____
19.	____	different	____
20.	____	stream	____
	____	Errors	____
	____	Scores	____

5 points each

Fourth-Reader Level

	Flash	*Stimulus*	*Untimed*
1.	____	spy	____
2.	____	fortune	____
3.	____	sheriff	____
4.	____	silence	____
5.	____	glanced	____
6.	____	breathe	____
7.	____	statements	____
8.	____	design	____
9.	____	pleasantly	____
10.	____	bacon	____
11.	____	courage	____
12.	____	islands	____
13.	____	western	____
14.	____	success	____
15.	____	trailed	____
16.	____	claimed	____
17.	____	knowledge	____
18.	____	peaceful	____
19.	____	rough	____
20.	____	guides	____
	____	Errors	____
	____	Scores	____

5 points each

Observations:

Mann-Suiter Developmental Word-Recognition Scoring Sheet (Form A)

NAME ______________________ DATE __________

√ = Correct √\ = Incorrect EXAMINER __________

Fifth-Reader Level				*Sixth-Reader Level*		
Flash	*Stimulus*	*Untimed*		*Flash*	*Stimulus*	*Untimed*
1. ____	naturally	____		1. ____	fleeting	____
2. ____	products	____		2. ____	poisoned	____
3. ____	defeated	____		3. ____	membership	____
4. ____	fought	____		4. ____	detained	____
5. ____	horrible	____		5. ____	medicine	____
6. ____	article	____		6. ____	summoned	____
7. ____	regarding	____		7. ____	licensed	____
8. ____	leisure	____		8. ____	malicious	____
9. ____	invitation	____		9. ____	liquids	____
10. ____	ancient	____		10. ____	obliged	____
11. ____	haze	____		11. ____	blonde	____
12. ____	shrill	____		12. ____	abandoned	____
13. ____	acquire	____		13. ____	partial	____
14. ____	scholar	____		14. ____	imagination	____
15. ____	prevent	____		15. ____	extensive	____
16. ____	salmon	____		16. ____	politics	____
17. ____	expensive	____		17. ____	cooperation	____
18. ____	whether	____		18. ____	scenes	____
19. ____	constantly	____		19. ____	negative	____
20. ____	emperor	____		20. ____	omitted	____
____	Errors	____		____	Errors	____
____	Scores	____		____	Scores	____
5 points each				5 points each		

Observations:

NAME ______________________________ DATE ____________

√ = Correct   √ = Incorrect   EXAMINER ____________

Seventh-Reader Level			Eighth-Reader Level		
Flash	*Stimulus*	*Untimed*	*Flash*	*Stimulus*	*Untimed*
1. ____	adequately	____	1. ____	prairies	____
2. ____	sojourn	____	2. ____	evident	____
3. ____	delighted	____	3. ____	nucleus	____
4. ____	waning	____	4. ____	antiquity	____
5. ____	grasped	____	5. ____	twilight	____
6. ____	vocation	____	6. ____	memorandum	____
7. ____	prominent	____	7. ____	whimsical	____
8. ____	preposition	____	8. ____	proportional	____
9. ____	exposition	____	9. ____	intangible	____
10. ____	subscribe	____	10. ____	formulated	____
11. ____	tremor	____	11. ____	ambitious	____
12. ____	height	____	12. ____	realize	____
13. ____	scientists	____	13. ____	ultimate	____
14. ____	individual	____	14. ____	financial	____
15. ____	persuade	____	15. ____	attitude	____
16. ____	approximate	____	16. ____	obviously	____
17. ____	environment	____	17. ____	oxygen	____
18. ____	compassionate	____	18. ____	visualize	____
19. ____	crisis	____	19. ____	surgery	____
20. ____	industrious	____	20. ____	fascinated	____
____	Errors	____	____	Errors	____
____	Scores	____	____	Scores	____
5 points each			5 points each		

Observations:

Table 5-2 Notations for Recording Responses

Stimulus Word	Notation	Meaning
see	√	Correct response
the	√^	No response or an incorrect response
sun	s-u-n	An attempt to reproduce the word phonetically
at	it/ate	Two wrong responses
where	when √	Corrected wrong first response
that	t/h/a/t	Student named the letters he or she saw but could not say the word or any part of the word.
duck	dk	What the student said he or she saw

SCORING INVENTORY

On the Developmental Word Reading Inventory, there is an allowance for a self-correction of errors. A response is counted accurate if

1. The student self-corrects during the timed exposure (the teacher must be sure to write down the initial response).
2. The student corrects the flash error during the untimed exposure. The error is counted only on the flash section of the test.

Note: Two scores should be obtained from each level test, one representing the student's flash vocabulary and the other his or her ability to identify words in an untimed fashion. Table 5.3 represents a score chart for flash and untimed words.

The scores on the Developmental Word Recognition Inventory can be plotted on the Developmental Reading Summary (Form 5-3, page 98).

Table 5-3 Score Chart for Flash and Untimed Words

Pre-Primer	Primer and Above
1 = 94%	1 = 95%
2 = 87%	2 = 90%
3 = 80%	3 = 85%
4 = 74%	4 = 80%
5 = 67%	5 = 75%
6 = 60%	6 = 70%
7 = 54%	7 = 65%
8 = 47%	8 = 60%
9 = 40%	9 = 55%
10 = 34%	10 = 50%

SPECIFIC WORD READING ERRORS

Word Reading Errors Primarily Due to Auditory Channel Problems

1. The student may be able to read letters and give names of letters but be unable to identify the sounds of letters (auditory-visual associative memory and/or auditory discrimination).
2. The student may take wild guesses at words with little or no relationship between the word seen and the word called (auditory-visual associative memory).
3. The student may substitute a synonym, such as *house* for *home* (auditory-visual associative mem ory).
4. The student may substitute one sound for another and read *bit* for *bet* (auditory discrimination).
5. The student may know the sounds but still be unable to blend them into words (auditory closure).

Word Reading Errors Primarily Due to Visual Channel Problems

1. The student may exhibit a slow rate of perception and be unable to read the word when it is flashed but be able to identify the word on the untimed presentation. Time makes the difference (rate of perception).
2. The student may discern only the beginning or the ending of a word and lose the middle (visual closure or rate of perception).
3. The student may reverse the letters in a word, for example, *was–saw, on–no* (usually visual memory, but also check visual discrimination and spatial).
4. The student may invert letters, for example, *me* for *we* (usually visual memory, but also check visual discrimination and spatial).
5. The student may fail to discriminate fine differences between letters and read *ship* for *snip* or *red* for *rod* (visual discrimination).
6. The student may add sounds to words, for example, reading *dogs* for *dog* (visual memory and/or misperception).
7. The student may try to sound words phonetically, exhibiting excessive hesitations (check visual memory). This problem can also be indicative of an oral expressive (retrieval) disorder in which the student knows the word but cannot retrieve the correct motor sequence.

In administering the Word Reading Inventory teachers should ask themselves the following questions: (1) What do the errors on the Developmental Spelling Inventory mean diagnostically? (2) Is the student making similar errors on the Developmental Word

Reading Inventory? (3) Am I observing the way he or she reads the words as well as trying to get a measure of his or her reading level?

Checking for Oral Language Development

Additional information can be obtained about the level of a student's word reading ability by testing the student's oral language development according to the following procedure:

1. After completing a level, the teacher can go back and select three words at random that the student has read successfully and ask him or her (a) to use the word in a sentence and (b) to tell what the word means. For example, on the PP3 list, the teacher asked a student to use the word *dog* in a *sentence*. He did it accurately and *S+* was written next to the word on the teacher scoring sheet. If the response had been wrong, the teacher would have marked *S−* next to the word. The teacher then asked the student the *meaning* of the word. The response was correct, so, *M+* was written next to the word on the teacher scoring sheet. Had the word been defined incorrectly, the teacher would have written *M−* next to it. Manual expressions of meaning are acceptable but should be noted.
2. Only three words should be used from each selection.
3. The Analysis of Errors worksheets (Chapter 6) contain a section on vocabulary that has been delineated into two basic *levels of conceptualization* for different grades: Concrete-Functional and Abstract. The *level of conceptualization* tells us how the student thinks. It is important for the teacher to know at what level the student is basically functioning so that the teacher can plan for an appropriate selection of materials and not overload the student with concepts that are too difficult.
   a. The Concrete-Functional level (*C − F*) includes any response that describes the quality, state of being, or function of the object to be defined. An essentially concrete-level response is that an apple is round. A response at the functional level is that an apple can be eaten.
   b. The Abstract level (*A*) includes any response that indicates a synonym, classification, or association. An abstract-level response is that an apple is a fruit.

The word meanings for any grade level can be classified according to the above-mentioned levels of conceptualization. They can be used in conjunction with the word meanings given in the Developmental Paragraph Reading Inventory (described later in this chapter), to aid the teacher in determining the student's overall level of responses. The teacher can then make the appropriate notation on the Analysis of Error Worksheets (Forms 6-1–6-4, pages 145–151).

Observable Behaviors

The following behaviors should be noted on the score sheet if they are present:

1. Tension or nervousness
2. Distractibility
3. Visual difficulties (ocular motor)
4. Hearing difficulties
5. Speech problems (stuttering, articulation, voice)
6. Bizarre responses

Developmental Paragraph Reading Inventory

The teacher can construct a Developmental Paragraph Reading Inventory (DPRI) from any basal reading series available. The DPRI is designed to do the following:

1. Determine the learner's independent, instructional, and frustration reading levels.
2. Identify specific types of word-recognition errors.
3. Estimate comprehension ability.
4. Determine the extent of the student's vocabulary.
5. Obtain information relative to the student's rate of performance.

DEVELOPING A DEVELOPMENTAL PARAGRAPH READING INVENTORY

1. Select any basal reading series and take a reading selection from the back one third of each of the levels. Be sure to get a representative variety to avoid extreme variations. The following readability formulas will aid you in choosing an appropriate selection: (a) For grades one through three, use the George Spache Formula; (b) for grades four through six use the Dale-Chall Formula; and (c) for grades seven and eight use the Fry Formula.[5]
2. Begin at the PP3 level and proceed to as high a level as necessary for your class. Table 5-4 will help you decide upon the appropriate number of words for each reading selection:

5. G. Spache, "New Readability Formula for Primary Grade Reading Materials," *Elementary School Journal* 53 (March 1953): 410–413; E. Dale and J. Chall, *A Formula for Predicting Readability* (Columbus: Bureau of Educational Research, Ohio State University), 1948; and E. Fry, "A Readability Formula That Saves Time," *Journal of Reading*" (April 1968): 513–518.

Figure 5-3 Mann-Suiter Developmental Paragraph Reading Inventory (Sample Teacher Scoring Sheet)

MOTIVATIONAL QUESTION: Have you ever seen a red dog? Find out what kind of a dog Jane and Dick saw in this story.

Pre-Primer 3 (29 words)

THE RED DOG

"Look, look," said Jane.

"See the funny little dog.

Can you see it?

It is red."

"I see it," said Dick.

"It is a toy dog."

Errors	0	1	2	3	4	5
Percentage	100	96	93	89	86	83

Detail	1.	What did Jane see? (a funny little dog, a red dog, or a toy dog)
Vocabulary		What does the word *little* mean? (small, etc.)
Main Idea	2.	Why did Jane call the little dog funny? (it was red)
Inference	3.	Where do you think the children were? (toy store, etc.)
Detail	4.	What kind of a dog did Dick say it was? (toy)

Errors	0	1	2	3
Percentage	100	75	50	25

3. Construct the teacher scoring sheet and the student's reading copy. An example of the teacher's scoring sheet of a PP3 selection is shown in Figure 5-3. The teacher's copy can be dittoed. The student's reading selection can be typed on a sheet of oak tag, on nonglossy white cardboard, on heavy white bond paper, or on pieces cut from manila folders. Use primer type for reading selections PP3 through first level.

Table 5-4 Correlation between Grade Level and Length of Reading

Level	*Words (Approximate)*	*Questions*
PP3	20–30	5
P	30–40	5
1	35–50	5
2^1	40–55	5
2^2	45–60	5
3^1	60–90	5
3^2	60–100	5
4	75–125	5
5	90–150	5
6	100–175	5

Note: The length of the sentences should be approximately the same length found in the appropriate grade level basal reader.

Writing Comprehension Questions for the Paragraph Inventory

Comprehension questions should be asked after every reading selection. The order of the type of questions (detail, main idea, vocabulary, or inference) should follow the sequence of the text; therefore, it will be different for each story. The questions for each selection should be based upon that selection. Below is a list of areas the questions should cover.

1. *Vocabulary Questions.*
   Example:
   a. What does the word _____ mean?

b. What is another meaning for the word ____ ?
c. What is a word that can be used in place of ____ ?

Note: Look for Concrete-Functional or Abstract Responses.

2. *Detail Questions.* Questions should be included that require the student to tell what something is or is not doing. These questions can describe a quantity, quality, state of being, or an action.
Example:
a. What did Jane see?
b. What color was the dog?
3. *Main Idea Questions.* One question in each selection should reflect the essence of the story or of the main character in the story.
Example:
a. Why was Ann excited?
b. Why did Bill's mother tell him not to go swimming alone?
4. *Inference Questions.* Questions of this nature should require the student to formulate a logical deduction from several bits of available information.
Example:
a. What time of day was it? (The story tells about shooting stars.)
b. How do we know that John was being teased? (The story describes the teasing of a blind boy.)

SCREENING PROCEDURES FOR THE DEVELOPMENTAL PARAGRAPH READING INVENTORY

1. Select a level at which the student can begin with a success before he or she ultimately fails. You can also begin at the highest level at which the student had 85 to 90 percent correct on the untimed section of the Developmental Word Reading Inventory.
2. Before the student begins, tell him or her that you will ask a few questions about the story when he or she has finished. (Do not allow the student to preread the selection silently.)
3. Hand the student the reading selection, read the motivational question to him or her, and ask the student to read out loud to you. Be sure the student reads the title of each selection.
4. Always ask the questions as soon as the reading is completed, and permit the student to hold on to the selection so that he or she can refer to it as necessary. We do not want to penalize the student for possible difficulties with memory. However, if unusual amounts of time are used to find information, this should be noted.

   Note: If the pupil fails to respond to the questions appropriately, he or she may be asked to "explain more fully" or to "tell me more," etc. Although lack of response is considered in the total scoring, probing questions are permitted. However, use good judgment in such instances.
5. Be sure to mark the correct and incorrect responses by each question as it is answered. If there are two or three parts to the answer, give credit for the correct portion answered. For example, "What did Mary do first? Next? And last?" Each part of this question is worth one-third of the credit.

   Note: Do not forget to record unusual answers. Customarily, vocabulary questions are not counted into the comprehension score.

SCORING PROCEDURES FOR THE DEVELOPMENTAL PARAGRAPH READING INVENTORY

Symbol Notation

As the student reads the selection, use the following symbols to record the types of word recognition errors made during the paragraph reading selection.

1. *Unusual phrasing, or word-by-word reading.*

   Example: A/ little black dog ran/ away/ from home.

   (Noted but not counted as an error.)
2. *Omitted words, phrases, or word endings.*

   Example: A little black dog ran away from home. He talked (and talked) to her. He talk(s) to her.

   (Counted as an error.)
3. *Substitutions.*

   Example: Mary walked over (above) the bridge.

   Write the substituted word above. (Counted as an error.)
4. *Additions of words, phrases, or endings.*

   Example: A little black doggy ran away from (the) home.

   (Counted as an error.)
5. *Repetitions.*

   Example: A little black dog ran away from home.

   A line is drawn indicating the portion repeated. (Noted but not counted as an error.)

6. *Mispronunciation of words.*
   Write *M* above the word.

   Example: "The big machine." The error is in placing the accent on the wrong syllable. Write out the errors. (Counted as an error.)
7. *Punctuation.*
   The student continues to read through the punctuation marks.

   Example: A little dog ran away He ran, etc.

   (Noted but not counted as an error.)
8. *Needs assistance.*
   If the student hesitates more than five seconds, write *P* above the word and pronounce it for the student. (Counted as an error.)
9. *Self-correction of errors.*

   Example: She saw a penny.

   (Noted but not counted as an error.)
10. *Hesitations.*

    Example: A little black dog ran h away.

    If the student hesitates noticeably, put an *h* before the word. (Noted but not counted as an error.)

Each of the errors can be scored as indicated. Sometimes the teacher has to use his or her judgment in scoring. A good rule of thumb is to score as an error anything that changes or distorts the meaning or intent of the selection.

Summary of Word Recognition Errors

The student makes an error when he or she

1. Omits a word
2. Substitutes a word
3. Adds a word
4. Mispronounces a word
5. Asks the examiner to pronounce a word

Note: Proper names are not counted as errors, as they depend upon experiential factors.

Scoring of Comprehension Questions

The teacher divides 100 by the number of questions, not including vocabulary questions, to get the value of each comprehension question. For example, if the first-level reading selection has 5 questions, including 1 vocabulary question, the teacher divides 100 by 4 to get the value of each question.

After the teacher obtains the percentage correct from each of the levels tested, he or she should record the scores on the Developmental Reading Summary Record (Form 5-3), under Reading-Comprehension. Both the word-recognition and comprehension scores should be plotted to get the level of performance.

Note: It is important that the teacher listen carefully and record accurately errors made by the student. Practice will help to develop this skill. One should not expect to be an expert after the first administration.

FINDING THE READING LEVELS

Frustration Level

The student performing at the frustration level reads with symptoms such as fingerpointing, tension, or hesitant word-by-word reading. Comprehension may be extremely low. The student is completely unable to handle the reading materials presented.

Instructional Level

At the instructional level, the student will be able to read with at least 93 percent accuracy of word recognition and with 75 percent or better comprehension. At this point, the teacher's help is necessary; but after being given the instruction, the student should be able to handle the material independently.

Independent Level

At the independent level, the student reads with ease. It is the level to be used in selecting supplementary reading material and library books. The student has at least 97 percent word recognition and 90 percent comprehension.

Summary of Scoring

1. Independent level: 97 percent and above correct oral reading and 90 percent and above comprehension
2. Instructional level: 93–96 percent oral reading and 75 percent and above comprehension
3. Frustration level: Below 93 percent oral reading and below 75 percent comprehension.

SILENT READING COMPREHENSION

Many teachers will not give a silent comprehension test because it is too time-consuming. However, for diagnostic purposes, it may be helpful to know the discrepancy between the student's oral and silent reading.

If a silent reading test is given, the teacher may want to average the scores between the oral comprehension and the silent reading comprehension in order to get a more approximate grade level.

LISTENING COMPREHENSION LEVEL (OPTIONAL)

The teacher can read more difficult selections to students after they have failed one to determine whether or not they can understand higher level material and discuss what they have heard. Such selections should be beyond their instructional level. The highest level at which they can understand 75 percent of the material would determine their probable level of comprehension. Many professionals believe a student should be reading at this level of understanding. The listening comprehension scores can be recorded on the Developmental Reading Summary Record.

SPECIFIC READING ERRORS

Reading Errors Primarily Due to Auditory Channel Problems

1. The student may mispronounce words, for example, read the word *chimney* as *chimley* (auditory acuity and/or discrimination).
2. The student may take wild guesses, with no relationship between the word seen and the word read (auditory-visual associative memory).
3. When stuck on a word, the student may not be able to sound it out (auditory-visual associative memory).
4. The student may be poor in blending sounds together to make words (auditory closure).
5. The student may use a synonym, for example, saying *mommy* for *mother* (auditory-visual associative memory).
6. The student may substitute words, such as *a* for *the* (auditory-visual associative memory).

Reading Errors Primarily Due to Visual Channel Deficits

1. The student may exhibit word-by-word reading or poor phrasing (rate of perception).
2. The student may be unable to keep his or her place and may skip lines or parts of lines when reading (visual figure-ground or ocular motor).
3. The student may add words that may or may not change the meaning, for example, adding the word *the* when it isn't there (visual memory and/or misperception).
4. The student may repeat parts of words, phrases, and sometimes whole sentences in an attempt to get the meaning (check receptive and expressive language).
5. The student may read through punctuation, distorting the meaning of what he or she reads (check receptive and expressive language).
6. The student may reverse words or letters (visual sequential memory and/or spatial).
7. The student may invert words or letters (visual-memory and/or spatial).
8. The student may look at the beginning of a word and then say some other word that starts in the same way, for example, *surprise* for *something.* If the student self-corrects, he or she may be only looking at initial consonants and configurations (rate of perception).

Observing Paragraph Reading Behavior

When facing unfamiliar words in a paragraph, does the student display any of the following behaviors:

1. Guesses without regard to any thought of the context read.
2. Seems unwilling to attempt to read and just waits for the teacher to say the word.
3. Seems willing to just skip the unknown word and go on.
4. Seems unable to sound out word parts and blends.
5. Tries to spell out the word he or she cannot read.
6. Makes little use of the context in attacking an unknown word.

In general, does the student behave as follows:

1. Disregards punctuation.
2. Doesn't pay attention to the story line.
3. Has a low meaning vocabulary—not adequate for the reading level under concern.
4. Makes no attempt to correct errors.
5. Exhibits frequent hesitations and makes sounds like uh. . . .
6. Drops his or her voice at the end of a sentence.
7. Reads word by word instead of in phrases or thought units.
8. Exhibits a negative and indifferent attitude. "Do I have to?"

Is there flash-untimed discrepancy or a wide range between the flash and untimed scores, with a much smaller sight vocabulary evident on the flash part of the testing? Students with this discrepancy are often slow in recognition, but able to work out the pronunciation. The untimed part of the test may be within the passing level, but the slow recognition or excessive sounding out will hinder the student in reading.

Some learners frequently substitute or add words in a paragraph, but that does not usually interfere with the overall sense and meaning. As long as it does not interfere with the meaning or understanding of the content there is no need for undue concern.

Mann-Suiter Developmental Reading Summary Record

The examiner should plot the scores for each area of reading on the Developmental Reading Summary Record (Form 5-3) to determine the student's present level of functioning. The procedure for plotting the scores is as follows:

1. Record the scores for *percentage word-recognition, correct flash,* in the appropriate boxes. These scores are used for diagnostic purposes only, giving information as to how quickly and how accurately a student perceives a word.
2. Record the scores for percentage *word-recognition, correct-untimed,* and the *percentage word-recognition, accuracy,* from the paragraph oral readings in the appropriate boxes. These two scores are averaged to give the *percentage word-recognition, average,* and are recorded in the appropriate boxes.
3. Record the *reading comprehension* and note the appropriate form. Then record the *listening comprehension* score if given.
4. Plot the final scores on the graph, indicating the level of functioning, such as PP3 or P, in the appropriate section—independent, instructional, or frustration.

Examples of Mann-Suiter Developmental Paragraph Reading Inventory (Form A)

The following inventory, made up of original stories, can be used to determine the reading levels of students. To administer the inventory, the teacher should follow the instructions given on page 93.

Note: Primer type is recommended in reproducing the student copies for primer through level one selections.

GENERAL READING SCREENING (GROUP AND INDIVIDUAL)

Three screens were developed in response to requests by many teachers for general reading screening that could be administered to more than one student at a time. This would enable teachers to determine during the first days of school the range of language skills in their classrooms. With the Mann-Suiter general reading screens the teacher can estimate the reading, written language development, and vocabulary comprehension levels of the students. More precise individual reading evaluations can then be administered where necessary.

Knowing the estimated range of variability will enable the teacher to plan for individual needs in reading, written language expression, and vocabulary acquisition.

The three language screens are the Mann-Suiter Word Reading Screen, the Mann-Suiter Vocabulary Screen, and the Mann-Suiter Silent Reading and Written Language Screen.

Mann-Suiter Word Reading Screen

The Mann-Suiter Word Reading Screen has been designed to be used with individuals or groups of students in grades 2 through 8. Reading level of the selections range from preprimer through grade 8.

RATIONALE

The purpose of the Mann-Suiter Word Reading Screen is to give the classroom teacher an approximate beginning reading level for each student. It will estimate the wide range of ability in the classroom and serve as an aid in selecting classroom material needed for the reading program.

This screen is particularly useful for group evaluation at the beginning of the school year. The following are suggested levels for beginning screening at particular grades.

Grade 2—Preprimer, Primer, First, and Second
Grade 3—Primer, First, Second, and Third
Grade 4—First, Second, Third, and Fourth
Grade 5—Second, Third, Fourth, and Fifth
Grade 6—Third, Fourth, Fifth, and Sixth
Grade 7—Fourth, Fifth, Sixth, and Seventh
Grade 8—Fifth, Sixth, Seventh, and Eighth

Note: The teacher may have to drop down to lower levels if there is a great deal of variability within a given class of students. Good judgment should be used.

ADMINISTERING THE MANN-SUITER WORD READING SCREEN

Each student in the class will need a copy of the Student Worksheet (Form 5-5, pages 111–113) for the level the teacher has selected to begin the screening. The lettered sections of the screen correspond to reading levels, as follows:

A. Preprimer
B. Primer
C. First
D. Second
E. Third
F. Fourth
G. Fifth
H. Sixth
I. Seventh
J. Eighth

The instructor should make sure that all the students have pencils and are ready. Detailed directions for administering the test are included on the Examiner's Copy and Answer Sheet (Form 5-6, page 114).

SCORING THE MANN-SUITER WORD READING SCREEN

Scoring is done on the Student's Worksheet. To the right of each worksheet is a column for the teacher to check if an error has been made. The student's approximate reading level is the last word he or she knew before missing three in a row.

If a student, for example, read all of the preprimer words, but knew only two or three of the primer words, his or her testing for placement in classroom materials would begin at the primer level. If another student knew four of the primer words, but none of the first-level words, he or she would be tested for mid-primer placement or be started in an easy first-level reading book.

To aid the teacher in determining the needs of the class, a Class Score Sheet (Form 5-7) has been developed. Before entering names on the Class Score Sheet, the teacher should organize the student's papers by score, ranking them from the lowest to the highest. When entering names on the Class Score Sheet, the teacher should enter the lowest first and proceed to the highest. A copy of the Class Score Sheet can be given to the librarian, who can use the estimated scores in teaching library skills and in helping individual students to select appropriate books and other materials. Figure 5-4 is an example of a completed Class Score Sheet.

Mann-Suiter Word Reading Screen
Class Score Sheet

Grade ____________ Date ____________

Name	A PP	B P	C I	D II	E III	F IV	G V	H VI	I VII	J VIII
1. Mary Smith	X									
2. Becky Rubin		X								
3. Johnny Jones		X								
4. Lisa Mason		X								
5. Danny ayres			X							

Figure 5-4 Completed Class Score Sheet

Form 5-3

MANN-SUITER DEVELOPMENTAL READING SUMMARY RECORD

NAME ______________________________ GRADE ______ AGE ______ DATE ______________

EXAMINER ______________________________

DEVELOPMENTAL WORD RECOGNITION AND READING INVENTORY

	PP3	*P*	*1*	*2¹*	*2²*	*3¹*	*3²*	*4*	*5*	*6*	*7*	*8*
1 % Word recognition, correct-flash												
2 % Word recognition, correct-untimed (*ut*)												
3 % Word recognition, accuracy–DPRI oral reading												
4 % Word recognition, average–UT and DPRI oral reading (2 and 3)*												
5 % Reading comprehension, form ____												
6 % Listening comprehension, form ____												

Average of the Untimed Word Recognition and the DPRI Oral Reading

Reading Comprehension

%	100	99	98	97	96	95	94	93	92	91	90	89	88	87	86
100															
95															
90	INDEPENDENT														
85															
80				INSTRUCTIONAL											
75															
70															
65							FRUSTRATION								
60															
55															
50															
45															

*Difficulties noted:

Frustration Level ________

Instructional Level ________

Independent Level ________

Form 5-4

MANN-SUITER DEVELOPMENTAL PARAGRAPH READING INVENTORY—FORM A (TEACHER SCORING SHEET)

NAME ______________________________ DATE ______________

GRADE ______________ EXAMINER ______________________________

MOTIVATIONAL QUESTION: Have you ever seen a red dog? Find out what kind of a dog Jane and Dick saw in this story.

Pre-Primer 3 (29 words)

THE RED DOG

"Look, look," said Jane.

"See the funny little dog.

Can you see it?

It is red."

"I see it," said Dick.

"It is a toy dog."

Errors	0	1	2	3	4	5
Percentage	100	97	93	89	86	83

Detail	1.	What did Jane see? (a funny little dog, a red dog, or a toy dog)
Vocabulary		What is the meaning of the word *little*? (small, etc.)
Main Idea	2.	Why did Jane call the little dog funny? (it was red)
Inference	3.	Where do you think the children were? (toy store, etc.)
Detail	4.	What kind of a dog did Dick say it was? (toy)

Errors	0	1	2	3
Percentage	100	75	50	25

NAME ______________________________ DATE ______________

GRADE ______________ EXAMINER ______________________________

MOTIVATIONAL QUESTION: Have you seen a baby animal? This story is about a cute baby animal that a little girl named Ann saw.

Primer (40 words)

THE BABY MONKEY

One day Ann went

for a walk in the zoo.

Soon she saw something.

"A baby monkey," said Ann.

"I see a baby monkey."

Then she saw Mary and Jimmy.

"Come see the baby monkey," called Ann.

Errors	0	1	2	3	4	5	6
Percentage	100	98	95	93	90	88	85

Detail	1.	Where was Ann walking? (in the zoo)
Main Idea	2.	Why was Ann excited? (she saw a baby monkey)
Detail	3.	How many children are in the story? (three)
Vocabulary		What is the meaning of the word *zoo*? (any acceptable answer)
Inference	4.	Why do you think Ann wanted Mary and Jimmy to see the baby monkey? (any acceptable answer)

Errors	0	1	2	3
Percentage	100	75	50	25

NAME ____ DATE ______________

GRADE ______________ EXAMINER ____

MOTIVATIONAL QUESTION: The family in this story went to a park. Read to find out what mother forgot to take with her.

First Reader (51 words)

FUN AT THE PARK

One hot day we went to a park to swim.

Other people were at the park, too.

"Let's get a hot dog on a bun," said Dick.

"I want ice cream," said Lisa.

"O-o-o-!" Mother cried.

"I left my money at home."

"I have some," said Dick.

Errors	0	1	2	3	4	5	6	7
Percentage	100	98	96	94	92	90	88	86

Detail	1.	What kind of a day was it? (hot)
Inference	2.	What time of day do you think it was? (afternoon, around noon, lunch time)
Main Idea	3.	What were the children planning to do at the park? (have fun, eat hot dogs, swim)
Inference	4.	How do you think Lisa felt when Mother said she forgot her money? (upset, sad, angry)
Vocabulary		What is the meaning of the words *hot dog*? (wiener, frankfurter, etc.)

Errors	0	1	2	3
Percentage	100	75	50	25

Mann-Suiter Developmental Paragraph Reading Inventory—Form A

NAME ______________________________ DATE ______________

GRADE ______________ EXAMINER ______________________________

MOTIVATIONAL QUESTION: Have you ever earned your own money? The children in this story wanted some money. Let's see how they decide to earn it.

2[1] Reader (55 words)

THE LEMONADE STAND

It was a hot summer day.

Bill and Ann wished they could make some money.

Ann said, "Why don't we have a lemonade stand?"

"I know where we can get some ice and lemons to make lemonade," said Bill.

"I'll ask John to help us," said Ann.

"He can get the ice."

Errors	0	1	2	3	4	5	6	7
Percentage	100	98	96	94	93	91	89	87

Vocabulary		What is the meaning of the words *lemonade stand*? (any acceptable response)
Main Idea	1.	Why did the children decide to have a lemonade stand? (to earn money)
Detail	2.	What kind of a day was it? (hot summer day)
Detail	3.	What did the children say they were going to get to make lemonade? (ice and lemons)
Inference	4.	What other things do you think they will need in order to make lemonade? (water and sugar)

Errors	0	1	2	3
Percentage	100	75	50	25

NAME ______________________________ DATE ______________

GRADE ______________ EXAMINER ______________________________

MOTIVATIONAL QUESTION: Have you ever looked at the stars at night? What do they look like to you? This story is about a boy and girl who saw something different in the sky one night.

2^2 Reader (61 words)

A VISITOR FROM OUTER SPACE

One night Ann and Bill were looking at stars.

"Look, Ann," said Bill. "Something flashed across the sky."

"I saw it too," said Ann.

"It must have been a shooting star."

"Where do shooting stars come from?" asked Bill.

"I don't know," said Ann.

"Let's ask fathei "

Father said, "They are burning rocks from outer space."

Errors	0	1	2	3	4	5	6	7	8
Percentage	100	98	97	95	93	91	90	88	87

Detail	1.	What were the children doing? (looking at stars)
Inference	2.	What time of day was it? (night)
Main Idea	3.	Why is this story called, "A Visitor from Outer Space"? (the visitor is the shooting star and it's from outer space)
Detail	4.	What did father say shooting stars were? (burning rocks)
Detail	5.	Where do shooting stars come from? (outer space)
Vocabulary		What is another word for shooting star? (meteor, falling star, etc.)

Errors	0	1	2	3
Percentage	100	80	60	40

NAME ______________________________ DATE ______________

GRADE ______________ EXAMINER ______________________________

MOTIVATIONAL QUESTION: Have you ever seen a big fire? This story tells about a very large fire and what a little girl thought would put it out.

3[1] Reader (70 words)

THE FIRE IN THE EVERGLADES

"There are many fires in the Everglades National Park," said the TV announcer.

"The fires are spreading to the Indian villages.

Smoke is clouding the sky.

The animals are being forced to leave their homes."

Ann thought, "If we only had some rain, then the animals would not have to run away.

I hope that it rains soon so the fires will be put out."

Errors	0	1	2	3	4	5	6	7	8
Percentage	100	98	97	96	95	93	92	90	89

Vocabulary		What is the meaning of the word *announcer*? (a person who announces information on the radio or TV)
Detail	1.	How did Ann find out about the fires? (TV announcer)
Detail	2.	What was clouding the sky? (Smoke)
Main Idea	3.	Why was everyone worried about the fire? (it was spreading, animals could get hurt, Indians endangered, etc.)
Detail	4.	Where was the fire? (Everglades National Park)

Errors	0	1	2	3	4
Percentage	100	80	60	40	20

Note: Everglades National Park is a proper name and therefore not counted as an error.

NAME ______________________________ DATE ______________

GRADE ______________ EXAMINER ______________________________

MOTIVATIONAL QUESTION: Would you go swimming if you were told not to? This is a story about a boy who disobeyed his mother and found himself in trouble.

3² Reader (96 words)

SWIMMING ALONE

It was a dark and cloudy day, but Bill went swimming alone in the rough water.

His mother had told him not to go because it was such a poor day for swimming.

Bill disobeyed her and went anyway.

He soon swam out over his head and realized in a panic that he could not get back to the shore.

Luckily, there was a woman on the beach who heard his screams for help.

A boat soon came to his rescue.

Bill did not disobey his mother again by swimming alone in rough water.

Errors	0	1	2	3	4	5	6	7	8	9	10
Percentage	100	99	98	97	96	95	94	93	92	90	89

Vocabulary		What is the meaning of the word *disobeyed*? (to refuse, or to fail to obey)
Detail	1.	What kind of a day was it? (dark and cloudy)
Detail	2.	Who went swimming with Bill? (no one)
Main Idea	3.	Why did Bill's mother tell him not to go swimming? (because it was such a poor day, rough water, dark and cloudy day)
Detail	4.	How was he rescued? (a boat)
Inference	5.	How do you think Bill feels now about swimming alone in rough water? (any logical answer)

Errors	0	1	2	3	4
Percentage	100	80	60	40	20

NAME ______________________________ DATE ______________

GRADE ______________ EXAMINER ______________________________

MOTIVATIONAL QUESTION: This story is about a dog who went to the movies.

4 Reader (124 words)

DUKE GOES TO THE MOVIES

Duke and his master went to the movies.

The manager said, "You can't take a dog in there.

It's against the rules."

"This is no ordinary dog," said Duke's master.

"He is well behaved and has a cóllar.

If he becomes noisy, we will leave."

After the show, the manager spoke to Duke's master.

He said that he was watching Duke and noticed that the dog wagged his tail

for the happy parts of the movie.

He yawned when it became dull and whined a little at the sad parts.

"What an amazing dog!" said the manager.

"Did he enjoy the movie?"

Duke's master said, "I think he may have been a little bored, since he read the book."

Errors	0	1	2	3	4	5	6	7	8	9	10	11	12
Percentage	100	99	98	98	97	96	95	94	93	92	91	91	90

Vocabulary		What is the meaning of the word *master* in this story? (his owner)
Detail	1.	Who didn't want to let Duke into the movies? (the manager)
Detail	2.	Why aren't dogs allowed in the movies? (against the rules)
Main Idea	3.	What made Duke an unusual dog? (wagged tail for happy parts, yawned when dull, whined when sad, read the book)
Inference	4.	Do you think the other people in the theatre were upset with Duke? (no—Duke made no loud noise)
Detail	5.	What did Duke do when he became bored? (yawned)

Errors	0	1	2	3	4
Percentage	100	80	60	40	20

NAME ______________________________ DATE ______________

GRADE ______________ EXAMINER ______________________________

MOTIVATIONAL QUESTION: Have you ever dusted furniture? Some people don't want theirs dusted. See what Mr. Bradshaw's reasons are for not dusting his furniture.

5 Reader (93 words)

LEAVE THE DUST ALONE

Mr. Bradshaw had an antique shop in a small New England town.

The dust was so thick you could hardly find your way around.

He used to repair old furniture and sell it to people from the big cities who

came wandering through his little shop.

People would ask, "How much for this beat-up old chair with the dust on it?"

They thought it was old and they had a bargain.

Many liked to rummage through the dust.

"The dustier the better," he would say to his wife.

Errors	0	1	2	3	4	5	6	7	8	9	10
Percentage	100	99	98	97	96	94	93	92	91	90	89

Vocabulary		What is the meaning of the word *rummage*? (to search through things)
Detail	1.	What kind of a shop did Mr. Bradshaw own? (antique shop)
Detail	2.	Where was the shop located? (small New England town)
Main Idea	3.	Why didn't Mr. Bradshaw want to dust his furniture? (wanted it to look old)
Inference	4.	Why do you think people liked the dusty old furniture? (they thought it was old and they had a bargain)
Detail	5.	Where did people come from who bought his furniture? (big cities)

Errors	0	1	2	3	4
Percentage	100	80	60	40	20

NAME ______________________________ DATE ______________

GRADE ______________ EXAMINER ______________________________

MOTIVATIONAL QUESTION: Have your friends ever teased you? Here's a story about someone who was teased and what he did about it.

6 Reader (138 words)

A SENSE OF HUMOR

Rosemary walked John to his classroom every day.
She was ten and he was only seven.
John was blind and when he got off the bus, he needed someone to escort him to his room.
Rosemary was crippled, but her handicap did not prevent her from traveling to school alone.
"What color is my blouse?" she queried one day.
"I don't know," exclaimed John.
"You can't see it," she retorted.
"It's lavender. What color is the ribbon in my hair?"
"I don't know," sighed John.
"It's crimson," she giggled,
"but you can't see it."
It was obvious that John was being teased, but he didn't lose his patience.
After thinking for a while, he said quite seriously,
"Rosemary, what color is my underwear? You don't know, do you?
That's because you can't see it."

Errors	0	1	2	3	4	5	6	7	8	9	10	11
Percentage	100	99	98	97	97	96	95	94	94	93	92	91

Detail	1.	Why did John need someone to walk him to class? (he was blind)
Detail	2.	How did John get to school? (bus)
Inference	3.	Do you think Rosemary was mean? (any rational answer)
Inference	4.	How do we know that John was being teased? (Rosemary's questions)
Main Idea	5.	What did John use to solve a situation that could have been serious? (An answer that infers humor or intelligence)
Vocabulary		What does the word *obvious* mean? (evident, apparent, clear)

Errors	0	1	2	3	4
Percentage	100	80	60	40	20

NAME ______________________________ DATE ______________

GRADE ______________ EXAMINER ______________________________

MOTIVATIONAL QUESTION: Rats create a worldwide menace. War on rats is a continuing struggle. Read this to find out why man is having so much trouble with rats.

7 Reader (199 Words)

HUMAN'S WORST ENEMY

Except for humans, rats are the most numerous and successful mammal on earth. Like the human, the rat is a generalized animal. This means that rats are able to eat almost anything and live anywhere. They are not specialized like the anteater or tree sloth. Generalization is the key to the rats' extraordinary adaptability.

The same species that lives in a burrow in a grain field in the United States or in an attic in Europe may inhabit the crown of a coconut palm in the South Pacific. The marsh that is a good place for growing rice is also a great place for rats.

Rats love the lush American suburbs of the south, too, with their abundance of fruit and nut trees. Here they nest in the trees and have literally filled the niche of the squirrel.

The dietary habits of humans and rats are almost identical, except that we eat by day and the rats eat by night. In a world haunted by threat of famine, rats will destroy approximately a fifth of all food crops planted. Wherever humans go, it seems the rat is sure to follow, sharing the food of their table.

Errors	0	1	2	3	4	5	6	7	8	9	10	11	12
Percentage	100	99	99	98	98	97	97	96	96	95	95	94	94

Vocabulary — What is the meaning of the word *dietary* in this story? (pertaining to diet or eating)

Main Idea — 1. Why are rats so successful and numerous? (they are a generalized animal adapting to any living conditions and food)

Detail — 2. What animals are mentioned as being specialized? (anteater and tree sloth)

Inference — 3. When people talk about rodent control they are really talking about human survival. What does this statement mean? (rats are increasing and eating the food needed to feed people)

Detail — 4. Are the dietary habits of man and rat exactly the same? (no, they are almost identical except that the rat eats by night)

Detail — 5. Why do rats love the lush American suburbs of the south? (abundance of fruit and nut trees)

Errors	0	1	2	3	4	5
Percentage	100	80	60	40	20	0

NAME ______________________________ DATE ______________

GRADE ______________ EXAMINER ______________________________

MOTIVATIONAL QUESTION: This story is about a very famous city called Pompeii that was destroyed in just a few hours. Let's read to find out what happened.

8 Reader (172 words)

POMPEII

In the brief space of a few hours a city, with a history dating back over seven centuries, disappeared. Pompeii was destroyed twice: first by an earthquake in 62 A.D., then by the eruption of Vesuvius in 79 A.D., which buried it under twelve feet of lava and ashes. The first time, it was almost entirely rebuilt. After the second disaster it was left to its fate.

The eruption of Vesuvius brought the life of that rich city of merchants and traders to an abrupt end one August morning, while the whole population was busily going about its daily business.

In a few seconds, after the first deafening roar, streams of lava, thrown up thousands of yards by the gas pressure in the volcano, were running down the slopes of Vesuvius at a giddy pace. Ashes and scalding clouds of gas, released by the burning lava, were carried by the wind onto the city, while the raging sea cut off any retreat from the coast. The fate of Pompeii was sealed.

Errors	0	1	2	3	4	5	6	7	8	9	10	11	12
Percentage	100	99	99	98	98	97	97	96	95	95	94	94	93

Vocabulary		What is the meaning of the word *raging* in this story? (extreme violence or intensity; fury)
Detail	1.	How was Pompeii destroyed the first time? (by an earthquake)
Main Idea	2.	What happened to seal Pompeii's fate? (the eruption of Vesuvius buried it under twelve feet of lava and ash)
Detail	3.	What did the winds carry onto the city? (ashes and scalding clouds of gas)
Inference	4.	Although the story doesn't say, the city of Pompeii was built very close to what kind of a mountain? (a volcano)
Detail	5.	Why couldn't the people escape in boats? (retreat was cut off by the raging sea)

Errors	0	1	2	3	4	5
Percentage	100	80	60	40	20	0

Form 5-5

MANN-SUITER WORD READING SCREEN STUDENT WORKSHEET

NAME ______________________________ DATE ____________

EXAMINER ______________________________

							Incorrect Responses
A	1.	green	brown	red	purple	black	______
	2.	yellow	black	orange	brown	blue	______
	3.	big	bad	pig	dog	bed	______
	4.	no	can	hot	on	not	______
	5.	had	house	have	horse	hop	______
B	1.	the	with	went	what	want	______
	2.	sleep	like	look	help	little	______
	3.	how	know	out	now	away	______
	4.	came	some	home	one	come	______
	5.	when	walk	white	where	while	______
C	1.	around	over	again	other	also	______
	2.	many	mother	money	moon	morning	______
	3.	thing	food	their	father	took	______
	4.	children	sleep	chicken	splash	chair	______
	5.	wash	work	would	under	wish	______
D	1.	head	heavy	hide	heard	hard	______
	2.	light	through	laugh	though	right	______
	3.	front	found	flew	floor	first	______
	4.	noise	never	nothing	next	nose	______
	5.	beauty	because	both	before	bath	______
	6.	drink	bring	built	draw	burn	______

Mann-Suiter Word Reading Screen Student Worksheet

NAME ________________________________ DATE ______________

EXAMINER ________________________________

						Incorrect Responses
E	1. since	storm	safely	surface	saddle	______
	2. gravel	greatest	grounded	grove	grass	______
	3. chief	clamp	careful	clothe	clown	______
	4. danger	different	drawn	delicious	different	______
	5. eight	ocean	empty	about	except	______
	6. beach	being	bench	bounce	broke	______
F	1. fortune	future	flakes	freight	flourish	______
	2. bacon	breeze	breathe	beetles	broad	______
	3. design	develop	distant	dainty	digest	______
	4. silence	sheriff	success	support	serious	______
	5. courage	claimed	concern	cooperate	crickets	______
	6. guide	glanced	guilty	glass	guard	______
G	1. naturally	nursery	ninety	number	necessary	______
	2. scholar	salmon	shrill	solemn	source	______
	3. article	acquire	ancient	ambition	accurate	______
	4. evolved	enormous	expensive	emperor	explore	______
	5. legend	leisure	lower	loosely	limb	______
	6. products	prevent	prairie	presence	profitable	______
H	1. fleeting	fluent	figure	flattery	famous	______
	2. licensed	liquids	literal	lenient	lingering	______
	3. partial	politics	poisoned	paragraph	plough	______
	4. spectacular	substance	scenes	summoned	scamper	______
	5. omitted	obliged	obvious	obsolete	obedience	______
	6. irrelevant	irregular	illicit	illusion	imitation	______

NAME ______________________________ DATE ______________

EXAMINER ______________________________

						Incorrect Responses
I	1. individual	industrious	impressive	intricate	induce	______
	2. prominent	preposition	persuade	pensive	precision	______
	3. exposition	environment	exhausted	equipment	evident	______
	4. adequately	approximate	attentively	administer	architect	______
	5. sojourn	subscribe	scientists	stimulating	standardize	______
	6. contend	commence	commission	contemporary	crisis	______
J	1. prairies	proportional	procession	permanent	proposition	______
	2. financial	formulated	fascinated	furnace	fraternity	______
	3. inducement	irrelevance	intangible	inadequate	immediately	______
	4. commerce	communion	content	contrasting	circumstances	______
	5. obviously	oxygen	obligation	ordinarily	oppress	______
	6. grotesque	grasped	glistening	granting	gondola	______

Form 5-6

MANN-SUITER WORD READING SCREEN

Examiner's Copy and Answer Sheet

Directions

1. Say, "Find letter *[supply letter]* and put your finger on number 1."
2. Say, "One, *[supply word]*, circle the word *[supply word]*." *Note:* Check to see if all the students understand the directions.
3. Give the students approximately 15 seconds to circle their choice before moving to the next word. Keep the rate of input constant for each word.
4. After having administered the first selection, before starting the next selection, remind the students to put their finger on the next letter to the left of the page. Continue through the screens selected.

A. Preprimer
1. red
2. black
3. bad
4. on
5. horse

B. Primer
1. went
2. help
3. away
4. some
5. while

C. First
1. other
2. many
3. their
4. splash
5. wash

D. Second
1. head
2. though
3. flew
4. noise
5. both
6. draw

E. Third
1. since
2. gravel
3. clothe
4. delicious
5. except
6. being

F. Fourth
1. flourish
2. beetles
3. design
4. serious
5. courage
6. guilty

G. Fifth
1. necessary
2. salmon
3. ancient
4. emperor
5. leisure
6. prairie

H. Sixth
1. fluent
2. lenient
3. partial
4. scenes
5. obedience
6. illicit

I. Seventh
1. intricate
2. persuade
3. exposition
4. approximate
5. standardize
6. commerce

J. Eighth
1. proposition
2. fascinated
3. irrelevance
4. circumstances
5. obviously
6. grotesque

Form 5-7

MANN-SUITER WORD READING SCREEN

Class Score Sheet

TEACHER ______________________ GRADE __________ DATE __________

	Name	A PP	B P	C I	D II	E III	F IV	G V	H VI	I VII	J VIII
1.											
2.											
3.											
4.											
5.											
6.											
7.											
8.											
9.											
10.											
11.											
12.											
13.											
14.											
15.											
16.											
17.											
18.											
19.											
20.											
21.											
22.											
23.											
24.											
25.											
26.											
27.											
28.											
29.											
30.											
31.											
32.											
33.											

Mann-Suiter Vocabulary Screen

The Mann-Suiter Vocabulary Screen is designed to be used as an individual or group oral language development assessment.

RATIONALE

The purpose of the Mann-Suiter Vocabulary Screen is to indicate which students may need help in vocabulary development. By third grade, vocabulary assumes an important role in reading. Often students are thought to have a problem with inference or main-idea questions. However, the real problem in many cases is an inadequate vocabulary.

Although the vocabulary selections begin with Level I words, the Mann-Suiter Vocabulary Screen is designed primarily to be used with those reading at the second grade level and is ideally suited for readers at the third grade level or above.

ADMINISTERING THE MANN-SUITER VOCABULARY SCREEN

The Mann-Suiter Vocabulary Screen should be administered to the whole class regardless of the individual reading levels of the students. An estimated oral language development level can be ascertained for each student, even those considered to be poor readers. Teachers should begin two grade levels lower than the grade of the students they are screening. To assess a third grade class at the first of the year, the teacher should begin with Level I and continue as necessary.

The screen should always be read by the instructor, who will use the Examiner's Copy (Form 5-8, pages 118–120) and Answer Sheet (Form 5-9). Every student will need a copy of the Student's Work and Score Sheet (Form 5-10, pages 122–124) and a pencil. The room should be quiet, and all students should indicate that they can hear the instructor.

The teacher should read the number first, asking the students to put their fingers on the number in order to keep the place. The teacher should then read the sentences clearly, just as they are written on the examiner's copy, pausing slightly between the sentence and each of the three choices. Sentences may be reread, if necessary, once more. The student circles his or her choice.

USE WITH INDIVIDUAL STUDENTS

The Mann-Suiter Vocabulary Screen can also be used for individual students. After administering the Mann-Suiter Developmental Reading Inventories, the teacher can screen the student with the Mann-Suiter Vocabulary Screen to estimate his or her level of language development. Some students read words they do not understand, and others understand words far above the level they can read. It is important to understand that performance can be erratic in some students; for example, a student may fail Level III and be borderline in Level IV. This information is diagnostic, and the student may require further assessment to find out the reason for the erratic performance.

SCORING THE MANN-SUITER VOCABULARY SCREEN

The Student's Work and Score Sheet is designed to indicate an estimate of the student's level of vocabulary development based on graded reading material.

All answers are marked either right or wrong in the score boxes to the right of the student's response.

For each level of Levels I through IV the following scoring is used:

1 error	pass
2 errors	borderline pass
3 errors	needs instruction

For each level of Levels V through VIII the following scoring is used:

1 error	pass
2 or 3 errors	borderline pass
4 errors	needs instruction

The student's score sheet would look like the example in Figure 5-5. The teacher marks P (pass), BP (borderline pass) or I (instruction) on the small line to the left of the score box.

Score

	Right	Wrong
	×	
	×	
	×	
		×
	×	
P	×	

Figure 5-5 Example of Student's Score Sheet for Vocabulary Screen

Mann-Suiter Vocabulary Screen
Class Score Sheet

Grade ___4___ Date ___Sept. 3___

Name	I	II	III	IV	V	VI	VII	VIII
1. Mary Smith	X							
2. Becky Rubin			X					
3. Johnny Jones					X			
4. Lisa Mason				X				
5.								

Figure 5-6 Example of a Class Score Sheet

CLASS SCORE SHEET

The Class Score Sheet (Form 5-11, page 125) can be used by the teacher in decisions about grouping students for teaching vocabulary. The chart indicates the levels of screening across the top and the students' names down the left side. The teacher can black in or mark with an X the level at which the students need instruction. (See Figure 5-6.)

Students passing at their grade level can be tested at higher levels to determine their vocabulary development.

Form 5-8

MANN-SUITER VOCABULARY SCREEN

Examiner's Copy

Directions for administrating. Read the sentences clearly, just as they are written, pausing slightly between the sentence and each of the three choices. Sentences may be reread once more if needed.
Note: Start each sentence with the number. Have the students put their finger on the number, then read the sentence and the choices. The student circles his/her choice.

Level I

1. Again — If we say a person is going again, we mean
   another time first time last time
2. Next — If we say something is next to something, we mean it is
   farthest away beside it distant
3. Many — If we say there are many people, we mean there are
   none two a lot
4. night — Another word for night could be
   morning evening noon
5. full — If we say something is full, we mean there is
   no more room there is room it is empty
6. left — The opposite of left is
   over right under

Level II

1. built — If something was built, it was
   constructed torn down given away
2. through — If we say someone is through with something, we mean he is
   starting it finished with it getting it
3. leaves — Leaves are a part of a
   car chair plant
4. whole — If we say you can have the whole thing, we mean you can have
   part of it all of it half of it
5. change — If you change something you
   keep it the same do nothing make it different
6. close — If you close something, you
   open it shut it break it

Level III

1. gravel — Gravel is
   an insect a mixture of sand and pebbles a lion's roar
2. stream — A stream is a
   beach brook planet
3. tribe — The word tribe refers to a group of
   cars people mountains
4. fasten — If we fasten something, we
   secure it unlock it turn it on
5. surface — The surface of something is its
   interior thickness exterior
6. grove — A grove is a
   tunnel small wooded area pond

Level IV

1. glanced — If you glanced at something, you
   looked quickly   gazed at it   didn't look
2. design — If you design something, you
   put it away   sketch an outline of it   rent it
3. guide — A guide is a person who
   farms   directs   follows
4. vacant — If a building is vacant, it is
   occupied   filled   empty
5. concern — If you show concern, you are
   angry   unfriendly   interested
6. interior — Interior refers to the
   outside of something   inside of something   top of it

Level V

1. shrill — a shrill sound is
   high and piercing   soft   musical
2. prevent — If we prevent something, we
   include it   stop it   move it
3. ancient — If something is ancient, it is
   modern   fresh   very old
4. acquire — If you acquire something, you
   sell it   obtain it   give it away
5. legend — A legend is a
   myth   poem   group of soldiers
6. evolved — If something evolved, it
   died   unfolded   was changeless
7. solemn — A solemn occasion is
   serious   gay   merry
8. yield — To yield is to
   gaze   take over   surrender

Level VI

1. detained — If someone is detained, he is
   moved on   held back   promoted
2. omitted — If something is omitted, it is
   left out   added   clipped on
3. partial — If someone is partial toward something, she is
   biased   unbiased   dangerous
4. summoned — If someone is summoned, he is
   exiled   sent away   sent for
5. artificial — If something is artificial, it is
   real   not genuine   genuine
6. source — The source of something is its
   beginning   end   course
7. erratic — If a person's behavior is erratic, it is
   frugal   pleasant   eccentric
8. debris — When we speak of debris, we are discussing
   brocades   broken rubbish   paintings

Level VII

1. tremor — If a person writes with a tremor, his writing shows
   strength quivering humor
2. sojourn — A sojourn refers to a
   temporary residence permanent residence shack
3. waning — A waning moon is
   growing diminishing waxing
4. compassionate — If a person is compassionate, he is
   merciful vague lonely
5. malignant — A malignant growth
   enhances life sustains life threatens life
6. pensive — If one is in a pensive mood, she is
   laughing crying reflecting
7. precise — If something is precise, it is
   modern vague clearly determined
8. intricate — An intricate pattern is
   complicated uneasy plain

Level VIII

1. whimsical — A whimsical idea is
   factual realistic capricious
2. ultimate — The ultimate truth. Ultimate here means
   challenging fundamental stimulating
3. obvious — If something is obvious, it is
   obscure waning apparent
4. ambitious — If someone is ambitious, she is
   lazy aspiring content
5. grotesque — If something is grotesque, it is
   oddly formed pleasing professional
6. articulate — If someone is articulate, he speaks with
   a brogue an accent distinctness
7. subside — If you are waiting for something to subside, you are waiting for it to
   go down go up move over
8. permanent — If something is permanent, it is
   contrasting unchanging changeable

Form 5-9

MANN-SUITER VOCABULARY SCREEN ANSWER SHEET

Level I

1. another time
2. beside it
3. a lot
4. evening
5. no more room
6. right

Level II

1. constructed
2. finished with it
3. plant
4. all of it
5. make it different
6. shut it

Level III

1. mixture of sand and pebbles
2. brook
3. people
4. secure it
5. exterior
6. small wooded area

Level IV

1. looked quickly
2. sketched an outline of it
3. directs
4. empty
5. interested
6. inside of something

Level V

1. high and piercing
2. stop it
3. very old
4. obtain it
5. myth
6. unfolded
7. serious
8. surrender

Level VI

1. held back
2. left out
3. biased
4. sent for
5. not genuine
6. beginning
7. eccentric
8. broken rubbish

Level VII

1. quivering
2. temporary residence
3. diminishing
4. merciful
5. threatens life
6. reflecting
7. clearly determined
8. complicated

Level VIII

1. capricious
2. fundamental
3. apparent
4. aspiring
5. oddly formed
6. distinctness
7. go down
8. unchanging

Form 5-10

MANN-SUITER VOCABULARY SCREEN
STUDENT'S WORK AND SCORE SHEET

NAME ______________________________ GRADE ________ DATE ________

EXAMINER ______________________________

Directions: Circle your choice.

Level I

				Score: Right	Score: Wrong
1. another time	first time	last time			
2. farthest away	beside it	distant			
3. none	two	a lot			
4. morning	evening	noon			
5. no more room	there is room	it is empty			
6. over	right	under	____		

Level II

				Right	Wrong
1. constructed	torn down	given away			
2. starting it	finished with it	getting it			
3. car	chair	plant			
4. part of it	all of it	half of it			
5. keep it the same	do nothing	make it different			
6. open it	shut it	break it	____		

Level III

				Right	Wrong
1. an insect	a mixture of sand and pebbles	a lion's roar			
2. beach	brook	planet			
3. cars	people	mountains			
4. secure it	unlock it	turn it on			
5. interior	thickness	exterior			
6. tunnel	small wooded area	pond	____		

NAME ____________________ GRADE ________ DATE ________

EXAMINER ____________________

Directions: Circle your choice.

Level IV

			Score: Right	Score: Wrong
1. looked quickly	gazed at it	didn't look		
2. put it away	sketch an outline of it	rent it		
3. farms	directs	follows		
4. occupied	filled	empty		
5. angry	unfriendly	interested		
6. outside of something	inside of something	top of it		

Level V

			Right	Wrong
1. high and piercing	soft	musical		
2. include it	stop it	move it		
3. modern	fresh	very old		
4. sell it	obtain it	give it away		
5. myth	poem	group of soldiers		
6. died	unfolded	was changeless		
7. serious	gay	merry		
8. gaze	take over	surrender		

Level VI

			Right	Wrong
1. moved on	held back	promoted		
2. left out	added	clipped on		
3. biased	unbiased	dangerous		
4. exiled	sent away	sent for		
5. real	not genuine	genuine		
6. beginning	end	course		
7. frugal	pleasant	eccentric		
8. brocades	broken rubbish	paintings		

Mann-Suiter Vocabulary Screen—Student's Work and Score Sheet

NAME ______________________ GRADE ________ DATE ________

EXAMINER ______________________

Directions: Circle your choice.

Level VII

				Right	Wrong
1. strength	quivering	humor			
2. temporary residence	permanent residence	shack			
3. growing	diminishing	waxing			
4. merciful	vague	lonely			
5. enhances life	sustains life	threatens life			
6. laughing	crying	reflecting			
7. modern	vague	clearly determined			
8. complicated	easy	plain	____		

Level VIII

				Right	Wrong
1. factual	realistic	capricious			
2. challenging	fundamental	stimulating			
3. obscure	waning	apparent			
4. lazy	aspiring	content			
5. oddly formed	pleasing	professional			
6. a brogue	an accent	distinctness			
7. go down	go up	move over			
8. contrasting	unchanging	changeable	____		

Form 5-11

MANN-SUITER VOCABULARY SCREEN
CLASS SCORE SHEET

TEACHER ______________________ GRADE ________ DATE ________

	Name	I	II	III	IV	V	VI	VII	VIII
1.									
2.									
3.									
4.									
5.									
6.									
7.									
8.									
9.									
10.									
11.									
12.									
13.									
14.									
15.									
16.									
17.									
18.									
19.									
20.									
21.									
22.									
23.									
24.									
25.									

Mann-Suiter Silent Reading and Written Language Screen

The Mann-Suiter Silent Reading and Written Language Screen (Form 5-12, pages 128–138) is designed to be used with individuals or groups. Selections range from primer reading level through grade 8. This group screen is particularly useful for teachers who have students in remedial or special reading groups. While the specialist may prefer to give an Individual Reading Inventory (page 85), the regular classroom teacher or any other trained individuals can share in the evaluation process by giving the group reading screen.

OUTLINE OF WRITTEN QUESTIONS

The reading format and the type of questions to be answered change slowly as the selections become harder.

Questions at the primer level are of the fill-in variety and only require one- or two-word written responses.

Three questions at Level I call for fill-in answers of one or two words, and three questions need sentence answers.

At Levels II and III, three questions can be answered by filling in a missing word, and two questions require a sentence answer.

At Levels IV through VI a few simple fill-in sentence responses are included, but others require more thought.

Questions at Levels VII and VIII require the drawing of conclusions.

PURPOSE OF WRITTEN QUESTIONS

The purpose of the range of questions is to indicate to the teacher the class's wide range of abilities in the written language area.

The fill-in questions indicate whether or not the student can handle detail-type questions. The manner in which the writing is done indicates whether or not the student uses cursive or manuscript writing. It also indicates whether or not the student can copy correctly.

For the questions requiring sentence answers, the teacher needs to stress that the student write sentences if he or she can. Some students will only be able to write the phrases copied from the page. A wide range of ability may be observed.

At Levels VII and VIII the learner will have to be a little more original in his or her response. The answers should be two or three sentences long. The teacher should note how the student deals with more complex tasks.

OTHER USES OF THE SCREEN

These Silent Reading Screens can also be used to evaluate oral reading. If a student has done poorly on a level he or she should have been able to complete successfully, the teacher can ask the student to read the selection orally. This may help the teacher determine what the problem may be. Just the story part of each page can be used for this purpose. The selection should be retyped on a card for the student to read. The scoring chart at the bottom of the student's duplicator sheet should be used for scoring the oral reading. Scoring procedures are the same as those used for the Mann-Suiter Developmental Paragraph Reading Inventory (pages 93–94).

As students progress in school, more and more of their work is dependent upon reading a selection or reading instructions and responding. Usually the response required is in writing. This Mann-Suiter Silent Reading and Written Language Screen, given the first days of school, will help a teacher quickly estimate the range of needs of the students.

ADMINISTERING THE MANN-SUITER SILENT READING AND WRITTEN LANGUAGE SCREEN

For grades four and below, the teacher begins testing by administering selections from the primer level and Level I to all students. The students begin at the same time and then bring their work to the instructor upon completion. The teacher notes the time of completion on the back of each student's paper. The teacher will then have an idea of who works quickly and who needs extra time. After checking the completed work, the teacher continues evaluating only those who did passing work. They should be given the Level II and Level III screens at the second sitting. Those doing passing work on those screens should be given the Level IV screen, and possibly the Level V screen, at the third sitting.

It is very important that the student be encouraged to write sentences wherever requested. Sentences should be checked for punctuation and grammar.

For grades five and above, the teacher should begin evaluating with the third grade silent reading screen and follow the program outlined above.

The teacher can check answers against the Answer Sheet (Form 5-13) provided with the test.

USE FOR INDIVIDUAL STUDENTS

The Mann-Suiter Silent Reading and Written Language Screen is especially valuable to the instructor working individually with a student. After administrating the Mann-Suiter Developmental Reading Inventories and determining the student's independent reading level, the teacher can give the silent reading screen for that level for a quick evaluation of written language skills and the ability to carry out a written task. This is an area seldom assessed in testing.

The Silent Reading and Written Language Screen can also be used with students who are unable to write. They can read the test silently and answer orally.

FAILURE AT THE INDEPENDENT READING LEVEL

When a student fails the Mann-Suiter Silent Reading and Written Language Screen at his or her independent level of reading, the instructor should have the student read it aloud to determine if he or she can answer the questions orally.

If there seems to be a serious problem with written work, it may be necessary to test down one level at a time to determine at what level the student can handle written responses.

LISTENING COMPREHENSION LEVEL

These screens can also be used to determine a student's listening comprehension level. Once a student's instructional reading level has been determined through use of the Mann-Suiter Developmental Reading Inventories, the evaluator can read more difficult selections to the student to determine the highest level at which the student can understand and discuss what he or she has heard. Thus a fourth grader, for instance, reading on a second grade level may understand the content of the material presented orally on a fourth or even fifth grade level.

SCORING THE MANN-SUITER SILENT READING AND WRITTEN LANGUAGE SCREEN

The Mann-Suiter Silent Reading and Written Language Screen Score Sheet (Form 5-14) is designed to indicate the student's comprehension and written language scores.

Scoring for the Comprehension Test

At the top of each Mann-Suiter Silent Reading and Written Language Screen is a place for the teacher to mark the number of wrong answers to the comprehension questions.

The number of wrong answers is then plotted on the Mann-Suiter Silent Reading and Written Language Screen Score Sheet. Scoring for each reading selection is explained on the score sheet, making it easy for the teacher to mark Pass, Borderline Pass, or Needs Instruction for each level attempted.

Figure 5-7 is an example of the comprehension portion of the score sheet.

Comprehension

Primer	☐ Silent ☐ Oral	Pass	Borderline Pass	Needs Instruction
1 error; pass 2 errors; borderline pass 3 errors; needs instruction				

Figure 5-7 Example of comprehension portion of score sheet for Silent Reading and Written Language Screen

The chart in Figure 5-7 indicates that the student who makes only one error is passing, and the teacher puts a check mark in the Pass column. If the student makes two errors, the check will be put in the Borderline Pass column. Borderline pass is the lowest level of acceptable performance. If the student makes three or more errors, the check will be put in the Needs Instruction column.

Testing is discontinued when a student reaches a level where instruction is indicated.

Scoring for the Written Language Test

This portion of the Mann-Suiter Silent Reading and Written Language Screen is designed to get a sample of the written language development of each student. All questions requiring sentence answers have been listed. The teacher should check whether the student answered the questions in phrases or sentences. A third column can be checked if there are punctuation or capitalization errors. (Do not be concerned about whether or not the answers are correct on this portion of the test.)

Figure 5-8 is an example of the Written Language portion of the scoring sheet.

The Mann-Suiter Silent Reading and Written Language Screen Score Sheet can be used for scoring oral comprehension by simply checking the box next to "Oral." Scoring would remain the same.

Written Language

Level I	Phrases	Sentences	Punctuation Errors
Questions 4.			
5.			
6.			

Figure 5-8 Example of written language portion of score sheet

Form 5-12

MANN-SUITER SILENT READING AND WRITTEN LANGUAGE SCREEN

NAME ____ DATE __________

GRADE ____________ EXAMINER ______________________________________

Level Primer

Both Selections 75 words

Number Wrong ____

DAN AND PAL

Pal is a little dog.

He is white with black spots.

Pal likes to play ball.

He likes to play with Dan.

Dan is a little boy.

Pal and Dan play.

They like to play ball.

1. Pal is a little ______________________ .
2. He has ______________________ spots.
3. Dan is a little ______________________ .
4. Dan and Pal like to ______________________ .

(Continued)

Level Primer (Continued)

THE ZOO

Dan likes to go to the zoo.

He likes to go with Ann and Tom.

They like to look at the birds.

They like to see the monkeys.

They like to eat hot dogs.

5. Dan, _______________ and _______________ go to the zoo.
6. They like to see the _______________ and _______________ .
7. They like to eat ______________________________ .

Scoring for optional oral reading

Errors	0	1	2	3	4	4	6	7
Percentage	100	99	97	96	95	93	92	91

NAME ______________________________ DATE ____________

GRADE ____________ EXAMINER ______________________________

Level I

79 words
Number Wrong ____

THE GIRLS

Ann and Mary are little girls. They walk to school together every day. On their way to school one day, Ann fell down. She got her dress dirty. Her pretty red hair ribbon was lost. She started to cry.

1. Ann and Mary are ______________________________.
2. Ann's dress got ______________________.
3. Ann lost her ______________________________.

(Continued)

Level I (Continued)

Mary tried to help Ann. She found Ann's hair ribbon and put it in her hair. It was not dirty. She helped Ann brush off her dress. Ann was not hurt, so the girls went on to school.

4. Was Ann hurt? ______________________________
______________________________.

5. What did Mary do with Ann's hair ribbon?
____
______________________________.

6. What did both girls do? ______________________________
____
______________________________.

Scoring for optional oral reading

Errors	0	1	2	3	4	5	6	7	8	9
Percentage	100	99	97	96	95	94	92	91	90	89

NAME ______________________________ DATE ____________

GRADE ____________ EXAMINER ______________________________

Level II

106 words
Number Wrong ____

THE WITCH

Once upon a time there was a pretty little witch named Bell. She loved to fly through the air on her magic broom. She had a large, black cat with green eyes that always went with her. His name was Tom, and he loved to ride on her broom, too.

1. Bell loved to fly through the ______________.
2. Tom loved to ride on the ______________.
3. Tom's eyes were ______________.

Bell always wore a pointed, black hat. She always wore a long, black cape that kept her warm. Tom did not need a coat and hat, for his thick fur kept him warm. Bell and Tom loved to ride through the sky on her broom. They always went riding when the moon was full.

4. What kind of a hat did Bell have? ______________________________.
5. When did Bell and Tom like to go riding? ______________________________.

Scoring for optional oral reading

Errors	0	1	2	3	4	5	6	7	8	9	10
Percentage	100	99	98	97	96	95	94	93	92	92	91

NAME ______________________________ DATE ______________

GRADE ______________ EXAMINER ______________________________

Level III

127 words
Number Wrong ____

NOAH'S ARK

Do you know who Noah was? I would like to tell you a story about him. Noah lived on the earth many, many years ago. We remember him today because he built a large wooden ark. An ark is a type of boat. Noah built the ark to keep animals in during a bad flood.

1. This story is about a man named ______________________.
2. Noah built a large wooden ______________________.
3. An ark is a type of ______________________.

Noah was told that it would rain for forty days and forty nights. It rained so hard that towns were washed away and all of the land was covered with water. Noah and the animals, however, were safe in the ark. When the rain stopped and the water went down, Noah and the animals went ashore again. They knew they were safe because they saw a rainbow in the sky.

4. How long did it rain? ____.
5. What happened to the towns in the heavy rain? ____.

Scoring for optional oral reading

Errors	0	1	2	3	4	5	6	7	8
Percentage	100	99	97	96	95	94	92	91	90

NAME ______________________________ DATE ____________

GRADE ____________ EXAMINER ______________________________

Level IV

99 words
Number Wrong ____

BILLY'S PET

Billy had a very unusual pet. It was what he did that made him so unusual. Billy had a dog that could read. Unlike most dogs, Pal just loved to curl up with a good book. He loved to read cowboy stories and, of course, anything about dogs. He was really an unusual pet!

1. Billy had an unusual ______________________.
2. His dog's name was ______________________.
3. Pal loved to read stories about ______________________ and ______________________.

Pal especially liked stories about Rin Tin Tin, a wonderful dog that did all sorts of brave things. In one story, Rin Tin Tin saved a young child from drowning. That was Pal's favorite dog story, and Rin Tin Tin was his hero.

4. Why was Rin Tin Tin Pal's hero? ____.

Scoring for optional oral reading

Errors	0	1	2	3	4	5	6	7	8	9
Percentage	100	99	98	97	96	96	95	93	92	91

NAME ______________________________ DATE ____________

GRADE ____________ EXAMINER ______________________________

Level V

122 words
Number Wrong ____

SHARKS

Everyone knows something about sharks, but not many people know how many different kinds there are. Altogether there are about 250 species. Of these, only a few are truly dangerous to man. When people speak of a man-eater shark, they are usually referring to the great white shark.

1. There are about 250 ______________________ of sharks.
2. Most of them are not ______________________.
3. The great white shark is considered ______________________.

Great white sharks eat a wide variety of fishes and other sea animals. They are also known to attack and kill men. They are the only sharks that have been proven to attack small boats. Luckily there are not a lot of great white sharks. However, they are found throughout the world in the warmer ocean waters. They are usually about 20 feet in length, although one specimen was recorded at 36½ feet.

4. Why are people afraid of great white sharks? ______________________
____
______________________________.

Scoring for optional oral reading

Errors	0	1	2	3	4	5	6	7	8	9	10
Percentage	100	99	98	98	97	96	95	94	93	93	92

NAME ______________________________ DATE ____________

GRADE ____________ EXAMINER ______________________________

Level VI

110 words
Number Wrong ____

OUR NATIONAL EMBLEM

The dashing grace, strength, and courage of the bald eagle have impressed men for ages. However, when the bald eagle was first suggested as our national emblem back in 1776 Benjamin Franklin opposed the selection. He preferred the wild turkey because it was a thrifty bird.

1. For ages men have been impressed with the ______________________ .
2. In 1776 the bald eagle was first suggested as our ______________________
3. Benjamin Franklin preferred ______________________ .

Franklin believed the eagle was a coward, a bully, and a thief. He didn't feel it was fit to represent our country. What men didn't know then was that eagles mate for life, eat mostly fish, and spend more time raising their young than any other bird. About six months of the adult eagle's year is devoted to raising its young.

4. Benjamin Franklin didn't like the bald eagle, but other men of his time did. Why did they select the bald eagle to be our national emblem? ______________________

____

____

Scoring for optional oral reading

Errors	0	1	2	3	4	5	6	7	8	9	10
Percentage	100	99	98	97	96	95	95	94	93	92	91

NAME ______________________________ DATE ______________

GRADE ______________ EXAMINER ______________________________

Level VII

200 words
Number Wrong ____

LONDON BRIDGE IS FALLING DOWN

London Bridge is falling down,
Falling down, falling down . . .

A very old tradition holds that this incident inspired the nursery rhyme.

Norway's Olaf the Stout distinguished himself as a Viking. According to legend, sometime around the year 1010 he led a fleet up the Thames River and pulled down London Bridge.

Viking ships were open. To protect his ships, Olaf covered them with roofs built of wood and wicker. When the fleet was ready, the Vikings rowed up the river. As they neared the bridge, arrows engulfed them, and such large stones were thrown down upon them that neither their helmets nor their shields could withstand the onslaught. Many of the Viking ships were greatly damaged under the great siege.

1. Olaf the Stout was a famous ______________________.
2. What did Olaf do to protect his ships? ____.

Some of the Viking ships had to retreat, but Olaf and his men rowed up under the bridge, tied ropes around the supporting posts, and then rowed their ships downstream as hard as they could. The posts were dragged along the bottom until they were loosened from the bridge. Because a large army stood on the bridge, with a great weight of stones and weapons, the bridge fell into the river when the posts were broken.

3. Why wouldn't Olaf and his Vikings be successful today? ____.

Scoring for optional oral reading

Errors	0	1	2	3	4	5	6	7	8	9	10	11
Percentage	100	99	99	99	98	98	97	97	96	96	96	95

NAME ______________________________ DATE ____________

GRADE ____________ EXAMINER ______________________________

Level VIII

180 words
Number Wrong ____

THE CHUCKWALLA

The chuckwalla is a strange-looking lizard almost 20 inches long that feeds exclusively on vegetation and is found in the deserts of western United States. The skin of the chuckwalla droops from its body in great folds and wrinkles; it has a sagging stomach and even a double chin. But it wears this oversize suit for a reason. Any severe fright sends it scurrying into a rock crevice where it inflates itself like a great balloon by gulping in mouthfuls of air. Wedged tightly among the rocks, the lizard is almost impossible to dislodge.

1. Where would you look for a chuckwalla? ______________________________.

2. How do you know the chuckwalla is not a meat eater? ______________________________

______________________________.

Like many desert lizards, the chuckwalla seeks shade or a burrow during the heat of day. Even though chuckwallas are cold-blooded creatures and need some sun to keep warm, they must guard against too much heat, for its effects would be lethal. Changes in the chuckwalla's skin color during the day help regulate its body temperature. In the cool morning, it turns dark to absorb more solar heat, but as the day warms it becomes progressively lighter to reflect the sun's radiation.

3. What does the author suggest is the reason for the chuckwalla's color shift?

____

____

____

____

Scoring for optional oral reading

Errors	0	1	2	3	4	5	6	7	8	9
Percentage	100	99	99	98	98	97	97	96	96	95

Form 5-13

MANN-SUITER SILENT READING AND WRITTEN LANGUAGE SCREEN ANSWER SHEET

Primer

Dan and Pal

1. dog
2. black
3. boy
4. play or play ball

The Zoo

5. Ann and Tom or Tom and Ann
6. birds and monkeys or monkeys and birds
7. hot dogs

Level I

The Girls

1. girls or little girls
2. dirty
3. hair ribbon or ribbon
4. No, she was not hurt.
5. She put it in her hair.
6. They went to school.

Level II

The Witch

1. air
2. broom
3. green
4. She had a pointed, black hat.
5. They went riding when the moon was full.

Level III

Noah's Ark

1. Noah
2. ark or boat
3. boat
4. It rained for forty days and forty nights.
5. The towns were washed away.

Level IV

Billy's Pet

1. pet
2. Pal
3. cowboys and dogs or dogs and cowboys
4. Rin Tin Tin did many brave things. He saved a child from drowning. (One or both of these ideas.)

Level V

Sharks

1. species
2. dangerous
3. dangerous to man or a man-eater shark
4. They are known to kill men and will attack a small boat. They are very large sharks. (Any of these ideas)

Level VI

Our National Emblem

1. bald eagle
2. national emblem
3. the turkey or wild turkey
4. The dashing grace, strength, and courage of the eagle impressed most men. (The eagle's other attributes were not known at that time.)

Level VII

London Bridge Is Falling Down

1. Viking
2. He had roofs built of wood and wicker.
3. The contrast between warfare then, with arrows and stones and boats able to pull a bridge down, and warfare today, with steel and concrete bridges and guns, should give students a chance for original writing.

Level VIII

The Chuckwalla

1. In the deserts of western United States
2. The chuckwalla feeds exclusively on vegetation.
3. The author suggests that changes in skin color during the day help regulate its body temperature.

Form 5-14

MANN-SUITER SILENT READING AND WRITTEN LANGUAGE SCREEN SCORE SHEET

NAME ______________________ GRADE __________ INSTRUCTIONAL READING LEVEL ________

EXAMINER ______________________________ DATE ______________

Comprehension

☐ Silent ☐ Oral	Pass	Border-line Pass	Needs Instruc-tion
Primer			
1 error; pass 2 errors; borderline pass 3 errors; needs instruction			
Level I			
1 error; pass 2 errors; borderline pass 3 errors; needs instruction			
Level II			
1 error; pass 2 errors; needs instruction			
Level III			
1 error; pass 2 errors; needs instruction			
Level IV			
1 error; borderline pass 2 errors; needs instruction			
Level V			
1 error; borderline pass 2 errors; needs instruction			
Level VI			
1 error; borderline pass 2 errors; needs instruction			
Level VII			
1 error; borderline pass 2 errors; needs instruction			
Level VIII			
1 error; borderline pass 2 errors; needs instruction			

Written Language

	Phrases	Sen-tences	Punctu-ation Errors
Primer			
Only one word answers at this level			
Level I			
Questions 4.			
5.			
6.			
Level II			
Questions 4.			
5.			
Level III			
Questions 4.			
5.			
Level IV			
Question 4.			
Level V			
Question 4.			
Level VI			
Question 4.			
Level VII			
Questions 2.			
3.			
Level VIII			
Questions 2.			
3.			

PLANNING LEARNING STRATEGIES

After having assessed the student's strengths and weaknesses using the Developmental Inventories, Screens, and selected supplemental evaluation, the teacher is ready to plan for appropriate educational strategies in two areas.

1. Developmental Skills Curriculum and Instruction
   The teacher will be planning for specific activities designed to provide instruction in the developmental skills. Weakness in these particular abilities, or learning correlates (Figure 1.4, page 10), prevents the student from efficiently learning the subject area skills of reading, writing, spelling, arithmetic, science, and social studies.
2. Subject Area Curriculum and Instruction
   Subject area skills as they are being defined here are the basic skills of reading, writing, spelling, arithmetic, science, and social studies.

Both developmental skills or abilities and subject areas must be considered in order to achieve a well-integrated program for the student. These two areas of curriculum and instruction will be discussed in the chapters that follow.

Chapter 6 Supplementary Evaluation and Data Recording

SUPPLEMENTARY EVALUATION

The supplementary evaluation section is designed to provide the teacher and others who are concerned with diagnosing the problems of learning-handicapped students with a list of commonly used tests related to the various areas of learning. Individuals involved with assessment may wish to reinforce their findings by using standardized tests that measure different learning characteristics in students. Professionals from other disciplines may already be using several of these instruments as a part of their basic testing battery. It is important that individuals who are responsible for defining and interpreting test data and communicating this information to teachers be able to relate this data directly to the findings attained through informal or developmental evaluation compiled by the teacher. Psychologists and special resource teachers who may be more knowledgeable and sophisticated in the area of evaluation, working together with regular classroom teachers, present a comprehensive approach to defining particular learning problems in students. The classroom teacher should become informed as to what the particular tests measure. This does not mean that expertise is required in all areas of evaluation but that the classroom teacher should at least have some basic understanding of the assessment devices presently being used in different educational settings. Each of the evaluation instruments indicated has source information listed in the Diagnosis-Student Assessment section of the Bibliography.

General Readiness

1. Anton Brenner Developmental Gestalt Test of School Readiness (Brenner, 1964)
2. Behavior Tests Used at the Gesell Institute (Ilg and Ames, 1964)
3. Boehm Test of Basic Concepts (Boehm, 1970)
4. Clymer-Barrett Pre-Reading Battery (Clymer and Barrett, 1969)
5. Early Detection Inventory (McGahan and McGahan, 1967)
6. Evanston Early Identification Scale (Landsman and Dillard, 1967)
7. First Grade Screening Test (Pate and Webb, 1966)
8. Kindergarten Evaluation of Learning Potential (KELP) (Wilson and Robeck, 1967)
9. Meeting Street School Screening Test (Hainsworth and Siqueland, 1969)
10. Metropolitan Readiness Tests (Hildreth, Griffiths, and McGauvran, 1966)
11. Predictive Index (deHirsch, Jansky, and Langford, 1966)
12. Preschool Attainment Record (Doll, 1966)
13. Pupil Rating Scale (Myklebust, 1971)
14. Screening Test of Academic Readiness (Ahr, 1966)
15. Screening Tests for Identifying Children with Specific Language Disability (Slingerland, 1962)
16. Valett Developmental Survey of Basic Learning Abilities (Valett, 1967)
17. Vane Kindergarten Test (Vane, 1968)

Auditory Modality

ACUITY
1. Audiometric Sweep Test

PERCEPTION
Discrimination
1. Auditory Discrimination Test (Wepman, 1958)
2. Boston University Speech Sound Discrimination Test (Boston University, 1955)
3. Goldman-Fristoe-Woodcock Test of Auditory Discrimination (Goldman, Fristoe, and Woodcock, 1970)
4. PERC Auditory Discrimination Test (Drake, 1965)

Closure
1. Auditory Closure Subtest of the Illinois Test of Psycholinguistic Abilities (Kirk, McCarthy, and Kirk, 1968)
2. Roswell-Chall Auditory Blending Test (Roswell and Chall, 1963)

IMAGERY (MEMORY-SEQUENCING)
1. Detroit Tests of Learning Aptitude, Subtests 6 and 13 (Baker and Leland, 1959)
2. Digit Span Subtest of the Wechsler Intelligence Scale for Children (WISC) (Wechsler, 1955)
3. Goldman-Fristoe-Woodcock Auditory Skills Test Battery (Goldman, Fristoe, and Woodcock, 1975)
4. Memory Subtest of the Illinois Test of Psycholinguistic Abilities (Kirk, McCarthy, and Kirk, 1968)
5. Sentences Subtest of the Wechsler Preschool and Primary Scale of Intelligence (WPPSI) (Wechsler, 1967)
6. Strauss and Lehtinen Ability to Produce Tapped Out Patterns (Strauss and Lehtinen, 1947)
7. Wepman Auditory Memory Span Test (Wepman, 1973a)
8. Wepman Auditory Sequential Memory Test (Wepman, 1973b)

Visual Modality

ACUITY AND OCULAR MOTOR
1. Keystone Visual Survey Telebinocular (Keystone View Co., 1958)
2. Ortho-Rater (Bausch and Lomb, 1958)
3. Snellen Chart (American Medical Association)
4. Spache Binocular Vision Test (Keystone View Co., 1961)

PERCEPTION
Discrimination
1. Frostig Developmental Test of Visual Perception (Frostig, 1963)
2. Marion Monroe Visual Test #1 (Ilg and Ames, 1964)
3. Metropolitan Readiness Test (Hildreth, Griffiths, and McGauvran, 1966)

Closure
1. Illinois Test of Psycholinguistic Abilities Visual Closure Subtest (Kirk, McCarthy, and Kirk, 1968)

Figure-Ground
1. Frostig Developmental Test of Visual Perception (Frostig, 1963)
2. Southern California Figure-Ground Visual Perception Test (Ayres 1966)
3. Strauss and Lehtinen Figure Background Cards (Strauss and Lehtinen, 1947)

IMAGERY (MEMORY-SEQUENCING)
1. Benton Revised Visual Retention Test (Benton, 1963)
2. Detroit Tests of Learning Aptitude, Subtests 9 and 16 (Baker and Leland, 1959)
3. Marion Monroe Test #3 (Ilg and Ames, 1964)
4. Memory for Designs Test (Graham and Kendall, 1960)

VISUAL-MOTOR (GROSS AND FINE)
1. Bender Visual-Motor Gestalt Test for Children (Bender, 1938; Koppitz, 1964)
2. Bruininks-Oseretsky Test of Motor Proficiency (Bruininks, 1978)
3. Detroit Tests of Learning Aptitude, Subtest 5 (Baker and Leland, 1959)
4. Developmental Test of Visual Motor Integration (Beery and Buktenica, 1967)
5. Draw-A-Man Test (Goodenough, 1926)
6. Frostig Developmental Test of Visual Perception (Frostig, 1963)
7. Harris Test of Lateral Dominance. (Harris, 1958)
8. Left-Right Discrimination and Finger Localization (Benton, 1959)
9. Lincoln-Oseretsky Motor Development Scale (Sloan, 1954)
10. Minnesota Percepto-Diagnostic Test (Fuller and Laird, 1963)
11. Purdue Perceptual-Motor Survey (Kephart and Roach, 1966)
12. Standardized Road-Map Test of Direction Sense (Money, Alexander, and Walker, 1965)

Language

1. Basic Concept Inventory (Engelmann, 1967)
2. Developmental Sentence Analysis (Lee, 1974)
3. Houston Test for Language Development (Crabtree, 1963)
4. Illinois Test of Psycholinguistic Abilities (Kirk, McCarthy, and Kirk, 1968)
5. Mecham Verbal Language Development Scale (Mecham, 1959)
6. Northwestern Syntax Screening Test (Lee, 1969)
7. Peabody Picture Vocabulary Test (Dunn, 1959)
8. Picture Story Language Test (Pronovost and Dumbleton, 1953)
9. Slingerland Screening Tests for Specific Language Disabilities (Slingerland, 1964)

SPEECH TESTS

1. A Deep Test of Articulation (McDonald, 1964)
2. Templin-Darley Tests of Articulation (Templin and Darley, 1960)

Social-Emotional

1. AAMD Adaptive Behavior Scales (Nihira, Foster, Shellhaus, and Leland, 1969)
2. Behavior Problem Checklist (Quay and Peterson, 1967)
3. Behavior Rating Scale (Burks, 1968)
4. Bender Visual Motor Gestalt Test for Children (Bender, 1938; Koppitz, 1964)
5. Children's Apperception Test (CAT) (Bellak and Bellak, 1949–55)
6. Devereaux Elementary School Behavior Rating Scale (Spivack and Swift, 1967)
7. Draw-A-Man Test (Goodenough, 1926)
8. House-Tree-Person (HTP) (Bieliauskas, 1963)
9. Pupil Rating Scale (Myklebust, 1971)
10. Thematic Apperception Test (TAT) (Bellak, 1954)
11. Vineland Social Maturity Scale (Doll, 1953)

DATA COLLECTION

Mann-Suiter Analysis of Errors Worksheets

After giving the Developmental Inventories and Screens, the teacher can indicate the errors on the Analysis of Errors Worksheets (Forms 6-1 through 6-4). Having done this, the teacher will be better able to determine how much, and what type of, additional testing is necessary before formulating any educational strategies for a given student. Some teachers will require more information, including standardized tests, before making any decisions. The question is not how much testing is adequate but, rather, how much information is needed in order to make a decision about changing or modifying the educational program for a particular student.

Mann-Suiter Diagnostic Worksheet

After completing the Analysis of Errors Worksheets and giving any additional tests, which tend to support or negate the findings of the Developmental Inventories, the teacher is ready to summarize the results. The Diagnostic Worksheet (Form 6-5, pp. 152–154) can be used to summarize all information gained through formal and informal evaluations. This summary will further aid the teacher in formulating educational strategies for a particular student.

Mann-Suiter Educational Profile

After completing the Diagnostic Worksheet, the teacher can indicate the strengths and weaknesses of a particular student by checking the various areas on the Educational Profile (Form 6-6) with the appropriate colored pencils and also write in the recommended task-level options. This concise report can also be used to describe the needs of a student to other school personnel. It should become a part of the student's cumulative record and be sent with the student when he or she transfers to another school.

Form 6-1

MANN-SUITER ANALYSIS OF ERRORS WORKSHEET

DEVELOPMENTAL SPELLING INVENTORY

NAME ______________________ SCHOOL ______________________

DATE ______________________ GRADE ______________ DATE OF BIRTH ______________

EXAMINER ______________________

(A check mark indicates difficulty)

Auditory Errors

1. Makes substitutions (*t* for *d, f* for *v, sh* for *ch*) ____
2. Omits vowels (*brd* for *bird*) ____
3. Omits second consonant in blends (*rut* for *rust*) ____
4. Uses synonyms (*house* for *home*) ____
5. Makes wild guesses (*yot* for *yes*) ____
6. No response ____
7. Confuses vowel sounds (*but* for *bat*) ____
8. Omits word endings such as *ed, s, ing* ____
9. Cannot remember spelling rules ____
10. Does not discern the middle of a word (*h--d*) ____

Visual Errors

1. Writes the beginning letters only ____
2. Makes reversals of words or letters (*b* for *d,* or *on* for *no*) ____
3. Uses inversions of letters (*m* for *w*) ____
4. Mixes capital and small letters (ba*B*y) ____
5. Spells phonetically (cannot revisualize) ____
6. Spells correct letters in the wrong sequence (*teh* for *the*) ____

General Observations

1. Has the learner isolated sound-symbol relationships (i.e., correctly associating a visual symbol with its auditory referent)? ____
2. Does the learner sequence visual symbols (letters) and sounds of letters (auditory)? ____
3. Can the learner estimate the number of letters in a word? ____
4. Does the learner use a logical system to arrive at the spelling of a word correctly or incorrectly? ____
5. What is the overall memory ability of the student? ____
6. Is there a great discrepancy between spelling ability and other academic skills such as reading? ____
7. Is spelling automatic to the student (spells words instantly, correctly or incorrectly), or has the learner developed a unique analytical attack for each word? ____

Mann-Suiter Analysis of Errors Worksheet—Developmental Spelling Inventory

NAME ____

(A check mark indicates difficulty)

8. How rapidly does the student relate the sound of the word or letters to the visual association in his or her mind? Does the visual image appear as a word or just isolated letters? Can the student verbalize what is happening in his or her mind's eye? ____
9. Is there a discrepancy between the student's ability to spell isolated words and his or her ability to spell phrases or sentences from dictation? ____
10. What does the student do with unfamiliar words that are not part of the reading program? ____
11. Is poor spelling disguised by illegible or unorthodox handwriting? ____
12. In written expression does the student, because of spelling difficulties, tend to substitute simple words for more complex words having the same meaning? ____
13. Is there a great discrepancy between short-term and long-term memory of how words are spelled, requiring a great deal of intermittent reinforcement throughout the school year? ____
14. Does the learner have right-left scanning eye movements during the reading process that may result in two-letter reversals in spelling? ____
15. Is there a residual spelling problem even after the student has learned to read, requiring a great deal of oral spelling sequencing in training to correct this faulty learning? ____
16. Is the student having difficulty associating the meaning of a word with the sounds or symbols that make up the spoken word? ____
17. Is the spelling improvement commensurate with reading improvement, or is there a residual spelling problem after reading improves? ____
18. Does the student appear to learn better with words of similar spelling patterns (e.g., *fat, cat, sat, mat*)? ____
19. Have hearing and vision been checked recently and found to be within normal limits? ____
20. Does the student improve with more teacher-directed spelling activities? ____
21. Has the student developed an emotional block to spelling due to continued failure and pressures from the home or the school? ____
22. What kinds of study skills does the student use for spelling in school and at home? ____
23. In evaluation, does the student select the spelled word from among choices (recognition) more easily than he or she spells the word (recall)? ____
24. Is the student being confused or overloaded by the introduction of too many different phonics skills in the spelling and reading programs? ____
25. Does the student spell better aloud than in writing? ____
26. Does the student learn more words when less words are required to be learned in a given period of time (slower rate of input)? ____
27. Does the student *chunk* (use syllables or parts of words), or does he or she spell letter by letter? ____
28. Does the student pronounce words correctly? ____

Other Errors

Form 6-2

MANN-SUITER ANALYSIS OF ERRORS WORKSHEET

DEVELOPMENTAL WORD READING INVENTORY

NAME ______________________ SCHOOL ______________________

DATE ______________ GRADE __________ DATE OF BIRTH __________

EXAMINER ______________________

(A check mark indicates difficulty)

Auditory Errors

1. Guesses completely ____
2. Knows letter names, but not sounds ____
3. Makes associative error (*house* for *home*) ____
4. Knows sounds, but cannot blend into words ____
5. Substitutes one sound for another ____

Visual Errors

1. Has slow rate of perception (falls flash, but gets untimed) ____
2. Sees beginning of word only or beginning and endings only on flash ____
3. Makes reversals (*was* for *saw*) ____
4. Uses inversions (*me* for *we*) ____
5. Does not discriminate fine detail (*ship* for *snip*) ____
6. Omits sounds from words (check auditory discrimination) ____
7. Adds sounds ____
8. Hesitates ____

Other Errors

Form 6-3

MANN-SUITER ANALYSIS OF ERRORS WORKSHEET

DEVELOPMENTAL PARAGRAPH READING INVENTORY

NAME ______________________ SCHOOL ______________________

DATE ______________ GRADE __________ DATE OF BIRTH ______________

EXAMINER ______________________

(A check mark indicates difficulty)

Auditory Errors

1. Mispronounces words ____
2. Makes wild guesses ____
3. Makes associative errors (*house* for *home*) ____
4. Knows sounds but cannot blend ____
5. Needs to have words pronounced by teacher ____
6. Substitutes (*a* for *the*) ____
7. Cannot sound the word *out* ____

Visual Errors

1. Makes reversals of words (*was* for *saw*) ____
2. Transposes words and phrases (*said John* for *John said*) ____
3. Uses inversions (*me* for *we*) ____
4. Uses repetitions ____
5. Loses place and skips lines ____
6. Omits words or word endings ____
7. Makes errors of visual discrimination (reads *ship* for *snip,* or *ear* for *car*) ____
8. Reads word by word ____
9. Reads through punctuation ____
10. Exhibits hesitations ____
11. Adds words or endings ____

General Observations

Are items 1–6 true of the student when he or she is facing unfamiliar words?

1. Guesses without regard to any thought of the context read. ____
2. Seems unwilling to attempt to read and just waits for the teacher to say the word. ____
3. Seems willing to just skip unknown word and go on. ____
4. Seems unable to sound out word parts and blends. ____
5. Tries to spell out the word he or she cannot read. ____
6. Makes little use of the context in attacking a word he or she does not know. ____

NAME ____

(A check mark indicates difficulty)

In general, are items 7–14 true of the student?

7. Disregards punctuation. ____
8. Does not pay attention to the story line. ____
9. Has a low meaning vocabulary—not adequate for the reading level under concern. ____
10. Makes no attempt to correct his or her errors. ____
11. Exhibits frequent hesitations and makes sounds like uh . . . ? ____
12. Drops his or her voice at the end of a sentence. ____
13. Reads word by word instead of in phrases or thought units. ____
14. Exhibits a negative and indifferent attitude ("Do I have to?"). ____
15. How does the student analyze problems and glean meaning? ____
16. Does the student have excessive body movements while reading? ____
17. Is the student penalized by slowness in reading? ____
18. Does the student prefer to read alone or in a group? ____
19. How does the student react to being tested? Will he or she respond to an alternative type of evaluation? ____
20. Does the student avoid reading? ____
21. Does the student read at home? ____
22. Does the student understand more after reading silently than after material has been read orally to him or her? ____
23. Does the student value reading? ____
24. Is the student's failure mechanical or is the student deficient in comprehension? ____
25. Does the learner substitute words that are appropriate in his or her dialect while reading? ____
26. Does the student appear tense or nervous? ____
27. Is the student easily distracted from the task? ____
28. Does the student have a speech problem (stuttering, articulation, voice)? ____
29. Does the student give bizarre responses? ____
30. Does the student hold the book at the appropriate length from eyes? ____

Other Errors

Mann-Suiter Analysis of Errors Worksheet—Developmental Paragraph Reading Inventory

NAME ____

(A check mark indicates difficulty)

Reading Comprehension

STUDENT'S READING LEVEL	____	____	____	____
1. Detail	____	____	____	____
2. Main Idea	____	____	____	____
3. Inference	____	____	____	____
4. Vocabulary	____	____	____	____
a. Primarily Concrete-Functional (*C-F*)	____	____	____	____
b. Primarily Abstract (*A*)	____	____	____	____

General Observations on Oral Reading

1. Phrasing ____
2. Fluency ____
3. Finger pointing ____

General Observations on Silent Reading

1. Uses fingers ____
2. Vocalizes ____
3. Makes remarks ____

Listening Comprehension

1. Grade level expectancy based on listening comprehension ____

Form 6-4

MANN-SUITER ANALYSIS OF ERRORS WORKSHEET

HANDWRITING

NAME ______________________________ SCHOOL ______________________________

DATE ______________________ GRADE ____________ DATE OF BIRTH ______________

EXAMINER ______________________________

Handwriting Errors	(A check mark indicates difficulty)
1. Is unable to copy accurately	____
2. Aligns letters poorly	____
3. Exhibits unorthodox joining of letters in cursive	____
4. Fuses letters	____
5. Changes hands	____
6. Writes from right to left	____
7. Fatigues easily	____
8. Forms letters poorly	____
9. Makes irregular size letters	____
10. Exhibits poor spacing	____
11. Uses heavy pressure	____
12. Grasps pencil too close to the point	____

Other Handwriting Errors

Written Language Errors

1. Phrases	____
2. Sentences	____
3. Punctuation	____

Other Written Language Errors

Form 6-5

MANN-SUITER DIAGNOSTIC WORKSHEET

NAME ______________________ SCHOOL ______________________

DATE ______________ GRADE ______________ DATE OF BIRTH ______________

EXAMINER ______________________

Auditory

	Strengths	*Average*	*Weaknesses*
Sensory (Acuity)			
Perception: Figure-ground			
Closure			
Discrimination			
Localization-attention			
Imagery: Memory			
Sequencing			

Visual

	Strengths	*Average*	*Weaknesses*
Sensory (Acuity)			
Perception: Figure-ground			
Closure			
Discrimination			
Imagery: Memory			
Sequencing			

Language

	Strengths	*Average*	*Weaknesses*
Visual Language Classification			
Visual Language Association			
Auditory Language Classification			
Auditory Language Association			
Manual Language Expression			
Alphabet Speech Screen (letter names and sounds)			
Verbal Language Expression			
Written Language Expression			
Nonverbal Symbolic Language			

NAME ______________________________

Conceptualization

	Strengths	Average	Weaknesses
Vocabulary essentially concrete-functional			
Vocabulary essentially abstract			

Listening Comprehension

	Strengths	Average	Weaknesses
Level at which student understands 50% or more of paragraphs read to him or her			

Motor

	Strengths	Average	Weaknesses
Fine motor (handwriting)			
Gross motor			

	Strengths	Average	Weaknesses
Spelling			
Reading			
Arithmetic			

Speech

	Strengths	Average	Weaknesses
Articulation			
Stuttering			
Voice			

Social Emotional

	Strengths	Average	Weaknesses
Aggressive-acting out/passive			
Sensitive-withdrawn			
Immature-dependent			
Psychotic-neurotic			
Delinquent-unorthodox			
Social Perception Disorders			

Mann-Suiter Diagnostic Worksheet

NAME ____

Control Factors

	Strengths	Average	Weaknesses
Distractibility			
Hyperactivity			
Perseveration			
Disinhibition			
Impulsivity			

Other

____________________			
____________________			
____________________			
____________________			
____________________			

Comments

Form 6-6

MANN-SUITER EDUCATIONAL PROFILE

Green √ = strong
Red √ = weak
Black x = average
Unmarked = not tested

NAME ______________ EXAMINER ______________ ADDRESS ______________

DATE OF BIRTH ______________ SCHOOL ______________ DATE ______________

TEACHER ______________ GRADE ______________ STUDENT'S HOME TELEPHONE ______________

Auditory

Sensory
Acuity ☐

Perception
Discrimination ☐
Localization and attention ☐
Figure-ground ☐
Closure ☐

Imagery
Memory ☐
Sequencing ☐

Visual

Sensory
Acuity ☐

Perception
Discrimination ☐
Figure-ground ☐
Closure ☐

Imagery
Memory ☐
Sequencing ☐

Motor

Fine ☐
Gross ☐
Spatial ☐
Left-right orientation ☐
Body image ☐

Academic Tasks

Reading ______________

Comprehension and Concept level (Concrete-Functional, C-F, or Abstract A) ______________

Writing (Handwriting and Expression) ______________

Spelling ______________

Arithmetic ______________

Other ______________

Language

Receptive
Visual language classification ☐
Visual language association ☐
Auditory language classification ☐
Auditory language association ☐

Expressive
Manual language expression ☐
Speech ☐
Verbal language expression ☐
Written language expression ☐
Nonverbal language ☐

Other ______________

Social-Emotional-Control

Aggressive-Acting Out ☐
Sensitive-Withdrawn ☐
Immature-Dependent ☐
Psychotic-Neurotic ☐
Delinquent-Unorthodox ☐
Social Perception Disorders ☐
Distractibility ☐
Hyperactivity ☐
Perseveration ☐
Disinhibition ☐
Impulsivity ☐

Chapter 7 Developmental Skills Curriculum

Included in this chapter are additional diagnostic information, a list of developmental skills or objectives for the language arts, and prescriptive activities in the following process areas:

1. Auditory channel
2. Visual channel
3. Language

The criterion-referenced list of developmental skills was prepared after an extensive analysis of elements that constitute the tasks of reading, writing, spelling, and speech (oral production).

The instructor will find the delineation of developmental skills with accompanying educational activities helpful in planning an individualized educational program for a student exhibiting one or more difficulties in the processing of information.

The skills are listed in estimated developmental order. This order was followed so that the skills could be used as a criterion-referenced sequence of objectives in the development of individual educational programs. These criterion-referenced objectives—which can be correlated with teacher observations, screens, and tests—are designed to suggest areas for developing specific curricular activities. They will provide a functional basis for the development of an individual education program for each student.

The developmental skills can be used as a guide to individual student assessment, curriculum planning, and material management in programs designed to accommodate to students exhibiting learning difficulties in different academic settings.

More specific utilization of the developmental skills includes the following:

1. Assessment devices of any type—informal as well as formal instruments—can be item-, area-, or subtest-analyzed and correlated with the specific behaviors within the list. This will enable the individuals doing the evaluation to identify the level of performance in specific tasks such as reading, writing, or spelling and to determine the prerequisite skills necessary to effectively perform those tasks. Example: Failure in the "matching" subtest of the Metropolitan Readiness Test suggests possible difficulties with visual discrimination tasks.
2. The list of developmental skills can function as a basis for programming. Once the deficit area (for example, visual discrimination) and level of difficulty are identified, curricula activities can be developed or compiled based on the particular skills to be mastered.
3. Material can be analyzed (for example, to find anything related to visual discrimination) and coded into the developmental skills system for more effective management.
4. The developmental skills can be used for setting up an accommodating classroom environment based on particular areas of learning, such as auditory, visual, or motor. These learning areas, or centers, based on the developmental skills classification can be applicable to any learning environment. Further uses, of the list of developmental skills will become evident through continued use within the classroom.

Each section describing a learning area contains a list of activities for school and home that can be used in conjunction with the list of developmental skills to reinforce the skill or ability of concern.

AUDITORY CHANNEL

Auditory-Sensory

DIAGNOSIS

1. *Observable Behaviors*
   a. Students may cup their ears to hear.
   b. Students may be restless and exhibit poor behavior.
   c. Students may have difficulty following directions.
   d. The students may consistently ask for repetitions.
   e. Students may turn their heads unusually when trying to listen.
2. *Mann-Suiter Screening*
   Mann-Suiter-McClung Developmental Checklist, pages 25–31.
3. *Supplementary Evaluation*
   a. Audiometric Sweep Test (formal).
   b. Request that students stand in the rear of the classroom. Covering your mouth, call their names in your usual voice. The students respond to their names by taking their seats (informal).
   c. Watch-Tick Test: from behind the student, hold a pocket watch approximately one inch from the student's ear. Place the watch to the ear intermittently, asking the student to raise a hand when he or she hears the ticking. Alternate putting the watch to the ear with putting a half dollar to the ear to see if the student is responding appropriately (informal).
4. *Developmental Concerns*
   Auditory Acuity: Difficulty in hearing may result from physical disorders. Auditory development is based on the integrity of the following systems.
   a. *The vibrator, or sound producer.* Loss of specific frequencies may prevent students from hearing certain sounds. For example, they may not hear teachers who have either low- or high-pitched voices.
   b. *The acoustic signal, or sound in the air.* A clogged-up ear canal will affect the ability to hear. Some young children are continually putting things into their ears. Ears should be checked periodically by the teacher for wax buildup and foreign objects. Excessive buildup of wax may affect hearing.
   c. *The mechanical signal, or eardrum and/or bones of the middle ear.* Damage to the eardrum itself or to the bones of the middle ear can result in mild to severe hearing loss and require the use of a hearing aid.
   d. *The hydraulic signal, or the inner ear fluid.* Inner ear infection can cause difficulty in hearing.
   e. *The electrical signal, or the cochlea nerve.* Damage to the cochlea nerve may result in moderate to profound hearing loss and is quite difficult to treat.

PRESCRIPTIVE ACTIVITIES

1. Refer students for an auditory examination.
2. Change the students' seats so that they will be closer to the source of sound. Avoid seating the students near noisy air conditioners, windows, or doors.
3. Face the students when giving directions. Many teachers talk to the chalkboard.
4. Amplification would be helpful.
5. Do not speak from behind the students.
6. Watch your rate and amount of speech, or verbal input.

Auditory-Perception

AUDITORY ATTENTION TO SOUND

Diagnosis

1. *Observable Behaviors*
   a. Students with this problem may be easily distracted by competing stimuli.
   b. Students may appear to be emotionally disturbed or mentally retarded.
   c. Some students have difficulty getting meaning from sound or speech and, therefore, do not attend to auditory stimuli.

Prescriptive Activities

1. Create an awareness of sound by amplifying.
2. Attract the students' attention by using toys and musical instruments.
3. Use a clicker or some other sound signal to get the attention of the students.
4. In severe cases, you may have to turn the student's head to the source of the sound.

AUDITORY (SOUND) LOCALIZATION

Diagnosis

1. *Observable Behaviors*
   a. The learner may have difficulty finding the source of sound or the direction from which it is coming.
   b. The learner may have difficulty in assigning specific voices to specific persons.
   c. Some teachers have their desk in the back of the room and give directions from behind students. Students need to find the teacher's voice before they can attend to directions. Face the students when speaking to them.
2. *Mann-Suiter Screening*
   Mann-Suiter-McClung Developmental Checklist, pages 25–31.
3. *Supplementary Evaluation*
   To identify this problem, perform a simple "snap test." Ask the student to close his or her eyes, then snap your fingers around the student's body and have the student point to the direction of the sound. A student who cannot point to where the sound is coming from may have problems with auditory localization, and further evaluation may be indicated.

Prescriptive Activities

1. Students should practice locating sounds of bells, noise makers, and voices around the room, first with sight and then blindfolded.
2. Have the students close their eyes and point to sounds coming from different directions. Make sounds in different parts of the room, and have the students identify the sound and its location.
3. Take the students to a noisy place such as a shopping center or park and let them listen to the sounds that are present (e.g., cars, birds). Ask the students to close their eyes and tell what they hear. Have them point to the location of sounds as you name them.
4. Have blindfolded students match the classmate with the voice.
5. Hide a sound-making device, such as a small radio, for the student to find.
6. Parents or guardians can play sound-finding games at home.

AUDITORY (SOUND) DISCRIMINATION

Diagnosis

1. *Observable Behaviors*
   a. Student cannot tell when sounds are the same or different.
   b. Students have difficulty with pitch, frequency, and intensity.
   c. Students have difficulty distinguishing human vs. nonhuman sounds.
   d. Students confuse similar sounding letters (e.g., *d/t*).
   e. Students have problems in learning phonics and in blending sounds.
2. *Mann-Suiter Screening*
   a. Mann-Suiter Auditory Discrimination Screen, page 50.
   b. Mann-Suiter-McClung Developmental Checklist, pages 25–31.
3. *Supplementary Evaluation*
   Optional or as deemed appropriate. Refer to additional tests listed in Chapter 6.

Developmental Skills (Criterion Reference)

The student will

1. identify from unseen choices the object that produces a particular sound.
2. identify from choices the picture of the object that produces a particular sound.
3. identify from choices of closed containers pairs of objects that sound the same.
4. identify from three or more closed containers the object that sounds different.
5. identify from choices the object that has the same beginning sound as the model presented orally.
6. identify from choices the rhythm that is the same as the model.
7. identify from printed choices the letter sound that is the same as, or different from, the model presented unseen by the instructor.
8. identify from paired words presented orally and unseen by the student the pairs that sound the same or different.
9. identify from choices the object or picture of an object that rhymes with the model.
10. identify from choices presented orally the word that rhymes with the model.
11. identify from choices of pictures of words within the reading vocabulary the word that rhymes with the model presented orally.
12. identify from choices the picture of an object that has the same beginning sound as the model presented orally.
13. identify from choices the object that has the same ending sound as the model presented orally.
14. identify from choices the picture of an object that has the same ending sound as the model presented orally.
15. identify from choices the object that has the same medial sound as the model presented orally.
16. identify from choices the picture of an object that has the same medial sound as the model presented orally.
17. identify from choices the picture of an object that has the same beginning blend as the model presented orally.

Prescriptive Activities

GENERAL ACTIVITIES

1. Select from the list of developmental skills the particular target skills that are to be mastered in the area of Auditory (Sound) Discrimination. These target skills become learning or behavioral objectives.
   Example Target: Auditory Discrimination 7—The learner will identify from printed choices the letter sound that is the same as, or different from, the model presented unseen by the instructor.
2. If the student fails to demonstrate success in the target skills according to predetermined criteria such as failing items assessed on a standardized test or failing school tasks requiring the skills, do the following:
   a. Select from the list of developmental skills the target skill (example: Auditory Discrimination 7) and other related or similar skills (6, 5, etc.) that are deemed appropriate for developing activities that will provide success and practice for higher level functions or skills (8, 9, 10, etc.). Select activities at lower levels (6, 5, 4, etc.) as necessary to insure success and provide an array of different activities that will reinforce the development of Auditory (Sound) Discrimination skills.
   b. Develop or select from other sources additional activities related to all of the specific Auditory (Sound) Discrimination skills listed (1–17). These activities can be coded into the system at the appropriate levels within the list of development skills.

SPECIFIC ACTIVITIES

1. Begin with the recognition and discrimination of grossly different sounds in nature, such as wind, rain, fire, and thunder.
2. Teach the student to discriminate and identify social

sounds within the environment (e.g., horns, bells, birds, dogs).

3. Make the student aware of the sounds of danger, such as trains, cars, and sirens.
4. Let the student listen to the subtleties of sound that are present in a quiet place such as a park or forest (wind, trees, water, birds, etc.).
5. Go on a sound hunt through the neighborhood, listening for as many different sounds as possible. Note the things that sound similar to each other, such as types of motors, birds, car horns.
6. Identify objects in the home that make sounds (such as electrical appliances, pets, people, plumbing, radio, television) and discuss how the sounds are made.
7. Provide musical instruments, toys, or other objects (e.g., bells, squeeze toys) for the student to manipulate, recognize, and discriminate sounds.
8. Pure tones will help the student discriminate pitch, frequency, intensity, and timbre.
9. After teaching grossly different sounds, move to finer and finer discriminations, using tuning forks, musical instruments, and other sound-making devices.
10. Play a record of different musical instruments and/or voices and have the learner identify the instrument (trumpet, piano, violin, drum, etc.) or the voice (man's, woman's).
11. Have the student match different objects or pictures of objects, such as animals or musical instruments, and their concomitant sounds.
12. Fill identical (size and shape) containers, in pairs, with the same amount of contents (pennies, rice, tacks, etc.). The student rattles the containers and matches those with the same sound.
13. Ask the student to match objects on a duplicator sheet with their respective sounds as presented on record or tape.
14. Have the learner draw objects that make a particular sound.
15. Say words to the student (such as, *cat, house, hat*) and ask which two rhyme. Or say, "I'm thinking of an animal that rhymes with *hat*." Include rhyming words used in the learner's reading program.
16. Say sentences with simple rhymes for the learner to repeat (*the fat cat is on a mat*).
17. Use pictures of objects from magazines or books for matching words in rhyming activities. Words representing the pictured objects can be presented orally or on tape and matched by the learner.

    Example: "Are these the same or different?"
18. Say four words and ask the student to indicate which one was different.

    go go so go
    very fairy very very
    hop hop hop hot
19. In teaching, do not teach similar sounding letters for contrast; for example, do not teach *p* and *b* or *f* and *v* together. Most important, do not overload in teaching. Sounds should be taught one at a time. Never introduce more than one new sound in a given day.
20. Collect objects with the same beginning, ending, or middle sounds for matching activities.
21. Use pictures from magazines for purposes of matching initial, middle, and ending sounds.
22. Activities can be prepared for many of the developmental skills listed (1–17) by using the following:
    a. pictures drawn on the chalkboard
    b. acetates on the overhead projector
    c. cutting and pasting of pictures from old workbooks and magazines
    d. small objects
    e. commercial records and tapes
    f. instructor-prepared tapes
    g. movable letters, clay letters
    h. sound instruments
    i. glasses containing varied amounts of water

AUDITORY FIGURE-GROUND

Diagnosis

1. *Observable Behaviors*
    a. Students may exhibit forced attention to sound, causing them to attend to extraneous noises in their environment.
    b. Students may find it difficult to attend to speech.
    c. By comparison to other students, these students may not be able to sit for long periods of time. They may appear to be distractible and hyperactive.
    d. A teacher may find that students obey the commands of the teacher next door.
    e. Students may not be able to focus on their own work and may tend to interfere when the teacher is working with another student.
2. *Mann-Suiter Screening*
   Mann-Suiter-McClung Developmental Checklist pages 25–31.

Developmental Skills (Criterion Reference)

The student will:

1. identify and state the different sounds he or she hears in a room or out of doors.
2. identify selected sounds in a room or out of doors.
3. identify verbal sounds from among other sounds.
4. identify from choices the picture of an object that represents a word presented amidst a background of noise.
5. follow directions on command that are presented amidst a background of noise.
6. identify from choices of musical themes hidden amidst a background of noise the theme that is the same as the model.

Prescriptive Activities

GENERAL ACTIVITIES

1. Select from the list of developmental skills the particular target skills that are to be mastered in the area of Auditory

Figure-Ground. These target skills become learning or behavioral objectives.

Example Target: Auditory Figure-Ground 5—The learner will follow directions on command that are presented amidst a background of noise.

2. If the student fails to demonstrate success in the target skills according to predetermined criteria such as failing items assessed on a standardized test or failing school tasks requiring the skills, do the following:

   a. Select from the list of developmental skills the target skill (example: Auditory Figure-Ground 5) and other related or similar skills (4, 3, 2, 1, etc.) that are deemed appropriate for developing activities that will provide success and practice for higher level functions or skills (e.g., 6). Select activities at lower levels (4, 3, 2, etc.) as necessary to insure success and provide an array of different activities that will reinforce the development of Auditory Figure-Ground skills.

   b. Develop or select from other sources additional activities related to all of the specific Auditory Figure-Ground skills listed (1–6). These activities can be coded into the system at the appropriate levels within the list of development skills.

SPECIFIC ACTIVITIES

1. Provide a place that is reasonably quiet where the students can get off by themselves for parts of the day.
2. Do not seat the students by the window, door, or noisy air conditioner.
3. Help the students select relevant from irrelevant sounds in the environment with eyes closed, then with eyes open.
4. Condition the students by introducing sound into the environment on a selective basis. Gradually add distracting noises while giving directions or telling a story. Have the students discuss what they heard.
5. Use tapes or records to help the students build in sound selectivity (ear phones can be used to screen out distraction).
6. Face the students when giving critical directions.
7. Regulate the rate of verbal input. Going slower makes a difference.
8. Drugs under *strict supervision* may help.

AUDITORY CLOSURE (BLENDING)

Diagnosis

1. *Observable Behaviors*

   a. The students cannot blend sounds into syllables and words.

   Example: They can read *c-a-t* in isolation but cannot put the sounds together to make the word *cat*.

   b. Students may not be able to put sounds together to make words that they hear orally.

2. *Mann-Suiter Screening*

   a. Mann-Suiter Auditory Closure (Blending) Screen, page 51.

   b. Mann-Suiter-McClung Developmental Checklist, pages 25–31.

3. *Supplementary Evaluation*

   Optional or as deemed appropriate. Refer to additional tests listed in Chapter 6.

Developmental Skills (Criterion Reference)

The student will

1. identify from choices the object that represents the word presented by the instructor as a sequence, or spaced group, of sounds or syllables.
2. identify from choices the picture of an object that represents the word presented by the instructor as a sequence, or spaced group, of sounds or syllables.
3. name a word by synthesizing the sounds (letters or syllables) presented by the instructor.
4. synthesize sounds presented by the instructor and identify from among choices the word that is represented by these sounds.

Prescriptive Activities

GENERAL ACTIVITIES

1. Select from the list of developmental skills the particular target skills that are to be mastered in the area of Auditory Closure (Blending). These target skills become learning or behavioral objectives.

   Example Target: Auditory Closure 3—The learner will name a word by synthesizing the sounds (letters or syllables) presented by the instructor.

2. If the student fails to demonstrate success in the target skills according to predetermined criteria such as failing items assessed on a standardized test or failing school tasks requiring the skills, the instructor can do the following:

   a. Select from the list of developmental skills the target skill (example: Auditory Closure 3) and other related or similar skills (2, 1, etc.) that are deemed appropriate for developing activities that will provide success and practice for higher level functions or skills (e.g., 4). Select activities at lower levels (2, 1, etc.) as necessary to insure success and provide an array of different activities that will reinforce the development of Auditory Closure (Blending) skills.

   b. Develop or select from other sources additional activities related to all of the specific Auditory Closure Blending skills listed (1–4).These activities can be coded into the system at the appropriate levels within the list of development skills.

SPECIFIC ACTIVITIES

1. The pushing together of anagrams, clay, and sandpaper letters will help the student "see" how sounds go together through physical blending.
2. Give the student a selection of toys or small objects. Slowly say the sounds of one of the objects (*c-a-t*). The learner will pick up the correct object.
3. Give the learner duplicator pages of pictures of objects. Slowly say the sounds of one of the pictures. The learner marks the correct picture.

4. Say the meaning of a word (an animal) and slowly blend the word (*c-a-t*). The learner says the word (*cat*). If the student gives an incorrect response, repeat (an animal, *c-a-t*, and then give him or her three choices. (Is it dog, cat, rat?)
5. Blend names of students in a group. The correct student raises a hand.
6. Have the learner listen to a sentence and complete the blended word. (I play with a *b-a-ll*).
7. Slowly say sounds to the student (*c-a-t*) and ask him or her to say the word. Use words within the student's daily experiences.
8. Tapes of word analysis and synthesis (e.g., *cat—c-a-t, c-at, cat*) are helpful. These can be put into games in which the student guesses the word from the sounds.
9. Say words with a sound omitted and ask the student to indicate the word. For example, "What word is this: *heli . . . ter* [*helicopter*]." A space is left (no sound) for the missing part.
10. Play word Bingo games by blending the words instead of calling them out.
11. Verbally indicate to the student a particular spelling pattern, such as *at, et,* and *op*. Then give the student a consonant sound, such as *c, p, f,* and ask the student to make a word. For example, say the spelling pattern *at.* "If I put a *c* [sound] in front of *at,* what word do I get—cat." Repeat the activity with the sounds *f, s, b.*
12. In teaching reading, build on spelling patterns (e.g., *at, am, an, op,* and *et*) rather than on nonsense syllables.
13. The music teacher can provide activities that will aid the student in listening to the blending of tones.
14. For additional blending activities refer to page 206.

Auditory Memory–Sequencing

DIAGNOSIS

1. *Observable Behaviors*

   a. Students may not be able to recall (a) nonverbal sounds such as bells, animal sounds, and horns and (b) verbal sounds such as letters, words, or sentences.

   b. Students may have difficulty in following a sequence of directions at home as well as in school.

   c. Students generally are able to understand and to recognize words, but they have difficulty retrieving them.

   d. The student's parents may report that the students never get correct telephone messages.

   e. Memory deficits will also probably be observed by the physical education teacher, music teacher, etc.
2. *Mann-Suiter Screening*

   a. Mann-Suiter-McClung Developmental Checklist, pages 25–31.

   b. Mann-Suiter Auditory Memory Screen, page 53.
3. *Supplementary Evaluation*

   Optional or as deemed appropriate. Refer to additional tests listed in Chapter 6.

DEVELOPMENTAL SKILLS (CRITERION REFERENCE)

The student will

1. follow one or more directions given orally.
2. orally imitate a word or a sequence of unrelated words.
3. imitate a sequence of related words or sentences presented orally.
4. imitate a sequence of digits presented orally.
5. be presented with a sequence of digits and then state the sequence in reverse order.
6. imitate a sequence of nonsense syllables.
7. imitate a sequence of letter names or sounds.
8. state the names of the days of the week and the months of the year.
9. Count from 1 to 100 by 1s, by 2s, by 5s, and by 10s.
10. Follow directions given orally in testing situations.

PRESCRIPTIVE ACTIVITIES

General Activities

1. Select from the list of developmental skills the particular target skills that are to be mastered in the area of Auditory Memory–Sequencing. These target skills become learning or behavioral objectives.

   Example Target: Auditory Memory–Sequencing 4 —The learner will imitate a sequence of digits presented orally.
2. If the student fails to demonstrate success in the target skills according to predetermined criteria such as failing items assessed on a standardized test or failing school tasks requiring the skills, do the following:

   a. Select from the list of developmental skills the target skill (example: Auditory Memory–Sequencing 4) and other related or similar skills (3, 2, etc.) that are deemed appropriate for developing activities that will provide success and practice for higher level functions or skills (5, 6, 7, etc.). Select activities at lower levels (3, 2, 1, etc.) as necessary to insure success and provide an array of different activities that will reinforce the development of Auditory Memory–Sequencing skills.

   b. Develop or select from other sources additional activities related to all of the specific Auditory Memory–Sequencing skills listed (1–10). These activities can be coded into the system at the appropriate levels within the list of development skills.

Specific Activities

1. Use activities that will enable the students to better remember through associations with picture clues.
2. Slow down the verbal input and reduce the number of directions given to the students.
3. Show a student five or six objects. Call out the names of two of them and ask the student to point to the objects in the sequence called. Increase the difficulty to six as deemed appropriate.
4. Give students a series of pictures and orally indicate the order in which they should be placed. Example: cat,

dog, elephant, snake. This activity can be varied to include reverse order naming. Provide the students with a sequence and have them indicate the sequence back in reverse order.

5. Use chunking exercises, for example, use telephone numbers to practice the grouping and rhythm of long sequences (e.g., 246-8392).
6. Have students listen to numerals and words and tell how many they heard.
7. Say simple phrases and then short sentences of five words (or less) for the learners to repeat (e.g. "the big, yellow ball," "the dog is black and white") in the correct sequence. Slowly expand the number of words in the sentences.
8. Present in sequence words that begin with the same letter or that have a common basis (such as fruit, parts of a house, things that are found in the bathroom) and have the students remember them and repeat them in the same sequence.
9. Have the students listen to records that ask them to perform certain actions.
10. Have the students follow commands by going through an obstacle course.
11. Perform a series of auditory acts (such as clap, stamp foot, and close door) with the students blindfolded, and then ask, "What did I do?" "What did I do first?" "Next?" etc. When the students perform, say, "What did you do?" etc.
12. Practice giving different kinds of test directions orally. Example: "Take out your pencil and paper and open your book to page 12." Begin with two or three directions (vary complexity as necessary).
13. Say a sequence of simple-to-complex directions for the learners to follow (e.g., "Open the drawer, take out two pencils, and put them on the table.") Begin with two directions and increase the number as the learners succeed.
14. Clap out rhythms with your hands or with a drum and have the learners repeat the sequence. For example, clap clap—clap clap—clap.
15. Play echo games. For example, whisper a word, a phrase, or a sentence to one student, who repeats it to the next student until it goes around the room.
16. Use sentence completion games. For example, the first student says, "On the way to school, I saw a ________." The next student repeats the sentence and adds one more thing.
17. Introduce the learners to simple poems. Increase the complexity of the poems, pointing out the rhyming elements.
18. Singing songs and telling jokes and riddles are helpful in developing memory.
19. Read a story to the learners. Stop on occasion and ask them questions about the plot or ask them to retell the story. If they forget details or become involved in unnecessary details, bring them back to the story by leading questions. Recall will vary depending on the selection, the student, and the time of day.
20. If the learners can write, ask them to follow simple directions by writing words, numbers, geometric shapes, etc. (e.g., "Write your name." "Draw three circles and two squares.")
21. Students should be encouraged to remember the names and/or birthdays of the members of their families and the other students in the class.
22. Encourage the students to remember their own telephone numbers and the numbers of other members of the family. They can learn these by grouping the numbers (---/--/--) or by clapping the sequence (clap clap clap/clap clap/clap clap).
23. Parents or guardians can play games such as, "What did you hear first? . . . next?" after visiting different places or by using noises in the home or neighborhood.
24. Send students to various rooms in the house and have them bring specified items (for example, a glass of water and a spoon). Begin with two directions and add others as the students improve.

Auditory Language Classification

DIAGNOSIS

1. *Observable Behavior*
   Students with an Auditory Language Classification difficulty often cannot understand difference and sameness by category classification of objects or concepts presented orally. For example, when a student is asked whether a puppy belongs with ship, hat, door, or dog, he or she cannot discern the correct classification of puppy belonging with dog.
2. *Mann-Suiter Screening*
   a. Mann-Suiter-McClung Developmental Checklist, pages 25–31.
   b. Mann-Suiter Auditory Language Classification Screen, page 61.
   c. Mann-Suiter Developmental Reading Inventories, pages 85–89.
3. *Supplementary Evaluation*
   Optional or as deemed appropriate to additional tests listed in Chapter 6.

DEVELOPMENTAL SKILLS (CRITERION REFERENCE)

The student will

1. indicate the object that does not belong from among choices presented orally.
2. name all the objects included in a particular classification, such as fruit, animals, and transportation.
3. name the category when presented orally with a group of objects that can be classified together.
4. name the situation when presented orally with characteristic components.
5. indicate how objects or situations presented orally are alike or different, utilizing concrete-functional analysis as a rationale.
6. indicate how objects or situations presented orally are alike or different, utilizing abstract reasoning as a rationale.

7. complete sentences given orally that form analogies that involve the classification of objects or situations.

PRESCRIPTIVE ACTIVITIES

General Activities

1. Select from the list of developmental skills the particular target skills that are to be mastered in the area of Auditory Language Classification. These target skills become learning or behavioral objectives.

   Example Target: Auditory Language Classification 4—The learner will name the situation when presented orally with characteristic components.

2. If the student fails to demonstrate success in the target skills according to predetermined criteria such as failing items assessed on a standardized test or failing school tasks requiring the tasks, do the following:

   a. Select from the list of developmental skills the target skill (example: Auditory Language Classification 4) and other related or similar skills (3, 2, etc.) that are deemed appropriate for developing activities that will provide success and practice for higher level functions or skills (5, 6, 7, etc.). Select activities at lower levels (3, 2, 1, etc.) as necessary to insure success and provide an array of different activities that will reinforce the development of Auditory Language Classification skills.

   b. Develop or select from other sources additional activities related to all of the specific Auditory Language Classification skills listed (1–7). These activities can be coded into the system at the appropriate levels within the list of development skills.

Specific Activities

1. For more severely involved students or very young children, begin with simple auditory (sound) activities to teach the concept of difference and sameness. Be sure the student verbalizes what the sound is as well as what it is not. The following sequence is recommended:

   a. Gross sounds—bells, drums, dogs, etc. First teach different and same for gross sounds (between bells and drums), then for classification (all bells and all drums).

   b. Gross sound recognition. Play records of different sounds and ask the student to identify the sounds.

   c. Contrasting gross sounds. Ask the student to tell you which is loud, louder, loudest, low, lower, lowest, high, higher, highest, etc. Vary sounds in frequency, intensity, pitch, and timbre. Try to get complete sentence responses if you can. Remember to have the student verbalize what is loud as well as what is not loud.

   d. Help the student identify beginning sounds of words that are different and alike, then ending sounds that are different and alike, and, finally, medial sounds (the most difficult to discern) that are different or alike.

2. Use classification analysis games. For example, say one word, such as *ball*. The student names as many types of balls as he or she can, such as football, baseball, and handball.

3. Engage the student in category games:

   a. Which one does not belong? A cat, a dog, an umbrella.

   b. What are all of these called together? A pear, a plum, a peach.

   c. How many vegetables can you name?

4. Classification activities such as the following can be developed around media.

   a. Use the overhead projector for visual and auditory language classification games.

   b. Use real objects and talk about how they are the same and/or different.

   c. Draw pictures on the chalkboard for classification activities.

   d. Listen to records of different objects that can be classified together.

   e. Make duplicator masters for simple to complex activities.

   f. From old workbooks or magazines, cut out pictures that can be used for classification activities. They can be laminated, if desired.

   g. Use a pocket chart of pictures of objects for classification activities.

   h. Purchase or make tapes that contain classification activities.

   i. Have students draw objects that belong to the same classification, such as fruit, vehicles, different types of shelter.

   j. Use pictures to teach not only what an object is but also what it is not, such as, big–not big; little–not little; around–not around; live–not live. These concepts should be verbalized by the student.

Auditory Language Association

DIAGNOSIS

1. *Observable Behaviors*

   a. Students with this difficulty are unable to understand noncategorical relationships between words presented orally. For example, when the students are asked whether a motor belongs with a door, water, lamp, or car, they cannot discern the correct association of motor with car.

   b. Students with association problems may have difficulty in deriving meaning from words. The students can hear, but cannot associate words with meaning and, therefore, do not understand.

   c. Students may have difficulty in relating the spoken or written word with the appropriate unit of experience. (Note: Sometimes this disorder in its severe form is referred to as *childhood aphasia*.)

   d. Students may be frustrated by conversation.

   e. Difficulty may be evident with descriptors such as adjectives and adverbs.

   f. Verbal expression, or spoken language, is often affected, as are reading, writing, and arithmetic. The students may not be able to carry out a series of directions (check auditory memory).

   g. These students have difficulty with figurative language. For example, the students may not understand such statements as "he was chewed out" or "he has had it."

h. Students may not be able to associate the *m* sound in *mother* with the *m* sound in *man,* causing difficulty in learning phonics. Students may not transfer the sound of *m* in one word to the sound of *m* in another word (check auditory memory). Ability to make this transfer is a critical skill for success in the first grade. Inability to make the transfer is an auditory-to-auditory language association problem.

i. Students may not be able to associate the sound of *m* with the symbol *m.* This is an auditory-to-visual association language problem. Ability to make this association is another one of the critical skills necessary for success in first-grade language arts.

2. *Mann-Suiter Screening*
   a. Mann-Suiter-McClung Developmental Checklist, pages 25–31.
   b. Mann-Suiter Auditory Language Association Screen, page 63.
   c. Mann-Suiter Developmental Reading Inventories, pages 85–89.
3. *Supplementary Evaluation*
   Optional or as deemed appropriate. Refer to additional tests listed in Chapter 6.

DEVELOPMENTAL SKILLS (CRITERION REFERENCE)

The student will

1. identify from among two or more choices of objects or words the one that begins with the same sound as the one indicated by the instructor.
2. listen to a word and its beginning sound and indicate another word that begins with the same sound.
3. identify from among choices of objects the one that represents the meaning of the word presented orally.
4. identify from among choices of pictures of objects the one that represents the meaning of the word presented orally.
5. identify an object that is described in detail.
6. identify a situation that is described in detail.
7. describe an object indicated by the instructor in terms of function.
8. describe a situation indicated by the instructor in terms of feelings.
9. identify from choices the picture that represents the meaning of a sentence presented orally.
10. identify from choices based on a paragraph or story read to him or her the correct responses to associations dealing with social or cultural relationships.
11. identify from choices based on a paragraph or story read to him or her the correct responses to associations dealing with geographic or spatial-temporal relationships.
12. identify from choices based on a paragraph or story read to him or her the correct responses to associations or relationships involving good judgment in life situations.
13. verbally state an appropriate response to riddles.
14. orally indicate a logical and rational completion to an incomplete sentence.
15. complete analogies stated as incomplete sentences and define the rationale behind the associative relationship.
16. appropriately and logically extend open-ended situations.
17. orally complete in a logical manner a sentence read as an incomplete phrase by the instructor.
18. orally complete in a logical manner paragraphs read as open sentences by the instructor.
19. explain absurdities read in sentences, paragraphs, or stories by the instructor.
20. explain or indicate the absurdity when presented orally with absurd situations.
21. listen to a paragraph or story and orally paraphrase it.
22. listen to a word and verbally state it in a complete sentence, using it in the context of concrete or functional terms.
23. listen to a word and verbally state it in a complete sentence, using it in the context of abstract terms.
24. restate grammatically incorrect sentences presented orally into grammatically correct statements using good syntax and formulation.
25. respond correctly to multiple-choice or true-or-false questions related to a paragraph or story read to him or her.
26. respond to detail questions related to a paragraph or story read to him or her.
27. respond to main-idea questions related to a paragraph or story read to him or her.
28. respond to inference questions related to a paragraph or story read to him or her.
29. respond to personal questions relating to life history and environment.
30. verbally indicate all the words that he or she can think of in a given period of time.

PRESCRIPTIVE ACTIVITIES

General Activities

1. Select from the list of developmental skills the particular target skills that are to be mastered in the area of Auditory Language Association. These target skills become learning or behavioral objectives.
   Example Target: Auditory Language Association 25—The student will respond correctly to multiple-choice or true-or-false questions related to a paragraph or story read to him or her.
2. If the student fails to demonstrate success in the target skills according to predetermined criteria such as failing items assessed on a standardized test or failing school tasks requiring the skills, do the following:
   a. Select from the list of developmental skills the target skill (example: Auditory Language Association 25) and other related or similar skills (24, 23, etc.) that are deemed appropriate for developing activities that will provide success and practice for higher level functions or skills (26, 27, 28, etc.). Select activities at lower levels (24,

23, 22, etc.) as necessary to insure success and provide an array of different activities that will reinforce the development of Auditory Language Association skills.
b. Develop or select from other sources additional activities related to all of the specific Auditory Language Association skills listed (1–30). These activities can be coded into the system at the appropriate levels within the list of development skills.

Specific Activities

1. In severe cases or with very young children make the students aware of sound as opposed to no-sound activities. Ask the students to raise their hands when they hear the sound of machines turned on or off.
2. Begin with simple nouns within the students' experience. Use concrete objects, then use pictures of objects. Show the object or picture and discuss as follows:
   a. The quality of an object—for example, "the pencil is hard," "it has lead," "it can be made of wood." Then remove the object from sight and discuss what the students have learned immediately.
   b. The action potential or state of being of an object—for example, "the pencil is used to write with; it is not alive." After the object has been removed, the students describe from memory what they have learned.
3. Matching games like the following should be used to develop associative skills.
   a. Match environmental sounds such as horns with concrete objects and with pictures of horns.
   b. Match animal sounds with pictures of animals.
   c. Match words with concrete objects and then with pictures of objects.
   d. Match words given orally with words printed on cards.
4. Collect and use records of rhyming words and let the students hear the difference and then the sameness.
5. Use activities in which the students have to identify the source of sounds—first with their eyes open and then with their eyes shut.
6. Build vocabulary, beginning with words within the students' experience only.
7. In the beginning, ask short questions requiring short one-concept answers.
8. Say a word and tell the students to clap their hands when they hear the correct word among other words.
9. At first, build phrases by combining different action words with the same noun (for example, the boy walks, the boy runs, the boy eats).
10. Train the students to describe objects or situations from memory. ("What does an apple look like?" "What does your room look like?")
11. The intent of the following activities is for the students to verbalize associations between objects. Eventually, they should be able to do this without the object present as well as they can with the object present. Games that involve symbol or object associations will enable the students to "see" relationships more readily. For example:
    a. What-goes-with-what games, such as "What goes with shoe?"
    b. "Does bird go with feather, iron, or mountain?"
    c. What-is-the-opposite-of games: "What is the opposite of big?" "What is the opposite of high?" "What is the opposite of in?" etc.
12. Ask the students simple riddles. For example, "What is white and hard and you can write on the chalkboard with it?"
13. Ask association questions about stories read to the students and about television programs.
14. Teach cause-effect associations by asking the students such questions as the following:
    a. "When you see dark clouds in the sky, and lightning and thunder, what will happen?"
    b. "Why can't dogs fly?"
15. Use phoneme association games. For example: "Think of a word that begins like *boy* and sounds like *tag*."
16. Build in appropriate affectional association and improve social perception by varying the emotional tone of the verbal responses to include anger, excitement, declaration, interrogation, apathy, and happiness.
    a. Use puppets and carry on a dialogue that expresses the gamut of emotions. After the dialogue, the students can select from a group of pictures the facial expressions that the puppets expressed.
    b. Play a record of verbal behavior expressing emotions. Stand behind a student, looking into a full-length mirror. As the emotions are expressed, you and the student should pattern, or pantomime, the behavior. A full-length mirror is good for developing social perception and language.
17. Discuss real-life situations with the students and alternative solutions to everyday problems. Example: "What do you do if a bigger student hits you?"
18. If the students can learn to play checkers or chess, these kinds of activities can help to develop cause-effect relationships.
19. Identify concepts in particular stories or in areas of curriculum such as science or social studies that deal with the following:
    a. Space
    b. Time
    c. Geography
    d. Social order
    e. Economy (money)
    f. Value system
    Discuss the concepts in concrete-functional terms, then discuss relationship in terms of abstract thinking.
20. Matching or comparing for associative learning for many of the developmental skills can be achieved by using the following media:
    a. Real objects
    b. Pictures of objects or situations from books and newspapers
    c. Overhead projector using acetates
    d. Chalkboard activities
    e. Duplicated sheets of paper
21. A field trip provides a good real-life experience for

developing associative relationships. For example, a camel seen at the zoo is also a means of transportation in many areas of the world.

22. Discuss situations that will enable the students to take things to their natural consequences. What can happen if . . . ?
23. Vocabulary building in terms of word meaning should be a part of everyday activities in all subject areas.
24. Science and social studies are good areas for developing associative learning. For example:
    a. Dual meaning of words or phrases.
    b. Cause-effect relationship in economics, war, industry, science, etc.
    c. Historical sequences and relationships.
25. Develop duplicator masters that require students to indicate things that go together.
26. Find activities in old workbooks that develop associative skills. These can be laminated for continued use.
27. Discuss how things are not related as well as how they are related.
28. Discuss concepts dealing with space-time relationships. ("How long does it take you to get home from school?" "How far is it from where you live to the shopping center?" "During what season or time of the year is your birthday?")
29. Describe funny or silly situations. ("The car flew over the bridge," or "The cat skated down the hill.") Ask the learner what is funny about the statement.
30. Say a word to the students and have them give the opposite—for example, big and ______ [little]; hot and ______ [cold].
31. Present a student with several objects (for example, pencil, comb, and spoon). Have the student follow a series of directions such as the following:

    Give me the pencil and the spoon.
    Give me both the comb and the spoon.
    Give me none of the three objects.
    Give me two of the three objects.
    Give me the largest [or smallest, heaviest, roundest, smoothest, etc.] object.
    Give me the ones that are not used to comb your hair.
    Give me the one you write with.

32. Ask the learners to listen to a story record, a television program, etc., and have them verbally summarize the plot or list the major events.
33. Read to the learners. As they listen to different stories, they will increase their vocabulary. Encourage them to form visual images of the action, places, or characters in the stories.

VISUAL CHANNEL

Visual-Sensory (Ocular-Motor Disorders)

DIAGNOSIS

1. *Observable Behaviors*
    a. Blinking.
    b. Crossed eyes.
    c. Clumsiness.
    d. Poor performance in physical education activities.
    e. Unusual head tilt in reading.
    f. Tearing, redness, or inflammation of eyes.
2. *Mann-Suiter Screening*
    Mann-Suiter-McClung Developmental Checklist, pages 25–31.
3. *Supplementary Evaluation (Visual Sensory)*
    Optional or as deemed appropriate. Refer to additional tests listed in Chapter 6.

DEVELOPMENTAL CONSIDERATIONS (CRITERION REFERENCE)

Ocular-Motor Disorders can occur in the following areas:

1. *Distinguishing light from no light.* The individual exhibits reduced sensitivity to light, which is a prerequisite for efficient visual perception.
2. *Seeing fine detail.* A student's disability in seeing fine detail can be determined through the Snellen Chart (American Medical Association) and a professional examination that measures visual acuity.
3. *Binocular fusion.* The student may experience double vision resulting from uneven vision whereby the bad eye interferes with the good eye. This condition can be diagnosed through the use of the (a) Telebinocular, (b) Ortho-Rater, or (c) Massachusetts Vision Test.[1]
4. *Convergence.* Convergence difficulties can be due to a muscular imbalance that interferes with the coordinated movement of the eyes, resulting in the inability to focus properly. Ocular-motor activities under the direction of a professional in this area should be considered.
5. *Scanning.* With scanning difficulties, the student may not be able to perform (a) natural zigzag scanning that may be required for looking at different things within the classroom; (b) visual pursuit or tracking of a moving object; or (c) the systematic learned eye movements that are required for reading.

Prescriptive Activities

1. Students should be seated in the front of the room for chalkboard work.
2. It is the responsibility of the school to follow up with the home if corrective lenses are needed.
3. Be aware of the nature and extent of the visual problem and its possible implications for different kinds of activities. A key factor is fatigue, which may occur in students with ocular-motor difficulties.
4. Undertake specific ocular-motor activities only with the specific instruction of a qualified professional in the area of vision and with permission of the parents.

1. *Keystone Visual Survey Telebinocular* (Meadville, Pa.: Keystone View Co., 1958); *Ortho-Rater* (Rochester, N.Y.: Bausch and Lomb, 1960); *Massachusetts Vision Test* (Boston: Massachusetts Department of Public Health, Welch Allyn, Inc., 1954).

Visual Perception (Recognition and Discrimination)

VISUAL DISCRIMINATION

Diagnosis

1. *Observable Behaviors*
   a. The students may know a word in one context but not when it is presented in a new situation.
   b. The students may have difficulty in matching shapes, geometric forms, or symbols (e.g., letters, numerals, words).
   c. The students may have difficulty in recognizing people when they change a characteristic of their physical appearance.
   d. The students cannot discriminate differences and sameness as pertains to objects and symbols.
2. *Mann-Suiter Screening*
   a. Mann-Suiter-McClung Developmental Checklist, pages 25–31.
   b. Mann-Suiter Visual Discrimination Screen, pages 40–41.
3. *Supplementary Evaluation*
   Optional or as deemed appropriate. Refer to additional tests listed in Chapter 6.

Developmental Skills (Criterion Reference)

The student will

1. match objects that are the same or different.
2. match objects that are not identical but similar in characteristics.
3. match pictures of objects that are the same or different.
4. match pictures of objects that are not identical but similar in characteristics.
5. match three-dimensional geometric solids.
6. complete inserts with a square, rectangle, circle, triangle, diamond, etc.
7. match pictures of geometric forms.
8. match three-dimensional wooden, plastic, felt, etc., letters.
9. match printed letters.
10. match three-dimensional wooden, plastic, felt, etc., numerals.
11. match printed numerals.
12. match three-dimensional wooden, plastic, felt, etc., words.
13. match printed words.
14. match words that are different but have similar parts, such as ending in *ing* or *ed* or beginning with the same letter.

Prescriptive Activities

GENERAL ACTIVITIES

1. Select from the list of developmental skills the particular target skills that are to be mastered in the area of Visual Discrimination. These target skills become learning or behavioral objectives.
   Example Target: Visual Discrimination 9—The learner will match printed letters.
2. If the student fails to demonstrate success in the target skills according to predetermined criteria such as failing items assessed on a standardized test or failing school tasks requiring the skills, do the following:
   a. Select from the list of developmental skills the target skill (example: Visual Discrimination 9) and other related or similar skills (8, 7, etc.) that are deemed appropriate in terms of developing activities that will provide success and practice for higher level functions or skills (10, 11, 12, etc.). Select activities at lower levels (8, 7, 6, etc.) as necessary to insure success and provide an array of different activities that will reinforce the development of Visual Discrimination skills.
   b. Develop or select from other sources additional activities related to all of the specific Visual Discrimination skills listed (1–14). These activities can be coded into the system at the appropriate levels within the list of development skills.

SPECIFIC ACTIVITIES

1. *Concrete level.* The students should verbally describe the differences and similarities between objects. (Note: Students should be allowed to hold the objects as they describe them.)
   a. Give the learners small objects to sort into containers (e.g., nuts, bolts, buttons, seeds, shells). Ask the learners to use only the thumb, index, and middle finger in picking up the objects.
   b. Show the learners three or more objects, such as two forks, a knife, and a spoon. Ask them to indicate which objects are alike. Use familiar items in the home (toys, buttons, fruit, cereal, crayons, tools, etc.).
   c. Show the learners two objects that are similar (e.g., toy cow and toy horse; pen and pencil; radio and television; fork and spoon). Ask the learners to tell how the objects are alike and then how they are different.
   d. Have the students use colored blocks to reproduce simple designs.
   e. Have the learners put different size objects into their respective containers (e.g., cards in envelopes, food in containers, objects in boxes)
2. *Pictures*
   a. Use activity (duplicated) sheets involving finding differences and similarities in pictures, such as matching a smiling pumpkin with the one that looks different or the same. The learners should verbalize what is different or the same and how it is different or the same.
   b. Use photographs or pictures from magazines to aid the students in discriminating difference and sameness between objects and forms
3. *Geometric Shapes*
   a. Use duplicated activity sheets involving discrimination of geometric shapes.
   b. Ask the students to place geometric insets into cut out shapes.
   c. Ask the students to find objects in the classroom or home that are of different size and shape.
   d. Have the students reproduce simple designs or

geometric shapes with toothpicks, pick-up sticks, etc. For example:

 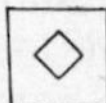

4. *Letters, Words, Phrases, and Numbers.* Develop activity sheets that facilitate the learning of differences and sameness in that order, using letters, words, then phrases or sentences.
   a. A student could find the letter that looks like *m* or the word that looks like *ship.* Matching activities can be done with anagrams of felt, wooden, or plastic letters.
   b. Ask the learner to match letter cards, f, or movable letters.
   c. Using duplicate sets of flashcards of vocabulary words learned at school, have the learner match like pairs.

   cat 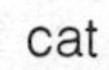

   d. Have the student match phrases and sentences that are different or the same.
   e. Ask the student to match numerals that are different or the same: 8694 / 4968 6948 8694.

OBJECT RECOGNITION (CENTRAL BLINDNESS)

Diagnosis

1. *Observable Behaviors*
   a. The students may not be able to recognize objects but can see, describe, and reproduce objects. (This condition may be due to cerebral dysfunction.)
   b. Sometimes the students may be able to recognize objects through touch.
   c. The students may have trouble integrating a visual stimulus into a uniform whole and may concentrate on the parts.
2. *Mann-Suiter Screening*
   a. Mann-Suiter-McClung Developmental Checklist, pages 25–31.

Developmental Skills (Criterion Reference)

The student will:

1. recognize and name familiar objects.
2. recognize and name familiar geometric forms.
3. recognize and name letters, words, and numerals that are within his or her experiential background.

Prescriptive Activities

SPECIFIC ACTIVITIES

1. Give the student a choice selection verbally ("Is it a ________, or ________, or ________?").
2. Have the students associate pictures or objects with sounds.
3. Have the students associate concrete objects or pictures with words.

FIGURE-GROUND DIFFERENTIATION

Diagnosis

1. *Observable Behaviors*
   a. Students may have difficulty in attending to the task assigned.
   b. Written work may be disorganized.
   c. Students may form letters incorrectly when forced to write on a crowded page.
   d. Students may have difficulty keeping their place while they read or copy material.
   e. Students may skip sections of tests or omit parts in the workbook.
   f. Students may have difficulty in completing work presented on a crowded paper.
   g. The most frequent complaint of the teacher is that the students "never finish their work."
   h. The students may have difficulty in distinguishing an object from the irrelevant background and holding the image while scanning the total pattern.
2. *Mann-Suiter Screening*
   a. Mann-Suiter-McClung Developmental Checklist, pages 25–31.
   b. Mann-Suiter Visual Figure-Ground Screen, page 37–38.
3. *Supplementary Evaluation*
   Optional or as deemed appropriate. Refer to additional tests listed in Chapter 6.

Developmental Skills (Criterion Reference)

The student will:

1. find partially hidden objects in different settings, such as classroom, playground, and home.
2. find an object or objects hidden amongst an unrelated background.
3. view a picture of an object and find and identify the same object fully exposed or partially hidden in an unrelated background.
4. locate and trace a design within a pattern or drawn on an unrelated background.
5. locate and trace over a picture of a geometric form on an unrelated background.
6. locate and name a symbol, such as a letter written on an unrelated background.
7. view a picture containing a letter, word or numeral and locate the requested symbol that is written within an unrelated background.
8. complete activities that require visually separating the foreground from the background, such as letters embedded in figures and color.
9. view a picture of an object and identify that object from among other objects by feeling them unseen in a bag or box.
10. locate and identify unseen objects in a bag or box, distinguishing them from other objects by feel and revisualization.
11. read material at his or her independent level without omitting words or lines.

12. complete work assignments within normal time limits and without becoming confused by the material provided.

Prescriptive Activities

GENERAL ACTIVITIES

1. Select from the list of developmental skills the particular target skills that are to be mastered in the area of Visual Figure-Ground. These target skills become learning or behavioral objectives.
   Example Target: Visual Figure-Ground 8—The student will complete activities that require visually separating the foreground from the background, such as letters embedded in figures and color.
2. If the student fails to demonstrate success in the target skills according to predetermined criteria such as failing items assessed on a standardized test or failing school tasks requiring the skills, do the following:
   a. Select from the list of developmental skills the target skill (example: Visual Figure-Ground 8) and other related or similar skills (7, 6, etc.) that are deemed appropriate for developing activities that will provide success and practice for higher level functions or skills (9, 10, 11, etc.). Select activities at lower levels (7, 6, 5, etc.) as necessary to insure success and provide an array of different activities that will reinforce the development of Visual Figure Ground skills.
   b. Develop or select from other sources additional activities related to all of the specific Visual Figure-Ground skills listed (1–12). These activities can be coded into the system at the appropriate levels within the list of development skills.

SPECIFIC ACTIVITIES

1. Locate and describe objects for the student in the street or playground.
2. Have the learner locate and describe objects that are partially hidden in the classroom or home.
3. Students can locate hidden objects and symbols in pictures, including geometric and other forms within their experience.
4. Hold up a book and read the title, pointing to each word as it is read. Use simple titles at first to help the students differentiate the word from the space. The students do not need to be able to read the words.
5. Put the color into the materials; do not overload the walls or the chalkboard with distracting color.
6. Place pictures of geometric forms, objects, letters, and words on newspaper or other backgrounds for the students to locate and identify.
7. Block out areas in workbooks so that the students will be able to attend better to specific tasks.
8. Provide various types of maps, globes, graphs, etc. Ask the learners to find products, places, or other specific information.
9. On field trips (nature hikes, factories, symphony concerts, etc.) aid the students in locating objects, people, or printed words.
10. Have the students locate specific items in a classroom terrarium or aquarium.
11. Provide books or encyclopedia pictures depicting animals, birds, and insects that are camouflaged by protective coloring and have the students locate and discuss them.
12. Have the students find specified information in reference books, classified ads, or telephone books. Encourage the students to gradually decrease the time in locating the information.
13. Have the students locate specific items in famous paintings. For example, locate the hidden animals in Henri Rousseau's paintings.

VISUAL CLOSURE

Diagnosis

1. *Observable Behaviors*
   a. Student may have difficulty blending letters into words visually.
   b. Students may be able to read the word *cat*, but if given the letters, they cannot put them together to form the word.
   c. The students may have difficulty in visualizing a "whole" and omit portions or details from objects or symbols.
2. *Mann-Suiter Screening*
   a. Mann-Suiter-McClung Developmental Checklist, pages 25–31.
   b. Mann-Suiter Visual Closure Screen, pages 42–46.
3. *Supplementary Evaluation*
   Optional or as deemed appropriate. Refer to additional tests listed in Chapter 6.

Developmental Skills (Criterion Reference)

The student will

1. put together pictures of up to five pieces.
2. put together puzzles of up to fifteen pieces.
3. assemble puzzles of over fifteen pieces.
4. assemble three-dimensional objects such as geometric forms or models of people, animals, cars, etc.
5. complete a partial picture of an object, thereby forming the whole object.
6. complete a partial picture of a geometric form, thereby forming the whole object.
7. identify the missing part from a picture of an incomplete object.
8. identify the picture of the object with the missing part, and the part missing, from among pictures of the same object with no missing parts.
9. locate and name the missing parts in pictures of incomplete objects.
10. complete dot-to-dot pictures.
11. identify, after viewing an incomplete object, the picture of the object as it would look completed.
12. name the completed objects when shown pictures of incomplete objects.
13. complete pictures of incomplete geometric forms by

writing or by using a finger or a pointer to indicate the missing lines.
14. complete an incomplete letter or numeral by writing.
15. identify the complete letter or numeral that is represented by an incomplete symbol.
16. *close,* or read a list of words with the letters spaced apart.

Prescriptive Activities

GENERAL ACTIVITIES

1. Select from the list of developmental skills the particular target skills that are to be mastered in the area of Visual Closure. These target skills become learning or behavioral objectives.
   Example Target: Visual Closure 13—Complete pictures of incomplete geometric forms by writing or by using a finger or a pointer to indicate the missing lines.
2. If the student fails to demonstrate success in the target skills according to predetermined criteria such as failing items assessed on a standardized test or failing school tasks requiring the skills, do the following:
   a. Select from the list of developmental skills the target skill (example: Visual Closure 13) and other related or similar skills (12, 11, etc.) that are deemed appropriate for developing activities that will provide success and practice for higher level functions or skills (14, 15, 16, etc.). Select activities at lower levels (12, 11, 10, etc.) as necessary to insure success and provide an array of different activities that will reinforce the development of Visual Closure Skills.
   b. Develop or select from other sources additional activities related to all of the specific Visual Closure skills listed (1–16). These activities can be coded into the system at the appropriate levels within the list of developmental skills.

SPECIFIC ACTIVITIES

1. Activities involving the completion of simple to complex puzzles: 2 pieces, 3 pieces, 5 pieces, 9 pieces, etc., can be used.
2. Have the learner assemble objects for art, science, and social studies lessons.
3. Show pictures of simple objects with parts removed or covered, and ask the learner to identify the missing parts.
4. Ask the learner to complete incomplete pictures or geometric shapes.
5. Draw simple dot-to-dot pictures for the learner to connect.
6. Teach the blending of letters this way:

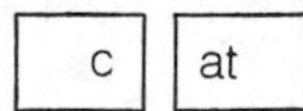

and not this way:

c	a	t

7. For additional blending activities refer to Chapter 8, page 206.

Visual Memory

DIAGNOSIS

1. *Observable Behaviors*
   a. The students may recognize the symbol when given a model but cannot recall it.
   b. The students often experience more difficulty in spelling and writing than in reading.
   c. The students cannot "see" things or symbols in their mind's eye.
   d. The students may be able to remember all of the parts but get them in the wrong sequence (*hpoe* for *hope*). (sequencing)
   e. The students may be erratic or variable in the way they sequence words, spelling the word *the*, for example, *the, hte,* or *teh;* or they may have a fixed wrong image, spelling the word *the*, for example, *teh* consistently. The latter problem appears to be more difficult to ameliorate. (sequencing)
2. *Mann-Suiter Screening*
   a. Mann-Suiter-McClung Developmental Checklist, pages 25–31.
   b. Mann-Suiter Visual Memory Screen, page 48.
3. *Supplementary Evaluation*
   Optional or as deemed appropriate. Refer to additional tests listed in Chapter 6.

DEVELOPMENTAL SKILLS

The developmental skills in the area of Visual Memory are separated into two parts: (1) Visual Memory–General and (2) Visual Memory–Sequencing.

Visual Memory–General (Criterion Reference)

The student will:

1. view a scene or a picture of a scene and name the things that are remembered.
2. describe from memory the characteristics of objects that are shown and then taken away.
3. view an object and identify it from among other objects after it has been removed.
4. view objects and name these objects after they have been removed.
5. view a group of objects and identify the object that has been removed from the group sight unseen.
6. view a group of objects and identify the object that has been added to the group sight unseen.
7. describe from memory the characteristics of pictures of objects that are shown and then taken away.
8. view a picture of an object and, after it is removed, identify the picture from among other pictures of objects.
9. view pictures of objects and name the objects after the pictures have been removed.

10. view pictures of objects and identify the picture of the object that has been removed sight unseen.
11. view pictures of objects and identify the picture of the object that has been added to the group sight unseen.
12. reproduce an object or geometric shape utilizing pencil and paper after the object has been removed.
13. identify a geometric figure, letter, or numeral from among choices after the model has been taken away.
14. write or construct out of clay a letter or numeral shown and then removed.
15. describe from memory the home, neighborhood, school, or other familiar place.

Visual Memory–Sequencing (Criterion Reference)

The student will:

1. imitate a series of one or more movements briefly demonstrated.
2. reproduce from a model a pattern utilizing beads, pegboards, blocks, etc.
3. reproduce a sequence of a pattern utilizing beads, pegboard, or blocks after the model has been shown and then removed.
4. when presented with a pattern of beads, pegs, blocks, etc., identify from choices the object that follows in order of sequence.
5. when presented with a picture of a sequence of objects, identify from choices the picture of the object that follows in sequence.
6. when presented with a picture of a sequence of objects, identify from choices the sequence that is the same.
7. reproduce from a model comprised of symbols such as letters or words a duplicate, using movable letters or writing.
8. when presented with a group of out-of-sequence pictures, arrange the pictures in the correct order.
9. reproduce a pattern from a model and then repeat the pattern two or more sequences, utliizing beads, peg board, blocks, etc.
10. reproduce a sequence of two or more letters, numbers, or words—using cards, movable symbols, or writing—after the model has been shown and then removed.
11. reproduce a sequence of two or more geometrical shapes after the model has been shown and then removed.
12. select from choices a sequence of letters, numbers, or words that is the same as the model that has been shown and then removed.
13. reproduce a sequence of pictures, using cards, after a sequence of pictures has been shown and then removed.
14. complete coded entries within a specific time period, given a sequence of samples as a model or guide: A = ○ ; B = □ ; C = △ ; etc.
15. select from choices the correct spelling of words that are within the independent reading vocabulary.
16. revisualize and spell words within the independent reading vocabulary, presented orally, by a written or verbal response.

PRESCRIPTIVE ACTIVITIES

Visual Memory–General

GENERAL ACTIVITIES

1. Select from the list of developmental skills the particular target skills that are to be mastered in the area of Visual Memory. These target skills become learning or behavioral objectives.
   Example Target: Visual Memory 5—The student will view a group of objects and identify the object that has been removed from the group sight unseen.
2. If the student fails to demonstrate success in the target skills according to predetermined criteria such as failing items assessed on a standardized test or failing school tasks requiring the skills, do the following:
   a. Select from the list of developmental skills the target skill (example: Visual Memory 5) and other related or similar skills (4, 3, etc.) that are deemed appropriate for developing activities that will provide success and practice for higher level functions or skills (6, 7, 8, etc.). Select activities at lower levels (4, 3, 2, etc.) as necessary to insure success and provide an array of different activities that will reinforce the development of Visual Memory skills.
   b. Develop or select from other sources additional activities related to all of the specific Visual Memory skills listed (1–15). These activities can be coded into the system at the appropriate levels within the list of development skills.

SPECIFIC ACTIVITIES

Basic to the amelioration process for students with memory problems is the concept that recall must follow recognition. In all activities, students are first asked to match or to pick out one from among others before they are required to use their recall abilities.

1. *Reinforcing Visual Memory with Tactual-Kinesthetic Associations.*
   Students with revisualization problems can be aided in their learning through the use of the tactual-kinesthetic modality. The students should be given an opportunity to establish a visual-tactual relationship by manipulating objects with their hands. Touch and body awareness will make them aware of difference and sameness at a more concrete level. The sequence of activities in Table 7-1 will be helpful to students who have difficulties with visual perception as well as with visual memory.
2. *Visual-Tactual Associations Using Shape as a Referent*
   a. Round and curved objects. Using spheres first, and then any round object available, do the following:
      (1) Let a learner take a suitably sized ball or sphere and cup it in her hands.
      (2) Draw attention to the way it looks and feels, how it fits into the palms of the student's hands.
      (3) Show the student that she can turn it in any direction and feel its roundness.
      (4) Call the student's attention to the fact that if her

Table 7-1 Sequence of Activities

Sequence in Teaching	*Visual–Tactual–Kinesthetic Associations*
Matching and comparing	The students match a felt, wooden, plastic, clay, or sandpaper letter to another felt, wooden, plastic, clay, or sandpaper object or symbol (letter, word, or numeral).
Tracing from a model	The students trace over a felt, wooden, plastic, clay, or sandpaper object or symbol with their fingers or walk or creep over a pattern.
Reproducing from a model. (pencil, pen, clay, wet sand, finger paint, etc.)	The students copy from a felt, wooden, plastic, clay, or sandpaper model of an object or symbol (letter, word, or numeral).
Reproducing without a model (pencil, pen, clay, wet sand, finger paint, etc.)	The students reproduce the object or symbol without the model present.

hands were large enough, they would fit around any ball and might even overlap.

(5) You could push a knitting needle through a ball to show that if the needle pierces the center of the ball from any point on the surface, the distance from point to center is always the same.

b. Straight-edged objects. Starting with a cube of wood or a styrofoam shape, do the following:

(1) Have a student take the shape into his hand to feel how it is unlike the sphere—it has straight edges and sharp corners that prick the palm.

(2) Let the student feel along the straight lines and measure with his fingers or with a ruler to see that the edges are all the same length.

(3) Use rectangular solids and have the student discover differences by looking at them and feeling them to see how they are unlike cubes.

c. Amelioration activities should include discrimination of shape, size, sequence, position, and color.

Note: Use concrete materials first, if necessary, then pictures, geometric shapes, letters, and words. Always proceed from that which is different to that which is the same.

3. Play memory games by describing objects or pictures of objects after they have been removed. Discuss the size, color, shape, function, and classification.
4. Help the learner practice describing objects or scenes from memory. ("What does your room look like?")
5. After trips to different types of stores, rides through scenic areas, viewing of television programs, etc., discuss what the students saw. Ask the students to draw pictures and include what they remember about a particular place.
6. Objects, animals, scenes, etc., used in science and social studies lessons can be examined, then removed and discussed.

Visual Memory–Sequencing

GENERAL ACTIVITIES

1. Select from the list of developmental skills the particular target skills that are to be mastered in the area of Visual Memory–Sequencing. These target skills become learning or behavioral objectives.

   Example Target: Visual Memory–Sequencing 11—The learner will reproduce a sequence of two or more geometrical shapes after the model has been shown and then removed.
2. If the student fails to demonstrate success in the target skills according to predetermined criteria such as failing items assessed on a standardized test or failing school tasks requiring the skills, do the following:

   a. Select from the list of developmental skills the target skill (example: Visual Memory–Sequencing 11) and other related or similar skills (10, 9, etc.) that are deemed appropriate for developing activities that will provide success and practice for higher level functions or skills (12, 13, 14, etc.). Select activities at lower levels (10, 9, 8, etc.) as necessary to insure success and provide an array of different activities that will reinforce the development of Visual Memory–Sequencing skills.

   b. Develop or select from other sources additional activities related to all of the specific Visual Memory–Sequencing skills listed (1–16). These activities can be coded into the system at the appropriate levels within the list of development skills.

SPECIFIC ACTIVITIES

1. *Activities Involving Auditory-Visual Associations*

   a. Listening and following directions. Ask the student to perform actions in certain sequences, such as the following:

   (1) Hopping, skipping, walking backwards, and walking forwards.

   (2) Going in different directions to various places, turning around, and touching objects with the left or right hand.

   (3) Tapping a sequence of sounds with the left or right foot or hand.

   b. Visual sequence and auditory associations.

   (1) Rhythm of motion related to sound can be developed by skipping, walking, running, and tapping to music.

   (2) Read sentences with rhymes, accenting the rhyming words. Ask the students to repeat in the same way as they point to the words; for example: The *cat* and the *rat sat* on a *mat*.

   (3) Say numerals in sequence, emphasizing the even

or odd ones as the students point to each one, for example:

$\underline{1}$ 2 $\underline{3}$ 4 $\underline{5}$ 6
1 $\underline{2}$ 3 $\underline{4}$ 5 $\underline{6}$

Have the students repeat the numbers that were emphasized.

(4) Give students practice in separating words into syllables so that they will hear and be able to repeat them in the proper order. This activity will help students with spelling, as well as with pronunciation, and will train them so that they will not be likely to make reversals or transpositions. For example, draw the syllables on the chalkboard or on paper, and have the students do the same. Have them say each syllable slowly as they do this. Start with two-syllable words and go to longer ones. This activity is called *chunking*, or *syllabication*.

walk ing
small er
po si tion
fol low ing

Chunk numbers the same way: have the students look at them, cover them, and see if they can repeat them, in groups, forwards and then backwards. This activity gives practice in sight recall.

2. Construct a simple pattern with beads, blocks, checkers, nuts, bolts, buttons, etc., for the learners to duplicate.
3. Show the learners a number of objects (begin with two or three and gradually increase the difficulty), remove them, and ask the learners to tell what they saw. Use familiar materials in the home (such as fruit, tools, cooking utensils, clothing, and toys).
4. Write a sequence of numerals, letters, or words on paper for the learners to copy, either by writing or by arranging cards.
5. Cut up simple comic strips or use sequence puzzles for the students to arrange in order.

Visual Language Classification

DIAGNOSIS

1. *Observable Behaviors*
   Students with a visual language classification difficulty often cannot understand differences and sameness by category classification of objects presented visually. For example, when the students are shown a picture of a pencil and asked whether it belongs with a picture of a pen, a ship, a hat, or a cup, they cannot discern the correct classification (in this case, the pencil belongs with the pen, since both are writing tools).
2. *Mann-Suiter Screening*
   a. Mann-Suiter Visual Language Classification Screen, pages 56–57.
   b. Mann-Suiter-McClung Developmental Checklist, pages 25–31.
3. *Supplementary Evaluation*
   Optional or as deemed appropriate. Refer to additional tests listed in Chapter 6.

DEVELOPMENTAL SKILLS (CRITERION REFERENCE)

The student will

1. sort objects (blocks, coins, beads, nuts, bolts, etc.) by shape, size, color, and position.
2. sort objects into categories and indicate how they are alike or different.
3. categorize pictures of objects and indicate how they are alike or different.
4. view pictures of objects and name those that can be grouped together, indicating the common characteristics or differences.
5. place objects or pictures of objects in front of a picture or model appropriate to the classification.
6. indicate, using pictures of objects, the single origin of several products (for example, paper, pencil, and piece of wood all come from a tree).
7. sort pictures of objects by function and state the rationale.
8. place pictures expressing different feelings into appropriate categories.
9. develop written lists of objects with common characteristics.
10. read paragraphs containing objects with common characteristics and then form written lists of objects by these specific characteristics.
11. read paragraphs at the independent level and respond, orally or in writing, to questions dealing with classification concepts.

PRESCRIPTIVE ACTIVITIES

General Activities

1. Select from the list of developmental skills the particular target skills that are to be mastered in the area of Visual Language Classification. These target skills become learning or behavioral objectives.
   Example Target: Visual Language Classification 7—The learner will sort pictures of objects by function and state the rationale.
2. If the student fails to demonstrate success in the target skills according to predetermined criteria such as failing items assessed on a standardized test or failing school tasks requiring the skills, do the following:
   a. Select from the list of developmental skills the target skill (example: Visual Language Classification 7) and other related or similar skills (6, 5, etc.) that are deemed appropriate for developing activities that will provide success and practice for higher level functions or skills (8, 9, 10, etc.). Select activities at lower levels (6, 5, 4, etc.) as necessary to insure success and provide an array of different activities that will reinforce the development of Visual Language Classification skills.
   b. Develop or select from other sources additional activities related to all of the specific Visual Language Classification skills listed (1–11). These activities can be coded into the system at the appropriate levels within the list of development skills.

Specific Activities

1. Begin with simple activities involving concrete objects, and teach difference and sameness. Using small plastic animals or real coins (pennies, nickels, dimes, and quarters), have the students match the animals or coins appropriately. The students should verbalize the difference and then the sameness as they point to each grouping and physically manipulate the objects. Along with teaching difference and sameness, teach what an object is and what it is not. This must also be verbalized by the students. For example, ask a student to show which coin in a group of coins is not a penny and tell why.
2. Repeat the preceding activities using color discs or blocks instead of coins. Color becomes the vehicle for teaching the concept of difference and sameness.
3. Difference and sameness can also be taught using position, size, and shape as a conceptual base. For example, "this one is facing up," "this one is shorter," "this one is round," etc. Remember, the objective is to make the student understand both the concept and the language of difference and sameness.

   Note: It is important for the teacher to determine whether or not the student has a perceptual (visual discrimination, etc.) problem to overcome in addition to a language difficulty.

4. The next step is to teach symbols by matching them in terms of difference and then sameness. First use plastic or wooden letters and words, then use printed letters and word cards.
5. Help the students look for and verbalize the common elements of concrete objects, including function. For example, pencils and pens are pointed and long, and they are both used in writing.
6. Involve the students in as much motor activity as possible. Permit them to manipulate objects as they verbalize difference and sameness, in that order.

   Note: For all areas of amelioration and dysfunctions, training should follow the sequence of levels listed below. Begin at the level that is most appropriate for the individual student, using (a) concrete objects, (b) pictures, (c) geometric forms, and (d) symbols, e.g., letters, words, and numerals.

7. After the students verbalize difference and then sameness at the concrete-functional level (what the object looks like and what you can do with it), move to the abstract level, using concrete objects first, then pictures. Hold up an apple and a pear, for example, and say, "These are both round. They are both good to eat. These are both fruit." The students should do likewise. The next step would be to hold up a picture of two items and have the students give similar classifications.

   Note: Many students functioning at the concrete-functional level in language development do not do well with tasks that require more abstract language abilities. The vocabulary sections of the Mann-Suiter Developmental Inventories will give the teacher information about the student's primary level of language functioning. Language in this sense becomes the tool of thinking or conceptualization.

8. Help the learners to classify objects or pictures.
   a. Household objects (tools, kitchen utensils, clothes, etc.) can be sorted into categories by the learner. Discuss the common characteristics.
   b. Pictures from trading stamp catalogs or magazines can be sorted into categories by the learner.
9. Show the learners a group of objects or pictures of objects and have them indicate the one that does not belong (such as apple, book, pear, peach).
10. Play a category game by naming three or four objects. The learner names the one that does not belong (bicycle, car, pencil, airplane).

Visual Language Association–Nonsymbolic (Object and Picture Level)

DIAGNOSIS

1. *Observable Behaviors*
   Students with this difficulty are unable to understand noncategorical relationships between objects presented to them visually. For example, when the students are shown a picture of bread and asked whether it belongs with a picture of butter, car, door, or crayon, they cannot discern the correct association. In this case, it is bread and butter.
2. *Mann-Suiter Screening*
   a. Mann-Suiter Visual Language Association Screen, pages 58–59.
   b. Mann-Suiter-McClung Developmental Checklist, pages 25–31.
3. *Supplementary Evaluation*
   Optional or as deemed appropriate. Refer to additional tests listed in Chapter 6.

DEVELOPMENTAL SKILLS (CRITERION REFERENCE)

The student will

1. point to the object or a picture of the object named by the instructor.
2. name the object or picture of an object pointed to or otherwise indicated by the instructor.
3. point to the size, shape, color, or position of the object or picture of an object named by the instructor.
4. name the size, shape, color, or position of the object or picture of an object indicated by the instructor.
5. place in the proper setting (picture or model) different objects or pictures of objects that represent the appropriate association.
6. place the object or picture of the object related to specific job roles in the appropriate setting (picture or model).
7. view a specific object or picture of an object and state where the object belongs.

8. view an object or a picture of an object and describe the object's function.
9. point to, or otherwise indicate from among choices, an object or picture of an object that goes with, or has a high degree of association with, the model.
10. view a model and sets of objects or pictures of sets of objects and state the association between the objects and the model.
11. view a picture of an object (model) and from among choices select the object that has the greatest degree of association with the model.
12. select from choices of pictures of objects and connect with a line, or otherwise indicate, those pictures of objects that go together.
13. select from choices of pictures of objects and connect with a line, or otherwise indicate, those pictures of objects that go together, stating the rationale for the association.
14. view a model or picture of a setting, identify the unrelated objects from among choices, and state the rationale.
15. view an object or a picture and complete in a logical manner an incomplete phrase or sentence stated by the instructor.
16. view a picture of an object or scene and create and express verbally a logical story.
17. view a picture of an object and select from choices the object that is the opposite of the model.
18. view a picture of a situation and select from choices the situation that is opposite of the model.
19. view a picture of an absurd circumstance or predicament and indicate verbally the absurdity.
20. view pictures of antecedents or components of a situation and state the outcome, indicating the cause-effect relationship.
21. view pictures of analogies and select from choices the analogy that is appropriate to the model.

PRESCRIPTIVE ACTIVITIES

General Activities

1. Select from the list of developmental skills the particular target skills that are to be mastered in the area of Visual Language Association at the nonsymbolic level. These target skills become learning or behavioral objectives.

   Example Target: Visual Language Association–Nonsymbolic 8—View an object or a picture of an object and describe the object's function.
2. If the student fails to demonstrate success in the target skills according to predetermined criteria such as failing items assessed on a standardized test or failing school tasks requiring the skills, do the following:

   a. Select from the list of developmental skills the target skill (example: Visual Language Association–Nonsymbolic 8) and other related or similar skills (7, 6, etc.) that are deemed appropriate for developing activities that will provide success and practice for higher level functions or skills (9, 10, 11, etc.). Select activities at lower levels (7, 6, 5, etc.) as necessary to insure success and provide an array of different activities that will reinforce the development of Visual Language Association skills.

   b. Develop or select from other sources additional activities related to all of the specific Visual Language Association skills listed (1–21). These activities can be coded into the system at the appropriate levels within the list of development skills.

Specific Activities

1. Build vocabulary by beginning with words within the student's experience.
2. Begin with concrete objects (for example, an apple), and have the student match the oral word with the single object first. Then ask the student to match the word with the appropriate object picked from a group of three or four objects. ("Give me an apple.")
3. Have students match oral words with pictures of objects within their experience. Begin with single words and match them to pictures, and then let the students match the word with the appropriate picture picked from a group of three or four different pictures.
4. Hold up familiar objects and have the students describe the quality and function of the objects. The students should be allowed to manipulate the objects as they describe them.
5. Hold up pictures of familiar objects and have the students describe the quality and function of the objects.
6. Try to get short-phrase or short-sentence responses from the students if they cannot give a long sentence, for example, "cotton," "soft cotton," "The cotton is soft."
7. Give the students directions by pointing or showing. For example, point to the door and motion for the student to close it.
8. Show the learners an object (shoe) and ask them to locate another object that goes with it (sock). If they cannot locate an object, provide a selection of three or more objects for the learners to select from. Discuss the associative relationships of the object.
9. Encourage the learners to use adjectives (such as soft, hard, big, little, red, fuzzy) to describe objects on a table or in a room, their clothes, etc.
10. Say sentences, leaving out a word, and have the learners supply the missing word (e.g., "The cotton feels ________.")
11. Take the learners on trips to parks, museums, places of historical significance, etc. Discuss the qualities of the objects or scenes viewed.
12. Play games (e.g., relay races) with the learners to teach verbs—walk, run, hop, skip, jump, etc.
13. On a hike with the learners, use adverbs and discuss their meaning (e.g., walk slowly, carefully, quickly, sadly, quietly, happily, noisily, etc.).
14. As a learner moves from room to room within the house, play riddles with him or her. (E.g., "I have four legs. I am not alive.")
15. Discuss the animals in stories (e.g., pelican, pig, rat, horse). On a trip to the library, examine pictures of the

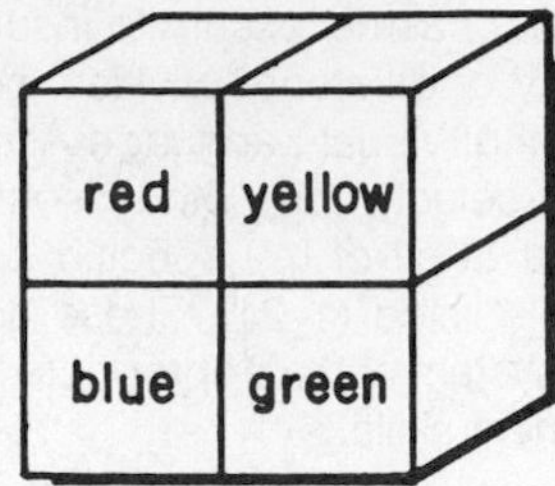

Figure 7-1 Block Pattern

animals in books and discuss their coloring, types, location, food, habitat, etc.

16. Develop simple analogies by using colored sheets of paper, blocks, or crayons. Say, "as green as." Go on a color hunt to find articles to complete the comparison.
17. Present the student with four blocks (Figure 7-1) and ask the following questions:
    What color blocks are on top?
    What color blocks are underneath?
    What color block is beneath the yellow block?
    What color block is beside the blue block?
    What color block is on top of the green block?

(*Note:* Slow down the rate and amount of input for all activities to avoid frustration.)

Visual Language Association–Symbolic (Letter, Numeral, and Word Decoding and Comprehension Skills)

DIAGNOSIS

1. *Observable Behaviors*
   a. Students may not be able to associate a word they can read with the appropriate unit of experience. These students are sometimes referred to as *word callers*. They can read, but do not understand.
   b. The students' verbal or written language and arithmetic may also be affected by this disorder in that they may not be able to associate words or numerals that they see with meaning.
2. *Mann-Suiter Screening*
   a. Mann-Suiter-McClung Developmental Checklist, pages 25–31.
   b. Mann-Suiter Alphabet Speech Screen, page 54.
   c. Mann-Suiter Developmental Word Recognition Inventories, pages 85–89.
   d. Mann-Suiter Developmental Paragraph Reading Inventory, pages 99–110.
   e. Mann-Suiter Word Reading Screen, pages 111–113.
   f. Mann-Suiter Silent Reading and Written Language Screen, pages 128–138.
   g. Mann-Suiter Vocabulary Screen, pages 118–124.
3. *Supplementary Evaluation*
   Optional or as deemed appropriate. Refer to additional tests listed in Chapter 6.

DEVELOPMENTAL SKILLS (CRITERION REFERENCE)

The student will

1. select from choices the object or picture of the object that begins with the same sound as the one indicated by the instructor.
2. select from choices the object or picture of the object that begins with the same sound as the word indicated by the instructor.
3. identify from choices the printed letter name or numeral indicated by the instructor.
4. identify from choices of printed letters the letter sound as indicated by the instructor.
5. identify from choices the printed letter blend as indicated by the instructor.
6. select from choices the object or picture of an object that ends with the same sound as the one indicated by the instructor.
7. select from choices the object or picture of an object that ends the same as the word indicated by the instructor.
8. select from choices the object or picture of an object that has the same middle sound as the one indicated by the instructor.
9. select from printed words the word that has the same middle sound as the one indicated by the instructor.
10. identify from among choices of objects or pictures of objects the one that represents the meaning of a word.
11. connect by marking or by other means words or columns of words that have associative relationships.
12. identify from choices the word that has the same or similar meaning as the one indicated by the instructor.
13. state a word that has the same or similar meaning as the word indicated by the instructor.
14. identify from choices a word within the reading vocabulary.
15. identify from choices a short phrase within the reading vocabulary.
16. identify from choices a sentence within the reading vocabulary.
17. identify from printed words the word that has an opposite meaning from the one indicated by the instructor.
18. state a word that has an opposite meaning from the word indicated by the instructor.
19. select from printed words the word that completes the analogy.
20. read a word or statement and orally complete the analogy.
21. formulate a complete sentence indicating in concrete-functional terms what a word read represents in terms of quality, state of being, or function.
22. read a sentence with words deleted (blank spaces) and select from choices the picture representing the word that can be inserted into the blank space.
23. read a sentence with words deleted (blank spaces) and select from choices the printed word that can be appropriately inserted into the blank space.
24. read a sentence with words deleted (blank spaces) and

insert a word in the blank space that will appropriately complete the sentence.
25. read grammatically incorrect sentences and restate them into grammatically correct statements.
26. read a paragraph or story at the independent level and orally paraphrase it.
27. read a paragraph or story at the independent level and correctly respond to questions relating to vocabulary or meaning of words.
28. read a paragraph or story at the independent level and correctly respond to questions relating to details of the story.
29. read a paragraph or story at the independent level and correctly respond to questions relating to the main ideas of the story.
30. read a paragraph or story at the independent level and correctly respond to questions relating to the inferences in the story.

PRESCRIPTIVE ACTIVITIES

General Activities

1. Select from the list of developmental skills the particular target skills that are to be mastered in the area of Visual Language Association–Symbolic. These target skills become learning or behavioral objectives.
   Example Target: Visual Language Association–Symbolic 14—The learner will identify from choices a word within the reading vocabulary.
2. If the student fails to demonstrate success in the target skills according to predetermined criteria such as failing items assessed on a standardized test or failing school tasks requiring this skill, do the following:
   a. Select from the list of developmental skills the target skill (example: Visual Language Association–Symbolic 14) and other related or similar skills (13, 12, etc.) that are deemed appropriate for developing activities that will provide success and practice for higher level functions or skills (15, 16, 17, etc.). Select activities at lower levels (13, 12, 11, etc.) as necessary to insure success and provide an array of different activities that will reinforce the development of Visual Language Association–Symbolic skills.
   b. Develop or select from other sources additional activities related to all of the specific Visual Language Association skills listed (1–30). These activities can be coded into the system at the appropriate levels within the list of development skills.

Specific Activities

1. To improve phoneme-grapheme relationships have the learner do the following:
   a. Sort objects according to the initial consonant sound.
   b. List words that begin or end with the same sound.
   c. Identify pictures or objects that have a specified medial sound (e.g., *a—cat, man*).
2. Refer to Chapter 8, page 198, for specific activities for developing sound-symbol relationships.
3. Read the definition of a word. Have the student hold up the appropriate word card.
4. Use the Cloze technique to complete sentences.
   The cat ______ over the chair.
5. Have the learner rewrite figurative speech or similies in order to understand meaning.
6. Use dictionary activities to discuss the multiple meanings of words.
7. Additional Comprehension activities are located in Chapter 8, pages 207–208 and 221–222.

Visual Language Association–Graphic (Writing)

DIAGNOSIS

1. *Observable Behaviors*
   a. Students exhibiting a disorder in this area of encoding have problems with writing in terms of using words to express concepts.
   b. Some cannot write a sentence that indicates a complete thought or write a paragraph on a theme.
   c. Others cannot write definitions of words or record in a meaningful sequence an event or real-life experience.
2. *Mann-Suiter Screening*
   a. Mann-Suiter-McClung Developmental Checklist, pages 25–31.
   b. Mann-Suiter Written Language Expression Screen, page 68.
3. *Supplementary Evaluation*
   Optional or as deemed appropriate. Refer to additional tests listed in Chapter 6.

DEVELOPMENTAL SKILLS (CRITERION REFERENCE)

The student will
1. write the letter name indicated by the instructor.
2. write the letter corresponding to the sound indicated by the instructor.
3. write the letter blend indicated by the instructor.
4. circle all the words known from word lists provided by the instructor.
5. write all the words known from word lists provided by the instructor.
6. write a complete sentence on a theme or word provided by the instructor, using words in the reading vocabulary.
7. write a paragraph on a theme provided by the instructor, using words in the reading vocabulary.
8. write an appropriate definition of a word within the reading vocabulary.
9. write a story on a theme provided by the instructor, using words in the reading vocabulary.
10. write a logical paragraph or story based on a picture of a scene, event, or real-life experience, using words within the reading vocabulary.
11. read a paragraph and write logical responses to questions related to the content.

12. read a paragraph and outline the main ideas in an appropriate and logical progression.
13. read a paragraph and write a statement summarizing the content.

PRESCRIPTIVE ACTIVITIES

General Activities

1. Select from the list of developmental skills the particular target skills that are to be mastered in the area of Visual Language Association–Graphic (Writing). These target skills become learning or behavioral objectives.
   Example Target: Visual Language Association–Graphic (Writing) 8—The learner will write an appropriate definition of a word within the reading vocabulary.
2. If the student fails to demonstrate success in the target skills according to predetermined criteria such as failing items assessed on a standardized test or failing school tasks requiring the skills, do the following:
   a. Select from the list of developmental skills the target skill (example: Visual Language Association–Graphic [Writing] 8) and other related or similar skills (7, 6, etc.) that are deemed appropriate for developing activities that will provide success and practice for higher level functions or skills (9, 10, 11, etc.). Select activities at lower levels (7, 6, 5, etc.) as necessary to insure success and provide an array of different activities that will reinforce the development of Visual Language Association skills.
   b. Develop or select from other sources additional activities related to all of the specific Visual Language Association skills listed (1–13). These activities can be coded into the system at the appropriate levels within the list of development skills.

Specific Activities

1. Many students appear to be nonreaders or limited in vocabulary acquisition. Norm-referenced, standardized tests measure only a sample of the words that can be read by the students. To gain a more accurate baseline of vocabulary (recognition), ask the students to circle all the words known from word lists (e.g., Mann-Suiter Reading and Spelling Screens, Mann-Suiter Everyday Word List) provided. Then ask the students to read the circled words. Count only the words read without hesitation. (For a more detailed description of the use of baseline information, refer to pages 7–8 and 209–210.)
2. For students having difficulty writing the definitions of words, ask them to draw a picture of what a word means first and then write about the picture.
3. Refer to Chapter 8 for additional written language activities.

Visual Motor-Gross

DIAGNOSIS

1. *Observable Behaviors*
   a. *General Gross Motor*
   (1) Students may have large muscle difficulties that hinder them in meeting the needs of everyday life.
   (2) Students may be poor in sports and appear clumsy and uncoordinated. This condition is especially debilitating because our culture esteems physical agility and participation in sports.
   (3) Students may not be able to throw a ball and may lose their balance easily.
   b. *Balance and Coordination*
   (1) Students may be clumsy or uncoordinated and appear to have poor body control.
   (2) Students may have problems in using both sides of their bodies simultaneously, individually, or alternately.
   (3) Students may use so much energy in trying to control their bodies that they do not pay attention to the more important aspects of learning or to what is happening in their environment.
   c. *Eye-Foot Coordination*
   Difficulty arises when students cannot get their eyes, feet, and thought processes to work together automatically or otherwise to control the movements of their bodies. Problems in this area will affect balance and coordination.
   d. *Body Rhythm*
   (1) Students may be continually out of step in marching activities.
   (2) These are the students who the teacher says, "Just do not do well in band or rhythm activities."
   (3) Students may not be able to follow a rhythm in singing.
2. *Mann-Suiter Screening*
   Mann-Suiter-McClung Developmental Checklist, pages 25–31.
3. *Supplementary Evaluation*
   Optional or as deemed appropriate. Refer to additional tests listed in Chapter 6.

DEVELOPMENTAL SKILLS (CRITERION REFERENCE)

The student will

1. crawl in an appropriate manner.
2. creep in an appropriate manner.
3. walk on a marked straight line without losing his or her balance.
4. walk on a board without losing his or her balance.
5. swing his or her arms in a coordinated manner when walking or running.
6. run on command or by imitating a peer or adult.
7. hop on command or by imitating a peer or adult.
8. skip on command or by imitating a peer or adult.
9. jump on command or by imitating a peer or adult.
10. throw a ball on command or by imitating a peer or adult.
11. catch a ball on command or by imitating a peer or adult.
12. climb a ladder on command or by imitating a peer or adult.
13. jump rope in a coordinated manner on command or by imitating a peer or adult.
14. perform physical-motor tasks appropriate to his or her age group, in a coordinated manner.
15. perform physical-motor tasks within normal time limits.

PRESCRIPTIVE ACTIVITIES

General Activities

1. Select from the list of developmental skills the particular

target skills that are to be mastered in the area of Visual Motor–Gross. These target skills become learning or behavioral objectives.

Example Target: Visual Motor–Gross 4—The student will walk on a board without losing his or her balance.

2. If the student fails to demonstrate success in the target skills according to predetermined criteria such as failing items assessed on a standardized test or failing school tasks requiring these skills, do the following:

a. Select from the list of developmental skills the target skill (example: Visual Motor–Gross 4) and other related or similar skills (3, 2, etc.) that are deemed appropriate for developing activities that will provide success and practice for higher level functions or skills (5, 6, 7, etc.). Select activities at lower levels (3, 2, 1, etc.) as necessary to insure success and provide an array of different activities that will reinforce the development of Visual Motor–Gross skills.

b. Develop or select from other sources additional activities related to all of the specific Visual Motor–Gross skills listed (1–15). These activities can be coded into the system at the appropriate levels within the list of development skills.

Specific Activities

1. *General Gross Motor*

a. Use swaying movements of the body. The learner imitates the teacher or a fellow student.

b. Games such as horse walk, leapfrog, seesaw, and pony ride are good.

c. Use rowing and climbing activities.

d. Use touch toes and Simple Simon games.

e. Use a large barrel open on both ends for the learner to crawl through. You can vary the barrel activity by turning the barrel slowly as the student crawls through.

f. Use jungle gym climbing devices.

g. A furniture dolly provides many activities for children in both the prone and seated positions.

h. Use running and jumping activities in the following ways: sideways, fast, slow, on heels, on toes, up and down steps, barefoot, squatting, and shuffling.

i. Use games such as the following:

(1) Call Ball. The students stand in a circle with one student in the center. The student in the center tosses the ball above his or her head while calling the name or a number assigned to a student in the circle. The student whose name or number was called tries to catch the ball. This student then takes the place of the student in the center. This game is also good for the development of eye-hand coordination.

(2) John Over the Ocean. The students stand in a circle with hands joined. One player, "John," stands in the center. The students walk around in a circle chanting:

> John's over the ocean.
> John's over the sea.
> John caught a ball.
> But he can't catch me.

As they say "me," the students squat quickly. "John" tries to tag a player before he or she squats down. If John is successful, the child whom he tagged becomes "John" and the game is repeated. This game is also good for the development of awareness of space and direction.

(3) Catch a Fish. Have the students sit in a circle. One student, standing in the center of the circle, is the fish. A student tries to hit the fish with a large ball, saying, "I'm going to catch a fish!" When the fish in the center is hit, he or she sits in the circle. The student who has hit the fish becomes the new fish. This activity is good for the development of awareness of space and direction and for eye-hand coordination.

(4) Stop the Ball. Use a volleyball. The students stand astride in a circle with feet touching their neighbors' on both sides. One student is "it" and stands in the center. He or she tries to roll the ball through the feet of any student in the circle. If successful, he or she takes the place of the student, and that student becomes "it." Students use only hands to stop the ball. This game is also good for the development of awareness of space and direction and for eye-hand coordination.

2. *Balance and Coordination*

a. Use balance-beam or walking-board activities.

b. Have the students walk and balance on their toes and knees.

c. Use ladder climbing activities.

d. Twist board activities are helpful.

e. Use walking, running, and jumping activities in the following ways: sideways, fast, slow, on heels, on toes, up and down steps, barefoot, squatting, and shuffling.

f. Provide for homolateral (both arms and legs together, as in pushing), unilateral (one side of the body, as in soldiers' walk), and cross-pattern (both sides of the body simultaneously, as in walking) activities.

g. Have the students stand, jump with legs apart, then jump pulling their feet together. This activity can be varied by having the students clap their hands over their heads as they jump with legs apart.

h. Rope and pole climbing are good exercises.

i. Play games such as the following:

(1) Walk the Tightrope. A wide line is drawn on the ground and the students pretend that it is a tightrope and they are the circus performers walking on it. The students could then become more daring acrobats as they hop, skip, or jump the line. This activity is also good for the development of basic body movement and eye-foot coordination.

(2) Duck, Duck, Goose. The students form a circle. One student, the "Duck," walks around the outside of the circle, touching the other students on the head while saying "Duck." When the Duck taps a student and says "Goose" instead of "Duck," the student tapped (the "Goose") chases the Duck around the circle. The Duck must get back to the Goose's place before being tapped by the Goose. If tapped, the Duck must go into the middle of the circle. The Goose becomes the next Duck. This activity is also good for the development of awareness of space and direction.

(3) Chicken and the Egg. The students place their heads on their desks, with their right hands open on

their desks. One student is the chicken and drops the egg (a piece of chalk) into the hand of a second student, who is seated. That student immediately gets up and tries to tag the chicken, who is safe if he or she can get back to the seat left open by the second student. This activity is also good for the development of the awareness of space and direction, eye-hand coordination, and fine muscle control.

(4) Jack in the Box. The teacher or a student says, "Jack is hiding down in his box until somebody opens the *lid*." The leader says the first part very quietly and slowly in order to build suspense. The students squat with their hands on their heads. They are holding the lid down on the box. When the leader says the word *lid*, they all spring up and jump with their legs apart.

(5) Camera Safari. Ask the students if they would like to go on a camera safari to take pictures of animals in Africa. Read or tell the story while the students listen and follow through with appropriate actions. The story is read like this: "Let's go on a camera safari. . . . Get your camera. . . . Get your film. . . . Get your hat. . . . Put it on. . . . Duck your head when you leave the tent. . . . Get into the land rover with your guide. . . . Drive across the bumpy ground. . . . See the tall giraffe. . . . Get your camera ready. . . . Stop the truck. . . . Focus your camera. . . . Snap the picture. . . . Drive on. . . . Stop. . . . I see a herd of elephants. . . . Move quietly through the tall grass. . . . Tiptoe. . . . Squat down low. . . . Get your camera ready. . . . Focus. . . . Snap, etc." Give many different directions to develop movement skills.

(6) Circle Around. Students form a circle. The teacher and students sing:

We circle around the desks
We circle around the room.
We circle around the toys,
On a Monday afternoon.
Whoops!

Very young students circle around to the right, hands joined. When they say, "Whoops!" they all jump up in the air and then crouch down together. Older students can circle right through the first two lines, then circle left on the last two, doing the same thing on "Whoops!" The teacher can substitute the appropriate name of the day of the week.

(7) Do What I Do. The teacher says or sings the following verse to the tune of "Old Macdonald Had a Farm" while doing a movement that the other players imitate:

This is what I can do.
Everybody do it too.
This is what I can do.
Now I send it on to you.

On the words, "Send it on to you," the teacher names, points to, or taps, a student, who then becomes the new leader. This game can be used to further the development of body image, space and direction, balance, and large muscle control.

3. *Eye-Foot Coordination*
   a. Have the students walk on masking tape: forward, backward, sideways, etc.
   b. Repeat number one using a balance beam.
   c. Place rope loops on the floor and have the students step into the loops.
   d. Have students roll a ball with their feet to another student.
   e. Have the students jump over a wriggling rope.
   f. Use jump rope activities.
   g. Use ladder walking activities.
   h. Play games such as the following:
      (1) Games such as hopscotch, kickball, and high jump are good.
      (2) Jumping the Stream. Draw two lines to represent the banks of the stream. The students run and jump over the stream. Anyone missing the jump and landing in the stream is sent "home" to put on dry shoes and socks. The student sits and pretends to do these things, then reenters the game. This game is also good for the development of space and direction and basic body movements.
      (3) Tire Obstacle Course. Place tires on the ground in a pattern for the students to step through. Time the students as they go through the course. Have them compete against their own best time first and then against each other.
4. *Body Rhythm*
   a. Clap as the students move fast and slowly, taking small steps first and then giant steps.
   b. Repeat the same activity with jumping.
   c. Music activities, including marching, are helpful for body rhythm.
   d. Allow students to use band instruments and lead the band after they have achieved reasonably good rhythm.
   e. Play games such as the following:
      (1) Freeze. Students move to the rhythm of music, walking, swaying, turning, etc. When the music stops, they must stop, or freeze, and hold whatever position they are in until the music starts again. This game is also good for the development of balance and basic body movement.
      (2) Mystery Music Leader. The students stand or sit in a circle. One student is selected to be "it" and leaves the room. The teacher chooses a student in the circle to be the Mystery Music Leader. Following the beat of a metronome or rhythm stick, the leader will switch the activity from clapping to finger snapping to head nodding, etc. "It" will come back into the room and have three guesses to name the leader. The leader becomes "it," and a new student is selected to lead a new beat.

Visual Motor–Fine

DIAGNOSIS

1. *Observable Behaviors*
   a. Students with fine motor coordination problems (or fine motor problems) have difficulty in getting their eyes,

hands, and thought processes to work together to achieve a given task.

b. The students' handwriting is often illegible.

c. The students may have problems in tasks requiring fine motor coordination, such as sorting, tying, buttoning, and cutting.

d. The students may be clumsy with some tools and avoid activities requiring their use.

e. Students may lack the finger strength necessary to carry out everyday activities.

f. Students may not be able to hold a pencil or write using fine motor movements.

g. Students may not be able to use eating utensils. This inability is related to difficulties with grasping. It is often observed in very young students who use the whole hand to pick something up instead of using the thumb and first two fingers as in a "three-draw chuck" (used in an electric drill).

2. *Mann-Suiter Screening*
   a. Mann-Suiter Visual Motor Screen, page 36.
   b. Mann-Suiter-McClung Developmental Checklist, pages 25–31.
3. *Supplementary Evaluation*
   Optional or as deemed appropriate. Refer to additional tests listed in Chapter 6.

DEVELOPMENTAL SKILLS (CRITERION REFERENCE)

The student will

1. not excessively drop things.
2. hold a pencil, pen, or crayon properly and with control.
3. tie shoes and button buttons on command or after demonstration by peers or adults.
4. develop handedness using one hand consistently,
5. reproduce geometric patterns—circle, square, triangle, or diamond—upon command or after demonstration by a peer or an adult.
6. draw a straight line from point to point on a chalkboard or paper vertically, horizontally, and on angles.
7. draw a circle counterclockwise.
8. color within boundaries.
9. cut following a straight line, curved line, circle, and square.
10. cut out pictures of objects.
11. copy letters, numerals, and words in manuscript from the chalkboard or desk in an acceptable (legible) manner.
12. copy sentences or paragraphs in manuscript from the chalkboard or desk in an acceptable (legible) manner.
13. copy sentences in manuscript from the chalkboard or desk, within normal time limits for his or her age group, in an acceptable (legible) manner.
14. copy letters, numerals, and words in cursive from the chalkboard or desk in an acceptable (legible) manner.
15. copy sentences or paragraphs in cursive from the chalkboard or desk in an acceptable (legible) manner.
16. copy sentences in cursive from the chalkboard or desk, within normal time limits for his or her age group, in an acceptable (legible) manner.
17. take dictation legibly in manuscript, within normal time limits, utilizing words at the independent reading level.
18. take dictation legibly in cursive, within normal time limits, utilizing words at the independent reading level.

Table 7-2 Motor Development Equipment

1. Paper and crayons	16. Mats
2. Small chalkboards	17. Blocks
3. Walking board	18. Whiffle ball
4. Balance board	19. Balloons
5. Ladder	20. Magnets
6. Twist board	21. Pegboard
7. Clothespins	22. Puzzles
8. Small bells	23. Work bench
9. Masking tape	24. Ring toss game
10. Rope	25. Clay
11. Geometric templates	26. Beads
12. Bean bags	27. Burlap and needles
13. Playground ball (eight inch)	28. Sewing and lacing boards
14. Ping pong ball	29. Finger paints
15. Rubber ball (three inch)	30. Rhythm band instruments
	31. Tape recorder

PRESCRIPTIVE ACTIVITIES

Table 7-2 lists motor development equipment that is available for the following activities.

General Activities

1. Select from the list of developmental skills the particular target skills that are to be mastered in the area of Visual Motor–Fine. These target skills become learning or behavioral objectives.
   Example Target: Visual Motor–Fine 7—The student will draw a circle counterclockwise.
2. If the student fails to demonstrate success in the target skills according to predetermined criteria such as failing items assessed on a standardized test or failing school tasks, requiring the skills, do the following:
   a. Select from the list of developmental skills the target skill (example: Visual Motor–Fine 7) and other related or similar skills (6, 5, etc.) that are deemed appropriate for developing activities that will provide success and practice for higher level functions or skills (8, 9, 10, etc.). Select activities at lower levels (6, 5, 4, etc.) as necessary to insure success and provide an array of different activities that will reinforce the development of Visual Motor–Fine skills.
   b. Develop or select from other sources additional activities related to all of the specific Visual Motor–Fine skills listed (1–18). These activities can be coded into the system at the appropriate levels within the list of development skills.

Specific Activities

1. Provide sorting, tying, and buttoning activities.
2. Clothespin hanging is helpful.

3. Use games such as pick-up sticks and bean-bag toss.
4. Young children can scribble with a crayon or pencil (do not overdo the activity). This can be varied with music.
5. Use sewing and lacing activities.
6. Use peg boards and form boards.
7. Use tracing activities.
8. Bead-stringing activities with varied designs help build in better discrimination.
9. Ball-bouncing and ball-throwing games are good.
10. Use a nail board with rubber bands to build designs and letters.
11. Use scissor activities with small squares of 4″ × 4″ heavy paper in the following sequence:

    a. Snipping off corners (one cut)

    b. Fringing (one cut)

    c. Fringing (two cuts without removing scissors)

    d. Cutting all the way across (no lines)

    e. Cutting following a line (straight)

    f. Cutting following a line (curved)

    g. Cutting following a circle

    h. Cutting following a square

    i. Cutting following a spiral (circular)

    j. Cutting following a spiral (square)

12. Use stencils and templates.
13. Tracing folds in paper is helpful.
14. Use dot-to-dot tracing games.
15. Have the student squeeze a ball.
16. Working with clay is a good activity. The students can roll out the thin long snakes to be used in making letters or numerals.
17. Use snapping and clapping finger games.
18. Face the student and move your finger in different directions (about two feet away) across the student's body. The student follows the finger with his eyes without moving his head. Go slowly at first.
19. Draw a line or design on the board and have the student trace and follow the finger or chalk with her eyes.
20. Establish a movement pattern with a flashlight or with a pointer and have the student verbalize while visually tracking the pattern: up, down, right, left, etc.
21. Fasten a ball to a string suspended from a stick and move it across the student's body in different patterns as the student follows it with his eyes.
22. Play games such as the following:
    a. Bean Bag Toss. Students toss bean bags into buckets or into any container with an opening. Place the container four to five feet from the students, increasing the distance as the children's ability increases. Numbers may be glued on the cans. Older students can keep score.
    b. Drop the Clothespin. From a standing position, students drop wooden clothespins into large-mouth bottles or containers. Make sure they hold the clothespin at waist height when dropping the pins.
    c. Ring Toss. Using rubber jar rings and coke bottles, or a commercial game, students throw the rings over the neck of the bottle. Here, again, numbers can be placed on the bottles, and older students can keep score.
    d. Elephant and Peanut. One student is selected to be the elephant. He sits on a chair in front of the other students, who are sitting at their desks. The elephant closes his eyes. His back is toward the other players. The elephant's peanut (an eraser or any other small article) is placed near the chair. A student selected by the teacher attempts to sneak up to the elephant and touch and pick up the peanut without being heard by the elephant. If the elephant hears someone coming, he turns to the person and says, "Roar." Then the player must return to his own seat, and another student tries. If that student picks up the peanut before the elephant hears her she becomes the elephant, and the game is repeated. The game can be varied by adding other animal names and sounds.

Note: Additional curriculum suggestions are provided in Chapter 8, in the section on handwriting.

Visual–Body Image

DIAGNOSIS

1. *Observable Behaviors*
   a. The students may have difficulty in relating themselves spatially to their environment. This can also be described as a lack of inner awareness of body as the physical parts of self relate to each other and to the physical environment.
   b. The students may have difficulty in locating different parts of their bodies when asked to do so.
   c. The students may have difficulty in organizing themselves to do a physical task such as moving furniture.
   d. The students may exhibit a faulty body image as indicated by distortions in the Draw-A-Person Test or in their human figure drawings. (Note: This is often developmental in young children.)
   e. The students may exhibit inadequate control of their bodies or clumsiness.
2. *Mann-Suiter Screening*
   Mann-Suiter-McClung Developmental Checklist, pages 25–31.
3. Supplementary Evaluation
   Optional or as deemed appropriate. Refer to additional tests listed in Chapter 6.

DEVELOPMENTAL SKILLS (CRITERION REFERENCE)

The student will
1. locate and name parts of the body on self.
2. locate, in pictures, body parts named by the instructor.
3. name body parts from pictures as indicated by the instructor.
4. draw a human figure with the body parts in proper position and in correct relationship.
5. point to, or otherwise indicate, symmetrical body parts on self.
6. point to the same body parts on an individual facing him or her.
7. place body parts on models of objects.

PRESCRIPTIVE ACTIVITIES

General Activities

1. Select from the list of developmental skills the particular target skills that are to be mastered in the area of Visual-Body Image. These target skills become learning or behavioral objectives.
   Example Target: Visual-Body Image 5—The learner will point to, or otherwise indicate, symmetrical body parts on self.
2. If the student fails to demonstrate success in the target skills according to predetermined criteria such as failing items assessed on a standardized test or failing school tasks requiring the skills, do the following:
   a. Select from the list of developmental skills the target skill (example: Visual-Body Image 5) and other related or similar skills (4, 3, etc.) that are deemed appropriate for developing activities that will provide success and practice for higher level functions or skills (6, 7, etc.). Select activities at lower levels (4, 3, 2, etc.) as necessary to insure success and provide an array of different activities that will reinforce the development of Visual-Body Image skills.
   b. Develop or select from other sources additional activities related to all of the specific Visual-Body Image skills listed (1–7). These activities can be coded into the system at the appropriate levels within the list of development skills.

Specific Activities

1. Outline the student's body on heavy construction paper, and have the student cut it out. The student can draw facial features and clothes on the cut out figure.
2. Students can outline each other, cut out the figures, and then try to match up the outlines with the corresponding persons.
3. The students can play Simple Simon games.
4. Have the student lie down flat with eyes shut. Stroke a part on one side of the student's body and have the student move, or otherwise indicate, the corresponding part on the other side.
5. Have the students verbalize the functions of different body parts.
6. Have the students compare body parts to those of each other, to those of dolls, and, finally, to those of a person in a picture.
7. Stand behind the student facing a full-length mirror and indicate body parts.
8. Pipe cleaners, clay, and wet sand are good for building figures.
9. Use activities that require the student to touch different body parts (hands, feet, etc.) to different objects in the room. For example, ask students to put their right hands on all the circles and their left hands on all the squares placed around the room.
10. Play games such as the following:
    a. Head, Shoulders, Knees, and Toes. The leader or teacher says the words, *head, shoulders, knees,* and *toes* in any desired sequence. A single student or a group must then touch the named parts in the order mentioned. The leader may state one order while demonstrating another order to see if the students can follow the spoken commands and not merely the actions. To vary this game, use different body parts and increase the number used as the ability of the students increases.
    b. Relay Games. Divide the students into two teams and place an object about twenty feet away from each team. The students must race around the objects. Give each pair of students competing against each other a direction involving body parts, such as "hop on one foot up and back," "hold your knees and walk up and back," or "put both hands on your head and skip up and back."

Visual–Spatial-Temporal

DIAGNOSIS

1. *Observable Behaviors*
   a. The students may not be able to judge how far or how near something is in relation to themselves.
   b. The students may not have developed sidedness or laterality. Therefore, they have problems with relating themselves to objects in space.
   c. The students may have problems in dressing.
   d. The students may have problems with directionality or object-to-object relationships in space. These problems result in difficulty with left-to-right orientation.
   e. The students may have difficulty telling time.
   f. Some learners cannot organize their thinking sequentially.
   g. The students may have difficulty in placing numerals in arithmetic or in numbering down the paper for a spelling test.
   h. The students may have a poor sense of direction, easily getting lost and often being unable to find their way home from familiar surroundings.
   i. The students may have difficulty in organizing a sequence of movements necessary to carry out a specific task. In some cases, this difficulty may affect the sequencing of letters or numerals, causing "reversals" or inversions. More often, they are a result of poor visual sequential memory.

j. Problems with words that denote space, like *before, after, left, right, in between,* and *beside*, may be evident.

2. *Mann-Suiter Screening*
   Mann-Suiter-McClung Developmental Checklist, pages 25–31.
3. *Supplementary Evaluation*
   Optional or as deemed appropriate. Refer to additional tests listed in Chapter 6.

DEVELOPMENTAL SKILLS (CRITERION REFERENCE)

The student will

1. lie flat on the floor without becoming anxious or disoriented.
2. estimate the size of objects in relation to each other.
3. deal functionally with the language of space, utilizing such words as *more, less, below, above, between, high,* and *low* correctly to indicate spatial relationships.
4. estimate the distance between objects.
5. estimate the distance between pictures of objects.
6. estimate the distance between geographic locations.
7. reproduce a design, using pictures or blocks, represented by a model or picture of a model.
8. state a logical rationale for indicating age.
9. estimate time for completion of simple tasks.
10. indicate appropriate relationships between time and space.
11. state the historical sequence, utilizing an appropriate time reference.
12. respond to written and oral questions in reading dealing with spatial-temporal relationships.
13. respond to written and oral questions in science dealing with spatial-temporal relationships.
14. respond to written and oral questions in mathematics dealing with spatial-temporal relationships.
15. establish left-to-right orientation.
16. establish a sense of direction with respect to orienting himself or herself within particular geographic locations.
17. learn to tell time.
18. number down on unlined paper in a manner indicating good spatial organization.
19. place numerals in their appropriate positions in arithmetic operations.
20. complete a maze using a pencil or a pointer.
21. mark routes or move a pointer through a map following oral or written directions.
22. construct a map and explain the relationships between geographical locations.

PRESCRIPTIVE ACTIVITIES

General Activities

1. Select from the list of developmental skills the particular target skills that are to be mastered in the area of Visual–Spatial-Temporal. These target skills become learning or behavioral objectives.
   Example Target: Visual–Spatial-Temporal 4—The learner will estimate the distance between objects.
2. If the student fails to demonstrate success in the target skills according to predetermined criteria such as failing items assessed on a standardized test or failing school tasks requiring the skills, do the following:
   a. Select from the list of developmental skills the target skill (example: Visual–Spatial-Temporal 4) and other related or similar skills (3, 2, etc.) that are deemed appropriate for developing activities that will provide success and practice for higher level functions or skills (5, 6, 7, etc.). Select activities at lower levels (3, 2, 1, etc.) as necessary to insure success and provide an array of different activities that will reinforce the development of Visual–Spatial-Temporal skills.
   b. Develop or select from other sources additional activities related to all of the specific Visual–Spatial-Temporal skills listed (1–22). These activities can be coded into the system at the appropriate levels within the list of development skills.

Specific Activities

1. Place a red arrow, made of tape, on the learner's desk as a reminder of the direction in which to proceed.
2. Give students clues by using color (magic markers) so that they will maintain proper placement in arithmetic. For example,

```
   32|8| (red magic marker)
 +  4|6|
   37|4|
```

3. Play obstacle course games with the students.
4. Fit the students' hands and feet into cutouts in different positions to develop handedness and laterality.
5. Use puzzles and geometric forms.
6. Provide experiences for the students to move through and verbalize the concepts of *in, on, down, over, out, up, beneath, beside,* etc.
7. Have the students verbalize a sequence of motor acts.
8. Let the students take time to organize their thoughts.
9. Let the students put different size cards into their respective envelopes as an exercise in spatial judgment.
10. To aid in spatial organization, ask the students to follow accurately a path bordered by blocks.
11. Ask, "How many steps do I need to take to get to the ____?"
12. Play games such as the following:
    a. Lions and Tigers. The players are in two groups: one called lions, the other tigers. Goal lines are marked across both ends of the playing area. Each group, in turn, stands on its goal line with the players' backs turned toward the other group. When a silent signal is given, the lions (or tigers) move quietly toward the other group's goal line. When they are within about ten to fifteen feet, the teacher calls, "the lions [or tigers] are coming." That is the signal for the tigers [or lions] to turn and chase, until the group is safe behind its goal line. Those who were tagged before reaching the goal line go with the students of the other team and become members of that team. Repeat with the other team. This

game is also good for the development of basic body movement.

b. Changing Partners. The players are grouped by twos. Partners stand back to back with elbows linked. One extra player does not have a partner. Upon a signal from the teacher, all players change while the extra player attempts to get a partner. One player will be left each time. The game is repeated with the player who is left without a partner giving the signal for the next change. This activity is also good for the development of body image.

LANGUAGE EXPRESSION

Motor Language Expression: Manual (Hand or Foot)

DIAGNOSIS

1. *Observable Behaviors*
   The students are unable to express manually the function of an object even though, when asked, they may be able to identify it from among other objects. For example, the students may be able to identify a hammer from among other objects, but not be able to show what to do with it manually.
2. *Mann-Suiter Screening*
   a. Mann-Suiter-McClung Developmental Checklist, pages 25–31.
   b. Mann-Suiter Manual Language Expression Screen, page 64.
3. *Supplementary Evaluation*
   Optional or as deemed appropriate. Refer to additional tests listed in Chapter 6.

PRESCRIPTIVE ACTIVITIES

1. Begin with real objects within the student's experience:
   a. Find out if the student knows the functions and movements of parts of his or her own body. Demonstrate first on your own body. Have the student imitate and verbalize the functions. For example, "My hands can hold, give, write, hit, stroke, clap," etc. "My eyes can open, close, see, blink, wink, squint, move from side to side and up and down," etc.
   b. Use things the student is familiar with, such as a pencil, which can write, poke, erase, tickle, scratch, roll, etc.
   c. Use things the student can manipulate, such as cars, fishing poles, footballs, pans, string, bucket, paper clips, a door, or a hose.

   Note: The process in teaching is imitation (do as I do), understanding (show me the one that writes, for example, from among three objects), then elicited responses (show me what this does). Teach the object, the word, and the function simultaneously, beginning with the concrete first, then going to pictures. (Some cautionary advice: Proceed slowly! Do not "jam" or "overload" the students with too much too fast. Leave them with a success.)
2. Pantomime the motion of hammering a nail and have the students pick up the real object (a hammer) from among three or four objects.

   Note: The above activities should also develop creativity and improve the language abilities of students.

Speech

DIAGNOSIS

1. *Observable Behaviors*
   a. The students may exhibit poor speech patterns and be unable to say words.
   b. The students have difficulty in retrieving the motor act of speech even if they have a model or can comprehend or recall.
   c. The students may have problems with execution or articulation, exhibiting omissions (leaving out initial, medial, or final sounds), substitutions (*wabbit* for *rabbit*), distortions (lisp, sloppy *s*, or a hissing sound), or additions (*sumber* for *summer*) of sounds and words.
   d. The students may use gestures and pantomime a great deal.
   e. In some cases, the tongue appears to be lost in the mouth during speech.
   f. Students will have difficulty imitating words, regardless of whom they are attempting to model.
2. *Mann-Suiter Screening*
   a. Mann-Suiter-McClung Developmental Checklist, pages 25–31.
   b. Mann-Suiter Alphabet Speech Screen, page 54.
   c. Mann-Suiter Speech Screen, page 65.
3. *Supplementary Evaluation*
   Optional or as deemed appropriate. Refer to additional tests listed in Chapter 6.

PRESCRIPTIVE ACTIVITIES

1. Make the students aware of sounds and the movements of the organs of speech by
   a. Using mirrors to illustrate positioning.
   b. Using touch to feel positioning as letters and words are formed (hands on face and throat).
2. Use additional clues, including
   a. Follow-the-leader games (i.e., look, listen, and imitate).
   b. Blowing, smiling, licking, and tongue movement activities.
   c. Peanut butter put in different places in the mouth to facilitate better tongue placement.
3. Establish a motor pattern by introducing sounds (c a t), reinforcing them with touch (feeling the organs of speech), and then converting them into a word (verbalization) by saying the word *cat*.
4. Give the student specific verbal directions for producing the sound or word. For example, "open your mouth, purse your lips, and blow" or "place your tongue between your teeth and force air through the opening."

5. Experiment with tactual-kinesthetic associations.
   a. Use a tongue depressor or lollipop to guide placement of the tongue.
   b. Overarticulate while the student feels your face.
   c. Have the students feel their own faces and throats as they speak.
6. Repeat the word correctly at first without correcting the student each time. Intermittent correction is appropriate. Use good judgment.

Verbal Language Expression

The students may be able to identify a hammer from among other objects presented visually. They may be able to show what can be done with it, but be unable to talk about it in a meaningful way or describe its function.

Note: Language reception must be checked first, since receptive disorders will invariably affect expression. Begin by finding out if the student understands the word (intact reception). This can be done by giving the student alternatives to choose from. ("Is this a crayon? Is this a hat? Is this chalk?") If chalk is the object and the student responds correctly, then the teacher can surmise that the student probably has an expressive language problem and not a receptive language disorder.

WORD RETRIEVAL

Diagnosis

1. *Observable Behaviors*
   a. The students exhibit difficulty in recalling or retrieving words for use in speaking.
   b. The students may not be able to express themselves in a complete sentence.
   c. The students may be able to repeat immediately after they hear a letter or word but be unable to recall after longer periods of time.
   d. The students may often use gestures and vocalization to make wants known.
   e. Retrieving words can sometimes be achieved when seeing or feeling the concrete object.
   f. The students can generally read better silently than orally.
   g. The students may have nonfluent speech that includes hesitations like stuttering.
   h. The students may not be able to sequence their thoughts or ideas.
   i. The students may use word substitutions such as *whatchamacallit, thingamajig,* or *gismo.*
   j. The students may emit strange sounds for words, such as "I foga da shugum" for "I swallowed the chewing gum." Find out if they can imitate the correct pronunciation.
2. *Mann-Suiter Screening*
   a. Mann-Suiter-McClung Developmental Checklist, pages 25–31.
   b. Mann-Suiter Verbal Language Expression Screen, page 67.
   c. Mann-Suiter Developmental Word-Recognition Screen, pages 85–89.
   d. Mann-Suiter Developmental Paragraph Reading Inventory, pages 99–110.
3. *Supplementary Evaluation*
   Optional or as deemed appropriate. Refer to additional tests listed in Chapter 6.

Prescriptive Activities

Note: Slow down the rate and amount of input. Wait for a response and do not rush the student. Reduce your demands for spoken language at first.

1. Give the students clues. Say, "do you mean," or give them the first letter of the word.
2. Have the students imitate single words presented verbally and associate them first with an object, then with a picture—for example, chalk (object-picture), pencil, etc. Then add qualifiers (adjectives and adverbs) in short phrases. Next, present sentences using objects then pictures of objects—for example: "Chalk is hard. I write with chalk."
3. Use cueing, such as "I write with a ______."
4. Use associative ideas, such as pairing: e.g., "bread and ______," "salt and ______."
5. Get the student to verbalize opposites and similarities of objects, then pictures.
6. Encourage the student to use words instead of gestures, and try to elicit short-phrase responses, then sentences.

SYNTAX AND FORMULATION

Diagnosis

1. *Observable Behaviors*
   a. Students with this difficulty have problems with the smooth and natural flow of the English language. They cannot structure thoughts into grammatically correct verbal units or sentences.
   b. The students may understand what you say but answer in single words or phrases with inadequate language structure.
   c. Syntax may be poor—e.g., students may omit words, distort the order of words, or use poor tense.
   d. The students may recognize correct sentence structure but not be able to reproduce a meaningful sequence themselves.
   e. The students may use telegraphic speech (e.g., mom—dad—me—go) in attempting to formulate a sentence.
   f. The students may have difficulty in expressing ideas or formulating sentences by using words.
2. *Mann-Suiter Screening*
   Mann-Suiter-McClung Developmental Checklist, pages 25–31.
3. *Supplementary Evaluation*
   Optional or as deemed appropriate. Refer to additional tests listed in Chapter 6.

Prescriptive Activities

1. Have the students verbalize their actions during meaningful play.
2. Use pictures and have the students name the pictured objects. They should use the word in a sentence and then develop a sequence of sentences about the object.
3. Elicit a response from the student by saying a sentence, leaving out a word, and having the student supply the missing word—for example, "I have a ______ ball."
4. Scramble word cards and then build sentences using the word cards.
5. Use sequential pictures, such as comic strips or sequence puzzles, and have the student verbalize the sequence of actions.
6. Make sequence puzzles based on simple stories or themes and have the student order them.
7. Ordering, or sequence of thought, can be taught by giving students two sentences in different order and asking them to give the correct sequence. For example:
   I ate my breakfast.
   I got up in the morning.
8. A sequence of amelioration activities such as the following may be helpful.
   a. *Restructuring verbal responses (imitation).* The student first repeats short sentences verbalized by the teacher indicating the correct tense. For example:
   Look at me.
   He looked at me.
   He is looking at me.
   The teacher can use the same sentences again, substituting different pronouns (e.g., *we, she*) or students' names. This activity can be reinforced by using associative clues such as pictures or filmstrips.
   b. *Understanding.* The student can indicate understanding by responding to (1) actions, (2) emotions, and (3) cause-effect relationships. For example, the student is asked questions based on pictures of actions (a boy running), emotions (a girl crying), and cause-effect relationships (a boy falling) that reflect the appropriate tense.
   Sample Activity: Understanding the verb *fall*. Show the student three pictures:
   A boy running.
   A boy tripping over a stone and falling.
   A boy on the ground.
   Say, "Show me the picture that means the boy is falling." The student repeats the sentence and indicates his or her understanding by selecting the correct response. (If the response is incorrect, repeat the sentence as necessary until it is understood.) Do the same thing with the picture of the boy on the ground. Say, "Show me the picture that means the boy has fallen."
   c. *Elicited Responses.* In this activity, the teacher provides a stimulus picture indicating (1) an action, (2) an emotion, and (3) a cause-effect relationship.
   Sample Activity: In expressing the verb *eat*, for example, show the student a series of cards, one at a time, of a puppy standing over a full bowl, a puppy eating, and a puppy standing over an empty bowl. Ask, "What is the puppy doing?" for each of these pictures. The student may reply with one word, a phrase, or a sentence. With practice, one-word and phrase responses should develop into sentences. Always repeat the response in a complete sentence even though the student may answer in one word. Vary the activities by giving the first sentences in a sequence and having the student give the next one or two sentences.

Written Language Expression

DIAGNOSIS

1. *Observable Behaviors*
   a. Students with problems in oral expressive language tend to write the way they speak.
   b. Those with retrieval problems are less consistent in their written errors than are those with difficulties in formulation. They may be unable to recall the visual image of a word that they cannot recall auditorily, and their written work may be somewhat better than their spoken language.
2. *Mann-Suiter Screening*
   a. Mann-Suiter-McClung Developmental Checklist, pages 25–31.
   b. Mann-Suiter Written Language Expression Screen, page 68.
3. *Supplementary Evaluation*
   Optional or as deemed appropriate. Refer to additional tests listed in Chapter 6.

PRESCRIPTIVE ACTIVITIES

1. Many of the educational procedures listed in the preceding sections could be used in the remediation of written language disorders. The only substitution would be to use written instead of oral exercises. Most of the work should involve the students at the particular level of their reading program and not their writing or speaking program.
2. Have the students write sentences and read them aloud. When an error is identified, provide a written model for them so that they can make the corrections on their papers.
3. The next step is to have them monitor their own written work by reading it aloud to themselves, checking every word as they say it. Much later, they will learn to reauditorize to themselves while scrutinizing printed words.
4. Write sentences containing one, then two, errors, read the sentences aloud, and ask the students if the sentences they heard are the same as the ones they see on a correct copy. For example, read these sentences one at a time:
   John went the story yesterday.
   The girl fell off him bicycle.
   Tomorrow we swimming in the pond.

The students' correct copy is as follows:
   John went to the store yesterday.
   The girl fell off her bicycle.
   Tomorrow we will go swimming in the pond.

5. Give students a group of word cards, speak a sentence (e.g., "The students are going to school."), and have the students reproduce the sentence with the cards. The students first arrange the words in the proper order and then copy the cards.

Note: Additional information and activities for written language expression can be found on pages 177–178 and 214.

Expressive Language in Arithmetic

DIAGNOSIS

1. *Observable Behaviors*
   a. Problems with retrieval will keep the students from quickly recalling numbers. They may recognize the correct number when they see it but be unable to say the one they want. Rapid oral drills are difficult for the students and should be avoided until the students have improved in retrieval.
   b. The students may not be deficient in understanding quantitative relationships and may do well in computation as long as it is written and not oral.

PRESCRIPTIVE ACTIVITIES

1. All oral work in both computation and problem solving should be reinforced by the open channel (i.e., tactual or visual) while the deficit area is being strengthened.
2. See Chapter 9 on arithmetic problems.

Nonverbal Language

Students with a nonverbal language difficulty have problems with assigning meaning to such nonverbal functions as art, religion, music, holidays, and patriotism. There is a language of art and music from which the students cannot derive meaning. Often, a nonverbal language disorder is accompanied by problems in the spatial area.

DIAGNOSIS

1. *Observable Behaviors*
   a. The students may have difficulty judging quantity (e.g., size, time, shape, and distance), as well as the seasons of the year.
   b. The students may not be able to understand religious symbols such as a Star of David, Cross, or Crescent Moon.
   c. The students may not understand the significance of the statue of "Iwo Jima" or the "Washington Monument."
   d. Although the verbal language of the students may be good, or even superior, they appear to have difficulty in formulating good judgment about things that are symbolic.
   e. The students may also exhibit difficulty with social perception involving nonverbal relationships with people.
2. *Mann-Suiter Screening*
   a. Mann-Suiter-McClung Developmental Checklist, pages 25–31.
   b. Mann-Suiter Nonverbal Symbolic Language Screen, page 70.

PRESCRIPTIVE ACTIVITIES

1. Begin by talking about things in the students' own environment. Do they keep things that they feel will bring them luck, such as a rabbit's foot or a special toy?
2. Talk about how we remember people (include monuments, statues, tombstones, etc.).
3. Begin with a simple painting or a patriotic song and talk about how the artist or composer may have felt when painting or writing the work. For example, discuss Francis Scott Key and the *Star-Spangled Banner.*
4. With the students, make a list of pictures and objects that have symbolic significance, then have the students verbalize the relationships.
5. Ask the students to match a list of holidays with the appropriate objects and pictures.
6. Talk about the history of particular symbols in the students' environment. How did flags become symbols? Discuss other symbols for countries or people (e.g., shields, seals, crests).
7. Have the students design and name their own family crests if they can.
8. Have students collect, label, and discuss emblems and badges representing different social organizations, such as scouting, the armed forces, and local clubs.
9. See the spatial disorder section (page 184) for activities in that area.

Inner-Language

Inner-language is the language with which one thinks. Inner-language serves to integrate experiences with a native spoken language. Inner-language can also be thought of as inner-speech. In this sense, inner-speech relates to thinking, while outer-speech provides for communication between people.

DIAGNOSIS

1. *Observable Behaviors*
   a. Some types of inner-language difficulties are a result of cerebral dysfunction.
   b. Inner-language conflict may result when students have incorporated as their native language a language other than standard English and cannot, or will not, integrate standard English as a functional language. The other language can be sign language, a foreign language, or a dialect.
   c. The students may think or solve problems in their native language even though they can speak fluent standard English.
   d. The students may have three different sounds for the same phonetic construct; for example, a student may

say, "bafroom" for *bathroom*, "mover" for *mother*, and "da" for *the*, all indicating three different sounds for *th*.

e. Some students have internalized the phonetic, or sound, system of a foreign language and have difficulty in learning the English phoneme-grapheme system.

PRESCRIPTIVE ACTIVITIES

1. In teaching initial reading, give the learners the best model possible. Say the word correctly and elicit it correctly from the students at least one time, no matter how they wish to pronounce it later on.
2. It is important not to correct students' speech constantly, as they will probably incorporate standard English speech patterns when they are ready to do so.
3. The students must be told explicitly that there is a universal English phonetic system common to all English-speaking people. For communication (verbal communication as well as reading and writing), they must learn that system. Otherwise, in order to communicate, they will have to teach their own code to anyone who doesn't know it. The learners must understand, for example, that there is a voiced and unvoiced *th* that is constant regardless of how they wish to pronounce it themselves.
4. Students should be taught that there is a language of the home, of the school, and of literature. They must learn to use each one appropriately.
5. Build on words based on the students' experiences first, and give the students many opportunities to verbalize their feelings and experiences. Teachers sometimes talk too much. Remember, the sequence in learning is verbal, reading, and writing. Activities under syntax and formulation are appropriate here.
6. Remember that the sound *t* is not "tuh"; do not add a vowel to a consonant when saying the sound, as this adds to the confusion.
7. Talk about the history of language and how people learned to communicate with each other both verbally and nonverbally.
8. Develop activities that involve the students in creating their own code so that they can see more readily the function of communication.

Chapter 8 Subject Level Curriculum

Students exhibiting difficulties in the language arts, science, and social studies areas will require a modified curriculum that considers both strengths and weaknesses in their abilities to process information. The suggested approaches to teaching reading, handwriting, spelling, science, and social studies in this chapter will enable the instructor to develop a more systematic curriculum for teaching these students. A good deal of attention is given to breaking down these specific tasks into their basic components. The following discussion on integrated learning will enable the instructor to better understand the nature of the task and to focus upon the particular levels on which the student may be presently functioning.

INTEGRATED LEARNING

Integrated learning can be described as the utilization of both mechanical-automatic skills and conceptual-thinking skills for success at academic tasks. Integration is possible for particular individuals to the extent that these abilities are intact and functional. Mechanical-automatic skills deal with levels of learning that do not involve meaning per se, such as sensory, perception, memory, motor, and spatial-temporal orientation. Conceptual or thinking skills relate to how individuals deal with their environment in terms of meaning, judgment, and ability to organize themselves and their daily life space effectively for survival in every aspect of our society. Some learners have deficiencies mainly in mechanical-automatic skills. Others are deficient primarily in conceptual or thinking abilities. Still another group may have problems in both areas. It is apparent, however, that in the teaching-learning situation, disabilities in one area will affect performance in the other area. The mechanical-automatic and conceptual-thinking areas of learning will be discussed in terms of performance in reading, writing, spelling, oral production (speech), and arithmetic. The following is an outline of the skills that are prerequisite to effectiveness in reading, writing, spelling, and oral production.

I. READING

Reading involves an automatic, natural flow that is the result of understanding the material presented.

A. Mechanical-Automatic Skills (M-A)

1. Sensory

Hearing and vision, the primary input channels, must be intact. If the integrity of these basic systems is damaged, a program that emphasizes alternative input systems must be developed (e.g., teaching deaf and blind children to read).

2. Perception

Auditory or visual recognition and discrimination of symbols (letters, words, and numerals).

Recognition of the nature of objects, geometric forms, and symbols (letters, words, and numerals).

Closure, the auditory or visual combining

of symbols (letters, words, and numerals).

Auditory or visual separation of foreground from background when decoding symbols (letters, words, and numerals).

3. Imagery (Memory)
   Auditory or visual memory for symbols (letters, words, and events).

   Auditory or visual sequencing of symbols and events.

   Auditory or visual associative memory relating visual symbols to their auditory referents.

B. Conceptual-Thinking Skills (C-T)
1. Meaning
   Receptive language classification and association at the concrete, functional, and abstract levels.

   Understanding associated with inference, details, main ideas, vocabulary, cause-effect relationships, cultural uniqueness, and concept load, which includes dealing with space, time, social order, geography, and economics.
2. Judgment
   Good common sense in dealing with everyday life situations, including problem solving behavior.

II. WRITING: EXPRESSIVE LANGUAGE

A. Mechanical-Automatic Skills (M-A)
1. Handwriting (Fine Motor)
   Grasp, control, spacing, legibility, speed in manuscript or cursive.
2. Copying
   Speed, accuracy, and eye movements related to desk work and chalkboard activities.

B. Conceptual-Thinking Skills (C-T)
1. Dictation
   Listening, writing in a sequence accurately.
2. Note Taking
   Listening, extrapolating main ideas, and writing in a meaningful sequence.
3. Creative Writing
   Elaborating on a theme, idea, or experience. Structuring thoughts and using imagery.
4. Grammatical Structure
   Indicating good syntax and formulation, which includes the use of correct tense, expression of ideas, and formulation of sentences.

III. SPELLING

A. Mechanical-Automatic Skills (M-A)
   Spelling isolated words *without meaning* to the student, given the understanding of the structure of English (e.g., Spanish word, *aqua* = *water*).

B. Conceptual-Thinking Skills (C-T)
   Spelling learned in context, such as words that have dual meanings (e.g., *sale* and *sail*). Meaning gives words a referent and aids in spelling.

IV. ORAL PRODUCTION (SPEECH): EXPRESSIVE LANGUAGE

A. Mechanical-Automatic Skills (M-A)
1. Articulation
   Functional and correct use of the organs of speech for oral production.
2. Word Retrieval
   Fluent speech with no hesitations, "blocking," or behavior like stuttering.
3. Flow and Clearness of Speech
   No stuttering or other defects that interfere with the natural flow of speech (oral production). Speech that does not call attention to itself.

B. Conceptual-Thinking Skills (C-T)
1. Grammatical Structure
   Speech that indicates good syntax and formulation, which includes using correct tense, ordering words, speaking in sequence, expressing ideas, and formulating sentences.

Implications for Teaching

It is important for all who are concerned with a student's welfare and academic performance in school to understand that deficiencies in any of the areas outlined in the preceding section have implications for every aspect of the learner's life. Problems in perception, memory, judgment, vocabulary, etc., will affect students not only in academic areas, but also in the way they deal with everyday life situations. And what students can do is just as important as what they cannot do. Emphasis must be placed on the positive by building on the students' strengths. The positive premise that the student can accomplish and can do things must permeate every aspect of diagnosis and curriculum.

Further, teachers in the early grades need to examine students' performances and formulate some ideas about what the children will do when they are in secondary school or even when they are adults, given that their learning patterns will not alter significantly. Likewise, educators at the secondary level must consider how a particular student must have performed as a young learner failing in school; they must remember that the student, through the years, was taught by many teachers using different techniques, few of which helped the student to become successful at academic tasks. Students do not come to us as blank slates. Most have experienced years of failure. Trusting relationships must be established through a better understanding of what the students can do and cannot do so that the teacher will be in a better position to avoid introducing more anxiety and failure into their lives. It is particularly important for educators to consider the students' performance and make some decisions that consider strengths as well as weaknesses, especially in terms of vocational implications. This is important at every level of education, beginning with that of the youngest child. The following discussion suggests how teachers can diagnose failures in the mechanical-automatic skills and conceptual-thinking skills and explains the implications of failure as they relate to reading, writing, spelling, oral production (speech), and arithmetic.

READING

1. The teacher must determine whether there is a discrepancy between students' ability to read words and their ability to conceptualize or glean meaning from the material presented. This can be accomplished by giving an oral comprehension examination, reading the paragraphs to the students and having them respond to the questions orally. If a discrepancy is evident, then the teacher must note which of the areas of learning is highest and which is lowest (mechanical-automatic skills or conceptual-thinking skills).
2. If mechanical-automatic skill areas of learning are the primary problem for the learner, then the teacher must consider the following:
   a. A significant part of the teaching should be concentrated on the development of basic word attack skills and vocabulary building (sight recognition).
   b. In testing students, the teacher must recognize that if learners cannot read the words, they cannot get the meaning of what is read. Therefore, their comprehension abilities may appear spuriously low.
   c. Students may be paying so much attention to reading words that they are not attending to the content, therefore, affecting the comprehension areas.
   d. The student may appear less adequate in the conceptual or thinking skill aspects of all testing that requires reading.
   e. There is a tendency to group youngsters with mechanical-automatic problems in the lower groups even though they probably should be in a higher group for the conceptual-thinking skills aspects of learning, such as science or social studies.
3. If the problem lies in the conceptual-thinking area, the teacher should consider the following:
   a. The student may be a word caller who cannot deal with the content in a meaningful manner.
   b. Failure or weakness in this area may affect other subject level learning, such as science and social studies.
   c. The student may have trouble with the language aspects of mathematics when required to do story problems.
   d. If the child is slow in conceptualizing with respect to meaning and judgment, the teacher should concentrate on that area.
   e. The teacher must be very much aware of the "concept load" of the material, or the type and number of the new concepts to be learned.
4. In situations where both mechanical-automatic skills and conceptual-thinking skills are low, both areas must be considered equally important in planning a program.
5. If students cannot read, they probably cannot spell, and both of these deficiencies will affect their writing activities.
6. The readability of textbooks in the subject level areas should be analyzed and matched up with the reading level of the students. Otherwise, the teacher may be introducing failure by using inappropriate materials.
7. The teacher should consider tying the reading, writing, and spelling programs in together so that the students are reinforcing the same vocabulary in different ways.
8. The special education teacher and regular classroom teacher can support each other by developing a reading program that focuses on the same vocabulary or includes a supportive vocabulary with the appropriate reinforcing activities.
9. The instructor who requires a great deal of reading of directions, library reading, reading in testing situations, oral reading, and copying from the chalkboard where reading is a primary factor is going to build in failure for the student who cannot read. Alternative input systems must be utilized in these cases to include oral directions, oral participation, oral examination, the use of tape recorders, and the utilization of the buddy system.
10. Reading as a skill is inextricably related to a student's self-concept, and the teacher must keep in mind that the student is constantly in situations

that result in embarrassment. The instructor should determine how he or she could prevent reading experiences that result in the diminished self-worth of the student while at the same time providing for rewarding reading experiences within the activities of daily school life.

WRITING

1. The teacher, utilizing the evaluation recommendations made on pages 35, 223, and 227–228, should determine the student's handwriting abilities.
2. The instructor should give the students a short lesson, requiring them to take notes, and then collect the notes. This will give the teacher a frame of reference for the students' note-taking skills.
3. The teacher can also check the students' notebooks to determine how they have been taking notes.
4. The teacher should read a short paragraph with words that are below the students' present grade level and ask them to write the dictation down word for word. This will give the teacher a basis for making judgments about how the students take dictation.
5. If students' handwriting is poor or they write slowly, the teacher can surmise that it will affect their ability to take dictation or copy from the chalkboard.
6. Many reading programs require a great deal of writing. Students whose handwriting is illegible or who cannot write in the small spaces may fail in the writing components of those programs.
7. Alternative output systems must be explored, especially by teachers who require a great deal of writing, copying from the chalkboard, and creative writing from students who cannot read or write. Alternatives include the following:
   a. Use of typing.
   b. Use of movable letters or word cards for creative writing and for developing grammatical skills.
   c. Development of a structured, individualized writing program that includes practice in handwriting and creative expression.

SPELLING

1. Students who have difficulty in reading should ordinarily not be spelling words they cannot read.
2. Spelling is difficult for some students who are good readers and should not be equated with reading ability in terms of grading.
3. Students who are primarily auditory learners and those who are primarily visual learners tend to make different types of spelling errors (e.g., pupils with good auditory processing abilities might use a more phonetic approach to spelling).
4. Many educators feel that spelling should be individualized and that spelling programs should be set up for each student. All students cannot be expected to learn the same words each week at the same rate to be regurgitated back on the Friday afternoon quiz, in many cases only to be promptly forgotten by Monday morning.

ORAL PRODUCTION (SPEECH)

1. Students with speech problems may be ridiculed by peers and pressured by parents, neighbors, and relatives. Many have experienced unhappiness, and some become reluctant to speak.
2. The teacher working with speech and language support services can be very helpful in helping the learner to develop better speech patterns through ongoing daily activities. This must be done carefully and under supervision so that the teacher does not reinforce the wrong behavior.
3. Sometimes children just don't want to talk to their teachers. Many of them will respond to a "show me" or "give me" request.
4. So-called nonverbal learners are found to be quite verbal when the teacher takes bus duty.
5. Children should not be penalized for "lack of oral participation," especially if the personality of the student indicates that limited oral expression is a matter of his or her choice.
6. There is a tendency to reward the "talkers" because in a sense they reinforce the teachers' behaviors.
7. Students with difficulties in oral expression tend to be neglected in many school situations.

ARITHMETIC

Problems in both the reading of words and the understanding of concepts will show up in arithmetic. The following need to be considered in planning a program:

1. It is axiomatic that reading problems will affect a student's ability to do story problems in arithmetic.
2. The readability of the textbooks may necessitate that the instructor rewrite directions and story problems at the appropriate instructional reading level of the student.
3. Teachers of young children should consider body awareness, directionality, and spatial-temporal orientation when teaching them measurement or when introducing words denoting directions (e.g., *up, down, over, below*).
4. Similarities and differences in numerals may con-

fuse young students experiencing difficulties in visual discrimination.

5. Students with spatial-temporal problems may have difficulty with the placement of numerals in complex problems and in telling time.
6. Deficits in eye-hand coordination or fine-motor coordination may interfere with sorting objects and writing numerals.
7. Even though computation is held constant, the complexity of the language can cause the learner to experience failure. For example:

   2 + 3 = 5
   2 dogs + 3 dogs = 5 dogs
   2 dogs + 3 cats = 5 animals
   John has 2 dogs and 3 bananas. Are there more animals than fruit?

8. The skills may be presented in a sequence that is inappropriate for some students.
9. The practice activities may not be reinforcing the skills most needed by the student experiencing learning problems in arithmetic.
10. Students may exhibit sequencing problems in their use of a numberline, in the formation of numbers, in left-right placement of numerals, and in the following of directions.
11. Reasoning (e.g., thinking logically, making predictions, drawing conclusions, and comparing) skills are prerequisite to measurement and to the solving of story problems.

Considerations for Programming

Following are some of the questions that must be asked by teachers and administrators when programming for students with learning difficulties:

1. What is the teacher's *modus operandi*? What does the teacher require of the student?
2. Does the teacher have strict standards?
3. Is there a tendency for the school to neglect the needs of certain kinds of students?
4. Does the teacher want to know more about why students do what they do?
5. Does the teacher try to accommodate the environment to the students or does the teacher expect the students to accommodate to his or her style of teaching?
6. How does the teacher individualize the way he or she deals with students' needs on a day-to-day basis?
7. Are learners who cannot read or write considered stupid?
8. What does the teacher do to decode students' learning characteristics, and afterward how does he or she set up an environment that promotes successful learning experiences?

READING: INITIAL AND REMEDIAL TEACHING APPROACHES

In examining the task of reading, we find many interrelated factors. Students, to become effective readers, must be able to do the following:

1. See a clear and unblurred image on a white field and hear the sounds of the letters and words (auditory-visual sensory input)
2. Distinguish one symbol from another and recognize the differences consistently (auditory-visual perception)
3. Remember the sounds or images of the symbols in sequence (auditory-visual memory)
4. Relate these symbols to meaning based on experience and synthesize the visual and auditory clues with the meaningful words for integrative learning (language-symbolization)
5. Do all of these things smoothly and with reasonable, efficient speed (input-output relationships)

Reading is a dynamic process in which perception, memory, language, and affect must function harmoniously with each other. Many educators feel that a unitary approach to teaching reading cannot be used for students exhibiting a variety of learning problems. Remedial plans must take into consideration the patterns of the students' strengths and weaknesses.

The recommendations made here are based upon a theoretical approach to instruction that focuses upon the needs of specific students or groups of students manifesting similar characteristics and problems. The teacher must be aware of, and program for, the learners' disabilities as well as their strengths. The strategy for remediation includes circumventing the major areas of difficulty for instructional purposes while simultaneously including work in these deficit areas. Since the same methodologies cannot be applied to every student, the teacher needs to adjust the program accordingly.

Even after teachers have formed a basic philosophy concerning reading, they frequently ask, "How and where do I begin to teach the learner?" Educators must learn to use all available materials and adapt them as necessary to the needs of the students who exhibit various disabilities.

The purpose of this section is to explore some

specific patterns or techniques for teaching that can be utilized and adapted to most of the available basic reading series or reading programs. The primary emphasis will be on instructional approaches to reading.

An approach to teaching reading to students with learning problems can be expressed in the following design:

Deficit Amelioration + Simultaneous Instruction = Integrative Learning

Although one objective of the educational plan, or strategy, for teaching is to raise the level of the problem areas, teaching to the deficits alone does not insure integration with all other areas of learning. Therefore, initial teaching or remediation of reading should begin by utilizing the students' strengths, permitting them initial success and satisfaction in learning.

Simultaneously, on the other hand, the teacher must include work in the areas of weaknesses. Time spent utilizing and developing strengths helps the students to gain a positive attitude and may result in an increased interest in the reading task. It then becomes easier to work with them on their weaknesses, especially when attempting initial reading instruction. This is true for students for whom failure has become the mode. The identification of problem areas through diagnostic teaching is accomplished by moving the learner through a structured process of assessment to determine the areas of breakdown.

At present, many teachers feel that they must teach fifty to one hundred sight vocabulary words before beginning work on phonics or analytical skills. They fail to consider that students with difficulties in the visual channel area, for example, may not be able to recognize, remember, or synthesize meaningfully what is presented to them visually. The effect of this disability may be an inability to learn by the sight-word approach, and students with this problem may find it difficult to learn even ten words as unique wholes. Reading instruction for those students should begin with the presentation of short visual units that can be blended into words using a basic phonic approach, along with simultaneous training in their problem (visual) areas. This approach to instruction helps them develop a needed sight vocabulary (associating sight with sound). The emphasis for instructional purposes is placed on a sound-memory or sound-to-sight approach.

On the other hand, a teacher may get a student who exhibits auditory channel difficulties in one or more of the areas of perception, imagery, or language. The reading instruction for this student should begin with a whole-word approach, providing the student can blend sounds. Many teachers using a basal-reading approach require that the student learn all the letter names and sounds prior to formal instruction. The student with auditory problems may find it difficult or even impossible to learn to read with this approach.

The basic concepts to keep in mind when planning a reading program are the following:

1. How much input can the learner take before breaking down or overloading (amount of input)?
2. How fast can the learner be taught before breaking down (rate of input)?
3. When is the best time of day to teach, and for how long—in short bursts or long sessions (optimal teaching time)?
4. With respect to language development, how can information be presented to learners in a developmental sequence?
5 What is the best input channel, or the open channel best utilized by the student to learn—for example, visual or auditory (sequence of input)?

Amount of Input

The teacher must remember that the goal is success—we do not want to leave the learner with a failure. Some teachers teach "just one more sound or word." That causes the learner to forget the other things that have been taught. The stabilization of vocabulary becomes irregular, and gaps may appear in the acquisition of skills. The learner may exhibit one or more of the following characteristics when the amount of input is not carefully controlled: anxiety, aggression, hyperactivity, lack of attention, and wild guessing when reading.

The teacher should ascertain the number of words learned within a given period of time to achieve 90 to 100 percent success. For example, if the instructor teaches two new words on Monday and the learner knows only one of them on Wednesday and seems to be losing vocabulary learned during the previous week, the amount of input may be contributing to failure. The instructor may have to introduce one new word at a session and then carefully monitor the type of repetitions required to ensure success. In the initial stages of word acquisition, the successful expansion of vocabulary is critical. It develops self-confidence in the learner and acts as a basis for building in new words and comprehension. The ability to recall words on a page will allow the learner to focus attention on comprehension and other skills.

Rate of Input

The rate of input of new concepts, vocabulary, letter sounds, and directions should be monitored carefully by the teacher. How fast the teacher speaks and gives directions may determine a student's successful acquisition of information. The instructor should teach without excessive verbiage. If pronunciation or accent is a concern, a tape recorder can be utilized to present vocabulary and phonetic elements, especially in initial teaching. Any teacher-made feedback program should be as uncluttered and cleanly produced as possible. When setting goals for the learner, the teacher must make sure that speed in completing material or trying to reach levels (primer, grade level) will not interfere with realistic progress.

Optimal Teaching Time

The concept to keep in mind is on-task learning. When is the optimal time the learner will attend to instructional input? For most students, the traditional morning language arts block of time is appropriate for reading skills. However, students with a short attention span may need shorter, more frequent teacher-directed input followed by successful reinforcement activities. Two or three concentrated five-minute instructional periods when the youngster is receptive to instruction may be more beneficial than a longer set period of time when the learner is too active or fatigued to learn.

Developmental Sequence

The teacher first has to determine the best possible approach to structuring and controlling the language input in terms of the learning needs of individual students. When the instructor initially presents vocabulary, concepts, and skills, directions should be simple. For some students, it may be more appropriate for the teacher to show a word card and say, "*cat*," instead of saying, "This is *cat*" or "Look at the new word *cat*."

The type of directions given by the instructor may influence successful responses by the student. Some nonverbal or reluctant students may not respond to the instructor's request for recall knowledge but will respond to a request for recognition responses. If the learner does not respond after being shown a word on a chalkboard or a card, the instructor has the option of requesting a recognition motor act from the learner rather than a recall verbal response. The instructor would say, "Give me *red*" or "Show me *red*." By getting a recognition response from the learner, the instructor at least knows that the student can select the appropriate word from among two or more choices, indicating a recognition level understanding of vocabulary. By probing for recognition responses, the instructor will have some idea about how much more repetition will be necessary to expand the vocabulary for particular students. Simultaneous with encouraging a verbal response, the instructor must develop the facility for verbal expression through a systematic approach utilizing a sequence of activities designed for this purpose.

Sequence of Input

While students with visual channel problems find it difficult to learn whole words because they may not be able to retain a visual configuration, students with auditory channel difficulties usually find this the easiest way to learn. Such students, even though they cannot associate a phoneme with a grapheme, can remember a visual sequence. This is evidence that supports the contention that auditory channel deficits are more debilitating than visual channel disabilities, especially with regard to reading.[1]

In planning for the various learning styles, it is necessary for the teacher to find a book series that can be adapted to the needs of the different students. While most basal-reading approaches can be adapted to the needs of students with reading disabilities, we have found the linguistic series to be most appropriate for students exhibiting processing disorders.

Certain of the linguistic series have much to offer students with learning difficulties. Linguistic books, however, have weaknesses as well as strengths. If the linguistic patterns are only introduced as sight words, students with the auditory channel problem (with the visual channel intact) will find it an easier way to learn to read; but students with visual channel problems may find it a more difficult way to learn, since they cannot retain a configuration of a whole word.

Some linguistic approaches, however, lend themselves to teaching students whether their deficits are visual or auditory or both. With just slight variations in the initial teaching approach, students with different problems can be in the same series of readers but on quite different individualized programs.

Since poor readers as a group have been traumatized by books, a book should not be used initially. It

1. N. Golden and S. Steiner, "Auditory and Visual Functions in Good and Poor Readers," *Journal of Learning Disabilities* 2 (1969):476–481.

should be introduced when the learners can read it; it should not be used to teach them to read.

Initial Teaching Approaches

The techniques discussed in this section are designed to guide the teacher in breaking down the various available linguistic approaches. Most of these approaches have the same basic format, and all the teacher needs to do is analyze the linguistic series in the manner illustrated in Tables 8-1 and 8-2 and then adjust the vocabulary in terms of the rate, amount, and sequence of input suggested for students exhibiting different learning problems. The first step is for the teacher to analyze the words in the series he or she intends to use.

1. List the words.
2. Note the spelling patterns these words follow.
3. See how rapidly the vocabulary is expanded.
4. Note the sight words and how fast they are introduced.

The second step is to analyze the introduction of letters of the alphabet.

1. Note what phonetic elements are to be taught and in what order.
2. Note the introduction of letters with similar auditory or visual discriminations. How have they been spaced? By spaced, we mean how and where they have been introduced in the reader. They should be spaced far enough apart to avoid unnecessary confusion for the student with an auditory or visual disability. For example:

    t and *d* spaced (aural)
    t and *f* spaced (visual)
    p and *b* spaced (aural and visual)

Note: In initial teaching, always select letters that do not look alike or sound alike. For best results, avoid teaching the following letters together: sound alikes (such as *p, b; k, g; t, v;* and *sh, ch*), look alikes (such as *b, d; f, t;* and *m, n*) and letters that can be inverted (such as *m, w; u, n*).

Two different linguistic approaches can be seen in the following examples (see Tables 8-1 and 8-2). After analyzing the sequence of steps in each of the two examples, the teacher should be able to develop a teaching plan based on both the disabilities and the intact learning channels of the student.

EXAMPLE SERIES A In this series, the teacher begins with the teaching of the long vowel sound *o* followed by the spelling pattern *op.* The student is not taught that *o* has different sounds but only that *o* in *no* says *o* and that the spelling pattern *op* says *op.* The intent is that spelling patterns should be taught through a simultaneous blending of the auditory and visual components. The rules that govern accentuation and syllabication are not taught at this time, but this is actually the student's beginning training in open and closed syllables.

EXAMPLE SERIES B In this series, the teacher starts with only short vowel sounds, teaching the spelling patterns *an, at,* etc. These spelling patterns can also be taught through a simultaneous blending of the auditory and visual components.

Visual Channel Problems

Learners with visual channel problems cannot, as a rule, retain the visual image of a whole word and need a more elemental or analytical approach to reading. If the student can blend sounds, the recommended method is to teach isolated sounds that can be blended into meaningful words. The basic approach is initially phonic oriented.

Note: The learners must have adequate auditory closure (blending) for this approach. This ability can be determined by using the Mann-Suiter Auditory Closure Screen (page 51).

TEACHING CONSONANT SOUNDS

Consonant sounds should be taught first. Look at the analysis of the series to be used. If an Example A (Table 8-1) series is used, teaching will begin with the consonants *n* and *g*; if an Example B (Table 8-2) series is used, teaching will begin with the consonants *m* and *p*.

It is important that the initial consonants that are presented to the student be different in both appearance and sound. Students with visual discrimination difficulties tend to confuse letters that appear similar. They may also fail to note internal detail (misreading *log* for *leg*) and have difficulty recognizing or remembering the different configurations of such words as *ship* and *snip.* Some exhibit inversion tendencies, such as misreading *m* for *w* and *u* for *n*.

The first step in teaching consonant sounds is to print the letters on 3″ × 5″ white cards in the presence of the students, preferably next to them or from behind them so that they can see you produce it in the correct position. The letters should not be reproduced while you are facing the students, because they will be getting a reversed image. All printing should be as

Table 8-1 Analysis of Linguistic Approach Used in Example Series A

Word List	Page No.	Spelling Patterns	Sight Words	New Letters Used
go, no	1	Long *o*	______	g, n
a	3	______	a	______
yes	4	______	yes	______
hop, mop	7	op	______	h, m
fog, log	11	og	______	f, l
I, me, he	15	Long *e*	I	______
she	17	Long *e*	______	sh
and	18	______	and	______
we	20	Long *e*	______	w
hen, ten	24	en	______	t

Table 8-2 Analysis of Linguistic Approach Used in Example Series B

Word List	Page No.	Spelling Patterns	Sight Words	New Letters Used
pan, man	1	an	______	p, m
a	2	______	a	______
ran	3	an	______	r
an	5	an	______	______
the	6	______	the	______
rat, fat	9	at	______	f
cat, see	11	at	see	c
I	12	______	I	______
can	14	an	______	______
sat	16	at	______	s

consistent as possible, done in heavy black ink and in lower-case letters. At this stage, teach the letter sounds only. It is usually best, initially, not to teach letter sounds in association with a key word (such as *b* for *boy*), as this may confuse the students.

Begin with a letter sound that cannot be distorted regardless of how long it is held, such as *m* or *n*. It is important that the consonant sound not be followed by a vowel sound verbally. For example, *t* should be said quickly and lightly, not drawn out into "tuh." If the sound is accented, for example, "puh" for *p*, it may be difficult for the students to learn to blend.

The second step is to hold the card up and say to the students, "This is 'm' [sound]." The students repeat the sound with you, then they say it alone. Ask the students to think of words that begin with the sound "m." Words can be repeated by the students after you carefully pronounce them (e.g., *man, mop, monkey*). Classification games can be introduced here, for example,"I am thinking of an animal that starts with the sound 'm'," or "How many things can you think of that start with 'm'?" After teaching the sounds of the two or three consonants you have selected, give a student one flash card (later the student will select the correct one from among others) and say, "Show me the *m*," or "Give me the *m*." This type of activity helps the learner build a strong association between the visual symbol and the auditory referent.

If a learner has difficulty making the auditory-visual association, such as sounding letters, introduce a tracing technique or use clay to form the letters. (Let the student roll the clay into a snake and then form the letters). If a tracing technique is used, the learner should trace his or her fingers over the letter while saying the sound. The following tracing options can also be useful:

1. Tracing letters on paper using finger paint.
2. Tracing letters that have been raised on paper. A

simple technique is to cut a piece of copper screening, 8″ × 10″, and bind the edges with electrical or masking tape. Place a sheet of newsprint over the screen, and then write on the paper with a black crayon. The student can then trace the raised letter with a finger.

TEACHING BLENDING

As soon as the students learn a few consonants and one vowel, they should be taught to blend those sounds into meaningful words. Nonsense syllables should not be used, and all words should be within the learners' spoken vocabulary. It is usually easiest to begin with nasal consonants and with words such as *an, man,* or *no*. As soon as the students are taught a word, they should be asked what it means. If possible, they should demonstrate the meaning with a motor response. They should then use the word in a sentence.

In teaching blending, you can place the letters on cards. Then the cards can be physically pushed together.

The following activities could be used by a teacher using Example Series A.

1. The learner is given a card with *o* on it, and he or she says "o." He or she is then given a card with an *n* on it. The two cards are then pushed together by the student while he or she says "n-o" and then "no."

   | n | o |

2. Plastic lower-case letters can be used in the same way. They should all be the same color.
3. Clay letters, made by the student, can also be used in the same way. The *o* is placed on the table, and the student moves the *n* beside it, saying "n-o" and then "no."

The following procedure could be used by a teacher using Example Series B.

1. The letters *a* and *n* can be presented together as a sight word or as a spelling pattern. Use cards that can be pushed together, plastic or wooden letters, or clay.
2. When the *an* pattern is understood, the letter *m* can be introduced to it to form the word *man*. The student should be taught to say "an," then the *m* over to the *an* and say "man."

Once the first words have been taught, the learners should be allowed to mix the cards or plastic letters up and then re-form the words they have been working on. In this way, they will experience analysis and synthesis. Always have the students say the spelling pattern and then add the new letter. For instance, the learner would say "an" and then move the *p* over and say "pan." An associative clue such as a picture drawn on the back of a word card by the student will help the student remember the word better.

TEACHING WORDS USING SPELLING PATTERNS

The next step will aid the learners in developing their sight vocabulary. They should be able to see spelling patterns more readily if taught in the following manner:

1. Place the spelling patterns and words on 3″ × 5″ white cards. Show the cards to the students, while saying the words, in the following sequence:

   | an |

   | man |

   | an |

   | pan |

2. Say "'an' [showing the *an* card] as in 'man'" (also showing the *man* card). Next, show the *an* card and say, 'an' as in 'pan' (showing the *pan* card). The students listen and imitate.

   Note: Some time may elapse before Step 2 is completed, as it takes some students longer to see these relationships.

3. When you feel that the students have mastered these two tasks, take away the cue card *an*, leaving just the whole words *man* and *pan*, and then ask the students to name the family and then the word. This may be quite difficult and require many repetitions; however, it is an important step in learning by this approach.

All of the teaching so far has been done without showing the learners the book. If the students were taught from Example Series A, for instance, they would know the words *go, no, a,* and *yes* before being introduced to the book. The mode inherent in this approach is success rather than failure. The sequence suggested in this approach can be called A → V plus TK, if necessary (Auditory → Visual plus Tactual-Kinesthetic.)

When success has been achieved with a few words, other word families can be introduced. These students cannot be expected to manipulate or revisualize the letters to form word families in their minds; therefore,

Figure 8-1 The House of e

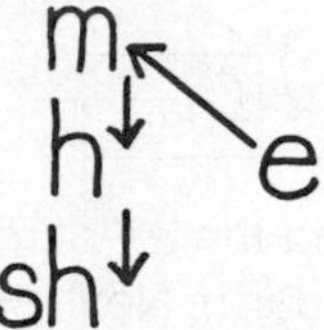

Figure 8-2 Word Building

Figure 8-3 Ditto Sheets

they must be shown how the patterns are similar. They need something concrete to manipulate in order to see exactly how the words are formed and changed. It will take much deliberate teaching, repetitions, and reinforcements before the students can be expected to see relationships between words.

Word families can be presented as members of a family living in a house together. Encourage the learners to draw a house at the top of their papers and to put the letter *e* in the doorway. Other members of the family are then printed under the house. Care should be taken to line up the family being taught. The house of *e* is shown in Figure 8-1.

Word families can also be presented with cards, raised screen letters, plastic letters, and clay. The word family can be brought to the learners' attention further by having them place the clay or plastic consonant letters in a column and then slide the single *e* down the line (as in Figure 8-2) while they say the words. Another approach to this exercise would be to have the students place three *e*'s in a row, then place the *m*, *h*, and *sh* in front of the *e*'s.

Prepare ditto sheets or acetates and have the learners trace or mark all of the words containing a specified spelling pattern (Figure 8-3).

Arrange charts or bulletin boards of houses (Figure 8-4). As new spelling patterns are added to the vocabulary, place word cards on the board.

If the students were learning from Example Series B, they would learn *pan, man, a, ran, an,* and *the* before seeing the book. Remember that the goal is success, as we do not want to leave the student with a failure. Don't teach "just one more sound or word." That "jams" or "overloads" the learners, causing them to forget the other things that have been taught.

TEACHING SIGHT WORDS

Sight words are taught in a way similar to that suggested for Example Series A—by tracing, by using

Figure 8-4 Bulletin Board

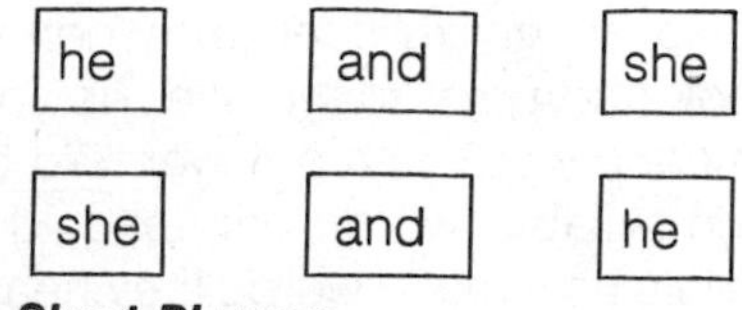

Figure 8-5 Short Phrases

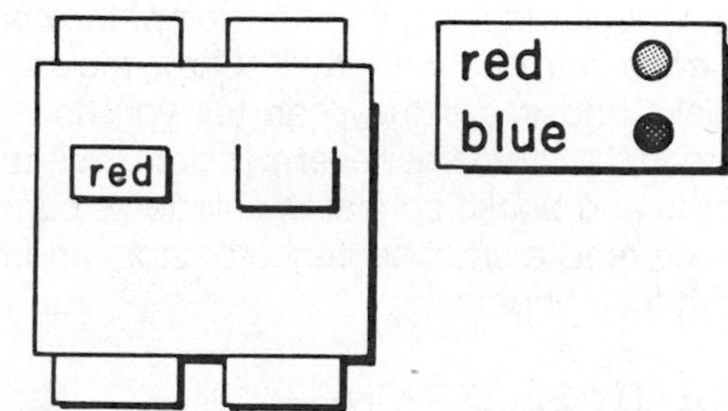

Figure 8-6 Tachistoscope

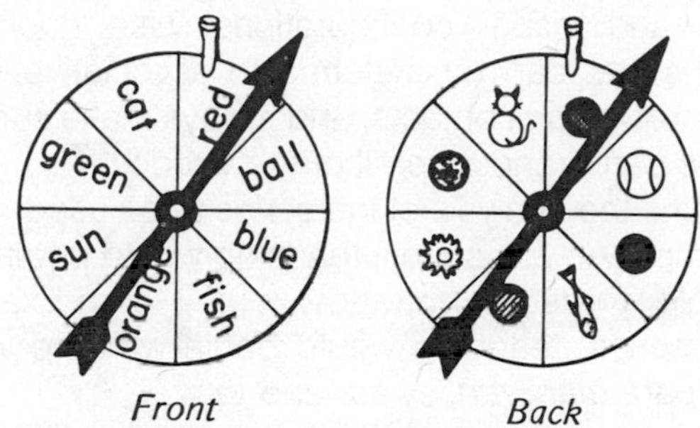

Figure 8-7 Spinner

cards, or by using clay, plastic, or wooden letters. It is recommended that sight words such as *is, and,* and *I* be taught first as whole words and then in phrases or sentences. For example, *and* can be taught with *he, me,* and *she.* Pin cards with the words *me, she,* and *and* on students and arrange them so that they make short phrases (Figure 8-5).

These phrases can be written on sentence strips and then cut up for the students to put back together. They can also be picture coded on the back for self-correction.

Other self-checking activities include the following:

Prepare a tachistoscope with a window and movable flap (Figure 8-6). On strips of cardboard prepare self-checking cards. The learner reads the word and checks by lifting the flap to see the associative picture clue.

Make or purchase a spinner with words on the front and colors or pictures on the back (Figure 8-7). The student spins the dial, reads the word, places a clothespin to mark the word, and self-checks on the reverse side.

Prepare vocabulary cards with the words on one side and the associative clue on the other (Figure 8-8).

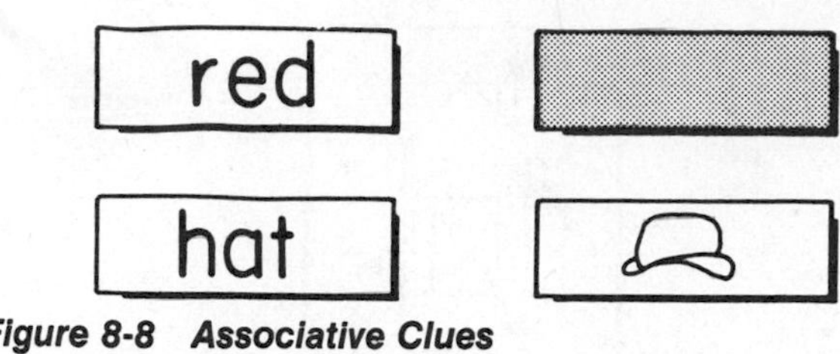

Figure 8-8 Associative Clues

Figure 8-9 Clue in Envelope

Prepare a cardboard envelope with the word on top and the associative picture on a card that slides out (Figure 8-9).

CONSONANT DIGRAPHS

Consonant digraphs should be taught as they are introduced in the reading series. For instance, in Example Series A, *sh* is introduced early. This is an isolated instance, so the digraph is taught without a lot of explanation to the student. The sound "sh" is easily said without distortion and poses little, if any, problem despite the longer visual unit.

CONSONANT BLENDS

When introducing students to two-letter consonant blends, encourage the students to think of both the sequence of the sounds and the form of the letters. Encourage them to think of the blends as a single unit, but keep them sounding out the letters individually until they are well established. For example, the *fl* in *fled* can be taught *f-l-e-d* initially. (Concrete materials should be used if needed.)

VOWELS

Terms like *long vowel sounds* and *short vowel sounds* should not be used, as they tend to confuse some students. Some students have great difficulty learning and applying rules. Present vowel digraphs such as *oa* and *ay* with a simple explanation such as, "When you see these two letters together they usually say ______."

A good deal of spelling and writing is used in the sight-word approach. As soon as the learners are able, they are encouraged to transfer from their clay figures, plastic or wooden letters, or cards to their own

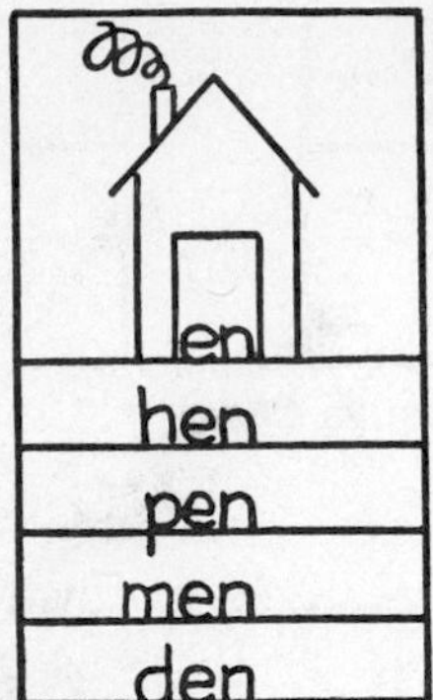

Figure 8-10 Word Family

written work. When teaching families, use lined paper cut into long strips, leaving room for the student to draw a house at the top and then to list the words in the family below (Figure 8-10).

After acquiring groups of basic sight words, the students should be encouraged to write short stories using these words. They can then cut pictures out to illustrate the stories and make their own collection. This will reinforce the learning and also increase the interest level.

Throughout the process, the students should always be encouraged to look for the like elements or spelling patterns within words. When they look at a word, they should see letter groupings that represent auditory patterns. It is important to remember that when using the intact channel as the primary input for instruction, the areas of disability must be simultaneously ameliorated during both the initial teaching period and the remedial program. The discrepancy between strengths and weaknesses must not be allowed to widen, and hopefully a decrease in weaknesses will become apparent with proper training. Many good commercial and homemade materials are available for the amelioration or strengthening of problem areas.

Auditory Channel Problems

Learners with auditory channel deficits usually learn better through the whole-word, or sight-word, approach. They find it difficult to relate symbols to their auditory counterparts and, therefore, cannot transfer the learning of sounds. These students usually must learn each new word as a unique entity, as they cannot relate part of a word to a whole. They need to make a direct association between the symbol and the experience for each word.

Make sure the students understand the relationship between the written and spoken word. To help develop awareness of auditory-visual correspondence, take a favorite book and point to the title. As you read the title, point to each word with a finger. (To begin with, titles with one-syllable words only should be used.) Ask the students how many words they heard. Say the title, letting the students count the words with fingers, and then ask how many words they saw. When the learners understand what you are doing, they should point to each word as you say it. Show the students other books and see if they can tell you how many words are in the title. Whenever possible, use matching records and books so that the students can listen to someone read a short sentence or story and follow along with their fingers.

VOCABULARY SELECTION

In selecting the students' beginning reading vocabulary, make sure that the words are within the students' range of experience and that they have different sounds and visual configurations. Use nouns or pronouns that can be matched to associative clues such as pictures of objects, and always make sure the students can pronounce all of the words.

Examine the analysis of the series to be used. If it is an Example A–type series, teaching would begin with the whole words *go, no,* and *yes*; if it is an Example B–type series, teaching would begin with the whole words, *pan, man, ran, a, an,* and *the*.

It is important to remember that one of the difficulties encountered with these students is teaching them discrimination of short vowel sounds. Many are unable to discriminate initial- or final-sound similarities or differences. Therefore, they cannot form generalizations that apply to new words and cannot break a word into syllables or individual sounds. Although the learners may know all of the sounds of the letters, they may be unable to blend them into words. The recommended procedure, therefore, is to work from the whole to the parts.

TEACHING SEQUENCE

The input sequence here is the whole word, then sounds, and then touch, or Visual → Auditory plus Tactual-Kinesthetic, if necessary. When you are sure the students can say the word and understand its meaning, concentrate on teaching them to match the word with a picture. It is not enough for the students to just listen and repeat the words; they must relate the word to a picture or other associative clue. Otherwise, they will be merely going from the auditory (sound) to the visual (word) and may not be tying it in with meaning. Anna Gillingham, who contributed so much to our knowledge of reading problems in children, stated that, "The constant use of association

Figure 8-11 Using Movable Letters.

of all of the following—how a letter or word looks, how it sounds, and how the speech organs feel when producing it—must be stressed."[2]

If an Example A–type series is used, the students in the reading group can play an integral part in illustrating the words. The students should always be involved actively. They can be given cards with the pronouns written on them; for example, a boy would be *he,* a girl *she,* and two children would share a card and be called *we*. The students should be encouraged to make up sentences using the words. The word *and* can be added, and the students can stand holding their cards and form themselves into phrases such as "he and she," "she and he," and "she and I." If an Example B type of series is used, pictures can be drawn on cards and used for matching with the printed word.

If students are still unable to read the words after thorough visual-auditory teaching, they should be introduced to a tactual-kinesthetic approach. Clay, tracing, and plastic or wooden letters are a few of the techniques that can be used.

In 1943, Grace Fernald said, "We find great individual differences in types of recall image."[3] She then went on to explain that for some children, seeing, hearing, and speaking must be reinforced with the concrete kinesthetic experience of handling and moving individual parts. Through the sense of touch, the students establish a mental concept that is strong enough to support their memory retention. However, we feel that the K and T in the Visual-Kinesthetic-Tactual approach should not be automatically introduced. They should be introduced only after failure with the intact channel alone. Introducing the tactual automatically may overstimulate and, in fact, confuse some students.

After the students have been taught their first basic sight vocabulary, word families can be presented to them exactly as they were introduced to the students with the visual and kinesthetic channel problem. Although many repetitions will be necessary for each new spelling pattern, that sequence of activities is necessary to help the students develop the ability to analyze and synthesize sounds. Most first grade phonics work is done orally and, therefore, is not appropriate for teaching these students. They need the simultaneous presentation of sound and visuals such as clay, plastic or wooden letters, and cards. When the learners have put their words into word families, immediately ask them if they see anything that is the same. They must then underline the spelling pattern that is being emphasized. (Visual reinforcement.) Next, have the students say the words to see if they hear the identical elements (tying the auditory to the visual), e.g., "top," "hop." The emphasis here is on the development of an awareness of consistent configurations. Exaggerate the sound you want the student to hear. The students must then exaggerate the sounds. Always use concrete materials that the students can manipulate so that they are continuously involved in doing, as well as looking and listening.

Movable letters are more effective when placed on a desk top chalkboard or on paper on a slant board so that the student can underline the pattern being emphasized. (Figure 8-11).

As the students start to learn the basic vocabulary, simultaneously work on improving auditory skills to prevent difficulties later on with spelling. In severe cases, if the problem areas are ignored, the auditory processing of data may become almost nonfunctional, so that the students may need to be taught like deaf students. It should be noted that some tests of auditory discrimination do not always identify a student whose primary disability is in perceiving sounds within words, such as the *and* in *hand*. A student's inability to do this often goes undetected for a long time. Teaching word families with concrete materials for manipulation and exaggerating the sound of letters

2. A. Gillingham and B. Stillman, *Remedial Training for Children with Specific Disability in Reading, Spelling, and Penmanship*, 2d ed. (Cambridge, Mass.: Educators' Publishing Service, 1969).
3. G. Fernald, *Remedial Techniques in Basic School Subjects* (New York: McGraw-Hill Book Co., 1943).

and words you are trying to teach will help the child with this type of problem. You may have to go back to simple auditory-discrimination activities with varying input, including nonsocial, nonverbal sounds (tones of different pitch, frequency, and intensity); social, nonverbal sounds (house and animal sounds); or social, verbal sounds (letters and words).[4]

For the learners who continue to have difficulty sounding letters, use techniques that will aid their internalization of the sounds. Remedial activities include using consonants that can be sustained, such as *m, s, sh, f, v, r,* and *l*. Ask the learners to say one sound, and then you say several sounds, including the one first given to the students. The students will hold up their hands when they hear "their" sound.

Learners with a problem in sounding letters need to concentrate on how the sound is formulated and how the lips and tongue are positioned. Mirrors can be used to help them see their mouth movements. Feathers or strips of paper can also be used to show the flow of air in the production of speech sounds.

Some students know all of the sounds but are unable to blend them. It is easier to blend syllables than single consonant and vowel sounds. It should be noted that difficulties may develop later when the students start to learn consonant blends such as *st* in *rust* and *ft* in *left*. Unless you deliberately teach the students to notice and pronounce the words correctly, they may leave out the *s* of *rust* and the *f* of *left*.

It is very important that these students hear the number of syllables in a word. Instill a consciousness of both the number and the order of sounds within the word. Always stress the rhythmic sequence of words, starting with one-syllable words, then going to two- and, finally, three-syllable words. Concrete materials for manipulation can be used effectively at this point. Only after the students are secure with the words and phrases they have learned should they be introduced to the book, especially if they have a long history of failure.

Golden and Steiner evaluated a group of students to determine possible differences in specific auditory and visual functions pertaining to good and poor readers of normal intelligence.[5] The results indicated that in this particular sample "poor" readers were lacking primarily in auditory rather than in visual skills. Golden and Steiner conclude that "the significance of these auditory skills may have been overshadowed and eclipsed by the amount of visual material made available to the teacher."

Auditory and Visual Channel Problems

Students with both auditory and visual channel problems should begin with the long vowel sounds first, as it is easier to discriminate between them than between the short vowel sounds. It is not enough, however, for these students to see, hear, and then say the word. Words must be matched with pictures or objects whenever possible and thoroughly reinforced with concrete material, such as clay, plastic, or wooden letters. Through the use of the tactual modality, the students will be able to feel and sense letters and words. This will also help the students achieve closure (blending) and eventually remember better. The learning process may be slower, and it may be some time before the teacher can really ascertain whether transfer has taken place with the student who has multichannel difficulties. These students usually need extensive work to help them hear similarities of initial and final sounds and to discriminate between the short vowel sounds. They often have difficulty forming generalizations about new words and exhibit problems in syllabication or individual sounds. They are generally unable to blend efficiently.

Tracing and writing are the manipulative aspects of reading that are a very necessary part of this program. The input sequence for these students emphasizes seeing how a word looks, listening to how a word sounds, and noticing how saying it feels by placing one's hand on one's face and throat. The students should become aware of how the word feels, then write it. This procedure implies using the Visual-Auditory plus Tactual modalities simultaneously.

Reading Skill Development Activities

WORD RECOGNITION

General sight vocabulary activities include the following:

1. Provide clay, movable letters, finger paint, and a typewriter, if available, for the learner to reproduce and reinforce the words in the reading program.
2. Encourage the learner to look for known words in books and magazines.
3. Help the learner to begin a picture dictionary using the words from the reading program.
4. Have the learner form sentences with the word cards and read them aloud.

4. D. Johnson and H. Myklebust, *Learning Disabilities: Educational Principles and Practices* (New York: Grune & Stratton, 1967).

5. Golden and Steiner, "Auditory and Visual Functions in Good and Poor Readers."

5. Give the learner a category and have him or her find all of the word cards for the category, or ask the learner to write the words. For example:

   Toys: ball, bat
   People: boy, she, he, we, mother, father, girl, baby, they
   Things to do: sit, hit, shop, go, hop, fish, run
   Rhyming words: cat – hat he – she fun – sun
   boy – toy bed – red pet – wet
6. If the learner has a picture dictionary, encourage him or her to write lists of animals, things that go, toys, etc.
7. Have the student cut out an interesting picture from a magazine, color his or her favorite picture in a coloring book, or draw a picture. Paste the picture on a larger sheet of paper. Have the student write a few sentences about the picture. Put the completed picture on a bulletin board or wall.
8. Use word cards to review vocabulary introduced in the learner's reading program.
9. Have the student write words on a magic slate. Later, the words can be easily erased.
10. On heavy cardboard, trace the letters of the alphabet (lower case). Cut them out. With a paint brush, paint on glue. Before the glue dries, pour on sand. After the glue dries, shake off the excess sand. The rough, beaded letters can be used for tracing as the learner reads or spells the reading vocabulary.
11. Provide lotto, concentration, or bingo word games to increase word recognition.

CONSONANTS AND BLENDS

The following activities will aid teachers, paraprofessionals, and peer tutors in the reinforcement of consonant sounds:

1. Small baskets, muffin tins, juice cans, egg cartons, plastic trays, coffee cans, or boxes can be labeled with the sounds to be reinforced (Figure 8-12). The learner picks up an object or picture of an object, says the beginning sound and the word, and places the object in the correct container.
2. Place a small card with a letter on it inside a face powder compact. The learner opens the compact, looks at the letter, then, looking in the mirror, produces the sound.
3. Use alliterative phrases or sentences to practice the repetition of an initial sound. Encourage older students to write their own phrases (e.g., Susan sang silly songs).

Figure 8-12 Labeled Containers

4. Accumulate coffee cans or other containers. Paste a letter on the outside of each container and have the student place in the containers pictures from magazines or concrete objects whose initial sounds correspond to the letters. (For example, all items that begin with *m* would go into the *m* container.)
5. Make letters from cookie molds, clay, or pipe cleaners, and have the learner identify them by giving the appropriate sound. ("That's an *m*.")
6. Have learners listen to words beginning with the same sound (for example, *hat, horse, happy*) and name other words beginning with the same sound. Vary the activity by saying three or four words that begin with the same sound and one word that does not (*man, monkey, car, marble*). The learners stop you when they hear the different word, or they name the different word after the sequence has been given.
7. Play a bingo-type game using letter sounds in place of numbers. The learner will indicate the sound while marking the letter.
8. Play "which sound does not belong" by producing three sounds (e.g., "s . . . s . . . f." The learner will indicate the sound that does not belong.
9. Have the learner locate and identify specified sounds of letters in newspapers and magazines.
10. From magazines or catalogs have the learners cut out pictures of words on their reading list. On one side of an index card, they can paste the picture: . On the other side, you print the word: ball . The learner can study these cards alone like flash cards by looking at the picture on the front of the card, saying the word, writing the word on paper and checking themselves. The cards can be kept in a box with alphabetical dividers. Use the cards for phonics review by having the learners put all the pictures with the same beginning sound into a pile (e.g., bat, boy, bird, ball).
11. Have the learner make sound posters by pasting cut- or torn-out magazine pictures of objects beginning with a specified sound, such as *m*, on a large sheet of paper or cardboard (Figure 8-13).

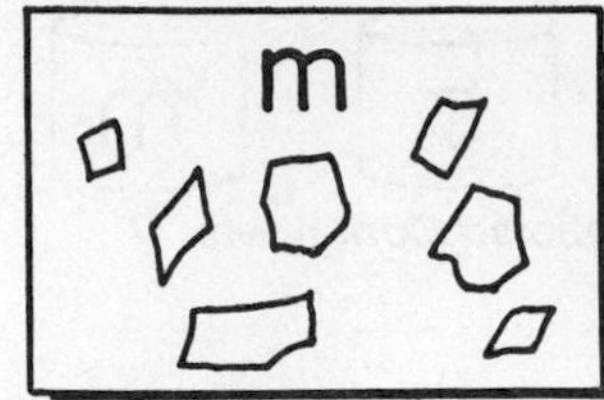

Figure 8-13 Sound Poster

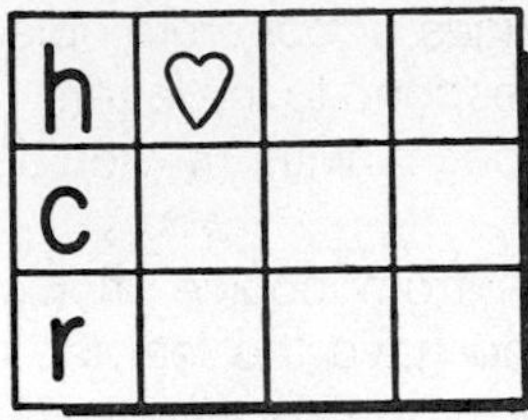

Figure 8-14 Sound Chart

Figure 8-15 Sound Cards

12. In the boxes of a chart, the learner pastes cutouts, or draws pictures, of objects beginning with the specified sound (Figure 8-14).
13. Have the learner place sound cards next to the picture of the object with the corresponding beginning sound (Figure 8-15).
14. Have the learner use pocket charts and small cards to review sounds (Figure 8-16).
15. Have the learner write the beginning sound that correctly completes a word that corresponds to a given picture (Figure 8-17).
16. To review an initial consonant sound previously introduced, write words (at the learner's independent reading level) beginning with that sound on the chalkboard or on an acetate to be used on the overhead projector. The student reads the word, underlines the initial consonant, and says the word again, emphasizing the beginning sound. (See Figure 8-18.)
17. Write a blend on a fill-in chart and have the student think of words that use the blend (e.g., *sn*), listing as many words as possible under the given categories (Figure 8-19). Point out the sequence of the sounds in consonant blends as well as the form of the letters. Pronounce the words containing blends correctly.

BLENDING

Students who continue to have difficulty in learning to blend will require additional blending (closure) activities. The following blending activities will aid the learner to develop the auditory, visual, and intrachannel (auditory to visual) skills necessary for efficiency in blending.

Figure 8-16 Pocket Chart

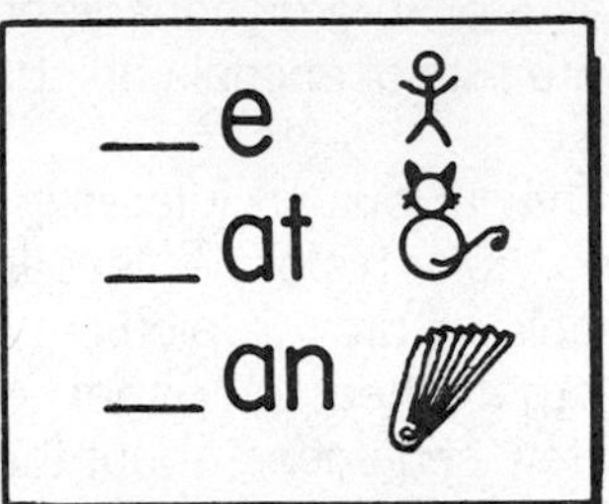

Figure 8-17 Word Completion

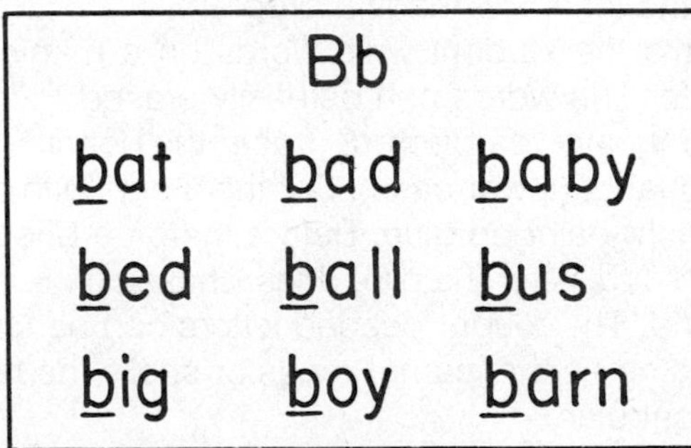

Figure 8-18 Initial Sound Review

Auditory Blending (Closure)

1. Have the students identify from two or more choices the object that represents the word presented by the instructor as a sequence, or spaced group of sounds oı syllables. ("Show me the bi . . cy . . cle, the c . . ar, the b . . a . . by.")
2. Ask the learner to identify from two or more choices the picture of an object that represents the word presented by the instructor as a sequence, or spaced group of sounds or syllables. ("Which one of these pictures has a d . . o . . g, a h . . . ouse, a tr . . ee?")
3. Have the learner name a word by synthesizing the sounds (letters or syllables) you have presented. ("What word do these sounds make: h . . app . . y, ch . . ick . . en, r . . a . . t?"

	Animals	Flowers	Clothes
sn	snail snake	snapdragon	sneaker

Figure 8-19 Blend Chart

4. Have the learner synthesize sounds you have presented and identify from among two or more choices the word that is represented by those sounds. ("Sh . . i . . p. Is it *slip, ship* or *snip*?")

Visual Blending (Closure)

1. Have the learner assemble simple to complex puzzles.
2. Have the student assemble three-dimensional objects such as geometric forms or models of people, animals, cars, etc.
3. Have the learner complete from two or more choices an open, or partial, picture of an object or geometric form, thereby forming the whole object. (Ask, "Which one of these goes with this picture?")
4. Ask the learner to identify the missing part from a picture of an incomplete object. (Ask, "What part of this picture is missing?")
5. Have the student locate and name the missing parts from pictures of incomplete objects. (Ask, "What is missing from the object in this picture?")
6. Have the learner view an incomplete object and then identify from two or more choices the picture of the object as it would look completed. (Ask, "See this? Which one of these pictures will it look like when it is finished?")
7. Have the learner name the completed objects when shown pictures of incomplete objects.
8. Have the student complete pictures of geometric forms, letters, or numerals with a pencil, or have the student use a finger or a pointer to show how the pictures can be completed.
9. Ask the student to identify from two or more choices the complete letter or numeral that is represented by an incomplete picture.
10. Have the learner identify from two or more choices the incomplete letter or numeral that is represented by a complete picture.
11. Have the learner identify from two or more choices the complete word that is represented by an incomplete picture. The words should be within the learner's reading vocabulary.
12. Have the student "close," or read a list of variably spaced words. (For example, c a t, co me, m other, ra t.) The words should be within the student's reading vocabulary.

COMPREHENSION

Main Idea

1. Play question-and-answer games to review lessons.
2. Ask the student to write titles for short paragraphs or headlines for newspaper articles.
3. Ask the student to write a sentence or a paragraph to explain political cartoons or comic strips.
4. Have a student read a story silently. You or another student can hold up one of the following cards:

What	When	Where	Who	Why

The learner will tell *what* the main ideas of the story are, *when* the story occurs (time of day, etc.), *where* the events take place, *who* the characters are, and *why* the events happen. For some learners simple sheets can be used to teach main ideas. (See Figure 8-20.)

5. Record short selections on a tape recorder. The learner will listen to a selection, shut off the machine, and write down the main ideas. The stu-

Who ______________________
____
____

What ______________________
____
____

Where ______________________
____
____

When ______________________
____
____

Why ______________________
____
____

Figure 8-20 Main Ideas

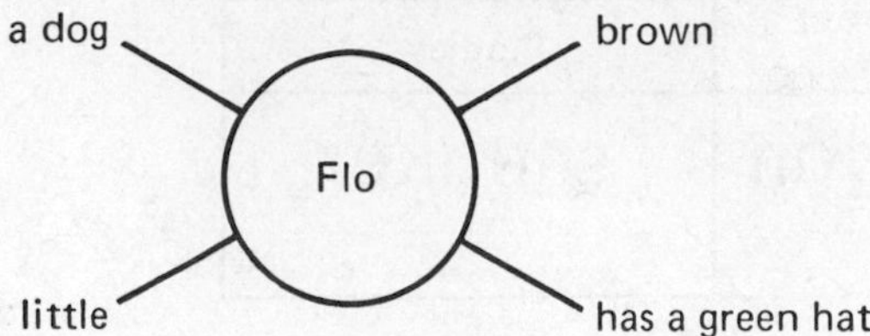

Figure 8-21 Subject and Details

dent can self-correct the list by listening to the instructor's summary of the main ideas.

Details

1. After the student reads a selection, ask him or her to print the subject of the selection, draw a large circle around the word, and list all the details about it that were mentioned in the passage. (See Figure 8-21.)
2. Have the student underline the details in a newspaper column.

Word Meaning

1. Ask students to pretend that they have to explain to a foreign visitor specified examples of colloquial or figurative speech (e.g., *backed out of a deal, green thumb*).
2. Give a definition of a word. The student circles the word on a page or holds up a word card.
3. If students cannot verbally express the meaning of a word, ask them to draw a picture to illustrate the meaning or multiple meanings.
4. Build the students' visual imagery by having them write what they see in their mind's eye when a word is said. Write lists of phrases to illustrate the word.

overcast dark, dreary day
grey clouds

Context Clues

1. On the chalkboard, a duplicator master, or the overhead projector, write incomplete sentences. Have the learner fill in the blanks with the correct words.

run fun sun

It is ______ to play with the dog.

The ______ is hot.

Can you ______ and jump?

2. Ask the learner to read the sentence and complete the missing word.

Maria is a little g ______.
The f ______ was in the pond.

Inference

1. Discuss the student's interpretation of a story in terms of truth or fantasy.
2. Let the student anticipate what will happen next in a story.
3. Use language association and classification activities. Refer to Chapter 7, "Developmental Skills Curriculum."
4. Have the learner list as many variations as possible for analogies.

as green as ______
grass
leaves
lettuce

5. First, discuss what kinds of questions will imply inference and list the key words usually found in those questions. Then, after a student has read a story silently, ask him or her to write questions to ask other students who have read the same material.
6. Refer to page 279 for developmental activities to help the student who has social perception problems and may be missing the emotional implications or humor in the story or the facial expressions in the illustrations.
7. Discuss cause-effect relationships. (What will happen if ______?)

ORAL READING

Students need a reason to read orally with a fluent, natural flow of speech. Provide the student with opportunities to read that will emphasize correct phrasing, intonation, voice, and punctuation.

1. Use vocabulary at the student's independent level for practice in oral reading.
2. Allow the student to read to peers or younger students at school. Encourage parents not only to read to their children but also to listen as much as possible when the child reads.
3. Reward oral reading by
   a. Autographing and signing the paper or booklet read.
   b. Using stickers, stars, punched holes, etc., to reward oral reading activities.
4. Older students can keep a log and evaluate progress on specific skills (e.g., "Read pages 16–17 in *Rocks Are Fun*. Phrasing much better.")
5. Use visual clues to aid in intonation, voice, and punctuation. For example, on a page of material, use colored pencils to mark the punctuation marks in red, the pauses in blue, etc. Underline words to be stressed.

6. Use a variety of media and materials to give the student practice in reading. Have the student
   a. Narrate filmstrips.
   b. Read phrases or sentences on a Language Master.
   c. Read into a tape recorder and play the tape back for evaluation.
   d. Read a newscast for a videotaped class program.
   e. Read a script for a puppet show.
7. Use phrase cards and tachistoscopic devices to aid the word-by-word reader

   (e.g., | This is | | a big bird. |).

8. Encourage creativity. Let the student read a commercial story or a poem onto tape and also record a musical introduction and sound effects.

DICTIONARY

1. List as many synonyms as possible for words.
2. Send old dictionaries home for students to use.
3. Keep a Quiz Box or list of questions for students to look up in a dictionary or other reference book.

A PERSONALIZED APPROACH TO READING

A modified experience approach to reading can be used for students who are beyond the initial stages in the elementary grades, as well as for secondary and adult students. Many students have come to dislike books because of continued failure in reading over a period of years. Teachers have found that it is difficult to get older students involved in reading by using a basal series whose concepts and format are far below the students' mental age or chronological age. These books are often referred to as baby books or kid books, and secondary-age poor readers, as a group, are reluctant to use basal readers from the primer level through level 4.

Alternative approaches that have been introduced by teachers include (1) linguistic series; (2) high interest–low vocabulary books; and (3) the experience method. Most of these techniques have built-in problems for older students.

1. The vocabulary of the high interest–low vocabulary books, in most cases, is too difficult for students reading below grade level three.
2. The experience approach requires a strong visual memory. Poor visual memory prevents students from learning in a basal series. Another factor that prevents their learning is that their motivation and interest are just not high enough to compensate for their poor word attack skills. They can hold just so much before their visual memory fails.
3. The linguistic series as a group, especially at the lower levels, appear to be too juvenile for many students. The linguistic approach, like the basal reading approach, requires the student to have a good visual-memory, even though the vocabulary is presented at a slower pace. The illustrations in the linguistics and basals are often too juvenile even if the stories are not. The interest level is often not appropriate for older students.

Some of the books in the Hilltop Series: An Individualized Program for Problem Readers[6] can be used with older students. The program was designed to provide reading material for learners who need successful learning experiences through a program of controlled language and reinforcement that is interesting and has elements of humor. The style of the illustrations was found to be appropriate for intermediate students who have a slower-than-average rate of learning as well as for students exhibiting learning difficulties.

A Linguistic-Based Experience Program

The following is a suggested modified experience method that incorporates a spelling pattern technique based on the linguistics approach to reading. This program is composed of four components plus a writing approach.

COMPONENT ONE—STUDENTS' PRESENT SIGHT VOCABULARY (WHAT DO THE STUDENTS HAVE?)

Experience has shown that students with anywhere near average intelligence acquire a sight vocabulary by merely attending school for a number of years. However, standardized testing may indicate that students have few words in their sight vocabulary, since much of their vocabulary may be composed of words that are not found on standardized tests. The first step in determining the students' actual sight vocabulary is to give them word lists, newspapers, books, etc., and have them circle or copy on paper the words they know. After the words have been checked, the students should list the words separately on 3″ x 5″ white cards. When they have completed this task, have them put an associative clue (such as a picture

6. P. H. Mann, R. M. McClung, and P. A. Suiter, The Hilltop Series: An Individualized Program for Problem Readers (Boston: Allyn and Bacon, 1977–1979).

or a short phrase using the word) on the back of the card. Let the students hold the stack of cards so that they can see that they have a "reading vocabulary." Many of these students are convinced that they cannot read; therefore, they develop a poor attitude toward books and, even more important, emotional barriers against learning to read. Therefore, it is recommended that students not receive a book until they can read it with 100% success. After the students have completed the stack of word cards they can read, they can put them into a small file box. The students should then be told that they are going to add many more words to their collection.

COMPONENT TWO—STUDENTS' INTEREST (WHAT DO THE STUDENTS LIKE?)

Develop a vocabulary made up of words dealing with an area of interest to the students. For example, if a student is interested in cars, make up a list of words that concern cars; make, type, parts, etc. Each student and the teacher should build a list together. As the students learn the words, they write them on 3″ x 5″ white cards with associative clues on the back and add them to their word collection. These words will be introduced *one at a time* into the writing program.

COMPONENT THREE—SPELLING PATTERNS

Introduce the students to spelling patterns such as *at*, *op*, and *an*. Teach these one at a time, along with the sounds of four or five consonants (such as *p*, *m*, *t*, and *g*) if the students do not already know them. The students then blend the sounds (consonants and spelling patterns) together to make words. The words are also written on 3″ x 5″ white cards and filed with those the students already know. The following is a list of spelling patterns and examples of combinations that can be derived therein. In teaching, the cards should be presented to the student like this:

[m][an] and not like this: [m] [an]

Consonant Vowel–Consonant ([C] VC). This pattern should be taught first. For example:

an – *m an, c an, p an, t an*
at – *c at, f at, s at, m at*
ap – *c ap, t ap, n ap, m ap*
ed – *w ed, b ed, l ed, T ed*
en – *t en, p en, h en, B en*

Following are other vowel–consonant spelling patterns:

ab, ad, ag, am
ed, eg, em, ep, et
ib, id, ig, im, in, ip, it
ob, od, of, om, on, op, ot
ub, ud, ug, um, un, up, ut

Begin with the following consonants, as they can be sustained without distortion for longer periods of time: *f, h, l, m, n, r, s,* and *v*. Then use such sounds as *b, g, t, d,* and *p*, and add the rest of the consonants as necessary. With the above consonant–vowel sound combinations, many words can be formed. By using word cards or plastic or wooden letters that the student physically pushes together and pulls apart, you can teach analysis and synthesis of words simultaneously. The same process is used with the patterns to follow. The student can be told that this is a spelling program.

Note: Digraphs and blends are added to the pattern in the same way as the initial consonants. (Again, if word cards are used, the letters should look like this: [ch][at] ; not like this: [ch] [at]) For example,

at – *ch + at = chat*
at – *fl + at = flat*

Following are other digraphs and blends that can be used with spelling patterns·

ch, cl, cr
dl, dr
fl, fr
gl, gr
pl, pr
sc, sh, sn, sm, sp, st
th, tr, tw
wh, wr

Consonant–Vowel Consonant (C V [C]). This is an alternate approach if Section 1 does not prove successful. For example:

ba – *ba d, ba t, ba g, ba m*
ca – *ca t, ca b, ca p, ca n*
da – *da d, da m, da b, Da n*
fa – *fa d, fa n, fa t, Fa b*

Other consonant–vowel spelling patterns include the following:

ma, na, pa, ra, sa, ta, va, wa
be, de, fe, ge, je, le, me, ne, pe, re, te, ve, ye
bi, di, fi, hi, ji, ki, li, mi, ni, pi, ri, si, ti,
vi, wi, yi
bo, co, do, fo, go, ho, jo, lo, mo, no, po, ro, so, to
bu, cu, du, fu, gu, ju, lu, mu, nu, pu, ru, su, tu, yu

By adding the consonants *f, h, l, m, n, r, s,* and *v* as before, and then *b, g, d,* and *p*, one can form many word combinations. Other consonants are added as necessary.

Consonant Vowel–Consonant–Consonant ([C] VCC). This pattern is taught next in the sequence. For example:

ash – *b ash, c ash, m ash, s ash*
ath – *b ath, m ath, p ath, r ath*
ang – *b ang, h ang, s ang, g ang*

Following are other vowel–consonant–consonant patterns:

esh, ish, ush
ath, eth, ith, oth
ing, ong, ung
ack, eck, ick, ock, uck
aff, eff, iff, uff
all, ell, ill, oll, ull
ess, iss, oss, uss
est, ist, ost, ust
ask, esk, isk, usk
asp, isp, osp, usp

Consonant blends and digraphs can be added as necessary to build many words.

Consonant Vowel–Consonant–Vowel ([C] VCV). This is the next phase in teaching spelling patterns. For example:

ike – *l ike, m ike, h ike, t ike*
ake – *m ake, t ake, b ake, f ake*

Following are other vowel–consonant–vowel patterns:

abe, ade, age, ame, ane, ape, ate
ede, ete
ibe, ide, ime, ine, ipe, ite
ode, ome, one, ope, ote
ube, ume, une, upe, ute

By adding the consonants mentioned previously as needed, you can add many new words to the student's list. These words can be filed on 3″ x 5″ white cards with associative pictures or phrases on the back. Digraphs and blends can also be added to the above vowel–consonant–consonant patterns to make words. For example:

ich – *wh* + *ich* = *which*
ush – *sh* + *ush* = *shush*
ing – *br* + *ing* = *bring*
th + *ing* = *thing*
ong – *th* + *ong* = *thong*

Other Spelling Patterns. Consonant digraphs and blends can be added to the following patterns to make words:

eel	ead	oad	all
eed	eak	oak	ain
eek	eam	oan	iad
een	ean	oat	ose
eep	eal		oum
eet	eap		use
atch	athe	ange	aste
etch	ethe	enge	este
itch	ithe	inge	iste
otch	othe	onge	oste
utch	uthe	unge	uste
anch	aint	lege	
ench	aize	ight	
inch	aise	ount	
onch	ease		
unch	east		

COMPONENT FOUR—ALTERNATIVE WORD LISTS

Words from different sources can be introduced into the reading program, one at a time. They can be taken from the following areas:

1. Everyday Word List
   An integral part of this program is the systematic introduction of words that are most common in everyday use. The Mann-Suiter Everyday Word List (Table 8-3) can be used for this purpose. As the students learn each word, they write it on 3″ × 5″ white cards, put an associative picture clue or phrase on the back, and put the cards in their file boxes. Introduce the words in phrases or sentences, not in isolation.
2. Short Phrase List
   Develop cards with short phrases and sentences for inclusion in the vocabulary building program. These should have associative picture clues on the back whenever possible. Phrases can be taken from the Mann-Suiter Developmental Phrase List (Table 8-4).
3. Subject Level Word List
   At the beginning of the semester or year, each of the subject level teachers can give the students a list of words they will need to learn (sight word and meaning) in order to succeed in that subject area. These words can be introduced into the reading program one at a time, associatively (e.g., words and phrases on word cards with pictures). This will enable the students to tie the reading program into the subject level areas.

Table 8-3 Mann-Suiter Everyday Word List

a	I	the
all	in	to
am	is	they
an	it	this
and	if	three
any		ten
are	jump	tell
at		two
	know	talk
be		then
been	look	that
big	like	too
blue	little	them
by	let	there
can	may	up
carry	many	
come	me	very
could	my	
	met	want
did		way
do	no	why
does	not	who
done		with
down	one	was
	once	will
eight	on	would
	of	what
for		where
four	play	when
	pretty	walk
get		went
go	run	
gone	ride	you
good	red	yes
got		your
going	see	yellow
green	some	
	so	
hop	said	
had	saw	
have	she	
he		
here		

COORDINATING THE COMPONENTS

The components should be coordinated as in Figure 8-22. Following is a sample lesson.

STEP 1—The Students Learn a Spelling Pattern. Present the words as whole words first, then show how they are broken down into consonants, digraphs, or

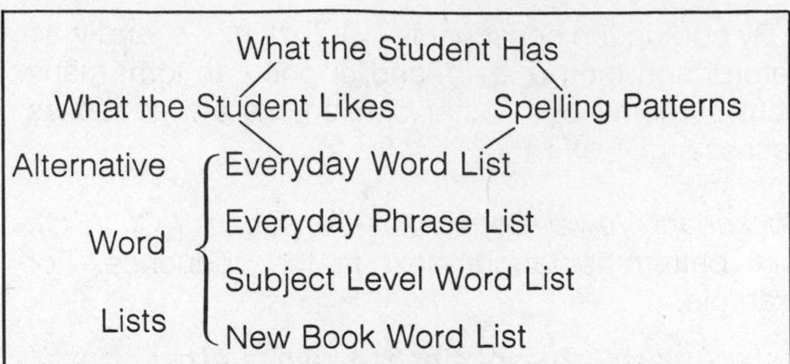

Figure 8-22 Coordinating the Components

blends and patterns. The student will need to see the same spelling patterns in each of the words. The sequence of teaching is as follows:

First: *cat* – whole word shown on a card or with anagrams
Second: *c at* – word broken down into sound and pattern on cards or with anagrams
Third: *cat* – whole word shown on a card or with anagrams

Note: Physical manipulation of cards or letters is important for students who cannot remember the patterns.

Next, line up the letters and words as follows so that the student can see the similarities.

(a)				(b)
at		at	at	c
cat	c	at	cat	m—at
mat	m	at	mat	p
pat	p	at	pat	f
fat	f	at	fat	

Mix up the letters and let the students build the words: *at, cat, mat, pat,* and *fat.* Have the students write the words on 3″ × 5″ white cards, put pictures or phrase clues on the back, and file the cards in their word boxes.

Note: The students should be tested the next day informally at their seats. Show them the word cards and ask them to identify the words. If they cannot, repeat the teaching process, letting them work for a longer period of time with the cards or plastic or wooden letters.

An alternative approach, to be used if the students do not appear to be stabilizing the words when they are introduced first as whole words, is the following:

First: *c at* – word broken down into sound and pattern on cards
Second: *cat* – whole word
Third: *c at* – word broken down again into sound and pattern (same as the first)
Fourth: *cat* – complete model

Table 8-4 Mann-Suiter Developmental Phrases

I

it is
a big hat
I see
I took
in a hat
the cat is
I had fun
I cut
the cup
the bus
look at the
I fed the
a cat is
I pet the
did he have
he can
she will get
do you see
he has a
I want a
the band is
I like that
it was a
I saw
I can find
I will
I play a
he sings a
I want to
I kick the
she took the
he likes to
we got the
he got a
she got five
he will ride
I found his
can you
do you
I will give
do you want
dad got a
I hear a
did he miss
we went to the
I like my
my name is
I live at
my eyes are
he took me
the room is
the kitten is
she is
I wish I

II

the ball is
a chicken is
I took that
my father is
my mother is
they are both
he drove a
father drove
this is my
she saw the
where are my
I put them
here they are
dad and I
the cow is
the house is
the boy has
a horse is
there are
can you see
is there a
I saw three
there were
one boy
two girls
is a car
he knows
I like a
the pony is
he rides a
I said
in the boat
at school
I found
a dime
his work
he has fun
at the farm
he helped
is one
Is pleased
with me
the train
come in
a ball game
he looks
to a game
the baby
the cat had
the cows are
he was
he let
his horse

III

we like
after school
it snowed
some stories
ask me
two trees
I am having
who worked
with them
would you
your room
we went
we can play
a game
we will walk
her father
a pretty doll
a new book
the children
to the farm
a black horse
a white rabbit
the little boy
we will walk
they were
a little baby
a white duck
a blue coat
when you come
to the tree
you will like
a small boat
a pretty girl
he would try
down the street
a yellow hat
went down
up the hill
the brown horse
a big house
a red bird
in the garden
into the water
the little chickens
my father knows
he would go
some cake
in the grass
to the barn
may I
I must try
on the chair
a baby pig
some brown cows

STEP II—The Students Learn Other Words Necessary for Writing a Sentence. Now that the students have learned four words based on spelling patterns, they and the teacher can incorporate them into functional use with other words the students know, words they like, and alternative words, as follows:

1. The teacher and students select out of all the words the students know the ones they need in order to write a sentence, paragraph, or short story. For example, a student may select from his or her file cards the words *the, is, a, red, he, she, and, has, car, his, have,* and *for*.

2. The teacher chooses words from an alternative word list (e.g., the Mann-Suiter Everyday Word List [Table 8-3]), introducing them one at a time and teaching them in a phrase or sentence, using a write-read approach.
3. The teacher allows the students to choose words they like (e.g., hot rod) and then teaches those words, one at a time, in a phrase or sentence, using a write-read approach.
4. The teacher combines the words from the first three categories with the four words based on spelling pattern (*cat, mat, pat, fat*).

STEP III—The Students Can Write Sentences and Then Paragraphs. Paragraph writing can be accomplished in three ways:

1. The teacher writes the first sentence and the student writes the next one, or vice versa. For example:
   Teacher: "Pat is a fat cat."
   Student: "The fat cat has a hot rod."
2. The student writes two sentences and the teacher writes the last one, or vice versa. For example:
   Student: "The cat is fat."
   Student: "He is with Pat in the hot rod."
   Teacher: "The red hot rod has a mat for the cat."
3. The student writes a whole paragraph based on the above vocabulary. For example:
   He has a hot rod. He is with Pat in his red car. Mat and Pat have the fat cat in the red car.

Words from each pattern should be developed into sentences, paragraphs, and then stories. In essence, the student is slowly developing a sight vocabulary.

(*Note:* Only one new thing should be introduced at a time, unless the students indicate through the learning process that they can cope with more.)

Step IV—The Students Can Develop Word Attack Skills through Oral Drill. Give the Mann-Suiter Alphabet-Speech Screen (page 54) to determine the students' sound-symbol relationship abilities (letter names and letter sounds). Note the production of the letter sounds. Are they "clean" or has there been faulty learning (e.g., "tuh" for *t*)?

Check to see if the students can blend (Mann-Suiter Visual Closure Screen [pages 42–46] and Auditory Closure Screen [page 51]).

Using the chalkboard, present a student with a spelling pattern and a consonant, as in Figure 8-23.

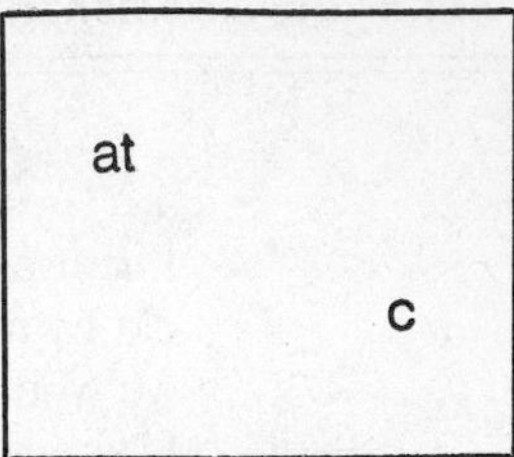

Figure 8-23 Spelling Pattern and Consonant

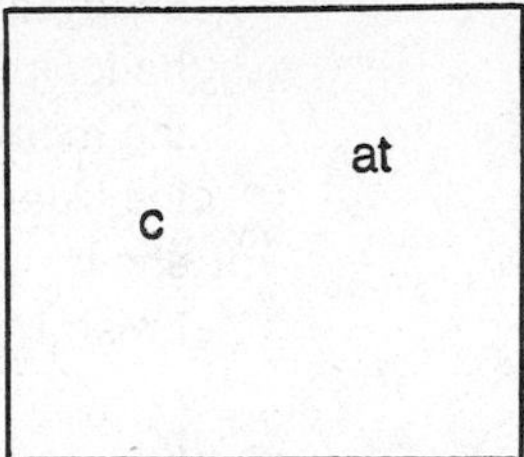

Figure 8-24 Consonant Closer to Spelling Pattern

Say, "If I put the "c" [letter sound] in front of the *at* [word], what word will it make?" If the student does not respond correctly, erase the *c* and place it closer to the pattern, as in Figure 8-24. Repeat the question. If the student still cannot respond, then place the *c* next to the *at*, making the word *cat*, and say, "See. C . . . at makes cat. You say it." Follow this with further blending activities, as blending is a problem area for the student. If the student responds correctly the first time, saying "cat," then say, "What word will be made if I put a "p" [sound] in front of the *at*?" If the response is "pat," then do the *f* sound and *m* sound. In teaching analysis and synthesis this way, *do not* use letter names, just letter sounds. (Letter names can be used in other situations.) When using letter sounds, be sure that they are used cleanly. *Do not* add a vowel sound on the end of a consonant (e.g., "tuh" for "t").

The same activity can be done without using a chalkboard in the following manner. Say, "Say the spelling pattern 'op.' " The student replies. Then say, "If I put an 'm' [sound] in front of 'op,' what word will it make?" A variation would be to say "op" and then "m" and then have the student make the word *mop*. Then say "p," and so on.

You will know that the student is beginning to develop analysis and synthesis ability when you write a pattern (e.g., *ate*) and, without your asking, the student says, "Mate, date, late."

The entire approach can be introduced to the students as a spelling or writing program. If the students do begin to expand their vocabulary, their reading will improve.

Step V—Students Can Develop New Sight Vocabulary by Adding Words from a New-Book Word List. The students and teacher can compare the students' baseline vocabulary (words they know) with the vo-

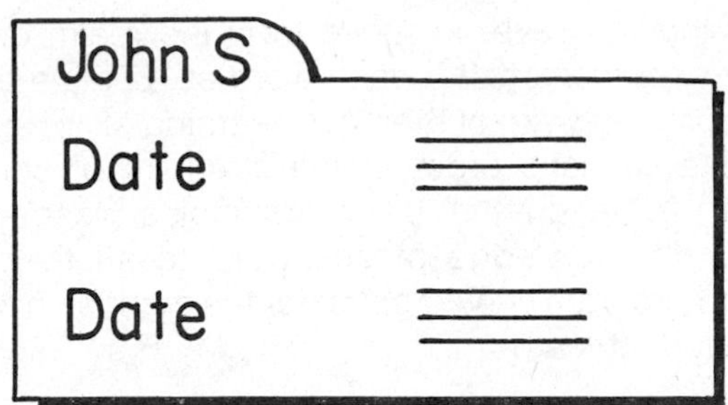

Figure 8-25

cabulary of a book they would like to read. Many readers have the vocabulary at the back of the book, so it is easy to compare the lists. Otherwise, a student may have to go through a book and make a list of all the words he or she cannot read. If the list of unknown words is too long, the book is too advanced for the learner. If the list is not too long, the words can be introduced into the reading program associatively, as in the previous examples. As the students learn the words through their write-to-read program, they can begin to read the books, reading only those pages that they can read with 100 percent success.

The students can put the new words on cards in a word box or write or type them on a folder. They should date each new word learned, or stabilized. (See Figure 8-25.) See pages 309–310 for alternative management systems for this kind of a program.

SPELLING

Spelling is a skill that can be developed with the reading program. Skill in reading does not necessarily assure skill in spelling, but it is axiomatic that most poor readers are also poor spellers. Spelling differs from reading in that spelling demands complete recall of the words to be spelled. It is recommended that the instructor select spelling words from the learner's independent reading vocabulary. If the learner has the fine motor skills to write the words, the reading, writing, and spelling activities can be coordinated.

In order to spell fluently, students must have the following:

1. A basic spelling vocabulary learned to the automatic level so that the students do not have to stop to think
2. Ability to apply spelling generalizations to unknown words
3. Knowledge of the contextual meaning of the word to be spelled (*ate, eight*)
4. A unique method of learning new words, which includes much practice in listening to, saying, and writing words
5. Knowledge of the consistency of letter-sound relationships in the English language

The following areas of inadequacy may affect spelling:

1. Speech problems associated with articulation or faulty patterns, such as saying "gonna" for *going*
2. Auditory problems with sound discrimination or memory-sequencing
3. Visual problems with symbol discrimination or memory-sequencing
4. Visual-motor problems affecting ability to make the correct motor pattern for a particular symbol (causing reversals, inversions, and inappropriate spacing)

For a spelling program to be successful, it must emphasize good study skills, good study habits, and motivation through success and interest.

At the turn of the century, spelling was taught by rote memorization. The assumption was that each word required a separate act of learning. Today, it is felt that students should be helped to identify patterns in words, such as the *and* in *sand* and *hand*. Students should be taught to apply these spelling patterns instead of using a different strategy for each word learned. This method takes advantage of the associative processes and stabilizes the patterns of spelling in the learners' minds. Eventually, this method must be converted as much as possible into more or less reflective behavior.

Prerequisite Skills

Students should have certain basic skills before beginning a spelling program. Too often, poor spelling is the result of learning inappropriate methods. In teaching spelling, make sure the students are able to discriminate sounds and articulate English speech sounds. Note cultural or speech deviations, and be realistic in your expectation for rapid change in this area. Students should also be able to discriminate visually between letters and be able to write upper and lowercase letters of the alphabet. They need sufficient strength and control of the fine muscles of the hand and arm to control and manipulate a writing instrument if a writing-to-reading-and-spelling approach is being used.

Auditory and visual memory-sequencing and closure skills are possibly the most crucial to spelling ability. To learn to spell fluently, students must be able to remember sounds of letters in isolation as well as how to blend them into whole words. Once the students' phoneme-grapheme relationship becomes consistent, they will be able to use the following skills:

1. Auditory-analysis (to hear a word as a whole and analyze it into separate sound units)
2. Auditory-synthesis (to hear separate speech sounds and blend them into a whole word)

After the auditory analysis and synthesis have been mastered, visual memory helps the students select the *c* for spelling *cat* rather than *k*. Later, they may learn the rule that the hard *c* sound is usually spelled as a *k* only when followed by *i* or *e*, and that the word *kangaroo* does not follow the rule because it is a foreign word. Students with memory problems have difficulty in remembering spelling rules. The students need a great deal of practice using words functionally, as in writing, before they can revisualize the words. If students in a spelling program are still visually or auditorily confusing *b*, and *d*, or *m*, and *w*, they may have difficulty moving from sheer rote memory to seeing the consistent language patterns that do exist in the English language. They should eventually hear and see that the *and* in *hand* is the same *and* that is in *sand*, without having to learn each word separately.

The goal of spelling instruction is to help the students develop as automatic a motor response as possible to the words they hear or visualize in their mind's eye. Developing an automatic motor response is different from taking a spelling test in that there are no external clues, such as using the word in a sentence; and the students must reauditorize the sequence of the sounds in their mind.

Recognizing a word in reading does not mean that the students have noticed it in sufficient detail to spell it correctly. Students need to develop a distinct image of the word so that they can recall it at will. Great differences are found in individual recall. Some people get only very vague images, or none at all, and actually remember words in terms of audio-images, recalling a word with sound (through lip and throat movements), or even with the movement of the hand in writing the word. Other people, with good visual memories, remember words by actually revisualizing the letters.

One of the prerequisites to good spelling is a distinct and accurate perception of a word and the ability to describe it in detail. Students with a learning difficulty must be taught through meaningful repetition until the process becomes so automatic that they can write the word without conscious attention to the details of its spelling.

All students have their own unique ways of learning, and if they are ever to move from the realm of rote memory, or memorizing each word as a single entity, they must be aware of their own learning style, as well as the systematic order in the structure of our language. To teach the basic principles needed for transfer of knowledge of one word to another, any spelling program should consider the manner in which each student learns.

Developing a Spelling Program

Besides a knowledge of how each student learns best, a teacher must have a spelling program that avoids introducing too many different vowel sounds at one time. The program should be simple, starting with letters and letter groups that most consistently represent the sounds of language.

Most commercial spelling programs are not applicable to students with learning problems because they are usually based on sets of words grouped around subjects. Little consideration is given to being consistent in the way words are presented.

Spelling programs could very easily follow the linguistic reading series presently available. By developing a language-spelling program around the reading series used, the teacher would be consistently using the same vowel sounds through writing, spelling, and reading activities. This would avoid the biggest problem most first graders face, which is "vowel cluttering." Occasionally, students are unable to develop their cognitive processing ability because too many different sounds of the same vowel are presented close together, causing vowel cluttering. (The *a* in *man* in the reading lesson becomes confused with the *a* in *Jane* on the same page and the *a* in *all* in the spelling lesson.) A combined reading-spelling program is also useful because reading should be reinforced through a motor response such as building words out of movable letters, which is also spelling.

With simple variations, most linguistic reading series follow a prescribed order of presenting words and can be an excellent outline for a spelling program. Most learners are ready for formal spelling when they have finished their first preprimers and can read simple CVC (consonant–vowel–consonant) pattern words without hesitation.

The following spelling program outline is recommended for first-level readers:

1. First introduce words of a simple CVC pattern (consonant–vowel–consonant). Have the students analyze them and then put them together using cards, plastic letters, or wooden letters.

2. Short vowel sounds should never be taught alone, but with a consonant (e.g., *c at*). The first spelling lesson could look like this:
   a. Select the family to be taught: *at*
   b. Select five CVC words (start with nouns if possible): *cat, bat, hat, mat, rat.*
   c. Include a simple sight word that can be used with the nouns in simple phrases: *a fat cat.*

   Note: The teacher should not try to teach all *at* words at one time.

The second spelling lesson would cover another short *a* family, such as *ad* with the CVC words *lad, mad, sad,* and *had,* plus the sight words *I* and *see*.

Note: Remain at each level until the students have attained absolute mastery. It is very important to overteach at this level to insure that the students have made these basic sound-symbol relationships.

In teaching lesson two, reach back into lesson one and continue to use the words in phrases. Introduce one short vowel sound at a time, including from three to five CVC words and one sight word in a lesson. After mastering the short vowels at this level, the student is ready to move on to more complex patterns. Introduce the following:

1. Words of a simple CVCC pattern, using short vowel sounds ending with a double *ff, ll, zz,* or *ss* (for example, *tiff, tell, buzz,* and *kiss*)
2. Words having two-letter blends with short vowels, such as *plan, blot, chat, bring,* and *clap*
3. Digraphs (*ch, th, sh, wh*) with short vowels, such as *chat, that, shop, shut,* and *when*
4. Three-letter blends with short vowels, as in *string, spring,* and *strap*
5. Long vowels (CVC words with an added *e*, such as *cap–cape; hat–hate; mat–mate*)
6. Long vowels with two-letter blends, as in *spade* and *stove*
7. Long vowels with digraphs, as in *shade* and *while*
8. Long vowels with three-letter blends, as in *stroke* and *strike*
9. Second sounds of *c, g,* and *s*, as in *city, garage, was*
10. *R*-controlled vowels, such as *ar, er, ir, or, ur*
11. Vowel digraphs, such as *ee* in *teen, ea* in *bread, ay* in *play*
12. Silent letters, such as *h* in *honest, t* in *listen,* and *k* in *knee*
13. Highly irregular words—impossible to decode—such as *said, the* and *was*
14. Root (base) words and affixes such as *re, de,* and *bi*
15. Words on the syntactic level of language, such as *bear–bare;* and *two–too–to*

In teaching spelling, always try to move from one known element to the new or unknown element, adding to the sound–symbol pattern already known.

How Does Each Student Learn Best?

Before teaching spelling, find out which combination of input produces the best output. The spelling suggestions given in textbooks are not suited to all students, and it is up to the teacher to help students understand that they do have an individualized method of learning how to spell.

Students who have difficulty in learning to spell should be taught spelling through their strongest channel. Sometimes students having trouble with spelling hide their spelling errors behind a facade of illegible handwriting.

Visual Channel Problems

Students with visual memory-sequencing problems may learn best through an auditory, or sound, spelling approach. The following methods are suggested:

1. Say the word, spell it, and then say it again. Next, have the student say the word and spell it. You repeat the sequence, and then have the student repeat it two or three more times before writing the word from memory.
2. Some students need a slightly different approach from method one. Say the word, spell it, and then say it again. Have the student write the word, and then you correct it. The student then writes it two or three more times and finally turns the paper over and writes it again.

Auditory Channel Problems

Students with auditory memory-sequencing problems may learn best through a more visual approach. The following methods are suggested:

1. Show the student the word on a card or list and say the word. Have the student look at the word, say it, spell it, and say it again. Remove the word and have the student spell it from memory. After spelling it two or three times more, the student writes it from memory and checks the word against the stimulus card.

2. Some students need a slightly different approach from method one. Show the word and name it. Have the student look at the word and then copy it on paper. The word is then covered and the student writes from memory and then checks it two or three more times. After spelling it two or three times more, the student writes it from memory and then checks the word against the stimulus card.

Both Auditory and Visual Channel Problems

Students who have problems with both auditory and visual memory-sequencing need a multisensory approach. The following method is suggested: Show the word on a card, name the word, and spell it out orally. Have the student look at the word, spell it, and then write it on paper. Cover the word. The student then spells it orally from memory several times, writes it from memory two times, turns the paper over, writes the word from memory, and checks it with the word card. Many repetitions may be necessary.

Note: Multisensory input is not always the best method for all students Find the simplest approach that appears to be the most productive for each learner.

Along with a visual-motor approach, include a great deal of practice in listening, saying words, and writing. Some of the manipulative material that can be utilized to reinforce spelling are these:

1. Three-by-five-inch white cards with associative picture clues on the back
2. Clay formed into letters
3. Plastic, wooden, felt, or beaded letters
4. Sand trays
5. Fingerpaint
6. Magnetic letters
7. Typewriter

Spelling Activities

As the number of words known increases, the learners may be evaluated through the dictation of longer word lists and more complex sentences. To prepare the learners for the tasks of listening, spelling, and writing lists of words or sentences, use the tape recorder. Many students are under great pressure to perform on a spelling test. By listening to the instructor's voice at a slower rate of dictation and with a smaller number of words, learners can be successfully prepared for group evaluation when the rate and amount are increased. After listening to the tape and spelling the words, the learners can listen to the words being spelled aloud and correct their own paper. If the words are not spelled aloud on the tape, the students can refer to a folder containing the list to check the answer, or they can work with a peer tutor or volunteer.

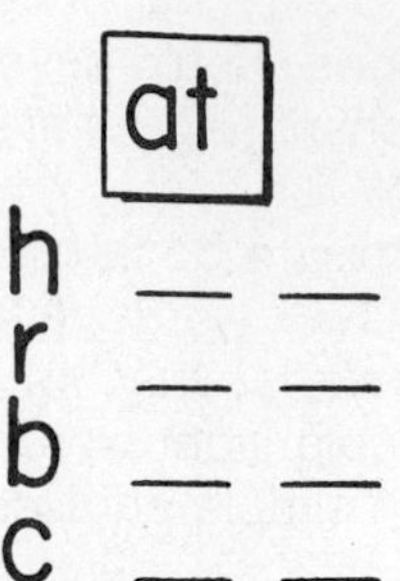

Figure 8-26

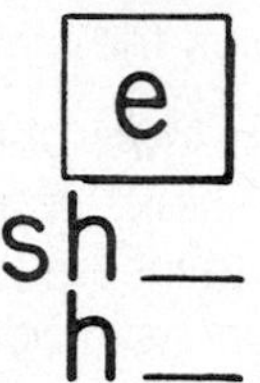

Figure 8-27

OPTIONS FOR EVALUATION AND PRACTICE

The following spelling activities will provide additional reinforcement. The students build words by using spelling patterns and consonants in combination with rebus (picture) or associative clues:

1. Write a list of incomplete words of a particular pattern on the chalkboard (Figure 8-26). The learner uses the spelling pattern card [at], writes the letters on the blank lines, and says the words.
2. Prepare acetates for use on the overhead projector, or make duplicator masters for the learner to complete (Figure 8-27). If the learners cannot write in the missing letter, they can use movable cardboard, wood, or plastic letters.
3. The learner completes words by writing or placing a movable letter on the line. The associative picture clue determines the correct response (Figure 8-28). The learner who cannot remember the correct sound to write on the line should be encouraged to use the self-checking vocabulary cards.
4. The learner recalls words using the patterns and then draws a picture of the word in the box beside the word (Figure 8-29). Nonsense words should not be encouraged. The learner who cannot recall all of

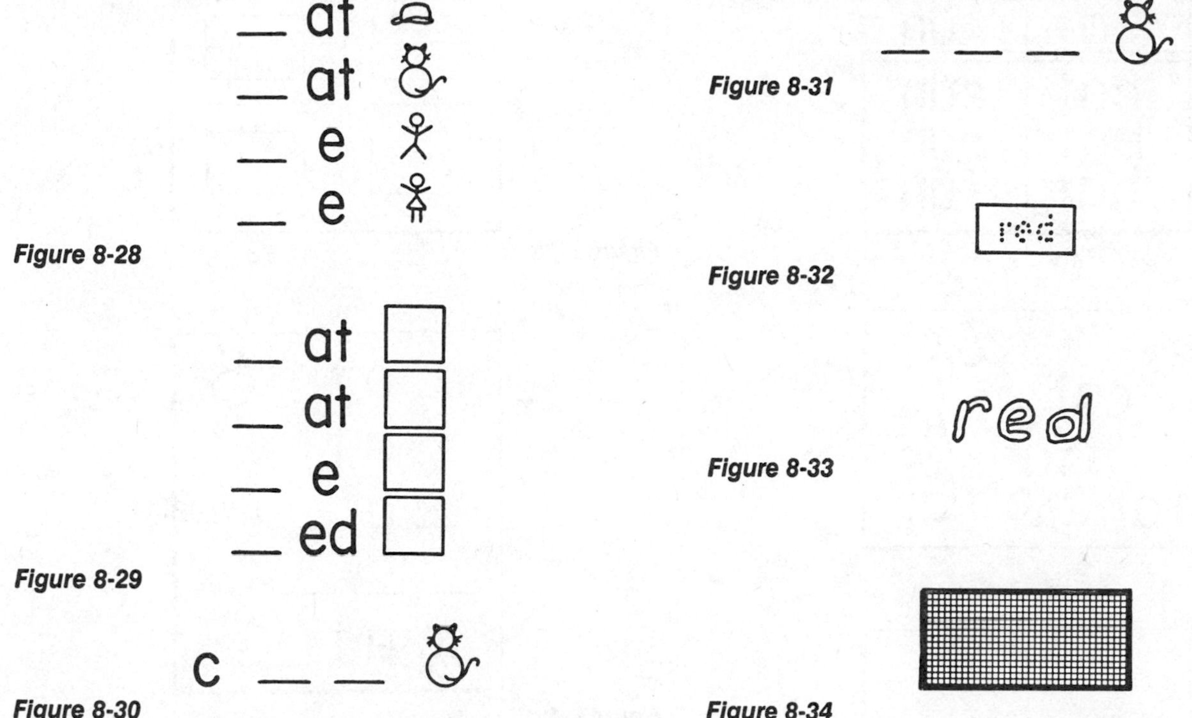

Figure 8-28

Figure 8-29

Figure 8-30

Figure 8-31

Figure 8-32

Figure 8-33

Figure 8-34

the words of a pattern can use the vocabulary word cards.

5. The learner has a word family card [at] on the desk, but no word cards. The instructor says, "Let's write *cat*." The learner can look at the card, if necessary, as an aid in working up to total recall of the word.
6. The instructor dictates, "cat." The students are shown the initial consonant and a picture (Figure 8-30) to aid them in revisualizing the word.
7. The instructor dictates, "cat." An associative picture (Figure 8-31) aids the learner in recalling the word.
8. The instructor holds up an object (e.g., cat) and the learner writes the word on the lines.

   ______ ______ ______

9. By the time short phrases, such as "a cat," are dictated, the learner has moved from completing the blanks to total recall.

TRACING AND WRITING IN SPELLING

1. Write a color word on a strip of cardboard. The learner traces it with a colored felt-tip pen (Figure 8-32).
2. Cover words that are to be traced with a piece of acetate. The learner traces them with a grease pencil.
3. Cover words that are to be traced with tracing paper. The learner uses a clipboard to hold the paper in place and traces the word with a pencil.
4. Fingerpaint can be used for tracing words.
5. Roll out thin strips of clay and form the letters of the word to be reviewed (Figure 8-33). The learner traces the word with a finger.
6. Prepare an 8″ × 10″ piece of copper window screening (Figure 8-34) by binding the edges with electrical or masking tape. (Plastic screen can be used, but it is softer, and the letters will not be as raised and as clear as they would be if copper screening were used.) Over the screen place a 5″ × 8″ piece of newsprint. (Notebook or typing paper can be used, but they are firmer, and the letters will not be as raised and as clear as they would be if newsprint were used.) Using a black crayon, write a word on the paper in plain manuscript or cursive. (The raised letters can be easily traced with the finger.) Say the word, then trace it, saying each part as you trace it, and then finish by saying the whole word. The student then says the word, traces it with a finger or fingers (saying each part of the word while tracing it), and then says the word. The student repeats this process as many times as is necessary (usually five times in the beginning), or until he or she can write the word correctly without looking at the copy. The word should always be traced with the student's finger or fingers, not a pencil.

at	un
cat	sun
bat	run
hat	fun

Figure 8-35

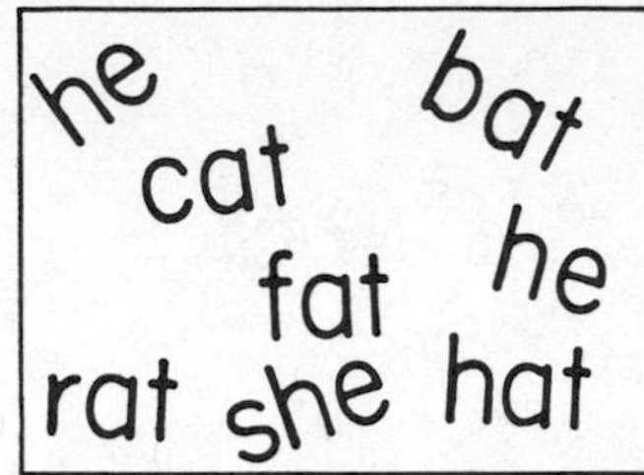

Figure 8-36

a red cat	a fat cat
a big hat	a rat

Figure 8-37

It is important that students trace until they can write the word without copy. The word should always be written as a unit. In case of error, the incorrect written form must be covered or crossed out. The student then looks at the word again and traces it, if necessary, before attempting to write it again from memory.

The student then writes the word again as a whole. Never allow a student to erase the incorrect part of a word and write in the correction. To be successful, the student must write the word as a whole. The very act of erasing and correcting single letters or syllables within the word breaks it up into meaningless parts.

As students trace words, they slowly develop the ability to learn them with fewer and fewer tracings. Eventually the students reach the stage where they can look at a word, say it to themselves, and then write it.

The following can be used on acetates for use on the overhead projector or on duplicator master activity sheets:

1. The learners will copy the *at* and *un* words in the appropriate column (Figure 8-35).
2. The learners will trace the *e* pattern in red and the *at* pattern in blue (Figure 8-36).

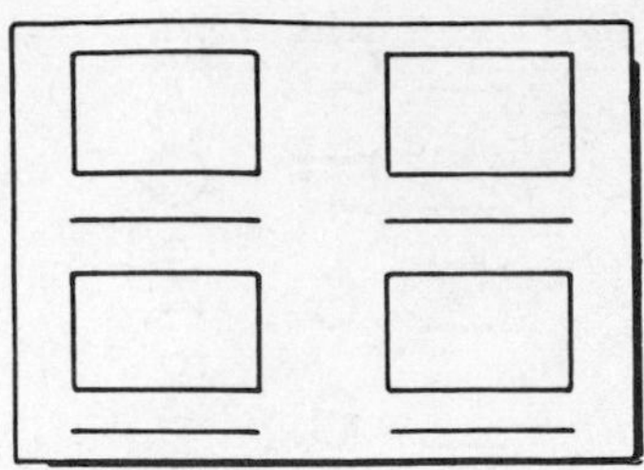

Figure 8-38

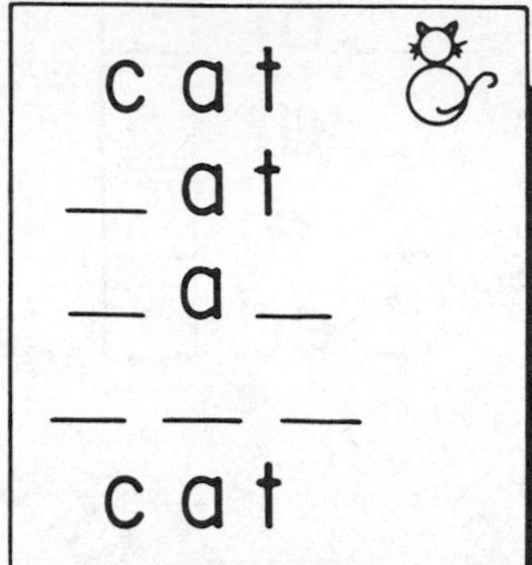

Figure 8-39

c a b

Legend

a = ☼ d = ∧
b = ≋ e = ∅
c = ✳ f = ≥

Figure 8-40

3. The learners will illustrate the phrases in Figure 8-37.
4. The learners will label pictures (Figure 8-38).
5. The learners will complete the words in Figure 8-39.
6. The learners will translate the spelling words into a code (e.g., an original code [Figure 8-40], the International Code, Braille, the Flag Code). The learners will decode exchanged codes and lists.

VISUAL MEMORY AND SPELLING. Use tachistoscopic devices, such as turning on and off the overhead projector to flash words. The learners look at the word, see it in their mind's eye, and then write it down.

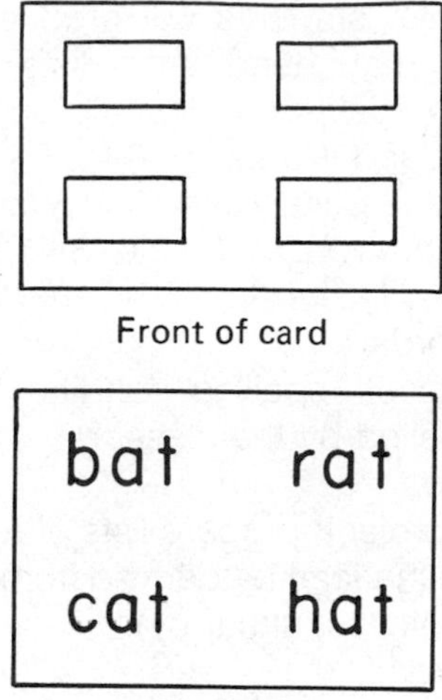

Figure 8-41

SELF-CHECKING SPELLING ACTIVITIES

1. The learners will cut out pictures of words on the spelling list and paste them on index cards 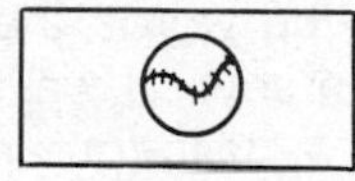 . On the other side of the card, they or the instructor will print the word **ball** .

   The learners can use these cards as flash cards by looking at the picture on the front of the card, saying the word, and then writing the word on paper, a small chalkboard, or an erasable slate. By turning the card over, they can compare the words and check their own spelling.

   The same cards can be kept in a recipe box containing alphabetical dividers. For a phonics review, the learners can put all the pictures beginning with the same sound behind the correct letter.

   As the students learn the order of the alphabet, they can arrange the word cards in alphabetical order.
2. The learners or the instructor can design self-checking spelling cards to review spelling patterns (Figure 8-41). On the front of the card draw or paste pictures to illustrate the words that contain a pattern. On the reverse side, write the words. The learners can exchange picture cards and spell the words illustrated.
3. Prepare cards for spelling patterns (e.g., *at, ed, et*). On the front of each card, write one pattern, on the reverse side of the card, write the words that have been introduced that include the pattern. (See Figure 8-42.)

   The learners write as many words as possible from memory and then turn the card over to self-check.

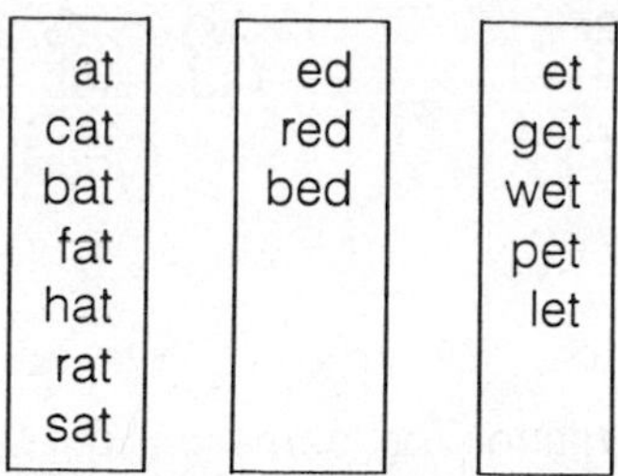

Figure 8-42 Reverse Side of Pattern Cards

Learners can take turns calling out the words on the reverse side of the cards, which the other students write or spell orally.

COMPREHENSION SPELLING ACTIVITIES

As words from the learners' reading program are incorporated into the spelling program, the instructor should review not only the correct pronunciation of the words, but also the meanings of the words. By using only the word cards with an associative clue on the reverse side and reading the words in the context of the reading material provided, the learners may not be fully aware of the multiple meanings of the vocabulary words. Therefore, a discussion of the various meanings of words and their uses in different types of sentences should be an integral part of the spelling lesson. The following activities can be utilized to reinforce comprehension skills:

1. Riddles. Write a list of the spelling words on the chalkboard. Say, "I am thinking of an animal that lives in a cave. What is it?" The learner says the word and spells it ("bat, *b-a-t*"). The students can take turns asking other riddles.
2. Missing Words. On the chalkboard, a duplicator master, or the overhead projector write incomplete sentences. The learner fills in the blanks with the spelling words

   run fun sun

   It is ______ to play with the dog.
   The ______ is hot.
   Can you ______ and jump?
3. Crossword Puzzles. The learner can design simple to complex crossword puzzles using the spelling words.
4. Classification. Dictate groups of spelling words. The learner will cross out the words that do not belong and will discuss the category. For example:

   birds dogs blue yellow

   cats ~~was~~ ~~is~~ red

   (animals) (colors)

Figure 8-43

5. Creative Writing. The learner will cut out an interesting picture from a magazine, color a picture in a coloring book, or draw a picture and paste the illustration on a larger sheet of paper. Then the learner will write a sentence or short paragraph about the picture, using the spelling words. Creative writing should be a relaxing activity with emphasis on getting ideas on paper first and later proofing for spelling. To aid the student who cannot spell the "other" words needed to write stories, prepare with the student or the class a chart of words that the student can read and may need for a particular topic. For example: Thanksgiving–turkey, Pilgrims, Indians.
6. Dictionary. Use the dictionary to discuss definitions, multiple meanings, synonyms, abbreviations, and plurals. The learner can use the information to design simple crossword puzzles.

PLURALS

Provide objects, pictures, and word cards for the learners to practice the concept of singular and plural. For example:

Place one toy dog and three toy dogs in groups (Figure 8-43).

By using the word cards, the students can label the groups.

If the cards have associative clues on the reverse side, they are self-checking.

Because the plural words are used in oral spelling tests or in sentence dictation, some learners may need practice in listening to the endings of words. Use a tape recorder to provide auditory experiences for the learners.

SPELLING OTHER WORD LISTS

As the learners become more proficient in spelling, they will need additional words to successfully complete reports, themes, etc. The following additional words can be used to expand the learners' spelling lists. Copies of these word lists can be placed in each student's spelling folder or spelling notebook.

1. Subject Level Words
   Prepare word lists from Science, Math, Social Studies. Older students will gradually add these words and may need such lists of words for themes.
2. Frequently Used Words
   Use the Mann-Suiter Everyday Word List (Table 8-3) and Phrase List (Table 8-4) for additional practice.
3. Irregular Words
   Prepare lists of "spelling bandits" that are most often misspelled by the class.
4. Similar Words
   As a class project, prepare lists of root words and other words that can be derived from the root (e.g., happy, happiness, unhappy).
5. Interest Words
   Some words are personalized according to the student's individual needs, interests, and hobbies.

METHODS THAT AID RETENTION OF SPELLING WORDS

Students with learning problems need a consistent review program to help them retain the words they have learned. Review can be done in several ways, either as an individual program or as a class (group) program.

Individual Approach

Give weekly tests (on Fridays, for example), and give review tests a few days later (on Mondays, for example) to see which words the student has remembered. Use the words the student did not retain, with a specified number of new words (the number would differ with each student), for that week's lesson.

Every four weeks give a review test of words taught to see which ones are still unknown, and include those with the ongoing program.

A student in this type of program would not be expected to learn a specified number of words in a given period of time and may not be expected to complete one grade's spelling book for the school year.

Classroom (Group) Approach. If the initial spelling test indicates that some students are still having trouble with words from the previous year, but their scores are not low enough to have them repeat a spelling level, the following method is one way of reinforcing spelling words from the previous grade. Using the previous grade's spelling book, write the words as they are presented (five to a card) on 5″ × 7″ index cards cut from tagboard or a manila folder. Number the cards in order and put them in a file for the students to use.

Regardless of the number of words normally presented in each lesson in the ongoing spelling program, begin by giving the students no more than five to seven new words a week while simultaneously requiring them to review one or two of the cards with the previous grade's words. Keep them moving as fast as possible through the review words while maintaining an ongoing program with the words at the next level. Some students will go faster than others.

HANDWRITING

Difficulties in handwriting fall into two main categories: (1) factors that are student based and (2) factors arising from an inadequate instructional program.

1. *Student-based difficulties*
   a. Lack of readiness for beginning writing may be a factor in that the student may exhibit fine motor dysfunction of the hands and fingers or poor eye-hand coordination.
   b. The student may have a visual acuity problem and need glasses.
   c. The student cannot grasp the pencil correctly or has an awkward writing position. He or she may have crippled hands or a spastic condition.
   d. The student may not have established a dominant hand. He or she may be switching from left to right.
   e. The student may have difficulty retaining visual symbols rather than having poor visual-motor coordination.
   f. The student may have an emotional problem that can easily show up in a deteriorating handwriting. He or she could also be physically ill.
   g. The student may have no interest in writing and be unwilling to practice. He or she may exhibit indifference to established minimum standards.
2. *Program-based difficulties*
   a. The student may have been started in a formal writing program before he or she was ready. Possibly the student is still undecided as to which hand to use.
   b. There could be insufficient interest on the part of the student due to undifferentiated group drill. The wrong positioning of paper might be a factor.
   c. Not enough care taken with initial teaching may have been a factor. The student may have been allowed to practice errors. Too much practice done without supervision can cause difficulties.
   d. A poorly planned transitional program from manuscript to cursive writing may be the cause of the problem in older students.

Screening for Developing a Writing Program in Primary Grades

Individual or group screening can be used to aid in determining the visual-motor and fine motor development of students.

A screening of visual-motor and fine motor skills serves the following purposes:

1. Indicates the students who lack readiness.
2. Identifies the students who have not developed a dominant hand and are still switching from left to right.
3. Indicates the students with a poor pencil grasp.
4. Identifies the students who have good visual-motor coordination and are ready for a full writing program.

Mann-Suiter Visual Motor Screen

Successful completion of the designs of the Mann-Suiter Visual Motor Screen (page 36) represents minimal standards for success in handwriting. Please note the normative data given on page 35. Give each student a copy of the screen and ask him or her to copy the designs to the left three times. This screen can also be used with groups. While the students are doing the screens, walk around the class, noting on a pad the left-handed students. Note the names of the students with a poor pencil grasp, especially the students who grasp the pencil too tightly or hold it back too far. This information can then be put on the screening sheets.

Readiness for Handwriting

For the younger students in kindergarten through first grade, training should begin with indirect preparation for writing. Fine motor dysfunction is not uncommon in these students; therefore, they need manipulative experiences designed to strengthen the muscles necessary for writing and pencil control.

TRAINING SEQUENCE

Activities that may help to develop fine motor skills necessary for writing are suggested below:

1. Cutting and manipulation of small objects such as knobs on puzzle parts, nuts and bolts, and caps on small bottles. Finger painting and clay modeling help to strengthen muscles for hand and finger control.

2. Solid, smooth, wooden geometric forms, △ ○ ▱, help the student to concentrate on different shapes and to feel, as well as to see, the difference between a square and a triangle, for example.
3. Templates or metal insets (#1 ⊡ #2 ⊡) will help perfect fine motor skills—hand and finger control. These can be used as follows:
   a. The learners start with frame #1 and trace around the inside with a finger. They then trace two or three times with a soft colored pencil or plastic crayon.
   b. Then, using a different colored pencil or crayon, the students fill in the center with short strokes ||| ↓ always made from top to bottom.
4. Scissor Activities. The cutting exercises outlined in Chapter 7, page 182, are helpful.
5. Material requiring coloring, cutting, and pasting can be used. Start with very-easy-to-color material that can be cut out and pasted. Slowly move into more difficult activities as the students progress.
6. Tracing sheets of interesting animals and objects makes a good individual activity. Clipboards and sheets of acetate or large plastic sheets that can be placed on a desk top can be used for tracing.
7. Duplicator master material requiring the student to connect dots to form a geometric shape or picture can be used.

GRASPING OF PENCIL

Good writing starts with proper grasping of the pencil. If the students cannot hold the pencil correctly, watch to see if they have trouble grasping other things. If they do have a problem, help them find a way to hold their pencils by using tape or a rubber band, putting the pencil through a rubber ball, or using any other aid. Be sure to place a note in the students' record indicating that they have been taught an unorthodox method.

In teaching students to hold a pencil, always give directions through their strongest learning channel and try not to combine the *VAT* (Visual, Auditory, Tactual) all at once. You may be overloading them with too much input.

1. *If the students have a visual deficit,* they ought to be taught through the auditory channel. The students should be given clear oral directions as to how to hold a pencil. They may need to keep their eyes shut as they grasp the pencil.
2. *If the students have an auditory deficit,* mark the pencil to show them where to hold it or else put some other "stop" in the proper place.
3. *If the students have an auditory-visual deficit,* ask them to close their eyes and then without talking, mold their hands around their pencils. Explain what you are going to do before doing it, and then explain again afterwards. Do not speak while you are molding the students' hands around their pencils.

Beginning Handwriting

In teaching a student how to write, you must be more direct, moving from large-scale gross movements to the necessary finer movements. The teaching process starts with the following:

1. Large templates that can be used at the chalkboard or on large sheets of paper (these help the student to feel, as well as to see, the differences between different geometric shapes)
2. Small templates that can be used at the desk
3. Scribble-scrabble on the blackboard, first with both hands and later with the dominant hand (for example, *eeee uuuu eee*)
4. Tracing over large printed letters, such as *a, b, c, d,* on a plasticized sheet using a washable crayon or grease pencil
5. Writing letters in a tray of damp sand with a finger, or writing in a tray of soft clay with a stick
6. Writing with a pencil on paper

Note: Be sure that the lines on the paper are clear.

Manuscript Writing

Manuscript writing is based entirely upon circles and sticks, or lines. Before starting to teach, consider the maturation level in terms of the previously mentioned skills of each of the students. Successful copying of circles is normative from about age 3. By first grade, it is important not only that the students can copy a circle but also that they produce it a specific way. By age 5, most girls can make a circle from the top down in a counterclockwise direction. For most boys this form is normative at 5½ years of age. After age 6, about 90% of both boys and girls start their circle from the top and go down in a counterclockwise direction. The one exception to this progression is left-handed students. Lefties may be as old as 9 years before a top-to-bottom counterclockwise circle is normative. The difficult part of making a circle is the return. The use of templates helps students to develop this ability.

Left-handed students' papers should always be turned so that the top points toward the right front corner of the desk. The students should also be taught

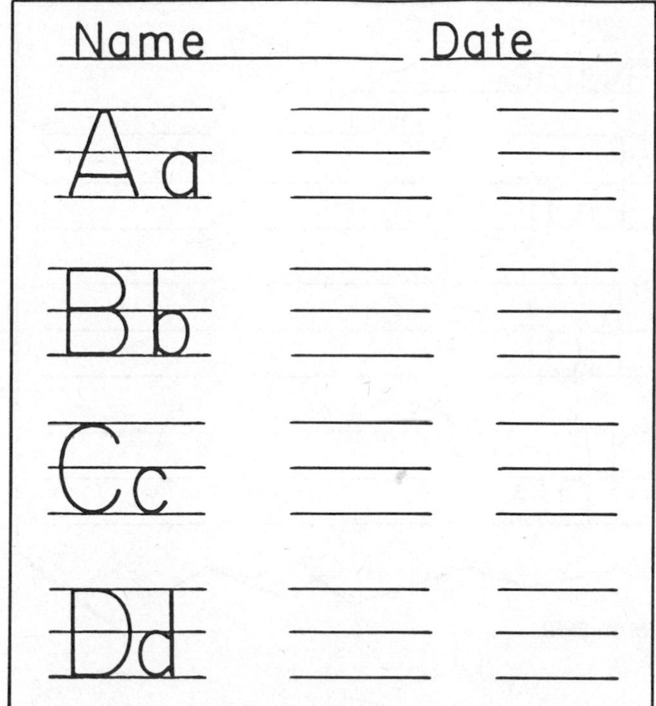

Figure 8-44 Sheet #1, Letters A-F

to grip their pencils farther away from the writing point than is normal for a right-handed student and to keep their hands below that which they are writing. (This prevents smearing and they can see what they have written.)

Physical comfort must always be considered, so the seating of left-handed students in the classroom is important. They should be seated at the left side of the room facing the chalkboard in order to copy material from the board more easily. Some students are slow in developing handedness. While dominant handedness is usually observable at the age of three, in some students it may not be fully developed until the age of eight.

WRITING THE ALPHABET. Many students have trouble learning to write the alphabet. The following are some suggestions for students at various stages of development.

Partial Alphabet Sheets. For students who have trouble both saying and writing the alphabet, the following method is suggested. Seven letters of the alphabet are taught at a time until they are known. (This number can be varied.) The students do *not* write the alphabet across the sheet, but down the page (Figure 8-44). This forces them to say the letters and write them in a sequence. After the students have written the alphabet down the sheet once, their work

Figure 8-45 Actual Size of the Letters and Lines

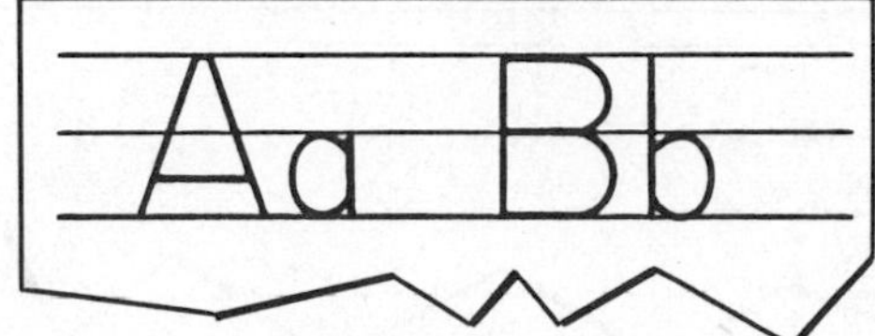

Figure 8-46

Figure 8-47

can be checked for accuracy so that they won't copy a poorly produced letter when writing down the second time. Figure 8-45 shows the actual size of the letters.

Copying the Whole Alphabet. For students who have learned to write the alphabet but still need practice, the following types of activities can be used.

1. In the activity in Figure 8-46 the students see the whole alphabet just as they have been taught it, and they copy to the immediate right of each pair of letters.
2. In the activity in Figure 8-47 the students see the alphabet delineated into capital and lowercase letters. The students copy the alphabet immediately below the written letters.
3. In the activity in Figure 8-48 the students see the alphabet written at the top of the sheet and copy it as a whole at the bottom. Activity sheets can be made with either capital or lowercase letters.

Figure 8-48

4. Students who successfully write the alphabet from memory can use activity sheets that require them to fill in missing letters.

Writing Must Have Meaning

As soon as possible, even at the readiness stage, writing should say something. Initially, students need to concentrate chiefly on learning the correct order of making the strokes. Right after this comes spacing. Whole words that have real meaning for the students and are easy to write are the best with which to start. Linguistic readers are well suited to this approach and will enable the students to begin writing that which they are already reading.

Until such time as the learners are able to write words from memory, they should have a copy or a model from which to write. The copy should be on the same kind of paper that the students use, although as the students improve they can copy phrases and sentences out of their reading books. Ten minutes at a time is usually enough writing for the younger students. Speed is never emphasized at this stage, and writing should always be supervised. Copywork from the chalkboard should be avoided in the early stages, because it forces constant refocusing of the eyes.

WORD ACTIVITY SHEETS

Begin with whole words that the students understand and that are easy to write. The beginning students should write from a model. The students should not just write words across the page. The words should be written one at a time *down* the page. (See Figure 8-49.) The words will have more meaning if the students have to stop and look at them before writing.

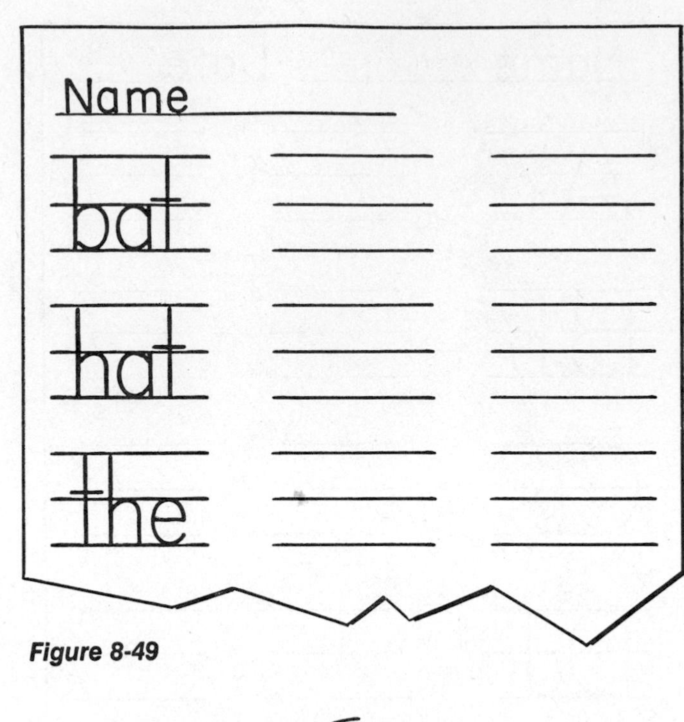

Figure 8-49

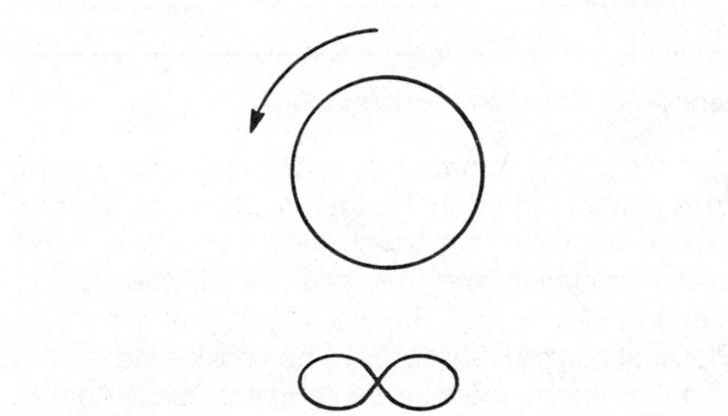

Figure 8-50

Cursive Writing

Many students experience difficulty learning to write in cursive. For students who are having problems, the following methods have been successful.

TRAINING FOR CURSIVE WRITING

1. Chalkboard Activity. The students begin with exercises at the chalkboard that can develop readiness for cursive writing. Begin with circles and figure eights (Figure 8-50), then go to *//*, *l's*, *e's*, and *le* combinations as fast as the students can handle them. Build in the strokes needed for the general writing program.
2. Chalkboards Used for Desk Work. Paint the designs shown in the preceding item on small chalkboards that the students can use at their desks.

The students can then practice by tracing over these smaller models.

3. Dittos or teacher-made activity sheets. For starting writing dittos and activity sheets can be used to teach the same designs as above. Encourage the student to write smaller. If writing smaller is too difficult at first, begin using first grade paper and then work toward the transitional paper and finally the third grade paper.

Students experiencing difficulty with initial attempts to make *lll* may need remedial practice with stencil forms. The following techniques are suggested.

1. Chalkboard Activity. Use chalk of different colors. Have the student make this stroke / with one color, then take the second color and complete the *l* (i.e., *l*). At this stage do not connect the *l's*.
2. Chalkboards Used for Desk Work. Use a desk chalkboard with the *l* pattern painted on it. Give the students two pieces of chalk of different colors and have them make the first stroke with one color, put it down, take the second color, and complete the tracing of the *l*. A pattern of smaller connected *l's* will help them feel the rhythm of the writing.
3. Dittos or Teacher-Made Activity Sheets. Use the same technique as in item 2, above. Colored pencils are used in place of chalk.

PROBLEMS IN CURSIVE WRITING

Any program, whether beginning or remedial, should stress good letter formation. The following letters cause the most trouble:

r that looks like an *n*
a that looks like an *o*
a that looks like a *u*
a that looks like a *ci*
e that looks like an *i*
i not dotted that looks like an *e*
b tnat iooks like an *li*
d that looks like a *cl*
t uncrossed and looped like an *l*

One very effective way to help students achieve better letter formation is to use connected print script (see Table 8-5, page 229). In *Language Skills in Elementary Education*, Paul Anderson gives detailed instructions on how this method can be used to help students in beginning cursive make the transition from manuscript to cursive writing.[7] This is also an excellent way of remediating a student who has developed poor writing habits.

Lowercase letters should be introduced first in the following order:

l, a, d, t, u, n, m, h, k
w, e, b, v, x, y, j, f, s,
p, r, c, i, g, o, q, and z.

The letters *b, e, f, k, r, s,* and *z* must be taught specifically. Capital letters are always practiced in usage. Always use whole words in this approach, and watch any word with an *n* in it, as this requires different spacing. Another letter that can cause confusion is *g*, as it changes with connections.

Handwriting Screen

Visual-motor skills generally develop early in most students and tend to be sequential. Three primary problem areas are evident in students exhibiting handwriting difficulties:

1. Poor quality, or illegible
2. Acceptable quality but below minimum standards when pressured by the requirement of speed
3. Extremely slow rate but acceptable quality

The teacher must identify early in the school year those students whose handwriting is illegible and of poor quality under normal daily conditions. Samples of the students' "best," fastest," and "usual" handwriting can be used for diagnostic purposes. Use materials that contain a vocabulary that is familiar to the students so they will have little difficulty with spelling or comprehension. Include sentences that contain all the letters of the alphabet. For example, "The quick brown fox jumps over the lazy dog."

1. *Usual Sample*. A sample of the student's usual work should be taken under conditions that are not fatiguing.

7. Paul Anderson, *Language Skills in Elementary Education* (New York: Macmillan, 1964).

2. *Best Sample*. Say to the student, "Write the sample three times. Take your time and do your best. This is to be your very best effort." There should be no time limit.
3. *Fastest Sample*. Say to the student, "Now I want to see how fast you can write. I am going to give you three minutes to write the sentence as many times as you can. I will tell you when to stop."

Now you have a basis for comparing handwriting. Since reading and writing are interrelated activities, you can utilize writing to reinforce reading.

The following should be considered in evaluating handwriting:

1. Can the student copy accurately?
2. Does the student align letters properly?
3. Does the student have an unorthodox joining of letters in cursive writing?
4. Does the student use neo-graphisms or squibbles that are not really letters?
5. Is there letter fusion such as writing *buck* for *brick*?
6. Does the student use the same hand consistently for writing?
7. Does the student write from left to right?
8. Does the student have poor spacing of letters and words?
9. Are the student's letters of irregular size?
10. Does the student's work show fatigue? For example, the last line may be noticeably,poorer than the first one.
11. Does the student exhibit poor letter formation (*d* like *cl*, *a* like *o*, *a* like *u*, *t* like *l*)?
12. Is the student unable to recall or retrieve the motor act of writing as a form of expressive language?

    Note: When evaluating an entire class, note the time it takes for each student to complete the task. (Some students can write well but take too much time.) This is important diagnostically in terms of determining the amount of written material that is required of a particular student in a given time.

Transitional Writing

In teaching transitional writing begin with the easier letters; you can add the difficult letters later one at a time:

1. First, print the word in manuscript.

all

2. Then connect the letters with a dotted line, using a colored pencil.

all at ant

The students then trace over the printed manuscript letter and the connecting dotted lines to form the cursive writing. Difficult letters should be written lighter than the colored dots and eventually fade out with successive tracings.

Note: Watch this problem with the letter *n*:

not pant

pan

The "n" in the middle or end of a word must have enough room in front of it for the extra hump needed in cursive.

Remediation techniques for writing that deteriorates under pressure are as follows:

1. The students should be observed as they write to see if they are doing it correctly. For instance, *i, j,* and *t* are dotted or crossed immediately in manuscript writing but not in cursive. Many students carry this habit over into cursive, and it slows them down.
2. If the students are writing correctly but tire too easily, desk templates should be used to help them develop more strength in the muscles needed for writing.
3. Extremely slow writers should be observed. If they are slow because they can't read the material they are copying and have to copy each letter almost stroke by stroke, they may have a reading problem and not a writing problem.

Handwriting for the Older Student

Students in the second grade and higher experiencing difficulty with either manuscript or cursive writing need a slightly different approach. In addition to col-

Table 8-5 Order of Presentation of Cursive Letters

Easier (level one)									
a	c	i	o	u	q	t	u	w	
Moderately Difficult (level two)									
e	d	g	h	j	l	m	n	p	y
More Difficult (level three)									
b	f	k	r	s	v	x	z		

lecting handwriting samples of those students, ask the following questions:

1. Was handedness changed at any time?
2. How much difficulty did the older student experience with beginning writing or cursive?
3. Is the student extremely nervous or emotional? Has the handwriting become either much larger or much smaller?
4. What is the student's general physical condition? Has the student been ill or suffered a seizure?
5. What is the student's ability to draw, color, and cut?
6. Does the student have difficulty in some other basic subject, such as spelling or reading?
7. Does the student have a negative attitude toward some or all school work?

If the handwriting problem is actually rooted in reading and spelling problems, then just trying to remediate the handwriting problem by itself will not usually be successful.

As already indicated in the handwriting discussion, there are three kinds of difficulties in handwriting:

1. Handwriting that is of poor quality, or illegible.
2. Handwriting that deteriorates under pressure of speed. (By the fourth grade, speed is gradually encouraged.)
3. Handwriting that is produced at too slow a rate.

The overall objectives for good handwriting are legibility and ease of writing. The single most important factor in determining the legibility of handwriting is letter formation. Next in importance is spacing.

The following are suggestions to help the older student practice cursive writing.

1. The students copy from material presented on the same activity sheet.
   a. Review sheets can be made for all capital letters. Students can then be given a complete review program including all of the sheets in order, or they can be given just the letters they are experiencing difficulty with.
   b. On the review sheet shown in Figure 8-51, the student first practices individual words and then copies a paragraph.
2. The students copy from a master copy to their own papers. Write a series of ten or twelve stories for the

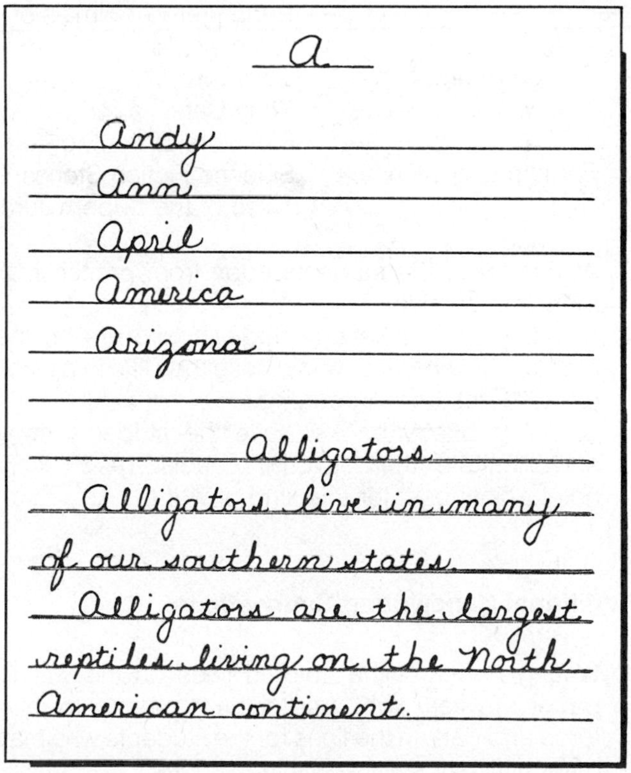

Figure 8-51

Figure 8-52

students to copy. The stories, written on regular classroom paper, are mounted on tag board. The students copy them on the same type of paper. Ditto pictures accompany each story. (See Figure 8-52.) When all of the stories of a group are completed, the pictures and stories are put together in a booklet to be taken home. The stories can be written on the approximate reading level of the students using them. The following subjects have proven popular:

For third and fourth	Animals of the Sea
	African Animals
	Endangered Animals of the World
For fourth and fifth	Early Aircraft
	Early Cars
	Monsters of the Movies
For fifth and sixth	Science Fiction Stories
	Tales of the Supernatural

3. At this level, the students copy from printed material into cursive.
   a. Many good joke and riddle books are on the market. The students copy those they like in a small (5″ x 7″) notebook in cursive.
   b. Using poetry books, have the students copy and illustrate their favorite poems. (A 5″ x 7″ notebook is best for this kind of work.)

Additional Handwriting Suggestions

1. *Writing Paper.* If the colored lines on the writing paper are very light, use colored pencils to reinforce and darken the lines for the students who may have difficulty staying within the lines.
2. *Directionality.* Place a dot or an arrow → to aid the learner in left-to-right progression in writing. An arrow can be placed in the upper left-hand corner of the chalkboard.
3. *Far-Point Copying.* Some learners may require successive approximations to successful copying of material from a classroom chalkboard. The following steps are suggested as the students copy material preferably at their own reading level. The students will
   a. copy phrases or sentences from a paper placed next to the writing paper
   b. copy material placed at the top of the desk or just above the writing paper
   c. copy material written on a portable chalkboard or an easel and placed directly in front of the learner
   d. copy material from a portable chalkboard or easel midway between the learner and the chalkboard
   e. finally, copy sentences from the chalkboard. The number of sentences successfully copied in an acceptable period of time should be noted. The amount of material should be carefully monitored.

Note: Incomplete, illegible assignments may be caused by many factors. When students are completing far-point copying from a chalkboard, an acetate on an overhead projector, a television monitor, etc., the following should be considered:

1. Is the model from which the students are copying neatly written and carefully spaced?
2. Do the students view the chalkboard from an appropriate angle? Do they have to turn around to see the material?
3. Is there a glare or shadows on the board caused by improper lighting, sunlight, mobiles, etc.?
4. Is the chalkboard, and therefore the printing, placed too high on the wall?

5. Are there too many distractors (e.g., excessively decorated bulletin boards, charts) in close proximity to the material to be copied?
6. Can the students read what they are copying?
7. Do the students have sufficient time to copy assignments?

4. *Practice*. Students should be encouraged to practice to a successful model. For example, if a student copies an *a*, say, "When your *a* looks like the model *a* or is your very best, stop." Some learners are required to copy to a failure when the number of times a letter is written is stressed more than the quality of the writing. Fifty *a*'s may result in too many *u*'s. For some students, ten minutes of writing may be the limit.
5. *Writing Tables*. Provide special tables for cursive writing.
   a. Slanted Tables. For some primary-age learners, provide a slanted desk top by raising the back legs of a table.
   b. Write-on tables. Attach a chalkboard or painted slate top to a desk to enable the student to use chalk directly on the surface of the desk.

LANGUAGE

Students need opportunities to experiment with words and express themselves freely in a nonthreatening environment. The learners should be encouraged to express themselves, even if they do so in nonstandard English. Constantly correcting a student's verbal expression often leads to the student's inhibiting any spontaneous language that may have been forthcoming. Some teachers feel that disadvantaged learners as a group do not have good communicative language, or are *nonverbal*. Away from school, the language the students use serve them well within their own social milieu, in most cases. It may not, however, help them to achieve success in what can be described as the language of school. This does not mean that students who appear to have a paucity of language in terms of standard English cannot "think" or learn to "think better." The function of the teacher is to expand the experiences of students, as well as to aid them in expanding their own minds. Help the students to derive greater meaning from experiences by perfecting their language acquisition skills.

Chapter 7 contains sections that further expand specific areas of language development. Included are a sequence of developmental skills, suggestions for diagnosis of the areas, and prescriptive activities. Refer to the following:

Auditory Language Classification, page 162
Auditory Language Association, page 163
Visual Language Classification, page 173
Visual Language Association–Nonsymbolic (Object and Picture Level), page 174
Visual Language Association–Symbolic (Letter, Numeral, and Word Level), page 176
Visual Language Association–Graphic (Writing), page 177
Language Expression, page 185
Verbal Language Expression, page 186
Written Language Expression, page 187
Nonverbal Language, page 188
Inner-Language, page 188

The following section contains activities and suggestions for language development that are most appropriately utilized with reading, writing, and spelling activities within the broader concept of language arts. As has been previously stated, the authors feel that there should be a close linkage between the subject level areas and language arts. The language arts skills should not be taught in isolation.

Suggested Teaching Strategies

The following is a description of how information can be presented to students in a developmental sequence. The following basic format for the presentation of information is applicable to all subject matter areas requiring language in terms of understanding and meaning. The format is designed to aid the teacher in determining the best possible approach to structuring and controlling the language input in relation to the learning needs of individual learners. The following components should be considered in building good concept formation in students: Level of Presentation, Level of Conceptualization or Ideation, and Serendipity.

LEVEL OF PRESENTATION

Concepts that lend themselves to physical representation can be taught using the following sequence of presentation:

1. Concrete objects or forms that can be manipulated by the students.
2. Pictures representing objects within the learners' experiences
3. Geometric shapes or forms
4. Symbols (such as letters, numerals, and words), the highest level of presentation

LEVEL OF CONCEPTUALIZATION OR IDEATION

Concrete-Functional (C-F). Many concepts can be presented in any of the above-mentioned forms, including objects, pictures, geometric shapes, and symbols. At a lower level of conceptualization, the language involving a particular concept can be defined as essentially descriptive or functional in nature (i.e., the word used tells us what the concept is, how it looks, what it is made of, what it does, what it does not do, and what can be done with it). This level of language can be termed concrete-functional or the analysis of concepts in a concrete-functional manner. An example of this level of conceptualization would be the following: The concept of *elephant* can be presented in concrete form, picture, shape, or word. It can also be described in concrete-functional terms such as "big," "heavy," and "it can carry people." Students who have language deficiencies should be introduced to concepts in terms of meaning by being presented with the concrete form first whenever possible. The language associated with the concept should be taught in a concrete-functional manner first.

Abstract (A). The concept *elephant,* to continue the example, which can be presented in different ways (concrete form, picture, shape, or word), should then be examined in an abstract sense. The appropriate sequence in teaching the concept *elephant,* for example, is to first teach how it is different from other things. After difference is understood, teach how it is the same as other things. For example, an elephant is different from a horse in size, shape, behavior, etc. It is the same as a horse in that both have four legs, a mouth, and two eyes, and they are both animals. The teacher can build in the meaning of the concept *elephant* at different levels by teaching simple, then complex, classifications and associations. This should be accomplished first visually by using visual associative clues such as a picture or object and then auditorily (through communication without the use of visual associative clues).

SERENDIPITY

Encourage students to look for relationships between concepts or functions of objects that may at first appear to be unrelated but will, if properly combined, result in something unique or different. Regard the following sequence in teaching:

1. Achieve good verbal behavior first, which may entail beginning with single words, then using short phrases, and finally using sentences.
2. Introduce the concept through reading activities.
3. Reinforce through writing.

Note: All students do not need to manipulate the concrete object in order to achieve understanding. A great deal depends upon which level of presentation the learner achieves the greatest amount of meaning and success from.

SAMPLE LESSON

The following is a sample language lesson dealing with the meaning of a specific concept that is within the student's range of experience.

1. *Concept.* Ball.
2. *Level of Presentation.* Object ball, picture of ball, shape of ball, or the word *ball,* depending upon the presentation level best suited to the needs of the student.
3. *Levels of Conceptualization.*
   a. *Concrete-Functional.* What does a ball look like and feel like? What is it made of? What can you do with it? What can you not do with it?
   b. *Abstract.* How is a ball different from a block, etc.?
   How is it the same as a circle, globe, etc.? (Classification)
   What goes with ball? (Simple association)
   Ball is to circle as block is to ______? (Complex association)

Written Expressive Language

For many students any form of written language expression will provoke reactions that range from fear and refusal to aggression. Essay tests, creative writing sessions, and science and social studies reports are often incomplete, of inferior quality, or ignored. The student may know the content, but be unable to express the ideas in writing. Multiple homework assignments that all require writing can cause an entire family to suffer.

Before giving subject level assignments, the teacher should first evaluate what is required for minimum success in a subject and how the student must respond to be successful. If the teacher requires note-taking, dictation, extensive copying from the chalkboard or overhead projector, essay tests, reports, and other forms of written expression, the student with learning problems is doomed to failure. This input-output discrepancy between the information received and answers returned must be considered.

Students with learning problems cannot be totally excused from written assignments, therefore the teacher must accommodate to their learning needs. The following should be considered:

1. Do students have a physical disability that will preclude all writing? If so, the instructor must consider allowing the students to dictate their thoughts to a volunteer, another student, their parents, etc. A tape recorder may be used by the students or the teacher to record key information or for testing purposes.
2. Are students deficient in spelling, handwriting, and written language skills? These students are often the most negative, since their papers not only look messy, but also lack the sentence formation, punctuation, syntax, spelling, etc., that are needed for success. They usually get the most red marks on limited attempts at writing. The instructor has to be concerned about the students' feelings and gradually build up a trusting relationship before the students will begin to feel secure in writing assignments. If the students are deficient in spelling, handwriting, and reading as well as in written expression, the grading and evaluation of the written expression must be considered. If the objective for a particular lesson is to have the students express their ideas on paper, then an alternative form of writing (e.g., typing or writing by a peer tutor) may have to be used. Bad handwriting and misspelled words may also need to be ignored in grading, with instructor comments pertaining primarily to the written expression. Sometimes the instructor has to work with the parents to prevent chastisement at home. Unless the parents realize why spelling errors were not corrected or poor writing excused, then the students run the risk of negative comments at home. During separate lessons, the instructor can begin to build up the mechanical skills of writing or spelling.
3. What are the students' strengths in written expression? Some students have spelling and handwriting skills as well as good imagery and can express very creative ideas in sentences. Those students, however, may require assistance in developing other kinds of skills (e.g., punctuation and grammatical structure). An integral part of developing written expression is activities that relate to the particular structural components (e.g., punctuation marks and capitalization). Table 8-6 is an outline of the structural components of written language expression that must be built directly into every aspect of writing as well as into the language arts curriculum. These concepts are taught both specifically in isolation and continually as a part of all writing activities.

Teaching Grammatic Structure

1. In oral reading activities, deliberately teach voice inflection. Read with the student and to the student to illustrate how certain forms of punctuation should be read. Use hand motions to indicate that the voice goes down at the end of sentences ending with periods and rises at the end of questions. Refer to page 208 for additional oral reading activities.
2. Indicate to the student the key words that are often found in certain types of sentences. For example, the interrogative words—*how, when, why, where,* and *who.* Use the students' reading vocabulary to give them practice in completing and writing different types of sentences. For example:
   a. I have a ______.
      I see a ______.
      He has a ______.
      What is ______?
      Who is ______?
      What has ______?
      What ______?
   b. Ask the students to use the reading or spelling words to write three sentences with a period and three with a question mark.
3. Dates can be written daily. To prevent repeated failure and copying of an incorrect response, carefully note during the first week of school the student who is making careless errors in writing the date.
4. Some form of daily practice may be required for students (even older students) who need to improve their use of capitalization and punctuation. This type of activity would be in addition to workbooks or other programmed material. For example, ask the student to write five sentences, each containing one of the following: a date, a name, a state, a quotation, or an exclamation mark. On the chalkboard write sentences without punctuation or capitalization. Spend five or ten minutes a day as a class to review previously taught skills and to discuss the correct responses.
5. If a student cannot write, use movable cardboard, magnetic, or plastic punctuation marks and word cards or sentence strips. If the materials are color coded, check to see if any of the students are color blind.

Note: For additional activities in the area of grammatical structure, see syntax and formulation, beginning on page 186.

Table 8-6 Grammatical Structure–Writing

Capitalization The student will capitalize	*Grade Levels* 1	2	3	4	5	6
Names of people	X					
Words used as names				Grandfather Mother	Aunt Sue	
Initials with names			X			
Titles of respect			Mr., Mrs., Ms., Dr., Miss	Pres., Gov., etc. Capt.	Judge	
Names of pets	X					
Sacred names				God, Jesus Our Father		
Days of the week		X				
Months of the year		X				
Holidays			X			
Places and things			Country Street State Park City School	Clubs Ocean Library River	Stores Wars Ships	
Words formed from place names				French American		
The word *I*	X			I'm		
Titles of books, etc.			X			
First word in sentence	X					
First word of direct quotation				X		
First word in greeting of letter			X			
First word in closing of letter			X			
First word in each line of poem			X			
Punctuation The student will place						
Period At end of sentence	X					
After initials of names			X			
After abbrev. of titles of respect		X				

Table 8-6 (continued)

Punctuation (continued) The student will place	1	2	3	4	5	6
Period After abbrev. of days				X		
After abbrev. of months				X		
After abbrev. of directions				X		
After abbrev. of states				X		
After abbrev. of other words; Blvd., St., Ave., R.F.D.				X		
At end of quotation				X		
Question Mark At end of sentence	X					
At end of direct quotation				X		
Exclamation Mark At end of sentence		X				
At end of direct quotation				X		
Commas Between month and year				X		
Between day of month and year			X			
Between day of week and month				X		
Following date in sentence				X		
Between city and state				X		
Between city and country				X		
After greeting of letter			X			
After closing of letter			X			
After names used in direct address (John,)				X		
After yes or no at beginning of a sentence				X		
To separate words in a series two words describing something					X	
three words naming something				X		
Between a direct quotation and the words preceding or following it					X	
Around interpolations (set, however, apart)				X		
After an "if" phrase					X	

Table 8-6 (continued)

Punctuation (continued) The student will place	Grade Levels 1	2	3	4	5	6
Apostrophe To combine two words (contraction)			X			
To form possessive of singular word				X		
To form possessive of plural word				X		
Quotation Marks Around a title in a sentence				X		
Around a direct quotation				X		
Colon After greeting in business letter					X	

Written Language Activities

The following writing activities can be used to incorporate the learner's reading and spelling vocabulary into a unified language arts program.

WORDS

1. Prepare duplicator masters or acetates for use on the overhead projector and have the learners trace and complete them (Figure 8-53).
2. Have the students write the singular and plural forms of words corresponding to the pictures on duplicator masters or acetates (Figure 8-54).
3. Ask the learners to use their vocabulary word cards to write pairs of rhyming words (Figure 8-55).
4. Have the learners use their word cards to write all of the words they can find for a specified category (Figure 8-56).
5. Write a spelling pattern (e.g., *at*) in a house. The learner will write all the words of that pattern on the lines below. (See Figure 8-57).

SENTENCES

1. For beginning writers, use sentence completion. For example:
   a. The learner copies from a model.
      The dog is ________. big, blue
   b. The learner uses vocabulary cards or a simple dictionary to complete a sentence.
      The dog is ______________.
   c. The learner writes original sentences.
      The ____________________.
2. Use the fill-in sections of the workbook or duplicator master pages as a writing lesson. After the sentences have been corrected, the learner can write or type them.
3. Have the learner start with a short sentence and add words to make longer and longer sentences. Example:

   I saw a dog.
   I saw a brown dog.
   I saw a little, brown dog.
   I saw a little, old, brown dog.
   He said, "I saw a little, old, brown dog."

4. Using a reading word list, write each of the words on a separate index card. Learners or teams of learners take turns drawing cards from the shuffled deck. Each player or team tries to form phrases or sentences. When the cards are all used, the players read each other's phrases or sentences. These can be used as a writing lesson.
5. Allow the students to use pictures in sentences in place of words they cannot spell.
6. Plan activities that require writing only a few sentences, such as the following:
   a. Greeting card messages for holidays
   b. "Fortune cookie" sentence strips to exchange with secret pals
   c. Sports cards to be illustrated with pictures from newspapers or magazines
   d. Dialogue for comic strips or cartoons
   e. Commercials or advertisement lines for products
   f. Short descriptions for travel posters
   g. Bumper stickers for desks
   h. Tongue twisters
   i. Riddles
   j. Messages on postcards

Salty	Salty	______
pet	pet	______

Figure 8-53

[picture: one cat]	cat
[picture: two cats]	

Figure 8-54

cat	hat	pet	wet
boy	toy	big	pig
day	play	go	so
shop	hop	hot	not

Figure 8-55

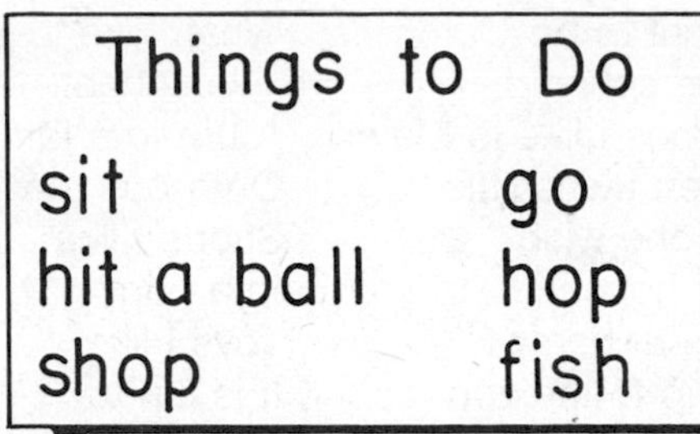

Figure 8-56

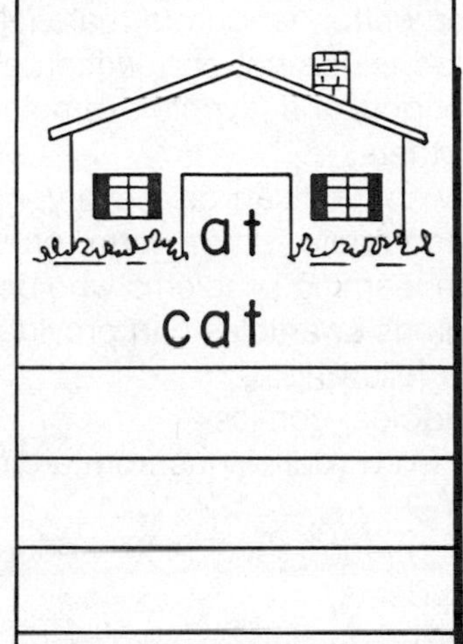

Figure 8-57

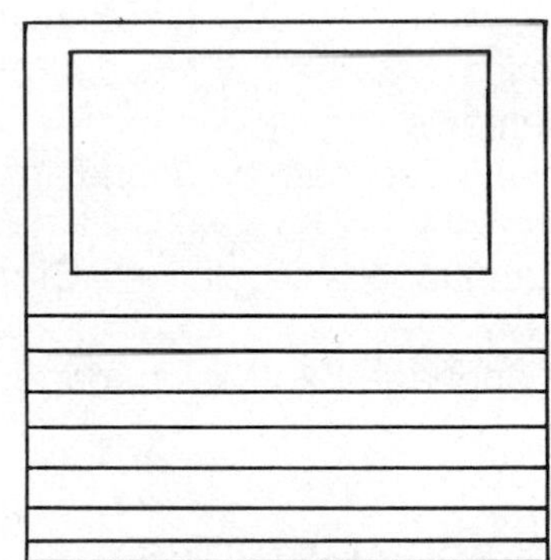

Figure 8-58

k. Button slogans—"We are first."
l. Captions for pictures on bulletin boards
m. Small books about a subject, with a picture and one or two sentences on a page
n. Labels for collections (rocks, shells, etc.)
o. Labels for photographs
p. Steps in an experiment
q. Answers to "famous faces" quiz involving pictures of television personalities

STORIES

1. The learners can draw characters from a book. They can then copy sentences from the book. (See Figure 8-58.)
2. Ask the learners to cut out an interesting picture from a magazine, color their favorite pictures from a coloring book, or draw a picture. Paste the picture on a larger sheet of paper. The learner will then write a few sentences about the picture.
3. Give the learners pictures. Encourage them to use their word lists for original stories. Assist with the spelling of additional words. If the students have difficulty with writing, they can dictate the story to another person or tell it into a tape recorder.
4. Have the learners prepare simple "About Me" booklets by writing sentences or drawing pictures to illustrate the following:

I wish I could	Mother
A trip to	Father

I want to be	What I like to do in school
After school I	A trip to a farm
Games I like to play	On a bus trip I saw
When I was little	Shops I like
My one wish	In a barn
Our house	Toys I like
Pets at home	It is fun to
A trip to the zoo	
I like to eat	

Older students can write autobiographies.

5. Encourage each student to have a notebook, diary, or folder for written language materials. Contributions should include not only written assignments, but also thoughts and favorite examples of material written by others.
6. A class newspaper can give everyone an opportunity to contribute some form of writing. The student with learning problems who usually avoids writing columns or articles can provide short items such as the following:
   a. Jokes, riddles, comics
   b. Mystery word (definitions from a dictionary)
   c. Sports
   d. Mystery person (short facts about classmates and new students)
   e. Math quiz
   f. Short book reviews
   g. Dear Aunt ______, Dear Wizard, hot-line types of columns
   h. Poems
   i. Short stories
   j. Advertisements
7. Additional activities can be found in chapter 7 under
   a. Visual Language Association—Graphic (Writing), page 177
   b. Written Language Expression, page 187

SCIENCE AND SOCIAL STUDIES

Before designing a science and social studies program for students exhibiting learning difficulties, the teacher must consider the following:

1. What are the student's strengths? Can the learner's ability to read, write, spell, or conceptualize ideas from the material to be covered be used as a strength to develop an understanding of the content area?
2. What is not intact? What areas of language are deficient to the extent that they prevent the learner from being successful in given tasks?

The student may have difficulty in basic decoding skills (sensory-perception), holding or remembering information (memory-sequencing), understanding vocabulary and integrating information (receptive language and conceptualization), or expressing ideas in a meaningful and grammatically correct manner (expressive language).

After the student's learning or cognitive style has been decoded (diagnosed), then the teacher must determine the following:

1. How can a science and social studies program be designed so that it will enable the learner to further develop in the areas of deficiency (e.g., perception, memory, language)? The developmental skills indicated in Chapter 7 can be applied here to identify specific areas. This will enable the teacher to plan science and social studies activities that relate to these skill areas.
2. How can the content areas (concepts, ideas, relationships) be presented in a manner that will enable the student to conceptualize the material and integrate the information given for purposes of expanding the knowledge base in these subject areas?

Considerations in Grade Level Planning

PROGRAMS FOR STUDENTS FROM MIDDLE OF GRADE 1 THROUGH GRADE 3

A science or social studies program for students beginning in the middle of grade one and going through the third grade should be based on an interest area. Dinosaurs, weather, seasons, seeds, and plants, for instance, are good subjects because there are usually enough concrete materials, visual aids, and library books about them to reach students through many mediums. At this level the students do not need to read the library books; they can look at the pictures.

Students at this level are easily involved in manipulative activities. Visual-motor activities that involve developing models for social studies and science projects by collecting, sampling, cutting, and pasting are naturally motivating to the learners. Nature studies (particularly out-of-doors activities) are excellent for developing interest in science projects.

Developing Visual Skills (Grades 1–3). With high interest science and social studies material, the visual skills taught students in kindergarten and beginning first grade can now be used to observe more carefully and notice the necessary details and sequencing in a film strip, for example, that is designed to teach them subject matter. The developmental skills program discussed in Chapter 7 can now be directed from purely training level activities to more practical application in the subject level areas.

If a student has difficulty with visual sequential memory, for example, the teacher can incorporate visual sequential memory activities into the science or social studies program. Example: Demonstrate a science experiment and ask the students what they saw first, second, and so on. The students can be required to remember details such as the color, shape, and size of items and the kinds of materials that were used in the experiment. Far-point copying and the ability to keep one's place on a sheet of paper can be developed through the science and social studies activities, as well as through the language arts program.

Developing Auditory Skills (Grades 1–3) The teacher as an input system now replaces cassettes and other taped auditory training material, and the student is slowly led through the subject area material into a teacher-oriented listening program. Students are expected to respond through listening, oral discussion, and written work. For the very young learner, the written response can be just one word written on a ditto sheet under a picture. The ideas or concepts behind the pictures on the ditto sheet are discussed orally first, developing listening skills, and then the word needed is put on the chalkboard for all to copy.

The student must listen and follow a sequence of directions. Listening is a prerequisite to understanding concepts and other language activities. The teacher must be constantly aware of how input is being delivered in terms of rate, amount, and sequence.

Developing Language Skills (Grades 1–3). The same concepts discussed in the language arts areas of Chapter 7 apply in the development of vocabulary for the subject level areas. Students must learn that many words have similar pronunciation but different meanings. This cannot be assumed. It must be taught explicitly and reinforced by using the concepts in many situations. Vocabulary development is an integral part of the language program. Lists of words made in the science and social studies areas and taught specifically in context through writing within the subject level area programs should be reinforced continually by the teacher who is responsible for the language arts areas. The teacher responsible for the reading program, for example, should be bringing the science, social studies, and arithmetic vocabulary that are necessary for success in those areas into the reading program. This is not to imply that the words are taught in isolation. The vocabulary of the subject level areas must be tied into the material that is being covered at a given time in those areas for it to have relevance for the learner. By second grade, words are increased and lead to phrases or sentences. By third grade, a student should be able to write a short paragraph of two or three sentences. Other language skills that begin to develop at this level as part of the science and social studies curriculum include:

1. classification or concept development
2. association at the concrete-functional and abstract levels
3. written expression, includes simple taking of dictation, note taking, beginning reporting (one or two sentences), and creative writing wherever appropriate

Developing Fine Motor Skills (Grades 1–3). The fine motor skills of coloring, cutting, and pasting developed in kindergarten and early first grade are an essential part of the early science and social studies program.

When a science or social studies project is completed, the students' papers should be made into simple booklets to take home. The booklet should be reviewed in class visually and orally, with the students participating in a page-by-page discussion. This will help them put the parts or segments of the project into a whole to achieve "closure." They will hear and see what they are learning in an organized fashion.

PROGRAMS FOR STUDENTS GRADES 4–5

A science or social studies program for students in grades 4 and 5 should emphasize the development of library and written language skills necessary for collecting information, keeping records, developing vocabulary and writing reports on a given subject. To successfully learn these skills, students should be reading on at least a middle second grade level, as little meaningful library material is written for the student below that level.

Auditory and Visual Skills (Grades 4–5). Students with learning problems generally find it difficult to learn from a teacher-directed demonstration program in science or social studies or a teacher-directed film strip or film-oriented program that requires them to learn by listening and watching, unless they were well trained in the lower grades.

Often the students' developmental skills in auditory or visual memory and sequencing are still low, and while the students may appear to be learning, a quick check will indicate that they are missing a lot.

A science or social studies program to meet the

needs of these intermediate students must include preparation before viewing a film and a highly structured discussion with written work immediately following the presentation. If time permits, a second showing of the film would be helpful. In these grades a good technique to use is to turn the sound off the second showing, asking different students to explain what they were watching. This type of activity needs to be followed with vocabulary development and written reports based on material collected from the library. The teacher cannot rush through the material, as rate, amount, and sequence of impact are critically important here.

Developing Fine Motor Skills (Grades 4–5) The fine motor skills of coloring, cutting, and pasting developed in the early grades are now replaced by free-hand sketching or tracing as students attempt to illustrate their material. Tracing requires visual-motor coordination and can usually be accomplished quite well by fourth and fifth graders.

Written Expression (Grades 4–5). In order to put the many parts together into a meaningful whole, all of the students' written work should be put together into a booklet and reviewed in class before it is taken home. Note taking, reporting and creative writing at this point becomes a major part of the students' program. Science and social studies are excellent for developing written and expressive language. The following should be considered:

1. Begin with short sentences. Check for punctuation.
2. Discuss grammatical structure and creative language with the students and, through writing (see Chapter 7, page 186), apply the principles of good syntax and formulation to the subject areas.
3. Move slowly into short and then longer paragraphs.
4. Reinforce and continue to be patient, for this aspect of language development is the most difficult one in which to achieve success. The students should illustrate their work (drawing pictures, etc.) whenever possible.

PROGRAMS FOR STUDENTS GRADES 6–8

To be successful in a science or social studies project at this level, the students need to have developed good visual, auditory, and motor skills to the point where they can read silently and follow directions or listen to an instructor and follow directions. Motor skills must be sufficiently developed to allow for the manipulation of material for writing. The library skills must be developed to the extent that the students can benefit from instruction on how to locate and use reference material. Written language skills must now enable the taking of notes and the writing of reports. This is a slow process and must be continually reinforced through the science and social studies program. *Practice* is a key word in this situation.

The students who are still at too low an academic level may find these projects extremely frustrating, as they may see that there is little they can do. The novelty of the new material may wear off. The teacher must assess the reading and written language levels of these students and gear the program to their abilities and needs. Screening as presented in the reading section of this Handbook can be used for this assessment. Teacher-made material and media using other approaches will need to be used here.

General Suggestions

The basic difficulty for students with learning problems is that if the class is using a textbook, they can't read it. Many social studies and science textbooks are written at a higher level of readability than the grade level for which it is written. In cases like this, if there is an overdependence on the textbook, many students will have to rely only on what they hear or see once in the classroom to get the lesson.

For students with learning problems, once is not enough. Following are some ways to let the students who need to hear and see something over again do so.

INTRODUCTION TO A SOCIAL STUDIES OR SCIENCE UNIT

If your introduction to a science or social studies unit is based on a common textbook used by all students in the classroom and includes an overview of the project and a discussion of the pictures in the book, tape it on a cassette recorder.

In the taped introduction tell the students which page to turn to and then give a brief description of the unit you are going to study. Go through the pictures page by page, pointing out things for them to notice or asking the questions you want them to think about. Cassette lessons of this type, to be effective, should not be longer than 10 minutes. Leave the book and cassette recorder in an area of the room or in the media center where they can be used by all students that want to listen and look again.

VOCABULARY EXPANSION

Because these students look but do not see, or hear but do not remember, repetition that leads to vocabulary expansion can be built into the program in the following ways:

A Unit on Farm Animals for First or Second Grade Students. Mount pictures of animals on tagboard and number them. On the cassette say, "Look at picture number 1," then pause, giving the child a chance to find it if it is out of order. Then say, "Number 1 is a picture of a baby cow. A baby cow is called a calf. This is a calf." Pause a few seconds and then go on. "Look at picture number 2. This is a picture of a baby horse. A baby horse is called a colt. This is a colt," etc.

When the animals have all been discussed, go back and review the pictures. Say, "Look at picture number 1. This is a calf." Or if there is time, say, "Look at picture number 1. What is it?" Leave time for the student to answer, and then say, "If you said calf, you are right."

A Unit on Birds for Third Grade Students. Picture cards of birds, numbered in the upper right corner, are all you need for this lesson in local bird identification. Proceed slowly through the cards, first giving the number and then the name of the bird. Hints on identifying marks can be given, but don't talk so much the students forget the name of the bird. When the birds have been shown, ask the students to spread the picture cards out in front of them and then, as you call out the bird's name, to pick the card up. Checking should take place on the tape. Say, "The cards should be in this order—card number 3, then 7," etc.

A Unit on Rocks and Minerals for Fourth Grade Students. Put items in an open box. Put numbers on each rock, using Scotch tape, and then proceed as above, giving the name of each specimen, mentioning something about it of interest (maybe comparing it to another specimen) but not talking too much. When finished, have the student spread the specimens out and then put them in order as their names are called or write down the numbers on a self-checking sheet. Checking should take place on the tape, as described in the preceding paragraph.

Additional Suggestions. Almost all science subjects lend themselves to this type of training. In a unit on weather, both instruments and cloud types can be taught. Names of plants, trees, animals, insects, and constellations have all been successfully taught this way.

TAPE SHORT BOOKS OR CHAPTERS OF BOOKS FOR EXTRA READING

This can be an incentive to the student unable to read well enough to use the classroom library books. The book and the tape should be together so that the student can follow along. Always indicate when to turn the page.

TAPE IMPORTANT PARTS OF THE CLASS TEXTBOOK

This will help students having difficulty reading the text.

TAPES AND FILMSTRIPS

Tape captioned filmstrips for the students that can't read them.

Make your own tape for a filmstrip that the class has already seen and heard. Many times there are other things in the filmstrip that you want them to notice (for example, filmstrips dealing with colonial America show different clothing and homes).

PROJECTS

A widely accepted premise suggests that science and social studies projects help develop participation. They can be extremely motivating to most students and are especially beneficial for further enhancing the language arts program in general. However, projects for the disabled reader or the student with learning problems require some modification. Projects are too often assigned or required based on reading and expressive language abilities or independent study habits. Good students who have the prerequisite skills plus some artistic or creative skills have little difficulty with such an assignment. But students with reading and writing problems may have difficulty, even if they know the science or social studies concepts, have an interest in the subject, and have creative skills. Therefore, projects for them should require more involvement and participation based on strengths. The activities should be to solve problems or to motivate thinking skills rather than to read and to write.

For some students, group-type activities can be arranged, with the composition of the group carefully balanced according to selected strengths. For example, if the group is doing an experiment and report on rocks, then each student can be assigned a specific contribution based on his or her strengths. For example:

1. The good reader reads and summarizes the textbook and other reference materials for the group.
2. The best printer or typist labels the rocks.
3. The artist prepares the charts, posters, or other visuals required in the project.
4. They all contribute to the written report (some through dictating ideas; others in writing). Everyone proofreads and checks the spelling.

5. The oral presentation and any other narrations (e.g., accompanying filmstrips or acetates for the overhead projector, introducing films) are based on strengths. There should not be undue pressure on students who stutter or are extremely shy to "participate" the first time they show an interest in a subject.

Gradually, the types of independent and small-group work will require students to assume more responsibility to produce quality material in their weaker areas. Prior to this, however, the students should plan how to get the assignment completed on time and with specific help if necessary. They may need a friend to help proof the first draft but the responsibility for the finished product is their own.

Chapter 9 Arithmetic

Arithmetic can be envisioned as both a symbolic language and a means of indicating spatial-temporal relationships. A number sense is built early in the development of most students, as many of the concepts that deal with space, form, distance, order, and time are learned by the students through their everyday interactions with people, especially their parents, siblings, and peers. Mother helps formulate math concepts during feeding time when she says "a little bit more" or "just one more bite," etc. Problems in dealing with number concepts may result from language disorders, inability to deal with spatial-temporal relationships, or other specific processing problems. Learning disabilities that affect reading, writing, and spelling tend to also affect arithmetic skills acquisition. No one basic task area can be considered in isolation in attempting to diagnose the problems of the learning-handicapped student.

VISUAL DISORDERS IN ARITHMETIC

1. The students may not be able to discriminate differences or similarities in size and shape (discrimination).
2. The learners may exhibit discrimination difficulties such as writing 3 for 8 or 2 for 5 (discrimination).
3. The learners may not be able to learn sets or groupings (closure or figure-ground).
4. The students may not be able to judge with accuracy spatial relationships that deal with distance and quantity (spatial).
5. The students may have difficulty in learning to tell time (spatial-temporal).
6. The students may ruin materials, books, garments, etc., because they try to force them into drawers or spaces that are too small. They may have difficulty in relating the size of an object to the appropriate container (spatial).
7. The learners may exhibit problems with the alignment and arrangement of numerals (spatial).
8. The students may overpour their glasses, have difficulty lining up buttons, and put too much food on their forks (spatial).
9. The students may have problems with body image as indicated by the Draw-A-Man Test. (spatial-body image).
10. The students may exhibit a poor sense of direction, getting lost easily, not being able to find different places in the school or neighborhood (spatial).
11. The learners may have difficulty with historical sequence and with geography that deals with maps and globes (spatial-temporal).
12. The students may have problems with right-left orientation and placement (directionality in arithmetic).
13. The students may have difficulty relating themselves to an object in space and appear awkward and clumsy in their attempts to perform a physical task (laterality).
14. The learners may have difficulty understanding cardinal and ordinal placement (memory-sequence, and/or spatial).
15. The students may exhibit reversals and write Ɛ

for 3, or inversions and write 6 for 9 (memory-sequence and/or spatial).

16. The learners may not be able to write numerals (visual-motor).

AUDITORY DISORDERS IN ARITHMETIC

1. The students may not be able to retain an auditory sequence of numerals (memory-sequence).
2. The learners may have difficulty with looking at a series of numerals while counting aloud (memory-sequence and visual scanning).
3. The students may exhibit difficulties with story problems that require them to assimilate and hold a great deal of information in their minds. (memory-sequence).
4. The learners may not be able to cope with rapid oral drills (memory-sequence).
5. The students may not be able to associate a numeral with its auditory referent (auditory-visual association).

LANGUAGE DISORDERS IN ARITHMETIC

Difficulties in receptive and expressive language that affect reading and writing will also affect the students' performance in arithmetic. The students may not be able to understand words that are associated with story problems. They may have difficulty with words or concepts that relate to space and time. They may have problems understanding process signs and words dealing with distance and measurement. Words such as *beside, further, in between, within, upside down,* and *next to* may be difficult for the students to conceptualize. Words with a dual meaning, such as *base, times,* and *equals* are difficult in that the students may not be able to handle both meanings of these words. They may not be able to retrieve numerals or words needed for arithmetical operations, or they may be unable to express themselves in terms of arithmetic in clear and sequential thought patterns.

RATIONALE FOR ASSESSMENT

The teacher should first determine the skills or operations that learners are expected to learn developmentally and that they will be expected to acquire at each particular grade level. This can be done by reviewing the state-approved scope and sequence arithmetic curriculum guides, by analyzing arithmetic text books, or by reviewing the developmental skills and the Mann-Suiter Grade Level Sequence (Form 9-1, pages 251–258). In this way the teacher will understand the developmental sequence in arithmetic and know where to begin in terms of teaching lower level skills or prerequisite critical arithmetic skills before attempting higher level, more formal operations. A textbook should not determine what is to be taught. It is only a guide and an aid in presenting predetermined concepts and materials that learners should be able to cope with at a specific instructional level. The textbook is helpful if the learners are ready for those tasks, having mastered the prerequisite skills to the particular operations presented in the textbook. It is important that assessment be geared toward identifying specific areas of strengths (acquired skills) as well as areas of weakness or deficits at the beginning of the school year so that appropriate programs can be set up for individual learners. This will help the teacher group students more effectively, as well as providing an initial basis of comparison for future work.

Developmental Arithmetic Skills

VISUAL DISCRIMINATION

The student will

1. complete a form board.
2. match shapes (objects) to models.
3. match pictures of shapes.
4. match pictures of numerals.
5. order objects by size.
6. order pictures of objects or shapes by size.

VOCABULARY, SPATIAL-TEMPORAL

The student will

1. understand the language of space (position), for example, *over, under, inside, behind, beside, between, below, more, less, top, bottom, in the middle of.*
2. understand the language of time, for example, *early, late, soon, now, yesterday, before, after, almost, today, tomorrow, long ago, young, old.*
3. identify objects that are close, closer, closest.

ESTIMATIONS

The student will

1. estimate size by comparing objects or pictures of objects (e.g., big/little, tall/short.)
2. estimate shape by comparing objects or pictures of objects.

3. estimate distance by comparing objects or pictures of objects.
4. estimate weight by comparing objects or pictures of objects.
5. estimate conservation of space.

SETS

The student will

1. match one to one.
2. match equivalent sets 00–00.
3. recognize sets 0–5.
4. order sets 1–5.
5. identify sets with more or less.
6. recognize sets 6–10.
7. understand the language of sets, such as *more, fewer, equal, unequal, equivalent, nonequivalent,* and *empty set.*
8. identify universal sets.
9. identify intersection of sets.
10. understand union of sets.
11. understand disjoint sets.
12. understand finite and infinite sets.
13. understand solution sets.
14. understand sets of ordered pairs.
15. identify null sets.
16. identify proper and improper subsets.

NUMERALS

The student will

1. match one to one.
2. count orally 0–10.
3. count orally and point 0–10.
4. count orally and point 0–50.
5. count orally and point 0–100.
6. identify the numerals 0–50.
7. identify numerals before and after 1–50.
8. identify the numerals 0–100.
9. write the numerals 0–10.
10. write the numerals 0–50.
11. write the numerals 0–100.
12. write the numerals 0–999.
13. write from dictation 0–999.
14. write numerals for objects or pictures of objects in sets.
15. write numerals for words.
16. name numerals for objects or pictures of objects in sets.
17. classify numerals as odd or even.
18. count and write by 2s to 100; 3s to 36; 4s to 48; 5s to 100; 10s to 200; 6s to 72; 7s to 84; 8s to 96; 9s to 108.
19. round off to nearest 10.
20. write expanded form for numeral $(a \times 10) + 6$.
21. give cardinal number of sets.
22. indicate place value 0–50.
23. indicate place value 50–100.
24. indicate place value beyond 100.
25. know, read, and write 1-, 2- and 3-place numbers.
26. rename through 50.
27. rename 50 through 100.
28. rename 100 through 500.
29. rename over 500.
30. indicate Roman numerals I–X.
31. indicate Roman numerals XI–L.
32. indicate Roman numerals C–M.
33. read and write to millions.
34. read and write to billions.
35. indicate an understanding of rounding of whole numbers.
36. classify numbers as composite, prime, or neither.
37. understand common factors and Greatest Common Factor (GCF).
38. identify multiples of numbers and Least Common Multiple (LCM).
39. understand integers.
40. understand negative numbers.
41. understand rational numbers.
42. understand base numeration.
43. understand primitive numbers.
44. understand scientific notation.

ORDINALS

The student will

1. understand first through fifth by marking objects in ordinal positions, first to fifth.
2. understand sixth through tenth by placing pictures in specified ordinal positions to tenth.
3. place and count objects in ordinal position first through tenth.
4. label pictured events according to ordinal sequence.
5. use ordinals over tenth in functional arithmetic.
6. read ordinals out of sequence.
7. understand ordinals to hundredths.

ADDITION

The student will

1. understand addition facts 1–10.
2. understand addition facts 11–20.
3. add facts vertically 1–10.
4. add facts horizontally 1–10.
5. add two digits, no regrouping.
6. add three digits, no regrouping.
7. complete number sentences with missing digits.
8. add two and three digits with regrouping.

9. add one to three digits and five addends with regrouping.
10. add two addends with five columns.
11. add three addends with four columns.
12. add four addends with four columns.
13. add equations.
14. add by endings.
15. understand vocabulary of addition.
16. average a series of numerals.
17. understand commutative property.
18. understand associative property.

SUBTRACTION
The student will

1. understand subtraction facts 1–10.
2. use number sentences with missing digits.
3. understand subtraction facts 1–20.
4. understand subtraction facts 1–20 horizontally and vertically.
5. subtract two digits, no regrouping.
6. subtract three digits, no regrouping.
7. subtract two and three digits with regrouping.
8. subtract two to four digits with regrouping.
9. subtract four and five digits with regrouping.
10. check subtraction by addition.
11. understand the vocabulary of subtraction.
12. understand 0.

MULTIPLICATION
The student will

1. count and write by 10 to 100, 5 to 50, 2 to 100.
2. count and write by 3 to 36; by 4 to 48; by 5 to 60; by 6 to 72; by 7 to 84; by 8 to 96; by 9 to 108; by 10 to 120; by 11 to 132; by 12 to 144.
3. multiply facts through 45.
4. multiply facts through 81.
5. multiply facts through 144.
6. multiply two digits by one digit.
7. multiply three digits by one digit.
8. multiply ten digits by one digit.
9. multiply three digits by three digits.
10. multiply four digits by three digits.
11. multiply multiples of 100, 1000.
12. multiply with regrouping.
13. understand vocabulary of multiplication.
14. identify prime numbers.
15. know modular multiplication.
16. understand square root.
17. understand cubes and cube root.
18. multiply numbers written in scientific notation.
19. multiply positive and negative integers.

DIVISION
The student will

1. divide facts through 45.
2. divide facts through 81.
3. divide facts through 144.
4. divide problems with remainder.
5. divide using multiples of 10.
6. divide 3/27.
7. divide 6/638.
8. divide 10/181.
9. divide 325/1942.
10. check answers by multiplication.
11. divide by two-digit divisor with quantity remainder.
12. divide by three-digit divisor.
13. understand vocabulary of division.
14. divide with fractions.
15. divide with decimals.
16. divide positive and negative integers.

STORY PROBLEMS
The student will

1. solve oral story problems involving 1 to 10 more.
2. solve oral story problems involving 1 to 10 less.
3. identify the process to be used in terms of key words in written story problems.
4. solve one-operation written story problems involving addition for 1–10.
5. solve one-operation written story problems involving addition for numbers over 10.
6. solve one-operation written story problems involving subtraction for 1–10.
7. solve one-operation written story problems involving subtraction for numbers over 10.
8. solve two-operation written story problems involving addition and subtraction for 1–10.
9. estimate the answers to written story problems.
10. solve two-operation written story problems involving addition and subtraction for numbers over 10.
11. solve one-operation written story problems involving multiplication for 1–10.
12. solve one-operation written story problems involving multiplication for numbers over 10.
13. solve one-operation written story problems involving division for 1–10.
14. solve one-operation written story problems involving division for numbers over 10.
15. solve two-operation written story problems involving multiplication and division for 1–10.
16. solve two-operation written story problems involving multiplication and division for numbers over 10.

17. solve two-operation written story problems involving combination of addition, subtraction, multiplication, and division for 1–10.
18. solve two-operation written story problems involving combination of addition, subtraction, multiplication, and division for numbers over 10.
19. solve simple written story problems involving fractions.
20. solve complex written story problems involving fractions.
21. solve simple written story problems involving decimals.
22. solve complex written story problems involving decimals.
23. solve simple written story problems involving percentage.
24. solve complex written story problems involving percentage.
25. solve simple written story problems involving combination of fractions, decimals, and percentage.
26. solve complex written story problems involving combination of fractions, decimals, and percentage.
27. write number sentences and equations for story problems and match equations to story problems.
28. solve story problems using concepts in measurement.
29. solve story problems using graphs.
30. solve problems dealing with time, work, rate, distance, and speed.

MEASUREMENT
The student will

1. understand and name days of the week in order.
2. understand and name months of the year in order.
3. tell time on the hour.
4. tell time on the half hour.
5. tell time on the quarter hour.
6. tell time on 5-minute intervals.
7. read symbols of time (6:00) and abbreviations (A.M., P.M., hr., min.) in time problems.
8. solve time problems.
9. read and understand words associated with time (*hour, half-hour, o'clock, past, after, leap year, fortnight, decade, scores, centuries, millenniums*).
10. read a digital clock.
11. determine age by computation from date of birth to present date.
12. understand temperature in degrees.
13. read Celsius or Fahrenheit scale thermometer.
14. solve temperature problems.
15. understand (convert) pint, quart, gallon (3 quarts = _______ pints).
16. use liter and milliliter.
17. understand (convert) half pint and half gallon.
18. solve problems with volume.
19. understand metric volume.
20. solve problems with metric volume.
21. understand ounce (oz.) and pound (lb.)
22. solve weight problems.
23. understand the vocabulary of weight comparisons (*full, empty, light, heavy, most,* and *least*).
24. know relationship of grams and kilograms.
25. solve metric weight problems.
26. understand inch, foot, yard, mile.
27. use centimeter to find lengths.
28. measure to closest unit of measurements (inch, etc.); for example, convert inches to feet.

$$\begin{array}{r} 28 \text{ inches} \\ +\ 40 \text{ inches} \\ \hline 68 \text{ inches} = 5 \text{ feet } 8 \text{ inches} \end{array}$$

29. solve standard distance problems.
30. understand metric distance.
31. solve metric distance problems.
32. understand standard dry measures.
33. use the calendar.
34. understand seasons.
35. find the perimeter of geometric shapes or objects.
36. find the area of shapes, rectangles, or objects.
37. find the diameter of shapes or objects.
38. understand time and climatic zones, belts, and standard time.
39. understand latitude and longitude.
40. read simple graphs (bar graph, line graph, pictograph).
41. read complex graphs.
42. read maps.
43. use solid measurements.
44. add and subtract measurements with regrouping, converting answers to simple form.
45. find area of triangle, circle, parallelogram.
46. find circumference.
47. understand ratio and proportion.

MONEY
The student will

1. identify penny, nickel, dime, quarter.
2. identify half dollar, etc.
3. compare value of coins (penny, nickel, dime, quarter, etc.).
4. substitute value of coins (e.g., 2 dimes + 1 nickel = 1 quarter).
5. know symbols $ and ¢.

6. do simple money problems (add, subtract, multiply, divide).
7. do complex money problems in dollar-and-cent notation.
8. identify change after a purchase.
9. add purchases and count out change.

FRACTIONS
The student will

1. divide shapes (objects) in half.
2. divide sets in half.
3. divide shapes and sets in quarters and thirds.
4. divide shapes and sets beyond one third.
5. add fractions with like denominators ($1/4 + 1/4 =$).
6. add fractions with unlike denominators ($1/2 + 1/3 =$).
7. add mixed numbers with like denominators ($2\,1/5 + 2\,1/5 =$).
8. add mixed numbers with unlike denominators ($3\,2/3 + 4\,1/4 =$).
9. add, renaming the sum ($6\,8/7 = 7\,1/7$).
10. add longer columns with same denominator ($5/8 + 3/8 + 2/8 =$).
11. add longer columns with different denominators ($3/8 + 2/6 + 1/3 =$).
12. subtract fractions with like denominators ($3/4 - 1/4 =$).
13. subtract fractions with unlike denominators ($4/6 - 1/3 =$).
14. subtract mixed numbers with like denominators ($6\,6/7 - 1\,1/7 =$).
15. subtract mixed numbers with unlike denominators ($3\,1/2 - 2\,1/6 =$).
16. subtract whole and mixed numbers with renaming ($8 - 5\,2/3 =$).
17. subtract mixed numbers with unlike denominators and renaming ($6\,1/8 - 2\,1/2 =$).
18. multiply fractions with like denominators ($1/3 \times 1/3 =$).
19. multiply fractions with unlike denominators ($2/3 \times 3/4 =$).
20. multiply simple fraction × whole number ($3/4 \times 11 =$).
21. multiply mixed number × whole number ($6\,2/3 \times 7 =$).
22. multiply mixed number × mixed number ($4\,1/2 \times 3\,2/3 =$).
23. multiply cancelling simple fraction × mixed number ($1/4 \times 2\,1/4 =$).
24. change mixed number to improper fraction by multiplication ($2\,3/4 = 11/4$).
25. change fraction to equivalent by multiplication ($2/3 = 6/9$).
26. understand inversion of fractions.
27. divide whole number by simple fraction ($6 \div 1/3 =$).
28. divide simple fraction by simple fraction ($1/2 \div 1/7 =$).
29. reduce to lowest terms ($4/8 = 1/2$).
30. change improper fraction to mixed or whole number ($12/7 = 1\,5/7$).
31. divide mixed number by simple fraction ($3\,2/3 \div 1/4 =$).
32. divide whole number by mixed number ($6 \div 4\,1/3 =$).
33. divide mixed number by mixed number ($3\,1/7 \div 2\,1/3 =$).
34. divide simple fraction by whole number ($3/4 \div 6 =$).
35. divide simple fraction by mixed number ($1/3 \div 2\,1/2 =$).
36. divide mixed number by whole number ($6\,3/8 \div 5 =$).

DECIMALS/PERCENT
The student will

1. identify place value.
2. compare decimals.
3. write decimals _____ tens + _____ tenths = ( ).
4. change decimals to fractions.
5. add and subtract decimals to tenths and hundredths.
6. add and subtract two-decimal numbers to hundredths.
7. multiply whole numbers by decimals.
8. understand, read, and write through billions.
9. extend meaning through millionths.
10. write decimal equations for proper and improper fractions.
11. multiply decimal by decimal.
12. divide by decimal number.
13. change decimal to fraction and then take percent.
14. compute fraction to percent.
15. compute percent to fraction.
16. compute percent to decimal.
17. compute percent of whole number.

GEOMETRY
The student will

1. identify and reproduce circles, squares, rectangles, triangles ○ □ ▭ △.
2. identify and reproduce ◇.
3. identify cone and semi-circle.
4. identify sphere and cylinder.
5. identify prism, pyramid, cube.

6. identify triangular and rectangular prisms.
7. identify tetrahedron.
8. measure angles.
9. identify straight and curved lines.
10. recognize line segments.
11. recognize congruent figures.
12. recognize intersecting curves.
13. identify labeled points.
14. identify rays, planes.
15. identify right angles.
16. identify parallel lines.
17. understand diameter and radius.
18. identify perpendicular and intersecting lines, planes, and line segments.
19. understand Pythagorean Theorem.
20. recognize polygons.
21. recognize right, congruent, and similar triangles.
22. measure triangles.
23. identify and draw angles, as well as isosceles and equilateral triangles.
24. recognize trapezoids.
25. identify optical illusions.
26. understand mean, median, mode.
27. measure exterior and interior angles.

SYMBOLS OF ARITHMETIC
The student will

1. understand + and − (addition and subtraction).
2. understand × and ÷ (multiplication and division).
3. understand < and > (*less than* and *greater than*).
4. understand = and ≠ (*equal* and *not equal*).
5. understand ″ and ′ (inches and feet).
6. understand . and % (decimal and percent).
7. understand _____ : _____ (time).
8. understand set notation: ∩ (intersection); ⊂ (subset); ⊃ (super subset); ∪ (union); ( ) (null); ∅ (empty).
9. recognize *n*° (degrees).

ARITHMETIC SEQUENCE AND INVENTORY

The Mann-Suiter Grade Level Arithmetic Sequence (Form 9-1) and Developmental Arithmetic Inventory (Form 9-2) can be used as follows:

1. The arithmetic sequence can be used to determine the skills necessary for success at a particular grade level. Items from the arithmetic inventory that measure these skills can be used by the instructor to assess these particular operations in learners. Further testing should be discontinued for the students who fail in the initial assessment. If students succeed in this initial evaluation, it indicates that they have at least the basic skills necessary for success in initial arithmetical operations at that grade level. The instructor can then continue to test to the limits of the learners' abilities with higher level items, stopping after a reasonable amount of failure. Assessment of this nature is designed to limit or reduce the amount of failure in testing. If students cannot count by ones to 10, it is unreasonable to expect them to count to 100 by fives.
2. An alternate approach in assessment would be to administer the entire inventory to all of the students and then relate the results to the particular skills that are outlined developmentally in the sequence chart. This will give the instructor a measure initially of a broader range of skills (strengths and weaknesses) in the learners.

Mann-Suiter Grade Level Arithmetic Sequence

The suggested developmental sequence indicates the extent to which particular skills should be introduced at certain grade levels. There is room for latitude in that some students will not have mastered certain arithmetic skills for their grade level and will need to have the curriculum adjusted accordingly. The teacher must be ready to drop down and build in the prerequisite skills for individual students. The developmental sequence chart is to be used as a guide and is designed to make it easy for the teacher to determine specific skills that need to be established for a particular grade level. The teacher can add items as necessary to the arithmetic sequence.

Mann-Suiter Developmental Arithmetic Inventory and Testing Kit

The Mann-Suiter Developmental Arithmetic Inventory (Form 9-2) and the Develop-Your-Own-Testing Kit (Form 9-3) are designed to aid teachers in determining strengths and weaknesses in the areas of arithmetic that involve both computation and problem solving. Information will also be gained in the area of spatial-temporal concept formation involving the critical skills necessary for success at higher levels of performance. The inventory and kit are flexible, adaptable to examining pre-school children or older students with higher mental processes.

Teachers can determine the performance skills of the students in their classes and utilize this information in preparing for the teaching of a particular arithmetical operation. They will also be better able to determine the extent to which spatial-temporal problems have affected the learning of arithmetic skills.

DIRECTIONS FOR ADMINISTRATION

1. Determine the arithmetic skills and sequence for a particular grade level by referring to the charts beginning on page 251.
2. From those charts, make a list of the prerequisite critical skills (previous level skills) related to this grade level sequence.
3. Choose the test items on the Mann-Suiter Developmental Arithmetic Inventory that pertain to the skills that you anticipate teaching.
4. Test initially using these items only.
5. Using more advanced items, test further only those students who have been successful in the initial testing. Evaluation in this way will reduce failure.
6. The inventory can also be used in its entirety for particular students.

Concept Teaching Sequence

It appears that number concepts need to be developed in a sequential manner. This consideration is particularly important when teaching students who have difficulties in processing information. In arithmetic, as in other areas of skill development, the level of presentation that appears to be most successful is the concrete one. This implies that the teacher must include a great deal of manipulative activities as part of the instructional program in each of the following developmental task areas:

VISUAL DISCRIMINATION (MATCHING)

Shape

1. Begin with small geometric solids and let the students feel and describe the differences and similarities between the various forms.
2. Use form boards, including metal insets or templates, to teach discrimination.
3. Pair off objects and forms, as in a Noah's ark.
4. Pictures or dittos of objects and geometric shapes can be used for matching purposes. Have the learner look for differences as well as likenesses.

Size

1. Use insets or "nesting material"—cans that fit into cans, barrels that fit into barrels, or boxes that fit into boxes.
2. Group cylinders, blocks, etc., by size.
3. Use different-size rods or wooden dowels.
4. Montessori material that can be used here includes the Pink Tower, the Brown Staircase, and Knobless Cylinders.
5. Use pictures of geometric shapes and objects for size differentiation.
6. Use graded insets, including objects or geometric shapes. For example: ● ● ● ● ●

GROUPING OR SETS

1. Begin with hula hoops and put objects inside.
2. Use regular dominoes: [: | ::] ; then proceed to dominoes with sets: [●● ● | ●●● ●]
3. Use figure-ground activities found on page 159.
4. Use matching sets of objects and forms printed on dittos. The learner will trace around identical objects or forms with the same color crayon.
5. Use tachistoscopic activities in which the teacher exposes groups of dots for short periods. Begin with widely separated dots and gradually move the dots closer together. Blocks or coins can be used in the same manner.

VOCABULARY OF SPATIAL-TEMPORAL RELATIONSHIPS

1. Use a concrete object (such as a toy monkey) and a box or some other container to teach concepts of space such as *over, under, inside, outside, below, above, beside, next, near, alongside.*
2. The same concepts can be taught using a toy squirrel and a cardboard tree.
3. Concepts of time can be taught using stories or real experiences such as field trips that include such words as *sooner, later, late, before, after, morning, afternoon, night, past, shortly afterward, almost,* and *often.*
4. Send students on an errand and time them. How long did it take to get there? Did it take more time to get back? Was it a long or short trip?
5. Parents can do many reinforcing activities during routine, day-to-day experiences at home or when traveling.

ESTIMATION

In all of the following activities, the students will be required to make judgments about spatial relationships without physically matching at first. After making an estimation, they can check for accuracy by manipulating the material or by other physical movements, such as pacing off the distance.

Form 9-1

MANN-SUITER GRADE LEVEL ARITHMETIC SEQUENCE
A

Grade Level	*One-to-One*	*Numerals*	*Sets*	*Ordinals*
K	Matches one to one Matches shapes (discrimination) ○ □ △ ◇ Vocabulary of space and position Estimates distance, height, and quantity Order by height	Matches one to one Writes 0–5 Identifies 0–10 Identifies before and after 1–10 Counts orally 0–10	Matches equivalent sets 00 = 00 Recognizes sets 0–5 Recognizes sets with more or less	Understands first through fifth
1st		Identifies 0–50 Counts orally 0–100 Counts and writes by 10s to 100 and 5s to 50 Writes 0–50 Knows place value 0–50 Renames 1s & 10s through 50 Identifies odd and even numbers	Recognizes sets 6–10 Knows language of sets	Understands sixth through tenth
2nd		Counts and writes by 2s to 100; 3s to 36; 4s to 48; 5s to 100; 10s to 200 Writes 0–100 Knows place value 50–100 Renames 50–100 Knows odd and even numbers	Identifies equivalent subsets	Reads ordinals through twelfth
3rd		Writes in sequence 1–999 Writes from dictation 1–999 Renames 10s to 100s Knows Roman numerals I–X Knows, reads, writes 1-, 2-, and 3-place numbers	Identifies equal sets	Understands ordinals to hundredths Reads ordinals through twentieth

Mann-Suiter Grade Level Arithmetic Sequence

A (continued)

Grade Level	One-to-One	Numerals	Sets	Ordinals
4th		Counts and writes by 6s to 72; 7s to 84; 8s to 96; 9s to 108 Knows place value to millions Knows Roman numerals XI–C Understands rounding of numbers to nearest 10	Identifies universal sets Identifies intersection of sets	Reads ordinals through thirtieth
5th		Reads and writes billions Knows Roman numerals C–M Understands rounding of whole numbers Identifies prime and composite numbers Understands common factors and Greatest Common Factors (GCF) Identifies multiples of numbers and Least Common Multiple (LCM)	Understands union of sets, disjoint sets, finite and infinite sets, empty sets	
6th		Understands integers, negative numbers, rational numbers, base numeration, place value to billions place	Understands solution sets, sets of ordered pairs	
7th		Understands primitive numbers, expanded number bases	Identifies null sets, proper and improper subsets, unequal sets	
8th		Understands scientific notation, absolute value, solving inequalities	Understands replacement set of a variable, set builder	

B

Grade Level	Addition	Subtraction	Story Problems	Geometry
K			Solves oral problems using "one more" Solves oral problems using "one less"	Recognizes and reproduces ○ □ ▭ △ Recognizes and reproduces straight and curved lines
1st	Knows facts 1–10 Adds facts 1–10 horizontally and vertically Adds 2 digits no regrouping	Knows facts 1–10 Subtracts 2 digits no regrouping Subtracts facts 1–10 horizontally and vertically	Solves written addition and subtraction problems 0–5	Recognizes and reproduces ◇ Recognizes line segments not closed curves
2nd	Knows facts 11–20 Adds 3 digits no regrouping Completes number sentences with missing digits	Knows facts 11–20 Subtracts 3 digits no regrouping Uses number sentences with missing digits	Solves written addition and subtraction problems through 20 1-step problems	Recognizes cone, semi-circle, congruent figures, intersecting curves, labeled points
3rd	Adds 2 and 3 digits with regrouping Adds by endings	Subtracts 2 and 3 digits with regrouping Checks by addition	Solves problems using + and − × and ÷ 2-step problems	Recognizes spheres and cylinders, rays, planes, right angles, parallel lines Understands diameter and radius
4th	Knows vocabulary Adds 1 to 3 digits and 5 addends with regrouping Commutative and associative properties expanded	Knows vocabulary Subtracts 2 to 4 digits with regrouping	Solves multiple-step problems + − × ÷ Writes number sentences Solves problems with averages	Recognizes prism, pyramid, cube, triangular & rectangular prisms and tetrahedron, perpendicular and intersecting lines, planes, and line segments

B (continued)

Grade Level	*Addition*	*Subtraction*	*Story Problems*	*Geometry*
5th	Adds 2 addends with 5 columns Adds 3 addends with 4 columns Adds 4 addends with 4 columns Adds equations Averages	Subtracts 4 and 5 digits with regrouping Understands 0	Solves multiple-step problems using fractions, decimals, ratio, measurement graphs (bar and circle)	Measures angles Understands Pythagorean Theorem Recognizes polygons Recognizes right, congruent, and similar triangles Measures triangles
6th	Adds Base 2	Subtracts Base 2	Solves problems dealing with time, work, rate, distance, and speed	Uses equations to find volume Finds perimeter and area Identifies and draws angles, isosceles and equilateral triangles
7th	Maintain concepts	Maintain concepts	Solves expanded story problems	Recognizes trapezoids, optical illusions, convex polygons, Classifies triangles Understands mean, median, and mode
8th	Maintain concepts	Maintain concepts	Solves expanded story problems	Proves triangles congruent through properties Measures exterior and interior angles Knows properties of circles, spheres, cylinders, cones, prisms, and pyramids

C

Grade Level	Standard Measurement	Metric Measurement	Symbols of Math	Multiplication
K	Understands simple comparison in length, size, and weight			
1st	Knows days of the week Tells time on the hour, half-hour, and day Knows temperature Knows pint, quart, cup Knows inch, foot, yard Knows weight Compares inch and half-inch	Uses centimeter to find lengths	Recognizes $+, -, <\ >$ $=$, and $\neq$	
2nd	Knows months of the year Relates inches to feet Knows gallon	Uses liter and milliliter	Recognizes $<\ >$, $=$, and $\neq$	Multiplies products through 25 Relates multiplication to repeated addition
3rd	Tells time in 5-minute intervals Tells time in quarter hours Converts inches, feet, yards Converts half-pint, quart Uses calendar, week, month Uses scale Measures to nearest ½ or ¼ inch Reads a digital clock Reads Celsius or Fahrenheit scale thermometer	Knows relationship of meters and centimeters, grams, and kilograms, liters and milliliters	Recognizes $\times, \div$, ″, and ′	Multiplies facts through 45 Multiplies 2 digits by 1 digit, 3 digits by 1 digit, 10 digits by 1 digit
4th	Finds perimeter of shapes Understands dry measures (weight) Understands volume, area, square inch, and square mile Converts one unit of measure to another	Uses scale to read kilograms	Uses letter *n* for missing number Recognizes metric symbols: cm, m, kg, and l Recognizes ∩ intersection of sets	Knows vocabulary Multiplies facts through 81 Multiplies multiples of 100, 1,000 Multiplies with regrouping

C (continued)

Grade Level	Standard Measurement	Metric Measurement	Symbols of Math	Mulitiplication
5th	Understands zones, belts, standard time Reads graphs (bar graph, line graph, pictograph) Solves time problems Finds area of squares and rectangles Uses solid measurements Reads road map Understands latitude and longitude	Shows metric comparisons Understands metric scale drawings Knows ratio of measures	Recognizes subset ⊂, super subset ⊃, union of sets ∪	Multiplies 3 digits by 3 digits Multiplies 4 digits by 3 digits Identifies prime numbers
6th	Finds approximation of area Finds area of triangle, circle Finds circumference	Understands approximation of area Knows abbreviations of metric units Converts to larger and smaller units	Recognizes %, π, c	Knows modular multiplication Knows lattice method of multiplication Knows square root Multiplies by 4 digits Multiplies with decimals and mixed fractions
7th	Finds the precision of a measurement Finds lateral and surface area Finds area of a parallelogram	Can write metric abbreviations in order: kilo, hecto, deca, deci, centi, milli Converts lengths to decimal measures	Recognizes null set ( ) Recognizes empty set ∅	Understands cubes and cube root
8th	Understands mass, conversion factors, ratio and proportion, hypotenuse and square root	Converts standard to metric measurement	Recognizes degrees n°, congruent figures ≅, absolute value |a|	Knows operations with approximate numbers Multiplies numbers written in scientific notation Multiplies negative and positive rational numbers Multiplies negative and positive integers

D

Grade Level	*Division*	*Fractions*	*Decimals/ Percent*	*Money*
K		Divides shapes in ½ Divides sets in ½		Identifies penny, nickel, dime
1st		Divides shapes and sets in ¼		Identifies quarters Compares value of penny, nickel, dime
2nd		Divides shapes and sets in ⅓		Knows symbols $ ¢ Substitutes money values: penny, nickel, dime, quarter Identifies change after purchase
3rd	Divides facts through 45 Divides problems with remainders Divides using multiples of ten	Divides shapes and sets in ½, ¼, ⅓		Compares money value 50¢ and $1.00 Adds and subtracts money problems
4th	Knows vocabulary Divides facts through 81 Divides $3\overline{)27}$ $3\overline{)638}$ $10\overline{)181}$ Checks answers by multiplication	Adds and subtracts fractions with like denominators Adds and subtracts fractions with unlike denominators Adds and subtracts mixed numbers		Adds purchases and counts out change
5th	Divides by 2-digit divisor with quotient remainder Divides 3-digit divisor Averages	Multiplies a whole number by a fraction, A fraction by a fraction, A mixed number by a whole number, A mixed number by mixed number	Identifies place value Solves decimal-fraction and equivalence Adds, subtracts, and reads and writes decimals to tenths and hundredths Adds and subtracts 2-decimal numbers to hundredths Multiplies whole numbers by decimals	

D (continued)

Grade Level	*Division*	*Fractions*	*Decimals/ Percent*	*Money*
6th	Divides by divisor with three or more digits Divides with fractions Divides with decimals	Divides fractions with like and unlike denominators Divides improper fractions Divides mixed numbers	Understands, reads, writes through billions Extends meaning through millionths Counts by tenths, hundredths, thousandths Adds and subtracts 2 decimals to thousandths Writes decimal equations for proper and improper fractions Multiplies decimal by decimal Divides by whole number or decimal number Computes percent of a number	
7th	Divides positive and negative integers	Simplifies expressions containing fractions Understands ratio and proportion Understands ratio and percent	Understands terminating and repeating decimals	
8th	Uses properties of division for rational numbers		Divides and multiplies decimals	

Form 9-2

MANN-SUITER DEVELOPMENTAL ARITHMETIC INVENTORY
(To be used for diagnostic purposes)

School ____________________

Teacher ____________________

Date ____________________

NAME ________________ DATE OF BIRTH ________ SEX ___ BI-LINGUAL YES ___ NO ___

ADDRESS ______________ GLASSES ______ HEARING AID ________

PERTINENT FACTS KNOWN IN PAST HISTORY ____________________

PREREQUISITES TO FORMAL ARITHMETIC: (LEVEL 1) YES NO

1. Place 4 cubes or blocks of different colors upright on a table in the suggested order and ask the following questions:
   a. Point to the blocks on the bottom . . . . ___ ___
   b. Point to the blocks on the top . . . . ___ ___
   c. Count all of them . . . . ___ ___
   d. Which color block is next to the blue block? . . . . ___ ___
   e. Which color block is above the green block? . . . . ___ ___
   f. Which color block is below the red block? (language) . . . . ___ ___

red yellow
blue green

2. Can the student match all of the following concrete insets correctly? (discrimination) (Note trial-and-error behavior) . . . . ___ ___
3. Does the student know the meaning of the words, *big, bigger, biggest,* and *small, smaller, smallest* when asked to compare three things of different size? (language) The teacher shows three circles and says the following:
   a. "Show me a big circle." (Count any of the bigger two correct) . . . . ___ ___
   b. "Show me a small circle." (Count any of the smaller two correct) . . . . ___ ___
   c. "Show me the biggest circle." . . . . ___ ___
   d. "Show me the smallest circle." . . . . ___ ___
4. Can the student place in order six cubes or cylinders based on increasing height? (spatial). ___ ___
5. Can the student count to ten pointing to each of 10 objects while counting? (one to one correspondence) . . . . ___ ___
6. Can the student estimate space by putting six different size cards in their respective envelopes? (spatial) . . . . ___ ___

   Note: For questions 7 and 9, ask parent for further information.
7. Does the student become confused and lost when taken away from a familiar environment, such as on a field trip? (spatial) . . . . ___ ___
8. Can the student be sent on an errand to an unfamiliar part of the school without getting lost? (spatial) . . . . ___ ___
9. Does the student ever exaggerate the size or shape of things? (spatial) . . . . ___ ___

10. Does the student know the concept of *less than*? (spatial). The teacher asks, "Which one has less?" [•.•] [:::] . . . . ___ ___
11. Does the student know the concept of *more than*? (spatial). The teacher asks, "Which one has more?" [•.•.] [:•:•:] . . . . ___ ___
12. Can the student reproduce the following geometric shapes with a pencil and paper?
    Age 2 ○ . . . . ___ ___
    Age 4 □ . . . . ___ ___
    Age 5 △ . . . . ___ ___
    Age 7 ◇ . . . . ___ ___

BASIC ARITHMETIC FUNCTIONS (LEVEL II)

13. Does the student know that 3 = 000, 4 = 0000, etc? (sets). . . . . ___ ___
14. Show the student a dime, two nickels, and a quarter, and say as you point to the dime, "Can you show me something that is the same as this?" (conservation of quantity) . . . . . . ___ ___
15. Does the student know that 5 = 3 + 2 or 4 + 1? (equivalence) . . . . ___ ___
16. Can the student tell you what comes before 5 or after 8? (spatial and/or memory) . . . . ___ ___
17. Can the student add or subtract in different positions? (spatial)

    $\begin{array}{r} 2 \\ +4 \\ \hline \end{array}$ . . . . ___ ___

    4 − 2 = ... ___ ___
    2 + 4 = ... ___ ___

    $\begin{array}{r} 4 \\ -2 \\ \hline \end{array}$ . . . . ___ ___

18. When shown incomplete numerals can the student identify them correctly? (Closure) . . . . . ___ ___
19. Does the student understand ordinal concepts? (first, second, last) (spatial and/or language) . . . . ___ ___
20. Can the student write numerals that you call out between one and one hundred? (auditory-visual association) . . . . ___ ___
    7 . . . . ___ ___
    13 . . . . ___ ___
    34 . . . . ___ ___
    65 . . . . ___ ___
    89 . . . . ___ ___
    96 . . . . ___ ___
21. Can the student reproduce the following on paper from memory? Expose the card for 4 seconds (visual memory) [5 2 7 4] . . . . ___ ___
22. Can the student fill in missing numbers on a 100-number board? (memory-sequence and/or spatial) . . . . ___ ___
23. Can the student tell you how many ones are in 25? (equivalence) . . . . ___ ___
24. Can the student tell you how many tens are in 76? . . . . ___ ___

COMPUTATION (LEVEL III)

25. Can the student add?
    a. Simple $\begin{array}{r} 4 \\ +3 \\ \hline \end{array}$ (7). . . . . ___ ___

    b. Complex $\begin{array}{r} 25 \\ +32 \\ \hline \end{array}$ (57) . . . . ___ ___

    c. Regrouping $\begin{array}{r} 28 \\ +54 \\ \hline \end{array}$ (82) . . . . ___ ___

26. Can the student subtract?
    a. Simple 5 −3 (2). . . . . ___ ___
    b. Complex 46 −32 (14) . . . . ___ ___
    c. Regrouping 37 −29 (8) . . . . ___ ___
27. Can the student multiply?
    a. Simple multiplication, ones. 4 ×3 (12) . . . . ___ ___
    b. Simple multiplication, 10s. 22 ×4 (88) . . . . ___ ___
    c. Complex multiplication, with carrying to 10s. 34 ×5 (170) . . . . ___ ___
    d. Complex multiplication, with carrying to 100s. 28 ×52 (1456). . . . . ___ ___
28. Can the student divide?
    a. Simple division: 3)9 (3). . . . . ___ ___
    b. Division with remainder, 10s. 4)15 (3 r 3). . . . . ___ ___
    c. Simple division with remainder, 100s. 6)248 (41 r 2). . . . . ___ ___
    d. Complex division with remainder, 10s. 22)75 (3 r 9). . . . . ___ ___
    e. Complex division with remainder, 100s. 429)1,240 (2 r 382). . . . . ___ ___

Fractions

29. Can the student tell you what part is shaded? . . . . ___ ___
    . . . . ___ ___
30. Can the student tell you what part is not shaded? . . . . ___ ___
31. Can the student show you ½? . . . . ___ ___

Time (Spatial)

32. Can the student tell time on the hour? 6:00 . . . . ___ ___
33. Can the student tell time on the half hour? 3:30 . . . . ___ ___
34. Can the student tell time on the quarter hour? 3:15 . . . . ___ ___
35. Can the student tell you how many days there are in a week?. . . . . ___ ___
36. Can the student tell you how many weeks there are in a month?. . . . . ___ ___
37. Can the student tell you how many weeks there are in a year? . . . . ___ ___
38. Can the student tell you how many months there are in a year? . . . . ___ ___

39. Can the student solve one-operation story problems (all third level or above and presented on printed cards in order of difficulty)?
    a. Bob had 6 marbles and he found 2 more marbles. How many marbles did he have altogether? (under 10 addition) (8). . . . . ___ ___
    b. Betty had 6 cookies, and her mother gave her 9 more cookies. How many cookies did she have altogether? (over 10 addition) (15). . . . . ___ ___
    c. A boy had 11 pennies and he gave his brother 5 pennies. How many did he have left? (simple subtraction) (6). . . . . ___ ___
    d. A girl spent 8 cents each for 3 candy bars. How much did she spend? (simple multiplication) (24). . . . . ___ ___
    e. A store had 24 new shirts and sold 11 of them. How many shirts were left? (complex subtraction) (13). . . . . ___ ___
    f. There were 16 pieces of candy to be divided among 4 boys. How many pieces of candy did each boy receive? (simple division) (4). . . . . ___ ___
40. Can the student solve two-operation, complex story problems?
    a. John bought 3 dozen toys at $5 a dozen. How much change should he receive from a $20 bill? (5) . . . . ___ ___
    b. If a man charged $10 for the first time he mowed your lawn and $5 per week from then on, how much would you pay for the first four weeks? (25) . . . . ___ ___

Form 9-3

DEVELOP-YOUR-OWN TESTING KIT

(For Use with Mann-Suiter Developmental Arithmetic Inventory)

Item	**Material**
1.	Use colored blocks for ages six and below and a 5″ × 8″ card colored with a magic marker for ages seven and above.

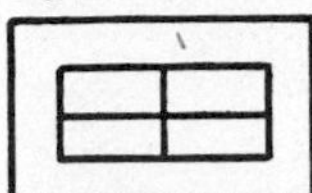

2.	Construct out of cardboard and color with a magic marker:

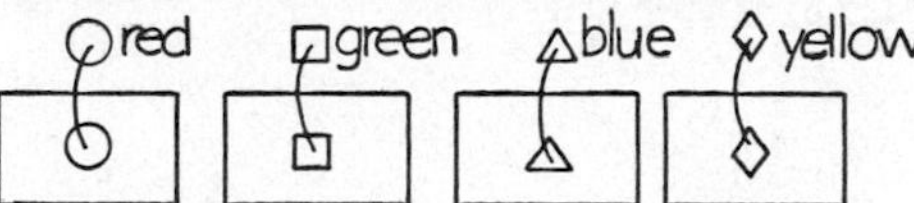

3.	Draw four different-size circles on a 5″ × 8″ white card:

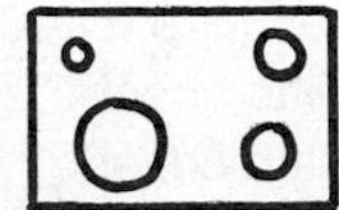

4.	Use six dowels or six pill boxes of different heights. Commercial materials can also be used.
5.	Use ten poker chips or ten pennies.
6.	Use six different-size cards with their respective envelopes.
10–11........	Use poker chips or pennies for ages six and below and 5″ × 8″ white cards with pictures of groupings for ages seven and above:

12.	Use insets from Item 2.
13.	Use blocks from Item 1 for ages six and below and 5″ × 8″ white cards with pictures of groupings for ages seven and above. (The same cards as in Item 10.)
14.	Use one dime, two nickels, and one quarter.
15.	Use a 5″ × 8″ card. Say, "Point to the ones that equal five." *Note:* The student must achieve 100% (2 correct and no wrong responses):

3+2 =
2+2 =
3+1 =
4+1 =

17.	Say, "How much is ______," pointing to each item in the order presented on the 5″ × 8″ white card:

$\begin{array}{r} 2 \\ +4 \\ \hline \end{array}$ 4-2=

$\begin{array}{r} 4 \\ -2 \\ \hline \end{array}$ 2+4=

18. .... Draw incomplete numerals on 3″ × 4″ cards.

5 2 4 9

Note: The student must achieve 100%.

19. .... Line up three blocks from Item 1, and have the student point.
20. .... Teacher's card is 3″ × 4″. The student writes on paper.

7-13-34-65-89-96

21. .... Place numerals 1″ apart on 5″ × 8″ card.

5274

22. .... Make or acquire a 100-number board.
25, 26. ...... Make a ditto sheet.
27, 28. ...... Make a ditto sheet.
29. .... Use 3″ × 4″ cards.
30. .... Use 3″ × 4″ cards.
31. .... Use 3″ × 4″ cards.
32. .... Use 5″ × 8″ cards. 6:00
33. .... Use 5″ × 8″ cards. 3:30
34. .... Use 5″ × 8″ cards. 3:15
39. .... Use six 3″ × 4″ white cards with one story problem typewritten per card.
40. .... Use two 3″ × 4″ white cards with one story problem typewritten per card.

Note: The story problems can be read by the students or the teacher and repeated if necessary. The students may look at the card and are also permitted to use pencil and paper if they desire.

Size

1. The students can estimate the size of other children in the class. Compare two students—"Who is shorter?" "Who is taller?" Then compare three or more students—"Who is the tallest?" "Who is the shortest?"
2. Ask the students to compare objects in terms of larger and smaller.
3. Place objects into various size piles and ask the students to rank them by size.
4. Use different size cards with their respective envelopes, and ask the students to estimate which card goes with which size envelope. Do not let the students physically manipulate the materials at first. Later, they can check for accuracy.
5. Give the students different size objects and different size containers, and let them estimate which object will fit into which container.
6. Have the students physically compare different size rods or dowels and rank them from smallest to largest.
7. Use ditto sheets that require the students to compare the relative size of lines and geometric forms.

Weight

1. Have the students hold and compare objects of different weights (begin with gross differences, then go to finer differences).
2. Ask the students to estimate the relative weights of objects without holding them. For example, "Which is heavier—a car or a bus?"
3. Using different piles of similar objects, the student should rank them by weight from lightest to heaviest.

Shape

1. Have the students estimate the fit of simple puzzle pieces.
2. Have the students use form boxes to make judgments about shapes.
3. Use ditto sheets that require the students to estimate shapes that interlock.

Distance

1. Ask students to estimate how many steps are required to go from one place to another (begin with short distances first).
2. Have students estimate how far they can throw a ball.
3. Have students estimate the relative distance of objects to themselves and from object to object in the classroom or outside of school. For example, "Which is closest to you—the tree or the fence?" "Which is further from the fence—the house or the telephone pole?"
4. Have students estimate the relative distance between a fixed point such as their homes or the classroom and other geographic locations that are familiar.
5. Use ditto sheets containing lines, geometric forms, or objects and have the students compare the relative distance of two or more objects from a fixed point, such as a small dot in the middle of the page, or from each other (begin with very simple comparisons).

COUNTING (ORAL)

1. Begin by teaching rote counting from one to five through songs such as "One Little, Two Little, Three Little Indians." (Later, count from one through ten.)
2. Follow the counting songs with Finger Plays. Begin with one to five and later count from one to ten.
3. Have the students do rote counting from one to ten.

COUNTING WITH MEANING (ONE-TO-ONE CORRESPONDENCE)

1. Begin by asking a student to give each student in the class a piece of paper or some other item that needs to be distributed.
2. Have the students fill a row of holes with pegs, beads, pebbles, or discs.
3. A variation of number two would be the addition of a drum beat as the learner performs each task.
4. Play Tea Time and have a student prepare settings of napkins, dishes, and utensils for a group of children who are already seated. A more advanced activity of this nature would be to prepare settings for a specific number of individuals who are not present.
5. Use paper dolls, and have the students give each one a costume.
6. Have the students match nuts and bolts and fit them together.
7. Use 2″ × 2″ cardboard squares, and have the students put wooden, plastic, felt, or magnetic numerals from one to five on each numbered square (later, from one to ten in each square). Begin as a matching exercise first and then go to rote memory.
8. Have the students count different groupings of students in the class.
9. Have the students count pennies, boxes, cylinders, stars in the flag, etc.
10. Have the students count things in the classroom by categories such as the number of pieces of chalk, erasers, and books on a shelf.

AUDITORY-VISUAL SYMBOL ASSOCIATION

1. Begin with wooden, plastic, felt, or magnetic numerals and have the students arrange them in order from one to five and later from one to ten. Say a numeral, hold it up, and have the students match by pointing to the correct one.
2. Have the students copy from a model as you say each numeral.
3. Have the students look in newspapers or magazines for numerals that they later can identify.
4. Use ditto sheets on which students circle all of one number while they say the number.
5. Use color-by-number games. Say a number and have the students color the area containing the number. The completed area colored by the students should form an identifiable design.

SYMBOL-VALUE ASSOCIATION (SETS)

1. Use Pop It Beads and say, "Show me one," etc.
   a. ●
   b. ● ●
   c. ● ● ●
2. Use the Maria Montessori formula as follows:
   a. Say, "This is (•) one."
      "This is (• •) two."
      "This is (• • •) three."
   b. Put beads in order.
   c. Say, "Show me one." ●
      "Show me two." ● ●
      "Show me three." ● ● ●
   d. Say, "Give me one." ●
      "Give me two." ● ●
      "Give me three." ● ● ●
   e. Make another set the same size as Item 1 above, and label as follows:
      Say, "This is [•]."
      "This is [• •]."
      "This is [• • •] "
3. Use a pegboard and have the students say the correct numeral as they match the number of pegs with the symbol equivalent. See Figure 9-1, for example.
4. Use beads, buttons, blocks, or coins to correspond with numerals from one to five (later from one to ten).

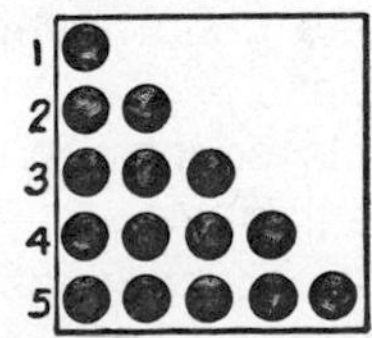

Figure 9-1

5. Have the students name things that come in twos, such as feet, eyes, ears, and hands; in threes, such as tricycle wheels, or a three-legged stool; in fours, such as dog's legs, chair legs, table legs, and car's tires; in fives, such as fingers, toes, pennies to a nickel, and points on a star.
6. Have the students make impressions of groups in clay, using pennies, beans, dowels, etc.
7. Have the students find pictures in magazines or books of different numbers of items.
8. Playing cards are good for learning and identifying sets.
9. Use small cans labeled from one to ten, with a corresponding number of ice-cream sticks or counters in them, to teach symbol-value associations (sets).

CARDINAL AND ORDINAL RELATIONSHIPS

1. Begin with three or four toy cars in a line near a toy house or a garage and ask the following questions:
   a. Which one is closest?
   b. Which one is farthest away?
   c. Which car is at the beginning of the line?
   d. Which car is at the end of the line?
   Note: As the learner responds, the teacher should say, "Yes, this is the first car, or second car, etc."
   e. Continue to ask questions about the third car, fourth car, etc.
2. Give the students number cards and teach the cardinal values of one to five first and the values to ten later. Have the students line up in groups of five or ten. When you call the cardinal number, the student with that number holds it up.
3. Play "office building" and decide on what floors certain things will need to go.
4. Label your bookshelves first, second, third, fourth, etc.
5. After the students can read the words, begin using cardinal directions when putting assignments on the chalkboard.
6. Use ordinal numbers in everyday activities in the classroom. For example, line up the class by saying, "Row one will line up first, row five will line up second . . ."

SIMPLE ADDITION AND SUBTRACTION

1. Teach alignment by using "see through" color pens (see Figure 9-2).
2. Use concrete materials such as rods to represent one or entire groupings (see Figure 9-3).
3. Write basic addition and subtraction number facts on small oak tag strips and place them in small drawstring cloth bags. The student can reach into

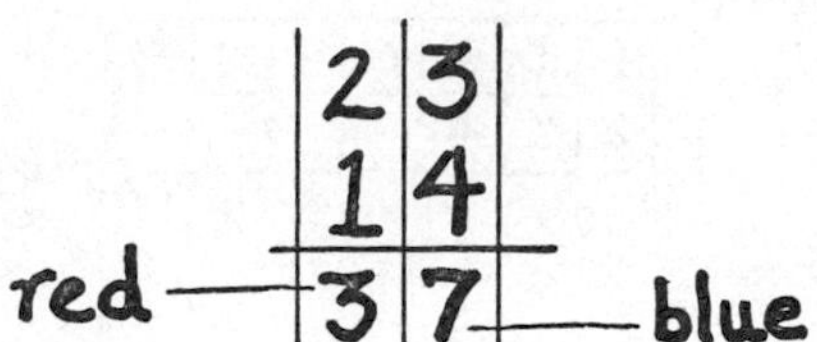

Figure 9-2

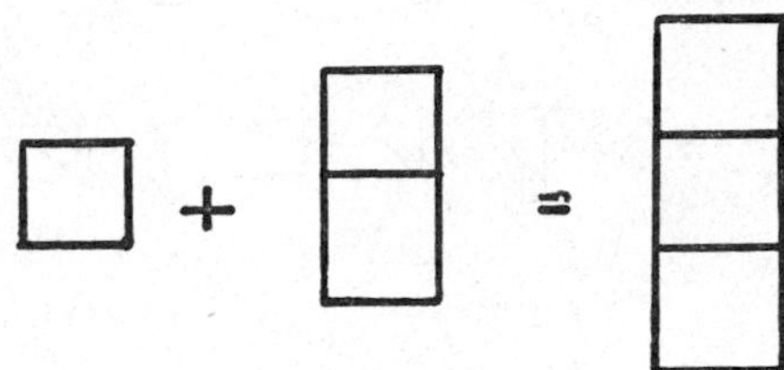

Figure 9-3

2+3= □+3=5 2+□=5 2+3=□

$\begin{array}{r}2\\+3\\\hline\end{array}$ $\begin{array}{r}\square\\+3\\\hline 5\end{array}$ $\begin{array}{r}2\\+\square\\\hline 5\end{array}$ $\begin{array}{r}3\\+2\\\hline \square\end{array}$

3-2= □-2=1 3-□=1 3-2=□

$\begin{array}{r}3\\-2\\\hline\end{array}$ $\begin{array}{r}\square\\-2\\\hline 1\end{array}$ $\begin{array}{r}3\\-\square\\\hline 1\end{array}$ $\begin{array}{r}3\\-2\\\hline \square\end{array}$

Figure 9-4

the bags and pull them out. Write the answers on the back of the cards to make them self-checking.

4. Using ditto sheets, teach addition and subtraction facts in all the ways shown in Figure 9-4.

SIMPLE MULTIPLICATION

1. Begin by teaching *skip counting,* for example, 2, 4, 6, 8, 10, 12, 14, 16, 18, 20, 22, 24.
   a. The students can begin with Pop It Beads or blocks and work simultaneously on small ditto sheets, on which are written the first and ending numeral (Figure 9-5). The students can count the beads and write the numerals, in that way checking their work.

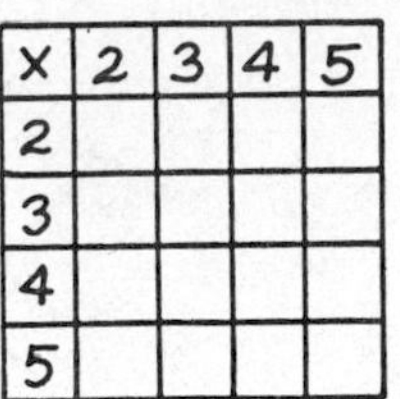

Figure 9-6

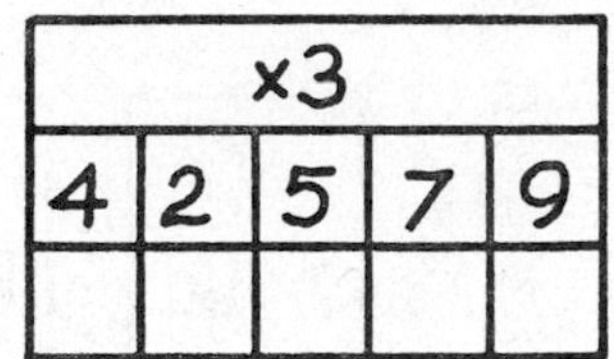

Figure 9-7

3×4= □×4=12 3×□=12 3×4=□

$\begin{array}{r}4\\\times 3\\\hline\end{array}$ $\begin{array}{r}4\\\times\square\\\hline 12\end{array}$ $\begin{array}{r}\square\\\times 3\\\hline 12\end{array}$ $\begin{array}{r}4\\\times 3\\\hline \square\end{array}$

Figure 9-8

   b. After the students have learned to skip count from two through ten, they can do larger ditto sheets with many different numeral combinations. Make up ditto sheets with blanks so they can be used for any numeral.
2. When the students have learned all of their skip counting, they can begin to use matrix sheets. The students can put the numerals across the top and down the left-hand side using different colored pencils (Figure 9-6). They can then fill in the matrix, working down or across. This will help them to see that 4 × 3, for example, is the same as 3 × 4.
3. Use ditto sheets with numerals on them. In the box at the top of the page put the multiplication fact you want the students to practice. See Figure 9-7, for example.
4. Teach multiplication in all of the ways shown in Figure 9-8.

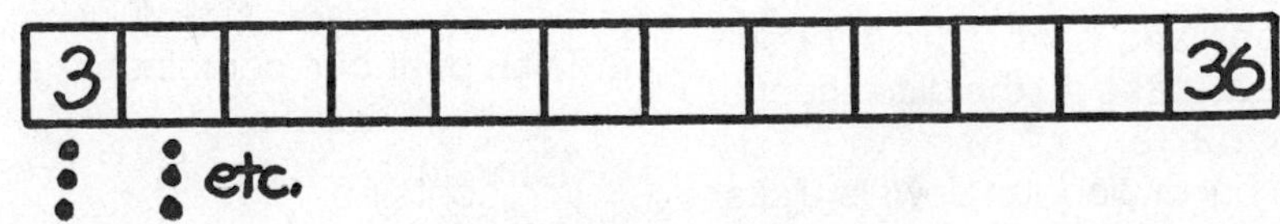

Figure 9-5

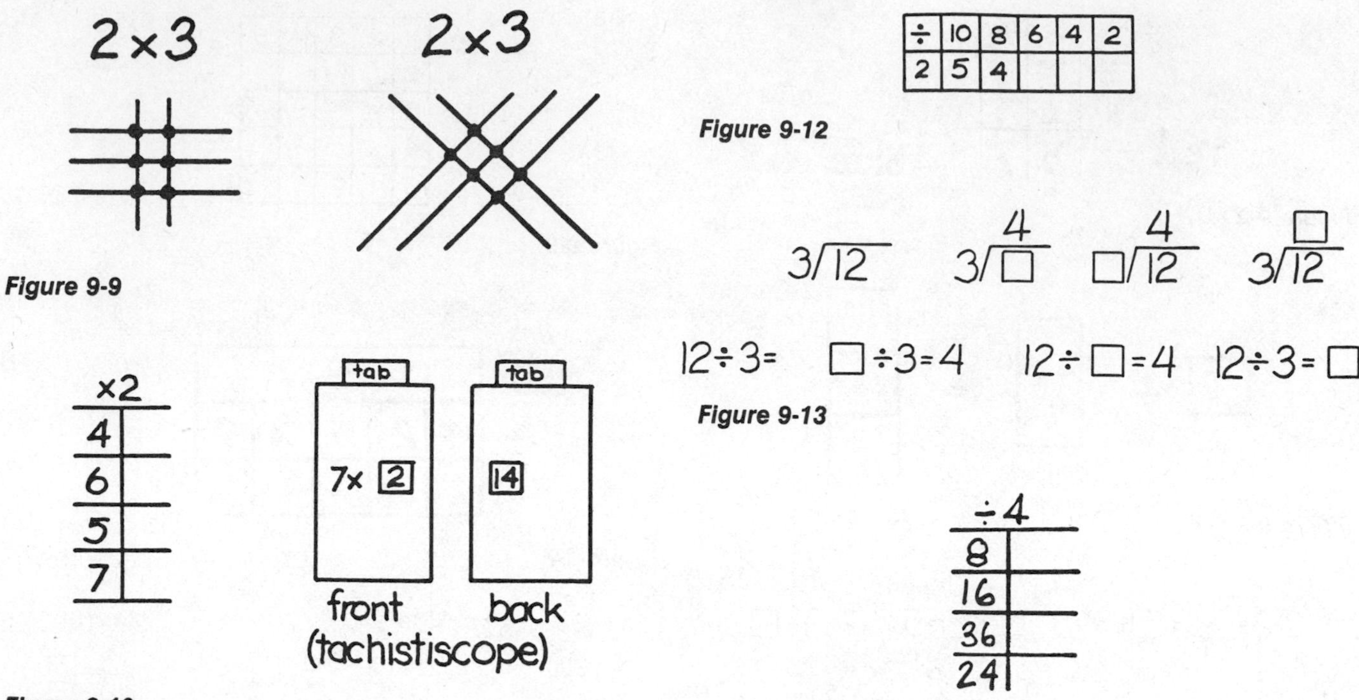

Figure 9-9

Figure 9-10

Figure 9-12

Figure 9-13

Figure 9-14

6÷2

| 1 | 2 | 3 | 4 | 5 | 6 | 7 | 8 | 9 | 10 | = 3 leaps

Figure 9-11

½ of (shape)
½ of or (set)

Figure 9-15

5. Have the students do arrays, whereby the student counts the intersections. (See Figure 9-9.)
6. Use multiplication drills. (See Figure 9-10.)

SIMPLE DIVISION

1. Have the students group Pop It Beads or blocks according to your directions. For example, "How many groups of 3 equal 6?"
2. Have a student distribute buttons or coins equally or with a remainder to fellow students.
3. Use a numberline to teach simple division with remainder. See Figure 9-11, for example.
4. Simple matrix sheets (Figure 9-12) can also be used to teach division.
5 Teach division in all of the ways shown in Figure 9-13.
6. Use simple drills, including the one in Figure 9-14.

SIMPLE FRACTIONS

1. Teach division of shapes and sets by using concrete objects, then repeat these on the ditto sheets. For example, see Figure 9-15.
2. Make a set of materials out of wooden dowels. Take a rod of 24-inch-long doweling and cut it into six 4-inch pieces. Leave four of the pieces whole to use for teaching division of sets and cut the other two pieces (one in half and one in fourths) to use in teaching division of shapes. The advantage of using wooden doweling is that the students can hold two or four pieces in their hands and put them together to see the whole, or they can line the four dowels up and see that ½ of 4 is 2. The dowels are also good for tracing around prior to working the problem.
3. After the students understand simple fractions using concrete objects, introduce them to ditto sheets.

CONSERVATION OF QUANTITY

1. Pour equal amounts of sand into two containers of the same size.

   Then pour one container of sand into another long, thin container ( ).

Finally, pour the contents of the second container into a short, wide container ( ). Ask the students to tell you which one has more sand. If they do not understand, reverse the process; then repeat it.

2. Use money to teach conservation of quantity, beginning with a nickel equals five pennies, two nickels equal a dime, or a nickel and five pennies equal a dime, etc.
3. Use rods or dowels to represent different sizes. There is also a great deal of commercial material available to teach this concept.
4. Count out twenty sticks with a student. Make four bundles of five sticks each. Take two bundles of five sticks and make one bundle of ten sticks. Tell the student that one bundle of ten sticks equals two bundles of five sticks. The student should check by counting. Then tell the student that one bundle of ten sticks and two bundles of five sticks equal the twenty sticks you started out with. The student should count to check.
5. Fill a small measuring spoon full of water. Suck up the water with an eye dropper. Count the drops as they are squeezed back into the spoon. Did the amount stay the same when it was put back in the spoon drop by drop?

PROCESS SIGNS

1. Begin by using wooden, plastic, sandpaper, or magnetic numerals, including process signs.
2. Blocks with numerals and process signs can also be used.
3. Use ditto sheets that include the forms shown in Figure 9-16.
4. Teach *greater than* and *less than*, using beads, blocks, or rods.
   Two is greater than one: **:>•** One is less than two: **•<:** The greater amount fits into the largest opening.
5. Use color-coded drawstring bags, each marked with a process sign, and in them put corresponding arithmetic problems on small oak tag strips. For example, a pink bag with a plus sign on it ( ) will contain pink strips of oak tag with addition problems.

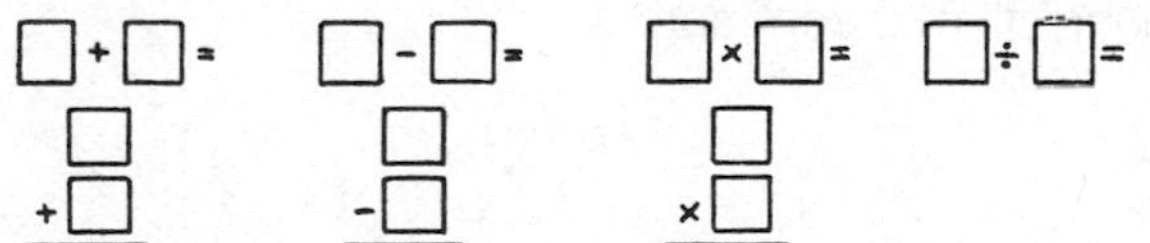

Figure 9-16

MEASUREMENT

1. Begin by rechecking the estimation ability of the student.
2. Use a yardstick and have the student measure the perimeter of the room.
3. Pour two pints of liquid into a quart jar and then four quarts into a gallon container.
4. Color each foot in a yardstick a different color.
5. The students can measure their desks and other areas of the room with a ruler.
6. Use ditto sheets and rulers (first with inches and later with half inches) and have the students measure lines of different length.
7. The students should draw their own lines and tell you how long they are.
8. Obtain a scale so the students can determine the relative weights of objects in the classroom.
9. The students should use a scale in order to better understand the concepts of equivalency. For example, sixteen ounces equal a pound.

MAPS AND GRAPHS

1. Use three-dimensional or raised forms to teach maps and graphs.
2. Use clay to teach land forms such as peninsular, isthmus, island, and lake.
3. Develop a globe by covering a balloon with papier mache and then painting it.
4. Draw simple maps of the classroom and have the students pace off and draw it to scale.
5. The students can draw maps of their bedrooms and then of their houses.
6. Older students enjoy designing their own treasure maps. This is an effective method of teaching the concepts of land forms, map legends, etc.
7. Graphs can be constructed from strips of oak tag and colored construction paper.
8. The students can graph their own progress in arithmetic and other subject areas.
9. The students can graph baseball and football scores, as well as scores in other sports and games.

Chapter 10 Social-Emotional Development

Behavior can be described in different ways depending on the training and orientation of the observer. Medical or psychiatric terms or labels for the most part tend to focus on descriptions of adult behavior or theories of ego development. Treatment in terms of a medical-psychiatric model focuses on more of what physicians can do by itemizing an array of alternatives which includes medication. In the psychoanalytical approach, the desired effect of treatment is to accomplish a change of behavior resulting from a restructuring of the personality of the individual. This type of treatment requires a great deal of time, a high level of training and resources, and is not practical for implementation in schools.

Behavior approaches to social-emotional maladjustment focus on the behavior that is manifested. The mode of treatment is to use a combination of techniques that will extinguish undersirable—or target—behaviors and elicit desirable behaviors. Student problems are defined in terms of target behaviors rather than by labels or constructs. The behavior management approach can be utilized by educators in any educational setting with a modicum of training. Teachers are concerned with behaviors that disrupt school activities or that inhibit learning in particular students.

Often students exhibit certain clusters of behavior that can be called symptoms or indicators of certain types of problems. Clustering of behavior suggests the following classifications:

1. Aggressive (acting out/passive)
2. Sensitive-withdrawn
3. Immature-dependent
4. Psychotic-neurotic
5. Delinquent-unorthodox
6. Social perception disorders
7. Control factors (distractibility, hyperactivity, perseveration, disinhibition, impulsivity)

These clusters of behavior are not mutually exclusive and sometimes overlap in particular individuals.

It is important to note that any of these behaviors can appear at one time or another in any individual. Our concern here is for the student who consistently exhibits patterns of behavior that interfere with learning in school. In viewing behavior, a great deal depends upon the frustration level and coping ability of the teacher. What is construed as problem behavior is to a large extent dependent upon the "eyes of the beholder." Terms such as *emotional disturbance* or *behavior problem* have different meanings to different people. Therefore, each case must be considered on its own merits, with consideration given to the attitudes and feelings of the teacher, the observable behaviors of the student, the environment in which all of this is taking place, and the dynamic interactions that occur among all of these factors.

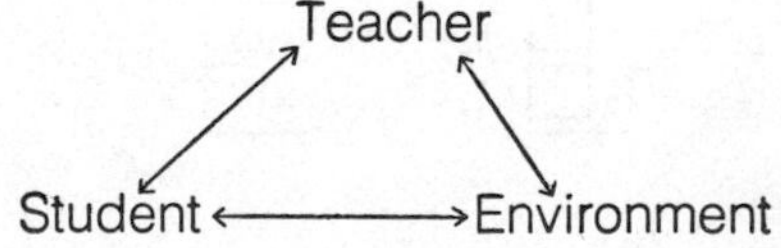

There are often many reasons for behaviors that are not easy to pinpoint. The teacher's responsibility is to probe, accepting relevant information and rejecting gossip, generalizations to particular students or groups, and teacher lounge psychiatry. Sometimes students react differently away from school. There are gray areas of behavior that are difficult to categorize and the parameters indicated in this chapter are there as guidelines for looking at different types of behavior.

The following descriptions of behavior can be easily used by the teacher to describe students who fall more into one category than into another and to focus on target behaviors to be modified. Procedures for dealing with these behaviors are also included. If teachers use categorical labels in discussing students or writing reports, they should define quite specifically what these labels or constructs mean and infer.

AGGRESSIVE (ACTING OUT/PASSIVE)

Behavior which could be described as aggressive can either be acting out or passive and perhaps can be an effect of many factors. Acting out behavior is particularly disturbing to the teacher because it tends to disrupt classroom activities and interferes with the teacher's ability to instruct. Acting out students are usually a problem to their peers as well as to the teacher and are easily identified. Passive-aggressive students are resistant to school activities and appear unmotivated. These students do not exhibit the anger of the acting out learners, but the rebellion and hostility are present nonetheless.

Observable Behavior: Aggressive (Acting Out/Passive)

The student

1. disrupts other children by moving about excessively and by being annoying.
2. is disrespectful or discourteous to peers or adults.
3. behaves in a compulsive manner.
4. is negative and does not do what is required of him or her.
5. is rough or noisy.
6. exhibits long periods of unhappiness.
7. is destructive to his or her own belongings.
8. does not complete assignments as requested.
9. indicates poor or bad feelings about school.
10. uses profanity excessively.
11. will not sit or stand still according to command.
12. will not stay with or complete a learning task within a normal time limit.
13. will not obey commands from authority figures.
14. is uncooperative in group learning or play activities.
15. fights with others without provocation.
16. is hot-tempered and flares up easily.
17. is undependable.
18. destroys the belongings of others.
19. behaves like a clown.
20. tests to extreme limits.

Discussion: Aggressive (Acting Out/Passive)

Aggressive-acting out students are sometimes destructive and may even hurt themselves or others. It is not unusual to hear similar complaints about them from students, teachers, administrators, support personnel, and even the parents themselves. Some students who have this type of behavior problem have been described as children who are "hurting" emotionally. They appear to be in a constant state of conflict. Acting out-aggressive students often come from hostile home situations. The parents may be rejecting or apathetic in their attitude toward the student. Poor or inadequate models may have resulted in ineffective socialization of the child. Children from these environments may not have learned to establish or develop trusting relationships. This can result in unsocialized behavior.

Some learners have a desperate desire for attention and require a great deal of "eye contact." Most teachers do not have the time to give individual attention to learners with this problem and may find that the students will do almost anything to get the teacher's attention or to engage in conversation. Attention-getting behaviors may take a negative form and the students may disturb other learners by making strange noises, breaking things, interrupting the teacher, and doing a myriad of other noxious things.

The inability to control aggressive impulses is one indicator among many of social immaturity in older students. Sometimes it appears to be an impossible task to try to control aggressive students who meet life situations with a frontal attack, often frightening parents, teachers, and peers with their bold actions and feelings of power. The teacher's initial impulse often is to strike back, to punish, and to get revenge. This in many cases reinforces the behavior rather than diminishing it. Aggressive-acting out students can often be found in the halls—sent there by the teacher—or in the principal's office. Teachers and parents may feel guilty about having punished these students. These are normal feelings, but care should be taken so the student will not perceive them.

Some parents condone or even admire and reward aggressive behavior. However, the school cannot let aggressiveness go beyond generally accepted normal limits. The students who disrupt learning, upset their classmates, and keep teachers in a state of anger and anxiety may require additional specialized attention, and this should be considered before expulsion from school is decided upon.

Aggression has many underlying causes, a few of which include:

1. a concomitant to failure in learning
2. organic brain dysfunction
3. reaction to treatment at home
4. symptom of repressed hostilities
5. a reaction to unmet needs

Passive aggressive learners may not appear to care, but there is usually an inner conflict where they are torn between simultaneous feelings of love and hate for parents and/or teachers. Parents who apply pressure beyond ordinary limits sometimes foster passive aggressive behavior in their children. These students may have an unconscious desire to fail in school and to hurt themselves through poor academic achievement. This may be one way of "getting back" at parents who have been very demanding.

Other factors relating to aggressive behavior include the following:

1. *Boredom.* The learners may become bored with school because they are not learning and cannot cope with the instructional program and the materials which may be beyond their grasp.
2. *The phenomenon of natural movement.* Children must move around, wrestle, or otherwise engage in body contact with each other as part of the natural developmental growth process. The "anxious" teacher who makes a "mountain out of a molehill" in these situations may create problems where none exist.
3. Coping behavior (panic and anxiety). Panic-coping is probably one of the most critical areas of concern in students who exhibit a processing problem or a learning disability. Pressure from parents, teachers, and peers can result in a continual state of frustration with accompanying anxiety. This anxiety can become specifically associated with a particular learning task such as reading, writing, or arithmetic. The students who fail in reading and at the same time receive a great deal of pressure to learn to read may become anxious and tense when asked to read from a book. They may even generalize this anxiety to all books. Perhaps students who are "book anxious" need to be taught to read away from books completely. They should be given a book only when they can achieve 100% success in terms of the reading vocabulary of that particular volume or section of a volume. The student must develop good coping behavior patterns in order to deal with continuous frustration in academic areas.

Treatment Considerations: Aggressive (Acting Out/Passive)

Following are some general suggestions to keep in mind when working with aggressive-acting out students.

1. In general, these students do not respond satisfactorily to the following:
   a. reasoning
   b. physical punishment
   c. excessive isolation
   d. withdrawal of privileges
   e. withdrawal of social reinforcement
   f. verbal and social rewards
2. The best treatment for aggressive-acting out students is, if possible, to anticipate the episode and remove the students from the situation for a short time, while directing them into another activity.
3. A "cooling-off" period is important. This means giving the students an opportunity to be off by themselves so they will have time to think about the situation and the ensuing results.
4. After a particular episode, place the student in a time-out room or corner. This should be an isolating, nonrewarding experience—not a reinforcement for aggression.
5. Aggressive students particularly need structure in their lives and boundaries delineated for them in terms of their behavior. They need to know just how far they can go. Therefore, limits must have a purpose and not just become a set of rules. Limits should be few at first, slowly increased, and verbalized to the learner in a simplified manner.
6. Organize the school day so that, through the planned unfolding of school activities, the students will have satisfied many of their unmet needs (e.g., need for approval, need for recognition, need for acceptance).
7. The teacher must be specific in giving directions. "Stop playing," or "Do your work," or "No talking," is not specific enough for the aggressive learner.
8. Since many of these students have a low frustration tolerance, allow them more time than usual for shifting from one activity to another.
9. Avoid frustrating the learners by having them do things that can be accomplished with at least some success.

10. Use self-checking materials and involve the students in projects so they will not become bored and get into trouble.
11. Provide stimulating and physically active, tension-releasing activities, doing things for the teacher in the classroom.
12. Students exhibiting hostility and aggression (active or passive) should have opportunities to displace this behavior through activities such as running (jogging), contact sports, arts and crafts, hammering nails into wood, using a punching bag, or gardening. Agriculture is an excellent vehicle for displacing aggression.
13. Introduce novel or attention-getting activities into the program.
14. Aggressive behavior may be a concomitant to hyperactivity. In this case the student should be permitted to leave his or her seat or engage in some other activity for a brief period of time to prevent aggressive episodes.
15. Utilize techniques which will help the student to delay or postpone gratification.
16. For the passive-aggressive student, it is important that the teacher not nag. The teacher should insist that the learner carry out short directions or assignments. The teacher will need to get him or her started.
17. Utilize the Premack principle and pair a low probability behavior (e.g., sitting in seat) with a high probability behavior (e.g., sitting in a favorite chair). The former should be strengthened.
18. In extreme cases, the length of the school day may need to be shortened. The student will only attend part of the day, to be increased accordingly.
19. Verbally aggressive students who ridicule others may require the following:
    a. separation from the group along with teacher-student discussion about the student's actions
    b. reward for not verbally disturbing the class
20. Look at antecedent behavior when fighting occurs in the classroom. Was the incident provoked by a student who has a pattern of fighting or by an accident-prone student with poor motor control?

SENSITIVE-WITHDRAWN

Students who can be described as fitting into the sensitive, withdrawn category may exhibit anxious or even depressed behavior. These students are generally shy, self-conscious and prefer not to be the "center of attention." They simply prefer not to call attention to themselves. The following are examples of some of the observable behaviors under this category.

Observable Behavior: Sensitive-Withdrawn

The student

1. exhibits feelings of insecurity.
2. becomes unhappy or cries easily.
3. likes to be left alone and withdraws from others.
4. becomes frustrated in everyday situations.
5. overreacts to the negative statements or behavior of others.
6. is anxious or fearful for no apparent reason.
7. does not participate in recreation or play activities with others.
8. is easily embarrassed or behaves in a self-conscious manner.
9. exhibits feelings of poor self-worth.
10. is shy in social situations.
11. is unable to be at ease and enjoy himself or herself with others.
12. exhibits little self-confidence.

Discussion: Sensitive-Withdrawn

In contrast to the aggressive-acting out students, the markedly sensitive, withdrawn students avoid situations that will place them in conflict and present a more passive acceptance of events in their lives. They are of concern to teachers who may perceive the students as unhappy and unable to develop because of poor social interaction or class participation. Their behavior is generally not considered "bad" or punishable, but is disconcerting to parents and teachers who reward and are in turn rewarded by social interaction. Teachers as a group are less sensitized to these types of students and, except for extreme cases, complain little about them. Some teachers, on the other hand, equate sensitive, withdrawn behavior with being "well behaved" and describe the student as "quiet" and "well mannered."

Generally, treatment for this type of student is focused on gradual desensitization, and strategies are employed to include the student in daily activities of school life. Some students are quiet and pretend to "play the game." They seem to be occupied with the required task. The student who is holding a book may be doing just that and nothing else. Therefore, in defining and charting task-related behavior, it is important to be certain that it is purposeful—rather than non-purposeful—task-related behavior that is observed. Withdrawn students may have more problems to overcome than those who are acting out. The acting-out learners are still, in most cases, fighting to survive, while the withdrawn learners may have already given up hope. It will take the combined effort of the school, the home, and the community in dealing with the total learner to facilitate any real changes in the behavior of these students.

Treatment Considerations: Sensitive-Withdrawn

The following are some general suggestions to keep in mind when working with sensitive-withdrawn students.

1. Condition the students to variable input (praise or punishment) slowly.
2. Involve the students in small group activities with one or two other students in the class.
3. Understand that these students may retreat for long periods from perceived negative interactions.
4. Be cognizant that these students may prefer familiar situations perceived to be "safe."
5. Give short assignments with built-in opportunities for free time and personal interaction.
6. In teaching situations, remember that these students do not want to be "singled out" and do not respond to forced participation.
7. Seat the students in an area that will present them with fewer opportunities for withdrawal and isolation.
8. Refrain from any intimidation or coercive tactics. These students are easily intimidated and respond negatively to coercion.
9. Do not rush the students. Give them an opportunity to respond at their own rate.
10. Avoid criticizing or reproaching the students in public.
11. Elicit appropriate behavior through the utilization of modeling techniques.
12. Strive for successive approximations to desired behavior.
13. Remember that the primary target behavior is to increase participation.
14. Provide opportunities for the students to express themselves in different ways (i.e., art, music, writing).
15. Don't back the students up against the wall so they may have to "lose face."
16. Reinforce the students consistently for even simple tasks at first, particularly individual efforts that are nonsolicited.
17. Avoid setting qualifications for participation that cannot be met by the sensitive-withdrawn students.
18. Use alternative methods to encourage verbal communication. Some students will not readily talk to parents, teachers, or peers, but may talk to hand puppets or over toy telephones or walkie-talkies.
19. If the withdrawn students appear to daydream excessively, provide structured interruptions (eye contact, touch, etc.) and rewards for completing assignments on time.
20. Some shy students are also perfectionists and may require private discussions with the teacher concerning realistic expectations in the classroom.

IMMATURE-DEPENDENT

Immature-dependent students often exhibit behavior inappropriate for their chronological age. These students require a great deal of patience and many opportunities to learn particular tasks in different situations before appropriate social behavior can be stabilized. Some of the observable behaviors for these students include the following.

Observable Behavior: Immature-Dependent

The student

1. requires constant direction and relies a great deal on others.
2. prefers to play or interact with younger people.
3. appears inactive or apathetic at inappropriate times.
4. needs a great deal of support and "stroking" from others.
5. has difficulty making decisions.
6. does not attend to activities that require a degree of concentration.
7. is easily influenced by others.
8. exhibits passive behavior.
9. appears absentminded or lost in thought to excess.
10. demands an unusual amount of attention.
11. continually complains of physical pains such as stomachaches and headaches.

Discussion: Immature-Dependent

Teachers sometimes lose patience with these children because they are so demanding of time and dependent upon them for every little thing. Some students cry easily, suck their thumbs or exhibit other immature behaviors. Some are continually complaining to the teacher about children who are picking on them, or they are observed constantly bickering with other students. Many tend to socialize with younger children and have difficulty getting along with their peers. They have problems with independent activities and require constant reassurance. Some students may cheat and/or lie to cover up their feelings. This is essentially a parent-child problem in terms of overdependence that transfers to the school. The concept to keep in mind in working with these students is independent functioning. All school activities should be geared to accomplish this by gradual increments to insure success. The students must learn to trust themselves and depend on their own judgment rather than only on the judgment of others. The teacher can insure success by calling on the students when they are sure the students know the right answers to the questions asked. Parents tend to control or direct the students' lives, permitting little opportunity for independent action or for "growing up." This classification or category of behavior is difficult to define.

Treatment Considerations: Immature-Dependent

These students need specific opportunities to learn socially acceptable behavior. The following are some general suggestions to keep in mind when working with immature-dependent students:

1. Provide a structured environment that will initially require monitoring and supervision.
2. Begin with simple or elementary activities or small assignments that will require the student to make decisions such as selecting between two choices and then gradually moving to more choices and longer assignments.
3. Provide many trials in different situations for learning acceptable social behavior.
4. Carefully consider rewards for independent activity and acceptable social behavior as part of the total treatment program.
5. Use both scheduled and spontaneous times for teacher-student or other adult-student private discussions about feelings. The adult can share expressions of concern, "I know how you feel . . ." These times can be used to plan for and encourage self-activiated and more independent behavior.
6. Include the students in activities that provide a creative expression of feelings (e.g., drama, art, music, crafts, writing).
7. Plan small groups where the students can work with peers and on occasion model another student's leadership.
8. Use structured group activities that involve a small group of students working on a carefully planned class project.
9. Involve the students in competitive games where they have a good chance for success.
10. Include the immature-dependent students in the assignment of responsibilities in the classroom (e.g., dusting erasers, leading the lines, caring for animals or plants, delivering messages, etc.).
11. Encourage participation in hobby clubs or special interest groups.
12. Discuss with parents or guardians activities that will increase the students' freedom to successfully perform independent tasks (e.g., going to sports events with friends, visiting other homes).
13. Gradually allow the students to confront disagreement with friends at school or at home. Avoid interceding for the students and interfering with situations in which they can begin to solve their own problems.

PSYCHOTIC-NEUROTIC

Services for students exhibiting behavior that is clearly psychotic or symptomatic of severe neuroses are limited in terms of public school programming. This category is not to be confused with those students who exhibit episodes of aberrant behavior but who for the most part function quite effectively in educational situations. It is the student who consistently manifests deep-seated, bizarre, aberrant, or fearful behavior that we are concerned about in terms of classroom management. The following are examples of behavior that fall into the category of being psychotic-neurotic in nature.

Observable Behavior: Psychotic-Neurotic

The student

1. exhibits inappropriate affect, such as laughing or crying at the wrong time.
2. exhibits unintelligible or strange speech patterns.
3. is not reality-oriented in mannerisms or speech.
4. tells lies excessively and tends to exaggerate greatly.
5. enjoys inflicting pain on self.
6. feels that people want to physically hurt him or her.

7. exhibits long periods of silence and almost complete withdrawal.
8. behaves in a bizarre manner.
9. exhibits compulsive behavior, such as excessive hand washing.
10. appears extremely nervous.
11. enjoys inflicting pain on others.
12. thinks everyone is talking about, and plotting against, him or her.
13. is fearful much of the time.
14. exhibits long periods of silence and withdrawal followed by extreme activity and excessive verbal behavior.
15. is extremely fearful about going to school.
16. has unreasonable fear of animals, heights, water, open places, etc.
17. has severe feeling of inferiority.

Discussion: Psychotic-Neurotic

The kinds of problems that are dealt with in this section are serious to the extent that they affect the emotional lives of the students so they cannot participate in or benefit significantly from much of school life. Many of these students experience uncontrolled anxiety that is devastating and debilitating. This calls for support and approaches that will reduce the suffering. Teachers working with specialists and parents can utilize appropriate techniques to reduce the anxious students. Generally, medical cooperation and supervision is part of the treatment program. Often medication is part of the overall treatment schedule.

Students who exhibit unreasonable fears, are not reality oriented, or exhibit bizarre behavior are not readily accepted by peers or teachers. Children who are severely disorganized, autistic, schizophrenic, or school phobic, for example, require specialized services in most cases. These services may be supplied by a total community service delivery system which includes mental health, special instructional programs, and other support services. Schools that do serve these youngsters through special programs require specialized or highly trained personnel. For many severely emotionally disturbed children, the process of treatment is long and the projected outcomes in terms of positive results are more limited than for the other categories. Disagreement exists as to the specific nature or causes of particular types of disorders such as autism, for example. In dealing with autism we have to rule out such factors as deafness and retardation. Some of these students will require life-long institutionalization or supervision. Many small or rural communities have had to combine resources in order to be able to provide services for these students.

Treatment Considerations: Psychotic-Neurotic

The following are some general suggestions to keep in mind when planning services for psychotic-neurotic students.

1. It is difficult to provide treatment for many disturbed students in regular school settings.
2. There are deep underlying causes for bizarre or aberrant behavior that require professional attention.
3. Some of these students will need trained teachers and require long term treatment.
4. Utilize a community-based mental health approach where available.
5. Some of these students may be able to function in academic settings within a limited school day.
6. Reinforce any successful school or home activity.
7. Teachers must recognize their professional limitations and not go beyond them in attempting specific treatments.
8. For *school phobic children* the following considerations are suggested:
   a. At first, allow the parent to attend school with the student for a limited school day (one-half hour, one hour, one and one-half hour). This is a process of desensitization.
   b. Alternate people who bring the student to school (i.e., father, teacher, grandmother, aunt).
   c. If necessary, allow the student to telephone home during the school day.
   d. Permit the student to bring to school objects to which he or she is particularly attached.
   e. Set up a schedule of reinforcement that includes other individuals in the school (i.e., school nurse, secretary, bus driver, cafeteria worker).
   f. Do not single out the student in an embarrassing manner.
   g. Use a variety of reinforcements on a continuous basis at first and reward the student for coming to school regularly.
   h. Provide the student with individual as well as group tasks that will gain approval from classmates.
   i. Include the student in high interest and stimulating activities (i.e., television, movies, trips).
   j. Seat the student close to the teacher.
   k. Let the student know that he or she was missed when absent from school.
   l. Speak to the student's parents or guardian on

the telephone when the student is at home, and praise the student's efforts.

m. Set up a schedule at home and in school and stick to it.

9. For *general fearfulness* consider the following:

a. Condition the student to animals (for example, a hamster) by successive approximation; the learner can stay in the same room, stand near the animal or touch it when held by the teacher, and finally hold and stroke it.

b. Discuss the causes and nature of things that frighten the student.

c. Do not force participation. Allow the student to set up his or her own goals each day.

d. The student can act out a fearful situation through role playing.

e. Avoid reminding the student of his or her fears. The idea is to reduce anxiety.

f. If the student is afraid of written tests, permit him or her to take oral tests.

10. *Depressed students* need the following considerations:

a. Establish a warm student-teacher relationship.

b. Insure success and inspire confidence in the student by freely praising him or her for successful efforts.

c. A busy student will have less time to become depressed.

d. Avoid timed tests or long drawn out assignments for depressed students.

e. Medication may be needed for depression and other emotional disorders.

11. *Violent behavior.*

a. The student should be separated from another student or from the group immediately.

b. If a student displays weapons and exhibits homicidal tendencies, school officials must attempt to remove the weapons. Parents and/or other authorities must be included in a staff meeting of the professionals who can provide immediate help in determining the cause of the behavior.

c. A student who shows excessive brutality and sadistic behavior should be referred by the classroom teacher to the personnel in the schools or community agencies that can provide diagnosis and treatment. Lines of communication, support, and follow-up to the classroom teacher should be established prior to the student's return to the classroom.

d. Students who inflict pain upon themselves will require specialized care and may need a variety of techniques including operant conditioning and individual counseling.

e. The student who makes comments about suicide should not be ignored. Prevention will require supervision and immediate attention by trained personnel.

DELINQUENT-UNORTHODOX

Delinquent-unorthodox students come from environments that foster the development of gangs and a gang philosophy of life.

These students for the most part do not exhibit disturbed social relationships. The behavior exhibited is quite realistic when considered within the circumstances or context of the local environment and the life-space of the individual. Unlike the other categories of behavior, the delinquent students may be quite well adjusted within the framework of their own peer group. Some examples of behavior follow:

Observable Behavior: Delinquent-Unorthodox

The student

1. exhibits variable habits of sleeping.
2. exhibits excessive loyalty to peers.
3. rejects figures representing authority.
4. is a member of a gang.
5. adheres to the gang's code of ethics and morality.
6. exhibits unorthodox social behavior.
7. steals in collaboration with others.
8. is often truant from school.
9. seeks the company of other delinquents.
10. does not express remorse for delinquent behavior.

Discussion: Delinquent-Unorthodox

The overriding concept in delinquent-unorthodox behavior is peer orientation and peer loyalty. Authority is something to oppose and schooling is not valued. As a group these students are more truant and tend to drop out of school at an earlier age than the average student. Security and recognition is sought from within the gang. Each member of the gang is under tremendous pressure from the group to conform to its own set of rules and regulations. This group loyalty is very difficult for the school to deal with, as a change in the behavior of the entire group is usually required before individuals within the group will respond to a more conformative style of life. These students are annoyed with problem situations which constrict or confine them. They are much less concerned about standard rules of right or wrong in terms of infractions which may result in guilt or remorse. It is difficult to orient the group away from delinquent behavior. In attempting to change the behavior of one individual we are in a sense asking him or her to "join us" and give up the gang. Without changing the environment, this is an extremely difficult task. It is also important to understand that we are dealing with varying degrees of "gangness," different types of behavior, and various degrees of affiliation.

Individual students may feel the need to engage in a personal battle with adults, whether they be parents, teachers, or others who represent authority figures. Many experienced teachers have learned that it is almost axiomatic that students will test limits in terms of interpersonal relationships. Sometimes opportunities for testing limits in different situations are not readily available in the home or community. In many instances where they are available in the students' out-of-school life, individuals who are important to them may not be consistent in the way they permit or react to testing. Students are generally uncomfortable with ambiguity or inconsistency and will force the teacher to deal or not to deal with different kinds of behaviors. It is the way the teacher deals with testing behaviors both initially and continually that makes the difference in many cases between the establishment of rapport or constant discontent in the learning environment.

Today, teachers are more aware of peer group loyalties than in previous years. This may be due to the effects of the media, such as television shows depicting "gang" life, and of recent changes in our society in the behavior of young people. Peer group loyalty is especially cogent with respect to youth group activity to achieve change in our society. This loyalty goes beyond the "I'll show you I'm brave and not chicken" kind of loyalty that commonly exists in gang psychology—and which, to some extent, has always existed as a developmental phenomenon in the growth process of most young people. Today, this posture or attitude is being observed more and more in children in the elementary schools.

In many situations, teachers misunderstand this form of exhibiting group loyalties as being hostility directed toward the teacher personally; some teachers have become fearful of students. In some instances, hostility truly is directed toward the teacher; however, if it is treated as hostility and returned in kind, it can result in unfortunate and unhappy situations for all involved.

Treatment Considerations: Delinquent-Unorthodox

The following are some general suggestions to keep in mind when working with delinquent-unorthodox students:

1. These students are primarily peer oriented.
2. They do not respond to an authoritative approach to changing their behavior.
3. These students generally exhibit behavior extremely inappropriate to school settings.
4. Their parents may be negligent and not provide enough socialization.
5. Street ideas override home or social values.
6. The behavior of most of these students tends to be resolved as they get older.
7. The school and community must channel these students' energies into socially acceptable activities.
   a. Develop a project to build a team clubhouse under supervision.
   b. Groups of students can repaint different areas within the school.
   c. A group of students can plant a vegetable and/or flower garden.
   d. Students can earn money for cleaning-up activities.
   e. Encourage the courts to force youthful offenders to repair damaged property.
8. Reinforce participation in the desired value system through involvement in school decision-making activities.
9. Insure success in school tasks.
10. Do not negate the power and loyalty of the group; focus attention on modifying the behavior of the group if possible.
11. Visit the home and discuss problems with the parents and the student.
12. Send a registered letter to parents if the student is consistently truant.
13. Competitive sports is one of the best ways of redirecting the delinquent student.
14. Counsel privately with the student assuring him or her that the discussions will be highly confidential.
15. A job after school may keep a delinquent student from getting into trouble.
16. For older students, a work/school program should be considered.
17. Provide opportunities for after school informal interactions or rap sessions.
18. Avoid using threats. They result in the opposite behavior more often than the desired behavior.
19. Sometimes it is best to ignore some behavior

instead of constantly being in conflict with the student.

20. Avoid open confrontation and show honest interest. Most importantly, be patient. It took years for the student's problem to develop and it will not disappear in a few weeks.
21. In serious situations, a gang leader may have to be separated from his or her followers. He or she should, however, be reinforced for on-task and appropriate behavior.

SOCIAL PERCEPTION DISORDERS

There is a group of students who have difficulty interpreting the social environment and dealing with social situations. Some of these students, even those that show high levels of intelligence, cannot formulate acceptable sound judgments. Their behavior is often perceived by peers and adults to be inappropriate and strange. The following are some of the observable behaviors under this category.

Observable Behavior: Social Perception Disorders

The student

1. misinterprets what he or she sees and gives the wrong response.
2. has difficulty with projective tests, such as the Thematic Apperception Test.
3. may be able to perceive individual objects, but fails to comprehend the meaning of their relationships.
4. may not derive meaning from gestures or expressions of others.
5. may not be able to size up a situation. For example, he or she may require constant interpretation while watching a TV show, watching a film, or listening to a story.
6. literally does not know enough to come in out of the rain.
7. is directed at home and rarely has opportunities to make up his or her own mind.
8. reacts inappropriately to situations, criticisms, and guidance from others.
9. has difficulty in understanding the subtleties in humor.
10. has difficulty in understanding figurative speech.
11. attends to the minor details instead of the major details in completing a task.
12. misreads emotions, moods, and attitudes of people.
13. misunderstands motives (why people do what they do).
14. fails to associate an incident with its implications for people and society.
15. consistently says the inappropriate thing at the inappropriate time.
16. does not understand facial expressions.
17. has difficulty in pretending or anticipating the outcomes in stories.

Discussion: Social Perception Disorders

Many of these students have difficulty making and keeping friends and endure more social rejection than do their age mates even though they may try hard to be accepted.

It has been noted that students with difficulties in this area tend to also have problems in perceptual-motor tasks, exhibit poor self-image and immature concepts of body image. Teachers have reported that these types of students are not emotionally disturbed, but lacking in emotional depth, and they appear to have a superficial understanding of the meaning of social situations. Characteristically, this kind of problem in social relationships will affect the learners in every aspect of daily life. It can occur with or without problems in other areas of learning and is found to be a most difficult area to deal with.

Treatment Considerations: Social Perception Disorders

The following suggestions should be considered when planning activities for the learner with social perception problems:

1. The teacher can train the student through the interpretation of good pictures or photographs. He or she should be careful not to overstimulate the learner with too much input and should begin with simple pictures.
2. The teacher should show the student action pictures.
3. The teacher can train the student with sequence pictures or comic strips—record the student's responses and lead him or her through by asking questions.
4. The teacher can build in good social perception through language experience utilizing the science curriculum and by helping the student understand cause-effect relationships.

5. The teacher should talk the learner through situations. Sometimes the student will not profit from imitation alone and will need an explanation of what he or she is doing.
6. Often the learner has good verbal ability, but cannot explain the significance of the action or sequence of actions in pictures. Use cartoons without the captions to elicit responses about the actions and the humor in the pictures.
7. Lead the student through and explain classroom or playground games especially those that involve gestures or verbal clues that appear to confound the learner.
8. Show the learner realistic pictures or photographs of children and adults who are expressing a particular feeling or emotion (e.g. anger, happiness, fear, sorrow). Have the student identify the feeling and then try to explain what led up to the feeling in the picture. Have the learner imitate the same feeling in a mirror. Finally, show the learner pictures in which more than one person is displaying emotions and ask the learner to discuss the significance of the scenes.
9. Use pictures of famous paintings and ask the student to explain what is happening, what happened before, what will happen next, where the action may occur, etc.

CONTROL FACTORS

Factors that affect control are those behaviors that originate from within the student and/or are precipitated by stimuli in the environment. These factors cause the student to exhibit atypical behavior or behavior that hinders him or her in terms of school adjustment and the acquisition of new concepts.

Distractibility

Distractibility can accompany deficits in the sensory, perceptual, memory, or language levels of learning or be related to emotional problems. The distractible learners exhibit intermittent attention. Further observations include the following:

Observable Behavior: Distractibility

The student

1. exhibits "forced attention" to extraneous stimuli within the environment and cannot attend to the task.
2. may respond to the teacher next door, following that teacher's directions.
3. may be distracted by visual or auditory stimuli or both.
4. is unable to focus his or her attention selectively.

Discussion: Distractibility

The distractible learners have difficulty attending to tasks for the same lengths of time that their peers do. They attend to irrelevant auditory and/or visual stimuli (e.g., hall or playground noises, air conditioners, moving mobiles, crowded colorful bulletin boards, flickering lighting) and are easily attracted away from designated tasks. Many of the concepts mentioned in Chapter 1 are appropriate for the distractible learners. The rate, amount, sequence, and optimal teaching moment for teaching should be considered. These learners fatigue easily; therefore, the types of classroom activities should be carefully scheduled. The learners may not listen attentively to a story after another auditory input lesson (e.g., listening to a lecture followed by a skill tape cassette). Additional factors that relate to distractibility include the motivation of the learner, the encouragement or incentives used to gain and keep the attention of the student, and the interest value of the task presented. The distractible student may also exhibit difficulties with vigilance (the ability to maintain concentration on a task). These less attentive learners are more apt to respond to extraneous stimuli than to the task required.

Treatment Considerations: Distractibility

1. The teacher should reduce the input or stimulus in the room.
2. Provide a place to "escape" from distraction. Study or learning cubicles or a big carton with little windows can be utilized to aid the student to stay on task. Many students should be encouraged to use the areas for independent activities. These areas must not be used for punishment too.
3. Put the distraction (color, etc.) into the material rather than on the walls.
4. The teacher should condition the learner by building in distraction (materials, bulletin board, etc.) a little at a time.
5. Involving the student in a motor act often reduces distraction. Manipulative materials such as clay, sand, wooden letters, felt letters, and finger paints are good.
6. Seat the student directly in front of the instructor.

7. Sometimes earplugs will help the student to concentrate on a specific task such as reading, or taking a test.
8. Separate the learner from the group and require him or her to do brief tasks that will be successful.
9. The student should complete a task and return the learning material immediately to its designated place.
10. To aid the student in completing all of the sections on a page, allow him or her to use a piece of paper to mask out one section at a time. A tachistoscopic device can be made by cutting a window in a piece of cardboard.
11. Material or activities should be presented to the learner in small units and evaluted as soon as possible after completion.
12. Utilize concrete material that will heighten the student's attention to the task.
13. Avoid giving the student vague assignments that involve dealing with a great deal of materials simultaneously.
14. The student should be able to envision both the beginning and the end of an activity.
15. Reduce verbal instructions as much as possible.
16. Such media forms as overhead projectors are useful in focusing the students' attention.

Hyperactivity

Students who are constantly on the move and have been described as hyperactive or hyperkinetic indicate a short attention span. They are continually shifting around in their seats, tapping their feet, playing with things, and creating a disturbance in the classroom. The learners appear to lack the inner control that is seen in the other students. Some of the behaviors to note under this category include:

Observable Behavior: Hyperactivity

The student

1. is constantly moving.
2. cannot control his or her movement and is unaware that it is occurring.
3. may fatigue earlier in the school day because of the hyperactivity.
4. may also be distractible. Both behavioral manifestations often go together.
5. has excessive movements even though he or she may be engrossed in a particular activity.

Discussion: Hyperactivity

Hyperactivity or hyperkinetic activity is one of the characteristics of brain-injured children. This does not imply that all hyperactive students are brain injured. Some students exhibit hyperactivity due to learning that occurs in situations that are noisy and overstimulating. The learners who have random movements are a problem in the classroom because they tend to take the other students off task. It is important for the instructor to get some indication of how long the students can stay on task. This can be charted. (See Form 10-1 [page 297] and Form 10-3 [page 303].)

Hyperactive students do not always have the same pattern of behavior. Some move more than others, some make distracting noises. Some students are very verbal and bright and are liked by their peers. Others are unhappy and are perceived in a more negative way. These students do not move about to gain the teacher's attention. Often they are unaware of the disturbing behavior. In young students some movement should be anticipated and considered normal. It is the atypical movement that should be noted; how much and when it occurs. Unfortunately, hyperactive students often are punished and isolated for their restless behavior and consequently are not in class enough to successfully learn or complete assignments.

These students require an overall reduced stimulus environment and a patient, structured teacher. Hyperactivity and/or distractible behavior can be modified by a highly supervised and well-managed program which could include a drug regimen. Drugs are just one alternative and must be highly controlled and monitored under strict supervision.

Treatment Considerations: Hyperactivity

1. Keep manipulative material away from the learner unless he or she is using the material for a specific activity.
2. The student should be given structured, high-attention tasks or activities (e.g., using a tape recorder).
3. Have the learner exercise or move about between activities. At specified times give the entire class a "visiting" break and encourage them to walk around, quietly talk to friends, sharpen pencils, etc.
4. Always follow a high stimulus activity such as music or physical education with a low stimulus activity (e.g., resting head on desk, playing a quiet game).

5. Allow the learner to rock in a rocking chair.
6. The young hyperactive student may work better on a carpet or in some other "low" environment than at a desk.
7. High stimulus clothing or jewelry on the instructor may interfere with the attention of the student.
8. The student could fold his or her hands or put them in pockets when quiet attention is required.
9. The teacher can cue the learner with a touch on the hand or shoulder or some other specified signal.
10. Put color or attracting devices into the learning materials instead of on too many bulletin boards.
11. Push the student to longer periods of attending and on-task behavior. Use Forms 10-1–10-3 (pages 297–298 and 303) to establish a baseline of time on task.
12. Reward on-task behavior with a system (e.g., stars, use of a favorite game, private time with the teacher).
13. Use contracts to specify desired behavior.
14. Through example and sometimes by discussing the problem directly with the class, teach the learner's peers how to ignore the active behavior.
15. Encourage the learner to participate in outside clubs or activities where the active behavior can be channeled into pleasant activities.
16. Plan alternative activities that will permit physical involvement during a lesson.
17. Avoid verbal attacks or commands in front of other students when the learner exhibits hyperactive behavior.

Perseveration

Once perseverating learners attend to a task they do not easily stop and transfer their attention to a different task. Since they have difficulty attending to differences, they tend to keep going with the first activity. The following behaviors may be noted in learners in this category.

Observable Behavior: Perseveration

The student

1. may say a word over and over.
2. cannot shift from one activity to another.
3. tends to repeat the previous response on tests.
4. may add all the problems in arithmetic, even though he or she can easily see that half of them are subtraction.

Discussion: Perseveration

Students who perseverate at first require monitoring of changes in tasks. Develop a system that will permit them gradually to divide a task into segments, note where changes occur, and make a transition smoothly into each section. Use short activities (i.e., addition, subtraction, multiplication problems) at the individual learner's level, so that the learner can attend to starting tasks, switching them, and then checking them. Everyone working with the students should be aware of the behavior and should be consistent in providing similar activities that will ensure success at the task as well as the development of self-monitoring.

Treatment Considerations: Perseveration

1. The student must learn to listen, wait, and then respond correctly.
2. Perseveration can be broken in many cases with a motor act. For example:

   John draws this: ○ .
   The teacher says, "John, give me your eraser." (motor act)
   "Now John, draw this: □ "

3. Another technique is to go to something else and then come back to the next task.
4. Red lines as a key to a change in directions or process are helpful for the student with this difficulty.
5. Warn the student that a change in activity is coming up.
6. "Simon says" or "Follow the leader" type of games can help the student to learn to shift behavior.
7. Physically move the student from the present task to the new activity.

Disinhibition

Learners exhibiting disinhibited behavior appear to have difficulty in shifting easily from topic to topic in conversation. They often give unusual responses to questions or have a jumbled sequence of thoughts. Past experiences are retrieved and inappropriately added to the train of thought.

Observable Behavior: Disinhibition

The student

1. gets carried away by his or her own thoughts.

2. gives inappropriate responses that are unrelated to the question asked.
3. cannot put on his or her "braking mechanisms," or control himself or herself.

Discussion: Disinhibition

These students need specific considerations in activities requiring the initiation and completion of an activity as well as verbal language expression. Instructions must be in detail, properly sequenced, and, in some cases, recorded by the student. To prevent the learner from making wild guesses and rushing through assignments, the teacher and learner should plan together how much time will be required for the task. The development of a success mode of behavior will depend on the length of the assignment and the student's ability to stay on task.

Treatment Considerations: Disinhibition

1. The teacher can help the student stay on the task or idea by touching him or her or by using such "breaking words" as "no" or "wait."
2. Give the student something to do with his or her hands (manipulatives).
3. The teacher should be calm and not appear irritated when giving directions.
4. Reward on-task behavior, and do not reward inappropriate behavior.
5. The instructor can plan specific steps with the learner to accomplish a particular activity.
6. Behavior modification techniques are found to be very helpful with disinhibited learners.
7. Do not accept a wild guess. Ask the student to rethink his or her response and come up with a better answer.
8. Purposeful activity that is verbally explained while being accomplished is a helpful technique to counteract disinhibition (e.g., John does simple tasks and explains what he is doing as he does it).
9. Plan small discussions that will train verbal interactions. Lead the student and help him or her focus thoughts through responses to questions.
10. Provide objects or pictures to help the student stay on the topic.
11. If the student's unusual responses appear to be interpreted by classmates and others as bad manners, use social situations to channel participation. Play "what will happen if" types of games to discuss manners, and appropriate verbal responses.
12. If the student confuses fantasy with reality when he or she responds, channel the creativity into projects that will have a theme or focus but will be enjoyable to the student. Puppet plays, role playing of book characters or historical figures, interviews, and similar activities can be used.

Impulsivity

Impulsive learners lack self-control and react too quickly. They make too many errors and appear to be less reflective than their peers. The following behavior is exhibited by these students:

Observable Behavior: Impulsivity

The student

1. quickly responds to questions before thinking out his or her answers.
2. is excessively talkative.
3. rushes into an activity before the instructor has completed the directions.
4. is impatient with repeated tasks and does not like to review old learning.
5. avoids anxiety and is unreflective in resolving problems.

Discussion: Impulsivity

If possible, the teacher should carefully chart the impulsivity of the learner and establish a baseline of behavior. Is there a pattern in the occurrence of his or her actions? The instructor should try to be as objective as possible in dealing with an impulsive student. Since the behavior may easily distract the teacher and other students, confrontations can occur. The instructor must be organized and anticipate the student's behavior. The instructor particularly serves as a role model for this category of students.

Treatment Considerations: Impulsivity

1. Set rules and limits for classroom activities.
2. Organize schedule, and/or state the steps the learner must take in making a transition from one activity to another.
3. Reward the student for self-monitoring the completion of assignments. If possible give immediate feedback to carefully completed tasks.
4. If the student has more than one teacher, then all

must attempt to coordinate steps in the completion of material.

5. The talkative student will need outlets for his or her behavior (e.g., reading into a tape recorder, telling stories to younger students, a chance to visit with other students during the day).
6. Refuse to accept wild guesses. Ask the student to verbally explain what he or she did and why.
7. Disguise review activities. The student has to see the value and quality of each lesson.
8. Avoid anger and derogatory remarks about the student's work. Keep folders of baseline work (e.g., samples of best handwriting) and ask the learner to compare his or her "sloppy" work with the "best" and then discuss a solution to the problem.
9. Provide short assignments with short, simple directions.
10. If the learner rushes through assignments, discuss the pacing and time restraints of a task.
11. Assign the learner to work with classmates as a peer tutor, with the responsibility of helping them check their work.
12. Discuss different solutions to problems to aid the student in seeing choices before he or she takes impulsive action.
13. Teach the student how to plan homework, to handle multiple assignments, and to effectively study independently.
14. Explain to the student how to handle frustration and errors. He or she needs to know that everyone makes errors, stops to evaluate what happened, and then proceeds to a better solution. The impulsive student needs to actually work through activities or problems that require reflective behavior.

BEHAVIOR MANAGEMENT

In viewing the whole concept of behavior management, the following general considerations are important.

1. The teacher should be primarily concerned with reinforcing good behavior. The teacher should be careful not to emphasize bad behavior by trying too hard to discourage it. The idea is to reward the student for the way he handles himself or deals with problems that come before or precipitate negative behavior. For example, rather than rewarding not fighting, the teacher rewards doing math or science, etc.
2. In reality, when we reward a student for not doing something bad, we are, in effect, reinforcing a subtle form of extortion. To reward a student for doing something that we want him or her to do (arithmetic) which replaces a negative or target behavior (fighting) that we don't want him or her to do, is really good business and is considered a form of free enterprise.
3. It is important that we think about getting out of the business of "paying off" for nonbehavior. The payoff sometimes leads to continued and greater payoffs. For example, one student stopping another student in a school hallway says, "You know, kids in this school are being beaten up on the way to school. For one dollar a week I can give you protection and guarantee that you will not be beaten up" (paying off for nonbehavior). After three weeks of payoffs, when the students meet again, the protector says, "Have you noticed how two of your friends got beaten up last week? They didn't have any protection. Since my expenses have gone up, I'm going to need two dollars a week from you" (continued and greater payoff).
4. It is important to recognize that "normal" is a relative term. Behavior management involves attending to different dimensions of behavior simultaneously and should consider all or any of the following:
   a. treatment for the student
   b. treatment for the teacher
   c. treatment of the environment
   d. any combination of 1, 2, or 3
   e. provide no treatment at all

   It appears that for most cases a, b, and c must be dealt with simultaneously in order to achieve a healthy emotional climate.

Specific Considerations in Behavior Management

1. Intracategory: Are we observing clusters of behavior which seem to fall into a particular category?
2. Intercategory: How much overlap in terms of observable behavior is there among the different categories of behavior?
3. Is the behavior occasional, what is the duration, and how severe is the episode?
4. Is the behavior chronic and what is the severity?
5. Can the teacher deal with the behavior within his or her present knowledge base and situation?
6. What are the resources available to help the teacher to improve the situation or to reduce the problem to a level where it can be dealt with effectively within the classroom by the teacher alone?

7. What alternatives are available that will enable the teacher to be able to deal with the problem behavior more effectively?

The remaining part of this chapter will deal with areas relating to specific techniques of behavior management. The underlying assumption in any behavior management program is that the individual imposing the treatment is also willing to change and to accept new ideas. This is not always the case. Many teachers are accustomed to dealing with problem behavior in "their own way" and are chary of trying alternative approaches. Many educators are resorting to physical punishment as a means of modifying behavior or of controlling students. It is said that education is presently the only profession that has the "legal" right to beat its clients into submission. The concept of power or control must be considered when we ask "To what purpose do we use what kinds of behavior management techniques?" "Do the students control us or do we control the students?" is a frequent question. What constitutes a loss of control? Does yelling and striking a student with a paddle constitute a loss of control? What about the whole matter of motive in dealing with behavior? Should we consider what motivates a student to behave as he or she does—or are we, as teachers, going to lash out at anything that disturbs us or that interferes with our perceived needs and goals?

Teaching Style

It is impossible to be what you are not. As an individual responsible for children, the teacher needs to ask himself such questions as "What sets me off or gets me uptight as a person?" Research has not indicated that one type of personality, a "permissive" person, for example, makes a better teacher than a person who is considered a "disciplinarian." It is difficult to ask a laissez-faire, permissive type of individual to suddenly change his or her way of life and become well-disciplined and structured, or vice versa. However, understanding oneself may result in a teacher being more ready to understand the conduct of learners as essentially an expression of their total experiences, rather than behavior that is directed only at the person in authority.

For the purposes of an operational definition, the area of behavior management shall be interpreted to mean a variety of treatment alternatives that can be installed in school settings. The underlying basis for approaches to behavior management is the utilization of good common sense and good judgment. If considered within the context of day-to-day school life, the implementation of behavior management techniques into any program will help the teacher to establish a better emotional climate for all learners.

Modifying Behavior

Behavior modification as an alternative treatment is based on the principle of rewarding desirable behavior and reducing or extinguishing undesirable behavior. It focuses on what a student says or does rather than emphasizing diagnostic categories. It involves a process by which behavior is observed and appropriate techniques to modify this behavior are imposed. It is generally felt that it is easier to deal with specific target behavior than it is to try to restructure a student's total personality. Difficulty with a straight behavior modification approach tends to occur when behaviors of different types appear in the same student or when different types of reinforcers are found to be unsuccessful. Time, self-discipline, and attention to detail on the part of the observer are important factors in behavior modification. Some teachers have difficulty dealing with these factors and, therefore, avoid behavior modification techniques. A behavior modification approach if appropriately utilized, however, can be successfully implemented in school settings.

ANALYSIS OF CONTINGENCY MANAGEMENT

The observer must be aware of the following aspects of student-teacher interaction.

1. Examine or observe the event (what happened?): Teacher says, "Class, may I have your attention?"
2. Analyze the action of the participant (who responded in what way?): The students stop talking and attend to the teacher.
3. Interpret the outcomes (what happened?): The teacher says, "That is good."

EVENT → ACTIONS → OUTCOMES

ACHIEVING DESIRED BEHAVIOR

Reinforcement

A stimulus that results in an increase or strengthening of the behavior it immediately follows is called a reinforcer. Praise or material rewards that result in desired behavior are reinforcers. Whether or not a particular stimulus is a reinforcer must be determined by observing its effects on the behavior it follows. In order to have maximum effect, the reinforcement must immediately follow the desired behavior. The immediacy of the reinforcement that follows the target behavior relates to how effective the reinforcement will be. Chastising a student two hours after a particular event is not as effective as doing it immediately after the episode. Complimenting or giving praise operates the same way. Reinforcement must be contingent on the target behavior. If you want the behavior to occur before you give a reward, then you are establishing a contingency. A reward for one student may have the opposite effect on another. The teacher saying, "Good work, Susan," may encourage Susan to stay on task. Saying "Good work" to John may, in effect, slow down or stop his efforts. Reinforcers, therefore, must be tested for individual children.

PRIMARY REINFORCERS. Things such as food, drink, warmth, and sexual stimulation that satisfy biological needs or needs that sustain life are called primary reinforcers. They do not depend on previous conditioning for reinforcing value.

SECONDARY REINFORCERS. Things like praise, toys, money, etc., that are not directly related to biological needs, are called secondary or conditioned reinforcers. Where primary reinforcers are paired with secondary reinforcers—such as giving praise with food—or when secondary reinforcers become desirable in and of themselves—such as praise alone—they can have strong reinforcing power in terms of modifying behavior. Some secondary reinforcers such as toys may be unimportant to some children and, therefore, have little or no reinforcing power. When a mother's touch is paired with food or drink the mother's touch can become a strong secondary reinforcer. Teachers usually use secondary reinforcers in school settings. Words, touch, body movement, or posture can have great reinforcing properties. There are always exceptions to the rule in that some students shun praise and others do not respond to competitive situations. Some reinforcers such as praise, touch, eye contact, etc., have a generalized effect on a wide range of behaviors.

TYPES OF REINFORCEMENT, There are two types of reinforcement: positive and negative. Both can increase or strengthen behaviors that follow. Neither should be confused with the concept of punishment.

Positive reinforcers include anything that is desired or needed by the student. Positive reinforcers tend to strengthen the response that has just occurred, making it likely that the response will reoccur. For example, William, working intently, gives the teacher his math paper and the teacher says, "Good work." That is a positive reinforcer. To be effective the positive reinforcer must follow immediately after the target behavior is achieved. Getting something good to eat contingent on desired behavior, is positive reinforcement because it tends to strengthen the response that follows. Teachers, too often, believe that behaving correctly is only what students are expected to do. They simply ignore good behavior. It is suggested that to encourage children to continue behaving well, we need to positively reinforce their good behavior and not just wait for them to misbehave. Students have been heard to say about certain teachers that it is extremely difficult to "Get a nice word out of him or her" or that "He is grouchy."

A *negative reinforcer* includes anything unpleasant or not desired by the student. Negative reinforcement involves taking away something noxious contingent upon the desired behavior. Negative reinforcers weaken the response that immediately precedes the onset of the negative reinforcer. This can occur in different ways.

1. Negative reinforcement strengthens the response that takes away the negative reinforcer.
2. Negative reinforcement also suppresses the behavior that brought on the negative reinforcer. For example, a student is reinforced for giving a response. By doing this he or she avoids punishment such as the case in which a teacher constantly yelled to keep the class quiet. The students responded by working quietly. Another case was the mother who nagged for better grades which motivated her child to get better grades. However, keeping quiet as in the first case or getting better grades in the second case may have reduced the yelling and nagging (punishment), but at the same time it tended to reinforce the behavior (yelling and nagging) of the person who is doing the punishing.

It is important to remember that negative reinforcement is a double-edged sword. We have many well-meaning, yelling teachers and nagging mothers who, while achieving their goals, become disliked by the children in the process.

Another consideration is the fact that while negative reinforcement results in an increase in the behavior that it follows, it is not to be confused with punishment. It is probably better to think of both positive and negative reinforcement as ways of modifying behavior and not worry too much about whether a particular response is negative or positive. Just think about the behavior that is occurring and the responses or consequences that is permitting it to continue.

REINFORCEMENT SCHEDULES

The four types of reinforcement schedules that are generally utilized include fixed ratio, variable ratio, fixed interval, and variable interval.

Table 10-1

	Fixed	Variable
Ratio	Fixed Ratio	Variable Ratio
Interval	Fixed Interval	Variable Interval

Fixed ratio: In this case reinforcement would occur after a specific number of responses. For example, after every three responses the student would be reinforced.

Variable ratio: Reinforcement in these situations would occur after a varying number of responses. For example, the student would be rewarded after one response, then after five responses, and then after three responses, with the number of responses between reinforcers averaging three.

Fixed interval: This involves reinforcement after a specific interval of time. For example, the student would be reinforced after a 10-second delay.

Variable interval: This involves reinforcement after different intervals of time. For example, the student would be reinforced after ten seconds, then after fifteen seconds, and then after five seconds, with the intervals averaging ten seconds.

It has been found that variable schedules of reinforcement produce more results than fixed ratios. It can be concluded that variable ratio reinforcement should produce the greatest response rate while the fixed interval would produce the least response rate.

HOW TO USE REINFORCERS

Reinforcers strengthen behavior and can be used to develop new skills. The following are some concepts to be considered.

1. Of all the reinforcers that are available to me, which will work with a particular child? Someone once said that "every student has his price." The reinforcer that works may be highly individualized.
2. How can I test for the most appropriate reinforcer? Observation of students at play and work are effective, or the teacher can talk to the student and probe for his likes and dislikes.
3. Does the same reinforcer function effectively at different times and in different situations? Ice cream, for example, may not be reinforcing in the winter for some students.
4. Secondary reinforcers work better if paired with food; for example, saying, "Good job, John" as he is given a bit of food and a pat on the back.
5. When can I take away the food and the pat and just rely on praise?
6. Tokens and food are good to start with, particularly when working with nonverbal children exhibiting a slow rate of development. Some of the more commonly used reinforcers include:
   a. A "time" or "clock stamp" can be used with a time clock. The teacher stamps small pieces of paper with the clock stamp and the number of minutes of on-task behavior is marked as indicated by the time clock that is left on the student's desk. The teacher then will write in the minute and hour hands that will indicate the amount of time that the student has worked at a particular task. This is later tallied and "time" is exchanged for tangible rewards.
   b. Token reinforcement, later to be exchanged for tangible rewards.
   c. Different colored stars to be later exchanged for toys, school supplies, or opportunities to play in a pleasant setting.
7. Reinforce the student only when he or she performs the desired behavior. Do not reinforce him or her randomly. In some cases you may want to reinforce successive approximations. For example, John could be reinforced for taking out his paper and pencil first, although the terminal behavior is to complete arithmetic problems copied from the chalkboard.
8. Do not reinforce any inappropriate behavior such as aggression or continually getting out of the seat.
9. Reinforce *immediately* after the desired behavior is completed.
10. Reinforce the student frequently and in small amounts, especially when you are teaching a new concept. Tokens or stars are small and can be given frequently in the lesson without losing their reinforcement value.
11. The Premack Principle can also be utilized in modifying behavior. For example, follow a low probability behavior such as taking out the garbage with a high probability behavior such as watching the T.V. or eating a favorite food. The latter (T.V. or food) should strengthen the former (taking out the garbage). Another example would be saying to students, "As soon as we put away the materials, we can have our snack, etc." The snack, in this case, may reinforce the putting away of materials.

Shaping

Sometimes students who are severe stutterers will not read aloud or answer questions orally in the classroom. In some cases they do not speak at all. How can we achieve the target behavior of attaining a modicum of verbal participation in classroom activities? *Modicum* is relative and must be defined specifically for each individual student. Shaping, in this case, means to reinforce successful approximations to the final target behavior by taking the student closer and closer to what we want, utilizing as a vehicle less threatening of nonthreatening situations. This may take a long time and require many interim steps. For the stuttering student the following is suggested:

1. Indicate privately to the student that you understand his or her problem and that while you will not force him or her to speak out loud (thereby relieving some of the student's anxiety), you are at the same time going to help him or her work through the problem.
2. We can then determine, with the student, situations in which he or she feels comfortable when speaking.
3. Through further approximations, in one-to-one interactions, determine with the student situations in which he or she will speak by choice. These situations should resemble general classroom activities. This could involve his or her speaking freely or responding to questions in a small group of two at first, then three, four, etc.
4. Finally, through reinforcing successive approximations, achieve the target behavior of class oral participation and continue intermittent reinforcements.

Modeling (Imitation)

Many educators believe that desirable as well as undesirable behavior patterns exhibited by students are a result of modeling after those of others. This occurs in different environments involving social interaction with people who constantly demonstrate certain behaviors. Kindness, patience, loudness, and punitive behavior, for example, are considered learned for the most part. Teachers need to be aware of their potential impact on students' behaviors in terms of their own modeling potential. Especially in the early grades, if the teacher is calm and warm, the students are likely to model or imitate these patterns of behavior. In utilizing modeling in modifying behavior, especially with the sensitive-withdrawn child, it is suggested that the teacher model desirable behavior with another student; i.e., reward another student for exhibiting the desirable behavior and then reward the target student for imitating the same behavior.

Imitation is an important skill to learn and a powerful tool in teaching new behaviors. The whole concept of imitation must be taught deliberately to those in whom it is not present, that is, in students who are unable to imitate. The teacher must present models that can be easily imitated and then praise the correct imitation or successive approximation to imitating the target behavior.

Prompting and Fading

Some students need to be shown or prompted to enable them to accomplish a particular task. The teacher may hold a student's hand and actually move it through the proper sequence in writing a manuscript "a" on the chalkboard, for example. The gradual lessening of direction and pressure from the teacher's hand will allow the student to take control. Finally, the teacher should slowly remove his hand as the student takes full control of the movement. This is one form of fading. Fading is the gradual withdrawal of support after the student has mastered each step or aspect of a specific event. This helps the student to achieve success and encourages further attempts at more difficult tasks. An example of prompting is when arrows are placed near a letter with a red dot (↓M), enabling the student to know where to start and in which direction to proceed when writing the letter M.

Generalization

Individuals are constantly reacting to new situations in a manner that is congruent with the way they responded to similar situations in the past. This is especially true if a particular set of behaviors was reinforced in the past. The greater the similarity between situations, the more generalized the response. Learning to ride a bicycle on one type of bicycle will enable the individual to ride other types of bicycles. The bicycle riding response will generalize itself to all bicycles. In terms of response generalization, it appears that in certain situations students will exhibit a generalized response to stress or happiness. An example would be the learner who, when happy, starts out by laughing but then makes funny noises and begins to jump up and down in his seat. The same response seems to occur each time.

Generalization is an important part of behavior management. We want behavior learned in the classroom to be generalized at home and to all social situations. Good manners at the table is an example of this phenomenon. Good behavior in the classroom should be generalized in the playground.

Deprivation and Satiation

Deprivation relates to the length of time since a reinforcer has been available to an individual. A game is more likely to be reinforcing after concentrated work such as reading or writing than immediately after a physical education class. An example of satiation is the situation in which a student is given too much of a particular reinforcement at one time and the value of the reinforcer is lost. Too much praise may make praise ineffective as a reinforcer. The teacher should vary reinforcers and learn to use generalized reinforcers, such as eye contact, effectively to control behavior. Continuous reinforcement, where every response is rewarded, is effective in acquiring good behavior. Intermittent reinforcement, however, is most effective in maintaining the desired behavior after it has been established.

WEAKENING BEHAVIOR OR PERFORMANCE

Punishment

Punishment can be verbal or physical and is used by many educators to decrease undesirable behavior. However, in particular students, it can result in an increase in more aberrant or more severe behavior. It may also not necessarily result in improved behavior. The student who is "paddled" may physically abuse or hurt another child or "get even" with the teacher through active or passive aggression. Punishment, for the most part, presents a moral and ethical issue, depending on the situation in which it is utilized. In certain critical or severe situations punishment may be necessary, particularly when injury or health may be at stake. For example, immediate punishment may be in order for the child who takes pills from the medicine cabinet and eats them or for the child who runs out in the middle of the street in front of cars. The following are considerations to keep in mind:

1. The child should understand in advance what he will be punished for.
2. Punish a child immediately after the behavior occurs, preferably, or while it is occurring, if possible.
3. Punishment should be consistent and accomplished with some objectivity.
4. Punishment should only be used in severe or critical situations where a quick change in behavior is necessary.
5. Continue to reinforce appropriate behavior. For example, praise a child for not going to the medicine cabinet without permission.
6. Use of punishment may lead not only to more aggressive behavior by the child, but also may result in the individual doing the punishing becoming accustomed to using physical punishment as a means of modifying behavior.

Overcorrection

Overcorrection as a technique for decreasing target behavior involves extending the treatment beyond the correction of a specific act. For example, the student who throws paper on the playground may be required to clean up the whole playground and perhaps sweep the halls. The following are important considerations:

1. The student must understand what behavior is being punished. In this case it is throwing paper on the playground.
2. The overcorrection procedure must be directly related to the undesirable behavior. Having him or her sweep up the halls may be too far away from throwing paper on the playground.
3. The overcorrection should require longer periods of time than the behavior being corrected.

The idea of work should never be construed as punishment.

Time-Out

Time-out is a form of punishment in which the opportunity for reinforcement is removed for a given time. The time is contingent upon a particular response from the student. For example, the teacher could isolate the student every time he or she does something that is undesirable. Seating the student in a corner by himself and not allowing anyone to talk to him is not a new concept in modifying student behavior. There are several important steps, however, to follow for maximum effect.

1. The student should know the rules regarding what behaviors will result in "time-out."
2. How long the student will have to be in a time-out situation should be clearly specified. (Probably not more than 5 minutes in most situations.)
3. Be consistent and use the time-out every time the undesirable behavior occurs.
4. Time-out areas should be supervised and the student should know the effects of getting out early without permission.
5. The activity should be carried out in an objective manner.
6. Time-out should be repeated if the student "fools around" or fails to do what is required.
7. At the end of the time-out continue to reinforce appropriate behavior immediately.

Response Cost

Response cost is a form of treatment where the student is penalized in some manner for undesirable behavior. Examples of response cost are fines, losing one's license, or having to give up something that is valued. The following are factors that should be considered.

1. The response cost must be specified. The fine, or whatever it is the student has to give up, should be

reasonable. Taking away six months of television for not doing homework for one night is not reasonable.

2. Time-out and overcorrection have been used successfully in educational settings. However, it is important to recognize that they are forms of punishment.

REALITY THERAPY

Reality therapy is based on the assumption that every student needs to experience love and a sense of worthiness. (Glasser, *Schools Without Failure*). The loss of love and the experience of trauma, by the same token, if experienced in the form of reduced self-esteem, will result in unhappiness and suffering. For some children, reading is a painful experience. Poor performance often results in loss of love and feelings of inadequacy. Educators have found that love, understanding, and support, in a verbal as well as physical sense, helps students to maintain a greater degree of frustration tolerance. This is particularly true when they fail in school tasks. In reality therapy the teacher is envisioned as a person who becomes involved in the learning process in an emotional as well as a physical sense. A humanistic approach to teacher-student interaction becomes the basis for sharing experiences and for delineating responsibility.

The teacher should be willing to give as well as accept love in a physical sense (i.e., touch, hug) and in a verbal sense, and to be aware of the effect of body language, and posture, on student behavior.

The essence of reality therapy involves giving students opportunities to evaluate their behavior and to select alternatives for themselves which will help them achieve their goals.

Individuals who are responsible for modifying the behavior of the students must support the children through a process of involvement.

The student is encouraged to face reality in terms of his or her own behavior and to verbalize his or her responsibilities.

Once the student makes the commitment to attain a particular goal, he or she is obliged to honor that commitment.

How It Works

1. Analyze the different opportunities for involvement with a particular student, such as reading and social studies.
2. Discuss with the student his or her present behavior in a particular area of involvement—reading, for example.
3. Insist that the student make a value judgment about his or her behavior.
   a. What am I doing?
   b. Is it helping me?
4. Help the student make a commitment to a plan or sequence that will change his or her behavior.
5. Help the student carry out the plan (follow-up).
6. Accept no excuses for failure. Instead, work the student through the activity or process as many times as necessary to achieve success (given that the goal is realistic and attainable by the student.)
7. Help the student reject unrealistic goals or behaviors and continue to encourage his or her involvement. For example:
   a. John cannot remember a sequence of directions. He gets out of his seat and talks to other children when the teacher gives an assignment.
   b. John talks about this situation with the teacher and admits that getting out of his seat and talking to other students will not solve his problem.
   c. Alternative solutions are worked out that include the teacher developing signals with John that will assuage his anxiety and indicate to him opportunities to get the directions again from the teacher or from a "buddy" student. John stated that with these changes he would not have to get out of his seat.
   d. When John forgets his commitment he is gently reminded and requested to recommit himself to the new behavior.
   e. The teacher will reinforce John for a success in his commitment and this will help to maintain the desired behavior.
   f. John soon learns that the teacher really loves him and does not want to punish him or to make him suffer or to "overload" him with too much input at one time.
8. Some regression in behavior must be expected by the teacher and treated accordingly without the student feeling loss of love or self-respect.
9. Another technique that can be utilized is the holding of class meetings. Meetings that are held in a circle can be a vehicle for making school experiences relevant to the students and to provide opportunities for them to develop confidence. The meetings may not provide opportunities to answer all questions, but they do provide a forum for examining alternatives. The following can be accomplished at meetings:
   a. Teachers can become more involved with an entire group of students.
   b. The students have an opportunity to indicate their attitudes and feelings.
   c. Students have opportunities to solve problems

and to work out possible solutions to social as well as academic concerns.

d. Teachers can learn how to probe to find out student concerns.

e. Since the basic thrust of such a meeting is problem-oriented, students learn how to focus on problems.

f. Students learn to respond to open-ended questions.

g. The leader learns how to develop an atmosphere in which children will not just give the kinds of answers that they think the leader wants to hear.

h. Meetings should be terminated with a commitment to finding alternative solutions to problems.

i. Students learn that there is "no one best way" of doing things that is appropriate for all people.

It is expected that by giving students an opportunity to discuss social problems as well as academic problems they will increase their probability of being successful in school tasks and therefore have better feelings about themselves while exhibiting self-initiated behavior. Proponents of reality therapy advocate eliminating present formalized grading systems and instead emphasizing the teaching of thinking skills and developing a problem-solving mode of behavior in students.

ADDITIONAL SUGGESTIONS AND SUMMARY

The following are additional general suggestions for behavior management.

1. Begin by structuring the environment to establish guidelines for yourself and for the students. This means delineating to the learners at the start of the school year, not only the dynamics of the learning environment in terms of their role, but, more importantly, the teacher's role both as an educator and as a human being. Young learners tend to see teachers as something "extra human." So do many parents. The students should understand that the teacher has "bad days" and "good days" and that he or she will exhibit anger and frustration as well as happiness and understanding. The teacher, at the same time, can indicate that he or she will try not to impose his or her personal unhappiness on the students, but, being human, situations could occur. At these times, the teacher would need the understanding of those around him or her. The reverse side of the coin will also hold true, and the teacher should indicate that he or she will try to be understanding when a student has a "bad day" and will indicate this to the student.
2. Rapport may be difficult or almost impossible to obtain with some children. In any case, the learner must be told explicitly (use good judgment) after a crisis situation that although his or her behavior threatens the entire learning situation, it will not be taken as a personal battle between him or her and the teacher. This tends to put the situation or episode on a more objective level. The teacher must permit testing within reasonable limits, but should not allow aberrant behavior to go beyond the established guidelines until tempers flare. In other words, don't wait five minutes until the situation gets completely out of hand before you step in. Know how far you can go with each child. A pat on the shoulder can send one student off on a rampage. Another child may need a great deal of "mothering" and "body contact." This is where reading the cumulative records and talking to the previous teachers is important. This information should not only tell you what to do, but what not to do with a particular student. The earlier in the year you get this information, the easier it will be for all parties concerned. Think out the concept of being there ahead of the student by understanding the nature of the problem and have some notion of how to deal with it.
3. The teacher may have to begin with "nonschool types of activities" in order to win the student back to learning. These include many of the readiness games at different levels which appear to be "play" but in reality are task-oriented. Some students have been "turned off" for too long. They should be reintroduced to formal academics gradually.
4. Reinforcement or punishment should not be postponed for long periods of time. Punishment, regardless of form, may get so far removed from the particular incident that it becomes meaningless.
5. The teacher should not get into a "social drama" with the student by backing him or her up against the wall with such statements as, "If you do that one more time you will leave my room and never come back." Few administrators will support such a statement and many students know this. It may result in your losing the respect of the other learners in the class. It is better to speak to the learner in private and agree on some strategy that will result in your both being better able to work together. During the student-teacher conference, it may be decided to include other people to help solve the problem, such as a counselor, the principal, parents, or even other teachers whose advice and objectivity may help improve the situation.
6. The teacher should provide for group and indi-

vidual opportunities to express feelings in a non-threatening environment. This can be accomplished by the teacher through structured group and individual counseling programs or by a counselor or psychologist, should one be available. Home-room counseling after school may be the best time to listen to students and work out problems.

7. A good behavior reinforcement or behavior modification program can be established whereby the individual is rewarded for successive approximations for a given task. The teacher should reward on-task behavior, for example, and should not in any way (positively or negatively) reinforce negative behavior.
8. The teacher might begin establishing better school–home relationships by sending home only that which the student can accomplish at his or her independent level. Another suggestion is to reduce or eliminate altogether the sending home of "red marked" poor papers which may further lead to poor parent–student–teacher relationships. The teacher should notify the parent through a telephone call or a short note when the learner has experienced success in school, either in academic tasks or in his or her social-emotional behavior.
9. Perhaps the most important principle to remember in behavior management is that although the material rewards are good, in many cases they will have limited transfer value. Success at the academic task must become rewarding in and of itself. Therefore, the teacher must provide for a success mode in learning academic tasks.

Observing and Charting

Observing and charting behavior has effects both on those observing and on the student whose behavior is being analyzed. These are:

1. Through counting the behavior under concern, the observer may find that it may not be happening as often as was believed.
2. It may be observed that the behavior occurs only at a certain time during the day or is precipitated by a particular situation. The observer may gain an understanding of why the behavior occurs.
3. The student may modify his or her own behavior merely by virtue of the fact that he or she now observes that someone is watching him or her and then writing things down (counting).
4. The student may relate a particular behavior with someone counting or charting and this kind of association may result in a change in behavior.

Observation and accurate recording of events or behaviors will give the teacher an idea of how often a particular behavior occurs. This can be accomplished easily by using a checklist. The teacher may want to note the amount of off-task or on-task activity that is occurring for a particular student. The frequency of the behavior can be charted to show how the student is performing over a period of time. It can then be determined if there is improvement, no change, or a decline in performance in terms of the student's behavior. The following are important in charting behavior:

1. Establish a baseline for particular behaviors by determining the current level of performance.
2. Estimate the time or duration of a particular behavior as well as how many times it occurs within a given period. For example, John may get off-task during a 30-minute reading period an average of five times for a given five-day period. He stays off-task an average of three minutes each time before going back to work.
3. Wherever possible have another observer check out and verify the results or count. Material needed will include a pencil, copies of the forms, and a stopwatch, regular watch, or clock. The Mann Student Observation Worksheet (Forms 10-1 and 10-2, pages 297 and 298) and the Graphing Worksheet (Form 10-3, page 303) can be utilized in observing and charting behavior.
4. The sequence involves pinpointing behavior, recording behavior, and then controlling the consequences or alternatives. It is suggested that the teacher discuss the findings of a particular behavior over a given period of time with the student. The teacher should attempt to arrive at an agreement with the student that this is an area of concern that needs to be improved.
5. If behavior is charted over a period of time, the teacher should discuss the progress or lack of it with the student. Reinforcement of improved or desirable behavior that has been charted should be accomplished on a continuous basis even after the undesirable behavior is no longer a problem. The teacher should continue to reinforce the desired behavior.

DETERMINING THE EFFECTIVENESS OF TREATMENT

The teacher needs to know if the intervention or treatment program has modified the behavior of the learner (in accordance with expectations). A logical method of determining this is to stop the treatment or return to a baseline mode and see if the desired

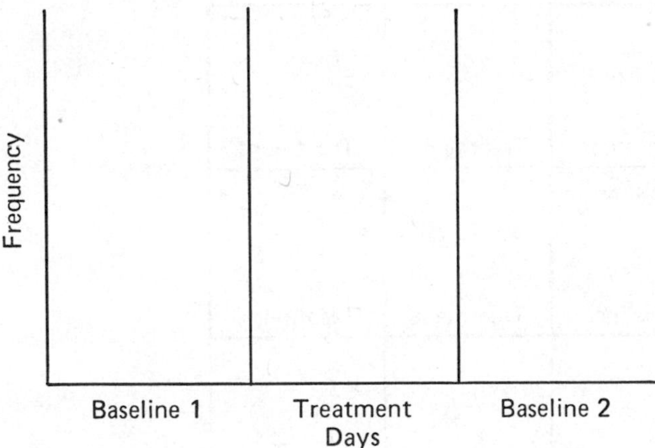

Figure 10-1 Design for Implementing Behavior Modifi cation Program

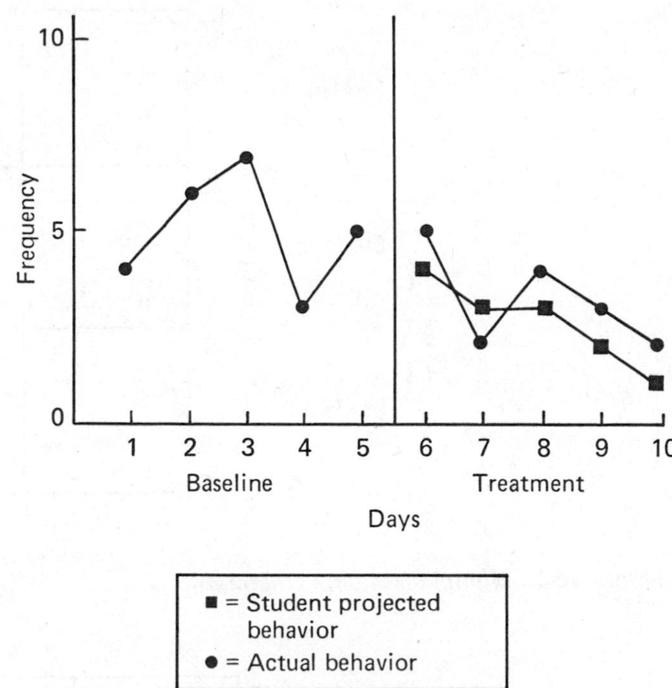

Figure 10-2 Chart of Student's Behavior

behavior is maintained. The basic design for implementing a behavior modification program is shown in Figure 10-1.

There are situations, such as in severe cases of aberrant behavior that is self-injurious or injurious to others, in which the teacher may not want to discontinue the treatment and return to a baseline mode. An alternate approach to using the basic ABA design is to chart the student's progress with his or her participation. (See Figure 10-2.)

1. The student notes that he or she is exhibiting the target behavior (talking out of turn) an average of five times during a science period each day for five days.
2. The student then specifies his own projected treatment plan that includes specifying the maximum number of times he will exhibit the target behavior for a five-day interval (treatment period).

   Example: Student, "I will try to talk out of turn (target behavior) less than five times each day." Using the baseline data as a guideline, the student states, "I will not talk out of turn more than four times on Monday, three times on Tuesday, three times on Wednesday, two times on Thursday, and one time on Friday." The teacher observes the student's behavior and records the incidence accordingly.
3. During the treatment period, the student and teacher chart the student's actual behavior (talking out of turn).
4. The process of charting enables the student to monitor his own behavior.
5. This approach lends itself very well to "contracting," where the student agrees in a written document to adhere to a schedule of behavior as outlined in a simple agreement contract.
6. After the treatment period, the student and the teacher review the results. The student indicates how the treatment period compares with the baseline period and then formulates new goals for the next period.

The students soon learn that they can control their own world. This technique is particularly appropriate for immature-dependent students who may discover that they can do a great deal to control their own destiny.

MULTIPLE BASELINE

Another alternative method for determining whether or not a particular treatment is effective is to examine antecedent behavior in several children simultaneously, establish a continuum of baselines, and apply a consecutive treatment program. Then comparisons will indicate whether or not the treatment has been effective. This approach is designed to determine the effectiveness of a particular reinforcer in a particular individual and often is difficult to interpret. (See Figure 10-3.)

1. The observer charts the concurrent baseline behavior of three students (five days).

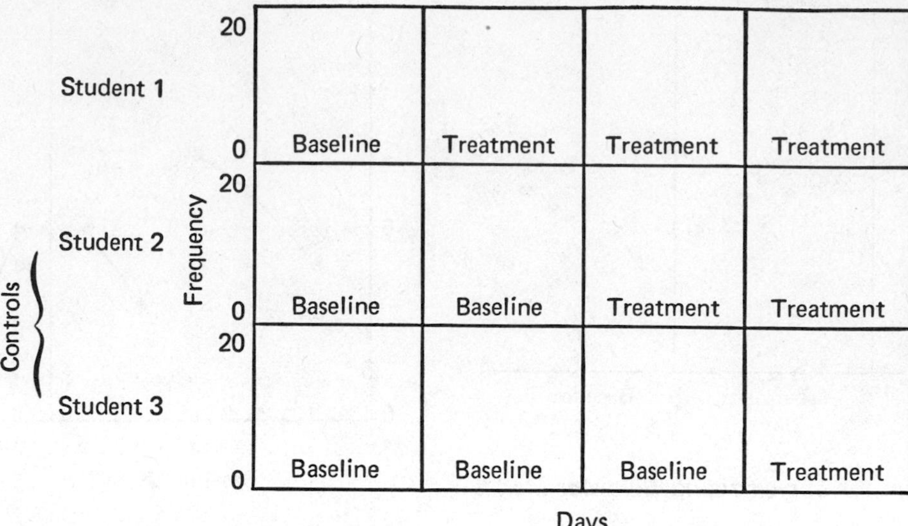

Figure 10-3 Multiple-Baseline Treatment

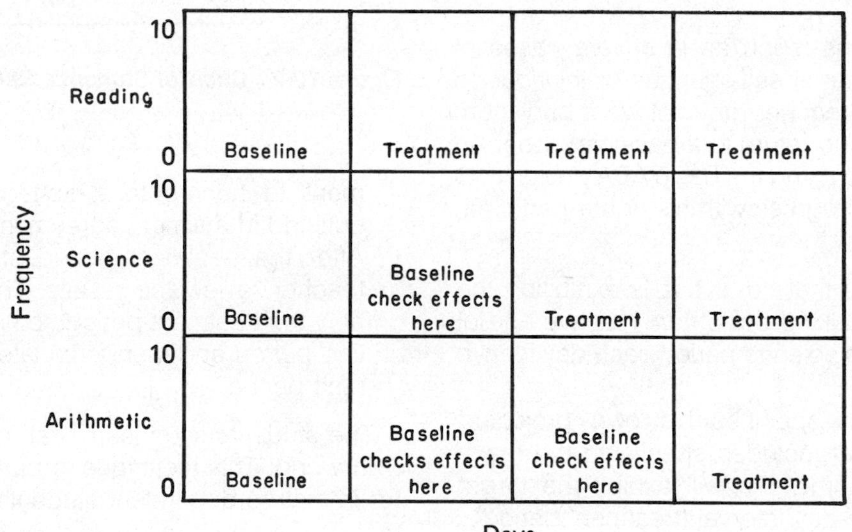

Figure 10-4 Behavior Generalization

2. After the first five days, treatment is applied to student 1 and baseline is continued for students 2 and 3.
3. At the end of the second week, student 2 receives the treatment along with student 1 as the observer continues to collect baseline data on student 3.
4. The third week student 3 receives the same treatment as 1 and 2.
5. After the fourth week comparisons are made between baselines and treatments for all three (1, 2, and 3) to determine the following:

   a. Did all three students improve while receiving the same treatment for a five-day treatment period?
   b. Was there no improvement in the behavior of any of the students using the same treatment?
   c. Was there a great deal of variability in treatment effects when comparisons are made of the three students?
   d. Was the treatment detrimental to the three students, causing a negative reaction?

Another approach to determining treatment effectiveness is to examine the generalization of treatment in one situation to other situations, as shown in Figure 10-4.

THE MANN STUDENT OBSERVATION WORKSHEET

The Mann Student Observation Worksheet is but one of many techniques available to teachers for the charting of observable data. The Observation Worksheet can be put on a clipboard for easy management. Following is a step-by-step analysis of how the Worksheet can be completed. The sample forms (Form 10-1 and Form 10-2) and Figures 10-5 and 10-6 (the case study of a particular student's observation and treatment program) should be referred to while reviewing this section.

1. *Name:* Student's name.
2. *Age:* The age can be listed by birthdate and number.
3. *Beginning Date—Ending Date:* The beginning date is the first day of observation and the ending date is the last day of observation.
4. *Teacher:* Teacher's name.
5. *Grade:* Student's present grade level.
6. *Observer 1—Observer 2:* The observer can be the teacher or any other person. If possible, it is good to have two individuals observing a student's behavior to see how they correlate for reliability.
7. *Check One: On/Off Task* or *Target Behavior:* The observer must decide whether he or she wants to focus on *On/Off Task* behavior and delineate the frequency of specific behaviors observed or to just focus in on one specific *Target Behavior.* Check *On/Off Task* when there are any behaviors that interfere with on-task activity. If *On/Off Task* is checked, it indicates that the observer desires to identify the behavior which is interfering with on-task behavior. Regardless of which area is checked, the observer must indicate under the *Behavior Desired* section the task involved and the target behavior.
8. *Obs. Nbr. (Observation Number):* 1 = first obs.; 2 = second obs.; 3 = third obs., etc. The number of observations will depend upon the frequency of the behavior. Low frequency behaviors will require longer periods of observation.
9. *Day and Date:* The day and date for each observation or group of observations is indicated.
10. *Observation Time:* Two time periods are recorded; the time the observation period begins and the time it ends.
11. *Nbr. of Beh. (Number of Behaviors):* If *On/Off Task* is checked, skip 11 and go to 12. See Example A. If *Target Behavior* is checked, it indicates that the observer will be counting the incidence of a particular behavior and marking the frequency of the behavior in the *Nbr. of Beh.* column. In this example the *Time Off-Task* and *Time On-Task* columns and the *Behavior Observed* sections would not be used. (See Example B.)
12. *Time Off-Task* and *Time On-Task:* When the observer checks *On/Off Task* behavior, he or she would skip the *Nbr. of Beh.* column and complete the columns for *Time Off-Task* and *Time On-Task,* and the *Behavior Observed* section. The *Time On-Task* and *Time Off-Task* behavior can be monitored in the following manner:
    a Use a stopwatch for exact timing or a wall clock or a wristwatch and record the interval of observation.
    b. The observer can time either *Time Off-Task* or *Time On-Task.* It is not necessary to observe for both. Record either *Time Off-Task* or *Time On-Task* and subtract from total time for other record.
    c. A trained aide, student teacher, or volunteer can also be an observer.
13. *Behavior Observed:* Observation of behavior requires a simple yes (√) or no (blank) response. Some observers prefer to use a yes (+) and no (−) type of notation. The observer is asked to judge which of the behaviors from this section are deemed to be problem areas. These problem areas can at some later time also be treated as *Target Behaviors.* Example B is an example of charting a *Target Behavior.* The important considerations to keep in mind are (1) to determine how much time the student is on or off task and (2) to pinpoint with reasonable accuracy the type of specific behavior the student exhibits when he or she is off task. Following are some definitions of *Behavior Observed:*
    a. Bothers Teacher
    The student who exhibits *excessive* direct contact with the teacher, verbally or otherwise. An example would be the student who continually leaves his seat to ask the teacher questions and/or often disturbs the teacher when he or she is working with other students.
    b. Bothers Students
    The student who continually annoys others with excessive verbal behavior or physical contact to the extent that it is obviously a nuisance type of attention-getting behavior.
    c. Talking
    Constant talking by the student to others in the class as well as talking out inappropriately in class.
    d. Playing
    The student may be involved in any kind of play, exhibiting verbally or through actions that he or

she is attending to toys, games, "fooling around" and other self-entertaining activity.

e. Bathr. (Bathroom)-Drink
This is interpreted as the student who does not have a physical problem but nevertheless goes to the bathroom and/or water fountain to excess.

f. Aggres. (Aggressive)-Fights
This refers to the hostile, angry student who may be fighting—not just playing in a manner that looks like fighting. The student may strike another individual, or break and throw things in anger.

g. Out of Seat
The learner is of concern because he or she is out of the seat constantly but not necessarily walking or running around the room. This student is off-task, and prefers to stand by his or her desk, sit on the floor, or do other things in other than the designated work area, i.e., at desk, table, etc.

h. Daydream-Sleep
This student may appear withdrawn and is, in fact, not attending to the task required by the teacher. He or she does not respond to questions or participate in class activities, appearing to be preoccupied with his or her own thoughts. Sleep refers to the student who is actually sleeping and not just resting his or her head for a few minutes. Check for physiological problems or lack of sleep at home.

i. Walk-Run
This involves *excessive* walking or running around the room and not just going to or coming from a work activity.

j. Does Other Work
The student who is involved in doing some other kind of school work, such as arithmetic during the reading period, and does not stay on the required task.

k. Other
The behavior should be specified in the allotted space and clarified in the *Comments-Treatment* section. It refers to any other behavior that is observed and deemed to be a problem to the extent that it interferes with or replaces on-task activity.

14. *Comments-Treatment:* In this section the observer would indicate the period of observation (P), i.e., P_1 = 5 days of observation, etc., and the following information:

    a. A summary of the *On-Task* and *Off-Task* time, a delineation of the *Behavior Observed,* and the treatment plan for the next period. If the observer has checked the box next to *Target Behavior,* then the incidence or frequency of the *Target Behavior* would be stated along with the treatment plan for the next period. (See Figures 10-5 and 10-6.)

15. *Dark Line Across:* A dark line across allows for and indicates the following:

    a. The end of a period and kind of data observed and indicated, i.e., baseline, treatment, etc.
    b. The totals for each of the columns in the observation areas for a particular period.
    c. The beginning of a new period and the kind of data that was observed and indicated for the new period.

MANN STUDENT GRAPHING WORKSHEET

After completion of the *Mann Student Observation Worksheet,* the data can then be recorded (graphed) on the *Mann Student Graphing Worksheet.* A *Worksheet* form (Form 10-3), Case Study Example A (Figure 10-7) and Case Study Example B (Figure 10-8) can be found on pages 303–305.

The *Mann Student Graphing Worksheet* should be thoroughly reviewed along with the information provided in this section.

The *Mann Student Graphing Worksheet* and the *Mann Student Observation Worksheet* can be utilized in the following manner:

1. to provide a graphic illustration of a student's observed behavior, treatment plan, and outcomes.
2. to describe a student's behavior when talking with parents, principals, or other appropriate individuals.

The following is an analysis of the *Mann Student Graphing Worksheet.*

1. The heading is the same as found in the *Mann Student Observation Worksheet.*
2. *Behavior Observed:* The observer transfers the *Behavior Observed* from the *Observation Worksheet* to the *Graphing Worksheet.*
3. The *Behavior Observed* section contains a coded symbol (letter) for each of the behaviors. This section contains a compilation of all of the cogent *Off-Task* behaviors.
4. The dark line separates the periods.
5. The graphs can indicate the following:

    a. One graph illustrates the frequencies of behavior for a particular interval of time.
    B.L. 1 (Baseline 1)
    C.R. (Continuous Reinforcement)
    V.R. (Variable Reinforcement)
    B.L. 2 (Baseline 2)
    b. The other graph can represent the plotting of the *Time On-Task* for a specified period of time.

Form 10-1

NAME: ______________________________ Beginning Date ____________________

AGE: ____________________ Ending Date ____________________

MANN STUDENT OBSERVATION WORKSHEET

On/Off Task and Target Behaviors

Teacher: ____________________ Grade: __________

Observer One: ____________________ Observer Two: ____________________

CHECK ONE: ☐ On/Off Task
☐ Target Behavior

Behavior Desired:

____

____

						BEHAVIOR OBSERVED											COMMENTS – TREATMENT
Obs. Nbr.	Day & Date	Observ. Time	Nbr. of Beh.	Time OFF Task	Time ON Task	Bothers Teacher	Bothers Student	Talking	Playing	Bathr./Drink	Aggres./Fights	Out of Seat	Daydream/Sleep	Walk – Run	Does Other Work	Other:	

NOTE: Draw a dark line to indicate end of period.

Form 10-2

NAME: ______________________ Beginning Date ______________

AGE: ______________ Ending Date ______________

MANN STUDENT OBSERVATION WORKSHEET (Continued)

OBSERVER: ______________________

Obs. Nbr.	Day & Date	Observ. Time	Nbr. of Beh.	Time OFF Task	Time ON Task	BEHAVIOR OBSERVED: Bothers Teacher	Bothers Student	Talking	Playing	Bathr./Drink	Aggres./Fights	Out of Seat	Daydream/ Sleep	Walk – Run	Does Other Work	Other:	COMMENTS – TREATMENT

NOTE: Draw a dark line to indicate end of period.

Figure 10-5

NAME: *Lisa Smith* Beginning Date *10-3-78*

AGE: *7-4-70 (8)* Ending Date *10-28-78*

EXAMPLE A
MANN STUDENT OBSERVATION WORKSHEET
On/Off Task and Target Behaviors

Teacher: *Mrs. L. Brown* Grade: *3*

Observer One: *Mrs. L. Brown* Observer Two:

CHECK ONE: ☒ On/Off Task
☐ Target Behavior

Behavior Desired: *stay on task during reading period*

Obs. Nbr.	Day & Date	Observ. Time	Nbr. of Beh.	Time OFF Task	Time ON Task	Bothers Teacher	Bothers Student	Talking	Playing	Bathr./Drink	Aggres./Fights	Out of Seat	Daydream/Sleep	Walk – Run	Does Other Work	Other:
						BEHAVIOR OBSERVED										
1	M. 10/3	9:30-10:30		50	10		✓	✓	✓			✓		✓		
2	T. 10/4	" - "		55	5		✓	✓	✓			✓		✓		
3	W. 10/5	" - "		40	20			✓				✓				
4	TH. 10/6	" - "		50	10		✓	✓	✓			✓		✓		
5	F. 10/7	" - "		50	10		✓	✓				✓		✓		
5	5 Days	5 Hours		245	55		4	5	3			5		4		
End period 1-baseline																
Begin Period 2-continuous reinforcement																
6	M. 10/10	9:30-10:30		35	25		✓	✓				✓		✓		
7	T. 10/11	" - "		20	40							✓				
8	W. 10/12	" - "		25	35			✓						✓		
9	TH. 10/13	" - "		30	30		✓	✓				✓		✓		
10	F. 10/14	" - "		20	40							✓				
5	5 Days	5 Hours		130	170		2	3				4		3		
End period 2- continuous reinforcement																
Begin period 3- variable reinforcement																

COMMENTS – TREATMENT

P1- off task; 245 minutes
On task; 55 minutes
Problem areas
Talking
Out of Seat
Bothers Students
Walk-Run
Playing
Treatment plan for P2 (5 days) continuous token reinforcement (colored discs) to be exchanged for school supplies for on task behavior i.e., group participation, silent reading, and other independent activities.

P2 - off task; 130 minutes
On task; 170 minutes
Problem areas
Talking - decreased
Out of Seat - decreased
Bothers students - decreased
Walk-run - decreased
Playing - decreased
Treatment Plan for P3 (5 days) Begin variable reinforcement (continue to use colored discs) and - add praise, smiles, etc. to reinforce on task behavior of reading, participation and other independent activities

NOTE: Draw a dark line to indicate end of period.

Figure 10-5 (continued)

NAME: Lisa Smith

AGE: 7-4-70 (8)

Beginning Date 10-3-78

Ending Date 10-28-78

EXAMPLE A
MANN STUDENT OBSERVATION WORKSHEET (Continued)

OBSERVER: Mrs. L. Brown

Obs. Nbr.	Day & Date	Observ. Time	Nbr. of Beh.	Time OFF Task	Time ON Task	Bothers Teacher	Bothers Student	Talking	Playing	Bathr./Drink	Aggres./Fights	Out of Seat	Daydream/Sleep	Walk – Run	Does Other Work	Other:
11	M. 10/17	9:30-10:30		35	25			✓				✓				
12	T. 10/18	" - "		30	30			✓								
13	W. 10/19	" - "		20	40							✓				
14	TH. 10/20	" - "		25	35							✓		✓		
15	F. 10/21	" - "		30	30			✓				✓				
5	5 Days	5 Hours		140	160			3				4		1		
End period 3-variable reinforcement																
Begin period 4 - new baseline																
16	M. 10/24	9:30-10:30		20	40							✓				
17	T. 10/25	" - "		35	25			✓				✓				
18	W. 10/26	" - "		30	30			✓				✓				
19	TH. 10/27	" - "		35	25			✓								
20	F. 10/28	" - "		15	45											
5	5 Days	5 Hours		135	165			3				3				
End period 4 - new baseline																
Continue social reinforcement																

COMMENTS – TREATMENT

P.3 - off task; 140 minutes
On task; 160 minutes
Problem Areas
Talking
Out of seat
Bothers students-eliminated
Walk-run- decreased
Playing-eliminated
Treatment plan for P-4 (5 days)
Establish a new baseline; reinforce with praise, smiles and remove token reinforcement.

P4 - off task; 135 minutes
On task; 165 minutes
Problem Areas
Talking
Out of seat
Bothers students-eliminated
Walk-run-eliminated
Playing-eliminated
Continue social reinforcement, i.e. praise, smile, touch, etc.

NOTE: Draw a dark line to indicate end of period.

Figure 10-6

NAME: Lisa Smith

AGE: 7-4-70 (8)

Beginning Date 11-1-78

Ending Date 11-25-78

EXAMPLE B
MANN STUDENT OBSERVATION WORKSHEET
On/Off Task and Target Behaviors

Teacher: Mrs. L. Brown

Grade: 3

Observer One: Mrs. L. Brown

Observer Two:

CHECK ONE: ☐ On/Off Task
☒ Target Behavior

Behavior Desired: Increase staying in seat during reading period

Obs. Nbr.	Day & Date	Observ. Time	Nbr. of Beh.	Time OFF Task	Time ON Task	Bothers Teacher	Bothers Student	Talking	Playing	Bathr./Drink	Aggres./Fights	Out of Seat	Daydream/Sleep	Walk – Run	Does Other Work	Other:
1	M. 11/1	9:30-10:30	20													
2	T. 11/2	" - "	18													
3	W. 11/3	" - "	22													
4	TH. 11/4	" - "	26													
5	F. 11/5	" - "	27													
5	5 Days	5 Hours	113													
End period 1 - baseline data																
Begin period 2 - continuous reinforcement																
6	M. 11/8	9:30-10:30	12													
7	T. 11/9	" - "	10													
8	W. 11/10	" - "	4													
9	TH. 11/11	" - "	6													
10	F. 11/12	" - "	6													
5	5 Days	5 Hours	36													
End period 2 - continuous reinforcement																
Begin period 3 - variable reinforcement																

COMMENTS – TREATMENT

P1 - Out of seat 113 times
Treatment plan for P2 (5 days)
continuous token reinforcement (colored discs) to be exchanged for staying in seat and doing on task activities i.e., group participation, silent reading and other independent activities.

P2 - Out of seat 36 times
Treatment plan for P3 (5 days)
Begin variable reinforcement (continue to use colored discs) and add praise, smiles, etc. to reinforce staying in seat doing on task activity, such as reading, participation and other independent activities.

NOTE: Draw a dark line to indicate end of period.

Figure 10-6 (continued)

NAME: Lisa Smith

Beginning Date 11-1-78

AGE: 7-4-70 (8)

Ending Date 11-25-78

EXAMPLE B
MANN STUDENT OBSERVATION WORKSHEET (Continued)

OBSERVER: Mrs. L. Brown

Obs. Nbr.	Day & Date	Observ. Time	Nbr. of Beh.	Time OFF Task	Time ON Task	Bothers Teacher	Bothers Student	Talking	Playing	Bathr./Drink	Aggres./Fights	Out of Seat	Daydream/Sleep	Walk – Run	Does Other Work	Other:
11	M. 11/15	9:30-10:30	8													
12	T. 11/16	" - "	7													
13	W. 11/17	" - "	5													
14	TH. 11/18	" - "	8													
15	F. 11/19	" - "	3													
5	5 Days	5 Hours	31													
End of period 3 - variable reinforcement																
Begin period 4 - new baseline																
16	M. 11/21	9:30-10:30	6													
17	T. 11/22	" - "	9													
18	W. 11/23	" - "	7													
19	TH 11/24	" - "	4													
20	F. 11/25	" - "	7													
5	5 Days	5 Hours	33													
End period 4 - new baseline																

COMMENTS – TREATMENT

P-3 - Out of seat 31 times
Treatment plan for P4 (5 days)
Establish a new baseline; reinforce staying in seat with praise, smile and touch and remove token reinforcement.

P4 - Out of seat 33 times
Continue social reinforcement, i.e., praise, smile, touch, etc.

NOTE: Draw a dark line to indicate end of period.

Form 10-3

NAME: ______________________ Beginning Date ______________

AGE: ______________ Ending Date ______________

MANN STUDENT GRAPHING WORKSHEET

On/Off Task and Target Behaviors

Teacher: ______________________ Grade: __________

Observer One: ______________________ Observer Two: ______________________

CHECK ONE: ☐ On/Off Task ☐ Target Behavior

Behavior Desired:

____

____

Period: ___	BEHAVIOR OBSERVED										
	Bothers Teacher	Bothers Student	Talking	Playing	Bathr./Drink	Aggres./Fights	Out of Seat	Daydream/Sleep	Walk – Run	Does Other Work	Other:
	CODE SYMBOL										
	a	b	c	d	e	f	g	h	i	j	k

Frequency: ______

Time: ______________

Frequency: ______

Time: ______________

Figure 10-7

NAME: Lisa Smith

AGE: 7-4-70 (8)

Beginning Date 10-3-78

Ending Date 10-28-78

EXAMPLE A
MANN STUDENT GRAPHING WORKSHEET

On/Off Task and Target Behaviors

Teacher: Mrs. L. Brown

Grade: 3

Observer One: Mrs. L. Brown

Observer Two: ____________

CHECK ONE: ☒ On/Off Task ☐ Target Behavior

Behavior Desired:

stay on task during reading period

Period:	BEHAVIOR OBSERVED										
	Bothers Teacher	Bothers Student	Talking	Playing	Bathr./Drink	Aggres./Fights	Out of Seat	Daydream/Sleep	Walk – Run	Does Other Work	Other:
	CODE SYMBOL										
	a	b	c	d	e	f	g	h	i	j	k
P1 1		✓	✓	✓			✓		✓		
2		✓	✓	✓			✓		✓		
3			✓				✓				
4		✓	✓	✓			✓		✓		
5		✓	✓				✓		✓		
P2 6		✓	✓				✓		✓		
7							✓				
8			✓						✓		
9		✓	✓	✓			✓		✓		
10							✓				
P3 11			✓				✓				
12			✓								
13							✓				
14							✓				
15			✓				✓				
P4 16											
17							✓				
18			✓				✓				
19			✓				✓				
20											
total		6	13	4			16		7		

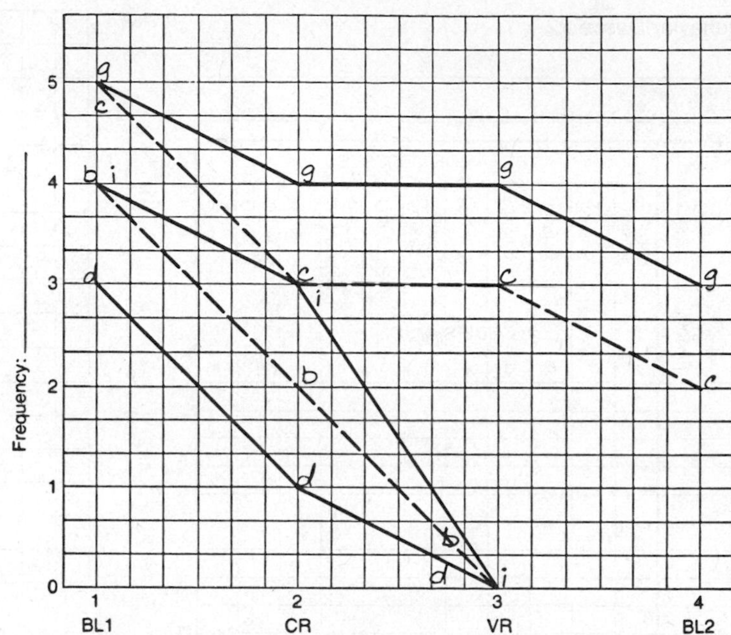

Time: Period (5 Days)

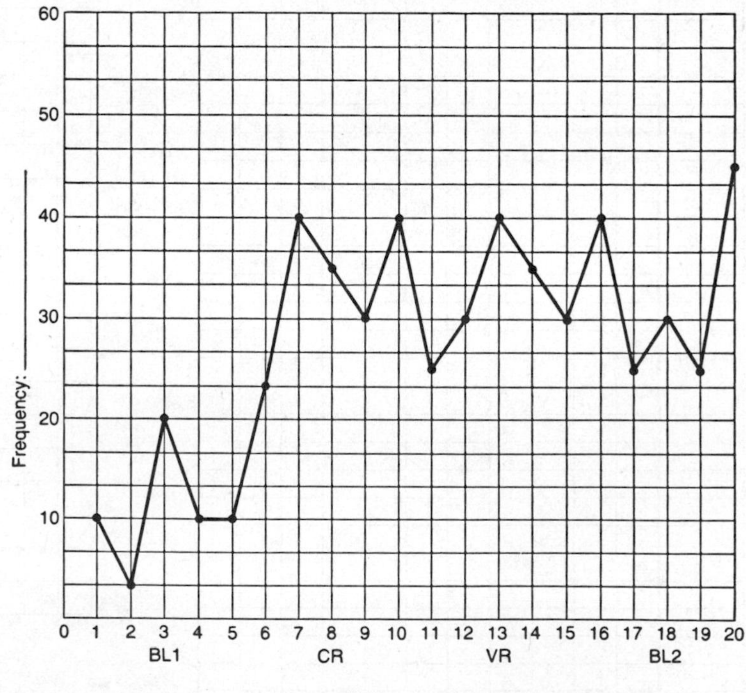

Time: Day (On task)

Figure 10-8

NAME: Lisa Smith

AGE: 7-4-70 (8)

Beginning Date 10-3-78

Ending Date 10-28-78

EXAMPLE B
MANN STUDENT GRAPHING WORKSHEET
On/Off Task and Target Behaviors

Teacher: Mrs. L. Brown

Grade: 3

Observer One: ______

Observer Two: ______

CHECK ONE: ☐ On/Off Task ☒ Target Behavior

Behavior Desired:

Increase staying in seat during reading period

Period: Day	a Bothers Teacher	b Bothers Student	c Talking	d Playing	e Bathr./Drink	f Aggres./Fights	g Out of Seat	h Daydream/Sleep	i Walk – Run	j Does Other Work	k Other:
P1 1											20
2											18
3											22
4											26
5											27
P2 6											12
7											10
8											4
9											6
10											6
P3 11											8
12											7
13											5
14											8
15											3
P4 16											6
17											9
18											7
19											4
20											7

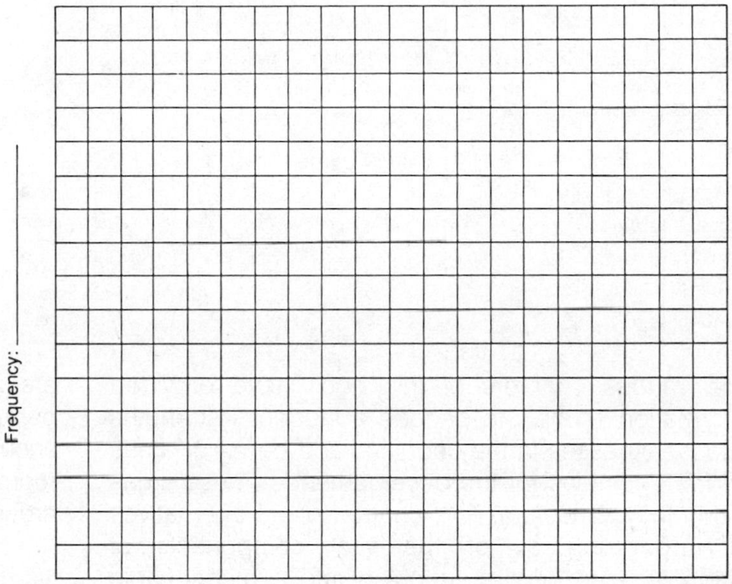

Frequency: ______

Time: ______

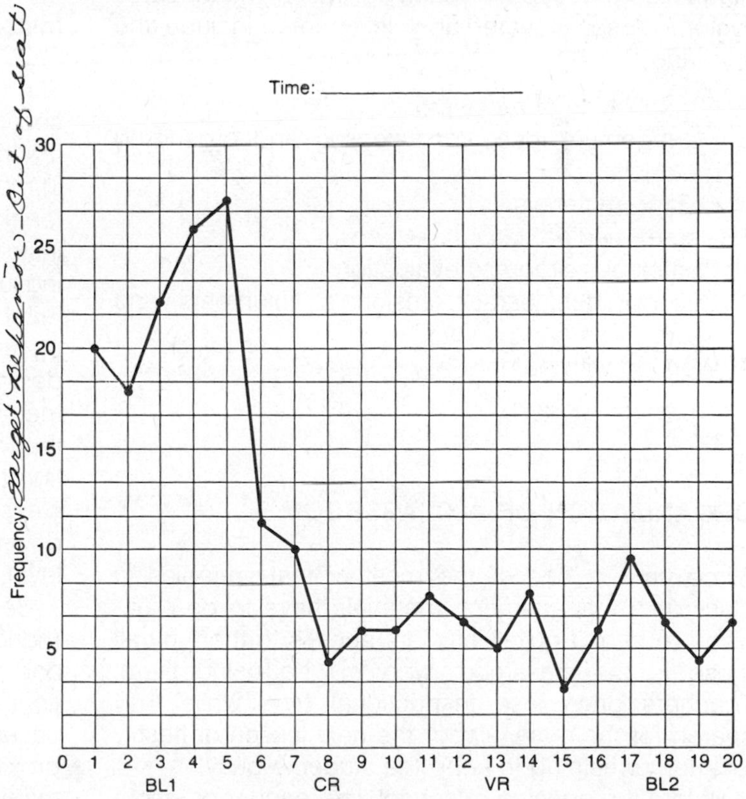

Frequency: Target Behavior—Out of seat

30, 25, 20, 15, 10, 5

0 1 2 3 4 5 6 7 8 9 10 11 12 13 14 15 16 17 18 19 20

BL1 CR VR BL2

Time: Day

Chapter 11 Educational Management

The various chapters of this book have provided information on how to decode a student's strengths and weaknesses in the cognitive and behavior areas and suggestions for the development of these areas within the curriculum. This chapter offers alternatives for organizing all of the vital components of diagnostic-prescriptive teaching into a manageable system. Areas covered in this chapter include the following:

1. Organization of a classroom
2. Management ideas for selecting and organizing materials
3. Coding materials
4. Use of media
5. Continuous progress evaluation
6. Use of aides, paraprofessionals, volunteers, and tutors
7. Working with parents

ORGANIZATION OF A CLASSROOM

Since time is one of the most critical variables in classroom management, materials have to be organized to permit quick, efficient access to them by all those in the classroom who will be using them. Teachers often lose instructional time while they search for the materials for the next lesson or hastily look for something to keep the students busy.

Before the opening of school, the teacher or teachers (if team-teaching is being used), as well as aides, paraprofessionals, and other support personnel, should plan the following major areas of the classroom: the instructional areas and the reinforcement areas.

Instructional Areas

The primary areas to draw on a floor plan first are the sections of the classroom from which the majority of teacher-directed activities will emanate. For example, in most elementary school classrooms, primary grade teachers have one area for small-group reading instruction. Because of the diversity of materials being used for students with learning problems, many teachers are using reading tables along with, or in lieu of, the more traditional reading circle of chairs. In designing such an area, the designer must consider the size and shape of the table, lighting, and noise. If the teacher will be seated for a portion of the instruction time, then lines of sight to all other areas of the classroom should be checked. The teacher should sit down and see what might impede eye contact at that level.

Regardless of what the major instructional areas are (handwriting, reading, arithmetic, science), the second consideration should be the location of instructional materials. The authors have found that bookcases, moveable carts, and closets in the closest proximity to the area should be organized with the materials most often used by the teacher. For exam-

Reading Level	Main Series	First Alternative	Second Alternative	A-V Feedback	Comprehension Workbooks	Phonics Workbooks	Cassettes	Specific Skill Worksheets	Games
PP^1									
PP^2									
PP^3									
PP^4									
Primer									
1^1									
1^2									

Figure 11-1 Analysis of Materials in the Classroom

ple, on a bookcase behind the instructional reading table, the instructor can place word cards, lesson plans, teacher's guides, workbooks, supplementary work sheets, pencils, pens, blank word cards, and phonics materials, plus a variety of other materials most often used during a directed reading session. Unless the teacher directs otherwise, the materials on these shelves are used primarily by the teacher.

Reinforcement Areas

After the major instructional areas are designated, then the remainder of the classroom space can be used by the students, individually or in groups, self-directed or instructor directed, to practice, evaluate, or review new information. Space can be allocated for the following areas:

1. Learning centers based on specific subjects with learning packets, or student-directed activities. For example, science materials and experiments.
2. Subject level areas that contain shelves, drawers, etc., with a variety of materials placed in somewhat of a developmental sequence and coded. For example, a handwriting section could have materials ranging from piece of material A 1 (clay to be squeezed to develop power in the hand) to A 40 (tracing stencils to develop cursive writing).
3. Areas that contain materials to develop processing skills (auditory, motor, visual, and language skills)
4. Interest areas such as a library center, games and recreation area, arts and crafts area
5. Areas for small-group or independent study (cubicles, carrels, booths)
6. Audiovisual area for listening stations, Language Masters, tape recorders, and typewriters

The students should know where things belong, how the classroom is organized, and what the various options are for individualized learning. When material is out, organized, and explained to the students, there is no excuse for a disorganized, messy classroom. Materials should be returned by the students to the places where they found them.

The reinforcement areas of a classroom should not be only a place for displaying materials or keeping students busy. There should be an integration of subject areas so that the students can experience the types of on-task activities that will be enjoyable, promote success, be a challenge, yet provide practice in the critical basic skills areas. For example, spelling games, word lists, and worksheets should be on the students' reading level and perhaps can also be the same words practiced in a handwriting lesson.

SELECTING AND ORGANIZING MATERIALS

How many and what kinds of materials are required in a regular classroom to effectively deal with the variability of students with learning and behavior problems? Before deciding what to buy or make, teachers must analyze the materials already available in a classroom or a school. For example, Figure 11-1 can be used in conducting a needs assessment for reading materials. The same general headings can also be used for the evaluation of other subject areas (e.g., science, math, spelling, social studies).

All of the materials listed are not required for a reading program, but a paucity or complete void in some areas may inhibit individualization of instruction. By going through such an evaluation, teachers may note the following:

1. Duplication of materials
2. Multiple use of materials
3. Which materials are the most and the least used
4. The percentage of self-checking or self-directed materials
5. Gaps in levels or skills
6. Location of materials
7. Condition and durability of equipment and materials
8. Which materials can be made by teachers, students, or volunteers

Reading Level

Considering the variability in most classrooms, many teachers would have to ascertain the availability of materials and the needs at several grade levels. It is important for the special teachers (e.g., reading, counseling, special education) and teachers from each grade level to work together to prepare a schoolwide chart of materials. The reading levels can be designated in a variety of ways. In Figure 11-1 the levels reflect a range from Preprimer 1 to first grade level². A wider range might have included Kindergarten readiness materials through a sixth grade level one reader (6¹). If the school is grouping on a system of levels (Level 1–20, etc.), then that designation can be plotted. The major consideration is to use a code that administrators, teachers, aides, student teachers, or parents can pick up and instantly understand, getting a feeling for what books preceded and which ones will follow a student's placement in a series. Therefore, the concept of readability must be used in a functional manner.

Main Series

The Main Series column in Figure 11-1 is for the state-adopted required-reading textbook, the preferred reading series, or the program that will be used as the major reading material in a classroom or school. This of course will vary widely from school to school, but most teachers have one or two most used reading series.

As a teacher or group of teachers fill in the chart, they should physically place the books in piles on tables. For example, the major series can be placed on a table next to labeled levels (PP1–First Grade). On the chart, the teachers may wish to actually write in the number of available books ("Book Title" – 56).

First and Second Alternative Series

Place on the table next to the major series, and note on the chart, the reading series that would be the first alternative, especially for students with learning problems who are experiencing failure in the main textbook series. This series is usually one that has features such as a slower rate of vocabulary acquisition, concepts that are more in keeping with the cultural or special comprehension needs of the students, or better workbooks. As a result of readability formulas or teacher feelings based on usage, the teacher tries this series first if the student cannot succeed in the major series.

It may be determined that there is no available backup series that is really appropriate for the students presently in the class; therefore, at this point, the teacher and the special teachers or curriculum specialists can begin to evaluate samples of other programs used in other schools.

Next to the samples of the first alternative series or program should be placed samples of the second, followed by all others in order of preference.

Audiovisual Feedback Equipment

The remaining columns in Figure 11-1 refer to categories of materials that supply many of the supportive, reinforcement types of activities that are more student directed. In the column for audiovisual feedback materials, such materials as the Language Master (Bell & Howell Inc.) can be listed. The teachers should list what and how many commercial or teacher-made cards are in good condition and available for use. Perhaps the school has a number of pieces of machinery in good working order, but no blank cards or many boxes of cards of the wrong lists of words, phrases, or sentences. Determining the availability of these types of machines and materials is important because they are valuable for individualized teaching of students who cannot use pencil-and-paper types of materials.

Comprehension Workbooks

Usually these materials are required after the student has acquired phonics skills or a vocabulary. Crucial factors include not only how many of various types of books are available, but also which ones are supportive to the students' ongoing major reading, writing, and spelling program. The readability level, concept load, size of print, illustrations, types of directions, and space for written responses, as well as the usability by volunteers, aides, peer tutors, and, of course, the students themselves, should be noted. It may be found that a few examples of many workbooks are available, but some students with reading problems and special handicapping conditions will "fall through the cracks" and not receive much reinforcement. It is at this point that the individual needs of students will point to appropriate new acquisitions.

Phonics Workbooks

Supplementary phonics workbooks should also be evaluated with regard to size of print, illustrations, usability, etc. Their potential for modification for use with the major reading series should be considered.

Cassettes

The availability of tape recorders, listening stations, and areas in the school or classroom for effective use of such equipment has to be evaluated (e.g., multiple electrical outlets and cubicles, study carrels, or other areas in which to use cassettes). Cassettes can be used for a variety of reinforcing activities (specific skills, phonics, recorded stories in readers, chapters in texts, library books, etc.).

Specific Skills Worksheets

In evaluating duplicator or printed worksheets, the instructors should consider the following:

1. Clarity and size of print
2. Appropriateness for grade level or skill being taught
3. Ease of student self-direction in use of material
4. Developmental sequence of the materials
5. Availability and organization of the material for use by teachers, aides, or students

Games

Puzzles, flash cards, card games, lotto games, etc., should provide both reinforcement and recreational value. Storage as well as durability should be noted.

Other Needs

After a needs assessment of all the major categories of materials, then the following can also be noted:

1. Other audiovisual material—films, filmstrips, projectors, overhead projectors, record players, records
2. Display boards—flannel boards, small chalkboards, magnetic boards, pocket charts
3. Manipulative reinforcers—moveable letters, tracing screens
4. Language development and phonics equipment—mirrors, commercial kits, puppets
5. Library books, magazines, reference books, and encyclopedias

CODING MATERIALS

The sophistication of the system for coding materials will vary with the reading level and grade level of the students. The following types of systems are suggested.

1. A rebus or picture-clue system can be used to help very young students find materials. For example, a picture of an ear can be put over a listening area, or a picture of the type of material can be placed on a shelf (puzzles, scissors, clay, pencils, paper, etc.).
2. Photographs of students performing a task can be placed in an area.
3. Areas can be numbered, with each number representing an activity.
4. If the students know the letters, then a combination of numerals and letters can be used. For example, section A (1–15) is puzzles, Section B (1–25) contains fine motor games, etc.
5. For older students, subject level words can be used (Science Lab, Private Office, Fun and Games, etc.).
6. Materials for older students can also be marked with a code (geometric colored designs ◇, ○, ▭, Indian designs ✳, ≋, ⋀⋀, etc.).

Codes become very helpful to peer tutors, aides, volunteers, and the student. The following techniques can be used to direct the student to the materials.

1. All of the duplicator masters can be run off and placed in folders coded with a "P4" for the fourth book in the reading series and numbered sequentially. Students who need reinforcement on specific

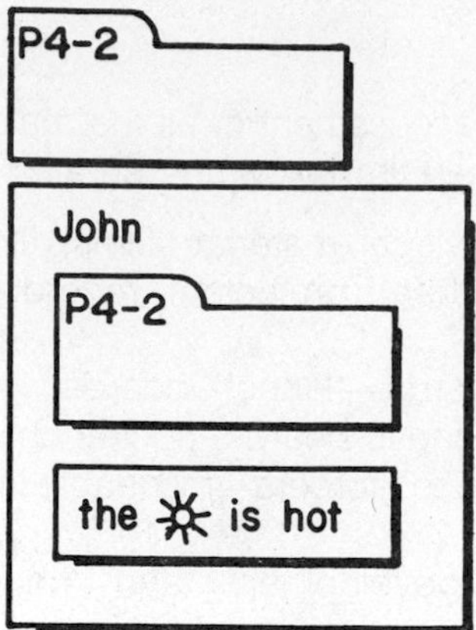

Figure 11-2

vocabulary words can be directed to the appropriate sheet through the use of a rebus or number form. (See Figure 11-2.)

Other activities using additional materials can be coded on the same sheet. On the illustrated sheet, the student may be directed next to the vocabulary cards to review a phrase used on the duplicator master.

Duplicator masters completed by the instructor, paraprofessional, volunteers, or older students can be placed in a separate answer folder. The learners can self-check their answers by matching them to the model.

2. Index cards or papers in folders can also be used to direct a student to an activity. For example, a series of codes for a specified period of time can be used (9/4/79–9/20/79—A-16, B-39, G-56, etc.).
3. The materials in a classroom can also be coded into a list of developmental skills. For example:

ITEM	*Developmental Skills*
30 1" multicolored blocks	Visual Discrimination – 5
	Visual Memory Sequencing – 2, 3, 4
	Visual Language Classification – 1

Making Material Self-Checking

The following are examples of how material can be made self-checking:

1. Color code or draw designs on the bottoms of puzzle pieces.
2. Laminate a duplicate of workbook or worksheet pages that have the answers written in.
3. Record answers to questions on tape that the students can listen to.
4. Write the answers on the back of flashcards.
5. For projects that require assembling or constructing of materials, place a completed model, or one at several numbered stages of development, in a container or cabinet for the learners to refer to when they have completed the task.

USE OF MEDIA

In spite of all the "specialists" we have in the area of media, in the final analysis it is the classroom teachers who play the most vital role in determining the use of media in the classroom. Not only do they make available different forms of media for their own and the students' use, but (even more important) they determine the emotional climate in which it will be used. The teachers who are fearful of using machines of one kind or another often impose these negative feelings upon the students in the classroom. The teachers who feel the equipment is special, to be used only on special occasions, will also influence how pupils think of it—as something unique, not basic learning equipment.

Very often, teachers develop in students a feeling that media of one kind or another are only to be used by adults—except for the "audiovisual helper." A similar fear—that special training is needed for the use of media—exists to some extent in teachers and often prevents them from using media effectively. Some schools perpetuate this fear by having one person purchase all or most of the materials for a school and then lock them up for "safe keeping."

Students should not always be told that this is what you can use and this is what you cannot touch. They can be taught to actually use the "machinery" while learning a specific task. Therefore, the task itself becomes the focal point, the media merely the vehicle to enhance the learning of the task. The students can be taught through involvement that an overhead projector is not very fragile, not a mystery, and not something that requires an adult operator.

There is a great deal available within the school and the classroom that teachers have not utilized. Many teachers are "material bound" by things that they have grown accustomed to using over the years—particularly textbooks. Pupils not able to learn by traditional methods must have the learning environment modified. In many cases, teachers should set aside those materials a pupil has tried and failed with, and try something new. Visuals and listening devices used appropriately as reinforcers to learning can aid the student at the learning task.

What is important is that pupils realize that the focus is on learning; using media effectively is only a means to that end. But we must teach students that using media is an "ordinary" thing to do. They must feel that every piece of material in the classroom is available to them to enhance their learning. This feeling can be instilled right from the start when students first enter school. That is when it is particularly important, since initial teaching or initial learning often sets the pattern for future behavior.

Such things as acetates, slides, and overlays are often a mystery to children. Some teachers, however, enhance understanding by producing these things as learning activities in the classroom and in this way provide experiences by which students can become involved in the actual development of material themselves. Becoming involved in the production of visuals, for example, may in and of itself enhance the learning situation, since pupils must know what to put on a visual before they can make one.

Many films produced for instructional purposes have a concept level much too difficult for some learning-handicapped students. Teachers must learn to analyze a film not only for its interest and content levels but also for its concept levels. For example, living in Florida, where it is tropical and low, students with spatial problems might find it difficult to comprehend mountains or the nature of the desert, even though aided by visuals. Teachers of these students will need to utilize a concrete object or experience along with the visuals. If you are going to show a film about mountains to these students, have them build models out of clay or other material. In using films for students with learning handicaps, first determine whether the rate, amount, and sequence of input is appropriate for the group. A great deal of time is wasted showing films or other visuals that have little or no relevance to the students viewing them.

One of the difficulties in present learning environments is that teachers are reluctant to record their own speech or the speech of their students. Tape recorders should be used by the teacher to record what is said so that students who are absent or unable to understand the lesson the first time it is presented can get another opportunity later on. Not only can media be used to enhance the instructional program or illustrate a point in a lesson, it can provide reinforcement through repetition.

Certain points need to be considered in determining the skills students need and the pursuant methods.

1. The teacher must determine the skills a student needs in order to succeed at the task to be presented.
2. The teacher must then determine which students do or do not have those skills.
3. After determining what the student needs in order to acquire the prerequisite skills, the teacher must utilize all of the media resources available to aid the student to develop them.
4. After the prerequisite skills have been developed, the teacher should enhance the learning of new skills through the use of media resources.

Analyzing a given instructional task in terms of these principles will enable the teacher to become more effective not only in determining the appropriate task, but also in deciding what method and media will be effective in carrying it out.

CONTINUOUS PROGRESS EVALUATION

The most effective type of continuous progress evaluation for classroom purposes is an ongoing system that enables the instructor to determine at a glance whether a particular skill area, such as vocabulary, is developing at the expected rate for a particular student. A vocabulary progress chart can be used in the following manner:

1. Administer a vocabulary pretest.
2. Write the names of the learners who will be using a particular book on the vocabulary progress chart (Form 11-1). Mark the boxes under those words that the learner correctly recognized on the pretest with ☒.
3. As new words are taught, mark the appropriate box, using the coding illustrated in Figure 11-3.
   a. On the day new words are introduced, mark the boxes with a ⧅. In the chart in Figure 11-3, the word *red* was introduced to John Jones; however, he cannot read it as yet.
   b. When the student has learned the word and can read it without hesitation, mark the box under the word with a ⧄. Lisa Mann was presented *red* and can now read the word ☒.
   c. Additional information can be coded on the same box. The top half of the box can be used to indicate when the student has learned to spell the word ☒. Becky Phillips can read and spell the word *red*. She can spell the word aloud or write it from dictation.
   d. To plot the mastery of a word, you may want to include information about the learner's ability to

Form 11-1

MANN-SUITER-McCLUNG VOCABULARY PROGRESS CHART

Instructor ____________________

Coding

- ☐ introduced word
- ☒ can read word
- ◩ can spell word
- ■ can read, spell, and write word

NEW WORDS

Name of Student

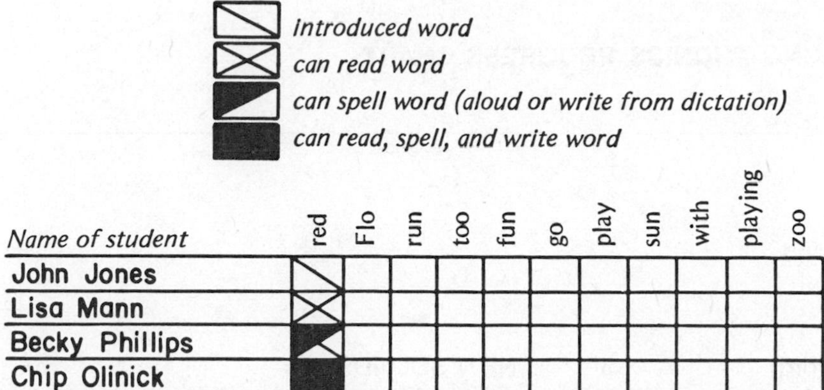

Figure 11-3

write the word (copy from a model). On the sample chart, the instructor completed the square by marking the lower half to indicate that the student can write the word. Therefore, by looking at the code, anyone reading this particular chart would understand that Chip Olinick can successfully read, spell, and write the word *red* . For an older student, the instructor may want to complete the box (from →) to indicate one of the following skills instead of just the ability to write the word: definition of the word, appropriate usage in a written or oral sentence.

4. The vocabulary progress charts can be put on clipboards or kept in your planning book for easy access.
5. By using the vocabulary charts for a designated period of time, you should gain an understanding of the learner's rate of progress. For example:
   a. The sheets could be dated to indicate a student's rate of progress for a five-day period. If all of the words introduced are not learned and the boxes show , then the progress should be carefully evaluated. The learner may require more repetitions, associative clues (pictures), or a reduction in the number of new words presented during a given period of time. If the lack of progress persists, the vocabulary, teaching techniques, and materials may require modification or substitution.
   b. Another student may know five out of seven new words at the end of the five-day period. By carefully noting the amount and rate of input, you can more accurately report student progress to parents and administrators.
6. Paraprofessionals, aides, and volunteer student helpers can use the information on the charts as a guide to the supportive activities that will reinforce the new vocabulary. For example, the sample chart indicates that John Jones needs word recognition activities, while Lisa Mann requires spelling reinforcement. In a well-organized classroom, while the teacher is working at the instructional level, supportive staff, including peer tutors, can utilize the educational materials to support the ongoing program.

Phonics Coding System

As you teach new sounds, mark the appropriate box on the phonics progress chart (Form 11-2), using coding illustrated in Figure 11-4.

introduced sound

can recognize sound (for example, "Show me **s** *.")*

can recall sound (for example, learner sees **s** *and gives sound)*

can use sound functionally in a word (for example, learner can read **sun** *and indicate sound analysis* s–u–n*)*

Name of student	s	z	g	w	-un	-et
John Jones						
Lisa Mann						
Becky Phillips						
Chip Olinick						

Figure 11-4

Form 11-2

MANN-SUITER-McCLUNG PHONICS PROGRESS CHART

Instructor ____

Coding

- introduced sound
- can recognize sound
- can recall sound
- can use sound functionally in a word

NEW SOUNDS

Name of Student															

MANN-SUITER-McCLUNG TEACHING CHART

Name MARY BROWN Date 6/9/79

Level 6 Instructor

Date	Page	Taught	Reinforced	Evaluated	Retaught
6/9	3	I am m	6/10, 6/11, 6/12	6/13	ok
6/10	4	help Matt	6/11, 6/12	6/13	ok
6/11	5	Nat and Nan at an n	6/12		
6/12			page 3, 4, 5		
6/13				page 3, 4, 5	at an

Figure 11-5

1. The sound s was introduced to John Jones; however, he cannot produce the sound as yet.
2. Lisa Mann can recognize the sound.
3. Becky Phillips can recall the sound.
4. Chip Olinick can use the sound functionally in a word.

John
9/4/75 Flo
run
her
9/6/75 too

Figure 11-6

Mann-Suiter-McClung Teaching Chart

To aid the teacher, tutor, or volunteer an ongoing teaching chart is included (Form 11-3). It follows the unit outline presented and provides an easy way to keep a record of what has been done and the areas found to be most difficult for the pupil.

The sample chart in Figure 11-5 shows that on June 9 the pupil did page 3 in the Reader/Workbook and was taught the words *I* and *am* and the sound of the consonant letter *m*. On June 10, the pupil did page 4 in the Reader/Workbook and was taught the words *help* and *Matt*. The words *I* and *am* and the sound "m" were reinforced. On June 11, three new words (*Nat, and,* and *Nan*), the sound of *n*, and two spelling patterns were introduced, and all prior learning was reinforced. On June 12th all prior learning was reinforced. On June 13th the pupil was tested and knew the words *I, am, help,* and *Matt* and the sound of *m*, but still needed work on *at* and *an*.

An ongoing chart of this type helps the instructor to constantly reinforce the words, spelling patterns, letter names, and sounds taught. It provides an easy way to keep track of what was taught, systematically reinforce it, evaluate the teaching, and reteach what is not known. A student's program can be slowed down or speeded up depending upon his or her ability to retain new teachings.

In addition to using progress charts, the instructor can assess daily and weekly vocabulary and skill acquisition by writing on the cover of a file folder the words, if any, the learner recognized on a pretest (Figure 11-6).

As new words are learned, they are added to the folder and dated. At periodic intervals, the instructor can have the learner read the words on the list. The instructor can get an idea of the learner's rate of progress by noting the dates and the retention of the vocabulary.

Monday is a preferable day for evaluation. The instructor will know which words from the previous week were learned and which ones must be reviewed. Lesson plans can be made or revised based on this information. If the learner will not give a verbal (recall) response when the card is shown, the instructor can place several cards on a desk or table and ask the child to "show" the word.

When the learner first arrives in the morning, the instructor can use word cards to go through a

Form 11-3

MANN-SUITER-McCLUNG TEACHING CHART

Name ______________________________ Date ______________

Level ______________ Instructor ______________________

Date	Page	Taught	Reinforced	Evaluated	Retaught

selected number of vocabulary words to check the learner's progress. For example, if five new words have been presented over a period of time, the instructor may wish to check these prior to introducing the next word. If the ongoing evaluation is done before the learner's scheduled reading instruction period, the instructor can provide a more successful lesson for the student.

USE OF AIDES, PARAPROFESSIONALS, TUTORS, AND VOLUNTEERS

Concerned parents and educators are setting up, or seeking, supportive services that will respond to the need for a broader utilization of reading and other programs with students. This development is in part due to the fact that teachers need additional support as they become involved in the process of trying to regulate programs in keeping with individual learners' rate and style of learning. Teachers who are concerned with truly individualized instruction recognize that there are different types of individuals who can support them effectively with students who require more specific kinds of remedial and corrective instruction.

Teacher-directed support personnel (e.g., tutors, paraprofessionals, and volunteers) provide an additional alternative to the general classroom management of both small and large groups. They provide an opportunity for the learner to become involved in a personalized manner with an individual other than the classroom teacher who will respond, on a one-to-one basis in most situations, to individual needs. The support person who is adequately trained and motivated will invariably respond to the emotional, as well as the educational, needs of the learner.

Before designating the paraprofessionals to a specified activity, the faculty should conduct a needs assessment to accurately pinpoint critical areas where additional personnel may need to be utilized. The use of support personnel can be divided into three classifications:

1. *Simultaneous Instruction.* Support persons in this class provide simultaneous support to the ongoing general classroom instruction of the teacher and may be called a *parallel teacher*.
2. *Task Specific Instruction.* Persons in this class would have expertise to work at specified tasks such as specific skill development in reading or math.
3. *Enrichment.* Persons in this class usually have skills or talents that would enable them to work with a wider range of students within a more flexible schedule of activities.

The competencies of the paraprofessionals and volunteers, as indicated on checklists, through questionnaires, during interviews, or in letters of recommendation, should be carefully analyzed by the administrators and selected faculty. After the strengths of the volunteers or paraprofessionals have been ascertained and the school-based needs have been determined, a training program for the supportive personnel may need to be planned. The training for different types of support personnel (e.g., paraprofessionals, aides, tutors, or volunteers) should be planned within the framework of how each group can most effectively be used.

Paraprofessionals will usually have the same time restraints as the teachers and are often full-time employees. They have to be aware of the general goals and curriculum of the school. They can work within a classroom with a teacher, function as a tutor in a resource room, or provide other specific services within the school.

Tutors have more mobility within the school and flexibility in terms of when and where they can work with students. Tutors may range from classroom peers, to older students teaching younger students, to certified personnel.

Volunteers' commitment to a school may not be long term, and their services are usually free; therefore, they are usually most productive in specified jobs. A successful volunteer program requires a coordinator who monitors the training and scheduling of the volunteers to meet the ongoing needs of the school. Volunteers can be a valuable asset to enrichment programs within a school for such activities as field trips, art, drama, and library projects.

Those assisting a teacher should know what to do, when to do it, where to do it, and how it should be done. The following should be considered in orientation sessions for supportive personnel:

1. The confidentiality of student records
2. How to keep the student on-task
3. How to repeat or review material in a successful, nonjudgmental manner
4. When to praise and types of appropriate reward systems
5. How to grade materials without writing negative remarks or drawing unhappy faces on papers
6. How to teach and promote good study habits
7. How to interpret directions on materials
8. How to record and monitor progress
9. How to spot-check progress daily, weekly, and monthly

10. How to interpret developmental sequences of skills or subject level sequences to know where to drop back if an activity fails
11. How to use audiovisual materials
12. How to work with students who may have special needs, disabilities, or handicaps that would require a modification of communication (e.g., for deaf or hard of hearing) or materials to be used.

Role of Support Personnel

The most effective program is one that is based on the premise that initially the support person and the learner must establish a friendly and helping relationship where both understand each other's role. Paraprofessionals and volunteers should be warm and responsive. If they are flexible and able to adapt to the needs of the students, a feeling of trust between the participants should emerge. The students then gain a sense of participation in the whole process and soon learn that although learning may not always be fun, there are rewards for attempting, as well as completing, the required tasks.

It is important for the support personnel to remember that the student may have not been completely successful in previous learning environments for extended periods of time. Since failure may have been a part of the student's academic life and in most cases was carried over to the home, the tutor must consciously strive for successes even if they are very small to begin with. Quick and dramatic results are rare. The learner, paraprofessional, teacher, and parents should understand this concept so that the program will not break down because of overexpectation. Neither the parents nor the support personnel must foster dependency by doing too much for the students. The students have to learn to cope with frustration.

Students who have failed may have experienced threats, embarrassment, conflict, boredom, or illness, to name only a few. They may have been held in low esteem by peers, teachers, parents, and siblings; therefore, it is not unreasonable for the tutor or volunteer to face some initial resistance as the students begin to evaluate themselves against a standard for success. The students may lash out verbally to try the tutor's sense of loyalty and trust. It is at this point that both the teacher and the supportive personnel must focus on the students' strengths as well as work on areas that need to be improved.

The students may not be communicative with strangers at first. Through careful observation, the paraprofessional has to know the students' interests and reaction to humor, as well as when to reward and offer praise. If the support personnel consistently plan and provide successful experiences, the students' attitude should become more positive, with concomitant improvement in their acquisition of knowledge.

Working with Students with Special Needs

All students will have unique problems for the tutor or volunteer to deal with; however, some students' "special needs" will require additional considerations and some modifications. The following suggestions may pertain to all students, but are especially important when the tutor works with handicapped students:

DEAF AND HARD OF HEARING STUDENTS

1. Use normal speech. Avoid excessive accentuation of the voice or facial distortion.
2. Face the students and avoid shadows on the face when speaking to them.
3. Use picture clues or write directions if necessary.
4. For lengthy directions or other oral material, tape record the information so that the students can then listen by amplification.
5. Be aware of similar-sounding words and use further examples.
6. Allow the students to use alternative responses to questions, such as pointing to the right answer.

PARTIALLY SIGHTED STUDENTS

1. Magnify the print, or retype the material by using a primary typewriter.
2. Tape record sessions with the students so that they can listen to the tape at a later time.

PHYSICALLY HANDICAPPED STUDENTS

1. If the students have difficulty writing, alternatives such as typing, use of moveable letters, or writing the answers for the students may have to be used.
2. Workbooks and other materials that require writing must be completed with some consideration for the students' abilities.

STUDENTS WITH A SLOWER RATE OF LEARNING

1. Consider the students' study skills and self-direction in the completion of tasks.
2. Provide repetition and review without showing the students that they have failed.
3. Regulate the amount of work that the students complete. Insure that they have successful experiences.

4. Use pictures, models, or other visual and auditory clues to help the students learn new material.
5. Consider the attention span of the students and avoid lengthy directions that will confuse them.
6. Set up an environment where the students can work without distractions.

WORKING WITH PARENTS

Parents need to understand that few children have just a single disability. It would be simple if a learner only had a reading problem or was hyperactive, but learning is a complex process, and learning difficulties overlap. It is, therefore, difficult to answer the simple question so often asked by parents, "What is wrong with my child?"

In many situations parents of students with learning and behavior problems have become adversaries of the school rather than advocates. A primary reason for this involves poor or negative communication between the home and the school. More important, it involves lack of access to school personnel who will assuage fears, indicate a rationale for what is being done, and include the home as part of the entire process of service delivery. The first assumption to be made is that all parents, regardless of socioeconomic status or cultural background, are concerned about their children. Few people will do for children what their parents will do. Parents have a right to be told the truth and to be given alternatives. Many parents want to know how to stimulate language and conceptual thinking in their children. The child-parent bond will help to support the parent's natural role as a teacher and model for the child.

The first contact by school personnel with parents should begin the process of shared responsibility and the establishment of trusting relationships that will be most beneficial for the student. The following suggestions are given to aid those who will be working with parents.

GENERAL SUGGESTIONS FOR PARENT-EDUCATOR INTERACTION

1. Present accurate information in a concise manner, using a handout or other visual reference as a basis for discussion, if possible.
2. Function as a good and understanding listener. Permit the parents or guardian to express their fears, concerns, and goals for the student openly.
3. Promote parent advocacy through collaborative, as well as independent, action. Permit the parents to indicate the things they can and want to do.
4. Set up a system or line of communication that guarantees accessibility. Specify when you will be available for future conferences or informal discussion by telephone.
5. Plan parent-teacher interaction within the framework of the cultural values of the community. There may be a pattern for how things are accomplished in certain communities.
6. Develop the concept of individualized education programs within the context of what is good education as well as for purposes of accountability.
7. Be prepared for confrontation when students fail, and have alternatives available for resolving adversary relationships into advocacy relationships.
8. Don't be afraid to deviate from traditional modes in working with parents. Guidelines are generally designed to guarantee only a minimum level of participation.
9. Emphasize that commitment as a concept in the development of individualized educational programming is a dual responsibility. Parents in a larger sense are also accountable to children and to the school.
10. Parents have a right to understand issues and to strive for guaranteed access, as well as to influence the planning, policies, and implementation of the educational program.
11. Do not use educational or testing jargon that is noncommunicative to parents.
12. Obtain the parents' consent for what the school is attempting to do in terms of placement and programming
13. Keep a log or anecdotal record of home visits and parent conferences. A checklist of all of the students' names and the date and reason for a contact with parents will provide an accurate record of which parents have or have not been contacted.
14. Involve the parents as ongoing observers of behavior at home. They can provide important information in the following areas:
    a. The learner's attitude toward school life, the teacher, and peers.
    b. Study habits and attitude toward specific subjects.
    c. Health information, especially if the student is receiving medical or psychological services. Report specific information regarding allergies, chronic conditions, or the use of medication.
    d. Hobbies, sports, or other interests where the student has a strength or is meeting success
    e. Sibling and other family relations.
    f. Recreational or other types of reading.
    g. When vacations will occur.

h. When there is an unusual break in the student's schedule or daily pattern (e.g., visits by relatives, baby sitters, for an extended period of time).

15. Involve the parent in school activities when it is feasible. Match the skills of the volunteer to the job requirement. If the parent can volunteer time in the school, provide training and experiences in the following:
    a. One-on-one or small group tutoring.
    b. Recreation, music, arts and crafts activities.
    c. Making materials that can be used in the classroom (e.g., work sheets, mounting pictures, reading material on audio tapes, games).
    d. Supervising students using audiovisual equipment in the resource center, library, or classroom.
    e. Small-group activities that provide someone for a student to talk to or for story telling, etc.
    f. Clerical work—duplicating.
    g. Health services within the training and school board guidelines.
    h. Community liaison for school projects.
16. If the parents cannot come to the school, but have expressed an interest in providing assistance, send the task to them. If the materials are sent home, the parents can cut out pictures, type, telephone other parents, make bookshelves, etc.

HOW PARENTS CAN HELP AT HOME

The parents must be assured that a student with learning difficulties can be helped by informed parents and teachers. In planning for the students' needs, the parents or guardians and the educators who will be involved with the students should attend to the following key areas:

1. The environment at home and at school may require more structure and some accommodation.
2. Controlling the learner may involve more consistent, yet loving, firmness. All those involved with the learner should consciously set good examples and fair standards.
3. Provision should be made at home and at school for successful experiences that will improve the learner's self-esteem. Each child is an individual and concern should be for his or her strengths as well as the weaknesses. Each student is special and has a unique way of learning.

Structuring the Environment. Children with learning difficulties respond to individuals in much the same way that other children do, but as a group they appear to function more effectively in more structured settings at home and in school. It appears that they often need more attention, more firmness, more clarity of instructions, more predictable outcomes, and more opportunity for success. They cannot be overloaded with too much to do at one time. Parents often fail to take these things into consideration.

Parents must become accustomed to the wide range in performance and the swings in mood that often occur. On some days the child will be alert, cooperative, and able to master the skills taught and on others he or she will be inept, sloppy, and remote, and learning unexpectedly appears to be gone. Sometimes these children are abnormally sensitive to minor changes in the environment: a visitor, the weather, or some new noise. They may also, on some days, be supersensitive to their failures and frustrations and appear to have lost all self-confidence.

Just as the school is structured, the children's home life should be structured. There should be a consistent wake-up time each morning and bedtime each night. Anxious children can be calmed if they know that things happen in a certain order. For example, bedtime is generally after bathing. If possible, meals should be served at regular times and TV, play, homework, etc., scheduled for specific times. Some students with learning problems have a very poor concept of time. They benefit from an orderly day. As they gain an appreciation of time and the progression of events during a day, they tend to become more self-directed.

Organizing the children's time can be a problem. Parents run the gamut from those who act as the social directors and car-pool drivers, scheduling every minute, to those who leave the children sitting endlessly in front of a television set. Certainly, during days when school is in session, parents have to be aware of the balance between play or recreation and time for homework. For many students with learning problems, prioritizing and completing homework is a disaster. Parents and teachers must carefully monitor the amount of time required for homework and the types of assignments that the children can successfully complete at home. Teaching the students how to study and presenting new material should be a function of school and not forced on the parents. The parents' commitment should be to provide guidance, support, and review for material presented in the class.

Parents should avoid asking their children to perform complex tasks at first. Responsibilities in the home should be within the capabilities of the students. Successful completion of one or two tasks for a few days or a week (e.g., placing silverware on the table and walking the dog) are more help to the parents and satisfying to the children than constant reminders of unfinished activities or chores.

Sudden decisions are often frustrating to the children. Instead of asking for immediate responses to questions (e.g., "What do you want for breakfast?") parents can help the children decide by giving them choices. It is often difficult for an impatient adult to wait for a child to make decisions.

Parents need to know that children with special needs will make greater demands on their time, energy, and understanding. Families can enjoy many pleasant recreation and learning experiences together, such as trips to the zoo or a museum. However, there will be times when the children will be left with neighbors, friends, or relatives. Such occasions should be planned and carefully explained to the children. Many learning-disabled students cannot tolerate the unexpected. They find solace in overorderliness and feel secure only when situations are quite reliably predictable. Highly distractible or hyperactive children are often unable to function properly or at all when presented with a stimulating new situation, such as a field trip or a new teacher. Parents must prepare the students for new situations.

Dealing with Behavior. Some of the children with learning disorders exhibit impulsive and other noxious behavior. In our society we have been taught to believe that a child's behavior is the result of upbringing, and when the child fails to meet society's expectations, not only the child but also the parents are to be blamed. Some parents are their own harshest critics. They blame their own child's failure on themselves. Some parents feel a vague sense of guilt about possible hereditary factors, or defective genes, and sometimes point out the same unusual behavior in a spouse or relative. This behavior is essentially pointless. Parents, for the most part, cannot take the blame for the impulsive, disruptive, aggressive, or antisocial acts of children with learning problems. Parents can, however, provide the children with the best model as well as good consistent training. At the opposite extreme are the parents who refuse to recognize their children's difficulties and feel that eventually "everything will be ok" or that they will "grow out of it."

Most frustrating to parents is the variability of behavior from one day or hour to another. This causes parents to feel "he could do better if he tried." At times, the child may be impudent, attention seeking, silly, or negativistic, behaving in any number of ways irritating and upsetting to teachers, peers, and parents. Regardless of age, overactive children are often unpopular with other children at home because of their unpleasant behavior or inability to compete. Because they are unpopular, they may continually be on the defensive. They may develop a short temper. When this is added to feelings of failure, they may develop an abrasive personality. The students may get into frequent fights at home, and other parents may exclude them from playing with their children. Instead of fighting, some children try to be the neighborhood clown. They try to win friends by giving them candy, money, or gifts that are out of proportion. Sometimes they even steal goods to give them away. It is difficult at these times to remember that the children are not willfully malicious; they are not the monsters they sometimes pretend to be. Teachers and parents must believe that sensible external controls, wisely imposed, will gradually take over and become internal controls and stay with the learners throughout life.

A learning disability does not justify lax controls and leniency. Some children feel that inconsistent discipline really means that their parents don't care enough about them to make them behave correctly. However, parents should not punish children for behavior that they cannot control, like clumsiness, excessive activity, short attention span, impatience, impulsiveness, or fear of trying something new.

The following are a few guidelines for parents:

1. Don't threaten punishment that is never carried out.
2. Make the punishment fit the act, and punish the same amount for the same act. Don't make a mountain out of a molehill.
3. Punishment should be prompt. Don't let children stew over it.
4. Avoid sermons and don't demand verbal assurance that the children will never do it again. Too much verbal behavior may overload the children and they will not attend to the specific concern.
5. Don't send children to bed as punishment. Keep this as a place of rest.
6. Stony silence or cold anger and then loving embraces should be avoided. Such actions confuse children and they may forget why they are being punished.
7. Encouraging good behavior is more beneficial than punishment.
8. Avoid at all costs belittlement or shaming, as it will affect a child's self-image.
9. Sometimes it is prudent to avoid being led into a long explanation and defense of actions to children when what they want requires a reversal of a decision.
10. Plan to gradually increase independence and freedom much as is done at school. When children are allowed to go to play outdoors, they know that if they misbehave, they will be called back to the house. The next day, they are given the

chance to try again. Start each day anew and avoid mentioning what was done, and why there was punishment, yesterday.

PROVIDING SUCCESSFUL EXPERIENCES

Parents and teachers need to work together to impose rules, standards, and controls, always remembering that in the end children have to become self-directed. With time, opportunity to grow, and understanding, most children can accomplish this. In the interim, however, the parents must expect the students to be sensitive to failures, especially when the students know they are not living up to expectations. If understanding is not forthcoming in this area, the students may develop a remarkably distorted self-concept and grow into adults who feel cheated, defective, or generally unworthy.

During the early sensitive years in school, most learners with problems cannot meet the academic challenge and experience their first failures. When placed in academic situations where they cannot measure up to expectations, they can be crushed. Self-esteem takes a severe blow as first teachers, then parents, and even the children themselves, begin to feel they are slow. Problems occur when other children in the neighborhood, and even in the family, quickly sense the differences in a child, but are not mature or gracious enough to overlook the weaknesses. Therefore, many of the children with disabilities have to learn to live with ridicule.

Some of the children suffer from inner conflicts, worries, and fears to the extent that they waste great amounts of energy that should be going into learning. Worries may concern physical size or weight, discord between parents, illness or death of someone in the family, more successful sisters and brothers, bad experiences in school, or a million or more other imaginary or real troubles. When a child suffers inner fears, those feelings lead to actions that are self-defeating. As schoolwork lags, the child may gain recognition through delinquent behavior that in an older student turns to truancy or other antisocial acts. Gradually, all progress in schoolwork stops, and we observe a socially maladjusted student.

This result can be avoided if the problem is caught early and the cycle of failure is stopped. It is important that the teacher find out what has changed at home to cause the child to worry, ruling out school-based difficulties first.

All children need to have experiences at school and at home that will give them opportunities for success. Success will induce feelings of security, of being important, and of being wanted. The students need to feel they are contributing and are needed. Parents need to be patient, understanding, and optimistic, but not overprotective. Sometimes families find that in accommodating to, and understanding, the needs of a child with learning problems they are more tolerant and cooperative. They tend to anticipate, or become sensitive to, difficulties in general and therefore avoid them. Other children in the family may begin to emulate the actions of the parents and become more thoughtful.

The following additional activities are suggested for parents, guardians, teachers, and others who are concerned about the students' feelings and self-concept.

1. Show the student pictures of people expressing various feelings (sadness, happiness, excitement, love, anger, pain) and have the student describe the feelings.
2. Role play feelings with the student by looking at facial expressions in a mirror.
3. Trace the body outline of the student on a large piece of wrapping paper. The student fills in the body parts (face, fingernails, etc.) and clothes. Discuss the concept of growth, physical health, and good feelings about oneself.
4. Allow five minutes each day for a personalized talk with the student. Discussions should center on the good things the child is doing in school and the child's interests, friends, and feelings.
5. Take the student through the family album, showing photographs of different members of the family and friends. Talk about the past history and experiences, hopes, and aspirations. Emphasize the learner's place in the social structure of the family. Slides can also be used for this activity.
6. If the student has a physical problem, discuss how it may impede certain activities, but emphasize the things he or she can do and ways the disability can possibly be overcome.
7. Children learn a lot about feelings from having pets and caring for them. Most pets have a quieting effect on children. They can be stroked, and feelings of genuine affection can be expressed.
8. When young children are reluctant to talk about problems, etc., use toy telephones, puppets, and walkie-talkies to communicate.
9. Discuss things that the child really enjoys (e.g., walk in the zoo, special food, friends, books, games, television shows). By knowing what the child likes to do, you can plan small rewards for special achievements.
10. Assist students in making something that can be

given to a grandfather, sibling, friend, senior citizen, etc. (e.g., food, art project). If they cannot make anything, encourage them to think of a project that would involve sharing their time (e.g., working in the yard, running errands).

11. After going to a movie or viewing a television program, discuss with the student the feelings of various characters and how they behaved in different situations.
12. Indicate something positive about any work the student brings home from school, regardless of how many errors are present.
13. The level of difficulty of any home activity should be so designed as to result in a successful experience for the student. People at home around the student can help the most by not assigning tasks that cause the student to feel discouraged and defeated. Failing children quickly blame themselves and soon refuse to try anything new. Simple activities that produce failure cause frustration and anger. Provide simple projects that can be completed in a short period of time. Start with things that are free or inexpensive and will not damage easily. Instead of an expensive paint set, let the child paint an old chair outdoors. Encourage the child to complete the entire process from gathering the materials, through doing the task, to cleanup activities.
14. Help the student learn to cope with frustration and failure. As students gradually enter competitive events or attempt new social interactions, the trust and support of their parents is crucial. A parent has to refrain from running interference and gradually guide the student into independent behavior. Be especially sensitive to activities where the child will receive peer pressure or comparison to other members of the family. For example, riding a bicycle is a difficult task for some children. Perhaps an understanding and trusting teenager has more stamina and patience to run around with a young child learning to ride than the parents.
15. Respecting the student's privacy contributes to stronger trusting relationships. Permit the student to have a private drawer or secret place to keep letters, diaries, etc.
16. Encourage activities that will provide things for the child to do with or without other children (e.g., rock collections, fishing, photography, nature activities).
17. Some students will require counseling or therapy sessions with personnel other than their parents or teachers. Older students especially may have misconceptions about the motives for involving psychologists, therapists, psychiatrists, counselors, etc. Careful communication must be established between the parents, the children, and the psychological services. The children need some explanation of why they are getting special attention.

Chapter 12 Individual Educational Programming

Many students with learning and behavior problems are in regular classrooms and may not require additional special services. Parent-teacher relationships are usually direct and only on occasion require involvement by administrators or other educators. However, the Education for All Handicapped Children Act of 1975 (P.L. 94-142), Section 504 of the Vocational Rehabilitation Act of 1973, state statutes, and judicial decisions now provide guidelines for students who will be receiving special education services through local and state agencies. These regulations directly involve the students and their parents or guardians. The students' teachers (regular teachers and specialists or resource personnel) will become involved in the development and implementation of an Individualized Educational Plan (IEP) for each student receiving special help. P.L. 94-142 defines an IEP as: ". . . a written statement . . . developed in any meeting by a representative of the Local Education Agency who shall be qualified to provide, or supervise the provision of . . . instruction . . . , the teacher, the parent or guardian . . . and when appropriate [the] child . . ." (Sec. 602[19]).

School districts will vary in their approach to developing both the process and the content involved in individual educational planning. The following suggestions for principals, teachers, and parents concerning the components of the IEP indicate

1. how the other chapters in the Handbook can be utilized within the context of any type of Individualized Educational Plan
2. commonalities and general areas for developing individualized programming that are specific for students requiring special services under P.L. 94-142 yet are also applicable to all students with learning and behavior problems.

COMPONENTS OF AN INDIVIDUAL EDUCATIONAL PLAN (IEP)

Components of an Individual Education Plan (IEP) include the following:

1. A statement of the present level of educational performance
2. A prioritized statement of annual and long-range goals
3. A statement of short-term instructional objectives
4. A statement of the specific special education and related services to be provided
5. Specification of the role of specified personnel responsible for IEP
6. A statement of the extent to which the student will be able to participate in least restrictive environment programs or the percentage of time in the regular classroom
7. Specification of the projected dates for the initiation of services and the anticipated duration of the services
8. Statement of the specific evaluation criteria for each of the indicated annual goals and a time line for determining whether instructional objectives are achieved

9. Recommendations for specific procedures/techniques, materials, etc., to include information relating to the learning characteristics of the student

Statement of the Present Level of Educational Performance

Principals' Roles. Although principals may not choose to sit in on all the mandatory conferences required in the process that will ultimately lead to individualizing a program for a student, they have major responsibilities in the entire process. First, a principal's attitude concerning students with special needs will influence all the personnel within a school. A positive feeling of advocacy by the principal for the access of handicapped students to education within the system may greatly aid in the development of support by all school personnel (secretaries, cafeteria workers, volunteers, teachers, bus drivers, etc.). The principal can facilitate the shared responsibility among staff that must occur for special services to be meaningful. Before the first meeting concerning a student, the principal, in cooperation with teachers and local school agency officials, should review the guidelines for an IEP. In many school districts, these guidelines are printed in a booklet for all schools to use. The principal or a designate must review with the faculty the due process procedures for the student; the confidentiality of all reports, meetings, or other communication concerning a student; the organizational plan for scheduling meetings with the members of the IEP team; and the forms that are required at various stages of developing an IEP. Since the principal is ultimately responsible with the teachers for the success of the student, the procedure for reviewing the plans for special needs students should be established. The principal must monitor to some degree the overall accountability of the program; therefore, lines of communication should be specified when the IEP process commences.

Teachers' Role. The types of teachers involved in the process of reevaluating either a student who is already receiving special services or a child who has been referred for special help will probably vary with the type of handicap or services required. In most instances, the regular classroom teacher, the special education teacher, or a psychologist or diagnostician will determine the mildly handicapped student's present level of educational performance. All of these professionals should understand their roles in the evaluation process. The regular teacher can provide observational data by using checklists such as the Mann-Suiter-McClung Developmental Checklist and information on academic performance by using the Mann-Suiter Spelling, Reading, Writing, Written Language, and Arithmetic Screens. Diagnosticians, special education teachers, and psychologists will provide the data from more comprehensive tests that will establish such areas as cognitive functioning, academic performance, and adaptive behavior. (Refer to Chapter 2, Introduction to Diagnosis, for a more detailed explanation of the process of diagnosis.)

Those who are involved in the evaluation process must particularly be aware of the following:

1. Have all of the due process procedures involving the parents or guardians been completed prior to an evaluation of the student?
2. Are all the required forms signed and on file?
3. Have the tests been carefully selected based on their validity?
4. Are the tests nondiscriminatory with regard to race or culture?
5. Is more than one type of test procedure being used?
6. Which tests are norm referenced and which ones are criterion referenced?
7. What kinds of observation, screening, or testing will each teacher or evaluator be using and is there a basic understanding of what the student will be required to do?
8. Who will inform the parents or guardians and the student about the evaluation process?
9. Will it be necessary to administer the test in the student's native language or other mode of communication?

During the IEP conference the present level of educational performance of the student must be clearly stated in language that the parents or guardians can comprehend. The teachers, especially the regular classroom teacher, must be prepared to present data of a student's strengths and weaknesses in a nonjudgmental manner.

Parents' Role. Parents are not passive receptors to the individualized educational plan. Before the initiation of the evaluation process, the parents must know why the testing is being done and what their rights will be during conferences and throughout every other phase of the development of the IEP. Parents can do the following:

1. Attend each meeting where the IEP will be planned, finalized, or reviewed
2. Have access to their child's records and secure copies

3. Ask for a reevaluation or seek an independent evaluation (The cost of such an outside evaluation should be determined before the evaluation.)
4. Receive a written copy of the IEP
5. Participate and provide information during IEP conferences (medical, family relationships, study habits at home, previous educational experiences)
6. Express fears and concerns and ask questions about the language used to describe their child's level of functioning
7. Request an interpreter if necessary
8. Request a due process hearing if dissatisfied with the process or the content of the IEP

Prioritized Statement of Annual and Long Range Goals

Principals' Role. Principals must determine the reality of the goals; defend their appropriateness with regard to grade level promotion, graduation, potential after-graduation employment, and other administrative rules or policies; and be prepared to mediate concerns of the parents or guardians and the instructional staff if the goals are unmet within a specified time.

Teachers' Role. Both regular and special education teachers must develop goals that encompass the academic and social-emotional needs of the student (for more severely involved students—special services). There has to be agreement that the student can achieve the goals. The developmental skills in Chapter 7 can be used in developing long range goals.

Parents' Role. Guardians or parents should be able to clearly understand the goals and should be encouraged to give additional suggestions before the final IEP is written.

Statement of Short-Term Instructional Objectives

Principals' Role. Principals should monitor the quality of the written instructional objectives and if necessary plan with their staffs the type of staff development meetings that will facilitate a more meaningful and manageable process. Principals must work carefully with their staffs to improve the paperwork load or time constraints that may inhibit the process.

Teachers' Role. The teachers must join in a collaborative effort to write the types of statements that can be measured and observed and are written in a language that everyone involved in the process can understand, including the student. The teachers should examine the scope and sequences of subject matter skills as well as such developmental skills lists as those included within this book in Chapter 7. The short-range goals must be attainable within a framework that permits modification once the process of instruction begins. Since parents and in some cases the student will attend IEP conferences, the teachers should be prepared to state the goals in terms of what the student knows and how the short-term goals in an IEP will build on those strengths.

Parents' Role. Parents have to agree to the goals and give additional suggestions or observations. The parents should not hesitate to question how the short-term goals will relate to the mastery of skills and how much instruction time or specialized, individualized time will be provided to achieve those goals. If possible, both parents should attend the conference to prevent misunderstandings in the reinterpretation of data. If either one of the parents or the child is not present, then the administrators and teachers present must be certain that the information will be interpreted to other family members in a positive way. Teachers and administrators must be especially sensitive to how children with special needs will be interpreted within their cultural milieu.

A Statement of the Specific Special Education and Related Services to be Provided

Principals' Role. Principals have to know what services will be provided by the school and what additional services may be secured from the community. They must mediate or know from whom to seek information if unrealistic services are either recommended by the committee or demanded by the parent. They or their designates must be knowledgeable about such services as transportation, mechanical devices, and services by ancillary teaching personnel (e.g., speech and therapy).

Teachers' Role. Regular and special education teachers must also be knowledgeable about what services are available within the system. The teachers must also consider how the services will blend into the students' ongoing programs and the long- and short-term goals. The committee members must avoid too many unrelated services that fragment the children to such a degree that the goals of their programs cannot be attained. If some of the support services to the regular teacher are not specifically funded, then the committee should examine the reliability and quality of such assistance as parent volunteers or peer tutors.

Parents' Role. The parents' responsibilities for at home follow-up should be clearly delineated. The parents can question the expertise of those giving services and should find out who will coordinate multiple services. The parent has the right to know whether one teacher will answer questions about all services or if each individual person must be consulted.

Role of Specified Personnel Responsible for IEP

Principals' Role. A system of communication for staff members and parents should be set up that will permit accessibility when unforeseen episodes or breakdowns in the collaborative effort occur. Principals have to have a clear understanding of the roles of their staff, especially such personnel as resource teachers who may perform a variety of tasks in many settings. A principal has to know the staff's strengths and weaknesses and must be prepared for conflict and know the steps to mediate and resolve adversary relationships. Encouragement and praise of staff, as well as solicitation of alternatives for improving the implementation of an IEP within a school, all add to good morale and more commitment from everyone to continue the extra effort that may be required in meeting the needs of the students.

Teachers' Role. Both regular and special teachers have to know how their work can aid students. Many organizational problems prevent a maximum use of their efforts. The following issues should be resolved in the role delineation of regular and special teachers:

1. When can they meet for ongoing evaluation? If they can't meet often because of conflicting schedules, then some other type of written communication should be planned.
2. Which teacher will communicate with the parents?
3. If the student's behavior deteriorates, what help is available and when?
4. How can schedule conflicts be avoided?
5. If the IEP has been written primarily by one teacher, can the other teachers successfully carry out their part of the long- and short-range goals?
6. What grading system will be used for the student? If the report card for the student with special needs is atypical, who informs the child and the parents?

Parents' Role. Parents need to know what to do at home. Both the regular and special teachers should coordinate homework activities and recommend specific tasks that will be reinforcing to the material presented in school but will not place children in conflict with their parents. Further suggestions for parents are included on pages 320–323.

Statement of Extent to Which the Student Will Be Able to Participate in Least Restrictive Environment Programs, or Percentage of Time in the Regular Classroom

Principals' Role. Every school should participate in an orientation session concerning services for handicapped children, what is required to receive such services, and what such terms as *least restrictive environment* mean. Working definitions will greatly aid the faculty in the planning process For example: Least restrictive environment is the place where handicapped students receive special services while, to the greatest extent appropriate, their education with nonhandicapped students is maximized. The staff has to do a needs assessment of what has to be changed to provide an environment that is in compliance with the law and that facilitates access and mobility within the school. The following should be considered:

1. Have physical barriers been removed (e.g., benches, plants, etc., in the hallways)?
2. Do all the students have access to classrooms, bathrooms, lunchroom, library, etc.? For example, can a wheelchair roll under the lunch tables or science lab tables?
3. Are signs that promote labelling removed (e.g., special class for retarded children)?
4. Are special classes placed throughout the school or are they all placed in one wing?
5. Have safety features in the school been accounted for? What happens during fire drills when a student is enroute from one teacher to another?
6. Does the entire staff understand special medical problems (e.g., seizures)?

The principal usually sets the example for labels within a school. Such words as "those children" are often picked up and repeated by secretaries or other building personnel.

Teachers' Role. Teachers are usually most concerned about the following·

1. Which subjects will be missed if a student goes to a special class, and how can that subject be made up?
2. How much extra time will the special needs child require?
3. What happens when other children ridicule a child?
4. How can a child receiving special services make the transition from room to room?

5. Who will do the grading when several teachers teach parts of the same subject (e.g., reading)?
6. How can information be coordinated to benefit the student (e.g., ongoing evaluation, improvement or failure in achievement, reporting to the parents)?
7. Will the time required to provide an individualized plan be excessive?
8. Where will the resource teacher best work with the student—in the regular classroom with the regular teacher or in a separate room?
9. What should the regular and special teachers know about each other's available resources?

Parents' Role. Parents need to know whom to talk to in the school about the students' progress, what the regular or special teachers will be teaching individually, and where those subject areas or special services will show up on a periodic evaluation or report card. Detailed lesson plans are not as critical to a parent as a realistic overview of what the students will be learning, when, and why. The parents need this outline in order to be able to ask the students and the teachers about the students' progress. Parents are also vitally concerned about the pressures the students will face as they spend more time in a regular classroom with achieving peers. For this reason, the students' strengths and potential for success should be documented in order to maintain self-confidence as well as academic progress. Parents should be given suggestions of what to do if the students have a minor setback in school (e.g., low grade on a test).

Specification of Projected Dates for the Initiation of Services and the Anticipated Duration of the Services

Everyone should keep good records and document the progress of the services. If it is evident that services will be either terminated or extended, the information leading to the decisions should not be a shock to the children or their parents.

Statement of the Specific Evaluation Criteria for Each of the Indicated Annual Goals and a Time Line for Determining whether Instructional Objectives Are Achieved

Principals' Role. Ongoing evaluations, which may include reports, conferences, and other communication completed on schedule, should facilitate continuity and improved services. Principals must allow teachers (regular and special) to admit failure or to ask for help if the student is not making the progress the committee anticipated. It is difficult to defend extended failure when intervening steps have not been used.

Teachers' Role. Teachers need to know how to evaluate goals and set up a continuous evaluation system. They must develop an informal system of daily or weekly spot-checking of progress, as well as methods of determining mastery of skills.

Parents' Role. Parents should receive written evaluation of their children's progress when appropriate. The parents should be encouraged to observe and evaluate the children's progress at home and provide information to the school.

Recommendations for Specific Procedures/Techniques, Materials, etc., to Include Information Relating to the Learning Characteristics of the Student

Principals' Role. As the financial broker of available resources, the principal often has to determine if the materials required by the teachers fit the existing budget categories. If a teacher needs materials that are atypical, then the principal must have a good understanding of additional sources of revenue (e.g., parents, clubs). The administrator has to have not only a knowledge of the appropriateness of educational materials, but also a management system for the materials in a building. How to effectively distribute, get multiple usage, modify, code, store, and avoid duplication are all important in cost-effective management.

Teachers' Role. Teachers are also concerned about the availability and classroom management of materials. A vital part of an IEP is how the student will acquire the prescribed skills and how much will be individualized. With class size, grouping, and time all impinging on individualization, the teachers need materials that can be made as student directed as possible. If teachers must share materials or the student has to use materials in a centrally located library, then the materials have to be coded and scheduled.

When teaching techniques or curriculum materials are atypical, then the instructor has to know how to make the transition from a supplementary to a major program. If the material is a game, then the students have to know why they are using it and perhaps what subject it applies to.

Parents' Role. As has been previously discussed, the parents are concerned about what to do at home to help the student. They are equally concerned that the curriculum for their children provide academic skills in keeping with the children's potential.

Appendix

MANN SELF-ASSESSMENT COMPETENCY INVENTORY (GENERIC)

MANN SELF-ASSESSMENT COMPETENCY INVENTORY (GENERIC) PART I

NAME ______________________________ DATE ______________________________

ADDRESS ______________________________ POSITION ______________________________

______________________________ TELEPHONE ______________________________

SCHOOL ______________________________

The following information reflects *my personal* need for training that will enable *me* to be *more effective* with:

(a) all the students within my area of responsibility, including
(b) students exhibiting a slower rate of development, learning problems, sensory impairments, behavior problems, physical disabilities, or any combinations of these and
(c) students who are gifted or talented.

I need

Diagnosis-Student Assessment (D-SA)

1. instruction in giving both formal and informal evaluation that relates more to specific instructional objectives.	No Need	1	2	3	4	5	Strong Need
2. to use different kinds of tests and screening devices with both individuals and groups of students.	No Need	1	2	3	4	5	Strong Need
3. information about different approaches to diagnosing students' needs.	No Need	1	2	3	4	5	Strong Need
4. participation in activities that involve the planning of a student assessment program.	No Need	1	2	3	4	5	Strong Need
5. information about how different individuals have implemented diagnostic programs in different types of educational settings.	No Need	1	2	3	4	5	Strong Need
6. experience in setting up and implementing a diagnostic program.	No Need	1	2	3	4	5	Strong Need
7. knowledge of the ways different individuals function as members of a diagnostic team.	No Need	1	2	3	4	5	Strong Need
8. to participate as a member of diagnostic teams where information is analyzed.	No Need	1	2	3	4	5	Strong Need
9. information about how diagnostic data should be interpreted to students, parents, and others in the community.	No Need	1	2	3	4	5	Strong Need
10. experiences communicating with parents in areas dealing with the diagnosis of their children.	No Need	1	2	3	4	5	Strong Need
11. knowledge of ways to evaluate the effectiveness of a student assessment program.	No Need	1	2	3	4	5	Strong Need
12. to develop instruments such as questionnaires that will evaluate the effectiveness of a diagnostic program.	No Need	1	2	3	4	5	Strong Need

Curriculum-Instruction (C-I)

13. information about ways to relate diagnostic data to different types of curriculum and instructional approaches.	No Need	1	2	3	4	5	Strong Need
14. to use different kinds of instructional materials and programs.	No Need	1	2	3	4	5	Strong Need
15. examples of how different individuals have designed individual instructional programs.	No Need	1	2	3	4	5	Strong Need
16. to design and make curriculum and instructional materials.	No Need	1	2	3	4	5	Strong Need
17. knowledge of different ways to implement individually planned educational programs.	No Need	1	2	3	4	5	Strong Need
18. to implement different instructional approaches in specific areas of curriculum such as reading and arithmetic.	No Need	1	2	3	4	5	Strong Need
19. instruction in how to be a part of a team that develops individual curriculum and instructional programs.	No Need	1	2	3	4	5	Strong Need
20. participation in interdisciplinary staff meetings where curriculum and instructional programs are designed for particular students.	No Need	1	2	3	4	5	Strong Need
21. information on how to interpret curriculum and instructional goals and objectives for students to their parents and other appropriate individuals.	No Need	1	2	3	4	5	Strong Need
22. to work with parents and members of community agencies in areas dealing with curriculum and instruction.	No Need	1	2	3	4	5	Strong Need
23. information about different kinds of data collection devices that can be used to evaluate the quality and effectiveness of curriculum and instructional programs.	No Need	1	2	3	4	5	Strong Need
24. to develop and use different kinds of evaluation devices to determine the effectiveness of curriculum and instructional programs.	No Need	1	2	3	4	5	Strong Need

Educational Management (EM)

25. information about different ways to organize the classroom and the school for more effective individualization of instruction.	No Need	1	2	3	4	5	Strong Need
26. to set up classrooms that are designed for more effective individualization of instruction.	No Need	1	2	3	4	5	Strong Need
27. to be shown models or designs of different kinds of learning environments.	No Need	1	2	3	4	5	Strong Need
28. to design and set up different learning environments.	No Need	1	2	3	4	5	Strong Need
29. information on how different educational management systems are implemented in different types of educational settings.	No Need	1	2	3	4	5	Strong Need
30. to implement different types of educational management systems, such as grouping for instruction.	No Need	1	2	3	4	5	Strong Need

31. to learn how teams of individuals plan and implement educational management programs for particular students.	No Need 1 2 3 4 5 Strong Need
32. experiences as a member of teams to develop educational management strategies for particular students.	No Need 1 2 3 4 5 Strong Need
33. knowledge about ways to communicate educational management strategies to students and their families.	No Need 1 2 3 4 5 Strong Need
34. to work with parents and members of community agencies where educational management programs are developed.	No Need 1 2 3 4 5 Strong Need
35. knowledge of ways different types of evaluation devices and techniques can be used for assessing the effectiveness of educational management programs.	No Need 1 2 3 4 5 Strong Need
36. to develop questionnaires and rating scales that can be used to determine the effectiveness of an educational management program.	No Need 1 2 3 4 5 Strong Need

Behavior Management (BM)

37. information about different types of behavior characteristics and ways to organize the classroom and the school for more effective behavior management.	No Need 1 2 3 4 5 Strong Need
38. to set up different types of behavior management programs.	No Need 1 2 3 4 5 Strong Need
39. to be shown examples of programs in the area of behavior management.	No Need 1 2 3 4 5 Strong Need
40. involvement in designing behavior management programs for different types of students.	No Need 1 2 3 4 5 Strong Need
41. knowledge of how different kinds of behavior management programs have been implemented in different types of educational settings.	No Need 1 2 3 4 5 Strong Need
42. to implement different types of behavior management techniques.	No Need 1 2 3 4 5 Strong Need
43. to be shown examples of how teams of individuals plan and implement an effective behavior management program.	No Need 1 2 3 4 5 Strong Need
44. experiences as a member of teams that develop behavior management programs for particular students.	No Need 1 2 3 4 5 Strong Need
45. knowledge of ways to communicate behavior management strategies to particular students, their families, and members of community agencies.	No Need 1 2 3 4 5 Strong Need
46. to work with parents and community service personnel in behavior management programming.	No Need 1 2 3 4 5 Strong Need
47. examples of how different types of evaluation techniques are used to evaluate the effectiveness of behavior management programs.	No Need 1 2 3 4 5 Strong Need

48. to develop evaluation procedures and instrumentation as well as to carry out the analysis necessary for determining the effectiveness of a behavior management program.	No Need 1 2 3 4 5 Strong Need

Special Education: School and Community (SE)

49. understanding of the concepts of *handicapped* and *disabled* and of the role and responsibility of the school in programming for handicapped and disabled learners in keeping with current legislation.	No Need 1 2 3 4 5 Strong Need
50. participation in activities that will result in a better understanding of what persons with special needs, including the gifted and talented, have to deal with in today's society.	No Need 1 2 3 4 5 Strong Need
51. information about different programs or instructional alternatives for students with special needs.	No Need 1 2 3 4 5 Strong Need
52. participation in activities with other educators to design educational programs for students with special needs.	No Need 1 2 3 4 5 Strong Need
53. knowledge about different approaches to programming for students with special needs within least restrictive environments.	No Need 1 2 3 4 5 Strong Need
54. participation in shared responsibility relationships with other educators in implementing educational programs for students with special needs.	No Need 1 2 3 4 5 Strong Need
55. knowledge of how educational teams approach the planning and implementation of programs for students with special needs.	No Need 1 2 3 4 5 Strong Need
56. participation in educational teams where individual educational plans are developed for students with special needs.	No Need 1 2 3 4 5 Strong Need
57. information on how to work with community agencies and with parents of students identified as having special needs.	No Need 1 2 3 4 5 Strong Need
58. experiences with parents of students with special needs and with members of community agencies, including special interest groups, who provide support services or are otherwise concerned with these students and their families.	No Need 1 2 3 4 5 Strong Need
59. information about how to evaluate programs for students with special needs in least restrictive environments.	No Need 1 2 3 4 5 Strong Need
60. participation in the evaluation of total program efforts for students with special needs.	No Need 1 2 3 4 5 Strong Need

MANN SELF-ASSESSMENT COMPETENCY INVENTORY (GENERIC) PART 2

NAME ______________________________ DATE ______________

Rank the items under each of the areas from 1 (*your highest priority of need*) to 10 (*your lowest priority of need*). Write the numbers next to the items.

Diagnosis-Student Assessment	*Rank*
Academic Achievement	____
Vocational-Interest Inventories	____
Social-Emotional Development	____
Use of Specialists (e.g., Psychologist, Special Education)	____
Observation-Screening Devices	____
Setting Up a Diagnostic Program	____
Continuous Progress Evaluation	____
Diagnostic Teams	____
Use of Parents, Aides, Tutors	____
Use of Specialized Tests	____

Curriculum-Instruction	*Rank*
Language Arts (e.g., Reading, Writing, Spelling, Speech)	____
Arithmetic	____
Science	____
Social Studies	____
Physical Education, Art, Music	____
Team Planning and Implementation	____
Use of Specialists (Reading, Special Education, etc.)	____
Use of Parents, Aides, Tutors	____
Vocational-Career Education	____
Prescriptive-Precision Teaching	____

Educational Management	*Rank*
Grouping, Grading, and Promotion	____
Use of Specialists (e.g., Special Education, Psychologists, Counselors)	____
Organizing Material	____
Use of Parents, Aides, Tutors	____
Classroom Organization (Open Classroom, Learning Centers, etc.)	____
Individualized Student Programs	____
Team Planning and Implementation	____
Managing Curriculum Systems	____
Student Self-Correction Devices	____
Student Inter and Intra Grade Mobility	____

Behavior Management	*Rank*
Team Planning and Implementation	____
Use of Specialists (e.g., Special Education, Psychologists, Counselors)	____
Use of Parents, Aides, Tutors	____
Behavior Modification	____
Group Dynamics	____
Individual Counseling	____
Contracting	____
Community Services (Mental Health, etc.)	____
Environmental Modification	____
Dealing with Disruptive Behavior	____

Mann Self-Assessment Competency Inventory (Generic) Part 1

Rank the items under each of the areas from 1 (*your highest priority of need*) to 10 (*your lowest priority of need*). Write the numbers next to the items.

Special Education: School and Community	*Rank*
Classification-Definitions; Causation-Characteristics	____
Historical Influences	____
Educational Provisions	____
Federal-State Legislation	____
Parents-Community	____
Attitudes-Sociality	____
Support Systems	____
Least Restrictive Environment (P.L. 94-142)	____
Due Process (P.L. 94-142)	____
Individual Educational Plan (P.L. 94-142)	____

Comments:

MANN SELF-ASSESSMENT COMPETENCY INVENTORY (GENERIC) PART 1 Summary Sheet

NAME ______________________________ DATE ______________

ADDRESS ______________________________ POSITION ______________

______________________________ TELEPHONE ______________

SCHOOL ______________________________

Legend:

a = information-knowledge systems
b = experience-activity systems
D-SA = Diagnosis-Student Assessment
C-I = Curriculum-Instruction
EM = Educational Management
BM = Behavioral Management
SE = Special Education
a + b = Maximum Value of 10
Total a + b = Maximum Value of 300

Diagnosis-Student Assessment

Area	a	b	a + b
D-SA 1	1	2	1 + 2
D-SA 2	3	4	3 + 4
D-SA 3	5	6	5 + 6
D-SA 4	7	8	7 + 8
D-SA 5	9	10	9 + 10
D-SA 6	11	12	11 + 12
TOTALS			

Curriculum-Instruction

Area	a	b	a + b
C-I 1	13	14	13 + 14
C-I 2	15	16	15 + 16
C-I 3	17	18	17 + 18
C-I 4	19	20	19 + 20
C-I 5	21	22	21 + 22
C-I 6	23	24	23 + 24
TOTALS			

Educational Management

Area	a	b	a + b
EM 1	25	26	25 + 26
EM 2	27	28	27 + 28
EM 3	29	30	29 + 30
EM 4	31	32	31 + 32
EM 5	33	34	33 + 34
EM 6	35	36	35 + 36
TOTALS			

Behavior Management

Area	a	b	a + b
BM 1	37	38	37 + 38
BM 2	39	40	39 + 40
BM 3	41	42	41 + 42
BM 4	43	44	43 + 44
BM 5	45	46	45 + 46
BM 6	47	48	47 + 48
TOTALS			

Special Education

Area	a	b	a + b
SE 1	49	50	49 + 50
SE 2	51	52	51 + 52
SE 3	53	54	53 + 54
SE 4	55	56	55 + 56
SE 5	57	58	57 + 58
SE 6	59	60	59 + 60
TOTALS			

Compilation

Area	a	b	a + b
D-SA			
C-I			
EM			
BM			
SE			
TOTALS			

Glossary

Abstract Level. A level of conceptualization or thinking that involves the ability to see relationships based on difference and sameness as they pertain to classification and association in all of life's experiences. An abstract response would be that an apple and an orange are both fruit.

Accommodation. Structuring the environment and the academic program to meet the needs of each learner so that the learner can be successful in every aspect of his or her school life.

Achievement Test. An instrument that is designed to determine the degree of knowledge acquired, and/or the level of development reached, within school tasks or a particular area of learning.

Acuity. A sensory-level function that pertains to keenness of sight, hearing, or touch. Acuity is a primary-level function in terms of input where learning is concerned.

Aggressive–Acting Out Behavior. Excessive behavior manifested as disorders of conduct such as being disruptive, negative, uncooperative, destructive, and unable to control agressive impulses.

Aggressive-Passive Behavior. Behavior that has as its basis inner conflict that results from simultaneous feelings of love and hate. It is manifested by poor academic performance.

Amount of Input. The quantity of information that is presented to the learner in a given period of time through any or all of the learning channels.

Analysis. The decoding of information. Analysis and synthesis are the essentials of an integrative system resulting in the formulation of concepts and in the constant evaluation and reevaluation of information.

Analytical Approach. A method of learning. In reading, the learner would begin with a configuration or the whole word and then break it down into its components or sound segments.

Aphasia. A disorder of language or symbolization resulting from neurological impairment that may affect areas of reception (comprehension of the spoken word) or expression. Persons with aphasia lose (partially or completely) their ability to speak, even though they know what they want to say.

Aptitude. The range or degrees of abilities necessary to function successfully in a particular system or situation.

Articulation. The execution of speech. Disorders of speech are manifested in omissions (leaving out sounds), substitutions (*teef* for *teeth*), distortions (lisping), and additions (*skippering* for *skipping*).

Associative Learning. The process of reinforcing learning by relating concepts or new learning to visual, auditory, or tactual associations. Associative learning enables the learner to stabilize (retain) that which has been taught. For example: a word is written on a card, and an associative picture clue is put on the back of the same card.

Attention. The act of focusing (attend) auditorily or visually on stimuli for a period of time without losing the context or content of that which is being presented.

Auditory Channel. All the processes involved in the auditory aspects of learning, including sensory (hearing), perception (localization, attention, discrimination, closure, figure-ground), imagery (memory-sequencing), and auditory language functions (classification and association).

Auditory Language Association. The understanding of noncategorical relationships between words or experiences presented orally. The individual can discern that *boat* goes with *water* rather than with *sky*.

Auditory Language Classification. The understanding of categorical relationships between words or experiences presented orally. The individual can discern that *apple* goes with *peach* rather than with *chair*.

Auditory-to-Auditory Association. The relating of a sound to a sound (phonemes). The student with the ability to make this association can relate the sound of *t* in *time* to the sound of *t* in *touch* and transfer the association to different situations. When presented with three toys, all of which begin with different sounds, the learner will identify the toy that begins with a specific sound indicated by the instructor.

Auditory-to-Visual Association. The relating of a sound to a symbol. The student with the ability to make this association can relate the sound of *m* or its letter name to the written symbol *m* and transfer this association to different contexts, such as an *m* in words printed on the chalkboard or on a paper on a desk.

Aural Processes. Processes that essentially involve hearing.

Balance and Coordination. The ability to use both sides of the body simultaneously, individually, or alternately.

Basal Reading Series. A program for teaching reading that incorporates a sight word vocabulary emphasizing a "look, say" approach within a system of readers, teachers' manuals, and supplementary material.

Baseline Data. Initial data that is based on the frequency of a particular behavior that is occurring, without treatment, within a given period of time.

Behavior Management. A total process that involves dealing effectively with the needs of learners in different educational settings while anticipating, planning for, and attending to, different dimensions of their behavior within a structured environment.

Behavior Modification. A system for controlling or modifying behavior that is based on the principles of operant conditioning. The reinforcement of desired learner behavior is accomplished through the understanding of contingencies, the manipulation of the environment, and the application of appropriate reward systems.

Binocular Fusion. The process of integrating the overlapping portions of the visual fields into a single set of visual information.

Body Image. The inner awareness of self in terms of the location of the parts of the body and their relationship to each other and to the environment.

Body Rhythm. The inner awareness of rhythm in body movement such as walking, running, marching, and keeping time to music.

Capacity. A ceiling that, in effect, places limitations on an individual's potential for achievement in the given areas of learning.

Cerebral Dominance. The dominance of one hemisphere of the brain over the other hemisphere. This is generally considered a prerequisite for the establishment of a preference for using the left or right hand in children.

Checklist. A means of delineating, through observational procedures, the specific areas of learning in order to provide a basis for preliminary decisions in programming and for further evaluation.

Closure. The auditory or visual formulation of a whole word from its component parts. In reading, this is called blending.

Cognitive Style. An individual's unique approach to dealing with new concepts or learning. It includes problem solving, adjustment to life situations, perception of parts-to-whole relationships (analysis) and whole-to-parts relationships (synthesis), and integration of the new information into the present knowledge base.

Compensatory Processing. The utilization of intact learning processes, or open channels, to compensate for deficient learning processes or correlates. If learners cannot remember what they hear, they can use visual or tactual associative clues to help them remember or retain what has been taught.

Conceptualization. The cognitive processing of information or experiences (thinking) at three basic levels:

1. *Concrete level:* A peach is round and has a fuzzy skin.
2. *Functional level:* The peach can be eaten or made into preserves.
3. *Abstract level:* A peach is a fruit.

Conceptual-Thinking Skills. Skills that relate to the interpretation and integration of information in terms of achieving meaning and understanding relationships. These skills include the ability to derive meaning from words, to understand concepts and cause-effect relationships, and to use good judgment.

Concrete Level. The level of thinking, conceptualization, or ideation at which experiences are primarily dealt with descriptively. For example, a pencil is made out of wood; it has lead and an eraser. The concrete level of presentation utilizes concrete objects in introducing concepts to learners.

Contingency Management. Management of the contingencies that involve events, actions, and outcomes for purposes of improving understanding of cause-effect relationships when dealing with the behavior of learners.

Continuous Progress. The rate and amount of learning achieved over an extended period of time. Continual monitoring (observation and documentation), utilizing charting procedures, enables ongoing comparisons of a learner's progress or lack of it in the given areas of learning.

Contracting. Agreeing, in a written document prepared by both the instructor and the learner, to adhere to a specific program or schedule of activities.

Control Factors. Factors that affect the control of learner behavior within the learning environment, a few of which are distractibility, disinhibition, and perseveration.

Convergence. The coordinated movement of the eyes that is necessary for focusing an image on the fovea.

Criterion-Referenced Measurement or Evaluation. A method of determining the level and quality of an individual's performance in relation to specific instructional objectives or criteria.

Critical Skills. Process-oriented skills that are critical for the acquisition of academic tasks, such as reading, writing, spelling, and arithmetic. For example, auditory discrimination is a prerequisite critical skill for learning phonics.

Cueing. A teaching technique used to aid learners with expressive language disorders to retrieve the correct word, e.g., "I kick with my ________?"

Decoding. Assigning meaning to experiences, including verbal behavior (speech, reading, and writing) and nonverbal behavior (gestures, expressions, and body movements).

Deficit Level. Level of learning at which a student is deficient in a specific ability or process. The deficiency is called a learning disability. These deficient processes keep the learner from succeeding at the skills of reading, writing, spelling, and arithmetic. A deficit in auditory discrimination may cause problems with phonics.

Delinquent-Unorthodox Behavior. Behavior, based on a "gang" psychology, that is acceptable and realistic for the peer group but unacceptable in school settings.

Deprivation. The length of time since a reinforcer has been available to an individual.

Developmental Inventories. Tests or checklists for measuring a student's level of functioning in reading, writing, spelling, and arithmetic. They indicate the student's independent, instructional, and frustration levels.

Developmental Skills. A sequence of functional skills that incorporate the process and content necessary for language acquisition, growth, and development. It is used to operationally define learning abilities.

Diagnosis. The analysis of specific strengths and weaknesses of the learner in the subject level areas of learning and the prerequisites, or subskills, that make up these subject level areas.

Directionality. The relationship of an object or point in space to another object or point in space. Difficulty in this developmental skill may result in left-right confusion in reading and writing.

Discrimination. A process under the category of perception that denotes the ability of the learner to discern likenesses and differences between sounds and between symbols.

Disesteemed Learners. Students who perform poorly in school tasks but are not learning disabled, mentally handicapped, or emotionally disturbed. These students fail in school for a variety of reasons and do not ordinarily receive special education services.

Disinhibition. Inability to control one's verbal behavior. For example, learners may get carried away by their own thoughts and offer unrelated responses to that which is being discussed.

Distractibility. "Forced attention" to extraneous stimuli, resulting in poor overall attention and reduced on-task behavior.

Encoding. The aspect of communication that involves output through the acts of motor language expression (manual, body movement, speech and handwriting), verbal language expression (retrieval, syntax, and formulation), and written language expression.

Equivalent Learning. Concepts, behaviors, or skills that are considered to be equally difficult to learn.

Expressive Language. A method of communicating by using words verbally, by writing, or by using gestures that describe or indicate a quality, a function, or a relationship.

Eye-Foot Coordination. Controls of foot movements through the coordination of the eye, foot, and brain, which operate in concert with each other at the automatic level of functioning.

Fading. Showing or prompting learners to enable them to accomplish a particular task, then gradually withdrawing support after they have mastered each step or aspect.

Faulty Learning Responses. Incorrect learning habits established to meet the demands of parents, teachers, and peers to achieve specific tasks. The student may develop an unorthodox pencil grip due to early inappropriate pressure and frustration with beginning writing.

Figurative Language. One of the integrative functions of auditory language association. Learners with problems in this area have difficulty understanding such phrases as "He blew up," meaning he was angry.

Figure-Ground. A sub-category of perception that involves the ability to separate at will what one wishes to attend to visually or auditorily (figure) from the surrounding environment (ground).

Fine Motor (Eye-Hand) Coordination. The purposeful coordinated movements of the hand and eye operating in concert with thought patterns to achieve a specific motor task such as writing, sorting, and sewing.

Fixed-Interval Reinforcement. Reinforcement after a specific interval of time. Example: A student would be reinforced for the first response after a ten-second delay.

Fixed Ratio Reinforcement. Reinforcement that occurs after a specific number of responses. Example: A student would be reinforced after every three responses.

Formal Tests. Tests that have been standardized and are administered under specified conditions, scored according to prescribed regulations, and interpreted in accordance with present criteria that establish reliability and validity.

Formulation. Organization of thought processes into concise patterns for smooth and natural flow of language in verbal expression and writing.

Frustration Level in Reading. The level at which the learner exhibits tension, hesitations, word-by-word reading, and low comprehension. Oral reading is below 93%, and comprehension is below 75%.

Generalization. The transfer of behavior from one situation to similar situations. The greater the similarity between situations the more probable the response.

Grapheme. The visual representation, or symbol, that includes letters, words, and numerals.

Gross Motor Movement. Movement that involves the balance, coordination, and large muscle activity required for efficiency in walking, running, skipping, jumping, and other physical activities.

Gustatory. Related to the sense of taste.

Handedness. The consistent use of one hand over the other.

Haptic Processing. The processing of cutaneous, or tactual (touch), and kinesthetic (body movement) information.

Hierarchial Learning. Concepts, behaviors, or skills, ordered from simple to complex and from easy to hard, that constitute a graduated system of prerequisites for learning higher level tasks.

High-Risk Students. Students who exhibit deficiencies in socialization and in the critical skills prerequisite to success in school tasks such as language arts and arithmetic. Basing their predictions on observation and other testing, examiners predict that these students will become failures in regular class settings as they are presently organized in most public schools.

Hyperactivity. An unusual amount of movement by a learner, considering the learner's age and the physical setting in which the excessive movement is taking place.

Hyperkinesis. Excessive motor activity or mobility.

Imagery. Overall memory including the ability to remember or retain both in sequence and out of sequence that which has been seen, heard, or felt for both long and short periods of time.

Immature-Dependent Behavior. Behavior characterized by a lack of the socialization that is appropriate for the individual's particular age group.

Impulsivity. A tendency to act on impulse, without considering the consequences of the particular act.

Independent Level. The level at which a student will work at ease without having to be under the constant direction of the instructor. In reading, for example, the learner will make less than four errors in one hundred consecutive words with 90% or better comprehension.

Individualized Instruction. An approach to teaching that is based on students' development, interests, abilities, and unique cognitive styles. It involves structuring the environment for each learner with respect to diagnosis, curriculum, educational management, and behavioral management.

Informal Tests. Evaluation that is based primarily on observing behavior. The tests must be scored and the results interpreted in relation to the population that the individual represents and the situation in which the tests are used. Reliability and validity are questionable.

Inhibiting Responses. Holding back or controlling motor expression or behavior because of pressure from parents, teachers, or peers. Learners may expend a great deal of energy, suffer anxiety, and even withdraw if they do not have opportunities to "act out," or "respond motorically," within a structured environment.

Inner-Language. The language of thinking used for the integration of experiences. A native language that can be labeled inner speech.

Input. Any information coming in through the auditory, visual, tactual, kinesthetic, olfactory, or gustatory modalities, the rate, amount, and sequence of which often determine success or failure in school.

Instructional Level. The point at which the teacher's aid is necessary. Following instruction, however, the learners should be able to continue with the material independently. In reading, they should be able to read with at least 93% accuracy in word recognition and 76% or better in comprehension.

Integrated Learning. The effective utilization of mechanical-automatic skills and conceptual-thinking skills for success at academic tasks.

Integration. The assimilation and organization of information and experiences into meaningful relationships that can be used by the learner to better understand self and the relationship of self to the total environment.

Kinesthetic Sense. The awareness of, and adjustment to, one's environment in terms of body movement. The potential for using body movement has not been fully explored in teaching children.

Language. The application of meaning to words and other symbols based on one's experiences; the act of expressing oneself through a motor act or through clear, sequential verbal thought patterns.

Language Arts. The aspects of school curriculum that deal with verbal behaviors, reading, writing, and spelling.

Laterality. The establishment of sidedness and the concomitant ability to relate oneself physically to an object in space.

Leverage Concepts and Skills. Concepts and skills that are partially learned and ready to be stabilized, or fully learned, with additional practice or instruction. They should be taught first in an instructional program.

Linguistic Approach to Reading. A whole-word approach that builds vocabulary on the basis of spelling patterns rather than nonsense syllables. For example, using a consonant-vowel-consonant pattern the consonant *c* combined with the spelling pattern *at* gives *cat*. The consonants *b*, *p*, *m*, etc., added to the same pattern, will give other words.

Listening Comprehension Level. The highest level at which learners can understand 75% of the material read to them.

Localization (Auditory). Locating the source and direction of sound. The learner may have difficulty in discerning that different people have different voices or that a particular voice is specific to one particular person.

Mainstreaming. Providing an instructional program for handicapped students in the least restrictive environment, emphasizing normalization and placement within regular class settings whenever appropriate and possible.

Manipulatives. Materials that involve the learner in a motor act. For example, the learner may build symbols out of clay, draw symbols in wet sand, or work with blocks or beads.

Manual Language Expression. A method of communication by which one expresses the function or quality of an object by using one's hands and other parts of one's body in meaningful gestures.

Maturational Lag. Slower-than-normal development in some of the critical areas of learning. Deficits in the physical, social-emotional, and cognitive processes, if not corrected, will hamper a student in the acquisition of academic skills, even if the student has near average, average, or above average intellectual functioning.

Mechanical-Automatic Skills. Skills that deal with different levels of learning, including sensory, perception, memory, motor, and spatial-temporal orientation.

Memory-Sequencing. The process of storing information for both short and long periods of time and the ability to retrieve this information when necessary and upon request. The effectiveness of this system is dependent on the integrity of the sensory and perceptual areas of learning, as well as the conceptual, integrative, and associative aspects of cognitive development.

Modality. Avenues of input, including auditory, visual, tactual-kinesthetic, olfactory, and gustatory approaches.

Modeling-Imitation. The learning of behavior by observing others demonstrate a response. Learners are likely to imitate, or model, behavior of valued persons in their lives.

Motor. Involving movement or muscular activity.

Multiple Baseline Method. A method of determining whether or not a particular treatment is effective by examining behavior in several individuals simultaneously, establishing a continuum of baselines, and then applying a consecutive treatment program.

Multisensory Approach. The utilization of many modalities, or avenues of input, simultaneously in teaching. The student will see, hear, and touch at the same time when presented a particular task.

Negative Reinforcer. Anything unpleasant or undesirable that strengthens a desired response by terminating or decreasing when that response occurs. Negative reinforcers weaken the undesirable responses that immediately precede their onset.

Nonverbal Language. The assigning of meaning to gestures and expressions (body language) as well as to such cultural phenomena as art, music, holidays, and patriotism.

Norm-Referenced Measurement. A method of comparing an individual's performance with the average performance of the population on which a particular measuring instrument was standardized.

Object Recognition. The integration of visual stimuli into a uniform, recognizable whole. Persons with a dysfunction in this area cannot recognize objects. They tend to focus on the parts.

Ocular Motor Involving Eye Movements. Movements required for visually examining the individual details of an object, for purposes of distinguishing light from no light, seeing fine detail, binocular fusion, convergence, and scanning.

Olfactory. Related to the sense of smell.

On-Task Behavior. Learner activity that is directed specifi cally toward the task as specified by the teacher and not extraneous to the task. For example, when the student is assigned the task of reading, he or she is doing more than just holding the book.

Open Channels. The intact channels (auditory, visual, or tactual-kinesthetic) that provide the learner with accurate information. An open channel includes the various processing levels of sensation, perception, imagery, and language. Helen Keller learned essentially through the tactual-kinesthetic approach (her open channel).

Optimal Teaching Time. The periods or times during the school day when the student is most receptive and responsive to participation in specific educational activities, such as reading and arithmetic.

Output. The processes involved in encoding, including motor responses (manual and body movement) as well as verbal responses (speech, syntax, and formulation).

Overcorrection. A technique designed to decrease undesirable behavior by extending the treatment beyond the correction of a simple act.

Overloading (Jamming). Giving the learner too much input too rapidly. One more spelling word or sound may result in forgetting. Students may fail at the task if they are required to "hold" too much information at a given time.

Overstimulation. Too much input for the learner to cope with, which may result in excessive motor activity, anxiety, poor attention, reduced learning, or any combination of these.

Panic-Coping. The continued attempt to deal with the frustrations imposed by the school and home in response to poor performance that results in anxiety and aggressive behavior.

Perception. A lower level of learning that can be described as more brain function in that it encompasses the subareas of discrimination, figure-ground, closure, and localization and attention as pertains to the visual and auditory processing of information.

Perseveration. The inability to use stop-and-go mechanisms efficiently. The learners tend to repeat an act when it is no longer appropriate. They may have difficulty in shifting from one activity to another. For example, they may repeat the previous response on tests.

Phoneme. The sound that is assigned to a symbol that may be used in different ways (e.g., the *p* in *pen* and the *p* in *spoon* are one phoneme.

Plateau. The level beyond which point the learner makes no significant progress in academic tasks.

Positive Reinforcer. Anything desired by the individual that tends to strengthen the response that has just occurred, making it likely that the response will reoccur.

Premack Principle. The following of a low-probability behavior, such as hanging up one's clothes, with a high-probability behavior, such as watching TV or eating a favorite food.

Prescriptive Teaching. An education program for individual learners that is based on data collected through specific diagnostic procedures.

Primary Reinforcers. Things such as food, drink, warmth, and sexual stimulation that satisfy biological needs, or needs that sustain life.

Psychoanalytical Approach. An approach to dealing with problem behavior that has as its underlying assumption the idea that to effect a change in behavior the individual must undergo a restructuring of the personality.

Psychotic-Neurotic Behavior. Behavior that appears fearful, compulsive, and emotionally exhausting or bizarre and clearly not oriented in reality. The individual displaying such behavior may be self-injurious or harmful to others.

Punishment. Verbal or physical retributive behavior designed to decrease undesirable behavior in the learner.

Rate of Input. How fast information is presented to the learner in a given period of time.

Readability. A formula that can be applied to written material to determine its grade placement.

Reality Therapy. A treatment approach that entails an analysis of opportunities for learner involvement in situations where the instructor makes value judgments about specific behavior and the learners commit themselves to a plan for a sequence of actions that will modify that behavior.

Reauditorization. The retrieval of auditory images.

Receptive language. The application of meaning to words based on experiences in terms of classification and association contingencies.

Reinforcer. A stimulus that results in an increase or strengthening of the behavior it follows. Praise or material rewards given to students are reinforcers if they result in desired behavior.

Reliability. Internal consistency and dependability of a test with respect to what it purports to measure.

Response Cost. A form of treatment in which the learner is penalized (e.g., fined) in some manner for undesirable behavior.

Retrieval. The recall of words for use in speaking and writing.

Revisualization. The recall of visual images, or the seeing of an image in the mind's eye.

Satiation. The overuse of a particular reinforcer to the extent that it loses its value, becoming ineffective.

Scanning. The natural zigzag movements of the eyes when shifting from image to image. This has also been referred to as *visual tracking* and *visual pursuit*. It involves the systematic learned eye movements required for reading.

School Phobia. An unrealistic and overwhelming fear of school settings that may be accompanied by severe anxiety and physical problems.

Screening. A part of the process of assessment that can provide a basis for initial teaching strategies as well as the basis for further in-depth and formal evaluation.

Secondary Reinforcers. Rewards like praise and tokens that are not directly related to biological needs. (Also called conditioned reinforcers.)

Sensation (Sensory). The lowest level of learning, at which the learners receive initial input through their auditory (hearing), visual (seeing), tactual-kinesthetic (feeling), olfactory (smelling), or gustatory (taste) senses.

Sensitive-Withdrawn. The classification of behaviors that is characterized by individuals who appear frustrated in everyday life situations, shy, self-conscious, and insecure and who indicate feelings of poor self-worth.

Sequence of Input. The order of input (visual-auditory-tactual), or presentation of information and material.

Sequencing. Remembering in order that which has been heard, seen, or felt for both long and short periods of time.

Shaping. Taking the learner closer and closer to the desired behavior by rewarding successful approximations in less threatening situations.

Social Perception. The ability to interpret, or glean meaning from, gestures and expressions or understand cause-effect relationships in social situations.

Spacing. The introduction of similar material or concepts far enough apart to avoid confusion of the learner:
t and *d* spaced (aural)
t and *f* spaced (visual)
p and *b spaced (aural and visual).*

Spatial Orientation. The ability of an individual to relate his or her physical self to the environment in terms of distance, size, position, and direction.

Suppression. The act of preventing an image from coming in from a less effective eye in order to avoid a double image. Suppression causes the less effective eye to become nonfunctional.

Symbolization. A synonym for language in that a symbol conveys meaning at both verbal and nonverbal levels.

Syntax. The way in which words are put together to form grammatically correct verbal units or sentences.

Synthesis (Reading). The act of blending, or the fusion of sounds into syllables and syllables into whole words.

Synthetic Approach to Reading. A part-to-whole approach beginning with letter sounds and then blending the sounds into words.

Tachistoscope. A device with which the instructor can control the presentation of visual material words) with precise time exposures.

Tactual. Related to the sense of touch.

Target Behavior. The behavior that is to be modified and the area to which the reinforcement program is directed.

Task Analysis. Analysis of the tasks of reading, writing, spelling, arithmetic, etc., into their basic elements or processes to determine the developmental skills that are prerequisite to their mastery.

Telegraphic Speech. A deficit in verbal language expression under the sub-area of syntax and formulation whereby the learner speaks as a telegram reads (e.g., hungry—give money—go eat).

Temporal Orientation. The ability to order and organize time efficiently.

Time-Out. A technique for modifying behavior by preventing its reinforcement for a given time. The learner is isolated every time he or she does something that is undesirable (target behavior).

Token Reinforcers. Objects, such as metal or colored discs, that are exchanged for tangible rewards.

Transition Writing Approach. A bridging technique that takes learners from manuscript to cursive writing by using connecting dots and tracing.

Treatment Period. The period (following the initial, or

baseline, period) during which the treatment program is implemented.

Understimulated. Having insufficient input, resulting in a poor learning environment where learners exhibit little motivation or interest.

Validity. The degree to which a test measures what it purports to measure.

Variable-Interval Reinforcement. Reinforcement after different intervals of time. For example, while working, the student gets a reinforcer after 10 seconds, then after 15 seconds, and then after 5 seconds, with the intervals averaging 10 seconds.

Variable Ratio Reinforcement. Reinforcement that occurs after a varying number of responses. For example, the student would be rewarded after 1 response, then after 5 responses, and then after 3 responses, with the number of responses between reinforcers averaging 3.

Verbal Language Expression. A sub-area under receptive language that includes word retrieval, syntax, and formulation.

Visual Channel. All of the processes involved in the visual aspects of learning, including sensation, perception, imagery, and language, as well as the related areas of visual motor integration.

Visual Language Association. The cognitive ability to understand noncategorical relationships between pictures of objects or experiences. The individual can discern that a picture of a pen goes with a picture of a pencil rather than with a picture of a bucket.

Visual Language Classification. The cognitive ability to understand categorical relationships between objects or experiences presented visually. The individual can discern that a picture of an airplane goes with a picture of a car rather than with a picture of a tree.

Visual Language Graphic Association. Expression that requires the learner to use words to express ideas, events, or concepts in writing in a meaningful manner, using grammatically correct sentence structure.

Visual Language Symbol Association. The use of symbols in the process of decoding (learning and communication), including relating letters to words and associating words to ideas and concepts.

Visual-Motor Coordination. The synchronization of the eyes with the movements of the hand and the thought processes of the brain. Efficiency of these three processes operating in concert with each other is required for handwriting and other motor tasks.

Word Caller. A learner who has mastered the mechanics of reading words but cannot apply meaning to the words based on his or her experiences.

Bibliography

GENERAL

Abeson, A.; Bolick, N.; and Hass, J. *A Primer on Due Process*. Reston, Va.: Council for Exceptional Children, 1976.

Aiello, B. "A Very Special Special Teacher." *Teaching Exceptional Children* 9: (1976):4–5.

Albert, R. S. "Toward a Behavior Definition of Genius." *The American Psychologist,* February 1975, pp. 140–151.

Anderson, E. M. *The Disabled School Child: A Study of Integration in the Primary Schools*. London: Methuen, 1973.

Ausubel, D. P., and Sullivan, E. V. *Theory and Problems of Child Development.* 2d ed. New York: Grune & Stratton, 1970.

Bachara, G. H., and Zaba, J. N. "Learning Disabilities and Juvenile Delinquency." *Journal of Learning Disabilities* 11, (1978):242–246.

Bangs, T. *Language and Learning Disorders of the Pre-Academic Child.* Englewood Cliffs, N.J.: Prentice-Hall, 1968.

Becker, W. C. *Parents Are Teachers.* Champaign, Ill.: Research Press, 1971.

Bereiter, C., and Englemann, S. *Teaching Disadvantaged Children in the Preschool.* Englewood Cliffs, N.J.: Prentice-Hall, 1966.

Berry, K. E. *Remedialdiagnosis*. San Rafael, Calif.: Dimensions Publishing, 1968.

Bertness, H. J. "Progressive Inclusion: The Mainstream Movement in Tacoma." In *Mainstreaming: Origins and Implications,* edited by M. C. Reynolds, pp. 55–58. Reston, Va.: Council for Exceptional Children, 1976.

Bijou, S. W. "What Psychology Has to Offer Education—Now." *Journal of Applied Behavior Analysis* 3 (1970):65–71.

Birch, H., ed. *Brain Damage in Children: The Biological and Social Aspects*. Baltimore: Williams and Wilkins, 1964.

Birch, H., and Belmost, L. "Auditory-Visual Integration in Brain-Damaged and Normal Children." *Developmental Medicine and Child Neurology* 20 (1965):135–144.

Birch, H., and Gussow, J. *Disadvantaged Children: Health, Nutrition and School Failure.* New York: Grune & Stratton, 1970.

Birch, J. W. *Mainstreaming: Educable Mentally Retarded Children in Regular Classes*. Reston, Va.: Council for Exceptional Children, 1974.

Birch, J. W. *Hearing Impaired Children in the Mainstream.* Reston, Va.: The Council for Exceptional Children, 1975.

Blatt, B., and Kaplan, F. *Christmas in Purgatory.* Boston: Allyn and Bacon, 1967.

Bloom, B. "Learning for Mastery." *Evaluation Comment,* vol. 1, May 1968. (Center for the Study of Evaluation, University of California at Los Angeles.)

Bloom, B. S.; Englehart, M. D.; Furst, E. J.; Hill, W. H.; and Krathwohl, D. R. *A Taxonomy of Educational Objectives: Handbook I, The Cognitive Domain.* New York: McKay, 1956.

Blumenfeld, S. L. *The New Illiterates—and How to Keep Your Child from Becoming One.* New Rochelle, N.Y.: Arlington House, 1974.

Boston, R. E. *How to Write and Use Performance Objectives to Individualize Instruction.* Vol. I, *How to Analyze Performance Outcomes.* Englewood Cliffs, N.J.: Educational Technology Publications, 1972.

Brickell, H. M. "Seven Key Notes on Minimal Competency Testing." *Educational Leadership* 35 (1978):551–557.

Bruce, W. "The Parents' Role from an Educator's Point of View." In *The Hearing Impaired Child in the Regular Classroom,* edited by W. H. Northcott. Washington, D.C.: A. G. Bell Association for the Deaf, 1973.

Bruner, J. *The Process of Education.* Harvard University Press, 1960.

Bryngelson, B., and Glaspey, E. *Speech in the Classroom.* 3d ed. Chicago: Scott, Foresman and Co., 1962.

Butts, R. F.; Peckenpaugh, D. H.; and Kirschenbaum, H. *The School's Role as Moral Authority.* Washington, D.C.: Association for Supervision and Curriculum Development, 1977.

Campbell, D. "Blind Children in the 'Normal' Environment." *Understanding the Child,* June 1955, pp. 73–76.

Cantrell, R. P., and Cantrell, M. L. "Preventive Mainstreaming: Impact of a Supportive Service Program on Children." *Exceptional Children* 42 (1976):381–385.

Career Education Current Trends in School Policies and Programs. Arlington, Va.: National School Public Relations Association, 1974.

Carrell, J. A. *Disorders of Articulation.* Englewood Cliffs, N.J.: Prentice-Hall, 1968.

Chalfant, J. C., and Scheffelin, M. A. *Central Processing Dysfunctions in Children: A Review of Research.* NINDS Monograph, No. 9. Bethesda, Md.: U.S. Department of Health, Education and Welfare, 1969.

Chomsky, N. *Aspects of the Theory of Syntax.* Cambridge, Mass.: MIT Press, 1965.

Clark, E. V. "Some Aspects of the Conceptual Basis for First Language Acquisition." In *Language Perspectives - Acquisition, Retardation and Intervention,* edited by R. L. Schiefelbusch and L. L. Lloyds. Baltimore: University Park Press, 1974.

Clark, G. M. "Career Education for the Mildly Handicapped." *Focus on Exceptional Children* 5 (1974):1–10.

Cruickshank, W. M., ed. *The Teacher of Brain-Injured Children.* Syracuse: Syracuse University Press, 1966.

Cruickshank, W. M. *Brain-Injured Child in Home, School, and Community.* Syracuse: Syracuse University Press, 1967.

Cruickshank, W. M., Bentzen, F.: Ratzeburg, F.: and Tannhauser, M. *A Teaching Method for Brain-Injured and Hyperactive Children.* Syracuse· Syracuse University Press, 1961.

Cruickshank, W. M., and Hallahan, D. P., eds. *Perceptual and Learning Disabilities in Children.* Vol. 1, *Psychoeducational Practices.* Syracuse: Syracuse University Press, 1975.

Dembinski, R. J., and Mauser, A. J. "What Parents of the Learning Disabled Really Want from Professionals." *Journal of Learning Disabilities* 10 (1977):578–584.

Deno, E. "Special Education as Development Capital." *Exceptional Children* 37 (1970):229–237.

DePauw, K. "Enhancing the Sensory Integration of Aphasic Students." *Journal of Learning Disabilities* 11 (1978): 142–146.

Dunlap, J. M. "Gifted Children in an Enriched Program." *Exceptional Children* 22 (1955):135–137.

Dunn, L. M. *Peabody Picture Vocabulary Test.* Minneapolis: American Guidance Service, 1959.

Dunn, L. M., ed. *Exceptional Children in the Schools: Special Education in Transition.* 2d ed. New York: Holt, Rinehart & Winston, 1973.

Dunn, L. M. Special Education for the Mildly Retarded—Is Much of It Justifiable? *Exceptional Children* 35 (1968):5–22.

Edgington, R. E. "SLD Children: A Ten-Year Follow-Up." *Academic Therapy* 11 (1975):53–64.

Egg, M. *Educating the Child Who Is Different.* New York: John Day Co., 1968.

Ekwall, E. E. *Diagnosis and Remediation of the Disabled Reader.* Boston: Allyn and Bacon, 1976.

Engelmann, S. E. "Relationship Between Psychological Theories and the Act of Teaching." *Journal of School Psychology* 5 (1967):93–100.

Federal Register, vol. 41 (Thursday, December 30, 1976), pp. 56966–56998. *Public Law 94–142.*

Fine, B. *Underachievers: How They Can Be Helped.* New York: E. P. Dutton & Co. 1967.

Frankenburg, W. "Increasing the Lead Time for the Preschool Age Handicapped Child." In *Not All Little Wagons Are Red,* edited by M. Karnes. Arlington, Va.: Council for Exceptional Children, 1973.

French, J. L. *Educating the Gifted: A Book of Readings.* New York: Holt, Rinehart & Winston, 1959.

Frierson, E., and Barbe, W., eds. *Educating Children with Learning Disabilities.* New York: Prentice-Hall, 1967.

Frostig, M., and Horne, D. "Marianne Frostig Center of Education Therapy." In *Special Education Programs Within the United States,* edited by M. Jones. Springfield, Ill.: Charles C Thomas, 1968.

Gallagher, J. *Teaching the Gifted Child.* 2d ed. Boston: Allyn and Bacon, 1975.

Gallistel, E. R. "Setting Goals and Objectives for LD Children—Process and Problems." *Journal of Learning Disabilities* 11 (1978):64–71.

Gardner, W. I. *Learning and Behavioral Characteristics of Exceptional Children and Youth: A Humanistic Behavioral Approach.* Boston: Allyn and Bacon, 1977.

Gartner, A.; Kohler, M. C.; and Reissman, F. *Children Teach Children: Learning to Read.* New York: Harper & Row, 1971.

Gearheart, B. R. *Learning Disabilities: Educational Strategies.* St. Louis: C. V. Mosby Co., 1973.

Gearheart, B. R. *Teaching the Learning Disabled: A Combined Task-Process Approach.* St. Louis: C. V. Mosby Co., 1976.

Gearheart, B., and Weishahn, M. *The Handicapped Child in the Regular Classroom.* St. Louis: C. V. Mosby Co., 1976.

Getman, G. *How to Develop Your Child's Intelligence.* Luverne, Minn.: G. N. Getman, O. D., 1962.

Glasser, W. *Schools Without Failure.* New York: Harper & Row, 1969.

Golden, N., and Steiner, S. "Auditory and Visual Functions in Good and Poor Readers." *Journal of Learning Disabilities* 2 (1969):476–481.

Goldhammer, K.; Rader, B. T.; and Reuschlein, P. *Mainstreaming: Teacher Competencies.* East Lansing: College of Education, Michigan State University, April 1977.

Good, T. "Which Pupils Do Teachers Call On?" *Elementary School Journal* 70 (1970):190–198.

Good, T., and Brophy, J. *Looking in Classrooms.* New York: Harper & Row, 1973.

Gordon, T., with Burch, N. *Teacher Effectiveness Training.* New York: Wyden, 1975.

Gorham, K. A. "A Lost Generation of Parents." *Exceptional Children* 41 (1975): 521–525.

Gourley, T. J., Jr. "Programs for Gifted Students: A National Survey." *Talents and Gifts,* June 1976, pp. 31–32.

Grotsky, J.; Sabatino, D.; and Ohrtman, W., eds. *The Concept of Mainstreaming.* King of Prussia: Eastern Pennsylvania Regional Resources Center for Special Education, 1976.

Grzynkowicz, W. *Meeting the Needs of Learning Disabled Children in the Regular Class.* Springfield, Ill.: Charles C Thomas, 1975.

Guilford, J. *The Nature of Human Intelligence.* New York: McGraw-Hill Book Co., 1967.

Hallahan, D. P., and Cruickshank, W. *Psychoeducational Foundations of Learning Disabilities.* Englewood Cliffs, N. J.: Prentice-Hall, 1973.

Hallahan, D. P., and Kauffman, J. M. *Introduction to Learning Disabilities: A Psycho-Behavioral Approach.* Englewood Cliffs, N. J.: Prentice-Hall, 1976.

Hammill, D., and Bartel, N. eds. *Educational Perspectives in Learning Disabilities.* New York: John Wiley & Sons, 1971.

Haring, N. G., and Bateman, B. *Teaching the Learning Disabled Child.* Englewood Cliffs, N. J.: Prentice-Hall, 1977.

Haring, N. G., and Krug, D. A. "Placement in Regular Programs: Procedures and Results." *Exceptional Children* 41 (1974):413–417.

Haring, N. G., and Schiefelbusch, R. L., eds. *Methods in Special Education.* New York: McGraw-Hill Book Co., 1967.

Haring, N. G., and Schiefelbusch, R. L., eds. *Teaching Special Children.* New York: McGraw-Hill, 1976.

Hebb, D. O. *The Organization of Behavior.* New York: John Wiley and Sons, 1949.

Hebb, D. O. "A Neuropsychological Theory." In *Psychology: A Study of a Science,* edited by S. Kock. New York: McGraw-Hill Book Co., 1959.

Hellmuth, J., ed. *The Special Child in Century 21.* Seattle, Wash.: Special Child Publications, 1964.

Hellmuth, J., ed. *Learning Disorders.* Vols. 1–4. Seattle, Wash.: Special Child Publications, 1965–1971.

Heron, T. "Maintaining the Mainstreamed Child in the Regular Classroom: The Decision-Making Process." *Journal of Learning Disabilities* 11 (1978):210–216.

Hewett, F. *The Emotionally Disturbed Child in the Classroom.* Boston: Allyn and Bacon, 1968.

Hewett, F. M., and Forness, S. R., eds. 2d ed. *Education of Exceptional Learners.* Boston: Allyn and Bacon, 1977.

Hildreth, G. H. *Educating Gifted Children at Hunter College Elementary School.* New York: Harper & Row, 1952.

Hull, F. M. and Hull, M. E. "Children with Oral Communication Disabilities." In *Exceptional Children in the Schools,* edited by L. M. Dunn. New York: Holt, Rinehart & Winston, 1973.

Hunt, J. McV. *Intelligence and Experience.* New York: Ronald Press, 1961.

Ilg, F., and Ames, L. *School Readiness: Behavior Tests Used at the Gesell Institute.* New York: Harper & Row, 1964.

Jackson, D. M., and Boston, B. O. "The Future of the Gifted and Talented." *The School Psychologist,* Summer 1976, pp. 4–15.

Janowitz, G. *Helping Hands.* Chicago: The University of Chicago Press, 1966.

Jansky, J., and deHirsch, K. *Preventing Reading Failure.* New York: Harper & Row, 1972.

Johnson, D., and Myklebust, H. *Learning Disabilities: Educational Principles and Practices.* New York: Grune & Stratton, 1967.

Johnson, D. W., and Johnson, R. T. *Learning Together and Alone.* Englewood Cliffs, N. J.· Prentice-Hall, 1975.

Johnson, G. O. "Special Education for the Mentally Handicapped . . . A Paradox." *Exceptional Children* 19 (1962):62–69.

Johnson, R.; Weatherman, R.; and Rehmann, A., eds. *Handicapped Youth and the Mainstream Educator,* Vol. 4 of Leadership Series in Special Education. Minneapolis: Audio Visual Library Service, University of Minnesota, 1975.

Jones, R. L., ed. *Mainstreaming and the Minority Child.* Reston, Va.: The Council for Exceptional Children, 1976.

Jones, V., ed. *Special Education Programs within the United States.* Springfield, Ill.: Charles C Thomas, 1968.

Jordan, J., ed. *Teacher, Please Don't Close the Door.* Reston, Va.: The Council for Exceptional Children, 1976.

Jordan, J.; Hayden, A.; Karnes, M.; and Wood, M., eds. *Early Childhood Education for Exceptional Children.* Reston, Va.: The Council for Exceptional Children, 1977.

Joyce, B., and Weil, M. *Models of Teaching.* Englewood Cliffs, N. J.: Prentice-Hall, 1972.

Kaplan, S. N. *Providing Programs for the Gifted and Talented: A Handbook.* Ventura, Calif.: Ventura County Schools, 1974.

Keogh, B. "What Research Tells Us About Mainstreaming." In *Mainstreaming: Controversy and Consensus,* edited by P. O'Donnell and R. Bradfield, pp. 25–38. San Rafael, Calif.: Academic Therapy, 1976.

Kephart, N. *Learning Disabilities: An Educational Adventure.* West Lafayette, Ind.: Kappa Delta Pi Press, 1968.

Kephart, N. *The Slow Learner in the Classroom.* 2d ed. Columbus, Ohio: Charles E. Merrill, 1971.

King-Stoops, J. "Critical Factors in Certain Innovative British Schools." *Phi Delta Kappan,* November 1974, p. 215.

Koppitz, E. *Children with Learning Disabilities: A Five Year Follow-up Study.* New York: Grune & Stratton, 1971.

Koppitz, E. M. "Special Class Pupils with Learning Disabilities: A Five-Year Follow-up Study." *School Psychology Digest,* Winter 1976, pp. 45–50.

Kotin, L., and Eager, N. *Due Process in Special Education: A Legal Analysis.* Cambridge, Mass.: Research Institute for Educational Problems, 1977.

Krager, J., and Safer, D. "Type and Prevalence of Medication Used in the Treatment of Hyperactive Children." *New England Journal of Medicine* 291 (1974):1118–1120.

Krathwohl, D.; Bloom, B.; and Masia, B. *Taxonomy of Educational Objectives: The Classification of Educational Goals. Handbook 2: The Affective Domain.* New York: McKay, 1964. Appendix A, pp. 176–185.

Kronick, D. "The Importance of a Sociological Perspective Towards Learning Disabilities." *Journal of Learning Disabilities* 9 (1976):115–119.

Lance, W. D. "Who Are All the Children?" *Exceptional Children* 43 (1976):66–76.

Lerner, J. *Children With Learning Disabilities.* 2d ed. Boston: Houghton Mifflin, 1976.

Lilly, M. S. "Special Education: A Teapot in a Tempest." *Exceptional Children* 37 (1970):43–49.

Lindsley, O. R. "From Skinner to Precision Teaching: The Child Knows Best." In *Let's Try Doing Something Else Kind of Thing: Behavior Principles and the Exceptional Child,* edited by J. B. Jordan and L. S. Robbins, pp. 2–11. Reston, Va.: The Council for Exceptional Children, 1972.

Lott, L.; Hudak, B.; and Scheetz, J. *Strategies and Techniques for Mainstreaming: A Resource Room Handbook.* Monroe, Mich.: Monroe County School District, 1975.

Love, H. D. *Educating Exceptional Children in Regular Classrooms.* Springfield, Ill.: Charles C Thomas, 1975.

Lovitt, T. C. "Applied Behavior Analysis and Learning Disabilities. Part I: Characteristics of ABA, General Recommendations, and Methodological Limitations." *Journal of Learning Disabilities* 8 (1975):432–443.

Lovitt, T. C. "Applied Behavior Analysis and Learning Disabilities. Part II: Specific Research Recommendations and Suggestions for Practitioners." *Journal of Learning Disabilities* 8 (1975):504–518.

McCarthy, J. J., and McCarthy, J. F. *Learning Disabilities.* Boston: Allyn and Bacon, 1969.

McLeod, P. *The Underdeveloped Learner.* Springfield, Ill.: Charles C Thomas, 1968.

McLoughlin, J. A., and Kass, C. "Resource Teachers: Their Role. *Learning Disability Quarterly* 1 (1978):56–62.

MacMillan, D.; Jones, R. L.; and Meyers, C. E. "Mainstreaming the Mildly Retarded: Some Questions, Cautions, and Guidelines." *Mental Retardation* 14 (1976): 3–10.

McNeill, D. *The Acquisition of Language.* New York: Harper & Row, 1970.

Mallison, R. *Education as Therapy.* Seattle, Wash.: Special Child Publications, 1968.

Mann, P. "Dyslexia, An Educator's View." *Florida Medical Association* 56 (January 1969):24–27.

Mann, P. "Learning Disabilities: A Critical Need for Trained Teachers." *Journal of Learning Disabilities* 2 (February, 1969):32–38.

Mann, P. H., ed. *Mainstream Special Education: Issues and Perspectives in Urban Centers.* Reston, Va.: The Council for Exceptional Children, 1975.

Mann, P. H., ed. *Shared Responsibility for Handicapped Students: Advocacy and Programming.* Miami: Banyan Books, 1976.

Mann, P. H. "Training Teachers to Work with the Handicapped." *The National Elementary Principal* 58 (1978):14–20.

Mann, P. H., and Barry, M. eds. *The Norfolk Experience: A Planning Design for Exceptional Child Component.* Washington, D.C.: National Teacher Corps, 1976.

Mann, P. H., Cawley, J. F.; Calder, C. R.; Ramanauskas, S.; Suiter, P.; and McClung, R. M. *Behavior Resource Guide.* Wallingford, Conn.: Educational Sciences, Inc., 1973.

Mann, P. H., and McClung, R. M. "A Learning Problems Approach to Teacher Education." In *Instructional Alternatives for Exceptional Children,* edited by E. Deno, pp. 11–21. Reston, Va.: The Council for Exceptional Children, 1973.

Mann, P. H., and McClung, R. M. "Perspectives for Staff Development: A Collaborative Design." In *The Range of Variability,* edited by S. Massey and R. Henderson. Durham, N. H.: New England Teacher Corps Network, 1978.

Mann, P. H.; McClung, R. M.; and Suiter, P. A. *Handbook of Suggestions for Tutorial Use.* Pathfinder: Allyn and Bacon Reading Program. Boston: Allyn and Bacon, 1979.

Mann, P. H.; McClung, R. M.; and Suiter, P. A. The Hilltop Series: An Individualized Program for Problem Readers. Boston: Allyn and Bacon, 1977–1979.

Mann, P. H.; McClung, R. M.; Suiter, P. A.; Cawley, J.; Calder, C.; and Ramanauskas, S. *Project Mainstream I and II.* Tulsa, Educational Progress Co., 1976.

Mauser, A. J. "As I See It: The Gifted Handicapped." *Talents and Gifts,* November 1975, p. 30.

Menyuk, P. *The Acquisition and Development of Language.* Englewood Cliffs, N.J.: Prentice-Hall, 1971.

Menyuk, P. *The Development of Speech.* Indianapolis: Bobbs-Merrill, 1972.

Mercer, J. R. "Cultural Pluralism and the Standardized Testing Movement." In *Ethical and Legal Factors in the Practice of School Psychology,* edited by G. R. Gredler. Harrisburg, Pa.: State Department of Education, 1974.

Miles, M. B. *Innovation in Education.* New York: Bureau of Publications, Teachers College, Columbia University, 1964.

Miller, R. B. "Task Analysis: Sources and Futures." *Improving Human Performance* 2 (1973):5–27.

Money, J., ed. *The Disabled Reader: Education of the Dyslexic Child.* Baltimore: Johns Hopkins Press, 1966.

Montessori, M. *The Montessori Method.* Translated from the Italian by Anne E. George. Cambridge, Mass.: Robert Bentley, Inc., 1965.

Mullins, J. B. "Integrated Classrooms." *Journal of Rehabilitation,* Vol. 37, no. 2 (1971), pp. 14–16.

Myers, P., and Hammill, D. *Methods for Learning Disorders.* 2d ed. New York: John Wiley & Sons, 1976.

Myklebust, H. *The Psychology of Deafness: Sensory Deprivation, Learning and Adjustment.* 2d ed. New York: Grune & Stratton, 1964.

Myklebust, H., ed. *Progress in Learning Disabilities.* Vol. 1. New York: Grune & Stratton, 1968.

Nagi, S. "Child Abuse and Neglect Programs: A National Review." *Children Today* 4 (1975):12–17.

Newcomer, P. "Special Education Services for the Mildly Handicapped." *Journal of Special Education* 14 (1977):85–92.

Northcott, W. H., ed. *The Hearing Impaired Child in a Regular Classroom: Preschool, Elementary, and Secondary Years.* Washington, D.C.: A. G. Bell Association, 1973.

Oakland, T. "Assessment, Education, and Minority-Group Children." *Academic Therapy* 10 (1974):133–140.

O'Donnell, P., and Bradfield, R. *Mainstreaming: Controversy and Consensus* San Rafael, Calif.: Academic Therapy Publications, 1976.

Parker, C. A., ed. *Psychological Consultation: Helping Teachers Meet Special Needs.* Reston, Va.: The Council for Exceptional Children, 1975.

Payne, J. S.; Kauffman, J. M.; Brown, G. B.; and DeMott, R. M. *Exceptional Children in Focus: Incidents, Concepts, and Issues in Special Education.* Columbus: Charles E. Merrill, 1974.

Payne, J. S.; Mercer, C. D.; and Epstein, M. H. *Education and Rehabilitation Techniques.* New York: Behavioral Publications, 1974.

Prouty, R., and McGarry, F. M. The Diagnostic/Prescriptive Teacher. In *Instructional Alternatives for Exceptional Children,* edited by E. Deno. Reston, Va.: The Council for Exceptional Children, 1972.

Rappaport, S., ed. *Childhood Aphasia and Brain Damage: A Definition.* Narberth, Pa.: Livingston, 1964.

Reger, R.; Schroeder, W.; and Uschold, K. *Special Education.* New York: Oxford University Press, 1968.

Renzulli, J. S. *New Directions in Creativity.* New York: Harper & Row, 1975.

Reynolds, Maynard C., and Balow, Bruce. "Categories and Variables in Special Education." *Exceptional Children* 38 (January 1972):357–366.

Reynolds, M. C., and Birch, J. W. *Teaching Exceptional Children in All America's Schools.* Reston, Va.: The Council for Exceptional Children, 1977.

Riesman, D. "Notes on Meritocracy." *Daedalus* 96 (1969): 905.

Riessman, F. *The Culturally Deprived Child.* New York: Harper & Row, 1962.

Ring, B. C. "Memory Processes and Children with Learning Problems." *Academic Therapy* 11 (1975):111–116.

Rosner, J. *Helping Children Overcome Learning Difficulties.* New York: Walker and Co., 1975.

Ross, A. O. *Psychological Aspects of Learning Disabilities and Reading Disorders.* New York: McGraw-Hill, 1976.

Russo, J. R., ed. "Mainstreaming Handicapped Students: Are Your Facilities Suitable?" *Education Digest* 40 (1975):18–21.

Sabatino, D. A., and Mauser, A. J. *Intervention Strategies for Specialized Secondary Education.* Boston: Allyn and Bacon, 1978.

Sabatino, D. A., and Mauser, A. J. *Specialized Education in Today's Secondary Schools.* Boston: Allyn and Bacon, 1978.

Sabatino, D. A.; Ysseldyke, J. E.; and Woolston, J. "Diagnostic-Prescriptive Perceptual Training with Mentally Retarded Children." *American Journal of Mental Deficiency* 78 (1973):7–14.

Siegel, E. *Helping the Brain-Injured Child.* New York: Association for Brain Injured Children, 1962.

Siegel, Ernest. *Special Education in the Regular Classroom.* New York: John Day Co., 1969.

Siegel, M. "Teacher Behaviors and Curriculum Packages: Implications for Research and Teacher Education." In *Handbook of Curriculum,* edited by L. J. Rubin. Boston: Allyn and Bacon, 1976.

Simches, R. F. "The Inside Outsider." *Exceptional Children* 37 (1970):5–15.

Simpson, D. *Learning to Learn.* Columbus: Charles E. Merrill Co., 1968.

Skinner,. B. F. *The Technology of Teaching.* New York: Appleton-Century-Crofts, 1968.

Smith, F. *Comprehension and Learning: A Conceptual Framework for Teachers.* New York: Holt, Rinehart & Winston, 1975.

Smith, R. M. *Clinical Teaching: Methods of Instruction for the Retarded.* New York: McGraw-Hill, 1968.

Smith, W. "Ending the Isolation of the Handicapped." In *The Range of Variability,* edited by S. Massey and R. Henderson. Durham, N. H.: New England Teacher Corps Network, 1977.

Solomon, B. "Using Videotape to Motivate the LD Student." *Academic Therapy* 11 (1976):271–274.

Special Education for Handicapped Children, First Annual Report of the National Advisory Committee on Handicapped Children. Washington, D.C.: Office of Education, Dept. of Health, Education, and Welfare, 1968.

Staats, A. *Learning, Language, and Cognition.* New York: Holt, Rinehart & Winston, 1968.

Stewart, C. J., and Cash, W. B. *Interviewing: Principles and Practices.* Dubuque, Iowa: Brown, 1974.

Stick, S. "The Speech Pathologist and Handicapped Learners." *Journal of Learning Disabilities* 9 (1976):509–519.

Strauss, A., and Kephart, N. *Psychopathology and Education of the Brain-Injured Child.* Vol. 1, *Progress in Theory and Clinic.* New York: Grune & Stratton, 1955.

Terman, L. M. *Mental and Physical Traits of a Thousand Gifted Children,* vol. 1. *Genetic Studies of Genius.* Stanford, Calif.: Stanford University Press, 1925.

Terman, L. M. "The Discovery and Encouragement of Exceptional Talent." *American Psychologist* 8 (1954):221–230.

Terman, L. M., and Oden, M. *The Gifted Group at Midlife,* vol. 5. *Genetic Studies of Genius.* Stanford, Calif.: Stanford University Press, 1959.

Terman, L. M. and Oden, M. "The Stanford Studies of the Gifted." In *The Gifted Child,* edited by P. Witty. Boston: D. C. Heath, 1951.

Tobias, S. "Achievement Treatment Interactions." *Review of Educational Research* 46 (1976):61–74.

Torgesen, J. K. "The Role of Nonspecific Factors in the Task Performance of Learning Disabled Children: A Theoretical Assessment." *Journal of Learning Disabilities* 10 (1977):27–34.

Torrance, E. P. *They Shall Create: Gifted Minority Children* (cassette, side 1). Reston, Va.: The Council for Exceptional Children, 1973.

Travers, J. *Learning Analysis and Application*. New York: Van Rees, 1965.

Valett, R. *Programming Learning Disabilities*. Palo Alto, Calif.: Fearon Publishers, 1969.

Valett, R. *Prescriptions for Learning*. Palo Alto, Calif.: Fearon Publishers, 1970.

Valett, R. *The Remediation of Learning Disabilities*. Palo Alto, Calif.: Fearon Publishers, 1974.

Wallace, G. "Interdisciplinary Efforts in Learning Disabilities: Issues and Recommendations. *Journal of Learning Disabilities* 9 (1976):520–526.

Wallace, G., and Kauffman, J. M. *Teaching Children with Learning Problems*. 2d ed. Columbus, Ohio: Charles E. Merrill, 1978.

Wallace, G., and McLoughlin, J. A. *Learning Disabilities: Concepts and Characteristics*. Columbus, Ohio: Charles E. Merrill, 1975.

Wasserman, E.; Asch, H.; and Snyder, D. "A Neglected Aspect of Learning Disabilities: Energy Level Output." *Journal of Learning Disabilities* 5 (March 1972):130–135.

Weinberg, R., and Wood, F., eds. *Observation of Pupils and Teachers in Mainstream and Special Education Settings: Alternative Strategies*. Reston, Va.: The Council for Exceptional Children, 1975.

Weintraub, F. J.; Abeson, A.; Ballard, J.; and LaVor, M. L., eds. *Public Policy and the Education of Exceptional Children*. Reston, Va.: The Council for Exceptional Children, 1976.

Wiig, E. H., and Semel, E. M. *Language Disabilities in Children and Adolescents*. Columbus, Ohio: Charles E. Merrill, 1976.

Wooden, H. E.; Lisowski, S.; and Early, F. "Volunteers, Head Start Children and Development." *Academic Therapy* 11 (1976):449–454.

Wright, H. F. *Recording and Analyzing Child Behavior*. New York: Harper & Row, 1967.

Young, M. *Teaching Children with Special Learning Needs*. New York: John Day Co., 1967.

Ysseldyke, J. E., and Salvia, J. "A Critical Analysis of the Assumptions Underlying Diagnostic-Prescriptive Teaching. *Exceptional Children* 41 (1974):181–195.

Diagnosis-Student Assessment

Adams, G. *Measurement in Education, Psychology, and Guidance*. New York: Holt, Rinehart, and Winston, 1964.

Adamson, G.; Shrago, M.; and Van Etten, G. *Basic Educational Skills Inventory: Math (Level A and Level B)*. Olathe, Kans.: Select-Ed., 1972.

Ahr, E. *Screening Test of Academic Readiness*. Skokie, Ill.: Priority Innovations, 1966.

American Medical Association. *Cardboard Snellen Charts for School Use*. Chicago.

Ayres, A. J. *Southern California Figure-Ground Visual Perception Test*. Los Angeles: Western Psychological Services, 1966.

Baker, H., and Leland, B. *Detroit Tests of Learning Aptitude*. Indianapolis: Test Division of Bobbs-Merrill Co., 1959.

Baldwin, A. Y. "Tests Can Underpredict: A Case Study." *Phi Delta Kappan* 58 (1977):620–621.

Bausch and Lomb. *Ortho-Rater*. Rochester, N.Y.: 1958.

Beery, K., and Buktenica, N.A. *Developmental Test of Visual Motor Integration: Administration and Scoring Manual*. Chicago: Follett Educational Corp., 1967.

Bellak, L. *Thematic Apperception Test*. New York: C. P. S. Co., 1954.

Bellak, L., and Bellak, S. *Children's Apperception Test*. New York: C. P. S. Co., 1949–1955.

Bender, L. *A Visual-Motor Gestalt Test and Its Clinical Use*. New York: American Orthopsychiatric Association, 1938.

Benton, A. *Left-Right Discrimination and Finger Localization*. New York: Hoeber-Harper, 1959.

Benton, A. *The Revised Visual Retention Test: Clinical and Experimental Application*. New York: Psychological Corp., 1963.

Bieliauskas, V. *The House-Tree-Person (H-T-P) Research Review*. Los Angeles: Western Psychological Services, 1963.

Black, F. W. "Achievement Test Performance of High and Low Achieving Learning Disabled Children." *Journal of Learning Disabilities* 7 (1974):179–182.

Blackhurst, A. E.; Cross, D. P.; Nelson, C. M.; and Tawney, J. W. "Approximating Noncategorical Teacher Education." *Exceptional Children* 39 (1973):284–288.

Boehm Test of Basic Concepts. New York: Psychological Corp., 1970.

Boston University Speech Sound Discrimination Picture Test. Boston: Boston University School of Education, 1955.

Brenner, A. *The Anton Brenner Developmental Gestalt Test of School Readiness*. Los Angeles: Western Psychological Services, 1964.

Bruininks, R. *Bruininks-Oseretsky Test of Motor Proficiency. Circle Pines, Minn.: American Guidance Services, 1978.*

Burks, H. F. *Behavior Rating Scale*. Los Angeles: California Association for Neurologically Handicapped Children, 1968.

Buros, O. K. *The Seventh Mental Measurements Yearbook*. Highland Park, N.J.: Gryphon Press, 1972.

Buros, O. K., ed. *Tests in Print II*. Highland Park, N.J.: Gryphon Press, 1974.

Bush, W. J., and Waugh, K. W. *Diagnosing Learning Disabilities*. Columbus, Ohio: Charles E. Merrill, 1976.

Cartwright, C. A., and Cartwright, G. P. *Developing Observational Skills*. New York: McGraw-Hill, 1974.

Clymer, T., and Barrett, T. *Clymer-Barrett Pre-Reading Battery*. Princeton, N.J.: Personnel Press, 1969.

Clymer, T.; Christenson, B.; and Russell, D. *Building Pre-Reading Skills: Kit A, Language.* Boston: Ginn and Company, 1965.

Connolly, A. J.; Nachtman, W.; and Pritchett, E. M. *KeyMath Diagnostic Arithmetic Test.* Circle Pines, Minn.: American Guidance Services, 1971.

Crabtree, M. *Houston Test for Language Development.* Houston: Houston Press, 1963.

Crites, J. W. *Career Maturity Inventory.* Monterey, Calif.: CTB/McGraw-Hill, 1973.

Cronbach, L. J.; Gleser, G. C.; Nanda, H.; and Rajaratnam, N. *The Dependability of Behavioral Measurements: Theory of Generalizability for Scores and Profiles.* New York: Wiley & Sons, 1972.

Cronbach, L. J., and Snow, R. E. *Aptitude and Instructional Methods.* New York: Irvington, 1977.

Cunningham, P. M. "Match Informal Evaluation to Your Teaching Practices." *The Reading Teacher* 31 (1977): 51–56.

Cunningham, R. "Developing Question-Asking Skills." In *Developing Teacher Competencies,* edited by J. Weigand. Englewood Cliffs, N.J.: Prentice-Hall, 1971.

Dale, E., and Chall, J. *A Formula for Predicting Readability.* Columbus: Bureau of Educational Research, Ohio State University, 1948.

deHirsch, K.; Jansky, J.; and Langford, W. *Predicting Reading Failure: A Preliminary Study of Reading, Writing and Spelling Disabilities in Preschool Children.* New York: Harper & Row, 1966.

Dixon, N. R. "Testing—Its Impact on Expectations, Practice, Accountability." *Educational Leadership* 35 (1978):294–297.

Doll, E. A. *The Vineland Social Maturity Scale.* Circle Pines, Minn.: American Guidance Service, 1953.

Doll, E. A. *Preschool Attainment Record.* Circle Pines, Minn.: American Guidance Service, 1966.

Drake, C. *PERC Auditory Discrimination Test.* Sherborn, Mass.: Perceptual Education and Research Center, 1965.

Drew, C. J. "Criterion-referenced and Norm-referenced Assessment of Minority Group Children." *Journal of School Psychology* 11 (1973):323–329.

Dunlap, W. P., and Thompson, C. S. "Diagnosing Difficulties in Learning Basic Math Facts." *Journal of Learning Disabilities* 10 (1977):585–589.

Dunn, L. M. *Peabody Picture Vocabulary Test.* Minneapolis: American Guidance Service, 1959.

Durrell, D. D. *Durrell Analysis of Reading Difficulty.* New York: Harcourt, Brace, Jovanovich, 1935. (2d ed., 1955.)

Durrell, D. D., and Murphy, H. A. "A Prereading Phonics Inventory." *The Reading Teacher* 31 (1978):385–390.

Engelmann, S. *Basic Concept Inventory.* Chicago: Follett Educational Corp., 1967.

Escovar, P. L. "Another Chance for Learning—The Assessment Class." *Teaching Exceptional Children* 9 (1976):2–3.

Feshbach, S.; Adelman, H.; and Fuller, W. W. "Early Identification of Children with High Risk of Reading Failure." *Journal of Learning Disabilities* 7 (1974):639–644.

Frostig, M. *Frostig Developmental Test of Visual Perception.* Palo Alto, Calif.: Consulting Psychologists Press, 1963.

Fuller, G., and Laird, G. "Minnesota Percepto-Diagnostic Test." *Journal of Clinical Psychology* 19 (January 1963):3–34.

Goldman, R.; Fristoe, M.; and Woodcock, R. *Goldman-Fristoe-Woodcock Test of Auditory Discrimination.* Circle Pines, Minn.: American Guidance Service, 1970.

Goldman, R.; Fristoe, M.; and Woodcock, R. *Goldman-Fristoe-Woodcock Auditory Skills Test Battery.* Circle Pines, Minn.: American Guidance Service, 1975.

Goodenough, F. *Draw-A-Person Test: The Measurement of Intelligence by Drawings.* Yonkers-on-Hudson, N.Y.: World Book Co., 1926.

Goodman, K. "Review of Reading Tests and Reviews." Ed. O. K. Buros. *American Educational Research Journal* 8 (1971):169–170.

Gorth, W. P., and Hambleton, R. K. "Measurement Considerations for Criterion-Referenced Testing and Special Education." *The Journal of Special Education* 6 (1972):303–314.

Graham, F., and Kendall, B. *Memory-for-Designs Test.* Missoula, Mont.: Psychological Test Specialists, 1960.

Greenwood, C. R.; Walker, H. M.; and Hops, H. "Issues in Social Interaction/Withdrawal Assessment." *Exceptional Children* 43 (1977):490–499.

Gronlund, N. E. *Preparing Criterion-Referenced Tests for Classroom Instruction.* New York: Macmillan, 1973.

Gronlund, N. E. *Measurement and Evaluation in Teaching.* New York: Macmillan, 1976.

Hainsworth, P., and Siqueland, M *The Meeting Street School Screening Test.* Providence: Crippled Children and Adults of Rhode Island, Inc., 1969.

Harris, A. *Harris Test of Lateral Dominance.* 3d rev. ed. New York: Psychological Corp., 1958.

Harris, O. *Goodenough-Harris Drawing Tests.* New York: Harcourt Brace Jovanovich, 1963.

Heathington, B. S., and Alexander, J. E. "A Child-Based Observation Checklist to Assess Attitudes Toward Reading." *The Reading Teacher* 31 (1978):769–771.

Herbert, J., and Attridge, C. "A Guide for Developers and Users of Observation Systems and Manuals." *American Educational Research Journal* 12 (1975):1–20.

Hildreth, G.; Griffiths, N.; and McGauvran, M. *Metropolitan Readiness Tests.* New York: Harcourt Brace Jovanovich, 1966.

Hillerich, R. L. "A Diagnostic Approach to Early Identification of Language Skills." *The Reading Teacher* 31 (1978): 357–364.

Hillson, M., and Bongo, J. *Continuous-Progress Education.* Chicago: Science Research Associates, 1971.

Hively, W., and Reynolds, M. C., eds. *Domain-Referenced Testing in Special Education.* Reston, Va.: Council for Exceptional Children, 1975.

Ilg, F., and Ames, L. *School Readiness: Behavior Tests Used at the Gesell Institute.* New York: Harper & Row, 1964.

Jastak, J.; Bijou, S.; and Jastak, S. *Wide-Range Achievement Test.* Wilmington, Del.: Guidance Associates, 1965.

Jedrysek, E.; Klapper, Z.; Pope, L.; and Wortis, J. *Psychoeducational Evaluation of the Preschool Child.* New York: Grune & Stratton, 1972.

Johnson, M., and Kress, R. *Informal Reading Inventories.* Reading Aids Series. Newwark, Del.: International Reading Association, 1965.

Kass, C. E. "Identification of Learning Disability (Dyssymbolia)." *Journal of Learning Disabilities* 10 (1977):425–432.

Keogh, B., ed. *Early Identification of Children with Potential Learning Problems.* New York: Grune & Stratton, 1972.

Keogh, B. K. "Psychological Evaluation of Exceptional Children: Old Hangups and New Directions." *Journal of School Psychology* 10 (1972):141–146.

Keogh, B. K., and Becker, L. D. "Early Detection of Learning Problems: Questions, Cautions, and Guidelines." *Exceptional Children* 40 (1973):5–11.

Keogh, B. K.; Tchir, C.; and Winderguth-Behn. A. "Teachers' Perceptions of Educationally High-Risk Children." *Journal of Learning Disabilities* 7 (1974):367–374.

Kephart, N., and Roach, E. *Purdue Perceptual-Motor Survey.* Columbus, Ohio: Charles E. Merrill, 1966.

Keystone Visual Survey Telebinocular. Meadville, Pa.: Keystone View Co., 1958.

Kirk, S.; McCarthy, J.; and Kirk, W. *Illinois Test of Psycholinguistic Abilities: Revised Edition, Examiners Manual.* Urbana: University of Illinois Press, 1968.

Koppitz, E. *The Bender Gestalt Test for Young Children.* New York: Grune & Stratton, 1964.

Koppitz, E. M. "Bender Gestalt Test, Visual Aural Deficit Span Test and Reading Achievement." *Journal of Learning Disabilities* 8 (1975):154–157.

Landsman, M., and Dillard, H. *Evanston Early Identification Scale.* Chicago: Follett Educational Corp., 1967.

Laten, S., and Katz, G. *A Theoretical Model for Assessment of Adolescents: The Ecological/Behavioral Approach* Madison, Wis.: Specialized Educational Services, 1975.

Lee, L. *The Northwestern Syntax Screening Test.* Evanston, Ill.: Northwestern University Press, 1969.

Lee, L. *Developmental Sentence Analysis.* Evanston, Ill.: Northwestern University Press, 1974.

Levine, M. "The Academic Achievement Test." *American Psychologist,* March 1976, pp. 228–238.

McDonald, E. *A Deep Test of Articulation.* Pittsburgh: Stanwix House, 1964.

McGahan, F. E., and McGahan, C. *Early Detection Inventory.* Chicago: Follett Educational Corporation, 1967.

Madden, R.; Gardner, E.; Rudman, H.; Karlsen, B.; and Merwin, J. *Stanford Achievement Test.* New York: Harcourt Brace Jovanovich, 1973.

Massachusetts Vision Test. Boston: Massachusetts Dept. of Public Health, Welch Allyn, Inc., 1954.

Massad, C. "Interpreting and Using Test Norms." *The Reading Teacher* 26 (1972):286–292.

Mecham, M. *Verbal Language Development Scale.* Minneapolis: American Guidance Service, 1959.

Mehrens, W. A., and Lehmann, I. J. *Standardized Tests in Education.* New York: Holt, Rinehart & Winston, 1969.

Meskauskas, J. A. "Evaluation Models for Criterion-Referenced Testing: Views Regarding Mastery and Standard-Setting." *Review of Educational Research* 46 (1976):133–158.

Metropolitan Achievement Tests. Tarrytown-on-Hudson, N.Y.: World Book Co., 1959.

Metropolitan Readiness Tests. New York: Harcourt Brace Jovanovich, 1950.

Michigan Picture Test and Thematic Apperception Tests. Chicago: Michigan Department of Mental Health, Science Research, 1953.

Miller, W. C. "Unobtrusive Measures Can Help in Assessing Growth." *Educational Leadership* 35 (1978):264–269.

Money, J.; Alexander, D.; and Walker, H., Jr. *A Standardized Road-Map Test of Direction Sense.* Baltimore: Johns Hopkins Press, 1965.

Murray, H. *Thematic Apperception Test.* Cambridge, Mass.: Harvard University Press, 1943.

Myklebust, H. *Development and Disorders of Written Language: Picture Story Language Test.* New York: Grune and Stratton, 1965.

Myklebust, H. R. *Myklebust Pupil Rating Scale.* New York: Grune and Stratton, 1971.

Nihira, K.; Foster, R.; Shellhaus, M.; and Leland H. *Adaptive Behavior Scales.* Washington, D.C.: American Association on Mental Deficiency, 1969.

Orton, J. *A Guide to Teaching Phonics.* Cambridge, Mass.: Educators Publishing Service, 1965.

Page, W. D., and Barr, R. D. "Use of Informal Reading Inventories." In *Help for the Reading Teacher: New Directions in Research,* edited by W. D. Page. Urbana, Ill.: ERIC Clearinghouse on Reading and Communication Skills: National Conference on Research in English, 1975.

Pate, J., and Webb, W. *First Grade Screening Test.* Circle Pines, Minn.: American Guidance Service, 1966.

Perceptual Forms Test. Winter Haven, Fla.: Winter Haven Lions Club, Publications Committee, 1956.

Peterson, W. *A Program for the Early Identification of Learning Disabilities.* Seattle: Special Child Publications, 1970.

Pikulski, J. "A Critical Review: Informal Reading Inventories." *The Reading Teacher* 28 (1974):141–151.

Popham, W. J., and Husek, T. "Implications of Criterion-Referenced Measurement." *Journal of Educational Measurement* 6 (1969):1–9.

Powell, G. C. "An Attitude Scale for Children." *The Reading Teacher* 25 (1972):442–447.

Prescott, G. A. "Criterion-Referenced Test Interpretation in Reading." *The Reading Teacher* 24 (1971):347–354.

Proger, B. B., and Mann, L. "Criterion-Referenced Measurement: The World of Gray Versus Black and White." *Journal of Learning Disabilities* 6 (1973):72–84.

Pronovost, W., and Dumbleton, C. "A Picture-Type Speech Sound Discrimination Test." *Journal of Speech and Hearing Disorders* 18 (1953):258–266.

Quay, H. C., and Peterson, D. R. *Behavior Problem Checklist.* Champaign, Ill.: Children's Research Center, 1967.

Renzulli, J. S., and Smith, L. H. "Two Approaches to Identification of Gifted Students." *Exceptional Children* 43 (1977):512–518.

Reyna, J., and Bernal, E. M., Jr. "Alternative Identification Strategies for Mexican American Youngsters at the Primary Level." *Talents and Gifts,* March 1976, p. 9 (Abstract).

Roach, E., and Kephart, N. *The Purdue Perceptual-Motor Survey,* Columbus, Ohio: Charles E. Merrill, 1966.

Roswell, F., and Chall, J. *Roswell-Chall Auditory Blending Test.* New York: The Essay Press, 1963.

Salili, F.; Maehr, M. L.; Sorensen, R. L.; and Fyans, L. J., Jr. "A Further Consideration of the Effects of Evaluation on Motivation." *American Educational Research Journal* 13 (1976):85–120.

Silvaroli, N. J. *Classroom Reading Inventory.* 2d ed. Dubuque, Iowa: William C. Brown, 1973.

Slingerland, B. *Screening Tests for Identifying Children with Specific Language Disability.* Cambridge, Mass.: Educators Publishing Service, 1962.

Sloan, W. *Lincoln-Oseretsky Motor Development Scale.* Los Angeles: Western Psychological Services, 1954.

Smith, R. *Teacher Diagnosis of Educational Difficulties.* Columbus, Ohio: Charles E. Merrill, 1969.

Smith, R. M.; and Neisworth, J. T. "Fundamentals of Informal Educational Assessment." In *Teacher Diagnosis of Educational Difficulties,* edited by R. M. Smith. Columbus, Ohio: Charles E. Merrill, 1969.

Spache, G. "New Readability Formula for Primary Grade Reading Materials." *Elementary School Journal,* 53 (March 1953):410–413.

Spache, G. *Spache Binocular Vision Test.* Meadville, Pa.: Keystone View Co., 1961.

Spivack, G., and Swift, M. *Devereaux Elementary School Behavior Rating Scale.* Devon, Pa.: Devereaux Foundation, 1967.

Strauss, A., and Lehtinen, L. *Psychopathology and Education of the Brain-Injured Child.* New York: Grune & Stratton, 1947.

Templin, M., and Darley, F. *The Templin-Darley Tests of Articulation.* Iowa City: University of Iowa Bureau of Research and Service, 1960.

Terman, E., and Merrill, M. *Stanford-Binet Intelligence Scale,* Boston: Houghton Mifflin, 1962.

Thorndike, R. L. "Mr. Binet's Test 70 Years Later." *Educational Researcher,* vol. 4, no. 5 (1975), pp. 3–4.

Valett, R. *The Valett Developmental Survey of Basic Learning Abilities.* Palo Alto, Calif.: Consulting Psychologists Press, 1967.

Valett, R. *A Psychoeducational Inventory of Basic Learning Abilities.* Palo Alto, Calif.: Fearon Publishers, 1968.

Vane, J. "The Vane Kindergarten Test." *Clinical Psychology* 24 (April 1968):1–34.

Wallace, G., and Larsen, S. *Educational Assessment of Learning Problems: Testing for Teaching.* Boston: Allyn and Bacon, 1978.

Wechsler, D. *Wechsler Intelligence Scale for Children: Manual.* New York: The Psychological Corp., 1955.

Wechsler, D. *Wechsler Preschool and Primary Scale of Intelligence: Manual.* New York: The Psychological Corp., 1967.

Wechsler, D. "Intelligence Defined and Undefined; A Relativistic Appraisal." *American Psychologist,* February 1975, pp. 135–139.

Wepman, J. *Wepman Auditory Discrimination Test.* Chicago: Language Research Associates, 1958.

Wepman, J. *Wepman Auditory Memory Span Test.* Los Angeles: Western Psychological Services, 1973 (a).

Wepman, J. *Wepman Auditory Sequential Memory Test.* Los Angeles, Calif.: Western Psychological Services, 1973(b).

Williamson, L. E., and Young, F. "The IRI and RMI Diagnostic Concepts Should Be Synthesized." *Journal of Reading Behavior* 6 (1974):183–194.

Wilson, J. A., and Robeck, M. C. *Kindergarten Evaluation of Learning Potential (KELP).* New York: McGraw-Hill Book Company, 1967.

Wisland, M. V. *Psycho-educational Diagnosis of Exceptional Children.* Springfield, Ill.: Charles C Thomas, 1973.

CURRICULUM AND INSTRUCTION

Adelman, H., and Taylor, L. "Two Steps Toward Improving Learning for Students with (and without) 'Learning Problems.'" *Journal of Learning Disabilities* 10 (1977):455–461.

Allen, R., and Allen, C. *Language Experiences in Reading.* Chicago: Encyclopedia Britannica Press, 1966.

Alvord, D. J. "Innovation in Speech Therapy: A Cost Effective Program." *Exceptional Children* 43 (1977):520–525.

Anderson, P. *Language Skills in Elementary Education.* New York: Macmillan, 1964.

Arena, J., ed. *Building Spelling Skills in Dyslexic Children.* San Rafael, Calif.: Academic Therapy Publications, 1968.

Armstrong, D. G. "Team Teaching and Academic Achievement." *Review of Educational Research,* 47 (1977):65–86.

Ashlock, Patrick. *Teaching Reading to Individuals with Learning Difficulties.* Springfield, Ill.: Charles C Thomas, 1974.

Ashlock, R. B. *Error Patterns in Computation: A Semi-Programmed Approach.* 2d ed. Columbus, Ohio: Charles E. Merrill, 1976.

Aukerman, R. C. *Approaches to Beginning Reading.* New York: Wiley, 1971.

Bailey, E. J. *Academic Activities for Adolescents with Learning Disabilities.* Evergreen, Colo.: Learning Pathways, 1975.

Balow, B. "Perceptual Activities in the Treatment of Severe Reading Disability." *Reading Teacher* 24 (1971):513–525.

Bannatyne, A. "Research Design and Progress in Remediating Learning Disabilities." *Journal of Learning Disabilities* 8 (1975):345–348.

Barrett, T. "Visual Discrimination Tasks as Predictors of First Grade Reading Achievement." *Reading Teacher* 18 (1965):276–282.

Barsch, R. *Achieving Perceptual Motor Efficiency*. Seattle: Special Child Publications, 1967.

Barsch, R. *Enriching Perception and Cognition*. Vol. 2, Seattle: Special Child Publications, 1968.

Bell and Howell, Inc. "Language Master." 7100 McCormick Road, Chicago, Ill. 60645.

Benthul, H. F.; Anderson, E. A.; Uteck, A. N.; Biggy, M. V.; and Bailey, B. L. *Spell Correctly*. Morristown, N.J.: Silver Burdett, 1974.

Benyon, S. *Intensive Programming for Slow Learners*. Columbus, Ohio: Charles E. Merrill, 1968.

Bloom, B. S. "New Views of the Learner: Implications for Instruction and Curriculum." *Educational Leadership* 35 (1978):563–576.

Bond, G. L., and Tinker, M. A. *Reading Difficulties: Their Diagnosis and Correction*. 3d ed. New York: Appleton-Century-Crofts, 1973.

Brogan, P., and Fox, L. K. *Helping Children Read*. New York: Holt, Rinehart & Winston, 1962. (Reprinted 1977.)

Building Handwriting Skills. Acadimic Therapy Quarterly. San Rafael, Calif.: Academic Therapy Publications 4 (Fall 1968): entire issue.

Building Spelling Skills. Academic Therapy Quarterly. San Rafael, Calif.: Academic Therapy Publications 3 (Fall 1967): entire issue.

Burmeister, L. E. *Reading Strategies for Secondary School Teachers*. Reading, Mass.: Addison-Wesley, 1974.

Burns, P. C. *Diagnostic Teaching of the Language Arts*. Itasca, Ill.: Peacock, 1974.

Burns, P. C., and Roe, B. D. *Teaching Reading in Today's Elementary Schools*. Chicago: Rand, McNally College Publishing Co., 1976.

Burrows, A. T.; Jackson, D.; and Saunders, D. O. *They All Want to Write*. 3rd ed. and New York: Holt, Rinehart & Winston, 1964.

Bush, C. L., and Huebner, M. H. *Strategies for Reading in the Elementary School*. New York: Macmillan, 1970.

Calfee, R.; Chapman, R.; and Venezky, L. "How a Child Needs to Think to Learn to Read." In *Cognition in Learning and Memory,* edited by L. Gregg. New York: John Wiley & Sons, 1972.

Carlson, R. K. *Writing Aids through the Grades*. New York: Teachers College Press, Columbia University, 1970.

Carlson, R. K. *Sparkling Words: Two Hundred Practical and Creative Writing Ideas*. Berkeley, Calif.: Wagner Printing Co., 1965, 1973 (distributed through the National Council of Teachers of English).

Carpenter, T. P.; Coburn, T. G.; Reys, R. E.; and Wilson, J. W. "Notes from National Assessment: Processes Used on Computational Exercises." *The Arithmetic Teacher* 23 (1976):217–222.

Cawley, J. F.; Goodstein, H. A.; Fitzmaurice, A. M.; Lepore, A.; Sedlak, R.; and Althaus, V. *Project Math: A Program of the Mainstream Series*. Wallingford, Conn.: Educational Sciences, 1976.

Chall, J. *Learning to Read: The Great Debate*. New York: McGraw-Hill Book Co., 1967.

Chall, Jeanne, and Feldmann, Shirley. "First Grade Reading: An Analysis of the Interactions of Professed Methods, Teaching Implementation, and Child Background." *Reading Teacher* 19 (May 1966):569–575.

Chaney, C., and Kephard, N. *Motoric Aids to Perceptual Training*. Columbus, Ohio: Charles E. Merrill, 1968.

Cheves, R. *Visual-Motor Perception Teaching Materials,* Boston: Teaching Resources Corp., 1967.

Cohen, S. A. Studies in Visual Perception and Reading in Disadvantaged Children. *Journal of Learning Disabilities* 2 (1969):498–507.

Copeland, R. W. *Mathematics and the Elementary Teacher*. 3rd ed. Philadelphia: Saunders, 1976.

Coughran, L., and Liles, B. *Developmental Syntax Program*. Austin, Texas: Learning Concepts, 1974.

Cramer, R. L., and Cramer, B. B. "Writing by Imitating Language Models." *Language Arts* 52 (1975):1011–1014.

Cratty, B. *Developmental Sequences of Perceptual Motor Tasks*. New York: Educational Activities, Inc., 1967.

Cratty, B. *Perceptual-Motor Behavior and Educational Processes*. Springfield, Ill.: Charles C Thomas, 1969.

Cratty, B. *Active Learning: Games to Enhance Academic Abilities*. Englewood Cliffs, N.J.: Prentice-Hall, 1971.

Cratty, B. *Movement Behavior and Motor Learning*. 3rd ed Philadelphia: Lea & Febiger, 1973.

Cratty, B. J. *Remedial Motor Activity for Children*. Philadelphia: Lea & Febiger, 1975.

Dale, P. S. *Language Development*. New York: Holt, Rinehart & Winston, 1976.

Daley, W. *Speech and Language Therapy with the Brain-Damaged Child*. Washington, D.C.: Catholic University of America Press, 1961.

Dallman, M. *Teaching the Language Arts in the Elementary School*. 3rd ed. Dubuque, Iowa: William C. Brown, 1976.

Dechant, E. *Diagnosis and Remediation of Reading Disability*. West Nyack, N.Y.: Parker Publishing Co., 1968.

Degler, L. S. "Using the Newspaper to Develop Reading Comprehension Skills." *Journal of Reading* 21 (1978): 339–342.

deHirsch, K.; Jansky, J.; and Langford, W. *Predicting Reading Failure: A Preliminary Study of Reading, Writing and Spelling Disabilities in Preschool Children*. New York: Harper & Row, 1966.

Delacato, C. *The Diagnosis and Treatment of Speech and Reading Problems*. Springfield, Ill.: Charles C Thomas, 1974.

Dickson, S. *Communication Disorders: Remedial Principles and Practices*. Glenview, Ill.: Scott Foresman, 1974.

Donlan, D. "How to Play 29 Questions." *Journal of Reading* 21 (1978):535–541.

Donofrio, A. F. "Grade Repetition: Therapy of Choice." *Journal of Learning Disabilities* 10 (1977):349–351.

Drader, D. L. "The Role of Verbal Labeling in Equivalence

Tasks as Related to Reading Ability." *Journal of Learning Disabilities* 8 (1975):154–157.

Duffy, G. G. "Maintaining a Balance in Objective-Based Reading Instruction." *The Reading Teacher* 31 (1978): 519–523.

Duffy, G. G., and Sherman, G. B. *How to Teach Reading Systematically*. New York: Harper & Row, 1973.

Duncan, E. R.; Capps, L. R.; Dolciani, M. P.; Quast, W. G.; and Zweng, M. J. *Modern School Mathematics: Structure and Use*. Rev. ed. Boston: Houghton Mifflin, 1972.

Dunlap, W. P. "An Attitudinal Device for Primary Children." *The Arithmetic Teacher* 23 (1976):29–31.

Dunlap, W. P., and House, A. D. "Why Can't Johnny Compute?" *Journal of Learning Disabilities* 9 (1976):210–214.

Dunlap, W. P., and Thompson, C. S. "Diagnosing Difficulties in Learning Basic Math Facts." *Journal of Learning Disabilities* 10 (1977):585–589.

Durkin, D. *Teaching Young Children to Read*. 2d ed. Boston: Allyn and Bacon, 1976.

Durrell, D. *Improving Reading Instruction*, pp. 200–201. Yonkers-on-Hudson, N.Y.: World Book Co., 1956.

Early, G.; Nelson, D.; Kleber, D.; Treegoob, M.; Huffman, E.; and Cass, C. "Cursive Handwriting, Reading and Spelling Achievement." *Academic Therapy* 12 (1976):67–74.

Ebersole, M.; Kephart, N.; and Ebersole, J. *Steps to Achievement for the Slow Learner*. Columbus, Ohio: Charles E. Merrill, 1968.

Edgington, R. "But He Spelled Them Right This Morning." *Academic Therapy Quarterly* 3 (1967):58–59.

Educational Products Information Exchange (EPIE). *Selecting and Evaluating Beginning Reading Materials. Report No. 62/63*. New York: Educational Products Information Exchange, 1973.

Educational Products Information Exchange (EPIE). *Analysis of Basic and Supplemental Reading Materials. Report No. 64*. New York: Educational Products Information Exchange, 1974.

Educational Products Information Exchange (EPIE). *Materials for Individualizing Math Instruction. Report No. 65*. New York: Educational Products Information Exchange, 1974.

Educational Products Information Exchange (EPIE). *Analysis of Elementary School Mathematics Materials. Report No. 69/70*. New York: Educational Products Information Exchange, 1975.

Educational Products Information Exchange (EPIE). *Selector's Guide to Bilingual Education Materials: Vol. 1, Spanish Language Arts*. New York: Educational Products Information Exchange, 1976.

Eisenson, J., and Ogilvie, M. *Speech Correction in the Schools*. 4th ed. New York: Macmillan, 1977.

Engelmann, T.; Osborn, J.; and Engelmann, T. *Distar Language: An Instructional System*. Chicago: Science Research Associates, 1969.

Estes, T. H., and Vaughan, J. L., Jr. *Reading and Learning in the Content Classroom*. Boston: Allyn and Bacon, 1978.

Ezor, E. L., and Lane, T. "Applied Linguistics: A Discovery Approach to the Teaching of Writing." *Language Arts* 52 (1975):1019–1021.

Farr, R., and Roser, N. "Reading Assessment: A Look at Problems and Issues." *Journal of Reading* 17 (1974):592–599.

Fellows, M. M. "A Mathematical Attitudinal Device." *The Arithmetic Teacher* 20 (1973):222–223.

Fernald, G. *Remedial Techniques in Basic School Subjects*. New York: McGraw-Hill Book Co., 1943.

Fink, W. T., and Carnine, D. W. "Control of Arithmetic Errors Using Informational Feedback and Graphing." *Journal of Applied Behavioral Analysis* 8 (1975):461.

Flesch, R. *How to Test Readability*. New York: Harper & Row, 1951.

Flesch, R. *Why Johnny Can't Read and What You Can Do About It*. New York: Harper & Brothers, 1955.

Freeman, F. *Guiding Growth in Handwriting: Evaluation Scale*. Columbus, Ohio: Zaner-Bloser Co., 1958.

Friedus, E. "The Needs of Teachers for Specialized Information on Number Concepts." In *The Teacher of Brain-Injured Children*, edited by W. Cruickshank. Syracuse: Syracuse University Press, 1966.

Fries, C. *Linguistics and Reading*. New York: Holt, Rinehart & Winston, 1963.

Fry, E. "A Readability Formula That Saves Time." *Journal of Reading* 11 (April 1968):513–518.

Gates, A. *Gates Reading Readiness Scales*. New York: Bureau of Publications, Teachers College, Columbia University, 1958.

Gentry, J. R., and Henderson, E. H. "Three Steps to Teaching Beginning Readers to Spell." *The Reading Teacher* 31 (1978):632–637.

Getman, G.; Kane, E.; Halgren, M.; and McKee, G. *Developing Learning Readiness: Teachers Manual*. St. Louis: Webster Division, McGraw-Hill Book Co., 1968.

Geuder, P.; Harvey, L.; Loyd, D.; and Wages, J., eds. *They Really Taught Us How to Write*. Urbana, Ill.: National Council of Teachers of English, 1974.

Gillespie, P. H., and Johnson, L. *Teaching Reading to the Mildly Retarded Child*. Columbus, Ohio: Charles E. Merrill, 1974.

Gilliland, H. *A Practical Guide to Remedial Reading*. Columbus, Ohio: Charles E. Merrill, 1974.

Gillingham, A., and Stillman, B. *Remedial Training for Children with Specific Disability in Reading, Spelling, and Penmanship*. 2d ed. Cambridge, Mass.: Educators' Publishing Service, 1969.

Gitter, L. *The Montessori Way*. Seattle: Special Child Publications, 1970.

Glaser, R. "Instructional Technology and the Measurement of Learning Outcomes." *American Psychologist* 18 (1963):519–521.

Glim, T. E., and Manchester, F. S. *Basic Spelling: A Rationale*. New York: J. B. Lippincott, 1975.

Goldstein, H. *The Social Learning Curriculum*. Columbus, Ohio: Charles E. Merrill, 1974.

Goodman, K. "Twelve Easy Ways to Make Learning to Read Difficult and One Difficult Way to Make It Easy." In

Psycholinguistics and Reading, edited by F. Smith. New York: Holt, Rinehart & Winston, 1973.

Goodman, Y. M. "Using Children's Miscues for Teaching Reading Strategies." *The Reading Teacher* 23 (1970):455–459.

Goodman, Y. M., and Burke, C. L. *Reading Miscue Inventory: Manual and Procedures for Diagnosis and Evaluation.* New York: Macmillan, 1972.

Goodstein, H. A. "Assessment and Programming in Mathematics for the Handicapped." *Focus on Exceptional Children* 7 (1975):1–11.

Greenspan, S.; Burka, A.; Zlotlow, S.; and Barenboim, C. "A Manual of Referential Communication Games." *Academic Therapy* 11 (1975):97–106.

Griffin, J. "I Can Say It, But I Can't Write It Down." In *Classroom Practices in Teaching English, 1975–1976: On Righting Writing,* edited by O. H. Clapp. Urbana, Ill.: National Council of Teachers of English, 1975.

Hanna, P. R.; Hodges, R. E.; and Hanna, J. S. *Spelling: Structure and Strategies.* Boston: Houghton Mifflin, 1971.

Harker, W. J. "Selecting Instructional Materials for Content Area Reading." *Journal of Reading* 21 (1977):126–130.

Harrigan, J. E. "Initial Reading Instruction: Phonemes, Syllables, or Ideographs?" *Journal of Learning Disabilities* 9 (1976):74–80.

Harris, L. P. "Attention and Learning Disorded Children: A Review of Theory and Remediation." *Journal of Learning Disabilities* 9 (1976):100–110.

Hatton, D.; Pizzat, F.; and Pelkowski, J. *Perceptual-Motor Teaching Materials, Erie Program 1.* Boston: Teaching Resources, 1967.

Haupt, E. J. "Writing and Using Literal Comprehension Questions." *The Reading Teacher* 31 (1977):193–199.

Hausserman, E. *Developmental Potential of Preschool Children.* New York: Grune & Stratton, 1958.

Herber, H. L. *Teaching Reading in Content Areas.* Englewood Cliffs, N.J.: Prentice-Hall, 1970.

Hollander, Sheila K. "Why's a Busy Teacher Like You Giving an IRI?" *Elementary English* 51 (September 1974):905–907.

Howes, V. M. *Individualization of Instruction.* New York: Macmillan, 1970. A book of readings.

Howes, V. M. *Individualizing Instruction in Reading and Social Studies.* New York: Macmillan, 1970. A book of readings.

Hoyt, K. B.; Evans, R. N.; Mackin, E. F.; and Mangum, G. L. *Career Education: What It Is and How to Do It.* 2d ed. Salt Lake City: Olympus, 1974.

Hoyt, K. B.; Pinson, N. M.; Laramore, D.; and Mangum, G. L. *Career Education and the Elementary School Teacher.* Salt Lake City: Olympus, 1973.

Huerta, V. "The Writes of Children." *Academic Therapy* 11 (1975):37–49.

Jackson, R. L., and Phillips, G. "Manipulative Devices in Elementary School Mathematics." In *Instructional Aids in Mathematics: Thirty-fourth Yearbook of the National Council of Teachers of Mathematics.* Washington, D.C.: National Council of Teachers of Mathematics, 1973.

Kagan, J. "Reflection-Impulsivity and Reading Ability in Primary Grade Children." *Child Development,* 36 (1965):609–628.

Kane, R. B.; Byrne, M. A.; and Hater, M. A. *Helping Children Read Mathematics.* New York: American Book Co., 1974.

Kaplan, P.; Kohfeldt, J.; and Sturla, K. *It's Positively Fun.* Denver: Love, 1974.

Karlin, R. *Teaching Elementary Reading: Principles and Strategies.* 2d ed. New York: Harcourt Brace Jovanovich, 1975.

Karnes, M. *Helping Young Children Develop Language Skills: A Book of Activities.* Washington, D.C.: The Council for Exceptional Children, 1968. (Pap. Ed. 1976.)

Kass, C. "Psycholinguistic Disabilities of Children with Reading Problems." *Exceptional Children* 32 (1966):533–539.

King, E. M. "Prereading Programs: Direct Versus Incidental Teaching." *The Reading Teacher* 31 (1978):504–510.

Kinsbourne, M., and Warrington, E. "Developmental Factors in Reading and Writing Backwardness." In *The Disabled Reader: Education of the Dyslexic Child,* edited by J. Money, pp. 59–71. Baltimore: Johns Hopkins Press, 1966.

Kirkland, E. R. "A Piagetian Interpretation of Beginning Reading Instruction." *The Reading Teacher* 31 (1978): 497–503.

Kottmeyer, W. *Teacher's Guide for Remedial Reading.* New York:McGraw-Hill, 1970.

Kottmeyer, W., and Claus, A. *Basic Goals in Spelling.* 4th ed. New York: McGraw-Hill, 1974. 5th ed. forthcoming.

Lankford, F. G., Jr. "What Can A Teacher Learn About a Pupil's Thinking Through Oral Interviews?" *The Arithmetic Teacher* 21 (1974):26–32.

Larrick, N. *Parents' Guide to Children's Reading.* 4th ed. New York: Pocket Books, 1975.

Laurendeau, M., and Pinard, A. *The Development of the Concept of Space in the Child.* New York: International Universities Press, 1970.

Lee, L. *Developmental Sentence Analysis.* Evanston, Ill.: Northwestern University Press, 1974.

Lee, L.; Koenigsknecht, R. A.; and Mulhern, S. T. *Interactive Language Development Teaching.* Evanston, Ill.: Northwestern University Press, 1975.

Lerner, J. W. "Remedial Reading and Learning Disabilities: Are They the Same or Different?" *Journal of Special Education* 9 (1975):119–131.

Levin, Beatrice J. "The Informal Reading Inventory." *Reading Improvement* 8 (Spring 1971):18–20.

MacDonald, J. D. "Environmental Language Intervention." In *Language, Materials and Curriculum Management for the Handicapped Learner,* edited by F. Withrow and C. Nygren. Columbus, Ohio: Charles E. Merrill, 1976.

McCroskey, R. L., and Thompson, H. W. "Comprehension of Rate Controlled Speech by Children with Special Learning Disabilities." *Journal of Learning Disabilities* 6 (December 1973):621–627.

McLeod, T. M., and Crump, W. D. "The Relationship of Visuospatial Skills and Verbal Ability to Learning Disabilities in Mathematics." *Journal of Learning Disabilities* 11 (1978):237–241.

Maring, G. H. "Matching Remediation to Miscues." *The Reading Teacher* 31 (1978):887–891.

Marquardt, T. P., and Saxman, J. H. "Language Comprehension and Auditory Discrimination in Articulation Deficient Kindergarten Children." *Journal of Speech and Hearing Research* 15 (June 1972):382–389.

Martin, W. D. "Measuring Children's Story Writing—II. *Language Arts* (52 1975):1023–1025.

Marzano, R. J. "Teaching Psycholinguistically Based Comprehension Skills Using a Visual Approach: A Proposal." *Journal of Reading* 21 (1978):729–734.

Mason, G. E., and Mize, J. M. Twenty-two Sets of Methods and Materials for Stimulating Teenage Reading. *Journal of Reading* 21 (1978):735–741.

Mason, J. M. "Refining Phonics for Teaching Beginning Reading." *The Reading Teacher* 31 (1977):179–184.

May, F. *To Help Children Read: Mastery Performance Modules for Teachers in Training.* Columbus, Ohio: Charles E. Merrill, 1973.

Mazurkiewicz, A. J., and Tanyzer, H. J. *Early-to-Read: i/t/a Program.* New York: Initial Teaching Alphabet Publications, 1966.

Minskoff, E., and Minskoff, J. G. "A Unified Program of Remedial and Compensatory Teaching for Children with Process Learning Disabilities." *Journal of Learning Disabilities* 9 (1976):215–222.

Moffett, J. *A Student-Centered Language Arts Curriculum, Grades K-13: A Handbook for Teachers.* 2d ed. Boston: Houghton Mifflin, 1976.

Morgan, R. F., and Culver, V. I. "Locus of Control and Reading Achievement: Applications for the Classroom." *Journal of Reading* 21 (1978):403–408.

Myers, C. A. "Reviewing the Literature on Fernald's Technique of Remedial Reading." *The Reading Teacher* 31 (1978):614–619.

National Council of Teachers of Mathematics. Instructional Aids in Mathematics: Thirty-fourth Yearbook. Washington, D.C.: National Council of Teachers of Mathematics, 1973.

Natchez, G., ed. *Children With Reading Problems.* New York: Basic Books, 1968.

Nelson, J. "Readability: Some Cautions for the Content Area Teacher." *Journal of Reading* 21 (1978): 620–625.

Newcomer, P., and Goodman, L. "Effective Modality of Instruction on the Learning of Meaningful and Non-Meaningful Material by Auditory and Visual Learners." *Journal of Special Education* 9 (1975):261–268.

Orton, S. *Reading, Writing and Speech Problems in Children.* New York: Norton, 1973.

Otto, W.; McMenemy, R. A.; and Smith, R. J. *Corrective and Remedial Teaching.* 2d ed. Boston: Houghton Mifflin, 1973.

Peskin, A., and Tauber-Scheidlinger, R. "Let Them Learn Their Way." *Academic Therapy* 11 (1976):301–311.

Peterson, D. L. *Functional Mathematics for the Mentally Retarded.* Columbus, Ohio: Charles E. Merrill, 1973.

Petty, W. T.; Petty, D. C.; and Becking, M. F.. *Experiences in Language: Tools and Techniques for Language Arts Methods.* 2d ed. Boston: Allyn and Bacon, 1976.

Quisenberry, N. L.; Blakemore, C.; and Warren, C. A.. "Involving Parents in Reading: An Annotated Bibliograpy." *The Reading Teacher* 31 (1977):34–39.

Ramey, C. T., and Smith, B. J. "Assessing the Intellectual Consequences of Early Intervention with High-Risk Infants." *American Journal of Mental Deficiency* 81 (1977):318–324.

Ringler, L. H., and Smith, I. L. "Learning Modality and Word Recognition of First Grade Children." *Journal of Learning Disabilities* 6 (1973):307–312.

Robinson, R. D., and Pettit, N. T. "The Role of the Reading Teacher: Where Do You Fit In?" *The Reading Teacher* 31 (1978):923–927.

Roswell, Florence, and Natchez, Gladys. *Reading Disability: Diagnosis and Treatment.* New York: Basic Books, 1971.

Sartain, H. W. "Instruction of Disabled Learners: A Reading Perspective." *Journal of Learning Disabilities* 9 (1976):489–497.

Shane, H., and Walden, J. *Classroom-Relevant Research in the Language Arts.* Washington, D.C.: Association for Supervision and Curriculum Development, 1978.

Shaw, H. *Spell It Right.* New York: Barnes & Noble, 1971.

Singer, H. "Active Comprehension: From Answering to Asking Questions." *The Reading Teacher* 31 (1978):901–908.

Smith, C. *Parents and Reading.* Newark, Del.: International Reading Association, 1971.

Smith, D. D., and Lovitt, T. C. "The Differential Effects of Reinforcement Contingencies on Arithmetic Performance." *Journal of Learning Disabilities* 9 (1976):32–40.

Smith, R. J., and Barrett, T. C. *Teaching Reading in the Middle Grades.* Reading, Mass.: Addison-Wesley, 1974.

Smith, S. E., Jr., and Backman, C. A., eds. *Teacher-Made Aids for Elementary School Mathematics: Readings from The Arithmetic Teacher.* Washington, D.C.: National Council of Teachers of Mathematics, 1974.

Spache, G. D. *Diagnosing and Correcting Reading Disabilities.* Boston: Allyn and Bacon, 1976.

Standal, T. C. "Readability Formulas: What's Out, What's In?" *The Reading Teacher* 31 (1978):642–646.

Stott, D. "Association of Motor Impairment with Various Types of Behavior Disturbance." *Journal of Learning Disabilities* 11 (1978):147–154.

Strang, R. *Diagnostic Teaching of Reading.* 2d ed. New York: McGraw-Hill, 1969.

Strange, M., and Allington, R. L. "Use the Diagnostic Prescriptive Model Knowledgeably." *The Reading Teacher* 31 (1977):290–293.

Stuart, M. *Neurophysiological Insights into Teaching.* Palo Alto, Calif.: Pacific Books Publishers, 1963.

Suiter, M., and Potter, R. "The Effect of Paradigmatic Organization on Verbal Recall." *Journal of Learning Disabilities* 11 (1978):247–250.

Summers, E., ed. *Reading Incentive Series.* St. Louis: Webster Division, McGraw-Hill Book Co., 1968.

Talmage, H., ed. *Systems of Individualized Education.* Berkeley, Calif.: McCutchan, 1975.

Tarver, S. G., and Dawson, M. M. "Modality Preference and the Teaching of Reading: A Review." *Journal of Learning Disabilities* 11 (1978):5–17.

Telegdy, G. A. "The Relationship Between Socioeconomic Status and School Readiness." *Psychology in the Schools* 11 (1974):351–356.

Thiagarajan, S. "Designing Instructional Games for Handicapped Learners." *Focus on Exceptional Children* 7 (1976):1–11.

Tiedt, I. M. *Individualizing Writing in the Elementary Classroom.* Urbana, Ill.: National Council of Teachers of English, 1975.

Tiedt, I. M., and Tiedt, S. W. *Contemporary English in the Elementary School.* 2d ed. Englewood Cliffs, N.J.: Prentice-Hall, 1975.

Tyler, J. L. "Modality Preference and Reading Task Performance Among the Mildly Retarded." *Training School Bulletin* 70 (1974):208–214.

Vance, H. B., and Hankins, N. E. "Teaching Interventions for Defective Auditory Reception." *Academic Therapy* 11 (1975):69–78.

Vandever, T. R., and Neville, D. D. "Modality Aptitude and Word Recognition." *Journal of Reading Behavior* 6 (1974):195–201.

Van Etten, C., and Watson, B. "Arithmetic Skills: Assessment and Instruction." *Journal of Learning Disabilities* 11 (1978):42–49.

Van Etten, C., and Watson, B. "Career Education Materials for the Learning Disabled." *Journal of Learning Disabilities* 10 (1977):264–270.

Van Etten, G. "A Look at Reading Comprehension." *Journal of Learning Disabilities* 11 (1978):30–39.

Van Riper, C. *Speech Correction: Principles and Methods.* 5th ed. Englewood Cliffs, N.J.: Prentice-Hall, 1972.

Veatch, J. *Reading in the Elementary School.* New York: Ronald Press, 1966. Describes individualized reading programs. 2d ed. Forthcoming.

Veatch, J.; Sawicki, F.; Elliott, G.; Barnette, E.; and Blakey, J. *Key Words to Reading: The Language Experience Approach Begins.* Columbus, Ohio: Charles E. Merrill, 1973.

Venezky, R. L. *Prereading Skills: Theoretical Foundations and Practical Applications.* Theoretical paper No. 54. Madison: Wisconsin Research and Development Center for Cognitive Learning, 1975.

Wallen, C. J. *Competency in Teaching Reading.* Chicago: Science Research Associates, 1972.

Watson, B. L., and Van Etten, C. "Materials Analysis." *Journal of Learning Disabilities* 9 (1976):406–416.

Waugh, R. P. "Relationship Between Modality Preference and Performance." *Exceptional Children* 39 (1973):465–469.

Westerman, Gayle S. *Spelling and Writing.* Sioux Falls, S. D.: Adapt Press, 1971.

Wiig, E. H.; Semel, E. M.; and Crouse, M. A. B. "The Use of English Morphology by High-Risk and Learning Disabled Children." *Journal of Learning Disabilities* 5 (1973):457–465.

Willows, D. M. "Reading Between the Lines: Selective Attention in Good and Poor Readers." *Child Development* 45 (1974):408–415.

Wilson, R. M. *Diagnostic and Remedial Reading for Classroom and Clinic.* 3d ed. Columbus, Ohio: Charles E. Merrill, 1977.

Wilson, R. M., and Geyer, J., eds. *Reading for Diagnostic and Remedial Reading.* Columbus, Ohio: Charles E. Merrill, 1972.

Wingate, M. E. *Stuttering: Theory and Treatment.* New York: Irvington Publishers, 1976.

Wisner, R. J. *Problem Solving Strategies for Elementary Mathematics.* A Scott, Foresman Monograph. Glenview, Ill.: Scott, Foresman, 1974.

Woodcock, R. W. *Peabody Rebus Reading Program.* Circle Pines, Minn.: American Guidance Services, 1967.

Younie, W. *Instructional Approaches to Slow Learners.* New York: Teachers College Press, 1967.

Zaner-Bloser Staff. *Creative Growth with Handwriting.* Columbus, Ohio: Zaner-Bloser, 1975.

EDUCATIONAL MANAGEMENT

Abrams, J. C., and Kaslow, F. "Family Systems and the Learning Disabled Child: Intervention and Treatment." *Journal of Learning Disabilities* 10 (1977):86–90.

Barksdale, M. W., and Atkinson, A. P. "A Resource Room Approach to Instruction for the Educable Retarded." *Focus on Exceptional Children* 3 (1971):12–15.

Bechtol, W. M. In *The Unit Leader and Individually Guided Education,* edited by J. S. Sorenson; M. Poole; and L. H. Joyal. Reading, Mass.: Addison-Wesley, 1976.

Becker, W. C., and Engelmann, S. *Teaching No. 1: Classroom Management.* Chicago: Science Research Associates, 1975.

Brown, V. "A Multipurpose Guide to the Organization and Management of the Learning Disabilities Program" *Journal of Learning Disabilities* 1 (1976):5–10.

Chalfant, J. C., and Foster, G. E. "Helping Teachers Understand the Needs of Learning Disabled Children." *Journal of Learning Disabilities* 10 (1977):79–85.

DeFever, K., and Plous, L. "Opening Up the LD Room, *Academic Therapy* 11 (1976):367–372.

Ehly, S., and Larsen, S. "Peer Tutoring in the Regular Classroom." *Academic Therapy* (1975–76):205–208.

Ehly, S. W., and Larsen, S. C. "Peer Tutoring to Individualize Instruction." *The Elementary School Journal* 76 (1976):475–480.

Gordon, S. "A Bill of Rights for Parents." *Academic Therapy,* 11 (1975):21–22.

Gordon, T. *Parent Effectiveness Training.* New York: Wyden, 1970.

Hassett, J. D., and Weisberg, A. *Open Education: Alternatives Within Our Tradition.* Englewood Cliffs, N.J.: Prentice-Hall, 1972.

Hudson, F. G., and Graham, S. "An Approach to Operationalizing the I.E.P." *Learning Disability Quarterly* 1 (1978):13–32.

Hull, R. E. "Selecting an Approach to Individualized Education." *Phi Delta Kappan,* November 1973, pp. 169–173.

Jenkins, J. R., and Mayhall, W. F. "Development and Evaluation of a Resource Teacher Program." *Exceptional Children* 43 (1976):21–29.

Keller, L. J. *Career Education In-Service Training Guide.* Morristown, N.J.: General Learning Corporation, 1972.

Klausmeier, H. J.; Rossmiller, R. A.; and Sailey, M. eds. *Individually Guided Elementary Education: Concepts and Practices.* New York: Academic Press, 1977.

Klosterman, D., and Frankel, J. "Tutoring Effectively." *Academic Therapy* 11 (1975):107–110.

Kunzelman, H. P. *Precision Teaching: An Initial Training Sequence.* Seattle: Special Child, 1970.

Lichter, P. "Communicating with Parents: It Begins with Listening." *Teaching Exceptional Children* 8 (1976):66–75.

McWhirter, J. J. "A Parent Education Group in Learning Disabilities." *Journal of Learning Disabilities* 9 (1976):16–20.

Martin, L., and Pavan, B. "Current Research on Open Space, Nongrading, Vertical Grouping, and Team Teaching." *Phi Delta Kappan* 57 (1976):310–315.

Mayhall, W. F., and Jenkins, J. R. "Scheduling Daily or Less-Than-Daily Instruction: Implications for Resource Programs." *Journal of Learning Disabilities* 10 (1977):159–163.

Paroz, J.; Siegenthaler, L. S.; and Tatum, V. H. "A Model for a Middle-School Resource Room." *Journal of Learning Disabilities* 10 (1977):1–9.

Rauch, S. *Handbook for the Volunteer Tutor.* Newark, Del.: International Reading Association, 1969.

Reger, R. "Resource Rooms: Change Agents or Guardians of the Status Quo?" *Journal of Special Education* 6 (1972):355–359.

Reger, R., and Koppman, M. "The Child-Oriented Resource Room." *Exceptional Children* 37 (1971):460–462.

Russell, R., and Kwiccinski, H. *A Program of Special Classes for Children with Learning Disabilities.* East Orange: New Jersey Association for Brain-Injured Children, 1967.

Sabatino, D. A. "An Evaluation of Resource Rooms for Children with Learning Disabilities." *Journal of Learning Disabilities* 4 (1971):84–93.

Scalon, R. G., and Brown, M. V. "Individualizing Instruction." In *Planned Change in Education,* edited by D. S. Busnell and D. Rappaport. New York: Harcourt Brace Jovanovich, 1971.

Sloman, L., and Webster, C. D. "Assessing the Parents of the Learning Disabled Child: A Semistructured Interview Procedure." *Journal of Learning Disabilities* 11 (1978):73–79.

Sorenson, J. S.; Poole, M.; and Joyal, L. H. *The Unit Leader and Individually Guided Education.* Reading, Mass.: Addison-Wesley, 1976.

Southwest Educational Development Laboratory. *Working With Parents of Handicapped Children.* Reston, Va.: Council for Exceptional Children, 1976.

Thelan, H. *Classroom Grouping for Teachability.* New York: John Wiley & Sons, 1967.

Torres, Scottie, ed. *A Primer on Individualized Education Programs for Handicapped Children.* Reston, Va.: Foundation for Exceptional Children, 1977.

Turnbull, A. P.; Strickland, B.; and Hammer, S. E. "The Individualized Education Program—Part 1: Procedural Guidelines." *Journal of Learning Disabilities* 11 (1978):40–46.

Turnbull, A. P.; Strickland, B.; and Hammer, S. E. "The Individualized Education Program—Part 2: Translating Law into Practice." *Journal of Learning Disabilities* 11 (1978):67–72.

Vallet, R. E. "The Learning Resource Center for Exceptional Children." *Exceptional Children,* 36 (1970):527–530.

Walker, J., ed. *Functions of the Placement Committee in Special Education.* Washington, D.C.: National Association of State Directors of Special Education, 1976.

Wallen, C. J., and Wallen, L. L. *Effective Classroom Management.* Boston: Allyn and Bacon, 1978.

White, O., and Liberty, K. "Behavioral Assessment and Precise Educational Management." In *Teaching Special Children,* edited by N. G. Haring and R. L. Schiefelbusch. New York: McGraw-Hill, 1976.

Worell, J., and Nelson, C. M. *Managing Instructional Problems.* New York: McGraw-Hill, 1974.

Yvon, B. R., and Vitro, F. T. "Become a Loser as a Parent." *Academic Therapy,* 11 (1976):467–471.

BEHAVIOR MANAGEMENT

Adams, E. "Perseveration—Some New Ideas." *Academic Therapy* 11 (1975–76):235–237.

Aiken, L. R., Jr., "Update on Attitudes and Other Affective Variables in Learning Mathematics." *Review of Educational Research* 46 (1976):293–310.

Axelrod, S. *Behavior Modification for the Classroom Teacher.* New York: McGraw-Hill, 1977.

Bany, M. A., and Johnson, L. V *Classroom Group Behavior.* New York: Macmillan, 1964, pp. 72, 73.

Becker, W. C. "Applications of Behavior Principles in Typical Classrooms." In *Behavior Modification in Education,* edited by C. E. Thorensen. Chicago: University of Chicago Press, 1972.

Bijou, S. Q. "Patterns of Reinforcement and Resistance to Extinction in Young Children." *Child Development* 28 (1967):47–54.

Block, G. H. "Hyperactivity: A Cultural Perspective." *Journal of Learning Disabilities* 10 (1977):236–240.

Brophy, J. E., and Good, T. L. *Teacher-Child Dyadic Interaction: A Manual for Coding Classroom Behavior.* Austin: The Research and Development Center for Teacher Education, The University of Texas, 1969.

Brophy, J. E., and Good, T. L. *Teacher-Student Relationship: Causes and Consequences.* New York: Holt, Rinehart & Winston, 1974.

Bryan, T. H. "Social Relationships and Verbal Interactions of Learning Disabled Children." *Journal of Learning Disabilities* 11 (1978):107–115.

Combs, A., ed. *Perceiving, Behaving, Becoming: A New Focus for Education.* Washington, D.C.: Association for Supervision and Curriculum Development, 1962.

Cowen, E. L.; Trost, M. A.; Lorion, R. P.; Dorr, D.; Izzo, L. D.; and Isaacson, R. V. *New Ways in School Mental Health: Early Detection and Prevention of School Maladaptation.* New York: Human Sciences, 1975.

Dinkmeyer, D. D. *Developing Understanding of Self and Others.* Circle Pines, Minn.: American Guidance Service, 1970.

Edgington, R., and Clements, S. *Indexed Bibliography on the Educational Management of Children with Learning Disabilities.* Chicago: Argus Communications, 1967.

Eron, L. D.; Huesmann, L. R.; Lefkowitz, M. M.; and Walder, L. O. "Behavior-Aggression." *American Journal of Orthopsychiatry* 44 (1974):412–423.

Eysenck, H. J. *Experiments in Behavior Therapy.* New York: Pergamon Press, 1964.

Fox, R. S.; Lippitt, R.; and Schmuck, R. *Pupil-Teacher Adjustment and Mutual Adaptation in Creating Classroom Learning Environments.* U.S. Department of Health, Education and Welfare, Office of Education. Cooperative Research Project No. 1167. Ann Arbor, Mich.: University of Michigan, 1964.

Fox, R. S.; Luszki, M. B.; and Schmuck, R. *Diagnosing Classroom Learning Environments.* Chicago: Science Research Associates, 1966.

Fox, R. S.; Schmuck, R.; van Egmond, E.; Ritvo, M.; and Jung, C. *Diagnosing Professional Climates of Schools.* Fairfax, Va.: NTL Learning Resources Corporation, 1975.

Friedland, S. J., and Shilkret, R. B. "Alternative Explanations of Learning Disabilities: Defensive Hyperactivity." *Exceptional Children* 40 (1973):213–214.

Futhans, F., and Kreitner, R. *Organizational Behavior Modification.* Glenville, Ill.: Scott, Foresman, 1975.

Gallagher, P. A. "Behavior Modification? Caution!" *Academic Therapy* 11 (1976):357–363.

Glasser, W. *Reality Therapy: A New Approach to Psychiatry.* New York: Harper & Row, 1965.

Glavin, J. P.; Quay, H. C.; Annesley, F. R.; and Werry, J. S. "An Experimental Resource Room for Behavior Problem Children." *Exceptional Children* 38 (1971):131–137.

Hall, R. V. *Behavior Modification: Application in School and Home.* Lawrence, Kans.: H & H Enterprises, 1971.

Hall, R. V. *Behavior Modification: Basic Principles.* Lawrence, Kans.: H & H Enterprises, 1971.

Hall, R. V. *Behavior Modification: The Measurement of Behavior.* Lawrence, Kans.: H & H Enterprises, 1971.

Hall, R. V. *Managing Behavior, Part 1.* Lawrence, Kans.: H & H Enterprises, 1971.

Hall, R. V. "Responsive Teaching: Focus on Measurement and Research in the Classroom and the Home." In *Strategies for Teaching Exceptional Children,* edited by E. Meyen, G. Vergason, and R. J. Whelan, pp. 403–415. Denver: Love, 1972.

Haring, N. "Application of Behavior Modification Techniques to the Learning Situation." In *Psycho-educational Practices,* vol. 1, edited by W. M. Cruickshank and D. P. Hallahan. Syracuse, N.Y.: Syracuse University Press, 1975.

Haring, N., and Phillips, E. *Analysis and Modification of Classroom Behavior.* Englewood Cliffs, N.J.: Prentice-Hall, 1972.

Haring, N., and Whelan, R., eds. *The Learning Environment: Relationship to Behavior Modification and Implications for Special Education.* Lawrence: University of Kansas Press, 1966.

Homme, L. E.; di Baca, P. C.; Devine, J. V.; Steinhorst, R.; and Richert, E. J. "Use of the Premack Principle in Controlling the Behavior of Nursery School Children." *Journal of the Experimental Analysis of Behavior* 6 (1963):544.

Jencks, S., and Peck, D. M. "Is Immediate Reinforcement Appropriate?" *The Arithmetic Teacher* 23 (1976):32–33.

Johnson, V. S. "Behavior Modification in the Correctional Setting." *Criminal Justice and Behavior* 4 (1977):397–428.

Johnson, V. S. "An Environment for Treating Youthful Offenders: The Kennedy Youth Center." *Offender Rehabilitation* 2 (1978):159–172.

Keogh, B. K., and Margolis, J. "Learn to Labor and to Wait: Attentional Problems of Children with Learning Disorders." *Journal of Learning Disabilities* 9 (1976):276–286.

Knaus, W., and McKeever, C. "Rational-Emotive Education with Learning Disabled Children." *Journal of Learning Disabilities* 10 (1977): 10–14.

Kounin, J. S., and Gump, P. V. *Discipline and Group Management in Classrooms.* New York: Holt, Rinehart & Winston, 1970.

Long, N. J.; Morse, W. C.; and Newman, R. *Conflict in the Classroom.* Belmont, Calif.: Wadsworth, 1971.

Lovitt, T. C. "Self-Management Projects with Children with Behavioral Disabilities." *Journal of Learning Disabilities* 6 (1973):135–150.

McDonald, F. J. "Behavior Modification in Teacher Education." In *Behavior Modification in Education: The Seventy-Second Yearbook of the National Society for the Study of Education,* edited by C. E. Thoresen. Chicago: University of Chicago Press, 1972.

McLaughlin, T. F. "Self-Control in the Classroom." *Review of Educational Research* 46 (1976):631–663.

Madsen, C. H., and Madsen, C. K. *Teaching/Discipline: A Positive Approach for Educational Development.* 2d ed. Boston: Allyn and Bacon, 1974.

Morse, W. C. "The Helping Teacher/Crisis Teacher Concept." *Focus on Exceptional Children* 8 (1976):1–11.

Pascal, C. E. "Using Principles of Behavior Modification to Teach Behavior Modification." *Exceptional Children* 42 (1976):426–430.

Poteet, J. A. *Behavior Modification: A Practical Guide for Teachers.* Minneapolis: Burgess, 1973.

Premack, D. "Toward Empirical Behavior Laws: 1. Positive Reinforcement." *Psychological Review* 66 (1959):219–233.

Prout, H. T. "Behavioral Intervention with Hyperactive Children: A Review." *Journal of Learning Disabilities* 10 (1977):141–146.

Quay, H. C.; Werry, J. S.; McQueen, M.; and Sprague, R. L. Remediation of the Conduct Problem Child in the Special Class Setting. *Exceptional Children* 32 (1966):509–515.

Rogers, C. R. *Client-Centered Therapy.* Boston: Houghton Mifflin, 1951.

Ross, D. M., and Ross, S. A. *Hyperactivity: Research, Theory and Action.* New York: Wiley, 1976.

Safer, D. J., and Allen, R. *Hyperactive Children: Diagnosis and Management.* Baltimore: University Park Press, 1976.

Schmuck, R. A., and Schmuck, P. A. *Group Processes in the Classroom.* Dubuque, Iowa: William C. Brown Co. 1975.

Shelton, M. N. "Affective Education and the Learning Disabled Student." *Journal of Learning Disabilities* 10 (1977):618–624.

Skinner, B. F. "Reinforcement Today." *American Psychologist* 13 (1958):94–99.

Staw, B. M. *Intrinsic and Extrinsic Motivation.* University Programs Modular Series. Morristown, N.J.: General Learning Press, 1976.

Sulzer, B., and Mayer, G. R. *Behavior Modification Procedures for School Personnel.* Hinsdale, Ill.: The Dryden Press, 1972.

Tharp, R., and Wetzel, R. J. *Behavior Modification in the Natural Environment.* New York: Academic Press, 1969.

Ulrich, R.; Stachnik, T.; and Mabry, J. *Control of Behavior,* vol 2. *From Cure to Prevention.* Glenview, Ill.: Scott, Foresman, 1970.

Valett, R. *Modifying Children's Behavior.* Palo Alto, Calif.: Fearon Publishers, 1969.

Valett, R. *The Psychoeducational Treatment of the Hyperactive Child.* Belmont, Calif.: Fearon Publishers, 1975.

Walker, H. M., and Buckley, N. K. *Token Reinforcement Techniques.* Eugene, Ore.: E-B Press, 1974.

Wolf, M. M.; Giles, D. K.; and Hall, R. V. "Experiments with Token Reinforcement in a Remedial Classroom." *Behaviour Research and Therapy* 8 (1968):51–84.

Wolf, M. M.; Hanley, E. L.; King, L. A.; Lachowicz, J.; and Giles, D. K. "The Timer-Game: A Variable Interval Contingency for the Management of Out-of-Seat Behavior." *Exceptional Children* 37 (October 1970):113–118.

Zifferblatt, S. M. "Behavior Systems." In *Behavior Modification in Education,* edited by C. Thoresen. Chicago: University of Chicago Press, 1972.

Index